The Art of Critical Reading

Brushing Up on Your Reading, Thinking, and Study Skills

Peter Mather | **Rita McCarthy**

Glendale Community College
Glendale, Arizona

McGraw Hill

Boston   Burr Ridge, IL   Dubuque, IA   Madison, WI   New York
San Francisco   St. Louis   Bangkok   Bogotá   Caracas   Kuala Lumpur
Lisbon   London   Madrid   Mexico City   Milan   Montreal   New Delhi
Santiago   Seoul   Singapore   Sydney   Taipei   Toronto

The McGraw-Hill Companies

McGraw Hill

THE ART OF CRITICAL READING: BRUSHING UP ON YOUR READING, THINKING,
AND STUDY SKILLS

Published by McGraw-Hill, a business unit of The McGraw-Hill Companies, Inc., 1221 Avenue of the
Americas, New York, NY, 10020. Copyright © 2005 by The McGraw-Hill Companies, Inc. All rights
reserved. No part of this publication may be reproduced or distributed in any form or by any means,
or stored in a database or retrieval system, without the prior written consent of The McGraw-Hill
Companies, Inc., including, but not limited to, in any network or other electronic storage or
transmission, or broadcast for distance learning.
Some ancillaries, including electronic and print components, may not be available to customers
outside the United States.

This book is printed on acid-free paper.

1 2 3 4 5 6 7 8 9 0 DOW/DOW 0 9 8 7 6 5 4

ISBN   0-07-241376-X (student edition)
ISBN   0-07-249999-0 (annotated instructor's edition)

President of McGraw-Hill Humanities/Social Sciences: *Steve Debow*
Senior sponsoring editor: *Alexis Walker*
Senior development editor: *Jane Carter*
Marketing manager: *Lori DeShazo*
Senior media producer: *Todd Vaccaro*
Project manager: *Catherine Iammartino*
Production supervisor: *Janean A. Utley*
Designer: *George Kokkonas*
Associate media project manager: *Meghan Durko*
Photo research coordinator: *Natalia C. Peschiera*
Photo researcher: *Inge King*
Art editor: *Katherine McNab*
Art director: *Robin Mouat*
Permissions editor: *Marty Granahan*
Cover design: *Laurie Entriger*
Cover image: ©John Van Hasselt/Corbis Sygma
Typeface: *10/13 Palatino*
Compositor: *The GTS Companies/York, PA Campus*
Printer: *R.R. Donnelley and Sons Inc.*

Library of Congress Cataloging-in-Publication Data

Mather, Peter.
    The art of critical reading : brushing up on your reading, thinking, and study skills / Peter
Mather, Rita McCarthy.
      p. cm.
    Includes index.
    ISBN 0-07-241376-X (student ed. softcover : alk. paper)—ISBN 0-07-249999-0 (annotated instructor's
ed. softcover : alk. paper)
    1. Reading (Higher education) 2. Critical thinking. 3. Study skills. I. McCarthy, Rita. II. Title.
LB2395.3.M27 2005
428.4'071'1—dc22
                                                                        2004042685

www.mhhe.com

About the Authors

Dr. Peter Mather Dr. Mather earned his B.A. in government from the University of Redlands, his first M.A. in African studies from the University of California, Los Angeles, his second M.A. in reading from California State University, Los Angeles, and his Ed.D. in curriculum and instruction from the University of Southern California. Before recently retiring, he taught reading at the secondary, adult education, and community college levels for approximately 30 years. While at Glendale Community College, he taught both developmental and critical and evaluative reading. He also taught American government and was the college director of the America Reads/Counts program. In addition to being a coauthor of the first and second editions of *Reading and All That Jazz,* he has published two articles in the *Journal of Reading.*

Ms. Rita Romero McCarthy Ms. McCarthy earned her B.A. in sociology and history from the University of California, Berkeley, and her M.A. in education from Arizona State University. She has taught at the elementary, secondary, and college levels. For the past 16 years, she has taught both English as a second language and various other developmental reading classes at Glendale Community College. In addition to being a coauthor of the first and second editions of *Reading and All That Jazz,* Ms. McCarthy has published articles in professional journals and other media; most of these have been concerned with the use of bibliotherapy. She has also published reading lists for beginning and remedial readers.

Brief Contents

Contents

Part 3   Interpreting What We Read   179

5   Inference   180

6   Figurative Language   218

10   Bias   336

Preface to the Instructor

In 1999, we published the first edition of *Reading and All That Jazz,* a textbook that uses the theme of jazz to highlight an exciting and engaged approach to reading and learning. This year, we are proud to present *The Art of Critical Reading,* a sequel to *Jazz* designed for more advanced courses in college reading.

Like *Jazz, The Art of Critical Reading* is designed to draw readers in with its engaging exercises and its reading selections, which are taken from a variety of sources: college textbooks, newspapers, magazines, and classic and contemporary literature. As with *Jazz,* the purpose of this book is to assist college students in developing the skills they need for reading, understanding, and critically evaluating textbooks and other college-level reading. While *Art* may be appropriate for a more advanced audience than is *Jazz,* it is still a book that will motivate and engage readers through its theme, its exciting reading selections, and its stimulating visuals and exercises.

Theme and Title

We chose art as the theme of this book because, like written texts, art is a form of communication. Like works of literature, works of art range from the easily understood to the enigmatic and thought provoking. In art, the viewer may dislike the unfamiliar, at least at first, but when he or she understands the "language" of art and its structure, the visual experience becomes richer. So, too, with written works. In the case both of written texts and art, the better a person understands the purpose and structure of the material, the more likely it is that that person will be able to interpret it accurately and enjoy it.

Art, like literature, sharpens our perceptions of life and requires us to re-examine our thoughts. Both artists and writers compose their works with a purpose in mind. And both artists and writers draw from their own personal experiences and backgrounds to convey their emotional or intellectual messages. Both viewers of art and readers of literature must bring their own perspectives to bear when engaged in evaluation and interpretation.

We emphasize the theme by introducing each chapter with a major work of art. We then ask students to consider the work of art so that they may reach a deeper understanding of it. To enhance the students' visual experience of the works of art included here, we also include a color insert that depicts these works in all their glory and includes journal prompts to encourage students to share their own colorful reflections with their teachers, classmates, and themselves. Throughout the text, we have included many carefully selected, provocative selections on a range of art-related topics, such as graffiti, public art, Egyptian artifacts, art theft, the Mona Lisa, and the Vietnam War Memorial. We conclude with a full-length chapter on art from a popular cultural anthropology textbook. Our hope is that students will find much material in *Art,* both visual and written, to stimulate and enrich.

Reading Selections and the Questions That Follow

The reading selections in this book were chosen, first, for their excellence. Many of the authors are famous or award winning. We also chose readings with contemporary relevance and interest. We made an effort to find selections that would broaden students' general knowledge about current events and be otherwise informative and useful. Finally, we sought readings that would appeal to a diverse audience. The selections address a wide variety of disciplines, from art to psychology to ethics to science. They also come from a wide variety of sources: while *The Art of Critical Reading* emphasizes textbook selections, it also presents other kinds of material students are likely to encounter in their college classes–works of literature as well as selections from magazines and newspapers.

While most of the selections are nonfiction, we also include poetry, fables, and cartoons. And although we emphasize contemporary material, we also include some classics. The one trait all the selections share is that they will enable students to clarify their own values as they experience events through someone else's eyes. Although most of the selections have not previously appeared in a reading textbook, instructors can use them with confidence, as they have been tested in our classes and in those of our colleagues.

The questions following the reading selections require the students to engage in recalling, understanding, interpreting, and evaluating. They come in various formats—multiple-choice, true-or-false, fill-in-the-blank, matching, discussion, and written-response questions. The objective questions are written in the style of questions asked on standardized tests such as the CLAST and the TASP. The open-ended questions for discussion and writing are included to give the students practice in analyzing, synthesizing, and evaluating. Such questions give students the opportunity to bring their personal experiences to bear, and they are organized in such a way as to lead the student to a greater understanding of the selections. Such questions rarely have a right or wrong answer; instead, they are meant to provoke discussion and encourage debate.

Organization of the Text

This book is organized along two dimensions. First, each successive part of the book focuses on different skills that an effective critical reader must master. Second, the book begins with a narrow perspective, focusing on students' personal experience, and then moves to increasingly broader perspectives, focusing in turn on interpersonal, social, national, and international issues. The book becomes increasingly challenging as it progresses, both in the selections presented and the critical reading skills taught:

- **Part 1 of this book is designed to capture the students' immediate attention and interest by discussing how to be successful in the college classroom.** Part 1 explores the skills likely to lead to a successful college experience. The mood of the selections is upbeat. Material presented in this section includes a review of a course syllabus, an overview of critical thinking skills, an introduction to study skills, a selection dealing with stress, tips on how to become a better speller, and strategies for combating procrastination. The Introduction in Part 1 is meant to be completed in the first week of class. The pretest and short written assignments that follow the selections will allow teachers to assess the skills of individual students and classes as a whole.

- **Part 2 reviews the basic skills needed for effective critical reading.** Focusing on the processes and structures of reading, Part 2 reviews skills that include identifying the topic, identifying the main idea and supporting details, and determining the author's purpose. Students practice recognizing and using transition words and patterns of organization, as well as identifying homonyms and other confusing words. The selections, which include fables, poems, and anecdotes, touch on themes of perception, motivation, risk taking, and ethics.

- **Part 3 emphasizes reading as an interpretive and analytical process.** The goal of Part 3 is to enable students to become proficient at reading between the lines. Topics introduced in Part 3 include inference, figurative language, and author's tone. Themes include animals and nature. Selections include material from such noted authors as Annie Dillard, Sandra Cisneros, Diane Ackerman, Farley Mowat, and Laura Hillenbrand (author of *Seabiscuit*).

- **Part 4 concentrates on developing critical reading and thinking skills.** Topics discussed include fact-and-opinion, the author's point of view, bias, propaganda techniques, and the structure of an argument. Selections cover such varied topics as health supplements, the Vietnam War Memorial, cultural literacy, and the Declaration of Independence and Bill of Rights. In Part 4, students are given an opportunity to evaluate evidence with material that covers two themes—death and dying, and animal experimentation— from varied perspectives.

- **Part 5 is devoted to improving study skills.** Throughout the book, we have introduced the student to study skills such as SQ3R, outlining, mapping, and annotating. Part 5 asks students to apply these skills to a complete chapter about art taken from a popular college anthropology textbook.

- **Part 6 is devoted to developing a college-level vocabulary.** It includes eight vocabulary units, each of which introduces students to a set of Latin or Greek word parts. Students learn college-level words associated with these word parts and then practice the word parts by means of verbal analogies and crossword puzzles.

- **The Appendices** address the skills needed to use a thesaurus and to interpret visual aids effectively. The section on visual aids—tables, charts, graphs, maps—is designed to be used as an independent unit or in conjunction with specific reading selections. A section on tips for spelling accurately is also included.

Organization of the Chapters

Each chapter begins with an overview of the chapter topic and a discussion of the key terms needed for understanding the topic, followed by short exercises designed to help the student understand and master the topic, and then by longer reading selections that further develop the topic. Introducing each of the longer reading selections is a section entitled "Getting the Picture," which is designed to engage the student with the subject of the upcoming selection. It is followed by a "Bio-sketch" of the author, which in turn is followed by a section entitled "Brushing Up on Vocabulary." Following the selections are a variety of exercises. Directions for longer written assignments, some of which will call for research by students, follow certain selections. Review tests are interspersed throughout the text to reinforce skills and remind students that while individual skills may be practiced in isolation, the reading process is cumulative.

The exercises in each chapter are sequential, progressing from relatively easy to quite difficult. These exercises use many different formats in order to maintain student interest. The instructor should feel free to pick and choose among the exercises in accord with the needs of particular students or classes. The exercises are designed so that the instructor can have the students work individually or in groups.

Special Features of *The Art of Critical Reading*

In addition to the wide range of readings and challenging questions that test and reinforce student learning, we've also included several special features that will reinforce skills crucial to succeeding in college:

- **Quotations in the margins that prompt student journal writing and discussion.** These quotations respond in provocative ways to reading selections and encourage students to reflect on the implications of what they have read.
- **Internet activities.** The Internet activities included in the text are directly related to the issues raised in the reading selections; some encourage students to delve more deeply into the lives and work of featured authors.
- **Study techniques.** We've included coverage of a variety of study techniques—from annotating and summarizing to outlining and mapping—to reinforce the basic skills students need to succeed in college.
- **Test-taking tips.** We conclude each chapter with tips for taking objective and essay exams. We also include a section on coping with test-taking anxiety.

Teaching and Learning Aids Accompanying the Book

Supplements for Instructors

- **Annotated Instructor's Edition (ISBN: 0-07-249999-0).** The Annotated Instructor's Edition contains the full text of the Student Edition plus answers to the objective exercises and some suggested answers to open-ended questions.
- **Partners in Teaching Listserv.** From current theory to time-tested classroom tips, this listserv and newsletter offer insight and support to teachers of developmental English from some of the most experienced voices in the field. To join, send an e-mail message with your name and e-mail address to english@mcgraw-hill.com.
- **Online Learning Center (www.mhhe.com/mather).** This password-protected site houses many resources for instructors, including:
    - **Instructor's Manual and Test Bank.** Available online for easy downloading, the Instructor's Manual and Test Bank, written by the authors of the textbook, are a robust resource providing innovative teaching tips, vocabulary quizzes, unit tests, supplementary activities, and useful connections to other resources, such as poems, movies, and political and cultural events.
    - **PowerPoint Slides.** Also available on the instructor's site are PowerPoint slides on which the instructional content of each chapter is summarized for overhead projection.

Supplements for Students

- **Online Learning Center (www.mhhe.com/mather).** Our companion website offers journal prompts for each chapter, links to direct students to reliable Web sources, search exercises to give students practice at finding reliable sites on their own, and much, much more.
- **Study Smart (www.mhhe.com/studysmart).** This innovative study-skills tutorial for students is an excellent resource for the learning lab or for students working on their own at home. Teaching students strategies for note taking, test taking, and time management, Study Smart operates with a

sophisticated answer analysis that students will find motivating. Available on CD-ROM or online, Study Smart is free when packaged with a McGraw-Hill text.

- **Word Works.** These Merriam-Webster and Random House reference works are available at low cost when ordered with *The Art of Critical Reading:*
  - *Merriam-Webster's Notebook Dictionary.* A compact word resource conveniently designed for 3-ring binders, *Merriam-Webster's Notebook Dictionary* includes 40,000 entries for widely used words with concise, easy-to-understand definitions and pronunciations.
  - *The Merriam-Webster Dictionary.* This handy, paperback dictionary contains over 70,000 definitions yet is small enough to carry around in a backpack, so it's always there when it's needed.
  - *Random House Webster's College Dictionary.* This authoritative dictionary includes over 160,000 entries and 175,000 definitions—more than any other college dictionary—and the most commonly used definitions are always listed first, so students can find what they need quickly.
  - *Merriam-Webster's Collegiate Dictionary & Thesaurus CD-ROM.* This up-to-the-minute electronic dictionary and thesaurus offers 225,000 definitions, 340,000 synonyms and related words, and 1,300 illustrations.
  - *Merriam-Webster's Notebook Thesaurus.* Conveniently designed for 3-ring binders, *Merriam-Webster's Notebook Thesaurus* provides concise, clear guidance for over 157,000 word choices.
  - *Merriam-Webster Thesaurus.* This compact thesaurus offers over 157,000 word choices, and includes concise definitions and examples to help students choose the correct word for the context.
  - *Merriam-Webster's Vocabulary Builder. Merriam-Webster's Vocabulary Builder* focuses on more than 1,000 words, introduces nearly 2,000 more, and includes quizzes to test the student's progress.
- **Novel Ideas.** These Random House and HarperCollins paperbacks are available at a low cost when packaged with the text:

  The Monkey Wrench Gang (Abbey); *Things Fall Apart* (Achebe); *The Lone Ranger and Tonto* (Alexie); *Integrity* (Carter); *The House on Mango Street* (Cisneros); *Heart of Darkness* (Conrad); *Pilgrim at Tinker Creek* (Dillard); *Love Medicine* (Erdrich); *Their Eyes Were Watching God* (Hurston); *Boys of Summer* (Kahn); *Woman Warrior* (Kingston); *One Hundred Years of Solitude* (Marquez); *Clear Springs* (Mason); *All the Pretty Horses* (McCarthy); *House Made of Dawn* (Momaday); *Joy Luck Club* (Tan); *Essays of E. B. White* (White).

For more information or to request copies of any of the above supplementary materials for instructor review, please contact your local McGraw-Hill representative at 1 (800) 338–3987 or send an e-mail message to english@mcgraw-hill.com.

Acknowledgments

No textbook can be created without the assistance of many people. First, we relied on the thoughtful reactions and suggestions of our colleagues across the country who reviewed this project at various stages:

Jesus Adame, El Paso Community College

Gertrude Coleman, Middlesex College

Marion Duckworth, Valdosta State University

Amy Girone, Arizona Western College

Suzanne Gripenstraw, Butte College

John Grether, St. Cloud State University

Lorna Keebaugh, Taft College

Sandi Komarow, Montgomery College

Mary D. Mears, Macon State College

Elizabeth Nelson, Tidewater Community College

Mary Nielsen, Dalton State College

Cindy Ortega, Phoenix College

Margaret Sims, Midlands Technical College

Marjorie Sussman, Miami-Dade Community College

Margaret Triplett, Central Oregon Community College

Richard S. Wilson, Community College of Baltimore County

Lynda Wolverton, Polk Community College

Cynthia Ybanez, College of Southern Maryland

In addition to our reviewers, our friends and collegues at Glendale Community College offered their thoughts and supported our efforts: Dave Gallett, Darlene Goto, Pam Hall, Reinhold Kiermayr, R. J. Merrill, Mary Jane Onnen, David Rodriquez, Rachel Segal, Nancy Siefer, Linda Smith, and Michael Vogt. Others who helped us were Joel Barez, Marilyn Brophy, Nancy Edwards, Cindy Gilbert, and Connie Holdread.

We'd also like to thank all the people at McGraw-Hill who worked to produce this text. First, there were our editors at McGraw-Hill: Sarah Touborg, our original editor, gave us the initial inspiration to write the book; our new editors, Alexis Walker and Jane Carter, followed the book each step of the way and gave us helpful criticisms and insights that were invaluable in developing the book. Our project manager—Cathy Iammartino—did a wonderful job coordinating all the tasks that had to be completed for this book to wind up in your hands. George Kokkonas handled the design process, Janean Utley oversaw the printing, Marty Granahan oversaw the text permissions, and Natalia Peschiera and Inge King worked on the photo program. Todd Vaccaro and Heather Severson helped us produce our terrific Online Learning Center. Also, our local McGraw-Hill sales representative, Sherree D'Amico, provided us with copies of the many textbooks that we have cited in the text.

To all the people who participated with us in creating this book, we offer our sincerest thanks.

Peter Mather
Rita McCarthy

Preface to the Student

"Everyone who knows how to read has it in their power to magnify themselves, to multiply the ways in which they exist, to make their lives full, significant, and interesting."

—Aldous Huxley

Art and reading both involve critical thinking. Artists, such as painters, sculptors, and photographers, engage in critical thinking as they go about creating a work of art. They think critically about the concept or idea or feeling they wish to convey and also about how best to express this perspective in the work of art. And viewers of a work of art must employ critical thinking in seeking to understand its meaning for the artist and for themselves. Similarly, authors think critically when working to communicate their thoughts in their writings, and readers think critically in seeking to understand an author's message and their own reaction to it. Art and reading share something else, too—they both involve specific skills that can be improved by effort and practice. Thus, the title of this book, *The Art of Critical Reading*.

The word *critical* derives from the Greek work *kriticos,* which means "is one who is able to judge." A critical reader is someone who is able to make judgments about a piece of writing. This process of making judgments involves understanding, interpreting, analyzing, and evaluating the written material.

So simply being able to read is only the starting point. To be a good reader, and a reader who can succeed at the college level, a person must possess the skills required to think critically about written materials. The purpose of this book is to teach you these skills and thus make you an effective critical reader and successful college student.

The first part of this book focuses on you as a person who wants to succeed in college. It discusses personal skills, such as setting goals, handling stress, and avoiding procrastination. The next part of the book broadens the focus to look at such topics as personal health and environmental concerns. The book then expands its focus further as it discusses political issues, such as those relating to the Declaration of Independence and the Bill of Rights, and social issues, such as cheating. Throughout the book, selections are drawn from the sorts of materials that you will encounter in other college courses, including excerpts from college textbooks, literature, newspapers, and popular fiction and nonfiction.

The following pages illustrate how this book works. Spending a few minutes getting to know the features and organization of the text will help you get the most out of *The Art of Critical Reading*.

Walkthrough

Chapter openers include a work of art and questions that will stimulate you to think critically about this work of art. These chapter openers will not only expose you to great works of art; they will also provide you with important opportunities to practice "reading" visuals critically.

Each chapter begins with an expanded explanation of the topic and a discussion of key terms needed to understand it. Short examples and exercises are included in these sections to help you master the topic and prepare you for the related readings that follow.

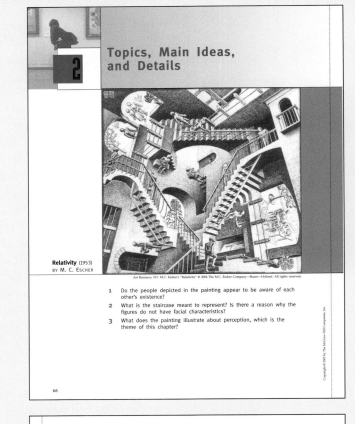

2 Topics, Main Ideas, and Details

Relativity (1953)
BY M. C. ESCHER

1   Do the people depicted in the painting appear to be aware of each other's existence?
2   What is the staircase meant to represent? Is there a reason why the figures do not have facial characteristics?
3   What does the painting illustrate about perception, which is the theme of this chapter?

66

Chapter 3 The Author's Purpose and the Rhetorical Modes   113

Purpose: _____   Clues: _____

Main Idea: _____

4.   In the traditional cultures of Asia, arranged marriages were the rule. Marriages were designed to further the well-being of families, not of the individuals involved. Marriage was traditionally seen as a matter of ancestors, descendants, and property. Supporters of these traditions point out that love is a fleeting emotion and not a sensible basis for such an important decision. However, most of these traditional cultures have a literature as well as a history full of love-smitten couples who chose death rather than marriage to the person selected by their respective families.

From Curtis Byer et al., *Dimensions of Human Sexuality*, 5th ed., New York: McGraw-Hill, 1999, p. 39.

Purpose: _____   Clues: _____

Main Idea: _____

An Introduction to the Rhetorical Modes

Highlight or underline the definitions of the key terms. Then write a paraphrase of each definition in the margin.

In longer reading selections, the main idea is often called the **thesis.** The thesis of an essay, just like the main idea of a paragraph, expresses the most important point the writer is trying to make. The thesis is sometimes called the *controlling idea,* because its primary purpose is to hold the essay or story together.

In the process of creating written work, most writers select a **rhetorical mode of writing** that helps them achieve their purpose. There are four primary rhetorical modes: *narration, description, exposition,* and *persuasion.*

Narrative

Material written in a **narrative mode** tells a story, either true or fictional. In narrative writing, the events of a story are usually ordered chronologically (by time).

Descriptive

With material written in a **descriptive mode,** the emphasis is on providing details that describe a person, place, or object. The writing may use figurative language and include material that appeals to one or more of the five senses. Descriptive writing most commonly deals with visual perceptions.

Expository

An author who is trying to explain something will likely use an **expository mode.** Expository writing explains ideas and how things work. It is more likely to be logical and factual. Much of the material that you read in your textbooks follows an expository mode.

Persuasive

Material written in a **persuasive mode** is meant to convince you of something. Persuasive writing tends to be about controversial topics. It presents an argument and offers evidence. It is writing that is considered to be biased.

Mixed

Sometimes an author will use more than one mode of writing. For example, the author might choose to write a piece that is both descriptive and narrative. This is called a **mixed mode** of writing and the organization may also be mixed.

Author's Purpose: To Inform

Read the following excerpt from *Understanding Psychology* by Robert S. Feldman. Feldman's purpose is to present information about motivation. His mode of writing is **expository.** Note the factual details that are intended to inform the reader.

The reading selections are preceded by a "Getting the Picture" section, which includes information that will help you understand what you are about to encounter. A "Bio-sketch" of the author follows; this section will provide you with information about the writer's life or writing experience. "Brushing Up on Vocabulary" sections will provide you with an overview of unfamiliar words in the selection.

The Comprehension Checkup following the reading selections consists of objective questions to test your understanding of what you have just read; the Vocabulary in Context exercises are provided to help you to build your word knowledge; "In Your Own Words" and "The Art of Writing" exercises ask you to reflect on and write about the selection you've just encountered, enriching your experience and giving you another opportunity to polish your skills; and the "Internet Activity" following the reading selection provides a jumping-off point for learning more about the topic or the author of the selection.

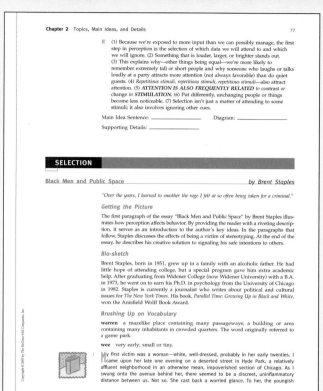

"Study Technique" boxes offer tips for mastering your college level work; these can be applied not only to the material you are encountering in this text, but in all your college courses.

388   **Part 4**   Reading Critically

STUDY TECHNIQUE 9
Venn Diagram

A Venn diagram is an illustration that shows similarities and differences between topics using a graphic of two overlapping circles. Notice the diagram below. In the circle on the left, characteristics specific only to Jefferson are listed; in the circle on the right, characteristics specific only to Adams are listed; in the overlapping area, characteristics shared by both Adams and Jefferson are listed.

Complete the Venn diagram comparing and contrasting Jefferson and Adams by listing more traits unique to each of these men and more traits they shared. Then write a paragraph comparing and contrasting the two men. You will find that it is much easier to write a comparison-contrast assignment after creating such a Venn diagram.

Jefferson
1. From Virginia
2. Wrote Declaration of Independence
3.

Both
1. Died on July 4, 1826
2. Denounced slavery
3.
4.
5.

Adams
1. From Massachusetts
2. Advocated Declaration of Independence
3.

SELECTION

Excerpt from *Benjamin Franklin: An American Life*   *by Walter Isaacson*

"The document Jefferson drafted was in some ways similar to what Franklin would have written."

Getting the Picture

Today, we remember Benjamin Franklin primarily for his inventions, such as bifocals and the lightning rod, and for his humorous sayings, such as "Early to bed, early to rise, makes a man healthy, wealthy, and wise." But in the course of American history he was much more than that, often providing the voice of reason to the "young hotheads." At the time of the writing of the Declaration of Independence, despite Franklin's being in poor health, his counsel proved invaluable.

Bio-sketch

Walter Isaacson, president of the Aspen Institute, has been the chairman of CNN and managing editor of *Time* magazine. He is the author of *Kissinger: A Biography,*

"Test-Taking Tips" at the end of each chapter provide helpful hints for mastering the process of taking an exam.

458   **Part 4**   Reading Critically

2. For an interview with Matthew Scully by Kathryn Jean Lopez of *National Review* Online, consult

www.nationalreview.com/interrogatory/interrogatory120602.asp

Think of five questions that you would like to ask Scully.

3. Use a search engine such as Google <www.google.com> or Yahoo <www.yahoo.com> to locate information about recent developments in the field of cloning. Summarize your findings.

TEST-TAKING TIP
Key Words That Often Appear in Essay Questions (Continued)

explain — to make clear, to give reasons. An explanation often involves showing cause-and-effect relationships or steps.

illustrate — to use a diagram, chart, or figure, or specific examples to explain something further.

interpret — to say what something means. A question that asks for an interpretation usually wants you to state what something means to you. What are your beliefs or feelings about the meaning of the material? Be sure to back up your position with specific examples and details.

justify — to give reasons in support of a conclusion, theory, or opinion.

list — to put down your points one-by-one. You may want to number each of the points in your list.

outline — to organize information into an outline, using headings and subheadings. Your outline should reflect the main ideas and supporting details.

prove — to demonstrate that something is true by means of factual evidence or logical reasoning.

relate — to discuss how two or more conclusions, theories, or opinions affect each other. Explain how one causes, limits, or develops the other.

review — to summarize or sometimes to summarize and then analyze critically.

summarize — to put down the main points; to state briefly the key principles, facts, or ideas while avoiding details and personal comments.

trace — to follow the course of development of something in a chronological or logical sequence. You will want to discuss each stage of development from beginning to end.

The Study Skills covered in Part 5 will reinforce the skills you've been learning throughout the book and will help you master the material you encounter in all your college courses.

The Vocabulary Units in Chapter 14 help you to build your vocabulary by showing you how to interpret words based on the common word parts of which they're made.

Chapter 14 Vocabulary Units

485

Vocabulary Units 1–8

Each of the following eight units will introduce you to important prefixes, suffixes, and root words, and give you vocabulary words using these word parts. Each unit will draw on what you learned in the previous units. You will find an exercise and a crossword puzzle at the end of each unit to reinforce your learning.

Unit 1

The following prefixes all indicate numbers:

uni—one	qua(d)—four	sept—seven
mono—one	tetra—four	hept—seven
bi—two	quint—five	oct—eight
di—two	pent—five	
du(o)—two		nov—nine
	hex—six	
tri—three	sex—six	dec, dek—ten

unify	to make or become a single unit.
unicameral	*-cam-* means "chamber." *Unicameral* is a legislative body made up of only one house or chamber.
bicameral	having two groups in the lawmaking body. The *bicameral* U.S. Congress is made up of the Senate and the House of Representatives.
univalve	having a shell composed of a single piece, such as a snail.
bivalve	having a shell composed of two parts hinged together, such as a clam or oyster.
monochromatic	of or pertaining to only one color, as in *monochromatic* pottery. It was obvious that Regis, who wore a gray tie, gray shirt, and gray slacks, preferred a *monochromatic* style of dress.
monogram	initials of a person's name in a design, such as are used on articles of clothing or stationery.
monolith	*-lith* means "stone," so a monolith is a single block or piece of stone of considerable size, sometimes carved into a column or large statue. The sphinx of Egypt is a *monolith.*
monotonous	sounded or uttered in one unvarying tone; lacking in variety. At the graduation ceremony, many were displeased with the keynote speaker because of his *monotonous* speaking style.
monocle	an eyeglass for one eye.
monorail	a single rail serving as a track for cars. Taking the *monorail* at Disneyland adds to the excitement.
monosyllabic	having only one syllable like "what" or "how."
biracial	consisting of or representing members of two separate races. Tiger Woods, whose mother is Asian and father is black, is *biracial.*
bipartisan	made up of or supported by two political parties. Support for education is *bipartisan.*

The Crossword Puzzles are fun exercises that will help you improve both your vocabulary and your reading comprehension.

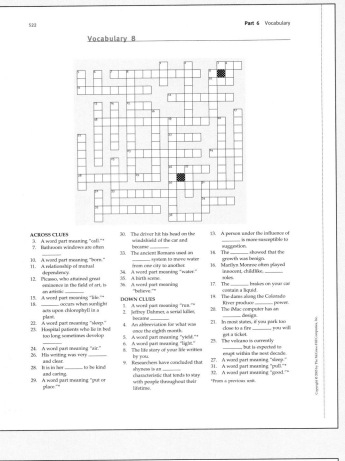

The Appendices will help you learn to interpret visual aids (like graphs, charts, and maps), use a thesaurus, master vocabulary word parts, improve your spelling, evaluate Internet sites, and write summaries that avoid plagiarism.

These features will serve as familiar guideposts and handy references as you make your way through the book. The structure will help you in understanding the book's content, even as the activities and exercises assist you in learning and remembering the material.

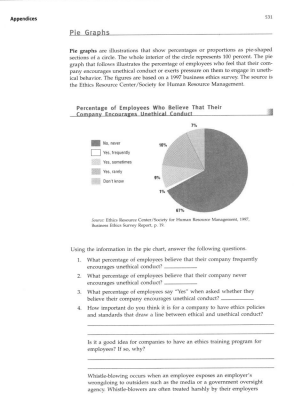

We hope that your experience using *The Art of Critical Reading* will be entirely successful. If you have comments or suggestions for improving the way this text-book works, we'd like to hear from you. Send an email to english@mcgraw-hill.com, and our editors will gladly pass it along.

The following short selection—"The Emperor and the Calligrapher" by Paul Freeman—will give you an opportunity to practice the skills you will be exposed to throughout the text. Not only will it require you to think critically about a piece of literature, it will also challenge you to practice your critical skills on a work of art. First, read the fable through carefully, and then consider the questions that follow.

Bicolored Rooster with the Cross of Lorraine (1945)*
BY PABLO PICASSO

*To see this work of art in color, turn to the color insert following page 260.

Réunion des Musées Nationaux/Art Resource, NY, Musée Picasso, Paris, France. © 2005 Estate of Pablo Picasso/Artists Rights Society (ARS), New York

The Emperor and the Calligrapher   *by Paul Freeman*

A long time ago in the emperor's court, there was a young apprentice calligrapher. The emperor called him to the throne and wished him well in his endeavors, and asked that he paint a rooster with some words along side it. The emperor asked the young man when he might have it, and the apprentice replied that he would like to have a year in which to prepare, and could he please be asked again.

The following year, the emperor called for the man to come to the throne, and asked him how he was coming along with the rooster and the words. The young man bowed politely and said that he was working on it diligently, but he was not ready, and would he please ask again in a year. This went on year after year for twenty years. By this time, the calligrapher was considered to be a master. The emperor called him to the throne again, but this time his tone was no longer peaceful. "I want this rooster *now*." but the calligrapher, no longer a young man, bowed politely and begged for six more months. The emperor reluctantly agreed, and at the end of six months, the calligrapher was again summoned and again asked for an extension. The emperor was furious. He gave the calligrapher one week and said if he did not have the rooster and the words at that time, the calligrapher would be executed.

At the appointed time, the guards brought the calligrapher with his ink stone, ink stick, water bowl, brush and roll of exquisite paper. The calligrapher centered himself, carefully regarded his tools, ground his ink in a nearly trance-like state, then bent over and with his whole body swept the brush upon the paper, and in a few strokes there was an incredibly beautiful rooster with the specified words.

"Calligrapher," the emperor cried out in amazement, "this took you just a few minutes to do! Why didn't you do this when I first asked it of you?"

The man bowed his head reverently, and, without looking up, replied, "My emperor, it took me over twenty years to learn how to do this so well and so quickly."

1   How would you express the moral of this fable?

2   How could this fable apply to your life?

3   How does Picasso's drawing of a rooster help you understand the role effort plays in doing something that looks effortless?

Just as the artist had to labor for a year to master drawing a perfect rooster in five minutes, we hope that the effort you put forth in your class now—reading selections and working carefully through the exercises in this book—will enable you to master the skills you will need to make your college career rewarding and successful.

Source: Courtesy of Paul Freeman, Pauline Sager, and the San Antonio Calligraphers' Guild and its Flourishes web site (at <www.axs4u.net/home/inksmith/sepfast01.htm>) as well as the newsletter of the New York Society of Scribes, where Paul Freeman published this version of the fable.

Part Learning How to Be a Successful Student

Introduction

The Scholar (1926)*
BY NORMAN
ROCKWELL

*To see this work of art in
color, turn to the color
insert following page 260.

Earl Derr Biggers — Austin Parker — Frank Ward O'Malley — Isaac F. Marcosson
Edwin Balmer and William MacHarg — Stephen Leacock — Henry Milner Rideout

1 What do you think the headmaster is saying about the young man?
Write your own caption.

2 What qualities do you think a successful student must have?

Some of you are just beginning college. Some of you have already taken college classes. Regardless of how much college experience you already have, this book is designed to help you become better at reading, understanding, and evaluating college level material. In this book, you will be given an opportunity to practice your reading skills on a variety of materials such as textbooks, journal and Internet articles, as well as selections from popular literature, fables, and poems. Along the way, you will learn how to be a critical reader. Critical reading goes beyond mere comprehension. It includes the ability to analyze and interpret what you read. Your college classes are designed to expose you to new information and ideas on many subjects. They are also meant to stimulate you to think critically about what you are reading and learning. This book will make you a better critical reader.

Portrait of a Successful Student

Once the women's basketball coach at our college asked us what it takes for a student to be successful in our reading classes. Our response was twofold—come to class and turn in all of the required work. This may not be a complete prescription for success in your college classes, but it's a big first step. Many students skip class. Some don't turn in all of their work on time. These students end up not learning as much as they could. They also end up doing poorly in their classes. Some will fail in these classes, and some will even drop out of college. You need to do some thinking about what sort of college student you want to be. Don't sell yourself short! Be the kind of student who always goes to class and always turns in assignments!

The following test is adapted from one found in a popular environmental science textbook. Take this test to help you assess how prepared you are to do well in college. Rate yourself on each question on a scale of 1 (needs improvement) to 5 (excellent). If you rate yourself below 3 on any item, think about what you need to do to improve and make yourself a stronger student.

_____ How strong is your commitment to be successful in your classes?

_____ How well do you manage your time (e.g., do you always run late or do you complete assignments on time)?

_____ Do you have a regular study environment that reduces distraction and encourages concentration?

_____ How effective are you at reading and note taking (e.g., do you remember what you read; can you decipher your notes after you've written them)?

_____ Do you attend class regularly and listen for instructions and important ideas?

_____ Do you participate actively in class discussions and ask meaningful questions?

_____ Do you generally read assigned chapters in the textbook before attending class so that you are not reading the chapters for the first time the night before the exam?

_____ Are you usually prepared before class with questions about material that needs clarification or that expresses your own interest in the subject matter?

_____ How do you handle test anxiety (e.g., do you usually feel prepared for exams and quizzes so that you are not terrified by them)?

_____ Do you actively evaluate how you are doing in a course based on feedback from your instructor and then make corrections to improve your effectiveness?

_____ Do you seek out advice and assistance outside of class from your instructors or their teaching assistants?

Test adapted from William P. Cunningham and Barbara W. Saigo, *Environmental Science*, 6th ed., New York: McGraw-Hill, 2001, p. 3. Copyright © 2001 McGraw-Hill. Reprinted by permission of The McGraw-Hill Companies, Inc.

Think about the following **A, B, Cs** of doing well in college.

A. **A**lways go to class.

B. **B**e at your class on time and don't leave early.

C. **C**omplete all of your work on time.

Learning Styles

Now that you have decided to always go to class, get to class on time, and complete all of your work on time, you need to think about learning styles. Not everyone learns the same way. We all have preferred learning styles, which are the ways that allow us to learn best. What are your preferred learning styles? Look at the descriptions of various learning styles below. Which of these learning styles apply to you?

Visual Learner

You learn best by seeing or visualizing information. You understand best by reading and looking at photographs, maps, charts, and picture puzzles. You might use flash cards to memorize material.

Auditory Learner

You learn best by hearing or listening to explanations. You understand best by listening to lectures, discussions, reading out loud, and even by listening to tape recorded material.

Logical Learner

You learn best by thinking through a subject and finding answers that make sense. You understand best by making connections between different thoughts and ideas as opposed to just memorizing material.

Tactile Learner

You learn best by doing. You need to be active. You understand best when you are learning through the use of physical activity. You are good at working with your hands and usually take copious notes from lectures. You might even learn best while walking around a room rather than sitting in a chair or at a desk.

Once you have determined your preferred learning styles, you need to think about applying what you have discovered to what you do as a student who wants to do well. How should you study to take best advantage of your learning styles? What major or classes best suit your preferred learning styles? Which teachers best suit your learning styles?

The Syllabus

An important part of any course is the syllabus. You will usually receive a syllabus from your instructor on the first day of class. The syllabus generally presents an outline of the requirements and objectives for the course as well as an explanation of the grading system. It often includes the dates for quizzes, tests, and the final exam. It might also include a list of assignments and their due dates. A good student will use this information to create a study plan. The class attendance policy may also be given. Will you automatically be dropped after a certain number of absences? Will your grade be reduced if you exceed an allotted number of absences? In the syllabus, you may find information you need to contact the instructor, such as office location, phone number, and e-mail address. In addition, the syllabus may suggest the instructor's primary teaching style. You might want to assess how well your preferred learning styles mesh with this style. An auditory learner might learn best from an instructor who presents material primarily through a lecture format. A visual learner might learn best when the instructor uses frequent PowerPoint presentations. The course syllabus lays down the ground rules and requirements for the class. By accepting the syllabus and taking the class, you are agreeing to abide by these rules and requirements. Keep your syllabus on hand so that you can refer to it easily.

Review of an Art History Syllabus

Take a look at the following syllabus from an art history class. Refer to the syllabus to answer the following questions with T for true and F for false.

_____ 1. Exam #2 covers chapters 3 and 4.

_____ 2. There are four exams each worth 25 percent of the final grade.

_____ 3. The instructor has five scheduled office hours per week.

_____ 4. The class covers art from the earliest times to the present.

_____ 5. Before each of the exams, the instructor will present a brief review.

ARH 101, section 1203   Dr. Pamela Hall
FA room 105   Faculty 03, room 107

PREHISTORIC THROUGH GOTHIC ART
Glendale Community College
Fall Semester 2002
Mon./Wed./Fri., 9:00–9:50 a.m.

COURSE REQUIREMENTS

Course Description: History of art from prehistoric through medieval period. Prerequisites: None. This course will survey the history of Western art from the prehistoric era to the early 14th century. Major monuments will be discussed, highlighting both their aesthetic qualities and cultural significance. Emphasis is placed on building a comprehensive understanding of art in its historical context.

Textbook: Laurie Schneider Adams, *Art Across Time,* vol. 1 (New York: McGraw-Hill, 2002), 2nd edition. *Art Across Time* is on sale in the bookstore and on reserve in the library. You are responsible for all assigned readings as indicated on the attached calendar. Readings should be completed before the topic is presented in class, enabling a better grasp of the lecture and a more informed participation in discussion.

Attendance: Much of the material for this course is based upon slides viewed and discussed in the classroom; accordingly, regular attendance is absolutely necessary. Students should be aware that it is virtually impossible to pass the course without attending class. If you must miss a class, please leave me a message. Six unexcused absences may result in your being dropped from the course.

Exams: There will be four exams, scheduled for Fri., **Sept. 27;** Mon., **Oct. 21;** Wed., **Nov. 20;** and Mon., **Dec. 16.** A brief review will precede each exam. Each of the exams will have the same format, and will consist of (1) identification of key works of art, (2) multiple-choice questions, and (3) short essays based on the readings and lectures. *Please note:* Make-up exams will *not* be given without prior consent (or, in case of illness, without a note from a physician) and will likely be a different format than the one given in class.

CALENDAR

Mon. **Aug.** 26		Overview	
Wed.	28	Prehistoric Art *Paleolithic*	Ch. 1
Fri.	30	Prehistoric Art *Neolithic, Bronze Age*	Ch. 1
Mon. **Sept.** 2		**Labor Day**	**No class**
Wed.	4	Ancient Near Eastern Art *Neolithic, Sumerian*	Ch. 2
Fri.	6	Ancient Near Eastern Art *Akkadian, Babylonian, Assyrian*	Ch. 2
Mon.	9	Ancient Near Eastern Art *Neo-Babylonian, Persian*	Ch. 2
Wed.	11	Egyptian Art *Pre-Dynastic, Old Kingdom*	Ch. 3
Fri.	13	Egyptian Art *Old Kingdom*	Ch. 3
Mon.	16	Egyptian Art *Middle Kingdom*	Ch. 3
Wed.	18	Egyptian Art *New Kingdom*	Ch. 3
Fri.	20	Egyptian Art *Amarna Period*	Ch. 3
Mon.	23	Egyptian Art *Tutankhamun*	Ch. 3
Wed.	25	Review	
Fri.	27	****Exam #1****	**Chs. 1–3**
Mon.	30	Aegean Art *Cycladic, Minoan*	Ch. 4
Wed. **Oct.** 2		Aegean Art *Minoan, Mycenaean*	Ch. 4
Fri.	4	Aegean Art *Mycenaean*	Ch. 4
Mon.	7	Greek Art *Introduction, vase painting*	Ch. 5
Wed.	9	Greek Art *Geometric, Archaic*	Ch. 5
Fri.	11	Greek Art *Early Classical*	Ch. 5
Mon.	14	Greek Art *High Classical*	Ch. 5
Wed.	16	Greek Art *Late Classical*	Ch. 5
Fri.	18	Greek Art *Hellenistic*	Ch. 5

			Review	
Mon.		21	**Exam #2**	**Chs. 4–5**
Wed.		23	Etruscan Art	Ch. 6
Fri.		25	Roman Art *Republican and Augustan*	Ch. 7
Mon.		28	Roman Art *Wall Painting and Early Empire*	Ch. 7
Wed.		30	Roman Art *Hadrian to Constantine*	Ch. 7
Fri.	**Nov.**	1	**Visit Phoenix Art Museum**	**No class**
Mon.		4	Roman Art *Late Empire*	Ch. 7
Wed.		6	Early Christian Art *Persecution Period*	Ch. 8
Fri.		8	Early Christian *Recognition Period*	Ch. 8
Mon.		11	**Veteran's Day**	**No class**
Wed.		13	Byzantine Art *Justinian Period*	Ch. 8
Fri.		15	Byzantine Art *Minor art*	Ch. 8
Mon.		18	Byzantine Art *Later Byzantine* Review	Ch. 8
Wed.		20	**Exam #3**	**Chs. 6–8**
Fri.		22	Early Medieval Art *Migration*	Ch. 9
Mon.		25	Early Medieval Art *Carolingian*	Ch. 9
Wed.		27	Early Medieval Art *Ottonian*	Ch. 9
Fri.		29	**Thanksgiving Holiday**	**No class**
Mon.	**Dec.**	2	Romanesque Art *architecture*	Ch. 10
Wed.		4	Romanesque Art *sculpture*	Ch. 10
Fri.		6	Romanesque Art *minor arts*	Ch. 10
Mon.		9	Gothic Art *architecture*	Ch. 11
Wed.		11	Gothic Art *sculpture and minor arts*	Ch. 11
Fri.		13	Proto-Renaissance Art *minor arts* Review	Ch. 12
Mon.		16	**Exam #4** 9.00–9.50 a.m.	**Chs. 9–12**

** This syllabus is subject to revision due to changing student needs, time constraints, or other unforeseen circumstances.**

Course Competencies: Upon successful completion of this course, you will be able to:
1. Identify stylistic characteristics of the various historical periods from the Prehistoric through the Middle Ages.
2. Define and use art historical terminology.

3. Identify various visual elements and explain how one uses these to analyze and evaluate works of art.
4. Identify key works by various painters, sculptors, and architects.
5. Critically compare and contrast various works of art.

Grading Policy: Each of the four exams is worth 25% of your grade. Please note that you must take all four exams to receive a passing grade. Final grades will be determined by the following computation:

Grade	Percent
A	90–100%
B	80–89%
C	70–79%
D	60–69%
F	0–59%

Attendance, class participation, and improvement will be considered in the event of borderline grades.

Extra Credit Option: You may improve your test grade(s) by *up to* five percentage points (i.e., from a 72 to a 77%) by submitting one of the following:
   a) a critical review of an Internet site related to a topic covered by the test
   b) a critical review of a recent (i.e., within three months) newspaper or magazine article related to a topic covered by the test.
In either case, your review should be typed; it must be submitted within two weeks of the return of test date to be considered. The extra credit option is *not* available with make-up exams.

Office Hours: Monday, Wednesday, Friday, 12:00–1:00; Tuesday, Thursday, 9:00–10:00; and by appointment. My office is located in the Faculty Office Building 03, room 107.

Please Note: If you have a disability that may have some effect on your work in this class and *for which you may require accommodations,* you need to notify the Disability Services and Resources office, located in TDS 100. The phone number is (623) 845-3080.

Review of Your Own Course Syllabus

Answer the following questions by looking at the course syllabus for your reading class.

1. Where is your instructor's office located? What are the office hours?

_____

_____

2. What is the attendance policy?

_____

_____

3. What is your instructor's policy on making up missed homework? Missed quizzes? Missed exams?

_____

_____

4. When is your first quiz? How many points is it worth?

_____

_____

5. Is extra credit available? If so, how can you earn it? How much is it worth?

_____

_____

6. Are you allowed to turn in assignments late? What are the rules governing late work?

_____

_____

7. What is the date for the final exam? What percent of the final grade is it worth?

_____

_____

8. Is there any indication of the instructor's primary teaching style? If so, how does it match up with your learning style?

_____

_____

9. Is anything missing from the syllabus that you would like to know about?

_____

_____

10. Compare and contrast your class syllabus with the syllabus for art history included above.
   a. What are some similarities between the two?

_____

_____

   b. What are some differences?

_____

_____

Internet Activity

Many textbooks have an Internet site. The website for *Art Across Time*, the textbook used in the art history class mentioned above, is:

http://highered.mcgraw-hill.com/sites/0072450061

Go to this website and see what additional resources are available. Are any of these resources potentially useful to you? Describe a feature that might prove useful if you were taking an art history class.

Crossword Puzzle

On the next page, you will find a crossword puzzle that will introduce you to the material covered in this book. The answers to many of the clues can be found in this book's preface to the student, the table of contents, and the index. The preface to the student appears on page xxi and describes what the book is about and why it was written. The table of contents shows you the major divisions of the book. The index, found at the back of the book, is an alphabetical listing of many important topics and the page numbers on which the information is located. Happy hunting!

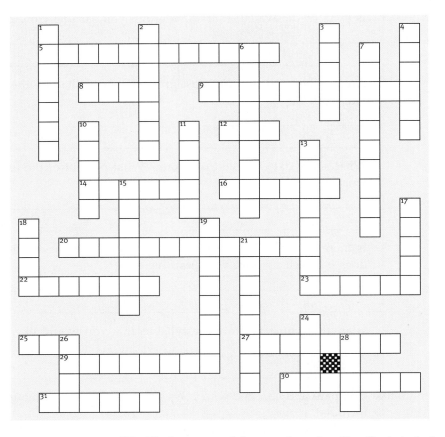

ACROSS CLUES

5. Chapter 4 discusses patterns of _____.

8. Patrick Buchanan wrote "The Death of the _____."

9. Charles Finney's selection discusses the western diamondback _____.

12. A discussion of similes, metaphors, and personification is found in Chapter _____.

14. The last name of the co-author of this book who attended the University of Redlands.

16. An author whose purpose is to _____ will provide readers with knowledge or information.

20. Marian Wright Edelman was born in the state of _____.

22. Chapter 2 discusses topics, main ideas, and _____.

23. One type of pattern of organization is called cause and _____.

25. According to Vocabulary Unit 1, the prefix for nine is _____.

27. The last name of the co-author of this book who has taught E. S. L. classes.

29. One type of pattern of organization is called _____ and illustration.

30. Study technique 6 is titled _____.

31. Figurative language compares two or more _____ things.

DOWN CLUES

1. "The Horse Fair" was painted by Rosa _____.

2. Most reading selections begin with a section titled "Getting the _____."

3. One type of logical fallacy is called _____ analogy.

4. Frida Kahlo was married to Diego _____.

6. Study technique 4 is titled _____.

7. Laura Hillenbrand wrote a book about the racehorse, _____.

10. Dave Barry writes for the _____ Herald.

11. Study technique 3 will teach you how to write summaries of _____ articles.

13. An author's purpose may be to _____ a reader or to try to change the reader's opinion.

15. If you learn by doing, your learning style would be called _____.

17. Chapter _____ discusses the difference between fact and opinion.

18. _____ stacking is one type of propaganda technique.

19. According to the Preface to the Student, the word "critical" came from the Greek word _____.

21. Michael J. Fox wrote the book _____.

24. _____ Ying Lin designed the Vietnam Veterans Memorial.

26. Study technique 9 will teach you how to make a _____ Diagram.

28. All chapters end with test-taking _____.

SELECTION

Commencement Address   *by Marian Wright Edelman*

"And do not ever stop learning and improving your mind, because if you do, you are going to be left behind."

Getting the Picture

The following selection is from a college commencement speech delivered by Marian Wright Edelman at Washington University in St. Louis, Missouri, on May 15, 1992. The eight lessons she mentions in the speech were meant to serve as "road maps" for graduating seniors. Because Edelman does not feel that she "has all the answers," students were urged to "ignore, revise, or use all or any of the lessons as they see fit." Edelman, who considers her life a testament to the American Dream, hopes that her words of advice might aid some in "developing a positive passion in life."

Bio-sketch

Marian Wright Edelman, the youngest of five children, was born in 1939 in Bennettsville, South Carolina. In the days when African-Americans were not allowed in city parks, Edelman's father built a park for them behind his church. Edelman graduated from Spelman College, a historically African-American college in Atlanta, went on to graduate from Yale Law School, and became the first African-American admitted to the Mississippi Bar. She has written many articles and books, including her autobiographical bestseller, *The Measure of Our Success: A Letter to My Children and Yours*. She is the founder and president of the Children's Defense Fund, has served on many boards, and has received numerous honorary awards. She is married to Peter Edelman, a professor at Georgetown Law School. They have three sons and two granddaughters.

Brushing Up on Vocabulary

free lunch   something acquired without due effort or cost. The term originated in the 1800s from the custom of taverns offering free food to their patrons to encourage them to buy drinks. Today *free lunch* is often used in a pejorative way.

cut corners   do something in the easiest or least expensive way; act illegally. The term was first used in the late 1800s. It originally meant to go around a corner as closely as possible so as to reduce the distance traveled, thereby saving time.

expediency   regard for what is advantageous rather than for what is right or just. The word *expediency* is derived from the Latin *expedire*, meaning "to free one caught by the foot."

illiterate   *illiterate* is derived from the Latin word *litera*, meaning "letter." So an *illiterate* is someone who does not know letters—that is, someone who lacks the ability to read.

integrity   adherence to moral and ethical principles; honesty. The word *integrity* is derived from the Latin *integer*, meaning "a whole number." The word later came to mean "in one piece."

Washington University

St. Louis, Missouri

May 15, 1992

1   ″I want to share a few lessons of life taken from a letter that I wrote to my own three wonderful sons. I recognize that you can take or leave these lessons, but you won't be able to say that you were never told them. Let me give you a few of them.

2   "The first lesson is, there is no free lunch. Do not feel entitled to anything you do not sweat or struggle for. Your degree will get you in the door, but it will not get you to the top of the career ladder or keep you there. You have got to work your way up hard and continuously.

3   "Remember not to be lazy. Do your homework. Pay attention to detail. Take care and pride in your work. Take the initiative in creating your own opportunity and do not wait around for other people to discover you or do you a favor. Do not assume a door is closed; push on it. Do not assume if it was closed yesterday that it is closed today. And do not ever stop learning and improving your mind, because if you do, you are going to be left behind.

4   "Lesson two is, assign yourself. Daddy used to ask us whether the teacher gave us any homework and if we said no, he said, well, assign yourself some. Do not wait around for somebody else to direct you to do what you are able to figure out and do for yourself. Do not do just as little as you can to get by.

5   "Do not be a political bystander or grumbler. Vote. Democracy is not a spectator sport. Run for political office. But when you do run and when you do win, don't begin to think that you or your reelection are the only point. If you see a need, do not ask, 'Why doesn't somebody do something?' Ask, 'Why don't I do something?' Hard work and persistence and initiative are still the non-magic carpets to success for most of us.

6   "Lesson three: Never work just for money. Money will not save your soul or build a decent family or help you sleep at night. We are the richest nation on earth with the highest incarceration rate and also with some of the highest drug addiction and child poverty rates in the world.

7   "Do not confuse wealth or fame with character. Do not tolerate or condone moral corruption or violence, whether it is found in high or low places, whatever its color or class. It is not okay to push drugs or to use them even if every person in America is doing it. It is not okay to cheat or to lie even if every public- and private-sector official you know does. Be honest and demand that those who represent you be honest. Do not confuse morality with legality. Dr. King once noted that everything Hitler did in Nazi Germany was legal. Do not give anyone the proxy for your conscience.

8   "Lesson four: Do not be afraid of taking risks or being criticized. If you do not want to be criticized, do not do anything, do not say anything, and do not be anything. Do not be afraid of failing. It is the way you learn to do things right. It doesn't matter how many times you fall down. All that matters is how many times you get up. Do not wait for everybody to come along to get something done. It is always a few people who get things done and keep things going.

9   "This country desperately needs more wise and courageous shepherds and fewer sheep who do not borrow from integrity to fund expediency.

10   "Lesson five: Take parenting and family life seriously, and insist that those you work for and who represent you also do so. Our nation mouths family values that we do not practice or honor in our policies.

11   "I hope that your generation will raise your sons to be fair to other people's daughters and share parenting responsibilities. I am the mother of three sons, so I have told them to 'share,' and not just help with, family life.

12   "I hope that you will stress family rituals and be moral examples for your children, because if you cut corners, they will too. If you lie, they will too. If you spend all of your money on yourself and tithe no portion of it for your university or civic

"The lust for comfort, that stealthy thing that enters the house a guest and then becomes a host, and then a master."

—Kahlillsibran

"To bring up a child in a way he should go, travel that way yourself once and a while."

—Josh Billings

causes or religious life, they will not either. If you tell racial or gender jokes or snicker at them, another generation will pass on the poison that our adult generation still does not have the courage to stop doing. Walk away from such jokes. Make them unacceptable in your presence.

13 "And let us not spend a lot of time uselessly pinning and denying blame rather than healing our divisions. Rabbi Abraham Heschel put it aptly when he said, 'We are not all equally guilty, but we are all equally responsible for building a decent and just America.'

14 "Lesson seven: Listen for the 'sound of the genuine' within yourself. Einstein said, 'Small is the number of them that see with their own eyes and feel with their own heart.' Try to be one of them.

15 "Howard Thurman, the great black theologian, said to my Spelman colleagues in Atlanta, Georgia, 'There is in every one of us something that waits and listens for the sound of the genuine in ourselves, and it is the only true guide you'll ever have. And if you cannot hear it, you will all of your life spend your days on the ends of strings that somebody else pulls.'

16 "You will find as you go out from this place so many noises and competing demands in your lives that many of you may never find out who you are. I hope that you will learn to be quiet enough to hear the sound of the genuine within your-self so that you can then hear it in other people.

"Knock the 't' off of the 'can't'."

—George Reeves

17 "Lesson eight: Never think life is not worth living or that you cannot make a difference. Never give up. I do not care how hard it gets; and it will get very hard sometimes. An old proverb reminds us that when you get to your wit's end, remember that is where God lives.

18 "Harriet Beecher Stowe said that when you get into a tight place and everything goes against you, till it seems as though you cannot hang on for another minute, never give up then, for that is just the place and the time the tide will turn.

19 "I do not care how bad the job market is. I do not care how hard the challenges seem to be. Hang in with life. And do not think you have to win or win immediately or even at all to make a difference. Sometimes it is important to lose for things that matter. And do not think you have to make a big difference to make America different.

20 "My role model was an illiterate slave woman, Sojourner Truth, who could not read or write, but she could not stand second-class treatment of women and she hated slavery. My favorite Sojourner story came one day when she was making a speech against slavery, and she got heckled by a man who stood up in the audi-ence and said, 'Old slave woman, I don't care any more about your antislavery talk than for an old fleabite.' And she snapped back and said, 'That's all right. The Lord willing, I'm going to keep you scratching.'

21 "So often we think we have got to make a big difference and be a big dog. Let us just try to be little fleas biting. Enough fleas biting strategically can make very big dogs very uncomfortable. I am convinced that together fleas for justice, and fleas in schools and religious congregations, and fleas in homes as parents com-mitted to a decent American society are going to transform our nation and make it un-American for any child to be poor or without health care in our rich land.

22 "Finally, let me just hope that you will understand that you cannot save your own children without trying to help save other people's children. They have got to walk the same streets. We have got to pass on to them a country that was better than the one that we inherited.

23 "What do you think would happen if every American, if every one of you, reached out and grabbed the hand of a child and committed yourself to seeing that no child is left behind? I hope that you will think about doing that, because everything that we hold dear as a people with faith depends on each of us committing to leaving no American child behind."

From *The Measure of Our Success* by Marian Wright Eldman, pp. 76–84. Copyright © 1992 by Marian Wright Eldman. Reprinted by permission of Beacon Press, Boston.

Comprehension Checkup

Multiple Choice

Write the letter of the correct answer in the blank provided.

_____ 1. Which of the following does Edelman consider key to career success?
   a. If you are special, someone will "discover" you.
   b. A good degree is all you need.
   c. Look at the big picture and ignore the details.
   d. Keep working hard.

_____ 2. Edelman would agree with which of the following?
   a. If someone asks you to do a task, and another task needs to be done as well, do both tasks without waiting to be asked.
   b. If you see a need, try to fill it.
   c. Don't do any more homework than you have to.
   d. Both a and b

_____ 3. With respect to parents and their children, Edelman would agree with which of the following statements?
   a. Parents should serve as moral role models for their children.
   b. Our nation takes family values seriously.
   c. Good parenting is not as important today as it was 50 years ago.
   d. Children are not likely to emulate their parents' attitudes and beliefs.

_____ 4. Edelman is passionate about
   a. trying hard and taking initiative
   b. the importance of leading a moral life
   c. protecting and helping children
   d. all of the above

_____ 5. Edelman mentioned in the excerpt that failure
   a. is to be avoided at all costs
   b. is the way that you learn to do things right
   c. is something you should be ashamed of
   d. is rarely experienced by successful people

_____ 6. Edelman would agree with which of the following?
   a. We should only care about our own children.
   b. How children are raised doesn't matter much for society.
   c. Our society should make a commitment to protecting and nurturing all of its children.
   d. How parents' behave doesn't have much affect on how their children behave.

_____ 7. Edelman is likely to admire those who
   a. spend all of their money on themselves
   b. donate money to charitable causes
   c. marry into money
   d. work hard to become powerful and famous

_____ 8. Edelman is likely to agree with which of the following?
   a. It's every man for himself.
   b. The end justifies the means.
   c. If corporate CEOs are lying, it's okay for you to lie as well.
   d. Lying and cheating to succeed are not acceptable.

True or False

Indicate whether the statement is true or false by writing T or F in the blank provided.

_____ 9. Edelman's role model was Sojourner Truth.

_____ 10. Edelman likely feels that one vote is relatively insignificant in the scheme of things.

_____ 11. Edelman agrees that people should try to avoid being criticized.

_____ 12. Edelman believes that something can be legal and still not be moral.

_____ 13. Edelman believes that it is important to listen to yourself.

_____ 14. Edelman believes that the easy path is the best one.

_____ 15. Edelman believes that the little contributions people make over time can make a big difference.

Vocabulary in Context

Look through the paragraph indicated in parentheses to find a word that matches the definition given below.

1. having a right or claim to something (paragraph 2) _____

2. confinement; imprisonment (6) _____

3. disregard; overlook; excuse (7) _____

4. power or agency to act for another (7) _____

5. just right; fittingly; appropriately (13) _____

6. a person who specializes in the study of divine things or religious truth (15) _____

7. associates; fellow members of a profession (15) _____

8. harassed with impertinent questions; shouting insults (20) _____

Choose one of the following words to complete the sentences below. Use each word only once. Be sure to pay close attention to the context clues provided.

| continuously | corruption | initiative | persistence | pinned |
| rituals | snickered | strategic | tide | tithe |

1. Despite many obstacles to her academic success, Estella refused to give in, and finally her _____ paid off with a $10,000 scholarship to the college of her choice.

2. Ruben took the _____ in collecting 10,000 signatures to get the proposal for a light-rail system on the ballot.

3. When Carrie got an F in English, she _____ the blame on everyone but herself.

4. Because she was _____ in pain from her leukemia, the doctor decided to try radiation as a palliative treatment.

5. Even though Marcus was on a fixed income, he was able to _____ a portion of his salary to his new church.

6. The audience _____ when the microphone went dead, but the politician continued with his speech completely unaware.

7. One of my daily _____ is a 45-minute walk with my friend Marilyn.

8. In many reality television shows, the players form _____ alliances in order to win.

9. The _____ turned against him, and he lost the election.

10. The new mayor's biggest job is to weed out _____ in govern-mental agencies.

Vocabulary in Context

Without using a dictionary, define the following phrases.

1. a political bystander (paragraph 5) _____

2. spectator sport (paragraph 5) _____

3. mouths family values (paragraph 10) _____

4. your wit's end (paragraph 17) _____

5. a tight place (paragraph 18) _____

6. hang in (paragraph 19) _____

7. second-class treatment (paragraph 20) _____

In Your Own Words

1. What is your personal reaction to each of Edelman's lessons? What do Edelman's lessons say about her as a person? What are Edelman's priorities in life?

2. The following is an excerpt from a speech given by President Theodore Roosevelt.

    "It is not the critic who counts;
    Not the man who points out
    Where the strong man stumbled,
    Or where the doer of great deeds
    Could have done them better.
    The credit belongs to the man
    Who is actually in the arena;
    Whose face is marred
    By dust and sweat and blood;
    Who strives valiantly;
    Who errs and comes up short
    Again and again;
    And who, while daring greatly;
    Spends himself in a worthy cause;
    So that his place may not be
    Among those cold and timid souls
    Who know neither victory nor defeat."

Which of Edelman's lessons does Roosevelt's speech support? In what ways is their advice the same?

The Art of Writing

1. Create a top-five list of suggestions of your own by drawing on knowledge that you learned the hard way. Include a short explanation for each of your choices. Try to give a personal anecdote illustrating each suggestion.

2. Colin Powell, secretary of state under George W. Bush, put together the following list of rules based on lessons he learned the hard way:

Colin Powell's Rules

1. It ain't as bad as you think. It will look better in the morning.

2. Get mad; then get over it.

3. Avoid having your ego so close to your position that when your position falls, your ego goes with it.

4. It can be done!

5. Be careful what you choose. You may get it.

6. Don't let adverse facts stand in the way of a good decision.

7. You can't make someone else's choices. You shouldn't let someone else make yours.

8. Check small things.

9. Share credit.

10. Remain calm. Be kind.

11. Have a vision. Be demanding.

12. Don't take counsel of your fears or naysayers.

13. Perpetual optimism is a force multiplier.

From Colin Powell, *My American Journey*, New York: Random House, 1995, p. 603. Copyright © 1995 Colin Powell. Used by permission of International Creative Management.

Write a paragraph explaining your reaction to each of Powell's rules. Write a description of Powell based on what these rules say about him.

Internet Activity

At the end of many reading selections, you will find one or more suggested Internet activities. Although we have checked each site, websites do come and go, and URLs change frequently. If the Internet site mentioned in the activity is no longer available, then use a search engine like Google <www.google.com> or Yahoo <www.yahoo.com> to find a similar site.

The website below gives you additional information about Marian Wright Edelman's background:

www.womenshistory.about.com

Visit this site, and then write a short paragraph about what you find interesting about Edelman's life.

Use a search engine like <www.google.com> or <www.yahoo.com> to locate information about one of the following individuals mentioned in Edelman's commencement speech: Sojourner Truth, Howard Thurman, Harriet Beecher Stowe, Dr. Martin Luther King, Jr., Albert Einstein, Rabbi Abraham Heschel.

What contributions did the individual you selected make to American society?

"The investigation of the meaning of words is the beginning of education."

—Antisthenes

Vocabulary Introduction

To be a successful college student, you need a college-level vocabulary. Improving your vocabulary will make you a better reader, speaker, and writer. Is there a painless way to improve your vocabulary? The answer is "No." Developing a college-level vocabulary requires effort. But there are some effective techniques that can help. These techniques are described below.

Context

When you come across an unfamiliar word in your reading, the first step you should take toward discovering its meaning is to look for context clues. The context of a word is what surrounds it and includes the sentence it appears in, other nearby sentences, or even the whole article. Try placing your finger over the unfamiliar word, and see if you can supply another word or phrase that gives the sentence meaning.

For example, see if you can figure out the meaning of the italicized word from the context of the sentence.

> Ellen's multiple sclerosis became increasingly *debilitating* to the point that she could no longer walk unaided and had to consider using a wheelchair.

You could go to the dictionary to look up the definition of *debilitating,* but you can probably guess from context clues that *debilitating,* at least as it appears in this sentence, means "to make feeble or weak."

Remember that if you are reading a light novel for enjoyment, the exact meaning of a word may not be as important as when you are reading a textbook.

Structure

The Greeks and Romans devised a system for creating words by putting together smaller word parts. To the main part of the word, which is called the root, they attached prefixes, which come before the root, and suffixes, which come after it.

This way of building words allows you to discover the meaning of a word by breaking it down into its parts. Knowing the meaning of the word's parts should help you decipher the word's meaning. Let's try an example:

> As a confirmed *misogamist,* it was unlikely Barry would be making a trip to the altar anytime soon.

The word *misogamist* has in it the word parts *mis* and *gam. Mis* means "hate" and *gam* means "marriage." So a *misogamist* is someone who hates marriage, or matrimony. In Chapter 14, we have included eight vocabulary units that familiarize you with more than a hundred word parts.

Dictionary

Often when people come across a word they don't know, their first impulse is to look it up in the dictionary. But this should be your last recourse for determining the meaning of a word. It's best first to try to determine a general meaning of the word by paying attention to context clues and word structure. If these techniques don't give you a sure enough sense of what the word means, then go to the dictionary to confirm or clarify the meaning. In the dictionary, you may find several different definitions for a particular word. You need to pick the one that fits the word in its sentence. Context clues will help you pick the right definition. For example, say that in your reading you come across the following sentence, and you don't know what the word *steep* means.

> To make good sun tea, you need to *steep* several tea bags in a large jar of water out in the sun for several hours.

You look *steep* up in your dictionary and find several definitions. The first definition may be "having an almost vertical slope." The second definition may be "unduly high; exorbitant." But it is the third definition, "to soak in a liquid," that seems to fit. So now you know that to make sun tea, you must let the tea bags soak in water.

Combination

In trying to determine the meaning of an unfamiliar word, you may need to employ all of these techniques in combination. Take the following example:

> Because of his *premonition* that he would not live to see his eighty-third birthday, he made the effort to say good-bye to all of his loved ones.

Look at the context, which suggests that the word has something to do with thoughts or feelings about the future. Now look at the word parts. *Pre* means "before" and *mon* means "warn." Now you are getting closer to the meaning in this sentence. The word *premonition* as used here has a meaning similar to "forewarning." Now go to the dictionary. You will find the definitions "impression that something evil is about to happen" as well as "strong feeling or prediction." Now you have a better grasp of what the word means. The man had a strong feeling warning him that he would be dead before his eighty-third birthday.

Homonyms

As part of our vocabulary study, we will also learn about homonyms. Although homonyms are not a technique for discovering the meaning of an unfamiliar word, we discuss them because misuse of homonyms is common. *Homo* means "same" and *nym* means "name." So homonyms are words or phrases with the same "name" or pronunciation, but different spellings or meanings.

Look at the following sentence:

> Because Tomoko *already* knows all of her colors and shapes and most of the letters of the alphabet, I'd say she's *all ready* for kindergarten.

In this example, *already* means "previously," and *all ready* means "completely prepared." People often confuse these two homonyms, as they do other homonyms. In the two sections on homonyms, you will learn how to use many homonyms correctly.

Verbal Analogies

A verbal analogy is an equation that uses words instead of numbers. Many standardized tests have sections that feature verbal analogies. Verbal analogies test not only your knowledge of vocabulary words, but also your ability to see relationships between words and the concepts the words represent. The verbal analogies in this text are presented in the following format:

> A : B :: C : D

This is read as "A is to B as C is to D." Here is a sample verbal analogy.

> day : night :: light : dark

This is read as "day is to night as light is to dark." The analogy indicates that the relationship between *day* and *night* and the relationship between *light* and *dark* are the same. The relationship is one of opposition. *Day* is the opposite of *night*, and *light* is the opposite of *dark*.

In this book, questions for verbal analogies will look like this:

day : night :: light : _____.

Your job is to find the word that fits into the blank. Here the answer is *dark*.

Word analogies can involve many kinds of relationships. Some common relationships that appear in word analogies are synonym, antonym, and cause-and-effect. Each vocabulary unit will introduce a new kind of word analogy. As we progress through the vocabulary units, the word analogies will become more difficult.

Thesaurus

A thesaurus, a special kind of word book organized by categories, enables you to refine your writing by helping you select precisely the right word for any given situation. Many of us use the same word over and over because we cannot think of an appropriate synonym. A thesaurus gives synonyms for the most common nouns, verbs, adjectives, and adverbs in the English language. In the following sentence, you can choose from any of the italicized synonyms to convey your meaning more precisely.

> As the famous fashion model made her way down the runway, the audience noted that she was extremely *slender, slim, svelte, lithe, skinny, lean, thin.*

You will learn about using a thesaurus in the appendix.

"The difference between the right word and the almost right word is the difference between lightning and the lightning bug."

—Mark Twain

Optimism and Success

According to Martin Seligman, a University of Pennsylvania psychologist, how people respond to setbacks—optimistically or pessimistically—is a good indicator of how well they will succeed in school, sports, and certain kinds of work. To test his theory, Seligman devised a questionnaire to screen insurance salesmen at the Metropolitan Life Insurance Company. Job applicants were asked to imagine a hypothetical event and then choose the response (A or B) that most closely resembled their own. Some samples from his questionnaire:

1. **You forgot your spouse's (boyfriend's/girlfriend's) birthday.**
   A. I'm not good at remembering birthdays.
   B. I was preoccupied with other things.
2. **You owe the library $10 for an overdue book.**
   A. When I am really involved in what I am reading, I often forget when it's due.
   B. I was so involved in writing the report I forgot to return the book.
3. **You lose your temper with a friend.**
   A. He or she is always nagging me.
   B. He or she was in a hostile mood.
4. **You are penalized for returning your income-tax forms late.**
   A. I always put off doing my taxes.
   B. I was lazy about getting my taxes done this year.
5. **You've been feeling run-down.**
   A. I never get a chance to relax.
   B. I was exceptionally busy this week.

6. **A friend says something that hurts your feelings.**
   A. She always blurts things out without thinking of others.
   B. My friend was in a bad mood and took it out on me.
7. **You fall down a great deal while skiing.**
   A. Skiing is difficult.
   B. The trails were icy.
8. **You gain weight over the holidays and can't lose it.**
   A. Diets don't work in the long run.
   B. The diet I tried didn't work.

Seligman found that insurance salesmen who answered with more Bs than As were better able to overcome bad sales days, recovered more easily from rejection, and were less likely to quit. In short, they were more optimistic. People with an optimistic view of life tend to treat obstacles and setbacks as temporary (and therefore surmountable). Pessimists take them personally; what others see as fleeting, localized impediments, they view as pervasive and permanent.

Optimism does have a downside, though. Unrealistic optimism can make people believe they are invulnerable and keep them from taking sensible steps to avoid danger. The recipe for well-being includes optimism to provide hope, a dash of pessimism to prevent complacency, and enough realism to understand the difference between those things we can control and those we can't.

From Martin E.P. Seligman, *Learned Optimism*. Copyright © 1991 by Martin E.P. Seligman. Used by permission of Alfred A. Knopf, a division of Random House, Inc.

Is Fred Basset an optimist or a pessimist?

Copyright © 2002 Tribune Media Services, Inc. Reprinted with permission.

Is it better for a student to be an optimist or a pessimist? Why?

SELECTION

Excerpt from *Lucky Man*   *by Michael J. Fox*

"These last ten years of coming to terms with my disease would turn out to be the best ten years of my life—not in spite of the illness, but because of it."

Getting the Picture

The following excerpt from Michael J. Fox's book, entitled *Lucky Man*, expresses Fox's optimistic spirit after being told that he had been diagnosed with Parkinson's disease. The book, published in 2002, describes how he learned to cope with Parkinson's disease and how he accepted the illness as a challenge and a positive factor in his life. Fox is an example of a person who sees a glass as being half-full rather than as half-empty.

Bio-sketch

Born Michael Andrew Fox in 1961 (Edmonton, Canada), Fox later added the "J" to his name in honor of actor Michael J. Pollard. Fox grew up loving hockey and even had dreams of one day playing the sport in the National Hockey League. Later, though, after experimenting with writing, art, and playing the guitar in rock-and-roll bands, he came to realize that he loved acting.

His first paid acting job was co-starring in a sit-com for the Canadian Broadcasting Corporation. At 18, he moved to Los Angeles and took a series of bit parts before winning the role of Alex P. Keaton on *Family Ties* in 1981. After earning three Emmy Awards and a Golden Globe award for his performances in that role, he left the show in 1989. Although diagnosed with Parkinson's Disease in 1991, Fox continued his acting career, starring in the TV show *Spin City* as well as in several films, including *Back to the Future, Doc Hollywood,* and *The American President.* He disclosed his condition in 1998 and retired from *Spin City* in 2000.

Although still strongly committed to acting, Fox has shifted most of his energies to the Michael J. Fox Foundation for Parkinson's Research, which he founded in 2000. He hopes the foundation can discover the cause and find a cure for Parkinson's disease by 2010.

Brushing Up on Vocabulary

Parkinson's disease   According to the Michael J. Fox Foundation's website, Parkinson's is a "chronic, progressive disorder of the central nervous system . . . Parkinson's disease has been known since ancient times. An English doctor, James Parkinson, first described it extensively in 1817. Symptoms of Parkinson's may include tremors or trembling, difficulty maintaining balance and gait, rigidity or stiffness of the limbs and trunk, and general slowness of movement." The cause of the disease is still unknown, as is the ability to predict who will get it.

missive   a written message or letter, originally from the Latin *missus,* meaning "send."

geek   a strange or eccentric person, probably from the Scottish word *geck,* meaning "fool."

A Wake Up Call   *Gainesville, Florida—November 1990*

1 I woke up to find the message in my left hand. It had me trembling. It wasn't a fax, telegram, memo, or the usual sort of missive bringing disturbing news. In fact, my hand held nothing at all. The trembling was the message.

2 I was feeling a little disoriented. I'd only been shooting the movie in Florida for a week or so, and the massive, pink-lacquered, four-poster bed surrounded by the pastel hues of the University Center Hotel's Presidential Suite still came as a bit of a shock each morning. Oh yeah: and I had a ferocious hangover. That was less shocking.

3 Even with the lights off, blinds down, and drapes pulled, an offensive amount of light still filtered into the room. Eyes clenched shut, I placed the palm of my left hand across the bridge of my nose in a weak attempt to block the glare. A moth's

wing—or so I thought—fluttered against my right cheek. I opened my eyes, keeping my hand suspended an inch or two in front of my face so I could finger-flick the little beastie across the room. That's when I noticed my pinkie. It was trembling, twitching, auto-animated. How long this had been going on I wasn't exactly sure. But now that I noticed it, I was surprised to discover that I couldn't stop it.

4   *Weird—maybe I slept on it funny.* Five or six times in rapid succession I pumped my left hand into a fist, followed by a vigorous shaking out. Interlocking the fingers of each hand steeple-style with their opposite number, I lifted them up and over behind my head and pinned them to the pillow.

5   Tap. Tap. Tap. Like a moisture-free Chinese water torture, I could feel a gentle drumming at the back of my skull. If it was trying to get my attention, it had succeeded. I withdrew my left hand from behind my head and held it in front of my face, steadily, with fingers splayed—like the bespectacled X-ray glasses geek in the old comic book ad. I didn't have to see the underlying skeletal structure; the information I was looking for was right there in the flesh: a thumb, three stock-still fingers, and out there on the lunatic fringe, a spastic pinkie.

6   It occurred to me that this might have something to do with my hangover, or more precisely with alcohol. I'd put away a lot of beers in my time, but had never woken up with the shakes; maybe this was what they called delirium tremens? I was pretty sure they would manifest themselves in a more impressive way—I mean, who gets the d.t.'s in one finger? Whatever this was, it wasn't alcoholic deterioration.

7   Now I did a little experimentation. I found that if I grabbed my finger with my right hand, it would stop moving. Released, it would keep still for four or five seconds, and then, like a cheap wind-up toy, it would whir back to life again. *Hmmm.* What had begun as a curiosity was now blossoming into full-fledge worry. The trembling had been going on for a few minutes with no sign of quitting and my brain, fuzzy as it was, scrambled to come up with an explanation. Had I hit my head, injured myself in some way? The tape of the previous night's events was grainy at best. But I didn't feel any bumps. Any pain in my head was from boozing, not bruising.

IRRECONCILABLE DIFFERENCES

8   Throughout the course of the morning, the twitching would intensify, as would my search for a cause—not just for the rest of that day, but for months to follow. The true answer was elusive, and in fact wouldn't reveal itself for another full year. The trembling was indeed the message, and this is what it was telling me:

9   *That morning—November 13, 1990—my brain was serving notice: it had initiated a divorce from my mind. Efforts to contest or reconcile would be futile; eighty percent of the process, I would later learn, was already complete. No grounds were given, and the petition was irrevocable. Further, my brain was demanding, and incrementally seizing, custody of my body, beginning with the baby: the outermost finger of my left hand.*

10   Ten years later, knowing what I do now, this mind-body divorce strikes me as a serviceable metaphor—though at the time it was a concept well beyond my grasp. I had no idea there were even problems in the relationship—just assumed things were pretty good between the old gray matter and me. This was a false assumption. Unbeknownst to me, things had been deteriorating long before the morning of the pinkie rebellion. But by declaring its dysfunction in such an arresting manner, my brain now had my mind's full attention.

11   It would be a year of questions and false answers that would satisfy me for a time, fueling my denial and forestalling the sort of determined investigation that would ultimately provide the answer. That answer came from a doctor who would

12   inform me that I had a progressive, degenerative, and incurable neurological disorder; one that I may have been living with for as long as a decade before suspecting there might be anything wrong. This doctor would also tell me that I could probably continue acting for another "ten good years," and he would be right about that, almost to the day. What he did not tell me—what no one could—is that these last ten years of coming to terms with my disease would turn out to be the best ten years of my life—not in spite of my illness, but because of it.

    I have referred to it in interviews as a *gift*—something for which others with this affliction have taken me to task. I was only speaking from my own experience, of course, but I stand partially corrected: if it is a gift, it's the gift that just keeps on taking.

13   Coping with this relentless assault and the accumulating damage is not easy. Nobody would ever choose to have this visited upon them. Still, this unexpected crisis forced a fundamental life decision: adopt a siege mentality—or embark upon a journey. Whatever it was—courage? acceptance? wisdom?—that finally allowed me to go down the second road (after spending a few disastrous years on the first) was unquestionably a gift—and absent this neurophysiological catastrophe, I would never have opened it, or been so profoundly enriched. That's why I consider myself a lucky man.

Comprehension Checkup

Multiple-Choice

Write the letter of the correct answer in the blank.

_____ 1. The reader may conclude that Michael J. Fox
    a. knew immediately that he had Parkinson's disease
    b. initially thought that he might have slept on his finger in an awkward position
    c. thought that his finger was trembling because he had been drinking alcohol to excess
    d. both b and c

_____ 2. Which of the following is true about what doctors told Fox?
    a. A doctor told Fox that he would only be able to continue acting for a few more months.
    b. A doctor told Fox that he had just 10 years to live.
    c. A doctor told Fox that he had an incurable neurological disorder.
    d. None of the above

_____ 3. Which of the following is true about Fox's reaction to his disease?
    a. He quickly adopted a siege mentality that has stayed with him for 10 years.
    b. He has always been cheerful about his disease.
    c. He now views his disease as a complete catastrophe.
    d. He now sees his disease as a special sort of gift.

_____ 4. What does Fox mean when he says, "I woke up to find the message in my left hand"?
    a. A friend had placed a letter in his left hand while he was sleeping.
    b. He awoke to find his left hand clutching a beer bottle.
    c. The trembling finger of his left hand was telling him something.
    d. His left hand was swollen from an unknown trauma that must have happened the night before.

_____ 5. What does Fox mean when he says, "my brain was demanding and incrementally seizing custody of my body"?
  a. His brain was starting to do things to his body that he could not stop.
  b. His brain was no longer obeying his wishes and demands.
  c. His condition was gradually getting worse.
  d. All of the above.

_____ 6. When Fox states that "efforts to contest or reconcile would be futile," he means that
  a. there is nothing he can do about the situation
  b. the situation is shocking
  c. given time and work the situation can be ameliorated
  d. both a and b

_____ 7. The overall feeling expressed in this selection could best be described as
  a. acceptance
  b. puzzlement
  c. bitterness
  d. despair

_____ 8. Which of the following proverbs best expresses the main idea of the selection?
  a. The bigger they are the harder they fall.
  b. Blood is thicker than water.
  c. When the cat's away the mice will play.
  d. Every cloud has a silver lining.

_____ 9. What does Fox do directly after he discovers his twitching little finger?
  a. makes a fist and then shakes out his fingers
  b. places his fingers behind his head
  c. spreads his fingers out in front of his face
  d. grabs his left finger with his right hand

_____ 10. Which of the following expresses how the author feels?
  a. Too much light was coming into the room.
  b. The unfamiliar surroundings were making him confused.
  c. Coming to terms with his disease has been a positive in his life.
  d. All of the above.

_____ 11. What implications does the phrase "mind-brain divorce" have for Fox?
  a. The mind is something different from the brain.
  b. His mind and brain had once cooperated well, but now were no longer doing so.
  c. When his mind tells his brain to make his body stop shaking, his brain does not obey.
  d. All of the above.

_____ 12. What are some of the things that Fox means when he calls his disease a "gift"?
  a. He means that it has brought only happiness in his life.
  b. He means that from his personal perspective it has been a gift.
  c. He means that it gave him the opportunity to begin a journey that has enriched his life.
  d. both b and c

True or False

Indicate whether the statement is true or false by writing T or F in the blank provided.

_____   1.   A doctor felt that Fox may have had Parkinson's disease for 10 years prior to its discovery.

_____   2.   Fox discovered his trembling when he was in the University Center Hospital.

_____   3.   Fox's finger kept moving when he held it.

_____   4.   Fox often woke up shaking after drinking.

_____   5.   Fox searched for a cause for his dysfunction for many months.

Vocabulary in Context

Determine the meaning of the following words from the context without using a dictionary. (The paragraph in which the word appears in the reading selection is indicated in parentheses.) Write your answers in your own words in the space provided.

1.   offensive (paragraph 3) _____

2.   pinkie (3) _____

3.   auto-animated (3) _____

4.   fuzzy (7) _____

5.   dysfunction (10) _____

6.   arresting (10) _____

7.   affliction (12) _____

In Your Own Words

Psychotherapist Alan McGinnis, author of *Power of Optimism*, says that optimists see themselves as "problem solvers and trouble shooters." According to McGinnis, the following qualities help optimists maintain a positive attitude while still being realistic:

- They look for partial solutions.
- They believe they have control over their future.
- They interrupt their negative trains of thought.
- They heighten their powers of appreciation.
- They are cheerful even when they can't be happy.
- They accept what cannot be changed.

In what ways has Michael J. Fox demonstrated the characteristics of an optimist?

The Art of Writing

In a brief essay respond to one of the following quotes:

1.   "Courage is resistance to fear, mastery of fear—not absence of fear." —Mark Twain

2.   "Courage is the price that life exacts for granting peace. The soul that knows it not, knows no release." —Amelia Earhart

What do you think the author means? Do you agree? Why or why not? How does the quote apply to the situation that Michael J. Fox faced?

Internet Activity

For information about Parkinson's disease and the Michael J. Fox Foundation for Parkinson's Research, go to its website:

> www.michaeljfox.org

Based on what you read there, write a paragraph about what's new in Parkinson's research.

Two other organizations dealing with Parkinson's are

- The Parkinson's Disease Foundation, www.pdf.org
- The National Parkinson Foundation, www.parkinson.org

Go to the website of one of these organizations, and write a paragraph about its mission and activities.

SELECTION

Excerpt from *Understanding Psychology*   *by Dennis Coon*

"Critical thinkers analyze the evidence supporting their beliefs and probe for weaknesses in their reasoning."

Getting the Picture

To succeed as a college student, you will need to be able to read, write, and think critically. The following selection from a popular introductory psychology textbook defines the process of critical thinking.

Bio-sketch

After earning a doctorate in psychology from the University of Arizona, Dennis Coon taught for 22 years at Santa Barbara City College in California. He recently returned to Tucson, Arizona, to teach, write, edit, and consult. Although he has written two college textbooks that have been used by two million students, his real passion is teaching introductory psychology classes.

Brushing Up on Vocabulary

empirical testing   gathering verifiable information from experience or experiments.

guru   a leader or person with some authority and respect. Originally a *guru* was a Hindu spiritual leader or guide.

anecdotal evidence   information gathered about a person through a series of observations rather than through systematic research. Teachers often collect anecdotal information about their students through firsthand observation.

Critical Thinking—Uncommon Sense

"Thought is the strongest thing we have. Work done by true and profound thought—that is a real force."

—Albert Schweitzer

1   Most of us would be skeptical when buying a used car. But all too often, we may be tempted to "buy" outrageous claims about topics such as "channeling," dowsing, the occult, the Bermuda Triangle, hypnosis, UFOs, numerology, and so forth. Likewise, most of us easily accept our ignorance of subatomic physics. But because we deal with human behavior every day, we tend to think that we already know what is true and what is false.

2   For these, and many more reasons, learning to think critically is one of the lasting benefits of getting an education. Facts and theories may change. Thinking and problem-solving skills last a lifetime.

3   In the broadest terms, **critical thinking** *refers to an ability to evaluate, compare, analyze, critique, and synthesize information.* Critical thinkers are willing to ask hard questions and challenge conventional wisdom. For example, many people believe that punishment (a spanking) is a good way to reinforce learning in children. A critical thinker would immediately ask: "Does punishment work? If so, when? Under what conditions does it not work? What are its drawbacks? Are there better ways to guide learning?"

4   The core of critical thinking is a willingness to actively evaluate ideas. It is, in a sense, the ability to stand outside yourself and reflect on the quality of your own thoughts. Critical thinkers analyze the evidence supporting their beliefs and probe for weaknesses in their reasoning. They question assumptions and look for alternate conclusions. True knowledge, they recognize, comes from constantly revising and enlarging our understanding of the world.

5   Critical thinking is built upon four basic principles:

6   1. *Few "truths" transcend the need for empirical testing.* It is true that religious beliefs and personal values may be held without supporting evidence. But most other ideas can be evaluated by applying the rules of logic and evidence.

7   2. *Evidence varies in quality.* Judging the quality of evidence is crucial. Imagine that you are a juror in a courtroom, judging claims made by two battling lawyers. To judge correctly, you can't just weigh the evidence. You must also critically evaluate the *quality* of the evidence. Then you can give greater weight to the most credible facts.

8   3. *Authority or claimed expertise does not automatically make an idea true.* Just because a teacher, guru, celebrity, or authority is convinced or sincere doesn't mean you should automatically believe them. It is unscientific and self-demeaning to just take the word of an "expert" without asking, "What evidence convinced him or her? How good is it? Is there a better explanation?"

9   4. *Critical thinking requires an open mind.* Be prepared to consider daring departures and go wherever the evidence leads. However, it is possible to be so "open-minded" that you simply become gullible. Critical thinkers try to strike a balance between open-mindedness and healthy skepticism. Being open-minded means that you consider all possibilities before drawing a conclusion; it is the ability to change your views under the impact of new and more convincing evidence.

A CASE STUDY OF CRITICAL THINKING

10   An anxious mother watches her son eat a candy bar and says, "Watch, it's like lighting a fuse on a firecracker. He'll be bouncing off the walls in a few minutes." Is she right? Will a "sugar buzz" make her son "hyper"? Does eating excessive amounts of

sugar adversely affect children's behavior? What are the implications of this claim? If it is true, children who eat sugar should display measurable changes in behavior.

11   *Anecdotal Evidence.*   What evidence is there to support the claim? It should be easy to find parents who will attest that their children become high-strung, inattentive, or unruly after eating sugar. However, parents are not likely to be objective observers. Beliefs about "sugar highs" are common and could easily color parents' views.

12   *Casual Observations.*   Perhaps it would help to observe children directly. Let's say you decide to watch children at a birthday party, where you know large amounts of sugary foods will be consumed. As predicted by the claim, children at the party become loud and boisterous after eating cake, ice cream, and candy. How persuasive is this evidence? Actually, it is seriously flawed. Birthday parties expose children to bright lights, loud noises, and unfamiliar situations. Any of these conditions, and others as well, could easily explain the children's "hyper" activity.

13   *Authority.*   For nearly 50 years, many doctors, teachers, nutritionists, and other "experts" have emphatically stated that sugar causes childhood misbehavior. Should you believe them? Unfortunately, most of these "expert" opinions are based on anecdotes and casual observations that are little better than those we have already reviewed.

14   *Formal Evidence.*   The truth is, parents, casual observers, and many authorities have been wrong. Dr. Mark Wolraich and his colleagues recently reviewed 23 scientific studies on sugar and children. In each study, children consumed known amounts of sugar and were then observed or tested. The clear-cut conclusion in all of the studies was that sugar does not affect aggression, mood, motor skills, or cognitive skills.

15   Studies like those we just reviewed tend to be convincing because they are based on systematic, controlled observation. But don't just accept the investigators' conclusions. It is important to review the evidence yourself and decide if it is convincing.

From Dennis Coon, *Introduction to Psychology: Gateways to Mind and Behavior,* 9th ed., pp. 23–25. © 2001. Reprinted with permission of Wadsworth, a division of Thomson Learning: **www.thomsonrights.com.** Fax 800-730-2215.

Comprehension Checkup

Fill in the blanks with details from the selection.

1.   Critical thinking refers to an ability to evaluate, compare, analyze, _____, and synthesize information.

2.   The core of critical thinking is a willingness to actively _____ ideas.

3.   _____ testing is needed to evaluate most ideas.

4.   The quality of the _____ must be critically evaluated.

5.   Even the evidence of an _____ must be evaluated.

6.   Critical thinkers must keep an open _____.

7.   The problem with anecdotal evidence is that people are not _____ observers.

8.   Casual _____ is not always reliable.

9.   An authority might want to offer an expert _____.

10.   You should _____ the evidence yourself to determine if it is convincing.

My Uncle Terwilliger on the Art of Eating Popovers   *by Dr. Seuss*

The late Theodore Seuss Geisel (1904–1991) was known to millions of readers (adult as well as children) as Dr. Seuss. In his lifetime, he wrote and illustrated over forty books, many of which are children's classics. Among the best known are *Horton Hears a Who, Hop on Pop, How the Grinch Stole Christmas,* and, of course, *The Cat in the Hat.* Critics praised his books, saying that he dispensed "nonsense with sense." After reading the poem below, explain the meaning in your own words. How does the poem relate to the previous selection?

My uncle ordered popovers
from the restaurant's bill of fare.
And, when they were served,
  he regarded them
with a penetrating stare. . .
Then he spoke great Words of Wisdom
as he sat there on that chair:
"To eat these things," said my uncle,
"you must exercise great care.
You may swallow down what's solid. . .
BUT . . . you must spit out the air!"

And . . . as you partake of the world's
  bill of fare,
that's darned good advice to follow.
Do a lot of spitting out the hot air.
And be careful what you swallow.

_____

_____

_____

_____

Life in College and Beyond

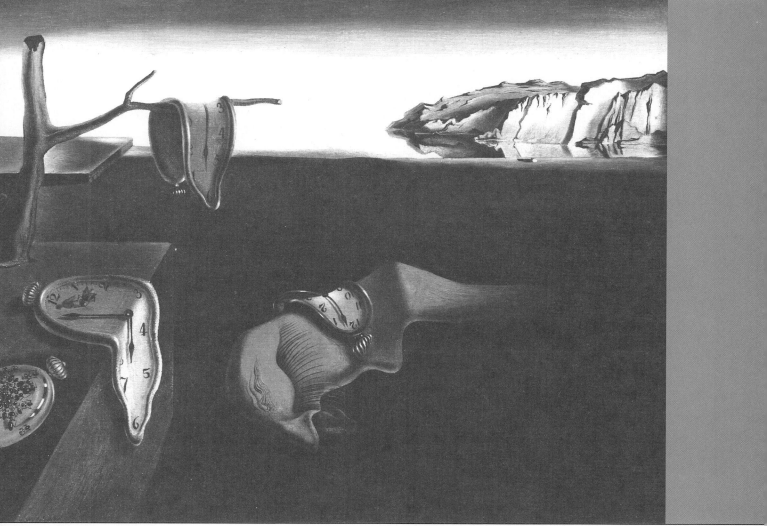

The Persistence of Memory, (1931)*

BY SALVADOR DALI

*To see this work of art in color, turn to the color insert following page 260.

1   What is your initial response to the painting? What overall impression does it create?

2   What do you think the limp or melting timepieces are meant to convey to the viewer? The landscape? The figure in the right foreground? What does the combination of elements in the painting suggest?

3   Answer the who, what, where, when, why, and how questions about this painting. Is there a main idea uniting these key details?

Portrait of a Successful Student (continued)

(continued)

STUDY TECHNIQUE 1

Underlining, Highlighting, Annotating

As you work through this book (and as you proceed through college), you will be introduced to a wide variety of reading selections. **Underlining or highlighting** important words or phrases in these selections will help you remember the authors' key points. When underlining or highlighting, be careful not to overdo. The goal is to mark just the important points to save you from having to reread. **Annotating,** another technique for helping you remember what you're reading, is particularly useful when reading textbook material. When you annotate, you write notes to yourself, often in the margins of the book. You might write down abbreviations or symbols to identify key ideas or terms. A list of things you might want to identify, with suggested abbreviations, appears in the next column.

> MI (main idea)
> T (thesis)
> S (summary)
> Ex (example)
> Def (definition)
> ? (questions, needs clarification)
> * (important point)
> KV (key vocabulary)

SELECTION

Excerpt from **Concepts in Health**   *by Paul M. Insel and Walton T. Roth*

"Respond ineffectively to stress, and eventually it will take a toll on your sense of wellness."

Getting the Picture

In this selection from a popular health textbook you are going to learn about stress and how you can lower it. After reading the bio-sketch and vocabulary sections, you will practice marking and annotating a section of a textbook. Look at the sample margin notes and underlining in the first section of the reading selection below, and follow this example in marking and annotating the remainder of the textbook material on stress.

Bio-sketch

Both writers of this textbook teach at the Stanford University Medical School. Paul M. Insel is an adjunct clinical associate professor in the Department of Psychiatry and Behavioral Sciences and Walton T. Roth is a professor of psychiatry and behavioral medicine. Roth is also the chief of psychiatric consultation services at the Veterans Administration Medical Center in Palo Alto.

Brushing Up on Vocabulary

hippocampus   a lower portion of the brain that consolidates short-term memories into long-term memories.

biological predispositions   tendencies or inclinations based on biology rather than background or experience.

STRESS: THE CONSTANT CHALLENGE

Ex As a college student, you may be in one of the most stressful periods of your life.
Ex You may be on your own for the first time, or you may be juggling the demands of college with the responsibilities of a job, a family, or both. Financial pressures
Ex may be intense. Housing and transportation may be sources of additional hassles.
Ex You're also meeting new people, engaging in new activities, learning new information and skills, and setting a new course for your life. Good and bad, all these changes and challenges are likely to have a powerful effect on you both physically and psychologically. Respond ineffectively to stress, and eventually it will take a toll
MI on your sense of wellness. Learn effective responses, however, and you will enhance your health and gain a feeling of control over your life.

TEST YOUR KNOWLEDGE

_____ 1. Which of the following events can cause stress?
a. taking out a loan
b. failing a test
c. graduating from college
d. watching a hockey game

_____ 2. True or false: About twice as many male college students as female college students report feeling frequently overwhelmed.

_____ 3. True or false: High levels of stress can impair memory and cause physical changes in the brain.

_____ 4. Which of the following may be caused or aggravated by stress?
a. headaches
b. irritable bowel syndrome
c. insomnia
d. high blood pressure

ANSWERS

1. *All four.* Stress-producing factors can be pleasant or unpleasant and can indicate physical challenges and the achievement of personal goals as well as what would commonly be perceived as negative events.

2. *False.* In recent surveys, about 20 percent of male and 40 percent of female college students report feeling frequently overwhelmed. Female college students are more likely to report financial worries, and they spend more time in potentially stress-producing activities such as volunteer work, housework, and child care.

3. *True.* Low levels of stress may improve memory, but high stress levels impair learning and memory and, over the long term, may shrink an area of the brain called the hippocampus.

4. *All four.* Stress—interacting with heredity, personality, social environment, and behavior—increases one's vulnerability to many health problems.

Everybody talks about stress. People say they're "overstressed" or "stressed out." They may blame stress for headaches or ulcers, and they may try to combat stress with aerobic classes—or drugs. But what is stress? And why is it important to manage it wisely?

Most people associate stress with negative events: the death of a close relative or friend, financial problems, or other unpleasant life changes that create nervous tension. But stress isn't merely nervous tension. And it isn't something to be avoided

MI—Stress usually associated with neg. events

at all costs. In fact, only death brings complete freedom from stress. Consider this list of common stressful situations or events.

- Interviewing for a job
- Running in a race
- Being accepted to college
- Going out on a date
- Watching a baseball game
- Getting a promotion

MI—Can be related to physical challenges, pers. goals

Obviously stress doesn't arise just from unpleasant situations. Stress can also be associated with physical challenges and the achievement of personal goals. Physical and psychological stress-producing factors can be pleasant or unpleasant. The actions you take in response to stress are influenced by your biological predispositions, past experiences, and current circumstances. While you cannot change who you are or what you've been through in the past, you *can* modify your current behavior and seek out people, places, and experiences that will improve your ability to deal with stress. In other words, what is crucial is how you respond, whether in positive, life-enhancing ways or in negative, counterproductive ways.

Can modify your behavior

WHAT IS STRESS?

Just what is stress, if such vastly different situations can cause it? In common usage, "stress" refers to two different things: situations that trigger physical and emotional reactions *and* the reactions themselves. We'll be using the more precise term **stressor** for situations that trigger physical and emotional reactions and the term **stress response** for those reactions. A date and a final exam, then, are stressors; sweaty palms and a pounding heart are symptoms of the stress response. We'll use the term **stress** to describe the general physical and emotional state that accompanies the stress response. A person on a date or taking a final exam experiences stress.

Each individual's experience of stress depends on many factors, including the nature of the stressor and how the stressor is perceived. Responses to stressors include physical changes and emotional and behavioral responses.

HOW HIGH IS YOUR STRESS LEVEL?

Many symptoms of excess stress are easy to self-diagnose. To help determine how much stress you experience on a daily basis, answer the following questions:

1. Are you easily startled or irritated?
2. Are you increasingly forgetful?
3. Do you have trouble falling or staying asleep?
4. Do you continually worry about events in your future?
5. Do you feel as if you are constantly under pressure to produce?
6. Do you frequently use tobacco, alcohol, or other drugs to help you relax?
7. Do you often feel as if you have less energy than you need to finish the day?
8. Do you have recurrent stomachaches or headaches?
9. Is it difficult for you to find satisfaction in simple life pleasures?
10. Are you often disappointed in yourself and others?

11. Are you overly concerned with being liked or accepted by others?

12. Are you concerned that you do not have enough money?

Experiencing some of the stress-related symptoms or answering "yes" to a few questions is normal. However, if you experience a large number of stress symptoms or you answered "yes" to a majority of the questions, you are likely experiencing a high level of stress. Take time out to develop effective stress-management techniques. Your school's counseling center can provide valuable support.

SYMPTOMS OF EXCESS STRESS

Physical Symptoms	Emotional Symptoms	Behavioral Symptoms
Dry mouth	Anxiety or edginess	Crying
Excessive perspiration	Depression	Disrupted eating habits
Frequent illnesses	Fatigue	Disrupted sleeping habits
Gastrointestinal problems	Hypervigilance	Harsh treatment of others
Grinding of teeth	Impulsiveness	Increased use of tobacco, alcohol, or other drugs
Headaches	Inability to concentrate	
High blood pressure	Irritability	Problems communicating
Pounding heart	Trouble remembering things	Social isolation

MIND/BODY/SPIRIT HEALTHY CONNECTIONS

Meaningful connections with others can play a key role in stress management and overall wellness. A sense of isolation can lead to chronic stress, which in turn can increase one's susceptibility to temporary illnesses like colds and to chronic illnesses like heart disease. Although the mechanism isn't clear, social isolation can be as significant to mortality rates as factors like smoking, high blood pressure, and obesity.

There is no single best pattern of social support that works for everyone. However, research suggests that having a variety of types of relationships may be important for wellness. To help determine whether your social network measures up, circle whether each of the following statements is true or false for you.

T F 1. If I needed an emergency loan of $100, there is someone I could get it from.

T F 2. There is someone who takes pride in my accomplishments.

T F 3. I often meet or talk with family or friends.

T F 4. Most people I know think highly of me.

T F 5. If I needed an early morning ride to the airport, there's no one I would feel comfortable asking to take me.

T F 6. I feel there is no one with whom I can share my most private worries and fears.

T F   7.   Most of my friends are more successful making changes in their lives than I am.

T F   8.   I would have a hard time finding someone to go with me on a day trip to the beach or country.

To calculate your score, add the number of true answers to questions 1-4 and the number of false answers to questions 5-8. If your score is 4 or more, you should have enough support to protect your health. If your score is 3 or less, you may need to reach out. There are a variety of things you can do to strengthen your social ties:

- Foster friendships. Keep in regular contact with your friends.
- Keep your family ties strong. Participate in family activities and celebrations.
- Get involved with a group. Choose activities that are meaningful to you and that include direct involvement with other people.
- Build your communication skills. The more you share your feelings with others, the closer the bonds between you will become.

"Without friends, no one would choose to live, though he had all the goods."

—Aristotle

From Paul M. Insel and Walton T. Roth, *Core Concepts in Health*, 9th ed., New York: McGraw-Hill, pp. 29–31, 43. Copyright © 2002 McGraw-Hill. Reprinted by permission of The McGraw-Hill Companies, Inc.

Comprehension Checkup

Multiple Choice

Write the letter of the correct answer in the blank provided.

_____   1.   An event that triggers stress is called a
   a. response
   b. stressor
   c. headache
   d. none of the above

_____   2.   Stress is best described as
   a. something completely under your control
   b. something rarely experienced by college students
   c. a physical and emotional response to a stressor
   d. a realistic and positive outlook on life

_____   3.   Which of the following could be a potential stressor?
   a. having to visit a relative you dislike
   b. failing a final exam
   c. the unexpected death of a relative
   d. all of the above

_____   4.   High levels of stress can
   a. aggravate high blood pressure
   b. contribute to insomnia
   c. both a and b
   d. improve memory

_____   5.   All of the following are correlated with high mortality rates except
   a. smoking
   b. social isolation
   c. marriage
   d. high blood pressure

True or False

Indicate whether the statement is true or false by writing T or F in the blank provided.

———— 6. Stress arises only from unpleasant situations.

———— 7. Excessive sweating may be a physical symptom of stress.

———— 8. Chronic stress can lead to heart disease.

———— 9. Healthy connections with others may play a role in the management of stress.

———— 10. Having good relationships with others is unlikely to contribute to wellness.

In Your Own Words

1. What is the difference between a stressor and stress? What are some of your stressors?

2. In what ways does the college experience contribute to the stress level of students?

3. Can stress be positive? Give an example of positive stress in your life.

4. What physical reactions does stress cause in the body?

5. Describe some healthy ways to deal with stress.

The Art of Writing

In a brief essay, respond to one of the items below.

1. Keep track of your own stress for several days. Try to determine what events are likely to trigger a stress response in you. Is your home life, work life, or school life the most stressful? Is your life more or less stressful than you expected?

2. Interview a friend or family member who seems to handle stress well. What strategies does this person use to successfully cope with stress?

Internet Activity

Stress has been linked to many illnesses. To find a list of the negative effects of stress on people's health, go to:

Top 20 Stressful Life Events

Death of a spouse

Divorce

Marital separation

Jail term

Death of a close family member

Personal injury or illness

Marriage

Fired at work

Marital reconciliation

www.stressless.com/AboutSL/StressFacts.cfm

Write a paragraph describing what you learned about stress and disease.
    Take the Quick Stress Assessment at:

www.stressless.com/AboutSL/StressTest.cfm

Use what you learn to evaluate how well you are handling your personal stressors.
    To find information on stress management, click on "Psychology at Work" on the American Psychological Association's Help Center:

http://helping.apa.org

Retirement

Change in health of family member

Pregnancy

Sex difficulties

New family member

Business readjustment

Change in financial status

Death of a close friend

Change to a different line of work

Change in number of arguments with spouse

Mortgage or loan for major purchase (home, etc.)

Reprinted from *Journal of Psychosomatic Research,* Vol. II, T.H. Holmes and R.H. Rahe, "The Social Readjustment Rating Scale," pp. 213–217. Copyright © 1967, with permission from Elsevier.

STRESS AT WORK

Most Stressful Jobs	Least Stressful Jobs
Air traffic controller	Bookkeeper
Customer-service or complaint worker	Civil engineer
Inner-city high school teacher	Forester
Journalist	Millwright
Medical intern	Natural scientist
Miner	Repairman
Police officer	Sales representative
Secretary	Telephone-line worker
Stockbroker	Therapist
Waiter	Toolmaker

Source: The American Institute of Stress.

SELECTION

Excerpt from The Art of Spelling   *by Marilyn vos Savant*

"Simply adopting more rigorous proofreading habits can eliminate many mistakes."

Getting the Picture

As college students, you will be required to write compositions. What you say in a composition is, of course, important. But how you say it is also important. So when you are writing for one of your classes, pay attention to such elements of a composition as word choice, grammar, punctuation, and spelling. Some students have a lot of trouble with spelling. In the following excerpt, Marilyn vos Savant provides practical tips and inspiration for dreadful spellers. As you read the selection, highlight the important information and make annotations in the margins.

Bio-sketch

Marilyn vos Savant is considered to have the world's highest IQ (228) and is so listed in *The Guiness Book of Records.* She writes the weekly "Ask Marilyn" column for *Parade Magazine.*

Brushing Up on Vocabulary

villain   a scoundrel; a cruel, malicious person involved in crime. The word originally meant "farmer or person of the soil." In the Middle Ages, the Latin word for "farm" was *villa* and the *villeins* who worked in the fields were half free, half slave. The great landowners looked down on the rough, crude, dirty farmers, and as a result the term acquired a negative meaning.

derision   ridicule; mockery. *To deride* is derived from the Latin prefix *de,* meaning "down," and the root *ridere,* meaning "to laugh." The literal meaning is "to laugh someone down."

innate   inborn. *Innate* is derived from the Latin word part *in,* and the root *natus,* meaning "born." It was believed that traits such as cheerfulness or generosity were inborn, or with you at birth.

demons   evil spirits; fiends. Originally, the Greek word *daimon* meant "a divine person." The word had a positive meaning and was associated with what we would now call a guardian angel. Later, as the Greeks and Romans were converted to Christianity, they were encouraged to cease worshiping their pagan gods and goddesses, so the word *daimon* came to mean an "evil spirit."

eureka   an interjection used as an exclamation of triumph at a discovery. Long ago in ancient Greece, King Hierro II gave some gold to a local artisan to make into a new crown. When the crown was delivered to the king, he found it to be lighter than he had expected and so he suspected the artisan of swindling him by substituting silver for gold. He sent for the Greek mathematician Archimedes and asked him to discover the truth. Archimedes came up with a solution to the problem while relaxing in his bath. Excited by his discovery, he rushed naked into the street, shouting "Eureka, eureka!" (Greek for "I have found it"). The artisan had indeed been cheating the king. *Eureka* is the motto of the state of California and refers to the discovery of gold in that state in 1849.

Man Sues over Misspelled Tattoo
Thursday, February 25, 1999
Roseville, MI (AP)

1   A man who used guesswork instead of a dictionary when getting a tattoo is now suing the tattoo parlor over the mistaken spelling of *villain.* Lee Williams was left with "villian" on his right forearm, but he didn't notice until a friend made fun of him, according to the Circuit Court lawsuit filed Wednesday. Williams, 23, is seeking $25,000 in damages against Eternal Tattoos. To cover up the mistake, he had plastic surgery which cost him $1,900 and left a "scar as long as his forearm," said his lawyer, Paul Clark. Williams, a student at Wayne State University and a former Marine, got the tattoo in 1996. Before the procedure, workers at the parlor debated how to spell the word, Clark said. Williams wasn't sure either, and they settled on "villian." Eternal Tattoos' owner, Terry Welker, said that the parlor has a policy of asking all customers how they want words spelled. He said if a customer agrees to a misspelling "that falls back on them, not the artist."

From Associated Press Information Services, 2/25/99. Reprinted with permission of The Associated Press.

2   Most spelling mistakes are not as financially costly as the one inflicted upon the unfortunate Mr. Williams, but they are often far more costly in other ways. Misspelled words in personal and business correspondence can result in derision worse than that Mr. Williams endured. Errors in written work limit your opportunities. They cause lower grades in school and negative feedback on the job and—perhaps worst of all—can keep you from getting a job in the first place. Bad spelling always reflects poorly on the writer, whether it's embedded in flesh or printed on a piece of paper. This is because we associate it with certain other (much more serious) negative attributes, like low intelligence, lack of education, and laziness.

3   A common excuse for not attempting to become a better speller is the argument that you "just can't spell" or that you aren't "a spelling person." Happily, research has shown that spelling is not an innate aptitude but a learned skill. Knowing that good—and bad—spellers are made, not born, is the first important step toward spelling improvement, because it allows us to take control of language in a way that we may not have fully realized was possible.

4   Another important thing to remember is that many spelling errors are the result of bad or nonexistent proofreading. Surprisingly, we actually know how to spell many of the words we misspell: the problem occurs when either a lack of confidence causes alternate spellings to be considered—and the wrong one is chosen—or the image of the word in the mind does not translate correctly to the page because of an untrained or confused "motor memory." Simply adopting more rigorous proofreading habits can eliminate many mistakes. As Sorsby points out, "No one knows how to spell every word, but everyone is capable of checking their work."

5   Something else worth knowing is that despite the chaotic appearance of our spelling system, most of the words we use on a regular basis follow some very learnable patterns. Improving your ability to recognize these patterns in more commonplace words is an enormous help in dealing with the less common, more difficult words we encounter. Also, realizing how few words we actually use from day to day—and how few of those actually cause us any spelling problems—makes the task of spelling improvement seem much smaller. Approximately 80 percent of the words we use are drawn from the same set of 1,000 basic, relatively regular words.

6   So, just how should you go about the task of improving your spelling. First and foremost, you must diagnose your problem. Understanding the reason you misspell certain words is a giant step on the road to spelling them correctly. And giving words personal significance is the best way to lock them into memory—after all, you don't misspell your own name or the names of close family members, do you?

7   To get close to your own spelling problems, you'll need to take two diagnostic tests: one to determine what types of spelling errors you most commonly make when writing and one to determine how good your proofreading skills are.

8   Once you've identified your errors, it'll be time to construct a list of your own personal spelling "demons": the words that you almost always misspell and have likely plagued you all your life. One encouraging note about this list: it's almost guaranteed that you will be pleasantly surprised by how few problem words you actually have, especially compared to how many you spell correctly all the time.

Diagnostic Test No. 1

What kind of speller are you?
Take this quiz to find out!
A fair speller will know which of these words is *not* spelled correctly:

   (1) aquainted

   (2) arguement

   (3) cantalope

   (4) congradulate

   (5) fourty

A good speller will know which of these words is *not* spelled correctly:

   (1) counterfeit

   (2) hygiene

(3) niece

(4) seize

(5) accommodate

An excellent speller will know which of these words are *not* spelled correctly:

(1) caterpiller

(2) changable

(3) harrass

(4) hemorhage

(5) reccommend

Diagnostic Test No. 2

Read through the following paragraph, jotting down in your notebook the numbers of the misspelled words as you spot them.

Its (1) finaly (2) that (3) time (4) again (5)—time (6) to (7) anounce (8) the (9) winner's (10) of (11) this (12) years (13) essaye (14) contest. (15) We (16) were (17) priveleged (18) enough (19) to (20) receive (21) allmost (22) fourty (23) fascinaiting (24) entrys, (25) and (26) nearley (27) all (28) of (29) them (30) were (31) concerning (32) personel (33) experiances. (34) It (35) ocurred (36) too (37) the (38) judges (39) that (40) perhapes (41) their (42) is (43) truth (44) to (45) the (46) old (47) addage: (48) "Great (49) minds (50) think (51) allike." (52) But (53) whatever (54) the (55) reason (56) for (57) the (58) repition (59) in (60) themes, (61) the (62) fact (63) remaines (64) that (65) each (66) indavidual (67) made (68) it (69) his (70) or (71) her (72) owne. (73)

Now check your list of misspellings with the one at the end of the selection. [see p. 44.] How did you do?

How to Spell Better

Learn a few rules. Focus on the rules that have few or no exceptions, and your spelling will improve quickly. For example: "Write i before e except after c, or when sounded like a, as in neighbor or weigh." Another example: The spelling of a word never changes when a prefix is added—as in necessary and unnecessary. [See the Appendix in this text for more spelling rules.]

Look it up. Don't bother using that old excuse, "How am I going to look up a word if I don't know how to spell it?" You know perfectly well you can find that word with a little effort! And when you have success, the feeling of *eureka!* will help imprint the correct spelling in your mind.

Don't use a spell-checker. When writing on a computer, don't use the spell-checker as you write or immediately afterward. Instead, place a question mark in parentheses—like this: (?)—directly following any word you are not sure you have spelled right. When you stop writing, go back and look up every one of those words in your electronic dictionary, correcting it yourself, and then removing the question mark. This will take only a few seconds for each word. After you finish, *then* run the spell-checker.

Train your motor memory. Memorizing movement is a part of what allows us to walk, talk, sign our names, or play the piano "by heart." You can become fixed in misspelling a word simply by doing so repeatedly, either by hand or typing. Correcting this motor memory is easy, although tedious. Just force yourself to write a word 10 times correctly each time you discover that you've written it incorrectly.

Pay attention to pronunciation. Although English is the least phonetic of all spelling systems, about 85 percent of the words are spelled the way they sound. How many times have you heard people say 'ek cetera' instead of 'et cetera?' Start listening to yourself, and you'll improve not only your spelling but also your speaking, which will make you sound better to others.

Like starting an exercise program, improving your spelling will be the toughest in the beginning. Unlike an exercise program, however, it will get easier and easier until you see almost no mistakes at all. At that point, you will be a good speller for life.

From Marilyn vos Savant, *The Art of Spelling: The Madness and the Method*, pp. 13–14, 151. Copyright © 2000 by Marilyn vos Savant. Used by permission of W.W. Norton & Company, Inc.

Comprehension Checkup

True or False

Indicate whether the statement is true or false by writing T or F in the blank provided.

_____   1. Mr. Williams has successfully resolved his lawsuit.

_____   2. Vos Savant believes that poor spellers should use a spell-checker as a first step in proofreading written material.

_____   3. According to vos Savant, in the area of spelling, "Practice makes perfect."

_____   4. Poor spelling can limit one's potential.

Multiple Choice

Write the letter of the correct answer in the blank provided.

_____   5. Vos Savant is most likely to agree with which of the following:
   a. Good spellers are born, not made.
   b. You can't look up a word if you don't know how to spell it.
   c. Problem words should be looked up in the dictionary.
   d. In English, at least 90 percent of the words are spelled the way that they sound.

_____   6. According to vos Savant, which of the following negative consequences are associated with being a poor speller?
   a. perceived by others as being lazy
   b. perceived by others as having low intelligence
   c. perceived by others as being poorly educated
   d. all of the above

_____   7. Which of the following activities is likely to improve our spelling according to vos Savant?
   a. being more vigilant in proofreading
   b. memorizing a few simple, reliable rules
   c. writing problem words correctly over and over
   d. all of the above

_____ 8. Vos Savant recommends that those trying to improve their spelling
should
a. pay attention to pronunciation
b. use a spell-checker as they write
c. have someone else proofread their essays
d. take a class in elementary phonics

Vocabulary in Context

Look through the paragraph noted in parentheses to find a word that matches the definition.

9. Qualities that are thought of as a natural part of some person or thing; characteristic (paragraph 2) _____

10. Fixed into a surrounding mass (2) _____

11. Confused or disordered (5) _____

12. Troubled, annoyed, or tormented (8) _____

In Your Own Words

Charles F. Kleber, president of Better Education Through Simplified Spelling, says that "the current irrational English spelling system is responsible, at least in part, for the nation's illiteracy problems, the dropout rate, crime, welfare dependence and drug and alcohol abuse." He is referring to the fact that in English one letter can stand for more than one sound. George Bernard Shaw once sarcastically asked why "fish" wasn't spelled "ghoti"—using the _gh_ from "enough," the _o_ from "women," and the _ti_ from "nation."

Despite these exceptions, vos Savant and most reading specialists contend that 80 percent of the most commonly used English words do follow reliable phonetic rules. Given the current complexity of the language, do you think children should be taught phonics (sound-symbol relationships) in the primary grades? Is this method likely to help create better spellers?

The Art of Writing

In a brief essay, respond to the item below.

Some people say the simplest remedy for poor spelling is to develop a good computer spell-checking program. But how much can a spell-checking program accomplish? Word processors don't flag correctly spelled words that are used incorrectly.

Internet Activity

To get viewpoints for and against the simplification of English spelling, consult the following two websites.
Simplified Spelling Society: www.les.aston.ac.uk/sss/

Society for the Preservation of English Language and Literature (SPELL):

www.mindspring.com/spellorg/

The Simplified Spelling Society wants to regularize English spelling, and SPELL wants to fight the misuse of the English language in the media. Report your findings.

ANSWERS TO SPELLING QUIZZES
DIAGNOSTIC TEST NO. 1

A Fair Speller?
All of the words are spelled incorrectly.

1. acquainted   2. argument   3. cantaloupe   4. congratulate   5. forty

A Good Speller?
All of the words correctly.

An Excellent Speller?
All of the words are spelled incorrectly.

1. caterpillar   2. changeable   3. harass   4. hemorrhage   5. reccommend

DIAGNOSTIC TEST NO. 2

Here are the numbers of the misspelled words and their correct spellings:

1. It's	23. forty	41. perhaps
2. finally	24. fascinating	42. there
8. announce	25. entries	48. adage
10. winners	27. nearly	52. alike
13. year's	33. personal	59. repetition
14. essay	34. experiences	64. remains
18. privileged	36. occurred	67. individual
22. almost	37. to	73. own

Critical Thinking and Problem Solving

A critical thinker must be ready to examine claims and assumptions. Just because support for a statement can be found on the World Wide Web doesn't make it true. Just because a famous person utters a statement doesn't make it true. Critical thinking requires an open and questioning mind and a thoughtful analysis.

Several problems are given below. They are meant to test your creativity and problem-solving abilities. To solve them, you need to look at each problem in a different way. Be cautious about making assumptions. The answers are on the following pages.

(a)   Nine dots are arranged in a square. Can you connect them by drawing four continuous straight lines without lifting your pencil from the paper?

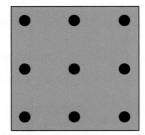

The nine-dot problem

(b)   Unscramble each set of letters to make a word that uses all the letters:

MEST   _____

LFAE   _____

DUB   _____

STKAL _____

OTOR   _____

LTEPA _____

Now try a new list:

FINEK _____

OPONS_____

KROF   _____

PUC   _____

SDIH   _____

LTEPA _____

(c)   See how many of the following questions you can answer correctly.

1.   Argentines do not have a fourth of July. T or F?

2.   How many birthdays does the average person have?

3.   A farmer had 19 sheep. All but 9 died. How many sheep did the farmer have left?

4.   Some months have 30 days, some have 31. How many months have 28 days?

5.   I have two coins that together total 30 cents. One of the coins is not a nickel. What are the two coins?

6.   If there are twelve one-cent candies in a dozen, how many two-cent candies are there in a dozen?

(d)   How many uses can you think of for a newspaper?

Answers

(a)   The nine-dot problem can be solved by extending the lines beyond the square formed by the dots.

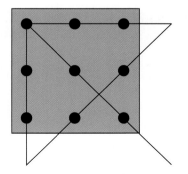

The nine-dot problem—
solved

(b)   Did you notice that the letters of the last item was the same in each group? In the first list (*stem, leaf, bud, stalk, root*), the item LTEPA is usually unscrambled as *petal*. In the second list (*knife, spoon, fork, cup, dish*), LTEPA is usually unscrambled as *plate*.

(c)   **1.** F. They have to have a fourth of July. They can't go from the third to the fifth. **2.** Each person has one "birthday" and the rest are celebrations. **3.** He has nineteen sheep. Nine are alive and ten are dead. **4.** All of the months have at least 28 days. **5.** The coins are a quarter and a nickel. One of the coins is not a nickel, but the other coin is a nickel. **6.** There are twelve.

(d)   Here are some starters. You can:
>   read it
>   write on it
>   line your garbage can with it
>   wrap packages with it
>   wipe your feet on it
>   lay it down on the floor before you paint
>   train your dog with it
>   make a kite out of it
>   wipe windows with it
>   use it to keep your head dry if it is raining
>   use it as a dustpan
>   and so on!

How is Garfield illustrating creative problem solving?

SELECTION

Overcoming Dyslexia   *by Betsy Morris*

"Charles Schwab was very strong in math, science, and sports (especially golf), which helped him get into Stanford. But anything involving English 'was a disconnect.'"

Getting the Picture

The article excerpted below describes individuals who used creative problem-solving techniques to overcome their personal limitations.

Bio-sketch

Betsy Morris, senior writer for *Fortune,* has firsthand experience with dyslexia. Her son Johnny was diagnosed with dyslexia at age 7. Over the years Morris learned a lot from watching Johnny deal with dyslexia. In particular, she came to admire his "patience, perseverance, and his ability not to give up when things don't come easily." Today, Johnny, now 12 years old, is doing well and has become a good reader. "I still hate math, though," he says.

Brushing Up on Vocabulary

dead-end a situation with no escape or solution. The term originated in the late 1800s and referred specifically to a passageway that has no exit, and so halts all progress.

perilously involving great risk; dangerous. The word *perilous* originated from the Latin *periculum,* which referred to the danger of going on a trip. Historically, travel was dangerous and uncomfortable, and as a result was "full of peril."

trivia matters or things that are unimportant or inconsequential. In Latin *tri* means "three" and *via* means "way." In ancient Rome, at the point where three roads crossed, the women would meet to talk and gossip on the way back from the market.

late-bloomer someone who matures after the usual or expected time. The term originally referred to roses that failed to bloom when they were expected to do so.

humility the quality or state of being humble or modest. The word comes from the Latin *humus,* or earth, and originally referred to people who prostrated themselves on the ground because they didn't think much of themselves.

1   Consider the following four dead-end kids.

2   One was spanked by his teachers for bad grades and a poor attitude. He dropped out of school at 16. Another failed remedial English and came perilously close to flunking out of college. The third feared he'd never make it through school—and might not have without a tutor. The last finally learned to read in third grade, devouring Marvel comics, whose pictures provided clues to help him untangle the words.

3   These four losers are, respectively, Richard Branson, Charles Schwab, John Chambers, and David Boies. Billionaire Branson developed one of Britain's top brands with Virgin Records and Virgin Atlantic Airways. Schwab virtually created the discount brokerage business. Chambers is CEO of Cisco systems. Boies is a celebrated trial attorney, best known as the guy who beat Microsoft.

4   In one of the stranger bits of business trivia, they have something in common: They are all dyslexic. So is billionaire Craig McCaw, who pioneered the cellular phone industry; John Reed, who led Citibank to the top of banking; Donald Winkler, who until recently headed Ford Financial; Gaston Caperton, former governor of West Virginia and now head of the College Board; Paul Orfalea, founder of Kinko's; and Diane Swonk, chief economist of Bank One. The list goes on. Many of these adults seemed pretty hopeless as kids. All have been wildly successful in business. Most have now begun to talk about their dyslexia as a way to help children and parents cope with a condition that is still widely misunderstood.

5   What exactly is dyslexia? The Everyman definition calls it a reading disorder in which people jumble letters, confusing *dog* with *god,* say, or *box* with *pox.* The exact cause is unclear; scientists believe it has to do with the way a developing brain is wired. Difficulty reading, spelling, and writing are typical symptoms. But dyslexia often comes with one or more other learning problems, as well, including trouble with math,

"You must have long-range goals to keep you from being frustrated by short-range failures."

—Charles C. Noble

auditory processing, organizational skills, and memory. No two dyslexics are alike—each has his own set of weaknesses and strengths. About 5 percent to 6 percent of American public school children have been diagnosed with a learning disability. 80 percent of the diagnoses are dyslexia-related. But some studies indicate that up to 20 percent of the population may have some degree of dyslexia.

A generation ago this was a problem with no name. Boies, Schwab, and Bill Samuels Jr., the president of Maker's Mark, did not realize they were dyslexic until some of their own children were diagnosed with the disorder, which is often inherited. Samuels says he was sitting in a school office, listening to a description of his son's problems, when it dawned on him: "Oh, shit. that's me." Most of the adults had diagnosed themselves. Says Branson: "At some point, I think I decided that being dyslexic was better than being stupid."

Stupid. Dumb. Retard. Dyslexic kids have heard it all. According to a March 2000 Roper poll, almost two-thirds of Americans still associate learning disabilities with mental retardation. That's probably because dyslexics find it so difficult to learn through conventional methods. "It is a disability in learning," says Boies. "It is not an intelligence disability. It doesn't mean you can't think."

He's right. Dyslexia has nothing to do with IQ; many smart, accomplished people have it, or are thought to have had it, including Winston Churchill and Albert Einstein. Sally Shaywitz, a leading dyslexia neuroscientist at Yale, believes the disorder can carry surprising talents along with its well-known disadvantages. "Dyslexics are over represented in the top ranks of people who are unusually insightful, who bring a new perspective, who think out of the box," says Shaywitz, codirector of the Center for Learning and Attention at Yale.

Dyslexics don't outgrow their problems—reading and writing usually remain hard work for life—but with patient teaching and deft tutoring, they do learn to manage. Absent that, dyslexia can snuff out dreams at an early age, as children lose their way in school, then lose their self-esteem and drive. "The prisons are filled with kids who can't read," says Caperton. "I suspect a lot of them have learning disabilities."

Dyslexia is a crucible, particularly in a high-pressure society that allows so little room for late-bloomers. "People are either defeated by it or they become much more tenacious," says McCaw. Don Winkler, a top financial services executive at Bank One and then at Ford Motor, remembers coming home from school bloodied by fights he'd had with kids who called him dumb. Kinko's founder, Paul Orfalea, failed second grade and spent part of third in a class of mentally retarded children. He could not learn to read, despite the best efforts of parents who took him to testers, tutors, therapists, special reading groups, and eye doctors. As young classmates read aloud, Orfalea says it was as if "angels whispered words in their ears."

In his unpublished autobiography, Orfalea says that to a dyslexic, a sentence is worse than Egyptian hieroglyphics. "It's more like a road map with mouse holes or coffee stains in critical places. You're always turning into blind alleys and ending up on the wrong side of town." He finally graduated but not before being "invited to leave . . . practically every high school in Los Angeles." One principal counseled his mother to enroll him in trade school, suggesting that Orfalea could become a carpet layer. His mother went home and tearfully told her husband, "I just know he can do more than lay carpet."

Charles Schwab was very strong in math, science, and sports (especially golf), which helped him get into Stanford. But anything involving English "was a disconnect." He couldn't write quickly enough to capture his thoughts. He couldn't listen to a lecture and take legible notes. He couldn't memorize four words in a row. He doesn't think he ever read a novel all the way through in high school. He was within one unit of flunking out of Stanford his freshman year. "God, I must be really dumb

"Faith is the substance of things hoped for, the evidence of things not seen."

—Hebrews 11:1

"Failure is delay, not defeat. It is a temporary detour, not a dead-end street."

—William Arthur Ward

in this stuff," he used to tell himself. "It was horrible, a real drag on me." So horrible that Schwab and his wife, Helen, created a foundation to help parents of children with learning disorders.

It was as if Schwab and the others were wearing a scarlet letter: "D" for dumb. Until about five years ago Chambers kept his dyslexia a secret. As CEO, he says, "you don't want people to see your weaknesses." One day a little girl at Cisco's Bring Your Children to Work Day forced him out of the closet. Chambers had called on her, and she was trying to ask a question before a crowd of 500 kids and parents. But she couldn't get the words out. "I have a learning disability," she said tearfully.

Chambers cannot tell this story without choking up himself. "You could immediately identify with what that was like," he says. "You know that pain. She started to leave, and you knew how hurt she was in front of the group and her parents." Chambers threw her a lifeline. "I have a learning disability too," he said. In front of the crowd, he began talking to her as if they were the only two people in the room. "You've just got to learn your way through it," Chambers told her. "Because there are some things you can do that others cannot, and there are some things others can do you're just not going to be able to do, ever. Now my experience has been that what works is to go a little bit slower. . . ."

15 It was the kind of coaching that proved crucial to nearly everybody we talked to: mentors who took a genuine interest, parents who refused to give up, tutors who didn't even know what dyslexia was. Winkler recalls that his parents refused to let their fear of electrocution stand in the way of his fixing every iron and toaster in the neighborhood. "I wired every teacher's house," he says. "I got shocked all the time." His parents owned a mom-and-pop shop in Phillipsburg, N.J. His mother cleaned houses to pay for his tutoring. Chambers, who read right to left and up and down the page, says his parents, both doctors, claim they never once doubted his abilities, even though he says, "I absolutely did." His parents' faith was important to him. So was his tutor, Mrs. Anderson. Even today Chambers remembers tutoring as excruciating. "It might have been once or twice a week," he says, "but it felt like every day." Nonetheless, he adds, "Mrs. Anderson had an influence on my life far bigger than she might have ever realized."

16 If you could survive childhood, dyslexia was a pretty good business boot camp. It fostered risk taking, problem solving, resilience. School was a chess game that required tactical brilliance. Schwab sat mostly in the back of the room. But he was conscientious and charming, and gutsy enough to ask for extra help. Boies took a minimum of math and avoided foreign languages and anything involving spatial skills. Orfalea worked out a symbiotic relationship with classmates on a group project at USC's Marshall Business School; they did the writing, he did the photocopying (and got the germ of the idea that led to Kinko's).

17 At Vanderbilt Law School, Samuels spent a lot of time in study-group discussions. "That's how I learned the cases," he says. His friends helped with the reading; he paid for the beer. Better than most people, dyslexics learn humility and how to get along with others. It's probably no accident that Kinko's, Cisco, and Schwab have all been on *Fortune's* list of the best places to work. "I never put people down, because I know what that feels like," says Branson, who seldom asks for a résumé either "because I haven't got one myself."

18 By the time these guys got into business, they had picked themselves up so many times that risk taking was second nature. "We're always expecting a curve ball," says Samuels. Schwab remembers how hard it was to watch his friends receive awards and become General Motors Scholars, Merit Scholars, Baker Scholars. "I was so jealous," he says. Later on, though, some of the prizewinners had trouble dealing with adversity.

19   If as kids, the dyslexic executives had learned the downside of their disorder inside out, as adults they began to see its upside: a distinctly different way of processing information that gave them an edge in a volatile, fast-moving world. "Many times in business, different is better than better," says Samuels. "And we dyslexics do different without blinking an eye."

Comprehension Checkup

Matching

Match the quotation with the speaker. Write the letter of the speaker in the appropriate blank. (Some speakers will be used more than once.)

(a) Richard Branson   (f) Paul Orfalea

(b) David Boies   (g) Charles Schwab

(c) Sally Shaywitz   (h) John Chambers

(d) Craig McCaw   (i) Donald Winkler

(e) Gaston Caperton   (j) Bill Samuels Jr.

_____ 1. "Many times in business, different is better than better, and we dyslexics do different without blinking an eye."

_____ 2. "It is a disability in learning. It is not an intelligence disability. It doesn't mean you can't think."

_____ 3. "Dyslexics are overrepresented in the top ranks of people who are unusually insightful, who bring a new perspective, who think out of the box."

_____ 4. "The prisons are filled with kids who can't read. I suspect a lot of them have learning disabilities."

_____ 5. "People are either defeated by it or they become much more tenacious."

_____ 6. "It's more like a road map with mouse holes or coffee stains in critical places."

_____ 7. "God, I must be really dumb in this stuff."

_____ 8. "You've just got to learn your way through it."

_____ 9. "I wired every teacher's house. I got shocked all the time."

_____ 10. "I never put people down, because I know what that feels like."

_____ 11. "We're always expecting a curve ball."

_____ 12. "At some point, I think I decided that being dyslexic was better than being stupid."

Multiple Choice

Write the letter of the correct answer in the blank provided.

_____ 1. Morris suggests all of the following about dyslexia *except*
        a. Dyslexia has nothing to do with IQ
        b. Typical symptoms of dyslexia are difficulty reading, writing, and spelling

c. Dyslexia is the same in all individuals

d. Dyslexia is not likely to be outgrown

_____ 2. What is the meaning of the word *devouring* as used in paragraph 2?

a. scrutinizing

b. collecting

c. tearing apart

d. taking in greedily with the senses or intellect.

_____ 3. What is the meaning of the word *snuff* as used in paragraph 9?

a. extinguish

b. suppress

c. crush

d. all of the above

_____ 4. *Crucible* in paragraph 10 refers to

a. a short-term effect

b. a temporary setback

c. a severe test or trial having a lasting influence

d. a momentous undertaking

_____ 5. As described in paragraph 10, a *tenacious* person is likely to be

a. persistent

b. capricious

c. infallible

d. disenchanted

True or False

Indicate whether the statement is true or false by writing T or F in the blank provided.

_____ 6. Chambers kept his dyslexia a secret because as CEO he felt that it was inadvisable to reveal his weaknesses.

_____ 7. One reason Chambers revealed his secret was because he felt a great deal of empathy for the little girl with the learning disability.

_____ 8. A *resilient* person is someone who is inflexible.

_____ 9. A relationship that is mutually beneficial to two parties could be called *symbiotic*.

_____ 10. As children, dyslexics can see the benefits of having dyslexia, but adults can see only the liabilities.

In Your Own Words

1. Dr. Mel Levine (professor of pediatrics at the University of North Carolina Medical School and an expert on learning differences) says, "schools reward well-roundedness, but so many of the most successful people have brains that are rather specialized." The dyslexic business leaders profiled in the *Fortune* magazine article by Betsy Morris all say that children should be allowed to specialize. For instance, Charles Schwab suggests that foreign language requirements should be abandoned and Paul Orfalea—trigonometry. What do you think? How much of the basic school curriculum should be modified to suit individual learners' needs?

2. Paul Orfalea recalls that as he was growing up his mother used to console him by saying that in the long run "the A students work for the B students,

the C students run the businesses, and the D students dedicate the buildings." What is your opinion?

3. Our current educational system places a great deal of emphasis on good grades and high test scores to the disadvantage of the dyslexic. Do you think the emphasis should be changed?

The Art of Writing

In a brief essay, respond to the item below.

> David Boies, in addition to being dyslexic himself, has two dyslexic sons. One graduated from Yale Law School despite childhood testing that indicated he would not be able to accomplish very much. Boies thinks our current educational climate does not allow for late-bloomers. "In this environment," he says, "you get children who think they are masters of the universe, and children who think they are failures, when they're 10 years old. They're both wrong. And neither is well served by that misconception."

Internet Activity

Consult two of the following websites and discuss information that you think would be helpful for parents of dyslexic children to know:

www.ldanatl.org/factsheets/dyslexia.html (Learning Disabilities Association of America)

www.Interdys.org (International Dyslexia Association)

www.NCLD.org (National Center for Learning Disabilities)

www.Schwablearning.org (Charles and Helen Schwab Foundation)

www.Cyberwink.com (Don Winkler's website)

www.Allkindsofminds.org (Mel Levine's Institute)

Vocabulary: Words in Context

One technique for discovering the meaning of unfamiliar words is the use of context clues. By paying attention to what an author is saying, we can often discover the meanings of words without having to look them up in the dictionary. As you will see, often our own background or experiences also will help us determine the meanings of unfamiliar words. Here are some common techniques for using context to determine the meaning of new words.

Definition

Sometimes a writer provides us with a definition of a word somewhere within the sentence or nearby sentences, especially if the word is one that we are likely to be unfamiliar with.

> Every year many people buy self-help audiotapes containing *subliminal* messages to help them relieve stress. These tapes contain messages that are supposedly below the level of human consciousness.

Subliminal here is simply defined as "below the level of consciousness."

Synonym

A synonym, which is another word with a similar meaning, may be used elsewhere in the sentence.

> Massages are thought to provide *therapeutic* benefits by relieving stress; however, their curative powers do not extend to all patients.

You can infer from this sentence that *therapeutic* and *curative* have similar meanings.

Antonym

Sometimes you can determine the meaning of a word by finding an antonym, a word with an opposite meaning, somewhere in the sentence.

> Juana's house was very well-maintained, but her sister's house was *dilapidated*.

You can see that the writer is making a contrast, and that well-maintained is the opposite of *dilapidated*.

Examples

Sometimes examples illustrate the meaning of a word.

> Terry has such *boundless* energy that even after working a full shift and taking care of her two small children, she still wants to go out dancing with her husband at night.

This example suggests to you that *boundless* means "infinite or vast."

Explanation

Sometimes a writer simply gives the reader an explanation of what a word means.

> The Russian gymnastic team was *disconsolate* after its loss to the Romanians. No amount of kind words from coaches and fans could raise the spirits of the young athletes.

The writer is telling you that the word *disconsolate* means persistently sad or unhappy.

Experience

This way of discovering the meaning of a word draws on your personal experience.

> Have you ever been seated next to someone in a restaurant whose *loquaciousness* on a cell phone made you ask to be moved to another table?

Perhaps you have experienced this or a similar situation, and you can infer that *loquaciousness* means "talkativeness."

Knowledge of Subject

Here you have just enough familiarity with the subject the writer is discussing to enable you to figure out the meaning of the unfamiliar word.

> Mark labored under the *delusion* that he could pass calculus without attending class or studying.

You can guess that Mark was fooling or *deluding* himself and that *delusion* is a "false or mistaken belief."

Combination

You can use a number of these strategies at the same time to decipher the meaning of a word.

> The man at the party was a real *introvert*. He sat quietly in a corner of the room by himself working a crossword puzzle.

Here you probably used explanation, experience, and familiarity with the subject to determine that *introverts* are persons who are much more focused on their own inner thoughts and feelings than on the social environment.

Context Clues: Exercise 1

Now define the following words, without consulting your dictionary. First, give your own definition for the italicized word, and then, indicate the method(s) you used to arrive at the definition. The first example is done for you.

1. Because Americans are eating better and have access to better medical care, their *longevity* is increasing.

   Definition: <u>length of life</u>

   Method(s) used: <u>example, knowledge of subject, explanation, maybe experience</u>

2. Nudists claim it is a *liberating* experience to be without the restrictions of clothes.
   Definition: _____
   Method(s) used: _____

3. Pictures of *emaciated* and starving children filled the news as the famine in the war-torn country continued.
   Definition: _____
   Method(s) used: _____

4. *Badgered* by her children's constant pleas for a big-screen TV, the young mother finally gave in.
   Definition: _____
   Method(s) used: _____

5. Walter's *obeisance* to his brother was a source of irritation to Nancy, who couldn't figure out why Walter always deferred to him.
   Definition: _____
   Method(s) used: _____

6. After her divorce, Reyna tried to *obliterate* all evidence of her former husband by throwing out his clothes, pictures, and CDs.
   Definition: _____
   Method(s) used: _____

7. Jonathan Swift, author of *Gulliver's Travels*, did not like people in the *aggregate*, but he could tolerate them as individuals.
   Definition: _____
   Method(s) used: _____

Context Clues: Exercise 2

Use context clues to determine the meaning of the italicized word. Circle the clue word(s).

1. Tomoko tried to *pacify* her young son by giving him a lollipop, but her efforts to satisfy him failed.

2. John Lennon of the Beatles had an *innate* talent for music, but despite his natural ability he still had to work hard to achieve success.

3. We have taken to calling our *inquisitive* neighbor "Mrs. Nosy Parker."

4. At his death, his property was distributed to his children in a just and *equitable* manner.

5. The doctor determined that constant ear infections had robbed the elderly woman of her *equilibrium*, so he prescribed a walker to help her maintain her balance.

6. Just as muscles can *atrophy* from lack of exercise, so too the mind can waste away from lack of use.

7. The *flippant* remark to his teacher earned Joel a detention. The teacher did not like Joel's joking attitude.

8. Many remarked about his *ostentatious* life style, but he refused to modify his showy ways.

9. Vincent was in a *pensive* mood, and he remained quietly thoughtful even while sitting in a noisy cafeteria.

10. Scientists have offered many explanations for why dinosaurs became *extinct*, but none of these explanations can fully explain their disappearance.

11. Venus Williams is an *agile* tennis player. Her coordination has saved many a shot.

Context Clues: Exercise 3

Use the context to determine the missing word. Briefly describe the clue or clues that you found.

1. Some students have a strong fear of success. They often "play dumb" with their friends or back away from winning in sports or school. Because success is perceived as stressful, they are more comfortable with _____.

   Clue: _____.

2. Both men and women are prone to fear of success. But women have an additional burden. If women define success as masculine, they are more likely to avoid it in order to be perceived as _____ by their peers.

   Clue: _____.

3. Avoiding success is not always undesirable. An overemphasis on achievement can be just as bad. In the United States there are many successful but unhappy workaholics. A truly successful life strikes a _____ between achievement and other needs. A happy medium is sometimes the best.

   Clue: _____.

4. What does it take to achieve great success? Many great Olympic athletes began with quite ordinary skills. It was their drive and determination that made them truly _____.

   Clue: _____.

5. Parents can raise high achievers by nurturing dedication and hard work. The parents of Olympic athletes supported their child's interest and emphasized doing one's _____ at all times.

   Clue: _____.

6. Most of us cannot achieve elite performance, but all of us can improve our everyday motivation. If you fail, regard it as a sign that you need to work _____, not that you lack ability.

   Clue: _____.

STUDY TECHNIQUE 2

SQ3R Study Method

SQ3R is a technique for reading and studying textbook material that was developed by Dr. Francis P. Robinson over 50 years ago. SQ3R stands for survey, question, read, recite, and review. Research shows that using the SQ3R method can help you improve both your reading comprehension and your grades.

A. **Survey** (Orient yourself to the assignment)
   1. Read introductory and summary paragraphs.
   2. Read headings and subheadings.
   3. Look at illustrations and tables.

At this stage, look at key parts of the article to achieve a general idea of how the article is structured and what it is all about.

B. **Question** (Find the main points)
   1. Ask who, what, where, when, why, and how?
   2. Contrast the material in front of you to previous material and to your background knowledge.
   3. Turn headings and subheadings into questions.

At this stage you will formulate questions about the material you would like to have answered.

C. **Read** (Read actively instead of passively)
   1. Look for answers to your questions.
   2. Underline or highlight key words or phrases.
   3. Make notes in margins.
   4. Summarize key points in your own words.

The goal of this stage is to read the material in an active, questioning, purposeful way. While you are reading, keep in mind the questions you have already formulated. Don't hesitate to read the material a second or third time. How often you should read something depends on how difficult it is. Reading something a second or third time is like seeing a movie over again—new details and meanings begin to appear.

D. **Recite** (Demonstrate your understanding of the material)
   1. Put the information you have learned into your own words.
   2. Recite the main points from memory.
   3. Organize the material through outlining, mapping, diagraming, or similar techniques.

Say the answers to your original questions either to yourself or out loud. Be sure you can recite the answers to the who, what, where, when, why, and how questions you orignally posed.

E. **Review** (Memory is improved by repetition)
   1. Review material frequently.
   2. Practice giving answers.

Just as you shouldn't hesitate to read material more than once, you shouldn't hesitate to test yourself on it more than once. Continual review is the key to learning material and remembering it.

Find Your Procrastination Quotient

FRANK & ERNEST® by Bob Thaves

FRANK & ERNEST reprinted by permission of Newspaper Enterprise Association, Inc.

Do you procrastinate? Do you wait until the last minute to accomplish a task, such as a homework assignment? Do you recognize yourself in the Frank and Ernest cartoon above? To assess your tendency for procrastination, take the test that follows. Look at the statements and circle the number that best applies.

1. I invent reasons and look for excuses for not acting on a problem.

   Strongly agree 4 3 2 1 **Strongly disagree**

2. It takes pressure to get me to work on difficult assignments.

   Strongly agree 4 3 2 1 **Strongly disagree**

3. I take half measures that will avoid or delay unpleasant or difficult tasks.

   Strongly agree 4 3 2 1 **Strongly disagree**

4. I face too many interruptions and crises that interfere with accomplishing my major goals.

   Strongly agree 4 3 2 1 **Strongly disagree**

5. I sometimes neglect to carry out important tasks.

   Strongly agree 4 3 2 1 **Strongly disagree**

6. I schedule big assignments too late to get them done as well as I know I could.

   Strongly agree 4 3 2 1 **Strongly disagree**

7. I'm sometimes too tired to do the work I need to do.

   Strongly agree 4 3 2 1 **Strongly disagree**

8. I start new tasks before I finish old ones.

   Strongly agree 4 3 2 1 **Strongly disagree**

9. When I work in groups, I try to get other people to finish what I don't.

   Strongly agree 4 3 2 1 **Strongly disagree**

10. I put off tasks that I really don't want to do but I know that I must do.

    Strongly agree 4 3 2 1 **Strongly disagree**

Scoring: Total the numbers you have circled. If the score is below 20, you are not a chronic procrastinator and you probably have only an occasional problem. If your score is 21–30, you have a minor problem with procrastination. If your score is above 30, you procrastinate quite often and should work on breaking the habit.

If you do procrastinate often, why do you think you do it? Are there particular subjects or classes or kinds of assignments on which you are more likely to procrastinate?

From Robert S. Feldman, *Power Learning*, 2nd ed., New York: McGraw-Hill, 2003, p. 44. Copyright © 2003 McGraw-Hill. Reprinted by permission of The McGraw-Hill Companies, Inc.

And One More Thing!

Many of us, despite our best intentions, are chronic procrastinators. We are forever putting off into the far, far distant future things that need to be accomplished today. Obviously, to be successful in school, as well as life, this bad habit needs to be changed.

SELECTION

Excerpt from *You Can Make it Happen*   *by Stedman Graham*

"Think about the successful people you know. Are any of them procrastinators?"

Getting the Picture

Practice your SQ3R techniques with this reading selection. Read the first paragraph, the first sentence of subsequent paragraphs, the subheadings, and the information in bold type. Then read the questions at the end. What do you already know about this topic? Did you know that procrastination can lead to health problems? College students who put off doing their assignments have more headaches, colds, and stomach pains than students who complete their assignments on time. Before you start reading, come up with some questions of your own. Then read the selection completely, at least once; articulate what you have learned; and, finally, review the material and answer your own questions.

Bio-sketch

In 1997, Stedman Graham, former professional athlete, founder of Athletes Against Drugs and, corporate and community leader, published *You Can Make It Happen: A Nine-Step Plan for Success*. The following is an excerpt from Chapter 9, "Win By a Decision."

Brushing Up on Vocabulary

procrastinate   to put off doing something unpleasant or burdensome until a future time

gridlock   a blockage; a paralysis. The word refers to a traffic jam, as at a busy intersection, in which no vehicle is able to move in any direction.

"Win By a Decision"

1 If you want to pursue a better life, you need a process and a method for making better decisions, a process that uses all of your creative and analytical powers, all the resources at your command. Big decisions require big thinking. Often, the only difference between you and someone you admire is that they have made the decision to make their lives better. There is a traditional African proverb that says, "If it is to be, it's up to me. . . ."

2 Napoleon Hill, author of the classic *Think and Grow Rich*, has noted that successful people make decisions quickly and firmly once they have reviewed all the information available. Unsuccessful people, he said, make decisions slowly and change them often. He claimed also that ninety-eight out of a hundred people never make up their minds about their major purpose in life because *they simply can't make a decision and stick with it*. I hope to help you change that percentage by becoming one of those people who can make good life decisions.

3 One of the biggest obstacles to the decision-making process is something I am very familiar with: procrastination. I come from a long line of procrastinators. It might have been longer, but they kept putting off having more of us. Some say that not

making a decision is a decision in itself, one with many implications. I've worked at overcoming my tendency to procrastinate, which is the tendency to put things off. One in five Americans is a chronic procrastinator, according to DePaul University professor Joseph R. Ferrari, coauthor of *Procrastination and Task Avoidance: Theory, Research and Treatment*. Ferrari has identified two types of procrastinators: the *arousal* type and the *avoidance* type. The first kind of procrastinator puts things off because they get a thrill out of doing things at the buzzer and in a last-minute rush. The second type puts things off to avoid them for a wide number of reasons ranging from fear of failure to simply wanting to avoid doing something they consider to be unpleasant. Those who procrastinate because they have a fear of failure believe that they are better off not trying than trying and failing. Mark Twain was the literary hero of procrastinators. His motto was *"Never put off till tomorrow what you can do the day after tomorrow."*

4   Here are a few other common phrases you'll hear from serious procrastinators:

This just isn't the right time to make that decision.

I have a few other important matters to deal with first.

My schedule just won't give me the time for that matter.

I've been meaning to get to that.

I'll tackle that when I've got more experience.

You wouldn't believe all the stuff I have to do before I can get to that.

Tomorrow, I promise you.

I just have to get away from all the distractions to focus on that.

I'm waiting to make a bigger move.

There is probably a safer (better, faster, easier) way of doing this. I'll wait for it.

5   Do any of these sound familiar to you? Procrastinators are creative in making excuses, even if they can't do anything else. The question they always get from people around them is "What are you waiting for. . . ?"

6   Decision-making gridlock is a serious problem if you are interested in pursuing your vision for a better life. Often, it is based in fear, whether your particular brand is fear of success or fear of failure or just fear of pulling your head out of the ground (or from wherever you might have stuck it). Think about the successful people you know. Are any of them procrastinators? Do they spend days looking before they leap? Or do they go after what they want? I was going to come up with a list to help you overcome this problem but . . . just kidding.

7   The self-defeating habit of procrastination is a fairly common trait. There are three theories as to why you put things off that are vitally important:

1. You are just lazy.

2. You are self-destructive.

3. You like being stuck because it brings you sympathy.

8   As you can tell, these theories do not paint a pretty picture of the procrastinator's personality. None of them really explains the problem or deals with it in a very logical manner. No one is born lazy. Only truly demented people enjoy causing pain and mental torment to themselves. Sympathy may be one form of attention, but it is hardly uplifting or inspiring.

9   Recent studies of procrastination have found that people who put things off as a matter of habit are often troubled with feelings of hopelessness, low self-esteem, guilt, or fear. Procrastination is also the province of perfectionists, who put things off because they are waiting for the perfect time to produce the perfect results.

10   Here are a few tips to help my fellow procrastinators out there get beyond their "but's" and past their "one day I'm gonna's."

Eight Small Steps for Getting Past Procrastination

11   1. *Take small bites.* Have you ever been to one of those Mexican restaurants that advertise Burritos As Big As Your Head? They aren't exaggerating, much. But you don't order one and then say, "I think I'll wait for a better time to eat this." No, you get to work on it. You don't try to do it in one huge bite, however; you eat that giant burrito one small bite at a time. This is not only good for digestion, it is good for decision making.

12   2. *Begin now!* Without even giving yourself time to think of excuses, sit down now and start the process and force yourself to keep at it for at least an hour. Set a time to pick up where you left off.

13   3. *Slam the door on critics.* If you feel that you can't make a decision because someone is holding you back, break free of that sense of helplessness and victimization. Sometimes you have to go against the sentiments of those around you in order to make decisions that open opportunities for yourself. You can't expect others to always share your vision. Don't let anything or anyone stand between you and your freedom to make decisions that improve your life. It is simply impossible to always reach a consensus.

"Whatever piece of business you have in hand, before stopping, do all the labor pertaining to it which can then be done."

—Abraham Lincoln

14   4. *Lighten up.* Procrastinators tend to take themselves far too seriously. You are significant only within a very limited scope. The world is not focused on your every move. The sun will still come up tomorrow. The stars will still shine tonight. No matter what you do, the future of the galaxy is not resting on your shoulders. If the thought of making a decision is weighing so heavily that you can't make it, you need to step away and regain perspective so that you don't take yourself so seriously. Do something to take your mind off the decision and to lighten your mood. Take a walk, visit a friend who cheers you up, read a comic novel, or take in a comedy at the movie theater or on television. Get out of that dark mood.

15   5. *Think of the carrot, not the stick.* Those who put things off sometimes do it because they focus on the difficulties and demands of taking an action rather than on the rewards that await them. Focus on the solution, not the problem. Keep your mind on the rewards and results of your decision rather than on the process itself. After all, how many times have you fretted and worried about doing something, only to discover that it was not nearly as painful as you had imagined? Don't dream of all the work involved; dream of the rewards you will reap when you have taken action and gone after what you want from life.

16   6. *Bring in a coach.* These days people have personal fitness trainers, personal bankers, personal speech coaches, personal accountants, personal nutrition advisers. Why not bring in a friend or family member to be your antiprocrastination coach? Give them a list of the things you need to do and order them to dog you until you do them. Provide the whip if you feel it is necessary. Drastic procrastination calls for drastic action.

17   7. *Live in the moment.* I knew of a fellow who came to the end of his life and realized that he had accomplished nothing that he had wanted to do. He lamented this fact to a friend of his, saying, *I don't know how I wasted my whole life.* The friend observed that he hadn't started out to waste his whole life. First, he had wasted a minute of it, then an hour, then a day, then a week, a month, a year,

a decade, and *then* his whole life. Take a clue, and do the opposite. Use up every minute, every hour, every day, until you have made the most of your entire life.

18 8. *Don't demand perfection.* Tell yourself there is not going to be a *perfect* time to get started, and that you don't have to be *perfect* in your performance. Compromise and start immediately and rough out the task, and then build upon it. No one is standing over your shoulder demanding that you make no mistakes. . . . You are far more likely to succeed if you work to please yourself, without feeling pressured to meet the standards of others.

Reprinted with the permission of Simon & Schuster Adult Publishing Group, from *You Can Make It Happen: A Nine-Step Plan for Success* by Stedman Graham, pp. 224–230. Copyright © 1997 by Graham-Williams Group. All rights reserved.

Comprehension Checkup

Fill in the Blanks

Drawing on what you learned from the selection, fill in the blanks with an appropriate word or phrase.

1. What is the selection about? _____

2. Of the eight tips presented by Stedman Graham, list the four that you find most helpful.

    a. _____

    b. _____

    c. _____

    d. _____

3. Name the two types of procrastinators.

    a. _____

    b. _____

4. There are three theories that attempt to explain why people procrastinate. List them below and give an example or illustration for each one.

    a. _____

    _____

    b. _____

    _____

    c. _____

    _____

Multiple Choice

Write the letter of the correct answer in the blank provided.

_____ 1. Graham would agree with which of the following:
    a. Successful people decide things impulsively.
    b. It's not possible to improve one's basic outlook on life.
    c. Procrastinators are capable of changing their decision-making habits.
    d. Before you decide on any important actions, carefully gather opinions from friends and family.

_____   2. All of the following are typical of procrastinators *except*
   a. taking a project one step at a time
   b. expecting perfection
   c. worrying about possible failure
   d. taking themselves far too seriously

_____   3. Graham suggests that procrastination can lead to
   a. feelings of hopelessness
   b. poor self-esteem
   c. guilt-ridden feelings
   d. all of the above

_____   4. What is the meaning of the word *demented* as used in paragraph 8?
   a. very fine
   b. easily hurt
   c. mentally ill
   d. spoiled

_____   5. According to Graham, procrastinators like which of the following excuses:
   a. I'll do it tomorrow!
   b. I'll wait for an easier way.
   c. I'm too distracted right now.
   d. All of the above.

True or False

Indicate whether the statement is true or false by writing T or F in the blank provided.

_____   6. According to Graham, many procrastinators have perfectionistic tendencies.

_____   7. Graham has probably never had a tendency to procrastinate.

_____   8. Graham suggests that many procrastinators should take themselves far less seriously.

_____   9. Some people procrastinate because they like the attention and sympathy such behavior brings.

_____   10. The word *lamented* in paragraph 17 means "celebrated."

Vocabulary in Context

Choose one of the following words to complete each of the sentences below. Use each word only once. Be sure to pay close attention to the context clues provided.

chronic	consensus	drastic	lamented	logical	scope
compromise	demented	fretted	literary	perspective	vitally

1. The _____ of a paperback dictionary that has 50,000 entries is far less than that of a hardback dictionary with 180,000 entries.

2. Her _____ neck pain was probably caused by a pinched nerve.

3. Marcy _____ about her son's withdrawn behavior and his sudden tendency to stay in his room all day.

4. Not many people realize that Steve Martin, the zany comedian, also has _____ talent and has published two well-received books.

5. Because the squabbling couple refused to _____ with each other, the marriage counselor recommended the dissolution of the marriage.

6. After the medical lab results came in, the doctor said that no _____ measures were necessary and instead advised a cautious wait-and-see approach.

7. In contrast to when I was a teenager, the _____ I now have on life is entirely different.

8. Many environmentalists say that it is _____ important that the United States reduce its dependence on fossil fuels.

9. At the funeral, many of those present _____ the loss of the young fireman who had given his life to rescue a little girl trapped inside a burning apartment.

10. The public defender argued that his client should not receive the death penalty because his client had a long history of mental problems and was _____.

11. Although Brian attends the biology class, he fails to attend the required lab sessions; therefore, it is _____ to assume that he might not pass the class.

12. It was the _____ of all members of my family that my decision to drop out of school was a mistake.

In Your Own Words

What is the main idea of this poem? How does the poem relate to the previous selection?

> Walk around feeling like a leaf
>   Know you could tumble any second.
>   *Then* decide what to do with your time.
>
> —*Naomi Shihab Nye*

The Art of Writing

In a brief essay, respond to the item below.

> Find something in your life that you feel needs improvement. Think about how you could go about making this improvement. Identify three specific things you could do that would move you toward your goal. For example: Your goal might be to lose 15 pounds. Your three specific actions might be (1) to go running three times a week, (2) to allow yourself no fast food on weekends, and (3) to substitute diet sodas for regular sodas. Decide how long you're going to stick to your three specific actions. Be sure to answer the following questions: What are you going to try to improve in your life? What specific actions are you going to take to reach your goal? How long are you going to persevere?

Internet Activity

Stedman Graham gives readers general pointers for dealing with procrastination. The University of Buffalo has put together a website to help students overcome procrastination:

> http://ub-counseling.buffalo.edu/stressprocrast.shtml#intr

Consult the site and list a few of the tips you find there.

TEST-TAKING TIP

Be Prepared

Sometime in the next few weeks you will take a test in one of your classes. Although this advice may seem obvious, you need to prepare for the test. Don't wait until late the night before to begin studying the material. That's too late. Following are some suggestions for preparing for the test.

1. Read the course material before it is discussed in class. Every evening review the day's class notes.

2. Practice the SQ3R method of studying. Annotate and highlight your textbook and class notes.

3. Begin reviewing for a test days in advance. If you learn best by listening, read the material out loud. If you learn best by seeing, make an outline of the material. If you learn best by being physically involved, copy your notes.

4. Find out what the test is going to cover. Your instructor may give you a study guide or sample questions. If not, put together your own study guide and sample questions. What points has the instructor emphasized? What do you think are the most important points?

5. Find out what kind of test it's going to be—multiple choice, true-false, short answer, short essay, or a combination. Knowing what to expect will guide your preparation and ease your anxiety.

The most important test-taking tip is—be prepared!

Discovering Meaning Through Structure

Topics, Main Ideas, and Details

2

Relativity (1953)
BY M. C. ESCHER

1   Do the people depicted in the painting appear to be aware of each other's existence?

2   What is the staircase meant to represent? Is there a reason why the figures do not have facial characteristics?

3   What does the painting illustrate about perception, which is the theme of this chapter?

Topics and Main Ideas

Most paragraphs are about a particular **topic** or **subject.** The topic is usually a single word or phrase and is often the noun that is mentioned most frequently in a paragraph. We can identify the topic by asking ourselves, "What is this all about?" or "Who is this all about?"

Paragraphs are supposed to be organized around a main idea with all sentences supporting this **main idea,** or key point, of the paragraph. The main idea can be identified by asking the question, "What key point does the author want me to know about the topic?"

The main idea may be directly stated in a paragraph—usually, but not always, in the first or last sentence—or it can be implied. When trying to find a main idea that is directly stated, it helps to remember that you are looking for a general statement, not a specific one. When main ideas are implied, you, the reader, are responsible for coming up with a general statement that unites the author's key details. This general statement should be no more than one sentence long.

Details are supporting sentences that reinforce the main idea. While the main idea is a general statement, supporting details provide specific information, such as facts, examples, or reasons, that explain or elaborate on the main idea.

As an illustration of the difference between main ideas and details, study the invitation below. The main idea of the invitation is the fact that a reception is going to be held. The details tell us who the reception is for and the date, time, and place it will occur.

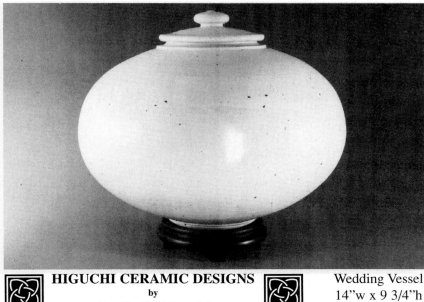

HIGUCHI CERAMIC DESIGNS
by
Jon Yukio Higuchi

Wedding Vessel
14"w x 9 3/4"h

Reprinted with permission of Jon Yukio Higuchi. Photo: Cheryl Miller

 Jon Yukio Higuchi "All Fired Up"

November 12 - December 5, 2002

Glendale Community College
Student Union Gallery

You are invited to an open Reception on:
Tuesday, November 12, 2002
6:00 p.m. - 8:00 p.m.

Glendale Community College
6000 West Olive/Dunlap Ave.
Glendale, AZ 85302

Sponsored by the Evening Students Association

Those supporting sentences that directly reinforce the main idea are called **major** supporting details, and those sentences that serve only to reinforce the major supporting details are called **minor** supporting details.

Read the following paragraph from *Gilbert's Living with Art* by Mark Getlein. The topic of the paragraph is perception.

1. In visual perception, our eyes take in information in the form of light patterns; the brain processes these patterns to give them meaning. The mechanics of perception work much the same way for everyone, yet in a given situation we do not all perceive the same things. The human eye cannot take in all available visual information. Our world is too complex, and we are constantly bombarded with an incredible range of visual images. To avoid overloading our mental circuits, the brain responds only to that visual information required to meet our needs at one moment.

The next paragraph contains a main idea sentence and a series of examples that support it. The topic of this paragraph, and the others that follow, is also perception.

2. It is easier to cope with our complex visual world if we simplify our perceptions and see according to our immediate needs. Suppose you are motoring along a busy street. Your eyes "see" everything, but what does your brain register? If you are the car's driver, you will see the traffic signs and lights, because awareness of such details is necessary. If you are hungry, your attention may be attracted by fast-food signs. If you are looking for a specific address, you will focus on building numbers and block out nearly everything else.

Identify the main idea sentence in paragraph 3 below.

3. Studies indicate that the brain is often more important than the eyes in determining what each of us sees as we move through the world. The brain's ability to control perception is obvious when we study ambiguous figures, such as the classic one reproduced here. When you first look at this drawing, you may see a white vase. Or you may see two dark profiles. Even after you have been made aware of the two images, you must consciously work at going back and forth between them. You can feel your brain shifting as it organizes the visual information into first one image and then the other.

Vase-profile illusion

Paragraph 3 expresses the main idea in the first sentence and then gives us an example that illustrates it.

To gain understanding of how main ideas and major and minor supporting details work together in a paragraph, read the following paragraph and study the outline that follows.

4. While perception can cause us to miss seeing what is actually present in the visual field, it can also do the reverse: cause us to "see" what is not present. The brain supplies information to create a kind of order it requires,

even though that information may not be recorded by the eyes. In the illustration of wavy forms you may see a perfect white circle, but there is no circle. There is only the illusion of a white circle created by breaks in the wavy forms. This is just another trick our brains play on us as part of the phenomenon of perception.

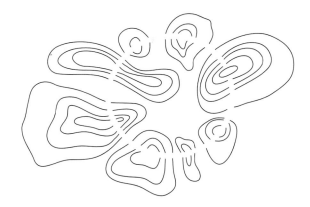

Wavy Forms

From Mark Getlein, *Gilbert's Living With Art*, 6th ed., New York: McGraw-Hill, 2002, p. 274. Copyright © 2002 McGraw-Hill. Reprinted by permission of The McGraw-Hill Companies, Inc.

Key: MI (main idea), MSD (major supporting detail), msd (minor supporting detail)

   I.   Perception can cause us to miss seeing what is there and can cause us to "see" what is not there. (MI)
      A.   The brain supplies information to create order in what our eyes see. (MSD)
          1.   You see a perfect white circle in the wavy forms. (msd)
          2.   In this way, our brains trick us. (msd)

It is wise to remember that while all paragraphs have a topic, not all paragraphs have main ideas. Some background or descriptive paragraphs, which are meant to set the tone or mood of a piece of writing, may not have any main idea at all.

Exercise: Locating Topics in Textbook Material

Locate the topic of each paragraph. Remember to ask the question, "Who or what is the paragraph about?"

1.   Tickets to athletic and artistic events are sometimes resold at higher-than-original prices—a market transaction known by the unsavory term "scalping." For example, a $40 ticket to a college bowl game may be resold by the original buyer for $200, $250, or more. The media often denounces scalpers for "ripping off" buyers by charging "exorbitant" prices. Scalping and extortion are synonymous in some people's minds. But is ticket scalping undesirable? Not on economic grounds. Both seller and buyer of a "scalped" ticket benefit and a more interested and appreciative audience results.

(From Campbell R. McConnell and Stanley L. Brue, *Economics*, 14th ed., New York: McGraw-Hill, 1999, p. 56.)

Topic: _____

During a one-month period in 2001, 30.7 percent of high school students had ridden in a vehicle driven by a person who had been drinking alcohol.

2. Alcohol consumption exacts an alarming toll on college students. Students who drink more frequently die in traffic accidents, receive citations for driving under the influence, damage personal or public property, argue or fight, attempt suicide, experience or commit sexual abuse, miss classes, receive failing grades, suffer academic probation, or drop out of college than do those who are not drinkers. Most campus rapes occur when the victim, the assailant, or both have been drinking.

From Clinton Benjamin, et al., *Human Biology*, New York: McGraw-Hill, 1997, p. 442.

Topic: _____

3. Anyone who has roomed with a noisy person, worked in a noisy office, or tried to study with a party going on in the next room can attest to the effect of noise on one's level of stress. Noise can raise blood pressure, increase heart rate, and lead to muscle tension. Noise has been found to be related to job dissatisfaction and to result in irritation and anxiety. Most disturbing is noise that constantly changes in pitch, intensity, or frequency. We may become used to more common and stable noise and almost ignore it. People who live near airports, for example, seem to not even hear the planes after a while. However, just because you become accustomed to the noise or are able to tune it out doesn't mean you are not being affected by it.

From Jerrold Greenberg, *Comprehensive Stress Management*, 6th ed., New York: McGraw-Hill, 1999, p. 76.

Topic: _____

4. In the traditional cultures of Asia, arranged marriages were the rule. Marriages were designed to further the well-being of families, not of the individuals involved. Marriage was traditionally seen as a matter of ancestors, descendants, and property. Supporters of these traditions point out that love is a fleeting emotion and not a sensible basis for such an important decision. Today, arranged marriages are still very common in India, in many Muslim nations, and in sub-Saharan Africa. However, it appears that this tradition is rapidly deteriorating, often in proportion to the degree of Western influence.

From Curtis Byer, et al., *Dimensions of Human Sexuality*, 5th ed., New York: McGraw-Hill, 1999, p. 39.

Topic: _____

"When people are bored, it is primarily with their own selves."

—Eric Hoffer

5. If you are like most people, you have indulged in fake listening many times. You go to history class, sit in the third row, and look squarely at the instructor as she speaks. But your mind is far away, floating in the clouds of a pleasant daydream. Occasionally you come back to earth: the instructor writes an important term on the chalkboard, and you dutifully copy it in your notebook. Every once in a while the instructor makes a witty remark, causing others in the class to laugh. You smile politely, pretending that you have heard the remark and found it mildly humorous. You have a vague sense of guilt that you are not paying close attention, but you tell yourself that any material you miss can be picked up from a friend's notes. Besides, the instructor is talking about road construction in ancient Rome and nothing could be more boring. So, back you go into your private little world. Unfortunately, fake listening has two drawbacks:

(1) You miss a lot of information, and (2) you can botch a personal or business relationship.

From Hamiton Gregory, *Public Speaking for College and Career*, 4th ed., New York: McGraw-Hill, 1996, p. 27.

Topic: _____

6. Despite our couples-oriented society, single-person households are outracing the growth of most other household types. The number of Americans living alone has increased 90 percent since 1970, much faster than the 12 percent growth in married couples. By 1990, nearly 23 million Americans were living alone, so roughly one of every four occupied dwelling units had only one person in it. Yet singles are hardly a monolithic group, with the divorced, widowed, and never-married constituting distinct groups of those aged 15 and older. The high incidence of divorce, the ability of the elderly to maintain their own homes alone, and the deferral of marriage among young adults have contributed to the high rate of increase in the number of single-person households.

From James W. Vander Zanden, *Sociology: The Core*, 4th ed., New York: McGraw-Hill, 1996, p. 306.

Topic: _____

Exercise: Locating Main Ideas in Textbook Material

Locate the main idea sentence of each paragraph. The main idea can be identified by asking the question, "What key point does the author want me to know about the topic?"

All excerpts from David G. Myers, *Social Psychology*, 7th ed., New York: McGraw-Hill, 2002, pp. 153, 156–157.

"Anxiety is fear of one's self."

—Wilhem Stekel

1. We infer our emotions by observing our bodies and our behaviors. For example, a stimulus such as a growling bear confronts a woman in the forest. She tenses, her heartbeat increases, adrenaline flows, and she runs away. Observing all this, she then experiences fear. At a college where I am to lecture, I awake before dawn and am unable to get back to sleep. Noting my wakefulness, I conclude that I must be anxious.

Main Idea: _____

2. James Laird instructed college students to pull their brows together and frown while experimenters attached electrodes to their faces. The act of maintaining a frown caused students to report feeling angry. Those students induced to make a smiling face reported feeling happier and found cartoons more humorous. We have all experienced this phenomenon. We're feeling crabby, but then the phone rings or someone comes to the door and elicits from us warm, polite behavior. "How's everything?" "Just fine, thanks. How are things with you?" "Oh, not bad. . . ." If our feelings are not too intense, this warm behavior may change our whole attitude. It's tough to smile and feel grouchy. When Miss Universe parades her smile, she may, after all, be helping herself feel happy. Going through the motions can trigger the emotions.

Main Idea: _____

3. Your gait can affect how you feel. When you get up from reading this chapter, walk for a minute taking short, shuffling steps with eyes downcast.

It's a great way to feel depressed. Want to feel better? Walk for a minute taking long strides with your arms swinging and your eyes straight ahead. Can you feel the difference?

Main Idea: _____

4. It appears that unnecessary rewards sometimes have a hidden cost. Rewarding people for doing what they already enjoy may lead them to attribute their doing it to the reward. This undermines their self-perception that they do it because they like it. If you pay people for playing with puzzles, they will later play with the puzzles less than those who play without being paid. If you promise children a reward for doing what they intrinsically enjoy (for example playing with magic markers) then you will turn their play into work.

Main Idea: _____

"Take away the cause and the effect ceases."

—Miguel de Cervantes

5. An old man lived alone on a street where boys played noisily every afternoon. The din annoyed him, so one day he called the boys to his door. He told them he loved the cheerful sound of children's voices and promised them each 50 cents if they would return the next day. Next afternoon the youngsters raced back and played more lustily than ever. The old man paid them and promised another reward the next day. Again they returned, whooping it up, and the man again paid them; this time 25 cents. The following day they got only 15 cents, and the man explained that his meager resources were being exhausted. "Please, though, would you come to play for 10 cents tomorrow?" The disappointed boys told the man they would not be back. It wasn't worth the effort, they said, to play all afternoon at his house for only 10 cents. This folk tale illustrates the result of bribing people to do what they already like doing; they may then see their action as externally controlled rather than intrinsically appealing.

Main Idea: _____

Exercise: Locating Supporting Details in Textbook Material

In previous exercises, we have seen that the main idea in a paragraph is frequently located at either the beginning or end of the paragraph. However, the main idea may also appear in other locations within a paragraph, such as in the middle, or at both the beginning and the end. Wherever the main idea is located, it must be supported by details. Most authors provide examples, illustrations, major points, reasons, or facts and statistics to develop their main idea. While a main idea can be either directly stated somewhere in the paragraph or implied, supporting details are always directly stated. The ability to recognize supporting details is of crucial importance in the reading process. Locating supporting details will tell you whether you have correctly identified the main idea.

For those of you who are visual learners, diagrams showing the development of a paragraph and the position of the main idea and supporting details might be helpful. The topic of each of the following paragraphs is perceptual organization.

After reading the explanation for each type of paragraph, write several key supporting details on the line provided.

From Richard Schaefer, *Sociology*, 3rd ed., New York: McGraw-Hill, 2000, pp. 54, 56, 158. Copyright © 2000 McGraw-Hill. Reprinted by permission of The McGraw-Hill Companies, Inc. Information for paragraph 5 is from Wayne Weiten, *Psychology Applied to Modern Life*, 6th ed., Belmont, CA: Wadsworth, 2000, p. 161.

Main Idea Sentence

Details

1. *Much of perception is based on prior experience.* For instance, Colin Turnbull tells of the time he took a Pygmy from the dense rain forests of Africa to the vast African plains. The Pygmy had never before seen objects at a great distance. Hence, the first time he saw a herd of buffalo in the distance, he thought it was a swarm of insects. Imagine his confusion when he was driven toward the animals. He concluded that he was being fooled by witchcraft because the "insects" seemed to grow into buffalo before his eyes.

In paragraph 1, the main idea is stated in the first sentence. The author states the main idea and then provides an example to illustrate it. A diagram of this type of paragraph would be a triangle with the point aiming downward. The main idea is represented by the horizontal line at the top.

Supporting Details:

_____

Details

Main Idea Sentence

2. A college professor was attacked by an actor in a staged assault. Immediately after the event, 141 witnesses were questioned in detail. Their descriptions were then compared to a videotape of the staged "crime." The total accuracy score for the group (on features such as appearance, age, weight, and height of the assailant) was only *25 percent* of the maximum possible. This incident dramatically demonstrates why witnesses to crimes so often disagree. *As you can see, impressions formed when a person is surprised, threatened, or under stress are especially prone to distortion.*

In paragraph 2, the author gives an example at the beginning and uses the main point to draw a conclusion. A diagram for this type of paragraph places the main idea at the bottom of the triangle.

Supporting Details:

_____

Details

Main Idea Sentence

Details

3. Harness yourself to a hang glider, step off a cliff, and soar. No matter how exhilarating, your flight still wouldn't provide a true "bird's eye" view. *Many birds see the world in ways that would seem strange to a human.* For example, pigeons, ducks, and humming-birds can see ultraviolet light, which adds an extra color to their visual palette. Homing pigeons and many migrating birds perceive polarized light, which aids them in navigation. The American woodcock can survey a 360-degree panorama without moving its eyes or head.

In paragraph 3, the author begins with an example, states the main idea, and then concludes with additional examples. Because the main idea is in the middle, the diagram resembles a diamond.

Supporting Details:

_____

_____

4. *Psychologists are gradually convincing lawyers, judges, and police officers of the fallibility of eyewitness testimony.* In one typical court case, a police officer testified that he saw the defendant shoot the victim as both stood in a doorway 120 feet away. Measurements made by a psychologist showed that at that distance light from the dimly lit doorway was extremely weak—less than a fifth of that from a candle. To further show that identification was improbable, a juror stood in the doorway under identical lighting conditions. None of the other jurors could identify him. The defendant was acquitted.

Main Idea Sentence

Details

Main Idea Sentence

Even in broad daylight, eyewitness testimony is untrustworthy. After a horrible DC-10 airliner crash in Chicago in 1979, 84 pilots who saw the accident were interviewed. Forty-two said the DC-10's landing gear was up, and 42 said it was down! As one investigator commented, the best witness may be a "kid under 12 years old who doesn't have his parents around." *These and other incidents are being used by psychologists to demonstrate to legal professionals the unpredictability of eyewitness testimony.*

In paragraph 4, the author begins with the main idea, provides detailed illustrations of it, and concludes with a restatement of the main idea. A diagram of this type of paragraph would have an hour-glass shape.

Supporting Details:

_____

_____

Main idea not directly stated

5.   Remember Evan, that bully from your elementary school? He made your nine-year-old life a total misery—constantly looking for opportunities to poke fun at you and beat you up. Now, when you meet someone named Evan, you notice that your initial reaction is negative and that it takes a while before you warm up to him. Why?

In paragraph 5, the main idea is not stated in any specific sentence. Instead, all of the sentences are working together to create a word picture in your mind. Because no one sentence is clearly the main idea, a diagram of this paragraph might resemble a square or a rectangle.

   Now practice what you have learned. Identify the main idea in the paragraphs below. Then draw a diagram of the paragraph and list some supporting details.

6.   In a literal sense, language may color how we see the world. Researchers Berlin and Kay have noted that humans possess the physical ability to make millions of color distinctions, yet languages differ in the number of colors that are recognized. The English language distinguishes between yellow and orange, but some other languages do not. In the Dugum Dani language of New Guinea's West Highlands, there are only two basic color terms—*modla* for "white" and *mili* for "black." By contrast, there are 11 basic terms in English. Russian and Hungarian, though, have 12 color terms. Russians have terms for light blue and dark blue, while Hungarians have terms for two different shades of red.

Diagram: _____

Main Idea: _____

Supporting Details:

_____

_____

_____

7.   We convey a great deal about how we feel in our facial expressions, but this can be a real problem when people of different cultures interpret facial expressions differently. Curious about cultural differences, researchers Tang and Shioiri decided to experiment by showing medical students in Japan and the United States photos of seven basic emotions: anger, contempt, disgust, fear, happiness, sadness, and surprise. They discovered that the two groups

agreed on only one facial expression: surprise. About 96 percent on both sides came to that conclusion.

Diagram: _____

Main Idea: _____

Supporting Details:

_____

_____

8. Journalist Naomi Wolf has used the term *the beauty myth* to refer to an exaggerated ideal of beauty, beyond the reach of all but a few females. When females carry adherence to "the beauty myth" to an extreme, they may develop eating disorders such as anorexia or undertake costly but unnecessary cosmetic surgery procedures. In a *People* magazine "health" feature, a young actress stated that she knows it is time to eat when she passes out on the set. Unrealistic standards of appearance and body image can have a destructive effect on young girls and adult women.

Diagram: _____

Main Idea: _____

Supporting Details:

_____

_____

Exercise: Identifying Main and Supporting Ideas and Diagramming Paragraphs in Textbook Material

The main idea sentence appears at different locations in the following paragraphs. Write the number of the main idea sentence on the line. Then draw a diagram of the paragraph and list numbers of the supporting detail sentences.

Information is from Ronald B. Adler and Neil Towne, *Looking Out/Looking In*, 9th ed., Fort Worth: Harcourt Brace, 1999, pp. 94–96, 114, 121.

A. (1) A person with high self-esteem is more likely to think well of others. (2) Someone with low self-esteem is more likely to have a poor opinion of others. (3) Your own experience may bear this out: Persons with low self–esteem are often cynical and quick to ascribe the worst possible motives to others, whereas those who feel good about themselves are disposed to think favorably about the people they encounter. (4) As one writer put it, "What we find 'out there' is what we put there with our unconscious projections. (5) When we think we are looking out a window, it may be, more often than we realize, that we are really gazing into a looking glass." (6) Our self concepts influence how we think about ourselves and interact with others.

Main Idea Sentence: _____   Diagram: _____

Supporting Details: _____

B. (1) We often judge ourselves more charitably than we do others. (2) When others suffer, we often blame the problem on their personal qualities. (3) On the other hand, when we're the victims, we find explanations outside ourselves. (4) Consider a few examples. (5) When *they* botch a job, we might think they weren't listening well or trying hard enough; when *we* make the mistake, the problem was unclear directions or not enough time. (6) When *he* lashes out angrily, we say he's being moody or too sensitive; when *we* blow off steam, it's because of the pressure we've been under. (7) When *she* gets caught speeding, we say she should have been more careful; when *we* get the ticket, we deny we were driving too fast or say, "Everybody does it."

Main Idea Sentence: _____   Diagram: _____

Supporting Details: _____

C. (1) At one time or another you've probably seen photos of sights invisible to the unaided eye: perhaps an infrared photo of a familiar area or the vastly enlarged image of a minute object taken by an electron microscope. (2) You've also noticed how certain animals are able to hear sounds and smell odors that are not apparent to humans. (3) Experiences like these remind us that there is much more going on in the world than we are able to experience with our limited senses; in fact, we're only aware of a small part of what is going on around us. (4) For instance, most people who live in large cities find that the noises of traffic, people, and construction soon fade out of their awareness. (5) Others can take a walk through the forest without distinguishing one bird's call from another or noticing the differences among various types of vegetation. (6) On a personal level, we've all had the experience of failing to notice something unusual about a friend—perhaps a new hairstyle or a sad expression—until it's called to our attention.

Main Idea Sentence: _____   Diagram: _____

Supporting Details: _____

D. (1) The kind of work we do often influences our view of the world. (2) Imagine five people taking a walk through the park. (3) One, a botanist, is fascinated by the variety of trees and plants. (4) The zoologist is looking for interesting animals. (5) The third, a meteorologist, keeps an eye on the sky, noticing changes in the weather. (6) The fourth companion, a psychologist, is totally unaware of nature, instead concentrating on the interaction among the people in the park. (7) The fifth person, being a pickpocket, quickly takes advantage of the others' absorption to make some money. (8) Our occupational roles shape our perceptions.

Main Idea Sentence: _____   Diagram: _____

Supporting Details: _____

E. (1) Even within the same occupational setting, the different roles that participants have can affect their perceptions. (2) Consider a typical college classroom, for example. (3) The experiences of the instructor and students often are quite dissimilar. (4) Having dedicated a large part of their lives to their work, most professors see their subject matter—whether French literature, physics, or speech communication—as vitally important. (5) Students who are taking the course to satisfy a general education requirement may view the subject quite differently: maybe as one of many obstacles that stand between them and a degree, maybe as a chance to meet new people.

Main Idea Sentence: _____   Diagram: _____

Supporting Details: _____

F. (1) Because we're exposed to more input than we can possibly manage, the first step in perception is the selection of which data we will attend to and which we will ignore. (2) Something that is louder, larger, or brighter stands out. (3) This explains why—other things being equal—we're more likely to remember extremely tall or short people and why someone who laughs or talks loudly at a party attracts more attention (not always favorable) than do quiet guests. (4) *Repetitious stimuli, repetitious stimuli, repetitious stimuli*—also attract attention. (5) ***ATTENTION IS ALSO FREQUENTLY RELATED*** to contrast *or* change *in* **STIMULATION.** (6) Put differently, unchanging people or things become less noticeable. (7) Selection isn't just a matter of attending to some stimuli; it also involves ignoring other cues.

Main Idea Sentence: _____   Diagram: _____

Supporting Details: _____

SELECTION

Black Men and Public Space   *by Brent Staples*

"Over the years, I learned to smother the rage I felt at so often being taken for a criminal."

Getting the Picture

The first paragraph of the essay "Black Men and Public Space" by Brent Staples illustrates how perception affects behavior. By providing the reader with a riveting description, it serves as an introduction to the author's key ideas. In the paragraphs that follow, Staples discusses the effects of being a victim of stereotyping. At the end of the essay, he describes his creative solution to signaling his safe intentions to others.

Bio-sketch

Brent Staples, born in 1951, grew up in a family with an alcoholic father. He had little hope of attending college, but a special program gave him extra academic help. After graduating from Widener College (now Widener University) with a B.A. in 1973, he went on to earn his Ph.D. in psychology from the University of Chicago in 1982. Staples is currently a journalist who writes about political and cultural issues for *The New York Times*. His book, *Parallel Time: Growing Up in Black and White*, won the Anisfield Wolff Book Award.

Brushing Up on Vocabulary

warren a mazelike place containing many passageways; a building or area containing many inhabitants in crowded quarters. The word originally referred to a game park.

wee very early; small or tiny.

1   My first victim was a woman—white, well-dressed, probably in her early twenties. I came upon her late one evening on a deserted street in Hyde Park, a relatively affluent neighborhood in an otherwise mean, impoverished section of Chicago. As I swung onto the avenue behind her, there seemed to be a discreet, uninflammatory distance between us. Not so. She cast back a worried glance. To her, the youngish

black man—a broad six feet two inches with a beard and billowing hair, both hands shoved into the pockets of a bulky military jacket—seemed menacingly close. After a few more quick glimpses, she picked up her pace and was soon running in earnest. Within seconds she disappeared into a cross street.

2   That first encounter, and those that followed, signified that a vast, unnerving gulf lay between nighttime pedestrians—particularly women—and me.

3   After dark, on the warrenlike streets of Brooklyn where I live, I often see women who fear the worst from me. They seem to have set their faces on neutral, and with their purse straps strung across their chests bandolier-style, they forge ahead as though bracing themselves against being tackled. I understand, of course, that the danger they perceive is not a hallucination. Women are particularly vulnerable to street violence, and young black males are drastically overrepresented among the perpetrators of that violence. Yet these truths are no solace against the kind of alienation that comes of being ever the suspect, a fearsome entity with whom pedestrians avoid making eye contact.

4   Over the years, I learned to smother the rage I felt at so often being taken for a criminal. Not to do so would surely have led to madness. I now take precautions to make myself less threatening. I move about with care, particularly late in the evening. I give a wide berth to nervous people on subway platforms during the wee hours, particularly when I have exchanged business clothes for jeans. If I happen to be entering a building behind some people who appear skittish, I may walk by, letting them clear the lobby before I return, so as not to seem to be following them. I have been calm and extremely congenial on those rare occasions when I've been pulled over by the police.

5   And on late-evening constitutionals I employ what has proved to be an excellent tension-reducing measure. I whistle melodies from Beethoven and Vivaldi and the more popular classical composers. Even steely New Yorkers hunching toward nighttime destinations seem to relax, and occasionally they even join in the tune. Virtually everybody seems to sense that a mugger wouldn't be warbling bright, sunny selections from Vivaldi's *Four Seasons*. It is my equivalent of the cowbell that hikers wear when they know they are in bear country.

From Brent Staples, "Black Men and Public Space" in *Ms. Magazine*, 1986. Reprinted by permission of the author.

Comprehension Checkup

Indicate whether the statement is true of false by writing T or F in the blank provided.

_____   1. In the essay, Brent Staples describes the intimidating effect he has on nighttime pedestrians.

_____   2. The first woman described in the essay perceived Staples as a threat to her safety.

_____   3. It does not bother Staples to be alienated from those he encounters on the streets.

_____   4. Staples has learned to stifle the anger he feels at being taken for a criminal because of his race.

_____   5. Staples monitors his movements to make himself appear less threatening to others.

_____   6. Staples behaves in the same manner whether dressed in casual clothes or business wear.

_____   7. Staples does not want to appear as though he is following someone when he enters a building.

_____ 8. When pulled over by a policeman, Staples is quick to express his anger and indignation.

_____ 9. Staples whistles classical music selections to indicate to others that he is unlikely to be a mugger.

_____ 10. Whistling classical music provides a measure of safety for Staples.

Vocabulary in Context

Each item below includes a sentence from the selection. Using the context clues from this sentence, determine the best meaning of the italicized words.

1. I came upon her late one evening on a deserted street in Hyde Park, a relatively *affluent* neighborhood in an otherwise mean, *impoverished* section of Chicago.

    affluent means _____

    impoverished means _____

2. As I swung onto the avenue behind her, there seemed to be a *discreet*, uninflammatory distance between us.

    discreet means _____

3. To her, the youngish black man—a broad six feet two inches with a beard and billowing hair, both hands shoved into the pockets of a bulky military jacket—seemed *menacingly* close.

    menacingly means _____

4. After a few more quick *glimpses*, she picked up her pace and was soon running in *earnest*.

    glimpses means _____

    earnest means _____

5. That first *encounter*, and those that followed, signified that a *vast*, unnerving gulf lay between nighttime pedestrians—particularly women—and me.

    encounter means _____

    vast means _____

6. They seem to have set their faces on *neutral*, and with their purse straps strung across their chests *bandolier-style*, they *forge* ahead as though bracing themselves against being tackled.

    neutral means _____

    bandolier-style means _____

    _____

    forge means _____

Vocabulary Practice

Using the context clues from each sentence below, choose the best definition for the italicized word, and write the appropriate answer letter in the blank.

_____ 1. The danger they perceive is not a *hallucination*. (paragraph 3)
    a. an illusion
    b. an aggravation
    c. an outrage

_____ 2. Women are particularly *vulnerable* to street violence. (3)
   a. hardened
   b. susceptible
   c. oblivious

_____ 3. Yet these truths are no *solace*. (3)
   a. comfort
   b. criticism
   c. contempt

_____ 4. The kind of *alienation* that comes of being ever the suspect (3)
   a. detraction
   b. correction
   c. separation

_____ 5. A fearsome *entity* (3)
   a. demonstrator
   b. being
   c. worker

_____ 6. Learned to *smother* the rage (4)
   a. instigate
   b. stifle
   c. create

_____ 7. Give a wide *berth* to nervous people (4)
   a. follow
   b. reality
   c. space

_____ 8. Calm and extremely *congenial* (4)
   a. angry
   b. sarcastic
   c. friendly

_____ 9. On late-evening *constitutionals* (5)
   a. demonstrations
   b. initiations
   c. walks

In Your Own Words

1. What kinds of things do you look for when you are trying to decide whether or not a stranger is threatening?

2. What steps do you take to make yourself less threatening to others when you are out late at night?

Internet Activity

Racial profiling occurs when people are treated differently because of characteristics that are associated with race, most prominently skin color. In the last few years, many discussions of racial profiling have appeared in the media, especially about racial profiling by law-enforcement agencies. Using an Internet search engine like Google <www.google.com> or Yahoo <www.yahoo.com>, explore the Internet to find discussions or articles about racial profiling. Write a paragraph describing what you learned about racial profiling. Based on what you learned, do you have an opinion about whether law-enforcement agencies should be allowed to engage in racial profiling?

SELECTION

The Look of a Victim   *by Loretta Malandro and Larry Barker*

Did you know that some people are more likely to get mugged than others because of their body language? To assess your "muggability rating," read the article below.

1   Little Red Riding Hood set herself up to be mugged. Her first mistake was skipping through the forest to grandma's house. Her second mistake was stopping to pick flowers. At this point, as you might remember in the story, the mean, heavy wolf comes along and begins to check her out. He observes, quite perceptively, that she is happy, outgoing, and basically unaware of any dangers in her surrounding environment. The big bad wolf catches these nonverbal cues and splits to grandma's house. He knows that Red is an easy mark. From this point we all know what happens.

2   Body movements and gestures reveal a lot of information about a person. Like Little Red Riding Hood, pedestrians may signal to criminals that they are easy targets for mugging by the way they walk. When was the last time you assessed your "muggability rating"? In a recent study two psychologists set out to identify those body movements that characterized easy victims. They assembled "muggability ratings" of sixty New York pedestrians from the people who may have been the most qualified to judge—prison inmates who had been convicted of assault.

3   The researchers unobtrusively videotaped pedestrians on weekdays between 10:00 A.M. and 12 P.M. Each pedestrian was taped for six to eight seconds, the approximate time it takes a mugger to size up an approaching person. The judges (prison inmates) rated the "assault potential" of the sixty pedestrians on a ten-point scale. A rating of one indicated someone was "a very easy rip-off," of two, "an easy dude to corner." Toward the other end of the scale, nine meant a person "would be heavy; would give you a hard time," and ten indicated that the mugger "would avoid it, too big a situation, too heavy."

4   The results revealed several body movements that characterized easy victims: "Their strides were either very long or very short; they moved awkwardly, raising their left legs with their left arms (instead of alternating them); on each step they tended to lift their whole foot up and then place it down (less muggable sorts took steps in which their feet rocked from heel to toe). Overall the people rated most muggable walked as if they were in conflict with themselves; they seemed to make each move in the most difficult way possible."

From Dr. Loretta Malandro and Dr. Larry Barker in *Nonverbal Communication*. Copyright © 1988 McGraw-Hill. Reprinted by permission of Dr. Loretta Malandro.

✔ Comprehension Checkup

Write the letter of the correct answer in the blank provided.

_____   1.   The main idea of paragraph 1 is expressed in the
                a. first sentence of the paragraph
                b. second sentence of the paragraph
                c. third sentence of the paragraph

_____   2.   The wolf is aware that Little Red will be easy to mug because
                a. she is an observant person
                b. she is oblivious to her surroundings
                c. she is a nature lover

_____ 3. The main idea of paragraph 2 is expressed in the
  a. first sentence of the paragraph
  b. third sentence of the paragraph
  c. fourth sentence of the paragraph

_____ 4. Persons convicted of assault were chosen to participate in the study because
  a. they were readily available
  b. they were not in a position to say no
  c. they knew what characteristics they had looked for in a potential victim

_____ 5. The body movements of the subjects most likely to be mugged indicate that
  a. they were well-coordinated
  b. they walked with a heel to toe motion
  c. they walked awkwardly

_____ 6. If someone is _unobtrusively_ videotaping, they are
  a. paying little attention to their subjects
  b. observing without calling attention to themselves
  c. interacting with those they are observing

Review Test 1:   Main Ideas and Details in Textbook Material

Each of the following groups contains a series of related statements: One of the statements gives a main topic, another statement gives a main idea, and two or more statements give supporting details. Identify the role of each statement in the space provided using the following abbreviations:

> **T** for Topic
>
> **MI** for Main Idea
>
> **SD** for Supporting Detail

1.

_____ a. Around 500 B.C., in what is today China, the ancient Scythians burned _Cannabis_ and inhaled the hallucinogenic smoke.

_____ b. The legendary Emperor Shen Nung recommended marijuana for the treatment of gout, absent-mindedness, female disorders, and constipation.

_____ c. The use of _Cannabis_ can be traced back to ancient China where the hemp plant was valued for its fiber and medicinal properties.

_____ d. Early history of _Cannabis_ in China

2.

_____ a. Hookahs, or water pipes, for smoking hashish were frequently found in bazaars and marketplaces.

_____ b. Arabic literature is replete with references to _Cannabis_, as can be seen in the famous _Thousand and One Nights_.

_____ c. Use of _Cannabis_ in the Muslim world

_____ d. The use of _Cannabis_ was commonplace throughout the Muslim world, including the Middle East and Africa.

3.

_____ a. Spread of *Cannabis* to France

_____ b. By the middle of the nineteenth century, Paris hashish clubs were frequent meeting places for intellectuals, writers, poets, and artists.

_____ c. Napoleon's troops, returning from a campaign in North Africa, first popularized hashish smoking.

_____ d. Then French intellectuals, who believed that the psychoactive properties of hashish enhanced their creative abilities, promoted the use of *Cannabis*.

_____ e. The use of *Cannabis* spread in France in the mid-1800's.

4.

_____ a. During the 1930s, American society began to turn against the use of *Cannabis* by passing laws and launching educational campaigns.

_____ b. The U.S. Congress enacted the Federal Marijuana Tax Act of 1937, which regulated the sale of *Cannabis* and resulted in its virtual elimination from the nation's pharmacopoeia.

_____ c. The Federal Bureau of Narcotics undertook an "educational campaign" to make the public aware of the dangers of marijuana use.

_____ d. The crackdown

5.

_____ a. *Cannabis* can damage lung tissue, much like nicotine.

_____ b. The effects of marijuana on the male reproductive system show decreased sperm production and decreased testosterone levels.

_____ c. Even moderate use of marijuana impairs learning, short-term memory, and reaction time.

_____ d. Adverse effects of marijuana use

_____ e. Studies have discovered harmful side effects of *Cannabis'* use.

6.

_____ a. Medical uses in chemotherapy and glaucoma

_____ b. While over the centuries, marijuana has been employed to treat numerous ailments, today it is used in contemporary medicine for the treatment of glaucoma and as an aid to chemotherapy.

_____ c. Marijuana can significantly reduce ocular pressure in patients with glaucoma.

_____ d. The side effects of chemotherapy, which include nausea, vomiting, and loss of appetite, are reduced by the use of marijuana cigarettes.

7.

_____ a. Perception of time and space may be distorted, and minutes may seem like hours.

_____ b. *Cannabis* has significant mind-altering effects.

_____ c. Marijuana and psychoactive effects

_____ d. For instance, marijuana is associated with a sense of euphoria and calmness.

Information from Estelle Levetin, *Plants and Society*, 2nd ed., New York: McGraw-Hill, 1999, pp. 336–339.

Paraphrasing

When you paraphrase something, you express the author's meaning in your own words. Often, you will substitute synonyms for some words (but you may have to leave the key words the same), and you will need to change the phrasing of the original passage. Usually, a paraphrase is shorter than the original passage, but it can also be the same length as the original or even longer.

The ability to paraphrase is important when you review ideas and also when you formulate an implied main idea. Here's an example with two possible paraphrases.

> Original: "The man who most vividly realizes a difficulty is the man most likely to overcome it." (Joseph Farrell)
>
> Paraphrase 1: The man who clearly recognizes a problem is the one likely to solve it.
>
> Paraphrase 2: You are more likely to solve a problem if you first recognize clearly that a problem exists.

The first paraphrase replaces key words with synonyms so it is very like the original and some teachers might consider this plagiarism. The second paraphrase is original because it not only replaces key words with synonyms, but also because it conveys the ideas without using the phrasing of the original.

Now try to paraphrase the passages below. Be sure that you use your own words and do not rely on the phrasing of the original. When you finish, check to make sure that you have captured the meaning of the original.

Exercise 1: Paraphrasing Quotations

Working in a group, paraphrase the following quotations. When you finish, check to make sure the meaning of both statements is the same.

1. Even if you're on the right track, you'll get run over if you just sit there. (Will Rogers)

     _____

     _____

2. One man's justice is another's injustice; one man's beauty another's ugliness; one man's wisdom another's folly. (Ralph Waldo Emerson)

     _____

     _____

3. A toe of the stargazer is often stubbed. (Russian proverb)

     _____

     _____

4. If we could read the secret history of our enemies, we should find in each man's life sorrow and suffering enough to disarm all hostility. (Henry Wadsworth Longfellow)

     _____

     _____

5. You are only what you are when no one is looking. (Robert C. Edwards)

_____

_____

6. I have always thought the actions of men the best interpreters of their thoughts. (John Locke)

_____

_____

7. Do not use a hatchet to remove a fly from a friend's forehead. (Chinese proverb)

_____

_____

8. The things which hurt, instruct. (Benjamin Franklin)

_____

_____

9. If a man deceives me once, shame on him; if he deceives me twice, shame on me. (Anonymous)

_____

_____

Exercise 2: Paraphrasing a Poem

Read the poem below carefully, noting the key words and main ideas. Then explain the meaning of the poem in your own words.

Six Men of Indostan   _by John G. Saxe_

It was six men of Indostan
  To learning much inclined,
Who went to see the elephant
  Though all of them were blind
That each by observation
  Might satisfy his mind.

The first approached the elephant
  And, happening to fall
Against the broad and sturdy side,
  At once began to bawl:
"Why, bless me! But the elephant
  Is very much like a wall!"

The second, feeling of the tusk,
  Cried: "Ho! What have we here
So very round and smooth and sharp?
  To me, 'tis very clear,
This wonder of an elephant
  Is very like a spear!"

The third approached the animal.
  And, happening to take

The squirming trunk within his hands
   Thus boldly up he spake:
"I see," quoth he, "the elephant
   Is very like a snake!"

The fourth reached out his eager hand
   And felt about the knee:
"What most this wondrous beast is like
   Is very plain," quoth he:
"Tis clear enough the elephant
   Is very like a tree!"

The fifth who chanced to touch the ear
   Said: "e'en the blindest man
Can tell what this resembles most—
   Deny the fact who can:
This marvel of an elephant
   Is very like a fan!"

The sixth no sooner had begun
   About the beast to grope
Then, seizing on the swinging tail
   That fell within his scope,
"I see," quoth he, "the elephant
   Is very like a rope!"

And so these men of Indostan
   Disputed loud and long,
Each in his own opinion
   Exceeding stiff and strong:
Though each was partly in the right,
   And all were in the wrong.

_____

_____

_____

_____

_____

_____

_____

_____

Exercise 3: Paraphrasing a Fable

Explain the meaning of the fable below in your own words.

The Cracked Pot

1   water bearer in India had two large pots, each hung on each end of a pole which he carried across his neck. One of the pots had a crack in it, and while the other pot was perfect and always delivered a full portion of water at the end of a long walk from the stream to the master's house, the cracked pot arrived only half full.

2   For a full two years this went on daily, with the bearer delivering only one and a half pots full of water to his master's house. Of course, the perfect pot was proud of his accomplishments, perfect to the end for which it was made. But the poor cracked pot was ashamed of its own imperfections, and miserable that it was able to accomplish only half of what it had been made to do. After two years of what it perceived to be a bitter failure, it spoke to the water bearer one day by the stream.

3   "I am ashamed of myself, and want to apologize to you."

4   "Why?" asked the bearer. "What are you ashamed of?"

5   "I have been able, for these past two years, to deliver only half my load because this crack in my side causes water to leak out all the way back to your master's house. Because of my flaws, you have had to do all of this work, and you don't get full value for your efforts," said the pot.

6   The water bearer felt sorry for the old cracked pot, and in his compassion he said, "As we return to the master's house, I want you to notice the beautiful flowers along the path."

7   Indeed, as they went up the hill, the old cracked pot took notice of the sun warming the beautiful wild flowers on the side of the path, and this cheered it some. But at the end of the trail, it still felt bad because it had leaked out half of its load, and so again the pot apologized to the bearer for its failure.

8   The bearer said to the pot, "Did you notice that there were flowers only on your side of the path, but not on the other side? That's because I have always known about your flaw and I took advantage of it. I planted flower seeds on your side of the path and every day while we walk back from the stream, you've watered them. For two years I have been able to pick these beautiful flowers to decorate my master's table. Without you being just the way you are, he would not have this beauty to grace his house."

> *"Accept the place divine providence has found for you."*
>
> —Ralph Waldo Emerson

Moral: Know that in our weakness we find our strength.

_____

_____

_____

_____

_____

_____

_____

Islamic Folk Stories   *by Nasreddin Hodja*

Nasreddin Hodja was born in Turkey in the early thirteenth century. He served as a religious leader (*imam*) and judge in his village. His folk stories are famous throughout the Middle East, Turkey, Hungary, Russia, and parts of Africa. All of his stories use humor to teach a fundamental lesson about human relationships and are designed to sharpen our perceptions of human failings.

After reading each fable, write the lesson or moral. Then reduce the key information in the fable to one sentence.

1   1. One day the Hodja and his son went on a short journey, the boy seated on a donkey. On the way they met some people coming in the opposite direction.

2   "That's modern youth for you," they said. "The son rides on a donkey and lets his poor old father walk!"

3   When they had gone, the boy insisted that his father take his place on the donkey. The Hodja mounted the donkey, and his son walked at his side. They met some more people.

4   "Just look at that!" they said. "There is a full-grown man riding on the donkey, while his poor little son has to walk!"

5   So, Hodja pulled his son on the donkey, too. After awhile, they saw a few more people coming down the road.

6   "Poor animal!" they said. "Both of them are riding on it and it is about to pass out."

7   "The best thing to do," said Nasreddin, when they had disappeared from sight, "is for both of us to walk. Then there can be no such arguments."

8   So they continued their way walking beside the donkey. It was not long before they met another group.

9   "Just look at those fools," they said pointing to the Hodja and his son. "They plod along in the heat of the sun, and their donkey takes it easy!"

10   "You will have learned, my boy," said the Hodja, when they had gone, "just how difficult it is to escape the criticism of wagging tongues!" (p. 21)

"Don't judge any man until you have walked two moons in his moccasins."

—Native American saying

Moral: _____

_____

Main Idea Sentence: _____

_____

_____

1   2. The Hodja was invited to an important banquet, and he went in his everyday clothes. No one paid any attention to him whatsoever, and he remained hungry and thirsty, and very bored. Eventually he slipped out of the house unobserved and made his way home. Here he changed into his best clothes, putting on a magnificent turban, a fine silk robe, and a large fur coat over all. Then he made his way back to the banquet.

2   This time he was welcomed with open arms. The host bade him sit beside him, and offered him a plate covered with the choicest delicacies.

3   The Hodja took off his fur coat and held it to the plate.

4   "Eat, my beauty!" he said.

5   "Sir, what are you doing?" exclaimed his astonished host.

6   "It was the fur coat, not the man inside, which conjured up these delicacies," replied the Hodja. "Let it then eat them!"

Moral: _____

_____

Main Idea Sentence: _____

_____

_____

1   3. A poor man was passing through Ak-Shehir with only a piece of dry bread between himself and starvation. As he passed by an eating house, he saw some very appetizing meatballs frying in a pan over the charcoal fire, and carried away by the delicious smell, he held his piece of dry bread over the pan in the hope of capturing some of it. Then he ate his bread, which seemed to taste better. The restaurant owner, however, had seen what was going on, and seizing the man by the scruff of his neck, dragged him off before the magistrate, who at this time happened to be Nasreddin Hodja, and demanded that he be compelled to pay the price of the pan of meatballs.

2   The Hodja listened attentively, then drew two coins from his pocket.

3   "Come here a minute," he said to the restaurant owner.

4   The latter obeyed, and the Hodja enclosed the coins in his fist and rattled them in the man's ear.

5   "What is the meaning of this?" said the restaurant owner.

6   "I have just paid you your damages," said the Hodja. "The sound of money is fair payment for the smell of food."

Moral: _____

_____

Main Idea Sentence: _____

_____

_____

From Charles Downing, *Tales of Hodja*. Copyright © 1964 Charles Downing, New York: Henry Z. Walck, Inc., 1965, pp. 21, 90–91, 44.

Formulating Implied Main Ideas in Textbook Material

Not all main ideas are directly stated. Sometimes we have to look closely at the details the author has provided in order to determine the main idea. In the paragraphs below, the main idea is implied, rather than stated. Read the paragraphs and try to identify the main idea. Then check to see whether you have identified it correctly.

From David G. Myers, *Social Psychology*, 7th ed., New York: McGraw-Hill, 2000, pp. 426–431, 433, 435–436. Copyright © 2000 McGraw-Hill. Reprinted with permission of The McGraw-Hill Companies, Inc.

1.   What do you look for in a potential date? Sincerity? Good looks? Character? Conversational ability? Sophisticated, intelligent people are unconcerned with such superficial qualities as good looks; they know "beauty is only skin deep" and "you can't judge a book by its cover." At least they know that's how they *ought* to feel. As Cicero counseled, "Resist appearance." However, there is now a cabinet full of research studies showing that appearance *does* matter. The consistency and pervasiveness of this effect is disconcerting. Good looks are a great asset.

"He had but one eye, and the pocket of prejudice runs in favor of two."

—Charles Dickens

The topic of this paragraph is appearance or looks. The implied main idea is: Looks matter, and people who believe that they do not are probably deceiving themselves.

In the next example, the topic is attractiveness and dating. To formulate the main idea, we must pay attention to the attitudes of both young men and young women as described in the paragraph.

2.   Like it or not, a young woman's physical attractiveness is a moderately good predictor of how frequently she dates. A young man's attractiveness is slightly less a predictor of how frequently he dates. Does this imply, as many have surmised, that women are better at following Cicero's advice? Or does it merely reflect the fact that men more often do the inviting? If women were to indicate their preferences among various men, would looks be as important to them as they are to men? Philosopher Bertrand Russell thought not: "On the whole women tend to love men for their character while men tend to love women for their appearance." To see whether indeed men are more influenced by looks, researchers conducted a series of experiments. The result: The more attractive a woman was, the more the man liked her and wanted to date her again. And the more attractive the man was, the more she liked him and wanted to date him again.

From the details presented, we can conclude that both men and women put value on opposite-sex physical attractiveness. Our implied main idea should be stated something like this:

> Main Idea: When it comes to dating, looks appear to matter as much to young women as to young men.

You can see that determining an implied main idea requires you to reduce all of the key information contained in the paragraph to one sentence.

In order to formulate the main idea, it is sometimes helpful, first, to identify the topic and then to ask *who*, *what*, *where*, *when*, *why*, and *how* about the topic. Read the following paragraph, and try to determine the main idea for yourself before checking the main idea provided.

3. Not everyone can end up paired with someone stunningly attractive. So how do people pair off? Judging from research by Bernard Murstein and others, they pair off with people who are about as attractive as they are. Several studies have found a strong correspondence between the attractiveness of husbands and wives, of dating partners, and even of those within particular fraternities. Experiments confirm this matching phenomenon. When choosing whom to approach in social settings, knowing the other is free to say yes or no, people usually approach someone whose attractiveness roughly matches their own.

    Who: men and women

    What: pair off

    Where: in social settings

    When: during interactions with each other

    Why: attempting to seek a good physical match

    How: by picking people as attractive as they are

The topic of this paragraph is the matching phenomenon. If we look at all the key details, our main idea will look something like this:

> Main Idea: People tend to pair themselves with others who are similarly attractive.

The next paragraph provides an explanation for couples who are not similarly attractive.

4. Perhaps this research prompts you to think of happy couples who are not equally attractive. In such cases, the less attractive person often has compensating qualities. Each partner brings assets to the social marketplace. The value of the respective assets creates an equitable match. Personal advertisements exhibit this exchange of assets. Men typically offer wealth or status and seek youth and attractiveness; women more often do the reverse: "Attractive, bright woman, 26, slender, seeks warm, professional male." Moreover, men who advertise their income and education, and women who advertise their youth and looks, receive more responses to their ads. The asset-matching process helps explain why beautiful young women often marry older men of higher social status.

    Who: men/women

    What: offer compensating qualities

    Where: in the social marketplace

    When: in relationships

Why: to achieve an equitable match

How: by bartering youth and beauty for wealth and status

When you put together these key details, you should arrive at a main idea that looks something like this:

Main Idea: Everyone brings assets to the social marketplace, and people choose partners who have similarly valuable assets.

Now look closely at these paragraphs discussing the social significance of physical attractiveness.

5. In an experiment, Missouri fifth-grade teachers were given identical information about a boy or girl but with the photograph of an attractive or unattractive child attached. The teachers perceived the attractive child as more intelligent and successful in school. Think of yourself as a playground supervisor having to discipline an unruly child. Might you show less warmth and tact to an unattractive child? The sad truth is that most of us assume what we might call a "Bart Simpson effect"—that homely children are less able and socially competent than their beautiful peers.

The main idea of this paragraph is directly stated in the last sentence because the "Bart Simpson effect" is illustrated by the remaining sentences.

In the next paragraph the main idea is implied because no one sentence is broad enough to cover all of the key details. Try formulating the main idea by expanding the first sentence.

6. What is more, we assume that beautiful people possess certain desirable traits. Other things being equal, we guess beautiful people are happier, sexually warmer, and more outgoing, intelligent, and successful, though not more honest or concerned with others. Added together, the findings define a physical-attractiveness stereotype: *What is beautiful is good*. Children learn the stereotype quite easily. Snow White and Cinderella are beautiful—and kind. The witch and the stepsisters are ugly—and wicked. As one kindergarten girl put it when asked what it means to be pretty. "It's like to be a princess. Everybody loves you."

Main Idea: We assume that beautiful people possess certain desirable traits, and we also assume that what is beautiful is good.

In the next few paragraphs, the topic and part of the main idea are provided for you. Use the *who, what, where, when, why*, and *how* strategy to complete the main idea.

7. Undoubtedly, there are numerous advantages to being beautiful. However, attraction researchers report there is also an ugly truth about beauty. Exceptionally attractive people may suffer resentment from those of their own sex. They may be unsure whether others are responding to their inner qualities or just to their looks, which in time will fade. Moreover, if they can coast on their looks, they may be less motivated to develop themselves in other ways.

Topic: The negatives of attractiveness

Main Idea: While there are many advantages to being beautiful, there are also

_____

8. To say that attractiveness is important, other things being equal, is not to say that physical appearance always outranks other qualities. Attractiveness probably most affects first impressions. But first impressions are important—

"Clothes and manners do not make the man; but when he is made, they greatly improve his appearance."

—Henry Ward Beecher

and are becoming more so as societies become increasingly mobile and urbanized and as contacts with people become more fleeting. Though interviewers may deny it, attractiveness and grooming affect first impressions in job interviews. This helps explain why attractive people have more prestigious jobs and make more money.

Topic: First impressions

Main Idea: Physical appearance doesn't always outrank other qualities, but it does affect _____

Exercise: Formulating Implied Main Ideas in Textbook Material

Who is attractive?

Each of the following paragraphs are concerned with attractiveness. Formulate the implied main idea for each paragraph.

1. Attraction has been described as if it were an objective quality like height, which some people have more of, some less. Strictly speaking, attractiveness is whatever the people of any given place and time find attractive. This, of course, varies. Even in a given place and time, people (fortunately) disagree about who's attractive.

Implied Main Idea: _____

_____

_____

2. What makes an attractive face depends somewhat on the person's sex. Consistent with men historically having greater social power, people judge women more attractive if they have "baby-faced" features, such as large eyes, that suggest nondominance. Men seem more attractive when their faces—and their behaviors—suggest maturity and dominance. People across the world show remarkable agreement about the features of an ideal male face and female face when judging any ethnic group. For example, "attractive" facial and bodily features do not deviate too drastically from average. People perceive noses, legs, or statures that are not unusually large or small as relatively attractive. Perfectly symmetrical faces are another characteristic of strikingly attractive people. So in many respects, perfectly average is quite attractive.

Implied Main Idea: _____

_____

_____

3. Women favor male traits that signify an ability to provide and protect resources. Males prefer female characteristics that signify reproductive capacity. Judging from yesterday's Stone Age figurines to today's centerfolds and beauty pageant winners, men everywhere have felt most attracted to women whose waists are 30 percent narrower than their hips—a shape associated with peak sexual fertility. When judging males as potential marriage partners, women, too, prefer a waist-to-hip ratio suggesting health and vigor. This makes evolutionary sense because a muscular hunk was more

likely than a scrawny fellow to gather food, build houses, and defeat rivals. But today's women prefer even more those with high incomes.

Implied Main Idea: _____

_____

_____

4. Let's conclude this discussion of attractiveness on an upbeat note. First, a 17-year-old girl's facial attractiveness is a surprisingly weak predictor of her attractiveness at ages 30 and 50. Sometimes an average-looking adolescent becomes a quite attractive middle-aged adult. Second, not only do we perceive attractive people as likable, we also perceive likable people as attractive. Perhaps you can recall individuals who, as you grew to like them, became more attractive. Their physical imperfections were no longer so noticeable. When people are warm, helpful, and considerate, they *look* more attractive. Discovering someone's similarities to us also makes the person seem more attractive.

Implied Main Idea: _____

_____

_____

5. Moreover, love sees loveliness. The more in love a woman is with a man, the more physically attractive she finds him. And the more in love people are, the *less* attractive they find all others of the opposite sex. "The grass may be greener on the other side, but happy gardeners are less likely to notice." To paraphrase Benjamin Franklin, when Jill is in love, she finds Jack more handsome than his friends.

Implied Main Idea: _____

_____

_____

SELECTION

Excerpt from *Dave Barry Is Not Taking This Sitting Down*   *by Dave Barry*

"My definition of a good sculpture is 'a sculpture that looks at least vaguely like something.'"

Getting the Picture

In this selection, Dave Barry is poking fun at modern art. Like much of the viewing public, he is not sure that nonrepresentational art is actually art at all.

Bio-sketch

Dave Barry is best known for writing his syndicated column for the *Miami Herald*. He is also a best-selling author. *The New York Times* called Mr. Barry the funniest man in America.

Brushing Up on Vocabulary

velveteen   a cotton fabric with soft velvet pile.

Pomodoro   Arnaldo Pomodoro was born in Italy in 1926. He has had many exhibitions in Italy, other European countries, and the United States. He is best known for his artistic stage designs and his modern sculptures located near public buildings.

1   Like many members of the uncultured, Cheez-It–consuming public, I am not good at grasping modern art. I'm the type of person who will stand in front of a certified modern masterpiece painting that looks, to the layperson, like a big black square, and quietly think: "Maybe the actual painting is on the other side."

2   I especially have a problem with modernistic sculptures, the kind where you, the layperson, cannot be sure whether you're looking at a work of art or a crashed alien spacecraft. My definition of a good sculpture is "a sculpture that looks at least vaguely like something." I'm talking about a sculpture like Michelangelo's *David*. You look at that, and there is no doubt about what the artist's message is. It is: "Here's a naked man the size of an oil derrick."

3   I bring this topic up because of an interesting incident that occurred recently in Miami. . . . Miami tends to have these interesting incidents, and one of them occurred a little while ago when Dade County purchased an office building from the city of Miami. The problem was that, squatting in an area that the county wanted to convert into office space, there was a large ugly wad of metal, set into the concrete. So the county sent construction workers with heavy equipment to rip out the wad, which was then going to be destroyed.

4   But guess what? Correct! It turns out that this was NOT an ugly wad. It was art! Specifically, it was Public Art, defined as "art that was purchased by experts who are not spending their own personal money." The money of course comes from the taxpayers, who are not allowed to spend this money themselves because (1) they probably wouldn't buy art, and (2) if they did, there is no way they would buy the crashed-spaceship style of art that the experts usually select for them.

5   The Miami wad is in fact a sculpture by the famous Italian sculptor Pomodoro (like most famous artists, he is not referred to by his first name, although I like to think it's "Bud"). This sculpture cost the taxpayers $80,000, which makes it an important work of art. In dollar terms, it is 3,200 times as important as a painting of dogs playing poker, and more than 5,000 times as important as a velveteen Elvis.

6   Fortunately, before the sculpture was destroyed, the error was discovered, and the Pomodoro was moved to another city office building, where it sits next to the parking garage, providing great pleasure to the many taxpayers who come to admire it.

7   I am kidding, of course. On the day I went to see it, the sculpture was, like so many pieces of modern taxpayer-purchased public art, being totally ignored by the actual taxpaying public, possibly because it looks—and I say this with all due artistic respect for Bud—like an abandoned air compressor.

8   So here's what I think: I think there should be a law requiring that all public art be marked with a large sign stating something like: "NOTICE! THIS IS A PIECE OF ART! THE PUBLIC SHOULD ENJOY IT TO THE TUNE OF 80,000 CLAMS!"

9   Also, if there happens to be an abandoned air compressor nearby, it should have a sign that says: "NOTICE! THIS IS NOT ART!" so the public does not waste time enjoying the wrong thing. The public should enjoy what the experts have decided the public should enjoy. That's the system we use in this country, and we're going to stick with it. . . .

Comprehension Checkup

1. What is the main idea of this selection? _____

_____

_____

True or False

Indicate whether the statement is true or false by writing T or F in the blank provided.

_____ 2. By calling Pomodoro "Bud," Barry is expressing respect for Pomodoro.

_____ 3. Barry has an appreciation for realistic sculpture such as Michelangelo's *David*.

_____ 4. When Barry refers to himself as a member of the "Cheez-It–consuming public" he means that his tastes are simple and unrefined.

_____ 5. The Pomodoro sculpture was almost destroyed by construction workers.

Agree or Disagree

Indicate whether Dave Barry is likely to agree or disagree by writing A or D in the blank provided.

_____ 6. Modern art is worthy of our respect.

_____ 7. Taxpayers rather than "experts" are better judges of art.

_____ 8. The more expensive a piece of art is, the more merit it has.

_____ 9. It is often difficult to tell the difference between modern art and junk.

_____ 10. The public, given a choice, would probably not select the modern art that is often on display outside public buildings.

Vocabulary in Context

Match the vocabulary word from the selection (on the left) with the most appropriate definition (on the right), and write the letter in the space provided. Refer to the paragraph in the selection for context clues.

_____ grasping (paragraph 1)   a. dollars

_____ certified (1)   b. extraterrestrial

_____ layperson (1)   c. nonexpert

_____ alien (2)   d. sitting

_____ squatting (3)   e. a large quantity

_____ wad (3)   f. comprehending; understanding

_____ convert (3)   g. change

_____ clams (8)   h. guaranteed; confirmed

In Your Own Words

Why does Barry mention that Dade County placed the sculpture next to a parking garage? Do you think that Barry considers a parking garage an appropriate location for the sculpture? Why?

The Art of Writing

In a brief essay, respond to the questions below.

Is there any public art in your area that became controversial? Why did it become controversial? Was it because of the cost? Was it because of the appearance of the artwork? Was it a combination of factors? How was the controversy resolved?

Internet Activity

Go to the *Miami Herald* website.:

www.miami.com.mld/miamiherald/

Click on Dave Barry's name, select a column by Barry, and print it. After reading the column, state Barry's main idea in your own words. List the details that Barry gives to support his main idea.

Study the cartoon "Eye of the Beholder." How does this cartoon illustrate Dave Barry's main idea?

_____

_____

_____

Eye of the Beholder

Copyright © 1997 Tribune Media Services, Inc. Reprinted with permission.

SELECTION

Excerpt from *Gilbert's Living with Art*   *by Mark Getlein*

"In this particular circumstance, the people for whom the art was intended chose to reject the art."

Getting the Picture

The proverb "beauty is in the eye of the beholder" implies that beauty is highly relative and that people will have varied opinions about what is actually beautiful.

What is pleasing to the eye of one of us is an eyesore to another. So too with art. People will have varied opinions about what constitutes art. In the selection below, taken from a popular art history textbook, the author Rita Gilbert describes a controversy over a work of modern art.

Bio-sketch

Rita Gilbert wrote her first edition of *Living with Art* in 1985. Her fourth edition of the book won a first-place award for outstanding design and production at the 1995 New York Book Show. Mark Getlein has taken over as author of this textbook. Getlein has written a variety of textbooks including *A History of Art in Africa* and *The Longman Anthology of World Literature*. As a painter, he is able to help students understand both the intellectual and practical processes of creating art.

Brushing Up on Vocabulary

dismantle   to take apart. *Dismantle* in Old French literally meant to divest of a mantle or cloak. *Dismantle* derives from the French word part *des,* meaning "off," and *mantler* meaning "to cloak." In Middle French *demanteler* meant to tear down the walls of a fortress.

integrity   the state of being whole or entire; honesty. *Integrity* derives from the Latin word *integer,* which means a whole number in mathematics.

Public Art

1   Rarely has the question "What is art?" caused such a public uproar as in a controversy that erupted in New York City in the early 1980s. At the center of the drama was a monumental sculpture by Richard Serra, entitled *Tilted Arc,* a 12-foot-high, 120-foot-long steel wall installed in a plaza fronting a government building in lower Manhattan.

2   Commissioned by the Art-in-Architecture division of the General Services Administration, *Tilted Arc* was part of a program that allocates 0.5 percent of the cost of federal buildings to the purchase and installation of public art. Soon after the sculpture's installation, however, the public for whom it was intended spoke out, and their message was a resounding *"That's* not art!" More than 7,000 workers in surrounding buildings signed petitions demanding the sculpture's removal. Opponents of the work had numerous complaints. *Tilted Arc,* they maintained, was ugly, rusty, and a target for graffiti. It blocked the view. It disrupted pedestrian traffic, since one had to walk all the way around it rather than straight across the plaza. It ruined the plaza for concerts and outdoor ceremonies. At a public hearing, one man summed up the opposition view: "I am here today to recommend its relocation to a better site—a metal salvage yard."

3   Artists, dealers, and critics rushed to the sculpture's defense. The sculptor himself argued vehemently against any attempt to move *Tilted Arc,* maintaining that it had been commissioned specifically for that site and any new location would destroy its artistic integrity.

4   The battle raged for many months, and while there were dissenting voices from all sides, it shaped up principally as a struggle between the art establishment (pro) and the general public (con). At last, in an unusual editorial, *The New York Times*—a newspaper that heavily supports the arts—took a stand. "One cannot choose to see or ignore *Tilted Arc,* as if it were in a museum or a less conspicuous public place. To the complaining workers in Federal Plaza, it is, quite simply, unavoidable. . . . The public has to live with *Tilted Arc;* therefore the public has a right to say no, not here."

5   This time the public won, and the question "What is art?" was answered by a kind of popular referendum, a majority decision. *Tilted Arc* was dismantled and removed in March of 1989.

6   Does this outcome mean that *Tilted Arc* is not art, or that it isn't good art? No, it does not mean either of those things. It means simply that, in this particular circumstance, the people for whom the art was intended chose to reject the art. And similar circumstances have, very likely, occurred since the earliest artists of prehistory began painting on the walls of their caves.

From Mark Getlein, *Gilbert's Living with Art*, 6th ed., New York: McGraw-Hill, 2002, p. 274. Copyright © 2002 McGraw-Hill. Reprinted by permission of The McGraw-Hill Companies, Inc.

✔ Comprehension Checkup

Multiple Choice

Write the letter of the correct answer in the blank provided.

_____   1. By choosing to use the words *uproar, controversy,* and *erupted* in the first paragraph the author implies that
             a. the public was moderately interested
             b. the sculpture provoked a swift and strong reaction
             c. unhappiness with the sculpture developed slowly

_____   2. From the context of paragraph 2, it can be determined that the word *resounding* most nearly means
             a. cheerfully expressed
             b. quietly voiced
             c. loudly uttered

_____   3. The public expressed all of the following misgivings about *Tilted Arc* except
             a. it disrupted vehicular traffic
             b. it was ugly and a target for graffiti
             c. outdoor ceremonies and concerts were no longer feasible

_____   4. A synonym for the word *vehemently* as used in paragraph 3 is
             a. ardently
             b. compassionately
             c. silently

_____   5. *The New York Times* took the following basic position in its editorial:
             a. Because the public and the federal workers could not avoid the sculpture, their opinion about whether it should stay counted for a lot.
             b. Because the sculpture could be disassembled and relocated elsewhere, it should be moved to a more welcoming location.
             c. Because it was commissioned specifically for the site and the sculptor opposed its removal, it should stay.

True or False

Indicate whether the statement is true or false by writing T or F in the blank provided.

_____   6. The author suggests that similar rejections of public art have occurred in the past.

_____   7. A *dissenting* opinion expresses an opposing viewpoint.

_____   8. A *conspicuous* place is one that is hard to find or see.

Tilted Arc (1981), Richard Serra
© 2005 Richard Serra/Artists Rights Society (ARS), New York

_____ 9. We can assume that *The New York Times* cast the deciding vote in the tiebreaker between the art establishment and the general public.

_____ 10. The sculptor felt that it was in the public's best interest to relocate the sculpture to a place where it would be enjoyed and appreciated.

In Your Own Words

1. Many artists argue that photographs can depict something lifelike far better than any painting can. They conclude that paintings should not be aimed at replicating reality. Do you believe that paintings should present lifelike portrayals of their subjects?

2. What makes a work of art good or successful? How important is it that a work of art display technical skill? Or does it count for more that it be imaginative or provocative?

3. Does a piece of art need to communicate a single clear message to be good?

4. What is your opinion of *Tilted Arc*? Should it have been dismantled?

The Art of Writing

In a brief essay, respond to one of the items below.

1. Do you agree with the conclusion drawn by *The New York Times* that the sculpture should be removed? Explain why.

2. Do you think that the public should always have the final say on whether a work of public art should be displayed or should remain on display? Why or why not?

STUDY TECHNIQUE 3

Summarizing Short Articles

Summarizing, or restating main ideas in your own words, is a skill you will be called upon to use both in your college classes and at work. In literature classes, for example, you may have to provide a brief summary of a story to show you've read and understood it or to provide your reader with the main points before you offer an analysis. In biology classes, you may have to provide a brief summary of an experiment before detailing the process and equipment you used. Later in life, you may also need to provide summaries. For instance, if you become a nurse you may need to summarize a patient's condition; if you become a sportswriter, you may need to summarize the action in a basketball game; if you become a police officer, you might need to summarize the events leading up to an accident.

When you write a summary, you need to present only the main idea and key supporting details in order of importance. Because it omits minor supporting details, a summary is much shorter than the original on which it is based. A good rule of thumb is that a summary should be one-fourth of the length of the original. A good way to identify key supporting details is to answer as many of the *who, what, where, when, why,* and *how* questions about the selection as apply. (Not all these questions will apply to every selection.) Remember, too, that the goal of a summary is brevity; in other words, always make sure that your summary contains only the main idea and key supporting details and does not include information more than once. Omit all trivia and repetition!

Also keep in mind that you are reporting the author's viewpoints and not your own. When writing a summary, never write something like "I feel" or "I think" or "It seems to me." What matters in a summary is what the author thinks. When reading over your summary, make sure you delete all expressions of your own thoughts and opinions.

You just read an excerpt from Mark Getlein's "Public Art." Try to write a summary of this excerpt. Begin by identifying the main idea.

Main idea: _____

_____

_____

_____

Now locate the main supporting details by answering as many of the question words as possible:

Who? _____

What? _____

Where? _____

When? _____

Why? _____

How? _____

Next, list five to six of the main supporting details in your own words.

1. _____

_____

2. _____

_____

3. _____

_____

4. _____

_____

5. _____

_____

6. _____

_____

You are now ready to draft your summary.

_____

_____

_____

_____

_____

_____

_____

_____

_____

After writing your summary, read it over. Delete any information that is not crucial to supporting the main idea. Delete any trivia or repetition and any expressions of your own opinion. Is your presentation of information logical? If not, reorganize the information in a more logical way. Now revise your summary.

Internet Activity

The National Endowment for the Arts, created by Congress in 1965, is an independent governmental agency that funds "projects of artistic excellence." One of its services is to publish articles on various topics related to the arts. One such article written by Marc Pally, entitled "The Enterprise of Process: Notes on Planning Public Art" (1998), provides guidance for making decisions about proposed public-art projects. You will find this article at:

http://www.nea.gov/resources/lessons/PALLY.html

Write a paragraph describing Pally's recommendations. Or write a paragraph explaining how Pally's recommendations might have led to better decision making about *Tilted Arc*.

Vocabulary: Homonyms and Other Confusing Words (Unit 1)

As you learned in the introduction, homonyms are words or phrases that sound the same but that have different spellings or meanings. In addition to homonyms, we have included in this section other troublesome words that you might need to practice. Mastering these words will help you make a good impression in written assignments.

The short poem below illustrates the importance of using words correctly. Can you spot the mistakes?

> English spelling can seam like a maize,
> And put won strait into a hays,
> Butt now never fear,
> The spell-checker is hear,
> And its sew well-deserving of prays.
>
> —*Anonymous*

allusion	A noun meaning "a casual or passing reference to something." *The author made an* allusion *to Aphrodite, the Greek goddess of love and beauty.*
illusion	A noun meaning "something that deceives by producing a false or misleading impression of reality." *The hikers, exhausted and suffering from dehydration, saw a lake up ahead of them. But as they got closer, they realized it was just a cruel* illusion.
alot	A mistake for a lot. There is no such word as alot.
a lot	"Many, much." *Peggy felt* a lot *better after getting a good night's sleep.*
allot	A verb meaning "to assign a portion." *Each heir to the family fortune was* allotted *an equal share of the estate.*
already	An adverb meaning "previously." *With just a few minutes left in the game, the Cardinals thought they had* already *won.*
all ready	"Completely prepared." *After gathering her supplies and buying her textbooks, Antoinette felt* all ready *to start school.*

Think about this sentence: She is *all ready* to go to the game because she is *already* dressed.

altogether	An adverb meaning "wholly, entirely." *"There is* altogether *too much violence in public schools," complained the president of the Parent Teacher Association.*
all together	"All at the same place or time." *The family reunion brought the family* all together.
censure	A verb meaning "strong disapproval or official reprimand." *The senator was* censured *because he had accepted campaign contributions from foreign countries.*
censor	A verb meaning "to examine for the purpose of suppressing or deleting." *The Harry Potter books by J. K. Rawling are being* censored *by school libraries across the country.*
cite	A verb meaning "to quote or mention in support." *You may need to* cite *your sources in your English term paper.*
site	A noun meaning "position or location." *The* site *of the Vietnam War Memorial is in Washington D.C.*
desert	A noun meaning "a dry sandy region with little or no plant life." *The Sahara Desert is the largest* desert *in the world.*

desert	A verb meaning "to leave without intending to return." *Marcia wanted to know how Jan could* desert *her husband after fourteen years of marriage.* (The pronunciation is the same as *dessert*.) Also, a noun meaning "deserved reward or punishment." *The attorney who had cheated many of his elderly clients out of their retirement funds received his just* deserts *when he was disbarred.* (The pronunciation is the same as *desserts*.)
dessert	A noun meaning "something sweet served at the end of a meal." *Is your favorite* dessert *cake, ice cream, or something else?*

Think about this sentence: Cactus candy is a delectable *dessert* that comes from *desert* cacti.

die	A verb meaning "to cease to live." *Most of our past presidents have already* died.
dye	A noun meaning "a coloring substance." *Did you use* dye *to change the color of your hair?* Also, a verb meaning "to color with a dye." *She* dyed *her hair shocking pink to go with her dress.*
emigrate	A verb meaning "to leave one country or region and settle in another." *Many people in the United States have ancestors who* emigrated *from Ireland.*
immigrate	A verb meaning "to come to a new country to settle." *Millions of people have* immigrated *to the United States in search of a better life for themselves and their families.*

Think about this sentence: Oksana's parents *emigrated* from Russia in 1944, *immigrating* first to France and then later to the United States.

fewer	An adjective meaning "not many," refers to number. *Fewer* is used before a plural noun. *There are* fewer *words in a paperback dictionary than in a hardbound one.*
less	An adverb meaning "not as much or as many." *Less* is used to refer to things that cannot be counted. *Many people feel that they should be spending* less *time at work and more time at home with their families.*
formally	An adverb meaning "marked by form or ceremony." *The young couple* formally *announced their engagement at a special dinner party.*
formerly	An adverb meaning "at an earlier time; in the past." *The candidate running for president was* formerly *a U.S. senator.*
its	A possessive pronoun meaning "the one or ones that belong to it." *The dog always knew where to find* its *bowl when it was time to eat.*
it's	A contraction for "it is or it has." *The dark clouds indicate that* it's *about to rain.*
later	An adverb or adjective meaning "coming after the usual or proper time." *Later* is the comparative form of *late*. *The students wanted to postpone the test until a* later *date.*

latter   An adjective meaning "being the second of two mentioned things." *Matt's parents said he could play only one sport in high school; when they gave him a choice between playing football or being on the track team, he chose the* latter.

Also, an adjective meaning "near to the end." *The use of the Internet became very popular during the* latter *part of the 1990s.*

Think about this sentence: Of the first two versions of his story, I prefer the *latter,* but the version he came up with *later* is the best of all.

lie   A noun meaning "something said that is not true." *Mary did not want to go to Cara's birthday party, so she told a little white* lie *and said she had to babysit that night.*

lie   A verb meaning "to say what is not true." *Perjury is* lying *under oath.*

Also, a verb meaning "to rest or recline; to exist in a horizontal position." *Lie* is an intransitive verb; that is, it cannot take a direct object. *The dog often* lies *on the couch even though she knows she is supposed to stay off the furniture.* The past tense of the verb *lie* is *lay: Despite having scolded her, she* lay *down there again yesterday.* The present participle of *lie* is *lying: I knew when she had been* lying *on the furniture, because it was covered with hair.* The past participle of *lie* is *lain: She had* lain *on the couch every day without reproach while my mother was visiting.*

lay   A verb meaning "to put down so as to rest on, in, or against something." Lay is a transitive verb; that is, it requires a direct object. *If I lay any more books there, the table will break.* The past tense of *lay* is *laid: I* laid *a book down on the table last week, and now I can't find it.* The present participle of *lay* is *laying: I have been* laying *my books on the table all week.* The past participle of *lay* is *laid: In fact, I had* laid *my books down in the same spot for weeks.*

Homonym Quiz

Drawing on what you've learned here, fill in the blanks with an appropriate homonym.

1. Margo was _____ late for work when she stopped to answer the phone.
       already/all ready

2. "Class," said Mrs Walker, "let's sing the last part one more time _____."
                                                    altogether/all together

3. The _____ of the disaster has been closed indefinitely.
       cite/site

4. He _____ from Brazil in 1948 and has not returned until recently.
   emigrated/immigrated

5. There were three _____ students in class today than on Tuesday.
               fewer/less

6. No one knew that the law student was _____ a convicted murderer.
                                   formally/formerly

7. _____ not a good day to visit Soon Yi. She's in bed with the flu.
   Its/It's

8. As he grew disenchanted with his work, he started arriving at the office
   _____.
   later/latter

9. Only fresh fruits or low calorie _____ are on my diet.
                           deserts/desserts

10. I just _____ that file down on the counter five minutes ago.
       lay/laid

Write a sentence of your own using *lain* correctly.

_____

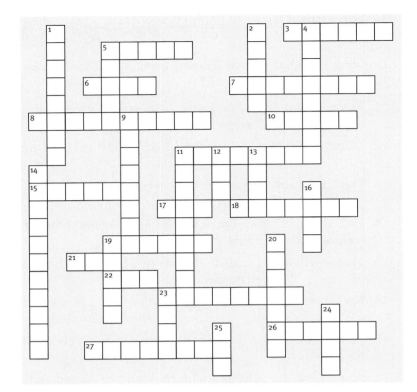

ACROSS CLUES

3. The student was _____ his backpack on the wrong desk.
5. Tim went to bed much _____ than he should have.
6. Mr. Tang _____ in the hospital after a lengthy illness.
7. The Senator was _____ because he made false statements to members of Congress while under oath.
8. _____ John Grisham has written eight successful novels.
10. Was the husband _____ to his wife about where he had been last night? Or, was he telling the truth?
11. Tina added a large mirror to her dining room to give the _____ of more space.
15. Sue and Anna are softball players. The former plays catcher and the _____ plays shortstop.
17. Too many children _____ by drowning in unsupervised swimming pools.

18. We usually eat a low-cal. _____ after a fattening meal.
19. The _____ is an area with an arid climate.
21. The workers were going to _____ the foundation for the house next week.
22. The cow gave birth to _____ first calf.
23. The movie was _____ before it was shown on TV.
26. Patty was _____ her hair to match her school colors.
27. Thailand was _____ called Siam.

DOWN CLUES

1. They were dressed _____ in tux and tails to go to the Winter Ball.
2. Some students would do better in college by taking _____ classes.
4. The author made an _____ to a character in *Romeo and Juliet*.
5. The woman was _____ on the ground when the paramedics arrived.

9. Juan _____ (d) from Mexico three years ago.
11. Many people now residing in other countries would like to _____ to the United States.
12. The officer told the suspect to _____ the gun down and put his hands in the air.
13. Every four years the Olympics are held at a different _____. In 2000, they were held in Australia.
14. The members of the class of 1980 will not be _____ again until the next reunion.
16. I should have eaten a lot _____ at our Thanksgiving dinner.
19. Should euthanasia be available for the _____?
20. Steve did not need to take college algebra because he had _____ taken it in high school.
23. Always make sure you _____ your references properly.
24. When he missed work, he _____ to his boss about being sick.
25. On St. Patrick's Day some people _____ their beer green.

TEST-TAKING TIP

Day of the Test

The day of the test has arrived. Make sure you have the proper equipment with you—pens, pencils, dictionary, blue books, and so on. Stay calm. By now you should have a good idea what's going to be on the test, and you should be prepared for it.

Now look at the test. Read through the whole test. Look on both sides of all the pages. How many questions are there? Think about how much time you want to devote to each question.

Always save time to check over your answers. Don't lose points because you accidentally skipped a question. And remember to write legibly and put your name on the test paper!

Don't be concerned if some people in the class finish the test much more quickly than you do. You don't know whether those students did well on the test or poorly.

The Author's Purpose and the Rhetorical Modes

The Oath of the Horatii (1784)*
BY JACQUES-LOUIS DAVID

*To see this work of art in color, turn to the color insert following page 260.

Photo: G. Blot/C. Jean. Louvre, Paris. Réunion des Musées Nationaux/Art Resource, NY

In the painting, three brothers are swearing an oath to their father to defeat their enemies or die for Rome.

1   What are the brothers receiving from their father?

2   Compare the postures and attitudes of the men to those of the women. How do the hands of the men and women express their respective attitudes?

3   What does the woman in black in the background of the painting appear to be doing?

4   Notice the three arches in the background of the painting. Where else does the artist repeat this theme of a group of three?

5   What do you think the artist's purpose was in creating this painting?

6   How does the painting illustrate risk-taking behavior?

7   What is the dominant color in the male grouping? What might that color represent?

Determining the Author's Purpose

Highlight or underline the definitions of the key terms. Then write a paraphrase of each definition in the margin.

Inform

———————————

———————————

Entertain

———————————

———————————

Persuade

———————————

———————————

———————————

Audience

———————————

———————————

Specific purpose

———————————

———————————

———————————

Most writers create a story, essay, article, or poem with at least one **general purpose** in mind. Because most writers do not directly state their general purpose, the reader must use indirect clues to determine it. We can identify the general purpose by asking the question, "Why did the author write this?" Usually, this purpose will fall into one of three broad categories: **to inform, to entertain, or to persuade.**

An author whose purpose is **to inform** will provide readers with knowledge or information. Ordinarily, the material will be presented in an objective, neutral fashion. Authors who write textbooks presenting factual material often have this purpose in mind. Articles in newspapers are also usually meant to inform.

An author whose purpose is **to entertain** will tell a story or describe someone or something in an interesting way. A piece of writing meant to entertain will often make an appeal to the reader's imagination, sense of humor, or emotions. Such writing may be either fiction or nonfiction. Witty, unusual, dramatic, or exciting stories usually have entertainment as their purpose.

Finally, the author's purpose may be to **persuade.** Persuasion goes beyond merely entertaining or providing information. This kind of writing tries to change the reader's opinions by appealing to emotions or intellect. If making an emotional argument, the author may use vividly descriptive passages designed to manipulate the reader's feelings. If making an appeal to intelligence, the author will employ logic and reasoning. Political literature is a common form of writing meant to persuade. Newspaper editorials ordinarily have persuasion as their purpose also.

Authors take into account their **audience** (those they are writing for) when they choose their **general purpose.** Writers of fiction usually want to entertain readers by creating interesting characters and stories. If an author writes an article for a wellness magazine, the general purpose will probably be to provide information promoting good health. If an author writes a letter to solicit campaign contributions for a political candidate, the general purpose will be to persuade people to give money.

In addition to a general purpose, authors also usually have a **specific purpose,** which reveals more detailed information about the article than the general purpose. Take the wellness example above. The general purpose is to inform. The specific purpose might be "to inform people about foods that protect against cancer."

Sometimes an author may have more than one purpose in mind. For instance, an author might want both to entertain and to persuade. Or the author might write an entertaining article that also provides information about something important. In these instances, usually one of the author's purposes will be primary. To determine the general and primary purpose, first identify the main idea and the key details that support that idea. Then note the author's choice of words. Is the vocabulary neutral and unbiased? Is it meant to influence our judgment in some way? Finally, note the source of the article or passage. Often the publication that the article or passage comes from will help you identify the author's primary purpose.

Read the paragraph below and identify the writer's topic, main idea, and general and specific purposes.

> The viewpoint, now gaining momentum, that would allow individuals to "make up their own minds" about smoking, air bags, safety helmets, and the like ignores some elementary social realities. The ill-informed nature of this viewpoint is camouflaged by the appeal to values that are dear to most Americans. The essence of the argument is that what individuals do with their lives and limbs, foolhardy though it might be, is their own business, and that any interference would abridge their rights. However, no civil society can survive if it permits each person to maximize his or her freedoms without

concern for the consequences of one's act on others. If I choose to drive without a seat belt or air bag, I am greatly increasing my chances, in case of an accident, of being impaled on the steering wheel or exiting via the windshield. It is not just my body that is jeopardized; my careening auto which I cannot get back under control, will be more likely to injure people in other autos, pedestrians, or riders in my car. The individual who chooses to act irresponsibly is playing a game of heads I win, tails the public loses. All too often, the unbelted drivers, the smokers, the unvaccinated, the users of quack remedies, draw on public funds to pay for the consequences of their unrestrained freedom of choice. Their rugged individualism rapidly becomes dependency when cancer strikes, or when the car overturns, sending the occupants to hospitals for treatment paid for at least in part by the public, through subsidies for hospitals and medical training. But the public till is not bottomless, and paying for these irresponsible acts leaves other public needs without funds.

From Amitai Etzioni, "When Rights Collide," in *Psychology Today*, October, 1977. Reprinted by permission of the author.

Topic:	Individual liberty vs. social responsibility
Main Idea:	No civil society can survive if it permits each person to maximize his or her freedom without concern for the consequence of one's act on others.
General Purpose:	To persuade
Specific Purpose:	Persuade us that there needs to be a balance between individual liberty and social responsibility

The following exercises will give you some practice in determining an author's general purpose.

Exercise: Determining the Author's Purpose

Label each sentence according to its general purpose: to inform (**I**), to entertain (**E**), or to persuade (**P**).

_____ 1.   Did you ever wonder how all the best athletes make sports seem so easy? The behind the back passes, the triple lutzes, the holes in one; on TV it looks so easy. We sit in our armchairs and say, "I could do that. How hard could it be?" The truth is, if we could do that, we'd be out there doing it. I think that if I had the talent, right now I'd be doing some triple lutzes. What is a lutz anyway? Are three of them a good thing? Do you have to do it in tights? Because if you have to do it in tights, I may have a problem with it.

From Tom Mather, *Voyages in the Toilet Dimension*, self-published, 1999, p. 35.

_____ 2.   Stealing goods from retail merchants is a very common crime; it constitutes about 15 percent of all larcenies. A recent survey in Spokane, Washington, revealed that every twelfth shopper is a shoplifter, and that men and women are equally likely to be offenders. Perhaps shoplifting is so frequent because it is a low-risk offense, with a detection rate of less than 1 percent. Shoppers are extremely reluctant to report shoplifters to the store management. According to one study, of those apprehended for shoplifting, approximately 45.5 percent are actually prosecuted. It is also estimated that men are slightly more likely than women to be shoplifters, and that 41 percent of offenders are white, 29 percent are black, and 16 percent are Hispanic. More than half of shoplifting events occur between the hours of 12:00 p.m. and 6:00 p.m. A study conducted in New South Wales with juvenile offenders in detention revealed that their reasons for shoplifting ranged from excitement, peer pressure, thrills, or fun; to obtaining clothes, food, or money for drugs or alcohol; to relieving boredom or stress.

From Frieda Adler, et al., *Criminology and the Criminal Justice System*, 5th ed., New York: McGraw-Hill, 2004, p. 292.

———— 3.   The Sound of Music: Enough Already

There was a time when music knew its place. No longer. Possibly this is not music's fault. It may be that music fell in with a bad crowd and lost its sense of common decency. I am willing to consider this. I am willing even to try and help. I would like to do my bit to set music straight in order that it might shape up and leave the mainstream of society. The first thing that music must understand is that there are two kinds of music—good music and bad music. Good music is music that *I* want to hear. Bad music is music that *I* don't want to hear. I do not under any circumstances enjoy hold buttons. But I am a woman of reason. I can accept reality. I can face the facts. What I cannot face is the music. Just as there are two kinds of music—good and bad—so there are two kinds of hold buttons—good and bad. Good hold buttons are hold buttons that hold one silently. Bad hold buttons are hold buttons that hold one musically. When I hold I want to hold silently. That is the way it was meant to be.

From Fran Lebowitz, *The Fran Lebowitz Reader*, New York: Vintage Books, 1994, pp. 137–138.

———— 4.   Cheating jeopardizes the basic fairness of the grading process. Widespread cheating causes honest students to become cynical and resentful, especially when grades are curved and the cheating directly affects other students. Cheating may also have long-term effects. Taking the easy way in college may become a habit that can spill over into graduate school, jobs, and relationships. And consider this: would you want a doctor, lawyer, or accountant who had cheated on exams handling your affairs? Cheating sabotages your own academic and personal growth. Don't cheat!

From John Gardner, *Your College Experience*, Belmont, CA: Wadsworth, p. 221.

Exercise: Identifying the Clues That Indicate the Author's Purpose and Main Idea

Read each of the following paragraphs to determine whether the author's primary purpose is (1) to entertain, (2) to persuade, or (3) to inform. Indicate the clues that enabled you to make your decision. In the space provided, write the stated or implied main idea.

1.   Put an alien creature from outer space in front of a television, and it would have very little idea of what family life is like in the United States. It would conclude that most adults are men, most adults are not married, almost no one is over age 50, very few adults have children, most mothers don't work for pay, and child care is simply not an issue. The fact is that *Friends, Third Rock from the Sun, Frasier, Ally McBeal*, and similar programs present fantasy lives that most households find fascinating, but not exactly true to their lives.

Eight out of 10 adults in the United States think that almost no TV family is like their own; nearly half find *no* TV family like theirs. Katharine Heintz-Knowles, a communications professor at the University of Washington, carried out content analyses of 150 episodes of 92 different programs on commercial networks over a two-week period. She found that of the 820 TV characters studied, only 38 percent were women, only 15 percent could be identified as parents of minor children, and only 14 percent were over age 50. Only 3 percent of the TV characters faced recognizable conflicts between work and family, and no TV family made use of a child care center.

Purpose: _____   Clues: _____

Main Idea: _____

2.   Good manners are back, and for a good reason. As the world becomes increasingly competitive, the gold goes to the team that shows off an extra bit of polish. The person who makes a good impression will be the one who gets the job, wins the promotion, or clinches the deal. Manners and professionalism must become second nature to anyone who wants to achieve and maintain a competitive edge. The lesson is this: You can have good credentials, but a good presentation is everything. You can't neglect etiquette, or somewhere in your career you will be at a competitive disadvantage because of your inability to use good manners or to maintain your composure in tense situations.

Purpose: _____   Clues: _____

_____

Main Idea: _____

_____

3.   If there's one thing this nation needs, it's bigger cars. That's why I'm excited that Ford is coming out with a new mound o' metal that will offer consumers even more total road-squatting mass than the current leader in the humongous-car category, the popular Chevrolet Suburban Subdivision—the first passenger automobile designed to be, right off the assembly line, visible from the Moon. I don't know what the new Ford will be called. Probably something like the "Ford Untamed Wilderness Adventure." In the TV commercials, it will be shown splashing through rivers, charging up rocky mountainsides, swinging on vines, diving off cliffs, racing through the surf, and fighting giant sharks hundreds of feet beneath the ocean surface—all the daredevil things that cars do in Sport Utility Vehicle Commercial World, where nobody ever drives on an actual road. Anyway, now we have the new Ford, which will be *even larger* than the Subdivision, which I imagine means it will have separate decks for the various classes of passengers. And it will not stop there. This is America, darn it, and Chevrolet is not about to just sit by and watch Ford walk away with the coveted title of Least Sane Motor Vehicle. No, cars will keep getting bigger. I see a time, not too far from now, when people will haul their overdue movies back to the video-rental store in full-size, 18-wheel tractor-trailers with names like The Vagabond. It will be a proud time for all Americans, a time for us to cheer for our country.

Purpose: _____   Clues: _____

_____

Main Idea: _____

4. In the traditional cultures of Asia, arranged marriages were the rule.
    Marriages were designed to further the well-being of families, not of the
    individuals involved. Marriage was traditionally seen as a matter of ancestors,
    descendants, and property. Supporters of these traditions point out that love
    is a fleeting emotion and not a sensible basis for such an important decision.
    However, most of these traditional cultures have a literature as well as a
    history full of love-smitten couples who chose death rather than marriage to
    the person selected by their respective families.

From Curtis Byer et al., *Dimensions of Human Sexuality*, 5th ed., New York: McGraw-Hill, 1999, p. 39.

Purpose: _____   Clues: _____

Main Idea: _____

An Introduction to the Rhetorical Modes

Highlight or underline the definitions of the key terms. Then write a paraphrase of each definition in the margin.

In longer reading selections, the main idea is often called the **thesis.** The thesis of an essay, just like the main idea of a paragraph, expresses the most important point the writer is trying to make. The thesis is sometimes called the *controlling idea*, because its primary purpose is to hold the essay or story together.

In the process of creating written work, most writers select a **rhetorical mode of writing** that helps them achieve their purpose. There are four primary rhetorical modes: *narration, description, exposition,* and *persuasion.*

Narrative

_____

_____

Material written in a **narrative mode** tells a story, either true or fictional. In narrative writing, the events of a story are usually ordered chronologically (by time).

Descriptive

_____

_____

With material written in a **descriptive mode,** the emphasis is on providing details that describe a person, place, or object. The writing may use figurative language and include material that appeals to one or more of the five senses. Descriptive writing most commonly deals with visual perceptions.

Expository

_____

_____

An author who is trying to explain something will likely use an **expository mode.** Expository writing explains ideas and how things work. It is more likely to be logical and factual. Much of the material that you read in your textbooks follows an expository mode.

Persuasive

_____

_____

Material written in a **persuasive mode** is meant to convince you of something. Persuasive writing tends to be about controversial topics. It presents an argument and offers evidence. It is writing that is considered to be biased.

Mixed

_____

_____

Sometimes an author will use more than one mode of writing. For example, the author might choose to write a piece that is both descriptive and narrative. This is called a **mixed mode** of writing and the organization may also be mixed.

Author's Purpose: To Inform

Read the following excerpt from *Understanding Psychology* by Robert S. Feldman. Feldman's purpose is to present information about motivation. His mode of writing is **expository.** Note the factual details that are intended to inform the reader.

SELECTION

Excerpt from *Understanding Psychology*   *by Robert S. Feldman*

"Most of the fundamental needs of life . . . can be explained reasonably well by the process of homeostasis."

Getting the Picture

Have you ever wondered what motivates people to quit smoking, to fight to get a diploma from college despite seemingly impossible odds stacked against them, or to engage in high-risk behavior like bungee jumping? This article helps answer these questions by explaining how motivation directs and energizes behavior. As you are reading the selection, practice your annotating skills by making notes in the margins.

Bio-sketch

Robert S. Feldman is a professor of psychology at the University of Massachusetts. Dr. Feldman has numerous scientific articles, books, and book chapters to his credit. His primary research interest is nonverbal behavior.

Brushing Up on Vocabulary

exemplify   to show by giving or being an example of

phenomenon   any fact, condition, or happening that can be either seen or heard and then described in a scientific way; an unusual or remarkable event or thing.

Motivation and Emotion

1   **Motivation** concerns the factors that direct and energize the behaviors of humans and other organisms. Psychologists who study motivation seek to discover the desired goals, or *motives,* that underlie behavior. Motives are exemplified in behavior as basic as drinking to satisfy thirst or as inconsequential as taking a stroll to get exercise. To the psychologist specializing in the study of motivation, underlying motives are assumed to steer one's choice of activities. The study of motivation, then, consists of identifying why people seek to do the things they do.

2   *In just an instant, John Thompson's life changed. That's all it took for an auger, an oversized, drill-like piece of farm equipment powered by a tractor, to rip off both of his arms when he slipped, falling against the rotating machinery.*

3   *Yet it was in the moments following the accident that Thompson demonstrated incredible bravery. Despite his pain and shock, he ran 400 feet to his house. Using the bone hanging from his left shoulder to open the door, he ran inside and dialed for help with a pen gripped in his teeth. When emergency crews arrived 30 minutes later, he told them where to find ice and plastic bags so that his severed arms could be packed for possible surgical reattachment. Thompson's rescuers came none too soon: By the time surgery could start, he had lost half his blood.*

"Always in a moment of extreme danger things can be done which had previously been thought impossible."

—General Erwin Rommel

"What makes life dreary is want of motive."

—George Eliot

4   What explains John Thompson's enormous motivation to stay alive? Like many questions involving motivation, this one has no single answer. Clearly, biological aspects of motivation were at work: He obviously experienced a powerful *drive* to keep himself alive before he lost so much blood that his life would drain away.

5   A **drive** is a motivational tension, or arousal, that energizes behavior in order to fulfill some need. Many basic kinds of drives, such as hunger, thirst, pain avoidance, and need for air and sleep are related to biological needs of the body. These are called *primary drives*. Primary drives contrast with *secondary drives,* in which no obvious biological need is being fulfilled. In secondary drives, needs are brought about by prior experiences and learning. Many secondary drives are related to learned motives for power, affiliation, approval, status, security, and achievement. Some people have strong needs to achieve academically and in their careers. We can say that their achievement need is reflected in a secondary drive that motivates their behavior.

6   We usually try to satisfy a primary drive by reducing the need underlying it. For example, we become hungry after not eating for a few hours and may raid the refrigerator, especially if our next scheduled meal is not imminent. If the weather turns cold, we put on extra clothing or raise the setting on the thermostat in order to keep warm. If our body needs liquids in order to function properly, we experience thirst and seek out water.

7   The reason for such behavior is homeostasis, a basic motivational phenomenon underlying primary drives. **Homeostasis** or "steady state" is the process by which an organism strives to maintain some optimal level of internal biological functioning by compensating for deviations from its usual, balanced internal state. Most of the fundamental needs of life, including the need for food, water, stable body temperature, and sleep can be explained reasonably well by the process of homeostasis.

8   Unfortunately, the process of homeostasis does not explain behaviors in which the goal is not to reduce a drive, but rather to maintain or even to increase a particular level of excitement or arousal. For instance, some behaviors seem to be motivated by nothing more than curiosity. Anyone who has rushed to pick up newly delivered mail, who avidly follows gossip columns in the newspaper, or who yearns to travel to exotic places, knows the importance of curiosity in directing behavior.

9   Similarly, many of us go out of our way to seek thrills through such activities as riding a roller coaster and steering a raft down the rapids of a river. In both of these cases, rather than seeking to reduce an underlying drive, people appear to be motivated to *increase* their overall level of stimulation and activity. In order to explain this phenomenon, psychologists have devised an alternative: arousal approaches to motivation.

10   According to **arousal approaches to motivation,** each of us tries to maintain a certain level of stimulation and activity. If our stimulation and activity levels become too high, we try to reduce them. But, if the levels of stimulation and activity are too low, we will try to *increase* them by seeking sensation.

11   People vary widely in the optimal level of arousal that they seek out, with some people needing especially high levels of arousal. For example, psychologists have hypothesized that individuals such as comic John Belushi, DNA researcher Sir Francis Crick, daredevil Evel Knievel, and bank robbers Bonnie and Clyde exhibited a particularly high need for arousal. Such people may attempt to avoid boredom by seeking out challenging situations.

12   It is not just the celebrated who pursue arousal; many of us characteristically seek out relatively high levels of stimulation. You can get a sense of your own characteristic level of stimulation by completing the questionnaire.

Do You Seek Out Sensation?

13   How much stimulation do you crave in your everyday life? You will have an idea after you complete the following questionnaire, which lists some items from a scale designed to assess your sensation-seeking tendencies. Circle either *A* or *B* in each pair of statements.

14   1. A. I would like a job that requires a lot of traveling.
      B. I would prefer a job in one location.

   2. A. I am invigorated by a brisk, cold day.
      B. I can't wait to get indoors on a cold day.

   3. A. I get bored seeing the same old faces.
      B. I like the comfortable familiarity of old friends.

   4. A. I would prefer living in an ideal society in which everyone was safe, secure, and happy.
      B. I would have preferred living in the unsettled days of our history.

   5. A. I sometimes like to do things that are a little frightening.
      B. A sensible person avoids activities that are dangerous.

   6. A. I would not like to be hypnotized.
      B. I would like to have the experience of being hypnotized.

   7. A. The most important goal of life is to live it to the fullest and to experience as much as possible.
      B. The most important goal of life is to find peace and happiness.

   8. A. I would like to try parachute jumping.
      B. I would never want to try jumping out of a plane, with or without a parachute.

   9. A. I enter cold water gradually, giving myself time to get used to it.
      B. I like to dive or jump right into the ocean or a cold pool.

   10. A. When I go on a vacation, I prefer the comfort of a good room and bed.
       B. When I go on a vacation, I prefer the change of camping out.

   11. A. I prefer people who are emotionally expressive, even if they are a bit unstable.
       B. I prefer people who are calm and even-tempered.

   12. A. A good painting should shock or jolt the senses.
       B. A good painting should give me a feeling of peace and security.

   13. A. People who ride motorcycles must have some kind of unconscious need to hurt themselves.
       B. I would like to drive or ride a motorcycle.

   Scoring Give yourself one point for each of the following responses: 1A, 2A, 3A, 4B, 5A, 6B, 7A, 8A, 9B, 10B, 11A, 12A, 13B. Find your total score by adding up the number of points and then use the following scoring key:

   0–3 very low sensation seeking
   4–5 low
   6–9 average
   10–11 high
   12–13 very high

15   Keep in mind, of course, that this short questionnaire, for which the scoring is based on the results of college students who have taken it, provides only a rough estimate of your sensation-seeking tendencies. Moreover, as people get older, their sensation-seeking scores tend to decrease. Still, the questionnaire will at least give you an indication of how your sensation-seeking tendencies compare with those of others.

From Robert S. Feldman, *Understanding Psychology,* 5th ed., New York: McGraw-Hill, 1999, pp. 326–327, 329. Copyright © 1999 McGraw-Hill. Reprinted by permission of The McGraw-Hill Companies, Inc.

Comprehension Checkup

What is the topic of this article? _____

What is the article's main idea? _____

_____

STUDY TECHNIQUE 4

Outlining

An outline is an orderly arrangement of ideas going from the general to the specific. An outline shows the relationship and importance of ideas by using a system of Roman numerals for main headings (I, II, III, etc.), capital letters for subheadings (A, B, C, etc.), and numbers for sub-subheadings (1, 2, 3, etc.). Whether you are using outlining to organize class notes or a reading selection, only the most important points should be included.

A partial outline of the previous selection follows. Complete the outline by filling in the missing information in your own words.

I. *Motivation* is defined as _____

_____

II. *Drive* is defined as _____

   A. *Primary drive* is defined as _____

_____

     1. An example of a primary drive is _____

_____

     2. Another example of a primary drive is ___

   B. *Secondary drive* is defined as _____

_____

     1. An example of a secondary drive is _____

_____

     2. Another example of a secondary drive is

_____

III. Reasons for Motivation

   A. *Homeostasis* is defined as _____

     1. An example of homeostasis is _____

_____

     2. Other examples of homeostasis are _____

_____

_____

   B. *Arousal* is defined as _____

_____

     1. An example of arousal is _____

     2. Another example of arousal is _____

_____

The Art of Writing

In a brief essay, respond to the questions below.

Think about yourself and try to identify your secondary drives. How would you describe them? How do they affect your behavior? Make sure you give some specific examples. For instance, you have a strong secondary drive to achieve. This has motivated you to increase your class load and graduate from college in just three years.

Author's Purpose: To Entertain

The following fable by Aesop has entertainment as its primary purpose. It is an example of the *narrative* mode of writing. Notice that the significant events of the story are told in chronological order.

The Country Mouse and the Town Mouse _____ *by Aesop*

"Gradually, when things seemed quiet, the country mouse crept out from his hiding place and whispered good-bye to his elegant friend."

Getting the Picture

Do you think that people who live in cities have a different perspective on life than people who live in rural areas? If you think this, what are some of the differences you see?

Bio-sketch

Aesop, a Greek slave, lived from about 620 to 560 B.C.E. According to legend, Aesop was eventually freed because the fables he told exhibited such great wisdom. As a free man he traveled to Athens, Greece, where he quickly made an enemy of the ruler and was condemned to death.

Many of Aesop's best fables draw parallels between animals and humans in order to illustrate key moral principles and universal lessons. Aesop is responsible for many familiar expressions that have survived to this day, such as "sour grapes," "don't cry over spilt milk," "actions speak louder than words," and "look before you leap."

Brushing Up on Vocabulary

morsel   a little bite. *Morsel* is derived from the Latin word *morsum*, meaning "bitten."

condescend   This word is derived from the Latin prefix *de* meaning "down," "down from," and "away." The meaning of "stoop to the level of inferiors" was first recorded in 1435. The fable states that "the town mouse *condescended* to nibble a little here and there." This means that the town mouse was "politely willing to do something that he thought was beneath his dignity."

rustic   The English language is almost always uncomplimentary to the "country cousin." *Rustic* is derived from the Latin word *rus,* meaning "open land, country." In 1585, it acquired the meaning "rough, awkward," and then in 1594 that of "simple and plain."

1   Once upon a time a country mouse, who had a friend in town, invited him to pay a visit in the country for old acquaintance's sake. After the invitation was accepted, the country mouse, though plain, coarse, and somewhat frugal, opened his heart and pantry to honor his old friend and to show him the proper hospitality. There was not a morsel which he had carefully stored that he did not bring forth out of its larder—peas and barley, cheese parings and nuts—with the hope that the quantity would make up for what he feared was wanting in quality to suit the taste of his elegant guest. In turn, the town mouse condescended to nibble a little here and there in a dainty manner while the host sat munching a blade of barley straw. In

2

their after-dinner chat the town mouse said to the country mouse, "How is it, my good friend, that you can endure this boring and crude life? You live like a toad in a hole. You can't really prefer these solitary rocks and woods to streets teeming with carriages and people. Upon my word of honor, you're wasting your time in such a miserable existence. You must make the most of your life while it lasts. As you know, a mouse does not live forever. So, come with me this very night, and I'll show you all around the town and what life's about."

Overcome by his friend's fine words and polished manner, the country mouse agreed, and they set out together on their journey to the town. It was late in the evening when they crept stealthily into the city and midnight before they reached the large house, which was the town mouse's residence. There were couches of crimson velvet, ivory carvings, and everything one could imagine that indicated wealth and luxury. On the table were the remains of a splendid banquet from all the choicest shops ransacked the day before to make sure that the guests, already departed, would be satisfied. It was now the town mouse's turn to play host, and he placed his country friend on a purple cushion, ran back and forth to supply all his needs, and pressed dish upon dish on him and delicacy upon delicacy. Of course, the town mouse tasted each and every course before he ventured to place it before his rustic cousin, as though he were waiting on a king. In turn, the country mouse made himself quite at home and blessed the good fortune that had brought about such a change in his way of life. In the middle of his enjoyment, however, just as he was thinking contemptuously of the poor meals that he had been accustomed to eating, the door suddenly flew open, and a group of revelers, who were returning from a late party, burst into the room. The frightened friends jumped from the table and hid themselves in the very first corner they could reach. No sooner did they dare creep out again than the barking of dogs drove them back with even greater terror than before. Gradually, when things seemed quiet, the country mouse crept out from his hiding place and whispered good-bye to his elegant friend.

3

"This fine mode of living may be all right for those who like it," he said. "But I'd rather have a crust in peace and safety than all your fine things in the midst of such alarm and terror."

Comprehension Checkup

True or False

Indicate whether the statement is true or false by writing T or F in the blank provided.

_____ 1. The country mouse would score high on the sensation-seeking scale.

_____ 2. The mice were filling a primary drive when they were interrupted by the revelers.

_____ 3. The country mouse probably has a strong secondary drive for security.

_____ 4. The late-night revelers entered the room quietly.

_____ 5. The town mouse's residence was lavishly decorated.

Multiple Choice

Write the letter of the correct answer in the blank provided.

_____ 6. What do the words *coarse, plain,* and *frugal* suggest about the country mouse?
    a. He is very lazy.
    b. He has a magnificent lifestyle.

     c. He lives a simple, thrifty life.

     d. He is likely to use obscenities.

_____ 7. A proverb is a traditional saying that offers advice or presents a moral. Which of the following proverbs best describes the attitude of the town mouse?

     a. You win a few, you lose a few.

     b. Absence makes the heart grow fonder.

     c. If you can't beat them, join them.

     d. Curiosity killed the cat.

_____ 8. Which of the following proverbs best describes the attitude of the country mouse at the end of the fable?

     a. Adventures are for the adventurous.

     b. It's best to be on the safe side.

     c. The early bird catches the worm.

     d. Both (a) and (b).

_____ 9. Which of the following best describes the town mouse's attitude toward the country mouse before their departure to the city?

     a. The country mouse is living his life to the fullest.

     b. The country mouse needs to have new experiences.

     c. The country mouse is very adventurous.

     d. The country mouse should stay right where he is because there's no place like home.

_____ 10. The town mouse and the country mouse crept _stealthily_ into the city. The most likely meaning of the word _stealthily_ is

     a. sneakily

     b. loudly

     c. obviously

     d. both (a) and (b).

Vocabulary in Context

Look through the paragraph indicated in parentheses to find a word that matches the definition below.

1. thrifty (paragraph 1) _____

2. place where food is kept or stored; pantry (1) _____

3. very full; swarming; abounding (1) _____

4. scornfully (2) _____

5. merrymakers (2) _____

6. searched thoroughly; plundered (2) _____

7. urged upon (2) _____

8. method; way of acting or behaving (3) _____

In Your Own Words

1. What is the main idea of the fable?

2. Working with a partner, paraphrase one of the paragraphs of the fable. Be sure to keep the characters and setting the same.

3. What is the significance of the ending of the fable? What is meant by the last sentence? Explain.

4. Determine which of the following proverbs is more likely to express the attitude of the country mouse. Explain your choice.

> "A life lived in fear is a life half-lived."
>
> "Better to be safe than sorry."
>
> "Nothing ventured, nothing gained."
>
> "Variety is the spice of life."
>
> "Acorns were good till bread was found."

The Art of Writing

In a brief essay, respond to one of the items below.

1. Are you more like the country mouse or the town mouse? Why?

2. Explain how the intrusion of the revelers and the barking dogs was a threat to the homeostasis of the mice. What do you see as the secondary drives of each mouse? Make reference to the previous article if necessary.

Internet Activity

The following website has a collection of more than 665 of Aesop's fables:

www.Aesopfables.com.

Select three fables you find interesting and print them. Think about the meaning of the fables and how the moral might apply to your own life. Describe your conclusions in a short paragraph.

Author's Purpose: To Persuade

The following is a poem by Judith Ortiz Cofer. The poem's purpose is to persuade and it is written in a persuasive mode.

Crossings   by Judith Ortiz Cofer

"Finally, you must choose between standing still in the one solid spot you have found, or you keep moving and take the risk."

Getting the Picture

What idea is Ortiz Cofer trying to convince us to accept? What course of action is she recommending?

Bio-sketch

Judith Ortiz Cofer was born in Puerto Rico in 1952 and is currently a professor of English and Creative Writing at the University of Georgia. A recipient of the O. Henry award for a short story, she has also published two volumes of poetry, *Peregrina* in 1986 and *Triple Crown* in 1987. *The Meaning of Consuelo* was published in 2003.

"To be alive at all involves some risk."

—Harold MacMillan

*Step on a crack.**
In a city of concrete it is impossible
to avoid disaster indefinitely.
You spend your life peering
downward, looking for flaws,
but each day more and more fissures
crisscross your path, and like the lines
on your palms, they mean something
you cannot decipher.
Finally, you must choose between
standing still in the one solid spot you
have found, or you keep moving
and take the risk:
Break your mother's back.

*"Step on a crack, break your mother's back"—a rhyme children say while they avoid stepping on the cracks in a sidewalk. Stepping on a crack is supposed to bring bad luck.

From Judith Ortiz Cofer, "Crossings," *Triple Crown: Chicano, Puerto Rican and Cuban-American Poetry*, Arizona State University: Bilingual Press, 1987. Copyright © 1987 Bilingual Press/Editorial Bilingue, Arizona State University, Tempe, AZ. Reprinted with permission.

In Your Own Words

Try to explain the meaning of the poem in your own words.

_____

_____

_____

_____

_____

_____

The next selection describes a painting by René Magritte. The mode of writing is **descriptive.** Do you think the author's purpose is to inform, entertain, or persuade?

SELECTION

Excerpt from *Interpreting Art*   *by Terry Barrett*

"The man in the picture is curiously unmoved. He seems neither startled, nor scared, not awed in the presence of such a mysterious phenomenon."

Getting the Picture

Study René Magritte's painting for a few minutes before you read the author's description of it. What message do you think the artist is sending by this picture?

René-Francois-Ghislain Magritte (1898–1967), a Belgian painter, began drawing as a child, attended art school as a young adult, and became a full-time painter in 1926 after a stint as a commercial artist.

At the age of 14, Magritte was horrified to find his mother's body in the river one night, her face covered by her nightgown. She had apparently committed suicide. Many of Magritte's well-known paintings depict people with covered or averted faces.

Magritte's art is well represented in museum collections around the world and is frequently reproduced in books, magazines, and on the Internet.

Bio-sketch

Terry Barrett, a professor of art education at Ohio State University, has been the recipient of a distinguished teaching award for courses in criticism and aesthetics in education. He has written four books, is an art critic in education for the Ohio Arts Council, and consults with museum educators.

Brushing Up on Vocabulary

Isaac Newton (1642–1727)   an English mathematician and physicist of the seventeenth century who gave a mathematical description of the laws of gravity. Supposedly the law of gravity occurred to him as he watched an apple fall from a tree.

William Tell   a legendary Swiss hero famous for his skill as an archer. Supposedly in the fourteenth century, he was forced to shoot an arrow through an apple that had been placed on top of his son's head; he succeeded, and his son lived.

Interpreting Out Loud

1   In *The Postcard*, I see a large green apple in the sky above the head of a man wearing a black coat and standing before a stone wall that is between him and a mountain range.

2   In my literal reading of the painting, I do not know whether the man (I assume, because of the haircut, that he is a man) is aware of the apple. The apple's placement is ambiguous, and I am not certain whether it is behind him, above his head, or in front of him. Perhaps I see the apple but he does not. Maybe the apple is in his imagination, and that is what I am seeing. Perhaps the apple imagines him!

3   I do not know in what kind of place the man is standing. Magritte gives no clues for the man's placement. He could be on the overlook of a mountain highway; he could have stepped from the stone room of a castle onto a balcony. The gray wall, though, is apparent. It is meticulously crafted of stone blocks and well kept. It separates him from the beyond, but it also protects him from the edge.

4   From the label, I can tell that the painting was made in 1960, but this does not tell me what year the painting depicts, though it does not seem to be set very long ago. The painting does not reveal the season of the year: the mountains are light gray and could be snow-covered; the air is clear. The scene looks chilly, and the man wears a coat, though it is the kind of coat that could be worn in summer or winter. The sun provides light, but I do not feel its warmth.

5   The man in the picture is curiously unmoved. He seems neither startled, nor scared, nor awed in the presence of such a mysterious phenomenon. He is stiff, his head straightforward. His face is not visible, but because his posture is so void of

La carte postale (The Postcard)* (1960), René Magritte

© 2005 C. Herscovici, Brussels/Artists Rights Society (ARS), New York

*Too see this work of art in color, turn to the color insert following page 260.

expression, I imagine that his face, too, is frozen in a vacant stare. Such cool aloofness, such dissociation and detachment, do not fit the eerie circumstance.

6   Magritte's handling of the paint is merely adequate for representing the scene in a realistic manner. He is not attempting effects that would fool the eye into believing that it is looking at an actual apple; nor is he trying to dazzle with his draftsmanship and painterly abilities. The compositional devices are straightforward: the apple and the human figure are centrally located along a vertical axis, while the apple dominates the upper area of the picture along the horizontal axis. The painting has directness about it. The painting does not seem to be at all about an artist's virtuoso display of technique in rendering the three-dimensional world in paint on a flat canvas. This is not a painting that is meant to trick the eye, but one meant to perplex the mind.

7   On the surface of the picture, the paint of the apple almost touches the paint of the man's hair. The man's coat collar aligns exactly with the top of the distant mountains, as if that horizon line could sever the man's head. There is ambiguity about foreground, middle ground, and background relationships. Which is closer to us, the top of the apple or the back of the man? The painting tests our tolerance of ambiguity. I think the apple takes the middle ground, the mountains the background, and the man the foreground, but I can't be sure.

8   Magritte's color palette is muted, the colors are cool, and the light green of the apple is the brightest hue. There is an indication of a light source coming from above and to the right of the figure and the apple. The light is likely from the sun although it could be the moon. Yeats wrote of "the silver apples of the moon, the golden apples of the sun." This painting feels more silver and moonlike than golden and sunlike. The feelings the painting evokes in me are of isolation, alienation, and loneliness.

"To be absolutely certain about something, one must know everything or nothing about it."

—Olin Miller

9 The apple carries with it many associations. There is the forbidden apple of wisdom in the Garden of Eden. There is the apple William Tell placed on his son's head, the apple that fell on Isaac Newton's head, the apple of my eye, and apple pie and motherhood.

10 The phrase "the apple of my eye" fits the painting if "my" refers to the man. The man does seem to see the apple; he could be the only one seeing it. Perhaps it exists only in the eye of his imagination. This would account for the strangeness of the scene: we can all imagine strange things, and we have all at one time or another believed one thing to be true, only to discover later that we had misperceived something.

11 Of all the associations with apples and *The Postcard*, the connection with Newton seems the most plausible. The most notable properties of this apple are its incongruously huge size, its placement in the sky, and especially its seeming ability to be airborne, suspended in denial of gravity. Therefore, the connection to Newton is strongest for me. Above all, the painting provides a test of anyone's tolerance for, or joy in, ambiguity.

From Terry Barrett, *Interpreting Art*, New York: McGraw-Hill, 2003, pp. 4–6. Copyright © 2003 McGraw-Hill. Reprinted by permission of The McGraw-Hill Companies, Inc.

Comprehension Checkup

True or False

Indicate whether the statement is true or false by writing T or F in the blank provided.

_____ 1. *The Postcard* was painted in 1950.

_____ 2. The season in the painting is winter.

_____ 3. The author considers the handling of the paint to be merely "adequate."

_____ 4. The author is uncertain whether the back of the man or the top of the apple is closer to the viewer.

_____ 5. The author assumes that the man is in the background.

_____ 6. The author characterizes the colors in the painting as warm.

_____ 7. When the author observes the painting, he experiences a feeling of loneliness.

_____ 8. An apple has multiple associations according to the author.

_____ 9. The author feels that the apple in the painting might have an association with Newton and gravity.

_____ 10. To the author, the painting is associated with ambiguity.

Vocabulary in Context

Match each word with its definition.

aloof	eerie	incongruously	muted	vacant
ambiguous	hue	meticulously	phenomenon	vertical

1. _____ something that is remarkable or extraordinary

2. _____ strange or weird

3. _____ reduced in intensity

4. _____ upright; lengthwise

5. _____ open to having several possible meanings

6. _____ lacking in thought; empty

7. _____ gradation or variety of a color

8. _____ taking or showing great care over minute details

9. _____ state of being reserved or reticent

10. _____ out of place; inappropriate

The Art of Writing

In a brief essay, respond to the item below.

Examine one of the paintings that appear at the beginning of each chapter. What do the details of the painting suggest to you? Make your description so clear that your classmates could pick this painting out from among others.

The next article discusses extreme sports. Read the article and think about its purpose and the rhetorical mode the author uses. Then answer the questions that follow.

SELECTION

Life On The Edge   *by Karl Taro Greenfeld*

"America has always been defined by risk; it may be our predominant national characteristic."

Getting the Picture

In recent years, the young and the fit have been besieged with invitations to participate in man-made "life tests." They are asked, "Do you have what it takes?" And told, "Just do it." Increasingly, reality movies and TV programs like *Survivor* occupy our national attention. As you are reading the article below, try to determine what's behind this preoccupation with testing the limits.

Bio-sketch

Karl Taro Greenfeld is a Japanese-American writer—author of *Speed Tribes: Days and Nights with Japan's Next Generation* (1994)—and editor for *Time* magazine's Asian edition.

Brushing Up on Vocabulary

acronym   a word formed by combining the initial letters or syllables of a series of words. It comes from the Greek *akros,* meaning "tip," and *onym,* meaning "name." Large numbers of *acronyms* first began to appear during World War I when WAAC (Women's Army Auxiliary Corps) and similar words were formed. The trend accelerated during World War II with terms such as RADAR (radio detecting and ranging). Some common acronyms are AIDS (acquired immunodeficiency syndrome), NAFTA (North American Free Trade Agreement), and MADD (Mothers Against Drunk Driving).

orgy   the word came to us from the Greek word *orgia,* which meant "secret ceremonies." The Greeks held nighttime religious rituals in honor of Dionysius, the

Greek god of wine. These *orgia* involved drinking, singing, dancing, and acts of sex. The current meaning is much the same except that the religious element has been eliminated.

bespeak   a British term meaning "to speak for or order in advance."

pandemic   an epidemic that spreads over a large area, possibly even worldwide. Comes from the Greek word *pandemos,* meaning "disease of all the people."

perilous   involving grave risk; hazardous; dangerous. A long time ago travel was a highly dangerous undertaking. The word *perilous* comes from the Latin *periculum,* which means "the danger of going forth to travel."

manifestation   clearly evident; an outward indication. From the Latin *manus,* which means "hand," and *festus,* which means "struck." Something that was *manifest* to the senses was something that could be touched or struck by the hand.

pansy   a dainty flower with velvety petals and a "thoughtful face." The word is derived from the French *penser,* meaning "to think." The word is also a slang term for an effeminate man.

contemplate   to consider thoughtfully. The ancient Roman priests carefully considered various signs or omens that were revealed to them inside the temples of their gods. *Contemplate* is derived from *con,* meaning "with," and *templum,* meaning "temple."

1   "FIVE . . . FOUR . . . THREE . . . TWO . . . ONE . . . SEE YA!" And Chance McGuire, 25, is airborne off a 650-foot concrete dam in Northern California. In one second he falls 16 feet, in two seconds 63 feet, and after three seconds and 137 feet he is flying at 65 m.p.h. He prays that his parachute will open facing away from the dam, that his canopy won't collapse, that his toggles will be handy, and that no ill wind will slam him back into the cold concrete. The chute snaps open, the sound ricocheting through the gorge like a gunshot, and McGuire is soaring, carving S turns into the air, swooping over a winding creek. When he lands, he is a speck on a path along the creek. He hurriedly packs his chute and then, clearly audible above the rushing water, lets out a war whoop that rises past those mortals still perched on the dam, past the commuters puttering by on the roadway, past even the hawks who circle the ravine. It is a cry of defiance, thanks, and victory; he has survived another BASE jump.

2   McGuire is a practitioner of what he calls the king of all extreme sports. BASE is an acronym for building, antenna, span (bridge), and earth (cliffs). BASE jumping has one of the sporting world's highest fatality rates: in its 18-year history, 46 participants have been killed. Yet the sport has never been more popular, with more than a thousand jumpers in the U.S. and more seeking to get into it every day.

3   It is an activity without margin for error. If your chute malfunctions, don't bother reaching for a reserve—there isn't time. There are no second chances.

4   Still, the sport's stark metaphor—a human leaving safety behind to leap into the void—may be perfect with our times. As extreme a risk-taker as McGuire seems, we may all have more in common with him than we know or care to admit. America has embarked on a national orgy of thrill seeking and risk taking. Extreme sports like BASE jumping, snowboarding, ice climbing, skateboarding and paragliding are merely the most vivid manifestation of this new national behavior.

5   The rising popularity of extreme sports bespeaks an eagerness on the part of millions of Americans to participate in activities closer to the metaphorical edge, where danger, skill, and fear combine to give weekend warriors and professional

athletes alike a sense of pushing out personal boundaries. According to American Sports Data, a consulting firm, participation in so-called extreme sports is way up. Snowboarding has grown 113 percent in five years and now boasts nearly 5.5 million participants. Mountain biking, skateboarding, scuba diving, you name the adventure sport—the growth curves reveal a nation that loves to play with danger. Contrast that with activities like baseball, touch football, and aerobics, all of which have been in steady decline throughout the '90s.

6

"Life has no romance without risk."

—Sarah Doherty, first one-legged person to scale Mt. McKinley

The pursuits that are becoming more popular have one thing in common: the perception that they are somehow more challenging than a game of touch football. "Every human being with two legs, two arms, is going to wonder how fast, how strong, how enduring he or she is," says Eric Perlman, a mountaineer and filmmaker specializing in extreme sports. "We are designed to experiment or die."

7

And to get hurt. More Americans than ever are injuring themselves while pushing their personal limits. In 1997, the U.S. Consumer Safety Commission reported that 48,000 Americans were admitted to hospital emergency rooms with skateboarding-related injuries. That's 33 percent more than the previous year. Snowboarding E.R. visits were up 31 percent; mountain climbing up 20 percent. By every statistical measure available, Americans are participating in, and injuring themselves through, adventure sports at an unprecedented rate.

8

Consider Mike Carr, an environmental engineer and paraglider pilot from Denver who last year survived a bad landing that smashed 10 ribs and collapsed his lung. Paraglider pilots use feathery nylon wings to take off from mountaintops and float on thermal wind currents—a completely unpredictable ride. Carr also mountain bikes and climbs rock faces. He walked away from a 1,500-foot fall in Peru in 1988. After his recovery, he returned to paragliding. "This has taken over many of our lives," he explains. "You float like a bird out there. You can go as high as 18,000 feet and go for 200 miles. That's magic."

9

America has always been defined by risk; it may be our predominant national characteristic. It's a country founded by risk-takers fed up with the English Crown and expanded by pioneers—a word that seems utterly American. Our heritage throws up heroes—Lewis and Clark, Thomas Edison, Frederick Douglass, Teddy Roosevelt, Henry Ford, Amelia Earhart—who bucked the odds, taking perilous chances.

10

Previous generations didn't need to seek out risk; it showed up uninvited and regularly: global wars, childbirth complications, diseases and pandemics from the flu to polio, dangerous products, and even the omnipresent cold-war threat of mutually assured destruction. "I just don't think extreme sports would have been popular in a ground-war era," says Dan Cady, professor of popular culture at California State University at Fullerton. "Coming back from a war and getting onto a skateboard would not seem so extreme."

11

But for recent generations, many of these traditional risks have been reduced by science, government, or legions of personal-injury lawyers, leaving Boomers and Generations X and Y to face less real risk. Life expectancy has increased. Violent crime is down. You are 57 percent less likely to die of heart disease than your parents; smallpox, measles, and polio have virtually been eradicated.

12

"The greater the difficulty, the more glory in surmounting it."

—Epicurus

Combat survivors speak of the terror and the excitement of playing in a death match. Are we somehow incomplete as people if we do not taste that terror and excitement on the brink? People are [taking risks] because everyday risk is minimized and people want to be challenged," says Joy Marr, 43, an adventure racer who was the only woman member of a five-person team that finished the 1998 Raid Gauloises, the grandaddy of all adventure races. This is a sport that requires several days of nonstop slogging, climbing, rappelling, rafting, and surviving through some of the roughest terrain in the world. Says fellow adventure racer and former Army Ranger Jonathan Senk, 35: "Our society is so surgically sterile. It's almost like our socialization just desensitizes us. Every time I'm out doing this I'm searching my soul. It's the Lewis and Clark gene, to venture out, to find what your limitations are."

13   Psychologist Frank Farley of Temple University believes that taking conscious risk involves overcoming our instincts. He points out that no other animal intentionally puts itself in peril. "The human race is particularly risk-taking compared with other species," he says. He describes risk-takers as the Type T personality, and the U.S. as a Type T nation. He breaks it down further, into Type T physical (extreme athletes) and Type T intellectual (Albert Einstein, Galileo). He warns there is also Type T negative, that is, those who are drawn to delinquency, crime, experimentation with drugs, unprotected sex, and a whole litany of destructive behaviors.

14   All these Type Ts are related, and perhaps even different aspects of the same character trait. There is, says Farley, a direct link between Einstein and BASE jumper Chance McGuire. They are different manifestations of the thrill-seeking component of our characters: Einstein was thrilled by his mental life, and McGuire—well, Chance jumps off buildings.

15   McGuire, at the moment, is driving from Hollister to another California town, Auburn, where he is planning another BASE jump from a bridge. Riding with him is Adam Fillipino, president of Consolidated Rigging, a company that manufactures parachutes and gear for BASE jumpers. McGuire talks about the leap ahead, about his feelings when he is at the exit point, and how at that moment, looking down at the ground, what goes through his mind is that this is not something a human being should be doing. But that's exactly what makes him take the leap: that sense of overcoming his inhibitions and winning what he calls the gravity game. "Football is for pansies," says McGuire. "What do you need all those pads for? This sport [BASE jumping] is pushing all the limits. I have a friend who calls it suicide with a kick."

16   When a BASE jumper dies, other BASE jumpers say he has "gone in," as gone into the ground or gone into a wall. "I'm sick of people going in," says Fillipino. "In the past year, a friend went in on a skydive, another drowned as a result of a BASE jump, another friend went in on a jump, another died in a skydiving plane crash. You can't escape death, but you don't want to flirt with it either." It may be the need to flirt with death, or at least take extreme chances, that has his business growing at the rate of 50 percent a year.

"Who does nothing need hope for nothing."

—J.C.F. von Schiller

17   Without some expression of risk, we may never know our limits and therefore who we are as individuals. "If you don't assume a certain amount of risk," says paraglider pilot Wade Ellet, 51, "you're missing a certain amount of life." And it is by taking risks that we may flirt with greatness. "We create technologies, we make new discoveries, but in order to do that, we have to push beyond the set of rules that are governing us at that time," says psychologist Farley.

18   That's certainly what's driving McGuire and Fillipino as they position themselves on the Auburn bridge. It's dawn again, barely light, and they appear as shadows moving on the catwalk beneath the roadway. As they survey the drop zone, they compute a series of risk assessments. "It's a matter of weighing the variables," Fillipino says, pointing out that the wind, about 15 m.p.h. out of the northwest, has picked up a little more than he would like. Still, it's a clear morning, and they've climbed all the way up here. McGuire is eager to jump. But Fillipino continues to scan the valley below them, the Sacramento River rushing through the gorge.

19   Then a white parks-department SUV pulls up on an access road that winds alongside the river. Park Rangers are a notorious scourge of BASE jumpers, confiscating equipment and prosecuting for trespassing. Fillipino contemplates what would

happen if the president of a BASE rig company were busted for an illegal jump. He foresees trouble with his bankers, he imagines the bad publicity his business would garner, and he says he's not going. There are some risks he is simply not willing to take.

From Karl Taro Greenfield, "Life on the Edge," *Time,* 9/6/99, pp. 29–36. © 1999 Time Inc. Reprinted by permission.

✔ Comprehension Checkup

True or False

Indicate whether the statement is true or false by writing T or F in the blank provided.

_____   1.   BASE jumping has an extremely low fatality rate.

_____   2.   Park Rangers are generally supportive of BASE jumping.

_____   3.   The BASE jumpers described in the article weigh many variables before deciding to perform a BASE jump.

_____   4.   Fillipino was reluctant to endanger his business interests with a jump off the Auburn bridge.

_____   5.   People who are Type T negative are attracted to unlawful activities.

Multiple Choice

Write the letter of the correct answer in the blank provided.

_____   6.   The author's primary purpose in writing this article was to
a. entertain the reader with a good story about Chance McGuire and friends
b. persuade people to try extreme sports
c. provide information about BASE jumping and other extreme sports
d. convince the reader that extreme sports should be outlawed

_____   7.   It is suggested in the article that
a. extreme sports will eventually be replaced by regular sports
b. extreme sports are responsible for many physical injuries
c. our national heritage is replete with stories of heroic individuals who took risks
d. both (b) and (c)

_____   8.   It is suggested in the article that
a. our ancestors faced real adversity in the form of disease and war
b. persons with Type T personalities especially enjoy challenges
c. some persons who do not face real adversity in their lives turn to extreme sports to fill this void
d. all of the above

_____   9.   What is the most likely meaning of *weekend warrior* as used in paragraph five?
a. a person who likes to take chances in the summer months
b. a person who encounters physical challenge and adversity on a daily basis
c. a person who works hard during the week and relaxes on the weekend
d. a person who engages in rigorous physical activity primarily on the weekend

_____ 10. Chance McGuire disparages those who
   a. have "gone in"
   b. participate in conventional sports
   c. believe paragliding is superior to BASE jumping
   d. take unwarranted risks

Vocabulary in Context

Using context clues provided, define the following words. Then consult your dictionary to see how accurate your definition is.

1. clearly *audible* above the rushing water, lets out a war whoop (paragraph 1)

    Definition: _____

2. If your chute *malfunctions*, don't bother reaching for a reserve (3)

    Definition: _____

3. a human leaving safety behind to leap into the *void* (4)

    Definition: _____

4. smallpox, measles, and polio have virtually been *eradicated* (11)

    Definition: _____

5. experimentation with drugs, unprotected sex, and a whole *litany* of destructive behaviors (13)

    Definition: _____

In Your Own Words

1. Have you ever tried an extreme sport? Do you think the benefits of participating in an extreme sport outweigh the risks? Based on the article, can you identify some common characteristics of those who participate in extreme sports?

2. Should the law place restrictions on extreme sports? What sorts of restrictions should apply?

3. Do you think that life is more risky today than it was 50 years ago? In what ways might contemporary life be more risky? In what ways might it be less risky?

The Art of Writing

In a brief essay, respond to the item below.

> "Extreme athletes put not only themselves in danger by their activity; rescue workers who rescue extreme skiers from avalanches and medical workers called on to helicopter-lift athletes in trouble out of the rugged terrain are also put at risk." Is this fair?

Internet Activity

To learn more about extreme sports, consult one of the following websites.

http://expn.go.com

http://www.adventuresports.com

http://www.extreme.com

http://espn.go.com/extreme/index.html

Summarize your findings.

Dean Dunbar, an extreme-sports enthusiast, has been an active participant in a variety of extreme sports despite a degenerative eye condition.

To read about Dunbar, go to www.awezome.com and click on Extreme Dreams. Summarize your findings.

Review Test 2: Context Clue Practice Using Textbook Material

Directions: Use the context to determine the meaning of the italicized word(s).

1. What are the odds that you'll be involved in some kind of violent act within the next seven days? 1 out of 10? 1 out of 100? 1 out of 1,000? 1 out of 10,000? According to George Gerbner, the answer you give may have more to do with how much TV you watch than with the actual risk you face in the week to come. Gerbner, former dean of the Annenberg School of Communication at the University of Pennsylvania, claims that heavy television users develop an exaggerated belief in "a mean and scary world." The violence they see on the screen *cultivates* a social *paranoia* that resists notions of trustworthy people or safe environments. (p. 344)

   cultivates: _____

   paranoia: _____

2. On any given week, two-thirds of the major characters in prime-time programs are caught up in some kind of violence. Heroes are just as involved as villains, yet there is great inequality as to age, race, and gender of those on the receiving end of physical force. Old people and children are harmed at a much greater rate than young or middle-aged adults. In the pecking order of "victimage," blacks and Hispanics are killed or beaten more than their Caucasian counterparts. Gerbner notes that it's risky to be "other than clearly white." It's also dangerous to be female. The opening lady-in-distress scene is a favorite dramatic device to *galvanize* the hero into action. And finally, blue-collar workers "get it in the neck" more often than white-collar executives. (p. 346)

   galvanize: _____

3. Not surprisingly, more women than men are afraid of dark streets. But for both sexes the fear of victimization *correlates* with time spent in front of the tube. People with heavy viewing habits tend to overestimate criminal activity, believing it to be ten times worse than it really is. In actuality, muggers on the street *pose* less bodily threat than injury from cars. (p. 348)

   correlates: _____

   pose: _____

4. Those with heavy viewing habits are suspicious of other people's motives. They subscribe to statements that warn people to expect the worst:

   "Most people are just looking out for themselves."
   "In dealing with others, you can't be too careful."

"Do unto others before they do unto you."
Gerbner calls this *cynical* mind-set the "mean world syndrome."
The Annenberg evidence suggests that the minds of heavy TV viewers become *fertile* ground for *sowing* thoughts of danger. (p. 348)

cynical: _____

fertile: _____

sowing: _____

5. Gerbner also explains the constant viewer's greater *apprehension* by the process of *resonance*. Many viewers have had at least one firsthand experience with physical violence—armed robbery, rape, bar fight, mugging, auto crash, military combat, or a lover's quarrel that became vicious. The actual *trauma* was bad enough. But he thinks that a repeated symbolic portrayal on the TV screen can cause the viewer to replay the real-life experience over and over in his or her mind. Constant viewers who have experienced physical violence get a double dose. (p. 349)

apprehension: _____

trauma: _____

6. Because advertising rates are tied directly to a program's share of the market, television professionals are experts at gaining and holding attention. Social critics *decry* the *gratuitous* violence on television, but Stanford psychologist Albert Bandura denies that aggression is unrelated to the story line. The scenes of physical violence are especially compelling because they suggest that violence is a preferred solution to human problems. Violence is presented as a strategy for life. (p. 369)

decry: _____

gratuitous: _____

7. On every type of program, television draws in viewers by placing attractive people in front of the camera. There are very few overweight bodies or pimply faces on TV. When the *winsome* star roughs up a few hoods to help the lovely young woman, aggression is given a positive cast.

winsome: _____

8. Using violence in the race for ratings not only draws an attentive audience, it transmits responses that we, as viewers, might never have considered before. The media expand our repertoire of behavioral options far beyond what we would discover by trial and error and in ways more varied than we would observe in people we know. Bandura says it's fortunate that people learn from *vicarious* observation, since mistakes could prove costly or fatal. Without putting himself at risk, Tyler Richie, a 10-year-old boy, is able to discover that a knife fighter holds a switchblade at an inclined angle of forty-five degrees and that he jabs up rather than lunging down. We hope that Ty will never have an occasion to put his knowledge into practice. (p. 370)

vicarious: _____

9. We observe many forms of behavior in others that we never perform ourselves. Without sufficient motivation, Ty may never imitate the violence he sees on TV. Bandura says that the effects of TV violence will be greatly

diminished if a youngster's parents punish or disapprove of aggression. Yet Ty also shares responsibility for his own actions. (p. 371)

diminished: _____

From Em Griffin, *A First Look at Communication Theory*, 2nd ed., New York: McGraw-Hill, 1994.

Vocabulary: Homonyms and Other Confusing Words (Unit 2)

loose	An adverb or adjective meaning "free or released from fastening or attachment." *The dog was running* loose *in the neighborhood instead of being on a leash.*
lose	A verb meaning "to come to be without." *If G. E. and Honeywell merge, Carol will probably* lose *her job.*
passed	A verb, the past tense of the verb *pass. The quarterback* passed *the ball to the tight end, who ran for a touchdown. The E.S.L. student* passed *the TOEFL exam. My grandfather* passed *away last year.* Each of these sentences uses the word passed as a verb expressing action.
past	A noun meaning "former time." *In the* past, *students used typewriters instead of computers.* Also, an adjective meaning "former." *One of our* past *presidents was Harry Truman.* Also, an adverb meaning "going beyond something." *Motel 6 is just* past *the Fashion Square shopping center.*

Think about this sentence: This *past* week has *passed* by quickly.

peace	A noun meaning "freedom from dissension or hostilities." *The United States would like Israelis and Palestinians to agree on terms for* peace.
piece	A noun meaning "a limited portion or quantity of something." *Do you want a big* piece *of pumpkin pie or a small one?*
personal	An adjective meaning "concerning a particular person." *Our* personal *lives are often quite different from our public lives.*
personnel	A noun meaning "the body of persons employed in an organization." *The airline employed a wide variety of* personnel, *including pilots, baggage handlers, and ticketing agents.*

"Peace is not an absence of war, it is a virtue, a state of mind, a disposition for benevolence, confidence, justice."

—Benedict Spinoza

Think about this sentence: Sometimes it is not a good idea to share too much *personal* information with other *personnel* in your office.

rain	Noun meaning "water that falls to earth in drops formed from moisture in the air." *It often seems like we have either too much or too little* rain.
rein	Noun meaning "a leather strap fastened to each end of a bit for guiding or controlling an animal." *The stagecoach driver held on tightly to the horses'* reins.

reign	A noun meaning "period of rule or government by a monarch." *The thousand-year* reign *of kings in France came to an end with the execution of King Louis the XVI.*
right	Adjective meaning "in accordance with what is good, proper, just." *The student circled the* right *answer on the quiz. After two years working as a waitress, Emily made the* right *decision to return to college.* Also, an adjective meaning "opposite of left." *At 18 months, Zachary uses his* right *hand to throw a ball.* Also, a noun meaning "something that is due to anyone by just claim." *The court gave Carl the* right *to see his daughter on weekends and holidays.*
rite	A noun meaning "a formal ceremony." *Fraternities have increasingly fallen into trouble with school authorities for having initiation* rites *that include hazing.*
write	A verb meaning "to form words or letters; to send a message in writing." *When did you first learn how to* write *your name?*
wright	A combining form meaning "a person who makes or builds something." *William Shakespeare is one of the most famous play*wrights.

Think about this sentence: It is *right* that we should attend the last *rites* of the well-known play*wright*.

stationary	An adjective meaning "not moving." *The cyclist bought a* sta-tionary *bike so that he could practice riding indoors during the winter.*
stationery	Noun meaning "writing paper." *The new bride bought special* stationery *to use for her thank-you notes.*
their	An adjective meaning "possession." *Their* apartment was *located near the college.*
there	An adverb meaning "direction." *Notice how the word* here *appears in the word* there. *The student union is over* there. Also, a pronoun used to begin a sentence or phrase. *There is an e-mail message waiting for you.*
they're	A contraction for "they are." They're *all packed and ready to go on their trip.*

Think about this sentence: *They're* supposed to be in class, so why do I see them over *there* talking with *their* friends.

tortuous	An adjective meaning "full of twists and turns." *Although it can be a grand adventure, rafting the* tortuous *Colorado River can also be dangerous.*
torturous	An adjective meaning "involving great pain or agony." *Prior to the use of local anesthetics, extracting a tooth was a* torturous *business.*
vain	An adjective meaning "having an excessively high opinion of oneself." *Carly Simon wrote a well-known song entitled "You're So* Vain." *Supposedly it's about Mick Jagger of* The Rolling Stones.

Also, an adjective meaning "futile." *The joint rescue effort was a* vain *attempt to free the sailors trapped in the submarine.*

vein	A noun meaning "any blood vessel that carries blood back to the heart from some part of the body." *Surface* veins *are often visible just under the skin.*
vane	A noun, a short form of weather *vane. The weather* vane *indicated the direction the wind was blowing.*
weather	A noun meaning "the state of the atmosphere with respect to wind, temperature, cloudiness, etc." *The dry* weather *during the summer led to many forest fires.*
whether	A conjunction used to introduce two or more alternatives. *It makes no difference to me* whether *or not he comes to the party.*
who	A subjective pronoun meaning "what person or persons or which person or persons." *I don't believe you did that paper all by yourself.* Who *helped you?* (Here *who* is the subject of the sentence.)
whom	A pronoun used as the object of a verb or preposition. *To* whom *do you want to give the money?* (Here *whom* is an object of the preposition *to.*) *Whom will you meet after the game.* (Here *you* is the subject of the sentence and *whom* is the direct object of the verb *meet.*)
who's	A contraction of "who is" and "who has." Who's *going with me to the movie tonight?*
whose	A possessive adjective meaning "done by whom or which or having to do with whom or which." Whose *car is this? Your lights are on! The Ford F-150 is a truck* whose *popularity is never in doubt.*
your	A possessive adjective meaning "belonging to you or done by you." Your *classes have been scheduled for mornings only, so that you can work in the afternoons.*
you're	A contraction for "you are." You're *on the list to receive tickets to the rock concert.*

Homonym Quiz

Directions: Fill in the blanks with an appropriate homonym.

1. The _____ department can't release _____ information.
   personal/personnel   personal/personnel

2. I don't like to teach in that classroom because the desks are all _____.
   stationary/stationery

3. You just got here. _____ not already thinking about leaving, are you?
   Your/You're

4. _____ going to do the grocery shopping this week?
   Who's/Whose

5. I found _____ car keys under the sofa cushion.
   your/you're

6. I don't know _____ the gym is open on Labor Day or not.
   weather/whether

7. Tina pleaded in _____ to get Sara taken away from her abusive mother.
   vain/vein/vane

8. The road into the mountains was becoming increasingly _____.
   tortuous/torturous

9. Farmers are worried about their crops because of too little _____.
   rain/rein/reign

10. How could you _____ your lunch money? You just had it in your hand.
    loose/lose

11. Write a sentence of your own using *passed* correctly.

   _____

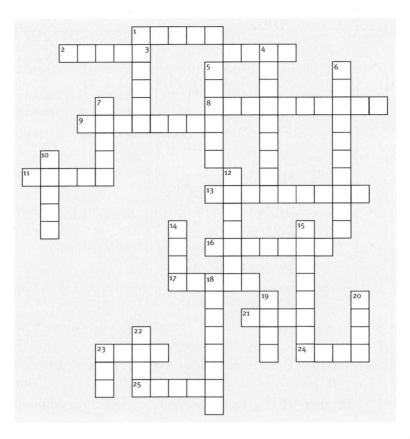

ACROSS CLUES

1. _____ car are we going to take?
2. Juan and Luz Garza purchased _____ new home in December.
3. Boot Camp is considered a _____ of passage for soldiers.
8. Objects are _____ unless moved.
9. The bus passengers were scared when the bus began its descent down the _____ mountain road.
11. The _____ treaty ending World War II was signed aboard the U.S.S. Missouri.
13. The _____ manager at Hewlett-Packard hired several new computer technicians.
16. Some people don't believe it matters _____ we have a Republican or a Democrat in the White House.
17. Is _____ going to be a test on homonyms tomorrow?
21. The cowboy saw a snake and pulled on his horse's _____ .
23. _____ going to win the World Series this year?
24. What are you going to do if you _____ your cleaning deposit on the apartment?
25. Some people think that "might makes _____ ."

DOWN CLUES

1. Arthur Miller, who wrote *Death of a Salesman*, is a famous play_____ .
4. Before the invention of the Aqualung, diving was _____ .
5. Jacob's uncle _____ away at the age of 90.
6. You might want to go to a _____ store to buy school supplies.
7. Katie hoped her _____ tooth would fall out quickly because she wanted money from the tooth fairy.
10. Queen Elizabeth II has had a long _____ .
12. The _____ outside was unbearably hot and humid.
14. The candidate admitted that he had made mistakes in the _____ .
15. You need to supply a list of _____ references when you apply for a job.
18. *Did Rosa's mother _____ from Peru or Colombia?
19. _____ s carry blood back to the heart.
20. The weather _____ indicated a strong wind from the north.
22. _____ chances of doing well in college are better if you attend class regularly.
23. _____ was our most intelligent president?

*Answer found in Homonyms (Unit 1)

TEST-TAKING TIP

After the Test Is Returned

After taking a test, think about what happened. Was it what you expected and prepared for? In what ways did it surprise you? Did it cover both lecture and textbook material? Or focus on one or the other? Think about how to change your approach to the course and the next test to take into account what you learned from the format of this test.

At some point, you will get your test back. Or you could ask to see it. This is another opportunity for you. Go over the test to see where your weaknesses are. What sorts of questions did you have the most trouble with? Many students have trouble with questions phrased in the negative, such as: Which of the following is not a valid conclusion that can be drawn from the evidence below? Did you have trouble with questions of this sort? If so, try to remedy this deficiency in your test preparation be-

fore the next test. You also need to go back and learn the material better that gave you trouble, because you may see questions about this material again on future tests, such as a mid-term or final exam.

If you did poorly on the test, you may want to make an appointment with the instructor to talk about it. Maybe you need to be working with the instructor or a tutor out-of-class. Or maybe you should become part of a study group. You might even be taking the course before you're ready for it and should take some other courses first.

The key point is to treat past tests as learning experiences for what they tell you about your test preparation, how you're doing in the course, and what changes you can make to do better. Above all maintain a positive attitude.

Transition Words and Patterns of Organization

Photo: Erich Lessing/Art Resource, NY

The Cardsharps

(1594)*

BY MICHELANGELO
MERISI DA
CARAVAGGIO

*To see this work of art in
color, turn to the color
insert following page 260.

1 What is the man in the background doing with his right hand?

2 What is the man to the right side of the picture doing behind his back?

3 What is the person to the left of the picture doing? Is he aware of what the other two people are doing?

4 What are your feelings about what's happening in the painting?

Transition Words

When you are reading it is important to pay close attention to **transition words.** These special words show the relationships between ideas within sentences and within paragraphs. Just as good drivers learn to watch the road ahead closely, using signposts or markers to make their trips easier and safer, good readers learn to pay attention to the author's transition words, making the writing clearer and more comprehensible.

Look at the sentences below. The addition of a transition word signaling a contrast makes a big difference in our ability to understand Juan's situation.

1. Juan was very eager to buy a new home. The thought of leaving the familiar surroundings of his apartment filled him with dread.

2. Juan was very eager to buy a new home. **However,** the thought of leaving the familiar surroundings of his apartment filled him with dread.

The first example doesn't really make a lot of sense. If Juan is so eager to buy a home, why is he filled with dread? The addition of the transition word in the second example makes the situation clear. Although Juan wants to buy a home, he is understandably reluctant to give up his safe and comfortable surroundings.

Now look at these two sentences.

1. Trent did poorly in his math classes. He decided to switch his major to economics.

2. **Because** Trent did poorly in his math classes, he decided to switch his major to economics.

The first example makes us guess at the relationship between the two sentences. The addition of the transition word clarifies this relationship.

Exercise: Using Transition Words

Below is a list of transition words, divided into groups by the information they convey. Review this list and then complete the exercises that follow.

TRANSITION WORDS

Words that can be used to show **classification or division (categories):**

break down	combine, combination	lump
category, categorize	divide, division	split
class and subclass	group, grouping	type
classify, classification	kind	

Words that can be used to show **cause and effect** relationships:

as a consequence	due to	result, resulting
as a result	for	since
because	for this reason	so
begin	hence	then
bring(s) about	lead(s) to	therefore
consequently	reaction	thus

TRANSITION WORDS (CONTINUED)

Words that can be used to show **comparison:**

all	both	like
and	in comparison	likewise
as	just as	similar, similarly

Words that can be used to show **contrast:**

although, though	(in) (by) contrast	on the other hand
but	in opposition	rather than
despite	instead	opposite
even so	nevertheless	unlike
however	on the contrary	yet

Words that can be used to show **steps in a process:**

after	finally	preceding
afterward(s)	first, second, third	process
at last	later	step
at this point	next	subsequently
at this stage	now	then

Words that can be used to show **examples:**

(for) example	specific	(to) demonstrate
(for) instance	specifically	(to) illustrate, illustration
(in) particular	such as	
particularly		

Words that can be used to **define:**

call, called	describe(s), described	refer(s) to
concept	label	term, terminology
define(s), defined	mean(s), meaning	
definition	name	

Words that can be used to show **chronological order:**

after	during	in the year(s)
always	earlier	later
any month (May, etc.)	era, period	next
any season (winter, etc.)	finally	preceding, previous
any time (12:00, etc.)	first, second, etc.	presently
any year (2003, etc.)	following	soon
at last	frequently	then
before	immediate, immediately	until
currently	in the meantime	when

Insert the appropriate transition word into the following sentences. Be sure your completed sentences make sense.

1. The tendency to explain most events in terms of oneself or one's environment is (definition) _____ *locus of control.*

2. Developed by psychologist Julian Rotter, the idea is that people fall into either of two (classification or division) _____: those with internal locus of control perceive that they are mostly responsible for what happens to them (both the good and the bad), while those with external locus of control consider their environment to be responsible.

3. Some evidence suggests that most of us are neither true internals nor true externals (contrast) _____ are a mixture of the two. Thus, we tend to see ourselves as responsible for our *successes* (contrast) _____ attribute our *failures* to our environment.

4. (example) _____, football players explain a win as being due to their athletic skills, but blame the condition of the field for a loss.

5. (comparison) _____, in games that combine skill and chance, winners easily attribute their successes to their skill and losers attribute their losses to chance.

6. When I win at Scrabble, it's (cause-and-effect) _____ of my verbal dexterity; when I lose, it's (cause-and-effect) _____ "Who could get anywhere with a Q without a U?"

7. Politicians attribute their success to (steps in a process) _____ their hard work, _____, their reputation, and _____ their strategy. They attribute their losses to factors beyond their control.

Locus of Control

Locus of control is the perception of the amount of personal control you believe you have over events that affect your life. In general, people with an **external locus of control** believe they have little control of the events in their life, whereas people with an **internal locus of control** believe they have a good deal of control of these events. Study the cartoon below. Do you think the cartoon illustrates someone who has an internal or external locus of control?

Frank and Ernest

FRANK & ERNEST reprinted by permission of Newspaper Enterprise Association, Inc.

To determine your locus of control, take the following test.

For each numbered item below, circle the answer that best describes your beliefs.

1. a. Grades are a function of the amount of work students do.
   b. Grades depend on the kindness of the instructor.

2. a. Promotions are earned by hard work.
   b. Promotions are a result of being in the right place at the right time.

3. a. Meeting someone to love is a matter of luck.
   b. Meeting someone to love depends on going out often and meeting many people.

4. a. Living a long life is a function of heredity.
   b. Living a long life is a function of following healthy habits.

5. a. Being overweight is determined by the number of fat cells you were born with or developed early in life.
   b. Being overweight depends on what you eat and how much.

6. a. People who exercise regularly make time for exercise in their schedules.
   b. Some people just don't have the time for regular exercise.

7. a. Winning at poker depends on betting correctly.
   b. Winning at poker is a matter of being lucky.

8. a. Staying married depends on working at the marriage.
   b. Marital breakup is a matter of being unlucky in having chosen the wrong marriage partner.

9. a. Citizens can have some influence on their governments.
   b. There is nothing an individual can do to affect governmental functions.

10. a. Being skilled at sports depends on being born well coordinated.
    b. Those skilled at sports work hard at learning their skills.

11. a. People with close friends are lucky in meeting people.
    b. Developing close friendships takes hard work.

12. a. Your future depends on whom you meet and on chance.
    b. Your future is up to you.

13. a. Most people are so sure of their opinions that their minds cannot be changed.
    b. A logical argument can convince most people.

14. a. People decide the direction of their lives.
    b. For the most part, we have little control of our futures.

15. a. People who don't like you just don't understand you.
    b. You can be liked by anyone you choose to like you.

16. a. You can make your life a happy one.
    b. Happiness is a matter of fate.

17. a. You evaluate how people respond to you and make decisions based upon these evaluations.
    b. You tend to be easily influenced by others.

18. a. If voters studied nominees' records, they could elect honest politicians.
    b. Politics and politicians are corrupt by nature.

19. a. Parents, teachers, and bosses have a great deal to say about one's happiness and self-satisfaction.
    b. Whether you are happy depends on you.

20. a. Air pollution can be controlled if citizens would get angry about it.
    b. Air pollution is an inevitable result of technological progress.

You have just completed a scale measuring locus of control. To determine your locus of control, give yourself one point for each of the following responses:

Item	Response	Item	Response
1	a	11	b
2	a	12	b
3	b	13	b
4	b	14	a
5	b	15	b
6	a	16	a
7	a	17	a
8	a	18	a
9	a	19	b
10	b	20	a

Scores above 10 indicate internality and scores below 11 indicate externality. Of course, there are degrees of each, and most people find themselves scoring near 10. "Internals" tend to take credit for their successes and accept blame for their failures. "Externals" credit the environment for their successes as well as blame it for their failures. What kind of person are you? Does your score reflect the way you typically think about yourself?

From Jerrold Greenberg, *Comprehensive Stress Management*, 6th ed., New York: McGraw-Hill, 1999, p. 124. Copyright © 1999 McGraw-Hill. Reprinted by permission of The McGraw-Hill Companies, Inc.

Internet Activity

The Discovery Channel has a website <http://health.discovery.com/tools/assessments.html> that includes several self-assessment tests in the areas of health, nutrition, personality, and locus of control. Go to the website and take a test that interests you. Then write a paragraph discussing your findings.

Some Common Patterns of Organization

Writers organize their supporting sentences and ideas using **patterns of organization.** Some common patterns of organization are:

1. Classification and division
2. Cause and effect
3. Examples and illustrations
4. Comparison and contrast
5. Listing
6. Steps in a process
7. Definition
8. Chronological order

A writer's chosen pattern of organization will affect the transition words that are used. In the sections that follow, we will discuss patterns of organization and the relationships between patterns of organization and transition words.

The reading selections in this chapter, dealing with ethical and unethical behavior, will give you an opportunity to study some of these patterns of organization and their associated transition words.

Classification or Division

Classification is the process of organizing information into categories. A category is created by noticing and defining group characteristics. The categories we create make it easier to analyze, discuss, and draw conclusions.

Often paragraphs are organized using classification. In the paragraphs below, the author organizes lying into three specific categories. This makes it easier for us to understand and remember the information being presented. Read the paragraphs and then study the outline that follows.

Lies, Lies, Lies

"No one means all he says and yet very few say all they mean."

—Henry Adams

St. Augustine identified eight **kinds** of lies, not all of them equally serious but all sins nonetheless. The number Mark Twain came up with, not too seriously, was 869. In practice, there are probably as many lies as there are liars, but lying can be roughly **classified** according to motive and context. No hard boundaries exist between these **categories,** since some lies are told for more than one purpose. Most lies fall within a spectrum of three broad **categories.**

1. Lies to protect others, or "I love your dress." Most "little white lies" belong here, well-intentioned deceptions designed to grease the gears of society. In this context, people want to be fooled. No one expects, and few would welcome, searing honesty at a dinner party. And the couple who leaves early, saying the babysitter has a curfew, would not be thanked by the hostess if the truth were told: "Frankly we're both bored to tears."

On rare occasions, lying to protect others can literally be a matter of life and death. Anne Frank survived as long as she did because those sheltering her and her family lied to the Nazis. The French Resistance during World War II could not have operated without deception. Military and intelligence officials will, as a matter of routine, lie to protect secret plans or agents at risk.

2. Lies in the interest of the liar, or "The dog ate my homework." Here rest the domains, familiar to everyone, of being on the spot, of feeling guilty, of fearing reprimand, failure, or disgrace, and on the other side of the ledger, of wishing to seem more impressive to others than the bald facts will allow. In this **category,** the liar wants to get away with something. If a lie turneth away wrath, or wins a job, or a date on Saturday night, why not tell it? Or so the theory goes.

3. Lies to cause harm, or "Trust me on this one." These are the lies people fear and resent the most, statements that will not only deceive them but also trick them into foolish or ruinous courses of behavior. Curiously, though, lying to hurt people just for the heck or fun of it is probably quite rare. Some perceived advantage prompts most lies. If there is no benefit in telling a lie, most people won't bother to make one up.

From "Lies, Lies, Lies," *Time,* 10/5/92, pp. 32–35. © 1992 Time Inc. Reprinted by permission.

    I. People differ on how many kinds of lies there are (MI)
        A.   St. Augustine—8 (MSD)
        B.   Mark Twain—869 (MSD)
    II. There are three basic categories of lies (MI)
        A.   Lies to protect others (MSD)
            1.   Little white lies (msd)
            2.   Lying to save lives (msd)
                a.   Anne Frank (msd)
                b.   Military and intelligence officials (msd)

  B. Lies in the interest of the liar (MSD)
   1. Lies to avoid failure and disgrace (msd)
   2. Lies to seem more impressive (msd)
  C. Lies to cause harm (MSD)
   1. Lies to deceive (msd)
   2. Lies to trick (msd)

Exercise: Classification and Division

Fill in the blank with an appropriate transition word from the list below. Some of the transitions words will fit in more than one of the sentences, but use each one only once. Make sure the sentence makes sense with the transition word you choose.

 category classes classify combine divide grouping split

1. According to criminologist Albert Cohen, we can _____ young urban males into three general categories.

2. The first _____ is called *corner boy,* because it describes a person who hangs out in the neighborhood with his peers, spending the day in some group activity such as gambling or athletics.

3. We can further _____ young urban males by identifying those individuals who are striving to live up to middle-class standards.

4. This _____ is referred to as *college boy.*

5. The final category, *delinquent boy,* can be _____ into two groups: those who eventually become law-abiding citizens and those who do not.

6. The *college boy* category is the smallest of the _____, while the *corner boy* is the largest.

7. According to Cohen, we can _____ all three groups to form a subculture that has its own norms, beliefs, and values that are distinct from those of the dominant culture.

Information from Freda Adler, et al., *Criminology,* 5th ed., New York: McGraw-Hill, 2004, p. 145.

Cause and Effect

In a cause-and-effect relationship, one thing causes another thing to happen. The second event is the effect or result of the first event. Try reading the following anecdote to locate cause-and-effect relationships.

It's Saturday morning. Bob is just about to set off on a round of golf when he realizes that he forgot to tell his wife that the guy who fixes the washing machine is coming around at noon. **So** Bob heads back to the clubhouse and phones home.
 "Hello," says a little girl's voice.
 "Hi, honey, it's Daddy," says Bob. "Is Mommy near the phone?"
 "No, Daddy. She's upstairs in the bedroom with Uncle Frank."
 After a brief pause, Bob says, "But you haven't got an Uncle Frank, honey!"
 "Yes, I do, and he's upstairs in the bedroom with Mommy!"
 "Okay, **then.** Here's what I want you to do. Put down the phone, run upstairs and knock on the bedroom door and shout to Mommy and Uncle Frank that my car has just pulled up outside the house."

"Okay, Daddy!"

A few minutes later, the little girl comes back to the phone.

"Well, I did what you said, Daddy."

"And what was the **result?**"

"Well, Mommy jumped out of bed with no clothes on and ran around screaming; **then** she tripped over the rug and fell down the front steps and she's just lying there. I think she's dead."

"Oh my God! And what was the **reaction** of Uncle Frank?"

"He jumped out of bed with no clothes on, and **then** he was all scared and **so** he jumped out the back window into the swimming pool. He must have forgotten that last week you took out all the water to clean it, **so** he hit the bottom of the swimming pool and is just lying there, not moving. He may be dead, too."

There is a long pause, **then** Bob says, "Swimming pool? Is this 854-7039?"

Now complete the followings sentences, inserting the effect of the given cause.

1. Because Bob forgot to tell his wife about the repairman, he _____.

2. Because the little girl informed Mommy and Uncle Frank that Daddy was home, they _____.

3. Because Bob called the wrong number, he _____.

Exercise: Cause and Effect

Fill in the blank with an appropriate transition word or phrase from the list below. Some of the transition words will fit in more than one of the sentences, but use each one only once. Make sure the sentence makes sense with the transition word you choose.

>   as a consequence   as a result   because   cause   therefore

1. _____ of skepticism about the validity of lie detector tests, many employers have turned instead to written "integrity tests."

2. Repeatedly, lie detectors have been proved to be unreliable indicators of lying. _____, the American Psychological Association has adopted a resolution stating that the evidence for the effectiveness of polygraphs "is still unsatisfactory."

3. The many sources of possible error in the use of lie detectors _____ operators to make mistakes when trying to judge another person's honesty.

4. _____ U.S. federal law bars employers from using polygraphs as screening devices for most jobs.

5. For now, _____, you can be assured that any secrets you may harbor will remain hidden.

Information from Robert S. Feldman, *Understanding Psychology*, 5th ed., New York: McGraw-Hill, 1999, p. 352.

Examples and Illustration

A paragraph of examples usually gives a general statement of the main idea and then presents one or more concrete examples or illustrations to provide support for this idea. The terms "example" and "illustration" are often used interchangeably, but an illustration can be thought of as an example that is longer and more involved. A main idea might be supported by only one "illustration." Many writers place the most important or convincing example or illustration either first, as an attention-getter, or last, as a dramatic climax.

The following paragraph provide an illustration of the main idea that most people are basically trustworthy.

"I think that we may safely trust a good deal more than we do."

—Henry David Thoreau

> How about some good news for a change? Something to consider when you are in a people-are-no-darn-good mood?
>
> Here's a phrase we hear a lot: "You can't trust anybody anymore." Doctors and politicians and merchants and salesman. They're all out to rip you off, right?
>
> It ain't necessarily so.

To **demonstrate,** a man named Steven Brill tested the theory, in New York City, with taxicab drivers. Brill posed as a well-to-do foreigner with little knowledge of English. He got into several dozen taxis around New York City to see how many drivers would cheat him. His friends predicted in advance that most would take advantage of him in some way.

One driver out of thirty-seven cheated him. The rest took him directly to his destination and charged him correctly. Several refused to take him when his destination was only a block or two away, even getting out of their cabs to show him how close he already was. The greatest irony of all was that several drivers warned him that New York City was full of crooks and to be careful.

You will continue to read stories of crookedness and corruption—of policemen who lie and steal, doctors who reap where they do not sew, politicians on the take. Don't be misled. They are news because they are the exceptions. The evidence suggests that you can trust a lot more people than you think. The evidence suggests that a lot of people believe that. A recent survey by Gallup indicates that 70 percent of the people believe that most people can be trusted most of the time.

Who says people are no darn good? What kind of talk is that?

From Robert L. Fulghum, *All I Really Need to Know I Learned in Kindergarten*, pp. 59–60. Copyright © 1986, 1988 by Robert L. Fulghum. Used by permission of Random House, Inc.

Exercise: Example

Fill in the blank with an appropriate transition word or phrase from the list below. Some of the transitions will fit in more than one of the sentences, but use each one only once. Make sure the sentence makes sense with the transition you choose.

example   for instance   particular   specifically   such as

1. A variety of strategies are useds to steal vehicles for financial gain. _____, the "strip and run" strategy occurs when a thief steals a car, strips it for its parts, and then abandons the vehicle.

2. Another _____ is the "scissors job," which occurs when scissors are jammed into certain ignition locks in mostly American-made cars, allowing the thief to start the car easily.

3. Some strategies involve deceit, _____ the "valet theft," which takes place when a thief dresses and poses as a valet attendant, opens the car door for the driver, takes the keys, and quickly drives away.

4. The "insurance fraud scheme," which occurs when a car owner reports his or her car stolen and hides the car for approximately 30 days, or until after the claim is paid, is another _____ strategy that involves deceit.

5. A combination of motor vehicle theft and robbery is _____ known as "carjacking."

Information from Freda Adler, et al., *Criminology and the Criminal Justice System*, 5th ed., New York: McGraw-Hill, 2004, p. 295.

Comparison-Contrast

"The study of crime begins with the knowledge of oneself."

—Henry Miller

A comparison shows similarities, while a contrast shows differences. Sometimes a writer both compares and contrasts at the same time. In the paragraphs that follow, the author compares and contrasts amateur and professional burglars and burglaries.

George Rengert and John Wasilchick conducted extensive interviews with suburban burglars in an effort to understand their techniques. They found significant **differences** with respect to several factors.

1. *The amount of planning that precedes a burglary.* **Unlike** amateurs, professional burglars plan more.

2. *The extent to which a burglar engages in systematic selection of a home.* Most burglars examine the obvious clues, such as presence of a burglar alarm, a watchdog, mail piled up in the mailbox, newspapers on a doorstep. **On the other hand,** more experienced burglars look for subtle clues such as closed windows coupled with air conditioners that are turned off.

In addition, Rengert and Wasilchick examined the use of time and place in burglary, and they discovered that time is a critical factor to all burglars, for three reasons.

Both amateur and professional burglars must minimize the time spent in targeted places so as not to reveal an intent to burglarize.

Also, opportunities for burglary occur only when a dwelling is unguarded or unoccupied, usually during daytime. (Many burglars would call in sick so often that they would be fired from their legitimate jobs, **while** others simply quit their jobs because they interfered with their burglaries.)

Further, burglars have "working hours." Many have time available only during a limited number of hours, particularly if they have a legitimate job. One experienced burglar stated that "the best time to do crime is between 8:00 and 9:00 a.m. when mothers are taking the kids to school." **In contrast,** another stated that the best time is in the middle of the afternoon when people are at work.

Information from Freda Adler, et al., *Criminology*, 5th ed., New York: McGraw-Hill, 2004, pp. 219–220.

Exercise: Comparison-Contrast

Fill in the blank with an appropriate transition word from the list below. Some of the transitions will fit in more than one sentence, but use each one only once. Make sure the sentence makes sense with the transition word you choose.

although   but   despite   even   nevertheless   while   yet

1. Our society seems to endorse one set of beliefs _____ glorifying just the opposite.

2. Examples of this glorification include Al Capone and Jesse James, who are in some ways cultural heroes _____ they were known criminals.

3. We have also glorified business executives, _____ we know that business executives are sometimes exploitative, as in the movie *Wall Street.*

4. We are dismayed by the amount of violence and crime in our society; _____ the television programs that play on these themes are the most popular.

5. _____ the fact that we condemn lying, politicians who tell the truth are rejected by voters.

6. We profess to be a country that cherishes our constitution and due process rights; _____, we clap and cheer in movie theaters when "Dirty Harry" types kill the "bad guys."

From Joycelyn M. Pollock, *Ethics in Crime and Justice*, 3rd ed., Belmont, California: Wadsworth, 1998, p. 18.

STUDY TECHNIQUE 5

Creating a Comparison-Contrast Chart

A comparison-contrast chart, like the one here, shows similarities, differences, or similarities and differences between two or more things. When studying closely related topics or reading texts that use the comparison-contrast pattern of development, consider creating a comparison-contrast chart to help you sort out and remember similarities and differences.

The comparison-contrast chart at right lists the differences and similarities discussed in the excerpt on suburban burglars on page 150. Completing this chart will help you learn the main supporting details discussed in the excerpt.

SUBURBAN BURGLARS

Differences

Amateurs	Professionals
1. Plan less	1. Plan more
2. Examine obvious clues.	2. _____

Similarities

1. Both must minimize time spent in targeted places.

2. Opportunities are usually best in the daytime.

3. _____

Review Test 3: Main Ideas, Details, Purpose, Patterns of Organization, Transitions

Read the following humorous poem and then answer the questions that follow.

Brushing Up on Vocabulary

Jesse and Frank James   outlaws in the nineteenth century who robbed trains and banks in spectacular style. It is believed that Jesse was killed by a member of his own gang.

vaudeville   a form of theatrical entertainment popular in the late nineteenth and early twentieth centuries that often included comedians, singers, dancers, and trained animals. Even though skits were short, audiences often pelted the performers with food when they didn't like the act.

Elizabeth Barrett Browning and Robert Browning   English poets of the nineteenth century. Elizabeth is best known as the author of the words, "How do I love thee? Let me count the ways," Robert is best known for his narrative poems, such as "My Last Duchess."

Crime at Its Best   *by Stoddard King*

Disgusted with crimes that are piffling and messy,
We think of the James brothers, Frankie and Jesse,
Who never degraded the clan of James
By writing "confessions" and signing their names.

When poverty hovered o'er Jesse and Frank,
They saddled their horses and held up a bank,
(A calling in which it is wrong to engage)
But they never appeared on the vaudeville stage.

Though Jesse was tough and his brother was tougher,
They never made readers of newspapers suffer
By reading the sob sisters' sorrowful sobbing
Of how they read Browning before going robbing.
The gang that they worked with was surely a bad one,
But as for smart lawyers, I doubt that they had one;
Insanity dodges they never were pleading,
And that's why their life makes such excellent reading.

A movie rights offer they'd both have resented,
(Provided that movies had then been invented).
So in spite of our virtue, it's hard to suppress
A sneaking affection for Frank and for Jess.

Stoddard King, "Crime At Its Best" from *Norton Book of Light Verse,* edited by Russell Baker, p. 202. Copyright © 1986 Russell Baker. Used by permission of W.W. Norton & Company, Inc.

1. What is the main idea of the poem? _____

    _____

2. What specific qualities does the author admire in the James brothers?

    _____

    _____

    _____

3. What does the author have to say about lawyers? _____

    _____

4. What does the title mean? _____

    _____

5. What commentary is the author making about our society? _____

    _____

6. What is the author's primary purpose—to entertain, to inform, or to persuade?

    _____

7. What pattern of development does the poem use? Point out transition words that the author used. _____

    _____

8. Write a paraphrase of one of the stanzas (in prose), making sure to retain the meaning of the poem.

Listing

When an author simply lists information without regard to order, the pattern of organization is referred to as listing or enumeration. Sometimes authors use numbers (1, 2, 3), letters (a, b, c) or bullets (•) to point out the individual items in the list. At other times, they say *first, second, third,* etc. or *in addition, next,* or *finally.* Often a colon will be used as punctuation at the start of a list. A variation of the word *follow* may indicate that a list is about to begin. In the excerpt below, the late columnist Ann Landers lists a series of "lies."

And The Third Biggest Lie Is . . . *by Ann Landers*

DEAR READERS:

A while back, I was asked to print the three biggest lies in the world. I was able to come up with only two: "I'm from the government and I'm here to help you," and "The check is in the mail."

I asked my readers if they could supply the third biggest lie. Thousands rose to the occasion. The mail was simply wonderful. Here's a sampling:

From Lebanon, Pa.: It's a good thing you came in today. We have only two more in stock.

Sparta, Wis.: I promise to pay you back out of my next paycheck.

Woodbridge, N.J.: Five pounds is nothing on a person with your height.

Harrisburg, Pa.: But officer, I only had two beers.

Hammond, Ind.: You made it yourself? I never would have guessed.

Eau Claire, Wis.: It's delicious, but I can't eat another bite.

Charlotte, N.C.: Your hair looks just fine.

Philadelphia: It's nothing to worry about—just a cold sore.

Mechanicsburg, Pa.: It's a terrific high and I swear you won't get hooked.

Dallas: The river never gets high enough to flood this property.

Manassas, Va.: The delivery is on the truck.

Tacoma, Wash.: Go ahead and tell me. I promise I won't get mad.

Billings, Mont.: You have nothing to worry about, honey. I've had a vasectomy.

Philadelphia: The three biggest lies: I did it. I didn't do it. I can't remember.

Chicago: This car is like brand new. It was owned by two retired schoolteachers who never went anywhere.

Boston: The doctor will call you right back.

Montreal: So glad you dropped by. I wasn't doing a thing.

U.S. Stars and Stripes: You don't look a day over 40.

Washington, D.C.: Dad, I need to move out of the dorm into an apartment of my own so I can have some peace and quiet when I study.

Windsor, Ont.: It's a very small spot. Nobody will notice.

Cleveland: The baby is just beautiful!

New York: The new ownership won't affect you. The company will remain the same.

Holiday, Fla.: I gave at the office.

Lansing, Mich.: You can tell me. I won't breathe a word to a soul.

Huntsville, Ala.: The puppy won't be any trouble, Mom. I promise I'll take care of it myself.

Minneapolis: I'm a social drinker, and I can quit anytime I want to.

Barrington, Ill.: Put the map away. I know exactly how to get there.

Troy, Mich.: You don't need it in writing. You have my personal guarantee.

Greenwich, Conn.: Sorry, the work isn't ready. The computer broke down.

Phoenix: I'll do it in a minute.

Elkhart, Ind.: The reason I'm so late is we ran out of gas.

Scarsdale, N.Y.: Our children never caused us a minute's trouble.

Detroit: This is a very safe building. No way will you ever be burglarized.

Glendale, Calif.: Having a great time. Wish you were here.

From Ann Landers. By permission of Esther P. Lederer and Creators Syndicate, Inc.

Steps in a Process

In the steps-in-a-process pattern, something is explained or described in a step-by-step manner. A transition word often introduces each step. Scientific writing commonly follows this pattern. In addition, anyone demonstrating how to make or do something will probably use this pattern.

In the paragraphs that follow, the author gives a step-by-step account of psychologist Lawrence Kohlberg's theory of moral development. The first two paragraphs are outlined for you as an example. Complete the outline of the third paragraph.

"Those who are too lazy and comfortable to think for themselves and be their own judges obey the laws. Others sense their own laws from within."

—Hermann Hesse

According to Lawrence Kohlberg, moral reasoning develops in **three stages.** In the **first stage,** the preconventional level, children's moral rules and moral values consist of do's and don'ts to avoid punishment. A desire to avoid punishment and a belief in the superior power of authorities are the two central reasons for doing what is right. According to the theory, until the ages of 9 to 11, children usually reason at this level. They think, in effect, "If I steal, what are my chances of getting caught and being punished?" According to Kohlberg, most delinquents and criminals reason at the preconventional level.

Most adolescents reason at **stage two,** the conventional **stage. At this stage,** individuals believe in and have adopted the values and rules of society. Moreover, they seek to uphold these rules. They think, in effect, "It is illegal to steal and therefore I should not steal, under any circumstances."

At the postconventional **level, the final stage,** individuals examine customs and social rules according to their own sense of moral principles and duties. They think, in effect, "One must live within the law, but certain ethical principles, such as respect for human rights, supersede the written law when the two conflict." This **level** of moral reasoning is generally seen in adults after the age of 20.

Information from Freda Adler et al., *Criminology,* 5th ed., New York: McGraw-Hill, 2004, p. 86.

I. There are three stages of moral reasoning.
   A. Stage one: the preconventional level
      1. Moral code of do's and don'ts
      2. Two reasons for doing what is right
         a. Avoid punishment
         b. Superior power of authority
      3. Ages 9–11
      4. Delinquents and criminals reason at this level.
   B. Stage two: the conventional stage
      1. Individuals have adopted society's moral code.
      2. Adolescents
   C. _____
      1. Individuals examine customs according to their own sense of moral values.
      2. Personal and ethical principles supersede _____.
      3. Adults after _____

Exercise: Steps in a Process

Fill in the blank with an appropriate transition word from the list below. Some of the transitions will fit in more than one of the sentences, but use each one only once. Make sure the sentence makes sense with the transition you choose.

    final   next   process   second   step   subsequently

Study Links Proficiency in Lying to Teen Popularity

Whether Pinocchio or a president, a liar can remain a beloved figure. In fact, a new research study suggests that the best teenage liars are often the most popular kids.

1. As a first _____, the study, conducted by Robert Feldman, a University of Massachusetts psychologist, looked at the nonverbal behavior of 32 young people ages 11 to 16.

2. At the _____ stage, the young persons' social skills were evaluated, yielding an assessment of their popularity.

3. _____, they were individually videotaped both lying and telling the truth about whether they liked a drink they had been given.

4. As a final step in the _____, 58 college students were asked to watch the videotapes and judge how much each teenager really liked the drink.

5. _____, researchers concluded that girls were better at lying than boys.

6. The _____ analysis showed a strong link between the most socially adept teenagers and the best deceivers.

Information from *The Arizona Republic*, 10/28/00.

Definition

A paragraph that uses definition will clarify or explain a key term. Definitions can be developed by providing dictionary meanings or personal meanings. They can also be developed through examples or by comparing and contrasting the key term with other terms.

In the paragraphs below, the authors of *Criminology* attempt to clarify the meaning of *burglary* by providing concrete illustrations, describing distinguishing characteristics, and comparing and contrasting this word to other similar words. Read the paragraphs and then study the map that follows.

Burglary

1   A "burg," in Anglo-Saxon terminology, was a secure place for the protection of one self, one's family, and one's property. If the burg protects a person from larceny and assault, what protects the burg? The burghers, perhaps. But there had to be a law behind the burghers. And that was the law of burglary, which made it a crime to break and enter the dwelling of another person at night with the intention of committing a crime therein. (Of course it had to be at night, because during the day the inhabitants could defend themselves, or so it was thought.) The common law defined "burglary" as:

2   The breaking and entering of the dwelling house of another person at night with the intention to commit a felony or larceny inside

3   By "breaking," the law **meant** any trespass (unauthorized entry), but usually one accompanied by a forceful act, such as cracking the lock, breaking a windowpane, or scaling the roof and entering through the chimney. The "entering" was complete as soon as the perpetrator extended any part of his or her body into the house in pursuit of the objective of committing a crime in the house. The house had to be a "dwelling," but that **concept** was extended to cover the "curtilage," the attached servants' quarters, carriage houses, and barns. The dwelling also had to be that of "another." And as we mentioned, the event had to occur at "night," which was **defined** as between sundown and sunup.

4   The most troublesome **term** has always been the "intention to commit a felony or larceny" (even a petty or misdemeanor larceny) inside the premises. How can we know what a burglar intends to do? The best evidence of intent is what the burglar actually does inside the premises. Any crime the burglar commits inside is considered evidence of criminal intention at the moment the burglar broke and entered the dwelling.

Information from Freda Adler, et al. *Criminology*, 5th ed., New York: McGraw-Hill, 2004, p. 310.

"The home of everyone is to him his castle and fortress, as well as his defence against injury and violence, as for his repose."

—Edward Coke

Exercise: Definition

Fill in the blank with an appropriate transition word or phrase from the list below. Some of the transitions will fit in more than one of the sentences, but use each one only once. Make sure the sentence makes sense with the transition you choose.

describe   is called   means   refers to   term

1.   The label "amateur thieves" _____ occasional offenders who take advantage of a chance to steal when little risk is involved.

2.   This _____ that most "amateur thieves" commit few crimes; some commit only one crime.

3. A person _____ a "professional thief" when he or she makes a career of stealing.

4. The term "professional thief" also is used to _____ persons who take pride in their profession, are imaginative and creative in their work, and accept its risks.

5. The _____ "larceny" refers to theft or stealing and is the most prevalent crime in our society.

STUDY TECHNIQUE 6

Mapping

Mapping is a technique you can use to organize material you are studying. Similar to outlining, it shows how the main points relate to each other. Unlike outlining, however, it is more visual and less formal. Visual learners may find this a more helpful technique than outlining.

The map below shows the major points, and how they relate to one another for the excerpt on burglary (page 156).

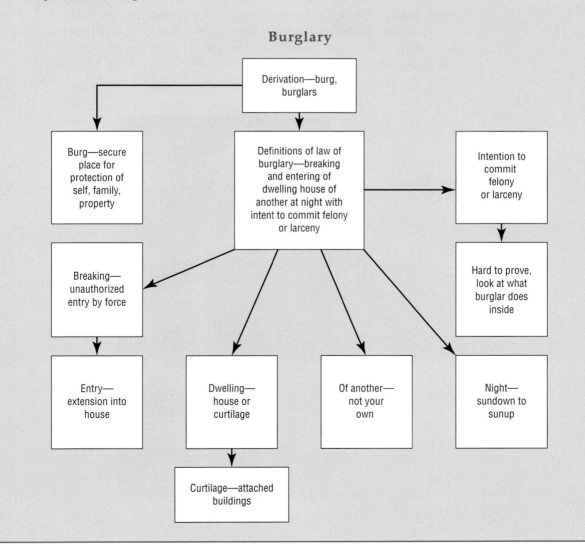

Burglary

Derivation—burg, burglars

Burg—secure place for protection of self, family, property

Definitions of law of burglary—breaking and entering of dwelling house of another at night with intent to commit felony or larceny

Intention to commit felony or larceny

Breaking— unauthorized entry by force

Hard to prove, look at what burglar does inside

Entry— extension into house

Dwelling— house or curtilage

Of another— not your own

Night— sundown to sunup

Curtilage—attached buildings

Chronological Order

The word *chronological* comes from the Greek root *chron,* which means "time." The chronological pattern of organization involves arranging events in the order in which they actually happened. For this reason, historical essays and other articles that are date-oriented are usually organized by this method. Paragraphs written with this pattern are usually very easy to recognize.

The following paragraphs are in the chronological pattern.

Brancusi's Bird: Manufactured Metal or Work of Art

"A work of art is an exaggeration."

—Andre Gide

A trial held in New York City in **1928** demonstrated just how hard it can be to agree on what constitutes "art." Edward Steichen, a prominent American photographer, purchased a bronze sculpture entitled *Bird in Space* from the Romanian artist Constantin Brancusi, who was living in France. In **1926,** Steichen imported the sculpture to the United States, whose laws do not require payment of customs duty on original works of art as long as they are declared to customs on entering the country. But when the customs official saw the *Bird,* he balked. It was not art he said: it was "manufactured metal." Steichen's protests fell on deaf ears. The sculpture was admitted into the United States under the category of "Kitchen Utensils and Hospital Supplies," which meant that Steichen had to pay $600 in import duty.

In **1927,** with the financial backing of Gertrude Vanderbilt Whitney, an American sculptor and patron of the arts, Steichen appealed the ruling of the customs official.

Bird in Space (1923), Constantin Brancusi

The Metropolitan Museum of Art, Bequest of Florence M. Schoenborn, 1995

The ensuing trial received a great deal of publicity. Witnesses discussed whether the *Bird* was a bird at all, whether the artist could make it a bird by calling it one, whether it could be said to have characteristics of "birdness," and so on. The conservative witnesses refused to accept the work as a bird because it lacked certain biological attributes, such as wings and tail feathers. The more progressive witnesses pointed out that it had birdlike qualities: upward movement and a sense of spatial freedom. The court decided in favor of the plaintiff. The *Bird* was declared a work of art, and Steichen finally got his money back.

In **today's** market a Brancusi *Bird* would sell for millions of dollars.

Information from Laurie S. Adams, *Art Across Time*, New York: McGraw-Hill, 1995, p. 5.

STUDY TECHNIQUE 7

Time Lines

A time line is a specialized way of organizing information. Time lines are useful when material needs to be organized chronologically by dates, such as in a history class, although they could also be useful in almost any other class too.

All that a time line does is list dates in chronological order along a line and then assign information to the dates. You can make a time line vertically (up and down) or horizontally (across). How specific you want to make a time line (that is, the number of dates and the amount of information you assign to each date) depends on the reading material and your needs.

Complete the time line with information from "Brancusi's Bird." Additional historical dates have been added to put the information in perspective.

1876	Birth date of Constantin Brancusi
1904	Brancusi moves to Paris
1926	_____
1927	_____
1928	_____
1957	Brancusi dies
1973	Edward Steichen dies

Exercise: Chronological Order

Fill in the blank with an appropriate transition word from the list below. Some of the transitions will fit in more than one of the sentences, but use each one only once. Make sure the sentence makes sense with the transition you choose.

> currently   finally   first   next   previously   then

1. _____, at Disney World, home of Donald Duck, Mickey and Minnie Mouse, Goofy, and their friends, illegal behavior is successfully controlled in an environment that does not have the sterile, fortresslike appearance so often associated with security.

2. The _____ security measure occurs at the parking lot with advice to lock your car and remember that you have parked at a particular lot, for example, "Donald Duck 1."

3. _____, with friendly greetings of "have a good time," watchful eyes surround visitors on the rubber-wheeled train into Never-Never Land.

4. The _____ line of defense is crowd control, which is omnipresent, yet unobtrusive, with signposts guiding you through the maze of monorails, rides, and attractions.

5. Physical barriers have _____ been strategically placed to prevent injury and regulate the movement of adults and children alike.

6. _____, Mickey Mouse and Goofy actors monitor movements, making Disney World one of the safest locations in the United States.

Review Test 4: Identifying Patterns of Organization in Textbook Material

Identify the pattern of organization by noting the transitional words.

1. Over the years, television has changed many sports. For example, the World Series is now played in chilly October temperatures at night on the East Coast and in late afternoon on the West Coast, thereby ensuring that the games will be shown on television during prime time in the eastern and central time zones. In another instance, professional basketball playoffs now include 16 of the 27 NBA teams, and the season stretches into June, providing TV with more high-rated games. And the National Hockey League has expanded the pauses in play following certain penalties to more than 30 seconds to allow time for commercials. (p. 31)

   Pattern: _____

   Clues: _____

2. For years, the National Association of Broadcasting (NAB) enforced restrictions on liquor advertising. First, NAB decreed that no hard liquor could be advertised on radio or television. Next, broadcasters were prohibited from showing anyone drinking beer or wine in a commercial; glasses could be hoisted, but no sipping was allowed. Finally, it was decided that currently active sports figures could not appear in beer or wine commercials. (p. 361)

   Pattern: _____

   Clues: _____

3. The tendency to blame the media for society's woes seems to be escalating. The general public seems convinced that media influences are creating and fostering antisocial behavior and are the reason for all that is wrong with society. These arguments are supported by members of Congress who have tried to curtail the violence on television, blaming it for the increase in violence in our cities. The end result was the introduction of the V-chip in television sets to allow parents to control the types of programs their children watch. (p. 6)

   Pattern: _____

   Clues: _____

4. The cyberpunks of the 1990s, racist groups such as skinheads and the Ku Klux Klan, Satan worshippers, and David Koresh's Branch Davidians often come to mind when we use the word *cult*. *Webster's Third New International Dictionary* includes in its definition of *cult*: "**a.** great or excessive devotion or dedication to some person, idea, or thing; **b.** the object of such devotion; **c.** a body of persons characterized by such devotion." Under this definition, *cults* can include a wide variety of devoted groups, including skateboard enthusiasts, baseball card collectors, and rockstar fan clubs. Long after the

Beatles split up and Elvis Presley died, *cultlike* followers have continued to worship these performers. The largest television-produced *cult* has been the "Trekkies," devoted followers of the *Star Trek* television series. Each year thousands gather at conventions, many of them dressed in *Star Trek* costumes complete with pointed plastic ears. (pp. 37–38)

Pattern: _____

Clues: _____

5. The largest circulating newspaper in the United States happens to be the *National Enquirer*. This popular publication's success can be traced back to 1952, when Generoso (Gene) Pope purchased the *New York Enquirer*. He immediately began filling the newspaper with stories about crime, sex, and violence. In 1958, Pope expanded the *Enquirer* into a national publication and began selling it in supermarkets. He toned down the sex and violence to appeal to a broader audience and began focusing on stories about celebrity gossip, government waste, psychic predictions, life-threatening accidents, and medical advice. At the conclusion of the O. J. Simpson murder trial in 1995, many news reporters across the nation begrudgingly conceded that the *Enquirer* had probably covered the story better than anyone else, and in fact had broken more stories than the regular news media outlets. Much of that credibility was lost in the final years of the 1990s as the *Enquirer* continued to print weekly stories accusing numerous people of being responsible for the death of JonBenet Ramsey of Colorado. Today, *National Enquirer* reporters are among the highest paid in the nation, and the paper covers major news events with teams of journalists and photographers. (pp. 175–176)

Pattern: _____

Clues: _____

6. During the Kosovo conflict in 1999, the Internet helped Americans find out what was happening. For instance, a 16-year-old reporter for Youth Radio in Berkeley, California, Finnegan Hamill, made news when he was receiving and broadcasting messages from a teenaged girl caught in that nation's violence. Hamill described the 16-year-old girl, known only as Adona, as a modern-day Anne Frank with a laptop. Her messages were like a diary, except in a real-time environment. Here is an example of what she wrote:

"Just from my balcony, I can see people running with suitcases and I can hear gunshots. A village just a few hundred meters from my home is all surrounded. As long as I have electricity, I will continue writing to you. Right now, I am trying to stay as calm as possible. My younger brother, who is 9, is sleeping now. I wish I will not have to stop his dreams." (p. 65)

Pattern: _____

Clues: _____

7. Getting a person to buy or rebuy a product involves far more than simply running an ad in a newspaper or a commercial on television. There are three main steps in the selling process: awareness, trial, and reinforcement. *Awareness* is the easiest step. Through repetition and other advertising techniques, consumers are made aware that a product exists. *Trial*, the second step, involves getting people to try the product by sending free samples

through the mail, handing them out in stores, giving away discount coupons, and offering price reductions. *Reinforcement* is the necessary third step to persuade users to buy the product again. (p. 351)

Pattern: _____

Clues: _____

8. The much anticipated fourth release of the *Star Wars* series, *Episode 1: The Phantom Menace*, may not have been as big a hit as expected, but it still managed to gross almost $430 million during its run in the United States. That was enough to make it the largest grossing film of 1999. But it was a small-budget independent film that generated a lot of talk—particularly on the Internet. In fact, Internet support and clever promotion helped the film, *The Blair Witch Project*, to crack the top-10 list of box-office hits during the final year of the twentieth century. The "documentary" film turned the movie industry on its ear, costing only $55,000 to make, a small portion of the *Star Wars* epic, yet grossing $141 million, enough money to become a cultural phenomenon. (pp. 217–218)

Pattern: _____

Clues: _____

From James R. Wilson, *Mass Media Mass Culture*, 5th ed., New York: McGraw-Hill, 2001, pp. 31, 361, 6, 37–38, 175–176, 65, 357, 217–218. Copyright © 2001 McGraw-Hill. Reprinted by permission of The McGraw-Hill Companies, Inc.

ADDITIONAL TRANSITION WORDS

Summary and Conclusion	Spatial Order	Emphasis	Concession
finally	above	as indicated	although
hence	below	as noted	despite
in brief	beyond	certainly without a doubt	even though
to conclude	center	here again	in spite of
in conclusion	front	It's important to remember	
in short	left	once again	
in summary	near	to emphasize	
over all	next to	to repeat	
so	on top	truly	
therefore	right	unquestionably	
thus	underneath		
to sum up			

Reversal	Addition
granted that	again
instead	also
nevertheless	and
still	another
unlike	as well as
yet	besides
	further
	furthermore
	in addition
	moreover
	too

While lists of transition words are helpful, the groupings of the words given in this section are not perfect, and many of these words may be used in more than one category. The only reliable way to determine the function of a transition word is by studying the context of the sentence and the paragraph.

COLLEGE STUDENTS' TOP 10 REASONS FOR CHEATING

When asked why they cheated, college students generally absolved themselves of responsibility, blaming their actions on the instructor or fellow students. Their responses also reflect concern about grades and time pressures.

Rank	Reason for Cheating
1.	The instructor assigns too much material.
2.*	The instructor left the room during the test.
2.*	A friend asked me to cheat, and I couldn't say no.
4.	The instructor doesn't seem to care if I learn the material.
5.	The course information seems useless.
6.*	The course material is too hard.
6.*	Everyone else seems to be cheating.
8.	I'm in danger of losing a scholarship because of low grades.
9.	I don't have time to study because I'm working to pay for school.
10.	The people sitting around me made no effort to protect their work.

*Tied

Source: Listing based on Valerie J. Haynes, George M. Diekhoff, Emily E. LaBeff, and Robert E. Clark, "College Cheating: Immaturity, Lack of Commitment and the Neutralizing Attitude," *Research in Higher Education*, 1986, Vol. 25, No. 4., pp. 347–354. Also in *CQ Researcher*.

Study the Calvin and Hobbes cartoon on the previous page.

1. What attitude about cheating does Calvin express? _____
    _____

2. What key point is being made in the cartoon? What is being criticized?
    _____

3. *To rationalize* means to justify behavior using reasons that appear to be good
    or valid but that do not reflect the true motivations. Explain how Calvin
    rationalizes cheating on a test. _____

SELECTION

School Cheating Scandal Tests a Town's Values   *by Jodi Wilgoren*

*"It began in December with a teacher's finding that 28 of 118 Piper High sophomores
had stolen sections of their botany project off the Internet."*

Getting the Picture

The article that follows describes what happened when a teacher gave high school
students a zero on an assignment after discovering that they had plagiarized.
Many educators believe that plagiarizing has become rampant on American cam-
puses. Donald McCabe and other professors at Rutgers University conducted a
2001 survey among approximately 4,500 high school students. In that survey,
70 percent of the students reported "seriously cheating at least once on written
work." Fifty-two percent reported "copying sentences from websites without
citing the source."

Bio-sketch

Jodi Wilgoren graduated from Yale University in 1992 with a major in history. After
writing for the *Los Angeles Times,* she became a national education correspondent
and general assignment reporter for *The New York Times.* Wilgoren is the Midwest
bureau chief for the *Times,* is responsible for the coverage of 11 states, and also
covered the 2004 presidential campaign.

Brushing Up on Vocabulary

tight-knit   well-organized or closely integrated.

clamped   became stricter or more repressive; put a stop to. The word *clamp* dates
from the mid-1900s and was originally a noun that referred to a device with
opposite sides or parts that could be brought closer together to compress
something.

empty nester   a parent whose children have grown up and moved out. The
expression alludes to a nest from which baby birds have flown.

flourishes   decorations or embellishments. The word *flourishes* derives from the
Latin word *florere,* meaning "to bloom."

1 Piper, Kansas, February 13—The Piper school board normally meets in a cozy conference room at district headquarters, but on Tuesday, folding chairs filled the purple-and-white elementary school gym to accommodate the overflow crowd.

2 More than 100 parents, students, and teachers skipped the basketball game at the high school next door to talk about the plagiarism scandal that has riven this tight-knit community 20 miles west of downtown Kansas City, Kansas, and become talk-show fodder as far away as Guam as a symbol of the decline in American values.

"Let the punishment fit the crime."

—Gilbert and Sullivan

3 It began in December with a teacher's finding that 28 of 118 Piper High sophomores had stolen sections of their botany project off the Internet. The students received zeroes and faced failing the semester. But after parents complained to the school board, the teacher, Christine Pelton, was ordered to raise the grades, prompting her resignation. Now, the community is angrily pointing fingers as they debate right and wrong, crimes and consequences, citizenship and democracy.

4 At Tuesday's meeting, Kay Miesner, who graduated from Piper High School in 1962—28 years after her father, 23 years before her son—told the board members who overruled Mrs. Pelton, "I know each and every one of you; I think you're all good people." But she said, "I think you made a mistake."

5 Someone yelled, "Yup," and the audience erupted. But Chris McCord, the board president, clamped the emotion, saying, "We'll have none of that."

6 Such tension is unusual here in Piper, a blue-collar bedroom community, in part because of young families drawn by the small school district.

7 Several teachers said that nearly half the high school's 31-member faculty plus its brand new principal planned to resign at year's end over the case, while parents fretted that the school's dwindling reputation might result in a decline in property values and disappearance of scholarship opportunities.

8 Mrs. Pelton, meanwhile, has become a kind of folk hero, with dozens of calls a day offering support—and jobs.

9 "It's not just biology, you're teaching them a lot more than that," Mrs. Pelton, 27, who had planned to resign this spring anyway to start a home-based day care center, said between television appearances the other day. "You're teaching them to be honest people, to have integrity, to listen, to be good citizens.

10 "We've got rules, and they've got to follow the rules," she added. "I'm not expecting more than what would be expected of them either at home or down the road."

11 Students, plagiarizers and nonplagiarizers alike, have already begun to feel the backlash.

12 A sign posted in a nearby high school read, "If you want your grade changed, go to Piper." The proctor at a college entrance exam last weekend warned a girl wearing a Piper sweatshirt not to cheat. A company in Florida faxed the school asking for a list of students—so it would know whom never to hire. At Tuesday's board meeting, as five television news crews rolled tape, a woman worried that the community had been "stamped with a large purple P on their foreheads for plagiarism."

13 The sophomore leaf project, an elaborate exercise in which students spend months collecting leaves and researching their origins, dates back a decade.

14 Mrs. Pelton, who came to Piper High in the fall of 2000 after a five-year program at the University of Kansas, sent an outline of the assignment home on the first day of school, along with her classroom rules (No. 7: "Cheating and plagiarism will result in failure of the assignment and parent notification. It is expected that all work turned in by the student is completely their own."), which students and parents had to sign.

15   Mrs. Pelton said she began to worry in October, when students' oral presentations, filled with big, unfamiliar words, sounded strangely similar. As she flipped through their projects a month later, she found the writing far more sophisticated than previous assignments. A plagiarism-detection website, turnitin.com, showed one in four were laced with lifted material.

16   The principal, Michael Adams, who declined to be interviewed, backed Mrs. Pelton's decision to give students zeroes, as did the superintendent. But after parents protested at the December 11 school board meeting, the superintendent, Dr. Michael O. Rooney, sent a memorandum home saying he had "reluctantly" directed Mrs. Pelton to deduct just 600 of 1,500 points from the plagiarizers' projects, and to cut its value in the overall grade from 50 percent to 30 percent.

17   Mrs. Pelton said a student told her, "We won."

18   Though teachers here say they begin discussing source citation in the fourth grade, some parents, of students with zeroes and those with A pluses, insist the students did not realize what they were doing was wrong (some say they thought the admonition was against copying from previous students' papers, not taking simple descriptions from research material). Failing a whole semester, they say, is too harsh.

19   "If your boss said to you, 'You were late one day this month so we're not going to pay you for the whole month,' is that fair?" asked Mary Myer, whose son, Mitchell, was not accused of cheating.

20   "Plagiarism is not a cut-and-dried issue," she added. "Somebody who gets in their car and hurts someone, we punish them differently than someone who goes out and shoots someone. Intent matters."

21   It is just the latest plagiarism revelation afflicting American high schools and colleges, aggravated by an Internet age in which research papers—as well as programs to detect cheating—can be downloaded by the dollar. A Rutgers University professors' survey of 4,471 high school students last year found that more than half had stolen sentences and paragraphs from websites, 15 percent handed in papers completely copied from the Internet, and 74 percent had cheated on a test.

22   On talk shows and the Internet, Piper's problems have been linked to recent admissions by the popular historian Stephen Ambrose that he failed to properly attribute passages; the resignation of George O'Leary, Notre Dame's football coach, after revelations that he falsified his résumé; and even alleged lying by executives at Enron.

23   Piper, a farming community founded in 1888 and annexed by the city of Kansas City, Kansas, in 1992, is defined by the four-school district of 1,300 students. Its headquarters doubles as the post office in an enclave without town hall or tavern; even empty nesters wear Piper purple to Pirates athletic events.

24   Many parents have expressed sympathy for the 75 percent of students who did not cheat, some of whom received lower semester grades in biology when the project they had slaved over suddenly counted less than they had anticipated. Some parents have even sent homemade cookies and nut bread to school in quiet solidarity with teachers.

25   "You can stand up for your kids when it's right, but when it's wrong, you can't bail your child out," said Diane Smith, who has a son in the freshman class and a daughter in middle school. "I don't think the board should have that much power; they really outstepped their boundaries."

26   Teachers, ever protective of the sanctity of their grade books, say the board has robbed their independence and professionalism. Instead of a lesson about the importance of honesty and originality, they say, students learned that complaining to higher powers mitigates punishment.

"Honesty's praised then left to freeze."

—Juvenal

27   "If I make a decision, I don't know if it's going to be backed up," said Angel Carney, a business teacher who submitted her resignation this week. "I had a disagreement with a parent the other day; right away she wanted to go over my head."

28   Even if no one ended up failing, students say they are paying the price. "Whatever you do will always come back to you," Amy Kolich, an 18-year-old senior, said when asked what she had learned from the situation. "In a way, to them, it didn't, but it came back to our school."

29   Piper High's handbook does not mention plagiarism specifically, but says the penalty for cheating, even a first offense, is no credit on the assignment. Administrators are now setting up a committee to handle conflicts over grades and collecting plagiarism policies from other schools.

30   Matthew Mosier, 16, spent hours on his botany project, gathering leaves from neighbors' farms, looking them up on the Web. His grandmother, a quilter, covered his three-ring binder in leaf fabric and embroidered his name on the cover. He bought fancy leaf paper at the Hobby Lobby to print out his reports.

31   Matt ended up with a D, the extra credit for his artistic flourishes washed out by the sentences Mrs. Pelton said he copied.

32   "Am I saying my son's perfect? No and hell no," said Kim Mosier, Matthew's mom, who was not among those who complained to the board but was pleased by the result. "We sat down with him and said, 'Did you plagiarize?' He said, 'No, Mom, I didn't.' I have to support him until they can prove him different.

33   "We hire that board, those teachers, that school, that principal—they work for us," she added. "Everybody has that opportunity that they should be questioned on a decision that they make."

 ## Comprehension Checkup

Matching

Match the quotation with the speaker. Write the letter of the speaker in the appropriate blank. (Some speakers will be used more than once.)

a. Angel Carney   e. Diane Smith

b. Kay Miesner   f. Amy Kolich

c. Chris McCord   g. Mary Myer

d. Christine Pelton   h. Kim Mosier

_____ 1. "I had a disagreement with a parent the other day; right away she wanted to go over my head."

_____ 2. "I'm not expecting more than what would be expected of them either at home or down the road."

_____ 3. "I don't think the board should have that much power; they really overstepped their boundaries."

_____ 4. "Whatever you do will always come back to you."

_____ 5. "I know each and every one of you; I think you're all good people." "I think you made a mistake."

_____ 6. "Everybody has that opportunity that they should be questioned on a decision that they make."

_____ 7. "Somebody who gets in their car and hurts someone, we punish them differently than someone who goes out and shoots someone."

_____ 8. "We'll have none of that."

_____ 9. "You're teaching them to be honest people, to have integrity, to listen, to be good citizens."

_____ 10. "Plagiarism is not a cut-and-dried issue."

Multiple Choice

Write the letter of the correct answer in the blank provided.

_____ 1. Which of the following best expresses the main idea of the selection?
a. After being ordered to raise the grades of some students accused of cheating, Christine Pelton resigned her position.
b. Some parents have begun to worry about declining property values.
c. The plagiarism scandal has engendered divisions in the once close-knit community of Piper.
d. Christine Pelton is experiencing a great deal of negative publicity because of the cheating incident.

_____ 2. The writer's main purpose in writing this selection is to
a. entertain the reader with an illustration of the old adage that cheating doesn't pay
b. persuade the reader that cheating is morally wrong
c. explain the cheating incident at Piper and its repercussions
d. describe the moral values of Christine Pelton

_____ 3. The author's use of the words "on Tuesday," "it began in December," and "at the December 11 school board meeting" is meant to demonstrate
a. cause and effect
b. chronological order
c. compare and contrast
d. simple listing

_____ 4. Which detail listed below from the selection is least relevant to the author's main idea?
a. Teachers say the board's decision has robbed them of independence.
b. Students complain that Piper High now carries a stigma of cheating that affects all of them.
c. Some parents feel that the board and the teachers work for them.
d. Matthew Mosier took advantage of his grandmother's skills as a quilter and seamstress to bolster his chances for a good grade on the project.

_____ 5. Which of the following best defines the word *fretted* as it is used in paragraph 7?
a. worried
b. kidded
c. suggested
d. stipulated

True or False

Indicate whether the statement is true or false by writing T or F in the blank provided.

_____ 6. According to the selection, the Piper school board normally meets at district headquarters.

_____ 7. Even before the incident, Mrs. Pelton was planning to leave Piper High.

_____ 8. One in four of the student projects submitted to Mrs. Pelton contained material that was not the student's own work.

_____ 9. Mrs. Pelton failed to make students aware of the consequences of cheating in her classroom.

_____ 10. The superintendent, after initially backing Mrs. Pelton, changed his mind.

Vocabulary in Context

Look through the paragraph indicated in parentheses to find a word that matches the definition below.

1. comfortable (paragraph 1)   _____
2. split apart (2)   _____
3. diminishing (7)   _____
4. negative reaction (11)   _____
5. warning (18)   _____
6. settled in advance (20)   _____
7. disclosures (22)   _____
8. condition of being strongly united (24) _____
9. sacredness (26)   _____
10. lessens in force or severity (26) _____

In Your Own Words

1. Most parents are naturally protective of their children, but they also want to teach them about taking responsibility for their actions. Do you think the parents described in the article were right to intervene?

2. Donald McCabe feels that many teachers are reluctant to address cheating directly in their classrooms. For McCabe, the Piper incident goes a long way toward explaining why teachers are so reluctant to follow through on punishment. McCabe says that "parents are going to complain to principals and the school board, and teachers feel there's no reason to believe they'll get support." Do you think that teachers should crack down on cheating? Has a similar incident occurred in a school system near you? Was the incident decided in the teacher's or the students' favor?

3. The Internet provides students with vast resources. In your opinion, where does using the Internet as a reference end and plagiarism begin?

4. Sue Bigg, a college consultant outside Chicago, says, "I'm afraid that a lot of this cheating comes from home, where the parents' modus operandi is success at any cost." What role do you think parental example plays in a child's decision to cheat?

5. Studies show that students who cheat are likely to make it a way of life. So it's no surprise that today's workplace is full of adults who lie about

everything from job experience to company earnings. Nearly three-quarters of job seekers admitted to lying on their résumés in a recent survey by SelectJOBS.com, a high-tech industry employment site. Offenses ranged from omitting past jobs (40 percent) to padding education credentials (12 percent). Is there anything employers might do to discourage cheating by job seekers?

The Art of Writing

In a brief essay, respond to one of the items below.

1. Have you ever cheated on something? If so, did you feel that your cheating was justified at the time the incident took place? Do you still feel that what you did was acceptable? Was your cheating similar to any incidents described in the article?

2. In the Piper incident, many students claimed they copied only a sentence or two and that they didn't know that this amounted to plagiarism. In fact, many students felt there were only so many ways to describe the characteristics of leaves. How would you have decided this case?

STUDY TECHNIQUE 8

Summarizing Longer Articles

In Chapter 2 you learned how to summarize a short article. Now you are going to apply the same principles to a longer article and summarize the article you just read about cheating at Piper High School. Summarizing is an important study skill. It will force you to identify the important points of what you have read and will reduce the amount of material you will have to review for a class discussion or exam. Summarizing simply means restating the main ideas and significant details of a reading selection in your own words. Remember that a summary should only include the author's opinions and not your beliefs.

To summarize, begin by identifying the main idea or thesis of the article. What is the most important point the author is trying to make?

Main idea or thesis: _____
_____
_____

Next, identify the main supporting ideas found in the article. Begin by answering as many of the who, what, where, when, why, and how questions that apply to the article. Remember to list important dates, events, and people involved. You may not be able to answer all of the questions.

Who? _____
_____

What? _____

Where? _____

When? _____

Why? _____
_____

How? _____

Now identify three to four main ideas with at least two details for each important point. Some of your information may be the same as what you wrote above. Each of these supporting main ideas may be either discussed in a particular section of the article or could be discussed at various points throughout the article.

Main idea 1: _____
_____

Detail 1: _____

Detail 2: _____
_____

Main idea 2: _____

Detail 1: _____
_____

Detail 2: _____

Main idea 3: _____
_____

Detail 1: _____
_____

Detail 2: _____

Main idea 4: _____
_____

Summarizing Longer Articles (continued)

Detail 1: _____

_____

Detail 2: _____

_____

You now have placed the important points of the article down on paper. Check what you have written down with another student in the class to make sure you have covered the most important information from the article.

After writing your summary, ask yourself whether you have put the ideas in your own words.

Then make sure you have included the significant main ideas and details you have listed above. Have you included any expressions of your own opinions? If so, delete them.

Give your summary a title so you will be able to locate it when you are ready to prepare for your exam, and keep it in your class notebook where you will know where to look for it.

After writing your summary, compare your version to the sample given in the appendix.

Internet Activity

Consult either of the following websites to get updated information on the ethical beliefs and practices of high-school and college students.

www.academicintegrity.org (Center for Academic Integrity)

www.josephsoninstitute.org (Josephson Institute of Ethics)

If available, print a recent ethics survey.

Review Test 5: Transition Words, Main Ideas and Supporting Details, and Vocabulary in Context

Transition Word Practice

Write the correct word(s) in the blank provided.

1. The actual burial vault of King Tutankhamum was opened in 1923. The coffin was made of 242 pounds of pure gold and was sculpted into a jeweled effigy of the king himself. When the mummy inside was unwrapped, it _____ was covered with jewels.
   a. despite
   b. truly
   c. also
   d. besides

2. _____, the mummy was in a state of extreme decay, possibly from use of excessive amounts of embalming oil. The lengthy embalming process, which took over 70 days to complete, included thoroughly washing the body, removing the internal organs, covering the body with sodium, drying it, coating it with resin, and wrapping it in linen. Finally, the pharaoh was ready to be displayed to the public.
   a. In spite of
   b. However
   c. Again
   d. As well as

3. The media was ecstatic _____ this was the first time that a pharaoh's tomb had been discovered reasonably intact in the Valley of the Kings. They

marveled at the precious objects the tomb contained, including gold sandals, rings, necklaces, bracelets, and amulets. And, in case the king wanted to travel, there were even two full-size gold chariots.
a. because
b. unlike
c. to emphasize
d. overall

4. _____ robbers had tunneled into King Tutankhamum's tomb shortly after he was interred, they had taken very little. About all they accomplished was to desecrate the holy site.
a. Again
b. Although
c. Underneath
d. Hence

5. _____, priests were called in to purify the site. They quickly resealed the tomb, and then they left behind curses to intimidate those who would attempt to enter the sacred shrine again.
a. In spite of
b. As noted
c. So
d. Yet

6. Inside the tomb over a hundred ushabti, three-foot-high statues of servants, were lined up _____ the king's body, ready to wait on him in death as they had waited on him in life.
a. as indicated
b. next to
c. further
d. right

7. King Tutankhamum ascended the throne at age 9, died at age 19, and never actually participated in a battle. _____, his tomb is crowded with images of him as a great warrior.
a. Yet
b. Finally
c. Here again
d. Thus

8. Tutankhamum became pharaoh after his childhood marriage to the daughter of the pharaoh Akhenaten. _____ his father-in-law Akhenaten, King Tutankhamum is not considered to be a great pharaoh.
a. Overall
b. Unlike
c. Furthermore
d. Without a doubt

9. _____, he was a totally innocuous one.
a. As well as
b. Once again
c. Hence
d. Instead

10. He has achieved fame solely _____ his tomb was discovered intact. Debris from other nearby tombs had covered the entrance hiding the tomb from view. _____ Carter removed the waste material on November 4, 1922, he discovered one stone step leading downwards. He uncovered 15 more steps and then a blocked doorway. As Carter slowly worked his way into

the tomb, he described it this way: "My eyes grew accustomed to the light, details of the room within emerged slowly, and gold—everywhere the glint of gold."

   a. again; Furthermore
   b. because; After
   c. nevertheless; Despite
   d. still; Once again

Excerpt from *Gilbert's Living with Art*   *by Mark Getlein*

"No matter who opens a tomb and takes away its contents, that person is violating the intentions of those who sealed the tomb originally."

Getting the Picture

How often does a person's most cherished dream come true? After 15 years of hard work, it happened to British archaeologist Howard Carter.

Brushing Up on Vocabulary

pillage   to rob or plunder. *Pillage* is derived from the Old French word *piller*, meaning "spoils or booty."

propriety   fitting or proper. *Propriety* is derived from the Latin *propietatem*, meaning "appropriateness."

perpetrator   person who carries out an evil, criminal, or offensive action. *Perpetrator* derives from the Latin word *perpetratus*, means "to bring into existence."

mummy   the dead body of a human being preserved by the ancient Egyptian process of embalming. The first step in this process was to remove the deceased's brain through the nostrils by means of a long hook. Next, the liver, lungs, intestines, and stomach were removed. All of the organs were then preserved in separate receptacles. The body was soaked in salt water for a lengthy period and thoroughly dried. Later the body was stuffed and then swaddled in clean strips of linen.

Whose Grave Is This Anyway?

1   When Howard Carter and his party opened the tomb of the Egyptian king Tutankhamum in 1922, there was rejoicing around the world. The tomb was largely intact, not seriously pillaged by ancient grave robbers, so it still contained the wonderful artifacts that had been buried with the young king more than three millennia earlier. Over the next several years Carter and his team systematically photographed and cataloged the objects from the tomb, then transported them to the Cairo Museum.

2   There is a certain irony in this story that raises complex ethical questions. Why are Carter and his party not called grave robbers? Why are their actions in stripping the tomb acceptable—even praiseworthy—when similar behavior by common thieves would be deplored? No matter who opens a tomb and takes away its contents, that person is violating the intentions of those who sealed the tomb originally. No matter what the motivation, a human body that was meant to rest in peace for all time has been disturbed. Should this not make us feel uncomfortable?

3   From the beginning some were uneasy about the propriety of unearthing Tutankhamum's remains. When Lord Carnarvon, Carter's sponsor, died suddenly from a mosquito bite, and several others connected with the project experienced tragedies, rumors arose about the "curse of King Tut." But Carter himself died peacefully many years later, and the talk subsided.

Howard Carter examining King Tut, 1922
NYT Pictures

4   Perhaps it is the passage of time that transforms grave robbing into archaeology. Carter would no doubt have been outraged if, say, his grandmother's coffin had been dug up to strip the body of its jewelry. But after three thousand years Tutankhamum has no relatives still around to protest.

5   Perhaps it is a question of the words we use to describe such ancient finds. We speak of Tutankhamum's "mummy," and mummy is a clean, historical-sounding word. Parents bring their children to museums to see the mummies and mummy cases. We can almost forget that a mummy is the embalmed body of a dead human being, pulled out of its coffin so that we can marvel at the coffin and sometimes the body itself.

6   Or, perhaps the difference between grave robbing and archaeology lies in the motives of the perpetrators. Common thieves are motivated by greed, by their quest for money to be made by selling stolen objects. Carter and his team did not sell the treasures from Tutankhamum's tomb but stored them safely in the Cairo Museum, where art lovers from around the world can see them. They were, in effect, making a glorious gift to the people of our century and centuries to come (while at the same time, one must point out, acquiring significant glory for themselves).

7   The basic issue is a clash of cultural values. To the Egyptians, it was normal and correct to bury their finest artworks with the exalted dead. To us, the idea of all that beauty being locked away in the dark forever seems an appalling waste. We want to bring it into the light, to have it as part of our precious artistic heritage. Almost no one, having seen these magnificent treasures, would seriously propose they be put back in the tomb and sealed up.

8   In the end, inevitably, our cultural values will prevail, simply because we are still here and the ancient Egyptians are not. After three thousand years, Tutankhamum's grave really isn't his anymore. Whether rightly or wrongly, it belongs to us.

Comprehension Checkup

(Answers can be found in the selection or the Transition Word Practice on pages 171–173.)

True or False

Indicate whether each statement is true or false by writing T or F in the blank provided.

_____ 1. Several people who were associated with unsealing the tomb died under mysterious circumstances.

_____ 2. King Tut's tomb was discovered close to its original condition.

_____ 3. Howard Carter was a British geologist.

_____ 4. Gold was featured predominantly inside King Tut's tomb.

_____ 5. The wondrous objects removed from King Tut's tomb were stored in the British Museum of Natural History.

Multiple Choice

Write the letter of the correct answer in the blank provided.

_____ 6. King Tut was a pharaoh who
   a. was relatively unimportant in Egyptian history
   b. died at an early age
   c. caused the death of Howard Carter
   d. both (a) and (b)

_____ 7. All of the following are true *except*
   a. The furnishings of King Tut's tomb were discovered largely intact
   b. In ancient Egypt, the burial of royalty was done in accord with elaborate rituals
   c. King Tut's coffin was made of pure gold
   d. Lord Carnarvon died before the discovery of King Tut's tomb

_____ 8. The contents of King Tut's tomb were
   a. resealed by Carter and Lord Carnarvon
   b. placed on display so that the public could view them
   c. sold to the highest bidder
   d. stolen by thieves and vandals

_____ 9. The ancient Egyptians
   a. buried their finest pieces of artwork with their dead
   b. took steps to embalm and preserve corpses
   c. tried to preserve royal tombs for eternity
   d. all of the above

_____ 10. The author of the article suggests all of the following *except*
   a. The passage of time transforms grave robbing into the study of archaeology
   b. Archaeologists offer opportunities to experience other cultures
   c. Archaeologists should stop invading and disturbing the burial sites of past civilizations
   d. King Tut's grave now belongs to humanity

Vocabulary in Context

Fill in the blanks using words from the following list. Use each word only once.

appalling	deplored	prevailed	sponsor
artifacts	heritage	propose	subsided
clash	marvel	quest	transformed
curse	precious	rejoicing	violating

1. After his anger _____, he was quick to apologize to his wife for his outburst.

2. Michael's mother _____ her son's slovenly ways because he failed to pick up anything in his room.

3. I would like to _____ a toast to the new bride and groom.

4. Having children _____ her life.

5. There was much _____ among the students when our team won the state football championship.

6. To someone who is dehydrated, a drop of water is very _____.

7. To determine whether _____ are genuine or fake without damaging them, scientists often use X-rays.

8. Be careful when you travel in foreign countries. You may be accused of _____ social customs you are unfamiliar with.

9. The amount of man-made debris that is found on beaches around the world is _____.

10. He was on a _____ to identify his son's murderer. Nothing would stop him until he fulfilled his goal of seeing the murderer behind bars.

11. When I failed to pay the fortune-teller for her advice, she placed a _____ on my children and my children's children.

12. Genealogy is important to people who want to trace their family _____.

13. When I look at the Eiffel Tower, I can only _____ at the amount of work that went into its construction.

14. We are looking for a _____ for our softball team. Are there any volunteers?

15. Do you think that a red blouse and an orange skirt _____?

16. She successfully _____ on her teenagers to pass up a vacation with friends and join the family on a car trip.

In Your Own Words

1. Do you think it's appropriate to investigate ancient grave sites for archeological purposes? Why or why not?

2. Do you think it's appropriate to display the bodies found in ancient graves in museums? Why or why not?

The Art of Writing

In a brief essay, respond to the item below.

In 2002, Zahi Hawass became the director of Egypt's Supreme Council of Antiquities. He has made it his mission to recover the ancient treasures of the

Egyptian people. In 1983, Egypt passed a law declaring all new finds to be Egyptian property. Previously, many artifacts belonged to the person who found them. Hawass and his staff have contacted museums around the world informing them of Egypt's readiness "to make the most strenuous efforts to reclaim illegally exported antiquities." Hawass hopes artifacts will be returned from many of the most illustrious museums in Europe, including the Louvre. As he says, "there is no statute of limitations on stolen masterpieces." He uses many weapons in his fight to recover Egypt's treasures, such as posting names on the Internet, taking museum board members to court, and barring foreign archeologists from working in Egypt. "Unfortunately, there is no 'curse of the mummies,'" he says. "I, however, am trying to fulfill that role."

Do you think museums should be compelled to return works of art that were taken many years ago from another country? What are some relevant considerations for whether antiquities should be returned to the country of origin? What if that country is politically unstable or near a place of tension and fighting? What about the many people who will no longer be able to visit the exhibits if they are moved a long distance away? How much opportunity will people have to learn about other cultures if countries begin taking back their antiquities?

Internet Activity

While the most famous mummies belong to the ancient Egyptians, other cultures and societies have also engaged in mummification. In 1995, the mummified body of a young Inca girl, probably a sacrificial victim, was discovered on the mountain of Nevado Impato. Evita Perón, the wife of Juan Perón, president of Argentina, died in 1952 and was embalmed. Her body disappeared in 1955 but was recovered and returned to Argentina in 1974, still perfectly preserved. Vladimir Lenin, the Russian revolutionary leader who died in 1924, is also preserved as a mummy. Today's more modern version of mummification uses cryogenics. Bodies are frozen in liquid nitrogen and then preserved in a steel container. Using an Internet search engine, such as Google or Yahoo, investigate the mummification or cryogenics process, and then write a short summary of your findings.

Do you believe in curses? When Howard Carter was warned that "death comes on wings to he who enters the tomb of a pharoah," he paid no attention. And yet his patron, Lord Carnarvon, died of a mosquito bite within days of unsealing King Tut's tomb. Other deaths quickly followed, including the death of a French scientist who visited the tomb shortly after its discovery, an X-ray specialist on his way to examine the mummy, and an American archeologist who died of a mysterious virus soon after a visit. Mere coincidences? What do you think? Check out the following websites and write a paragraph arguing your position on whether there was a curse. Be sure to use transition words in your paragraph.

http://www.civilization.ca/civil/egypt/egtut04e.html
http://unmuseum.mus.pa.us/mummy.htm
http://www.mummytombs.com/egypt//kingtut.htm

TEST-TAKING TIP

Dealing with Test-Taking Anxiety

While the key to success in test taking is generally adequate preparation, you also need to maintain a positive attitude and stay relaxed. Take the following test to help you determine whether anxiety over test taking may be interfering with your ability to get a good grade.

Test Anxiety Scale

To assess your test-anxiety level, rate yourself from 1 to 5 on each of the following statements.

> 1—never   2—rarely   3—sometimes
> 4—often   5—always

1. I have trouble sleeping the night before a test.

1	2	3	4	5

2. I have visible signs of nervousness right before a test (sweaty palms, shaky hands).

1	2	3	4	5

3. I have butterflies in my stomach or feel nauseated before a test.

1	2	3	4	5

4. I am irritable and hard to be around before a test.

1	2	3	4	5

5. I worry about how others are doing on the test.

1	2	3	4	5

6. My mind goes blank during the test, or I am unable to recall information.

1	2	3	4	5

7. I have difficulty choosing answers.

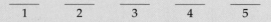

1	2	3	4	5

8. I make mistakes on easy questions or put answers in the wrong places.

1	2	3	4	5

9. I am always afraid that I will run out of time.

1	2	3	4	5

10. I remember the information that I forgot after I have turned in the test.

1	2	3	4	5

If you gave yourself five or more 4s or 5s, you may be highly anxious about tests. In that case, you should try the following relaxation techniques:

1. Take several long, deep breaths to calm yourself. After a few minutes, close your eyes and imagine a favorite place. Make this mental scene as detailed as you can.

2. Try to relax your whole body, starting with your feet. Work your way up through your body—your legs, torso, chest, arms, neck, head, and face.

3. If permissible, suck on a piece of hard candy.

4. View the test as an opportunity for self-discovery and not as a win/lose proposition.

If you feel that your anxiety is overwhelming, get help from your college counseling center.

Part 3

Interpreting What We Read

The Horse Fair,

(1853)*

BY ROSA BONHEUR

*To see this work of art in color, turn to the color insert following page 260.

1   Where on this picture is Bonheur trying to focus the viewer's attention?

2   What is it in this picture that indicates that horses are being exhibited for the benefit of potential buyers?

3   Who do you think the people on the hill, in the upper-right corner of the picture, are?

4   What is your reaction to the way the two white horses in the foreground have been portrayed? Are they portrayed realistically?

5   What does the painting tell us about the reaction of the horses to the way they're being treated?

Introduction to Inference Skills

A good reader makes educated guesses based upon observable details. We use our intuition and experiences to create a likely interpretation of what is happening in a story, while being careful that our interpretation is logical and realistic. The detective stories by Arthur Conan Doyle featuring the fictional detective, Sherlock Holmes, clearly show the reasoning process in drawing inferences. Holmes's extraordinary powers of observation and deduction enable him to solve mysteries that baffle lesser detectives. His companion is Dr. Watson, who records his many successes. The following excerpt from *A Study in Scarlet* is narrated by Watson.

"I wonder what that fellow is looking for?" I asked, pointing to a stalwart, plainly dressed individual who was walking slowly down the other side of the street, looking anxiously at the numbers. He had a large blue envelope in his hand, and was evidently the bearer of a message.

"You mean the retired sergeant of Marines," said Sherlock Holmes.

"Brag and bounce!" thought I to myself. "He knows that I cannot verify his guess."

The thought had hardly passed through my mind when the man whom we were watching caught sight of the number on our door, and ran rapidly across the roadway. We heard a loud knock, a deep voice below, and heavy steps ascending the stair.

"For Mr. Sherlock Holmes," he said, stepping into the room and handing my friend the letter.

Here was an opportunity of taking the conceit out of him. He little thought of this when he made that random shot. "May I ask, my lad," I said, in the blandest voice, "what your trade may be?"

"Commissionaire, sir," he said, gruffly. "Uniform away for repairs."

"And you were?" I asked, with a slightly malicious glance at my companion.

"A sergeant, sir, Royal Marine Light Infantry, sir. No answer? Right, sir"

He clicked his heels together, raised his hand in salute and was gone.

"How in the world did you deduce that?" I asked.

"Deduce what?" said he, petulantly.

"Why, that he was a retired sergeant of Marines."

"It was easier to know it than to explain why I know it. If you were asked to prove that two and two made four, you might find some difficulty, and yet you are quite sure of the fact. Even across the street I could see a great blue anchor tattooed on the back of the fellow's hand. That smacked of the sea. He had a military carriage, however, and regulation side whiskers. There we have the marine. He was a man with some amount of self-importance and a certain air of command. You must have observed the way in which he held his head and swung his cane. A steady, respectable, middle-aged man, too, on the face of him—all facts that led me to believe he had been a sergeant."

From Arthur Conan Doyle, *A Study in Scarlet*, New York: Berkley Books, 1975, pp. 25–28.

"All of us are watchers—of television, of time clocks, of traffic on the freeway, but few are observers. Everyone is looking; not many are seeing."

—Peter M. Leschak

Now study the Gary Larson cartoon on the top of the next page. Just as Sherlock Holmes used clearly observable details to make his deduction about the retired sergeant, the hunter/sleuth is using the same type of detail to determine

THE FAR SIDE® By GARY LARSON

"See how the vegetation has been trampled flat here, Jimmy?
That tells me where a deer bedded down for the night. After a
while, you'll develop an eye for these things yourself."

THE FAR SIDE® By GARY LARSON

that a deer has "bedded down for the night." Is the hunter using all the available clues? Which ones has he ignored?

You can see how you have to be good at drawing inferences to understand cartoons. In the "safari" cartoon be sure to look for all the clues that are provided for you. What do you think happened to the hunter?

Barney   *by Will Stanton*

"Poor Barney is dead and soon I shall be the same."

Getting the Picture

Most critical readers make inferences as they go along and then as they are provided more clues by the author, either reject these inferences or subject them to further analysis. At the conclusion of the story, they assemble all of these valid inferences, just as you must do in the following science fiction tale.

1 *August 30th.* We are alone on the island now, Barney and I. It was something of a jolt to have to sack Tayloe after all these years, but I had no alternative. The petty vandalisms I could have forgiven, but when he tried to poison Barney out of simple malice, he was standing in the way of scientific progress. That I cannot condone.

2 I can only believe the attempt was made while under the influence of alcohol, it was so clumsy. The poison container was overturned and a trail of powder led to Barney's dish. Tayloe's defense was of the flimsiest. He denied it. Who else then?

3 *September 2nd.* I am taking a calmer view of the Tayloe affair. The lonely life here must have become too much for him. That, and the abandonment of his precious guinea pigs. He insisted to the last that they were better suited than Barney to my experiments. They were more his speed, I'm afraid. He was an earnest and willing worker, but something of a clod, poor fellow.

4 At last I have complete freedom to carry on my work without the mute reproaches of Tayloe. I can only ascribe his violent antagonism toward Barney to jealousy. And now that he has gone, how much happier Barney appears to be! I have given him complete run of the place, and what sport it is to observe how his newly awakened intellectual curiosity carries him about. After only two weeks of glutamic acid treatments, he has become interested in my library, dragging the books from the shelves, and going over them page by page. I am certain he knows there is some knowledge to be gained from them had he but the key.

1. What kind of animal do you think Barney is? _____

2. What does the narrator infer about Tayloe's relationship to Barney? _____

    _____

3. What has Barney gained since Tayloe's dismissal? _____

    _____

4. What can we infer is the likely intent of the scientific experiments? _____

    _____

5 *September 8th.* For the past two days I have had to keep Barney confined and how he hates it. I am afraid that when my experiments are completed I shall have to do away with Barney. Ridiculous as it may sound there is still the possibility that he might be able to communicate his intelligence to others of his kind. However small the chance may be, the risk is too great to ignore. Fortunately there is, in the basement, a vault built with the idea of keeping pests out, and it will serve equally well to keep Barney in.

6   *September 9th.* Apparently I have spoken too soon. This morning I let him out to frisk around a bit before commencing a new series of tests. After a quick survey of the room he returned to his cage, sprang up on the door handle, removed the key with his teeth, and before I could stop him, he was out the window. By the time I reached the yard I spied him on the rim of the well, and I arrived on the spot only in time to hear the key splash into the water below.

7   I own I am somewhat embarrassed. It is the only key. The door is locked. Some valuable papers are in separate compartments inside the vault. Fortunately, although the well is over forty feet deep, there are only a few feet of water in the bottom, so the retrieving of the key does not present an impossible problem. But I must admit Barney has won the first round.

1. Why does Barney dispose of the key in this manner? _____

_____

2. What has Barney accomplished by getting rid of the key? _____

_____

3. Do you think Barney is aware of the writer's intentions toward him? _____

8   *September 10th.* I have had a rather shaking experience, and once more in a minor clash with Barney I have come off second best. In this instance I will admit he played the hero's role and may even have saved my life.

9   In order to facilitate my descent into the well I knotted a length of three-quarter-inch rope at one-foot intervals to make a rude ladder. I reached the bottom easily enough, but after only a few minutes of groping for the key, my flashlight gave out and I returned to the surface. A few feet from the top I heard excited squeaks from Barney, and upon obtaining ground level I observed that the rope was almost completely severed. Apparently it had chafed against the edge of the masonry and the little fellow perceiving my danger had been doing his utmost to warn me.

10   I have now replaced that section of rope and arranged some old sacking beneath it to prevent a recurrence of the accident. I have replenished the batteries in my flashlight and am now prepared for the final descent. These few moments I have taken off to give myself a breathing spell and to bring my journal up to date. Perhaps I should fix myself a sandwich as I may be down there longer than seems likely at the moment.

1. What conclusion does the scientist make about the probable cause of the accident? _____

_____

2. Why does he assume Barney is a hero? _____

_____

11   *September 11th.* Poor Barney is dead an soon I shell be the same. He was a wonderful ratt and life without him is knot worth livving. If anybody reeds this please do not disturb anything on the island but leeve it like it is as a shryn to Barney, espechilly the old well. Do not look for my body as I will caste myself into the see. You mite bring a couple of young ratts and leeve them as a living memorial to Barney. Females—no males. I sprayned my wrist is why this is written so bad. This is my laste will. Do what I say an don't come back or disturb anything after you bring the young ratts like I said. Just females.

Goodby

From Will Stanton, "Barney," from *Fifty Short Science Fiction Tales.* Copyright © 1951 Will Stanton.

1. Who is the likely writer of this last journal entry? _____

2. What specific requests does this writer make? _____
_____

3. Why does the writer want everyone to stay away? _____
_____

4. Would a sprained wrist account for the sudden grammatical and spelling errors? _____

5. How did Tayloe's dismissal benefit the final author? Why was it essential for him to remove Tayloe from the scene? _____
_____

6. What parts of this story are the opposite of what you expected them to be?
_____

7. Which group is the author poking fun of in this story? _____

8. In what ways do you think Stanton would like to see this group be more responsible? _____
_____

Vocabulary in Context

Using the context clues below and in the reading selection, choose the best definition for the italicized word, and write the appropriate answer letter in the blank. You may use your dictionary if necessary.

_____ 1. *petty* vandalisms (paragraph 1)
a. subordinate
b. small, minor
c. peevish

_____ 2. simple *malice* (1)
a. spite
b. charity
c. sickliness

_____ 3. cannot *condone* (1)
a. amplify
b. make dense
c. excuse

_____ 4. something of a *clod* (3)
a. lump of clay
b. a large heavy shoe
c. an oaf

_____ 5. *mute* reproaches (4)
a. muffle the sound
b. silent
c. shared

_____ 6. only *ascribe* (4)
a. attribute
b. restrain
c. occupy

_____ 7.   violent *antagonism* (4)
     a. unknown
     b. anxiety
     c. hostility

_____ 8.   *frisk* around (6)
     a. search for concealed weapon
     b. romp
     c. dive

_____ 9.   *commencing* a new series of tests (6)
     a. starting
     b. assuming
     c. preserving

_____ 10.   *facilitate* my descent (9)
     a. make superficial
     b. make easier
     c. make worthy

_____ 11.   a *rude* ladder (9)
     a. elemental
     b. ignorant
     c. crude

_____ 12.   *chafed* against (9)
     a. irritated
     b. fretted
     c. rubbed

_____ 13.   prevent a *recurrence* (10)
     a. repercussion
     b. repetition
     c. restoration

_____ 14.   *replenished* the batteries (10)
     a. stocked
     b. perfected
     c. replaced

_____ 15.   final *descent* (10)
     a. birth, lineage
     b. step downward
     c. devalue

A Remote-Controlled Rat: Using Robotics, Researchers Give Upgrade to Lowly Rats; Study Sees Job for Rodents at Disaster Sites
by Kenneth Chang

Getting the Picture

The previous selection described a very intelligent rat who in the end was able to best a scientist. The selection below describes an ongoing experiment with rats, to harness their native abilities.

1   Providing a biological twist to robotics, scientists have fitted live rats with remote controls to guide them through mazes, past obstacles, and even up trees by typing commands on a laptop computer up to half a mile away.

2   The approach, which takes advantage of an animal's innate ability to do things like climb over rocks, could ultimately be applied to inspecting a disaster area, said the scientists, who report their findings in May's issue of the journal *Nature*.

3   "An animal, especially a rat, has much greater facility for getting around a difficult terrain" than would a robot engineered from scratch, said the senior author of the paper, Dr. John K. Chapin, a professor at the State University of New York's Downstate Medical Center in Brooklyn.

4   The researchers do not commandeer the rat's brains and directly command the animals, zombielike, where to go. Rather, they take advantage of well-worn techniques of training animals by providing rewards.

5   The difference is that in the rats, both the stimuli and the reward are piped directly into the brain, and both can be sent by radio signals from some distance away.

6   Three wires were implanted into the brain of each rat. A pulse of current along one wire stimulated a region of the brain that made the rat feel as if its left whiskers had been touched.

7   A second wire led to the sensing region of the right whiskers. The third was connected to the part of the brain's pleasure center, the medial forebrain bundle.

8   The researchers trained the rats to turn left or right when they felt a stimulus in the corresponding whiskers, rewarding them with a pulse of euphoria in the pleasure center.

9   Strapped on the rat is a tiny backpack containing the antenna for receiving radio signals and a small microprocessor that dispenses the electrical pulses to the rat's brain. The researchers also attached tiny video cameras to get a rat's eye view.

10   Pressing the keys on the researchers' laptop computer sent the radio commands to the rat: the J key to steer the rat left, L to turn it to the right, and K to provide the reward.

11   The researchers also used a joystick like that used in video games to guide the rats up ladders, down stairs, and across narrow ledges.

12   Unlike robots, animals can quickly adapt to a new terrain. The researchers were able to take the rats, which had never been outdoors, and make them climb trees, scurry along branches, turn around and come back down.

13   "Our robot friend was astounded," Dr. Chapin said. "He knew what it would take to have a machine climb a tree having never seen a tree, having never come close to solving that physical problem."

14   That versatility could find use in search-and-rescue operations, Dr. Chapin said.

15   While robots can survive high temperatures, toxic chemicals, and even tumbles of several stories in height, remote-controlled animals might be able to penetrate through tiny spaces that robots cannot.

16   Dr. Robin R. Murphy, director of the Center for Robot-Assisted Search and Rescue who helped coordinate the use of robots at the World Trade Center wreckage, described the research as "very interesting," but added, "I don't think it's appropriate for search and rescue."

17   The rats would be easily distracted by blood or remains, Dr. Murphy said, adding, "Unfortunately, a lot of this is what rats usually treat as food." Human rescuers and victims would be disconcerted by the sight of rats scurrying around.

18   "The rats could scare weakened victims to death," Dr. Murphy said.

19   But she added that remote-controlled animals might be of use in less chaotic environments, like searches for land mines.

20   Dr. Chapin said he thought many of the problems could be solved.

21   A wireless computer network could ferry data between a pack of rats so that if one rat were out of direct radio contact with the operator, its signal could still be transmitted through the network, Dr. Chapin said.

22   And over time, perhaps people could learn to like rats.

23   "Maybe if it becomes widely known there are these rescue rats," Dr. Chapin said, "people wouldn't be scared."

From Kenneth Chang, "A Remote-Controlled Rat," *New York Times*, May 2, 2002, p. A20. Copyright © 2002 by The New York Times Co. Reprinted with permission.

The Art of Writing

In a brief essay, respond to one of the items below.

1. What can you infer about Dr. Chapin's feelings about the experiment? Does he think it likely that rats could be used in search-and-rescue missions? What does Dr. Murphy believe about the feasibility of using rats in rescue operations? Cite specific details from the selection to support your conclusions.

2. Other scientists weighed in with their opinions when this study was first published. One scientist concluded that he thought "rat-patrols" were certainly feasible and it was "better them than us." Howard Eichenbaum, professor of psychology at Boston University, said that while it was certainly cheaper to turn a rat into a robot than attempt to build a robot to function like a rat, he worried about the ethics of the situation. "We're talking about making animals behave like machines," he said. Finally, some scientists worried that this new "rat technology" could fall into enemy hands. If so, these so-called "robo rats" could be guided into government buildings where they could act as suicide bombers. Respond to each of these opinions by the experts and give your own opinion.

Drawing Inferences from Textbook Material

After reading the excerpts from the college textbooks below, choose the statement that can be directly inferred from the material, and write the appropriate answer letter in the blank.

Ethical Issues

As a graduate student in sociology at Washington State University, Rik Scarce studied radical environmental and animal-rights activists who sometimes break the law to dramatize their cause. When a group calling itself the Animal Liberation Front claimed responsibility for a raid on a university laboratory, in which 23 mink, mice, and coyotes were released and hydrochloric acid was poured on computers (causing an estimated $150,000 in damage), Scarce was subpoenaed to appear before a grand jury. Scarce acknowledged that he knew a prime suspect in the case quite well, but refused to answer any further questions. He argued that testifying about his sources not only would cause environmental activists to refuse to speak with him, curtailing his own research, but also would affect the sociological research effort as a whole. Sources would be less likely to trust other social scientists, and social scientists might shy away from controversial research that required confidentiality. Scarce went to jail rather than violate his commitment to confidentiality.

"You are remembered for the rules you break."

—Douglas MacArthur

From Craig Calhoun, *Sociology*, 7th ed., New York: McGraw-Hill, 1997, p. 42.

_____ 1. We can infer that
   a. the judge in this case was not persuaded by Scarce's argument.
   b. the courts agree that information collected during sociological research is confidential.
   c. Scarce actually knew nothing about who had raided the laboratory.
   d. just as journalists are allowed to protect their sources, so are sociologists.

A Friend Named Bo

Any of us would be lucky to have a friend such as Bo. Bo is a wonderful companion, loyal and giving unselfishly of time and affection. He is ever-ready to help, and in return, he asks for little.

But Bo was trained to be this way.

Bo is a 5-year-old golden retriever and labrador mix, a dog trained to be a helpmate to his owner, Brad Gabrielson. Gabrielson has cerebral palsy, and he has little control over his muscles. Yet with the help of Bo, Gabrielson can lead a life of independence.

Bo's abilities are many. If the doorbell rings, he answers the door. If Gabrielson drops something, Bo will pick it up. If Gabrielson is thirsty, Bo brings him a drink. One time, when Gabrielson fell, Bo left the apartment, went across the hall to a neighbor's door, where he scratched and barked. When the neighbor proved not to be home. Bo went upstairs to another neighbor's apartment.

When that neighbor—who had never encountered Bo before—came to the door, Bo led him downstairs, carefully tugging his hand. As the neighbor helped Gabrielson, Bo stood careful watch at his side. Said Gabrielson later, "On my own, I would have had to lie there . . . until my fiancée got home six hours later." But, he continued, "Bo came over and licked my face, to make sure I was all right, that I responded. Then he went to look for help." And Gabrielson stopped worrying.

From Robert S. Feldman, _Understanding Psychology_, 5th ed., New York: McGraw-Hill, 1999, p. 184.

_____ 2. We can infer that
   a. Gabrielson fell as a result of his own carelessness.
   b. Gabrielson stopped worrying because he knew that his fiancée would turn up shortly and take care of him.
   c. Gabrielson stopped worrying because he trusted that Bo would find help.
   d. Gabrielson stopped worrying because his cell phone was nearby.

Fiddler on the Mud

What lives in mud, feeds on mud, and finds mates by calling and waving across the mud? But, of course—fiddler crabs, creatures remarkable in many ways but best known as the ultimate experts in mud.

The many species of fiddler crabs (Uca) are inhabitants of mud and sand flats in estuaries and other sheltered coasts. Fiddlers are deposit feeders. They feed at low tide, using their pincers to scoop mud up into the mouth. The detritus in the mud is extracted with the help of brushlike mouth parts. Water is pumped from the gill chambers into the mouth to make the lighter detritus float and thus help separate it from the mud. The detritus is swallowed, and the clean mud is spat out on the substrate in neat little balls.

Fiddlers are active at low tide and retreat into their burrows at high tide. Each burrow has an entrance (revealed by the neat little balls of mud around it) that the occupant can plug when the tide comes in. At the next low tide, crabs emerge from home to feed and do whatever healthy, active fiddlers like to do.

Fiddlers have an interesting sex life. Males feature one tremendously enlarged claw, either right or left. It is brightly colored or highlighted with markings in many species. Females have a much smaller pair, which is used in feeding, as in the case of the males' small pincer. Males use their claw to advertise their sex—to tell females they mean business and to threaten any other males that may be in their way. They wave the claw at low tide on territories established around their burrows. Males entice any interested females into their burrows, and a female may visit a few pads before deciding on a particular one. Males often fight for prospective mates. They fight very carefully: A lost claw means disaster. It takes many molts to regenerate one that is big enough to get the crab back in action, and crabs whose claws are too small or that don't have the right moves can get pretty lonely!

In those areas coinhabited by several species of fiddlers, waving is used to prevent a male from attracting females of the wrong species. Some species wave up and down, others sideways. The angle and frequency of waving also vary, and bowing, fancy steps, and other body movements may form part of the ritual. Some beat the claw on the ground, and males of many species even produce sound by vibrating a joint of the large claw. It pays to advertise!

From Peter Castro in *Marine Biology*, 3rd ed., New York: McGraw-Hill, 2000, p. 249. Copyright © 2000 McGraw-Hill. Reprinted by permission of The McGraw-Hill Companies, Inc.

_____   3. We can infer that
   a. the small pincer is useful to female fiddler crabs, but not to males.
   b. both sexes of fiddler crabs use the small pincer for feeding.
   c. male fiddler crabs use the small pincer to attract female fiddler crabs.
   d. a male fiddler crab can quickly regenerate a large claw.

_____   4. We can infer that
   a. the male crab makes use of his large claw to attract female crabs of the right species.
   b. male fiddler crabs threaten other male fiddler crabs with their large claw.
   c. you can tell the species of a male fiddler crab by how it waves its large claw.
   d. all of the above

_____   5. We can infer that
   a. the fiddler crab's diet consists of mud.
   b. the fiddler crab's diet consists of the detritus that is extracted from mud.
   c. larger, stronger fiddler crabs eat smaller, weaker ones.
   d. fiddler crabs extract nutrition from sea water.

Devotion to Animals

Hinduism is distinctive among world religions for its kindness to animals. A devout Hindu does not kill or eat animals. Cows often wander along Indian streets, and cars and taxis take care to drive around them. Furthermore, visitors to some Hindu temples may find monkeys and even mice well fed and running free. Several extremely popular gods, such as Ganesha and Hanuman, have animal features; and gods such as Shiva and

Vishnu are regularly portrayed in the company of their animal companions. A Shiva temple would often be thought incomplete without a statue of Nandi, the bull who is Shiva's vehicle.

This devotion to animals in Hinduism has several possible origins: an ancient deification of certain animals, such as the elephant and tiger; the desire to neutralize dangerous or mischievous animals, such as the snake, rat, and monkey; and even a sense that human beings and animals have the same origin (a belief also common in oral religions). Belief in reincarnation has undoubtedly also played a role. When they see animals and insects, many Hindus see prehuman beings who in their spiritual evolution will eventually become human themselves. This brings a feeling of closeness to nonhuman forms of animal life.

Among the animals, cows receive special veneration. In rural India, to have a cow is to have milk and butter, fuel (dried dung), and the warmth and comfort associated with household pets. With a cow, one is never utterly destitute. Affection for the cow may represent a vestige of earlier matriarchal society—hinted at by the commonly used term *gau mata,* "mother cow." (The fact that Muslims butcher cows is a source of terrible friction between the Hindus and Muslims in India.)

From Michael Molloy in *Experiencing the World's Religions: Tradition, Challenge and Change* 2nd ed., New York: McGraw-Hill, 2002, pp. 88–89. Copyright © 2000 McGraw-Hill. Reprinted by permission of The McGraw-Hill Companies, Inc.

_____ 6. We can infer that
a. Hindus generally view animals as evil.
b. Hindus are ordinarily protective of animals.
c. a Muslim is unlikely to eat cow meat.
d. ownership of a cow in Hindu society is a terrible burden.

No Cattle, No Dignity

Along with the rest of their country, the Dinka of Sudan have been involved in a war that has torn apart the nation since 1955. Before the war caused institutions to collapse in southern Sudan, the Dinka were the south's richest and proudest tribe. They were high court judges, civil administrators, and doctors, as well as farmers and cowherds. But the loss of cattle changed all that. Cattle stood at the heart of virtually every important tradition and ceremony in Dinka life. Cattle has always been the Dinka's highest form of wealth, but the war caused the loss of many herds. The loss has caused the Dinka to change their myths and adopt new sources of food. The loss of cattle has also changed marriage. An offering of cattle to the bride's family was traditionally the central transaction at a dowry celebration. Nowadays the negotiations are still held, but they are about handshakes and pledges. There is no livestock available to change hands. Despite the loss of life and land caused by war, the loss of cattle may represent the biggest impact of the war on the Dinka. A change in this single part of culture has caused changes throughout the culture.

From Michael Hughes in *Sociology: The Core*, 6th ed., McGraw-Hill, 2002, p. 50. Copyright © 2002 McGraw-Hill. Reprinted by permission of The McGraw-Hill Companies, Inc.

_____ 7. We can infer that
a. sheep serve an important ceremonial function in Dinka society.
b. the destruction of war has not touched the Dinka's cattle herds.
c. the loss of cattle has had a devastating impact on Dinka society.
d. dowry exchanges in Dinka culture still feature an exchange of cattle.

"I consider myself a Hindu, Christian, Moslem, Jew, Buddhist, and Confucian."

—Gandhi

"There is nothing permanent except change."

—Heraclitus

Venomous Snakes Are Few

Modern snakes and lizards make up 95 percent of living reptiles. Snakes evolved from lizards during the Cretaceous period and became adapted to burrowing. They lack limbs, so their prey must be subdued and swallowed without the benefit of appendages for manipulating food. Most snakes, like the boas and pythons, are powerful constrictors, suffocating their struggling prey with strong coils. Smaller snakes, such as the familiar garter snakes and water snakes, frequently swallow their food while it is still alive. Still others use toxic saliva to subdue their prey, usually lizards. It is likely that snake venom evolved as a way to obtain food and is used only secondarily in defense.

There are two major groups of venomous snakes. Elapids are represented in the United States by the coral snakes, which inhabit the southern states and display bright bands of red, yellow (or white), and black that completely encircle the body. In these snakes, the fangs, which are modified teeth, are short and permanently erect. The venom is a powerful neurotoxin that usually paralyzes the nervous system. Actually, coral snakes are responsible for very few bites—probably because of their secretive nature, small size, and relatively mild manner.

Vipers, represented in the United States by pit vipers such as the copperhead and cottonmouth and about 15 species of rattlesnakes, make up the remaining venomous snakes of the United States. They have a sophisticated venom delivery system terminating in two large, hollow, needlelike fangs that can be folded against the roof of the mouth when not in use. The venom destroys the victim's red blood cells and causes extensive local tissue damage. These snakes are readily identified by the combination of heat-sensing facial pits, elliptical pupils in the eyes, and a single row of scales on the underside of the tail. None of our harmless snakes has any combination of these characteristics.

First aid for snakebite is not advised if medical attention is less than a few hours away; application of a tourniquet, incising the wound to promote bleeding, and other radical treatments often cause more harm than good. The best method of treating snakebite is through the use of prescribed antivenin, a serum containing antibodies to the venom. A hospital stay is required because some people are allergic to the serum.

Most people are not aware that snakes are perhaps the greatest controllers of disease-carrying, crop-destroying rodents because they are well adapted to following such prey into their hiding places. Also, snakes are important food items in the diets of many other carnivores, particularly birds of prey such as hawks and owls. Their presence in an ecosystem demonstrates the overall health of the environment.

From Sylvia Mader in *Biology*, 7th ed., New York: McGraw-Hill, 2001, p. 631. Copyright © 2001 McGraw-Hill. Reprinted by permission of The McGraw-Hill Companies, Inc.

_____ 8. We can infer that
   a. it is difficult to distinguish elapids from vipers.
   b. coral snakes are responsible for the majority of poisonous snake bites in the United States.
   c. snakes perform an important function in their ecosystems.
   d. a tourniquet should always be applied to a snakebite to keep venom from reaching the heart and causing cardiac arrest.

Drawing Inferences from Literature

The Life and Death of a Western Gladiator

by Charles Finney

"When autumn came the men decided to look for the rattler's den and execute mass slaughter."

Getting the Picture

The essay that follows is a classic. Charles Finney describes the life-and-death cycle of the western diamondback rattlesnake. Pay particular attention to how well suited the diamondback was to the environment before the arrival of man.

Bio-sketch

Charles Finney (1905–1984) was born in Sedalia, Missouri. He attended the University of Missouri and worked for the *Arizona Daily Star* in Tucson, Arizona, in various writing capacities from 1930 to 1970. His most famous book, *The Circus of Dr. Lao,* earned the 1935 National Booksellers Award for the most original novel. In addition to his other novels, he contributed short stories to various magazines such as *The New Yorker* and *Harpers.* This short story, "The Gladiator," has been selected for publication in nine literature anthology textbooks.

Brushing Up on Vocabulary

nemesis   an unconquerable opponent or rival. The word is derived from the ancient Greek goddess of divine retribution. The goddess *Nemesis* punished the pretentious with her mighty sword.

chaparral cock-roadrunner   a large (2-foot-long) terrestrial cuckoo residing in the arid regions of the western United States, Mexico, and Central America.

to homestead   to acquire or settle on unclaimed land. A law was passed in the 1860s that offered up to 160 acres of land to any man who paid a registration fee, lived on the land for five years, and cultivated or built on it.

flank   the side of an animal or person between the ribs and the hip.

rendezvous   an agreement to meet at a certain time or place. The word is borrowed from Middle French and literally means "to present yourself."

1   He was born on a summer morning in the shady mouth of a cave. Three others were born with him, another male and two females. Each was about five inches long and slimmer than a lead pencil.

2   Their mother left them a few hours after they were born. A day after that his brothers and sisters left him also. He was all alone. Nobody cared whether he lived or died. His tiny brain was very dull. He had no arms or legs. His skin was delicate. Nearly everything that walked on the ground or burrowed in it, that flew in the air or swam in the water or climbed trees was his enemy. But he didn't know that. He knew nothing at all. He was aware of his own existence, and that was the sum of his knowledge.

3   The direct rays of the sun could, in a short time, kill him. If the temperature dropped too low he would freeze. Without food he would starve. Without moisture he would die of dehydration. If a man or a horse stepped on him he would be crushed. If anything chased him he could run neither very far nor very fast.

4   Thus it was at the hour of his birth. Thus it would be, with modifications, all his life.

5   But against these drawbacks he had certain qualifications that fitted him to be a competitive creature of this world and equipped him for its warfare. He could exist a long time without food or water. His very smallness at birth protected him when he most needed protection. Instinct provided him with what he lacked in experience. In order to eat he first had to kill; and he was eminently adapted for killing. In sacs in his jaws he secreted a virulent poison. To inject that poison he had two fangs, hollow and pointed. Without that poison and those fangs he would have been among the most helpless creatures on earth. With them he was among the deadliest.

6   He was, of course, a baby rattlesnake, a desert diamondback, named *Crotalus atrox* by the herpetologists Baird and Girard and so listed in the *Catalogue of North American Reptiles* in its issue of 1853. He was grayish brown in color with a series of large dark diamond-shaped blotches on his back. His tail was white with five black crossbands. It had a button on the end of it.

7   Little Crotalus lay in the dust in the mouth of his cave. Some of his kinfolk lay there too. It was their home. That particular tribe of rattlers had lived there for scores of years.

8   The cave had never been seen by a white man.

9   Sometimes as many as two hundred rattlers occupied the den. Sometimes the numbers shrunk to as few as forty or fifty.

10   The tribe members did nothing at all for each other except breed. They hunted singly; they never shared their food. They derived some automatic degree of safety from their numbers, but their actions were never concerted toward using their numbers to any end. If an enemy attacked one of them, the others did nothing about it.

11   Young Crotalus's brother was the first of the litter to go out into the world and the first to die. He achieved a distance of fifty feet from the den when a Sonoran racer, four feet long and hungry, came upon him. The little rattler, despite his poison fangs, was a tidbit. The racer, long skilled in such arts, snatched him up by the head and swallowed him down. Powerful digestive juices in the racer's stomach did the rest. Then the racer, appetite whetted, prowled around until it found one of Crotalus's little sisters. She went the way of the brother.

12   Nemesis of the second sister was a chaparral cock. This cuckoo, or roadrunner as it is called, found the baby amid some rocks, uttered a cry of delight, scissored it by the neck, shook it until it was almost lifeless, banged and pounded it upon a rock until life had indeed left it, and then gulped it down.

13   Crotalus, somnolent in a cranny of the cave's mouth, neither knew nor cared. Even if he had, there was nothing he could have done about it.

14   On the fourth day of his life he decided to go out into the world himself. He rippled forth uncertainly, the transverse plates on his belly serving him as legs.

15   He could see things well enough within his limited range, but a five-inch-long snake can command no great field of vision. He had an excellent sense of smell. But having no ears, he was stone deaf. On the other hand, he had a pit, a deep pockmark between eye and nostril. Unique, this organ was sensitive to animal heat. In pitch blackness, Crotalus, by means of the heat messages recorded in his pit, could tell whether another animal was near and could also judge its size. That was better than an ear.

16   The single button on his tail could not, of course, yet rattle. Crotalus wouldn't be able to rattle until that button had grown into three segments. Then he would be able to buzz.

17   He had a wonderful tongue. It looked like an exposed nerve and probably was exactly that. It was forked, and Crotalus thrust it in and out as he traveled. It told him things that neither his eyes nor his nose nor his pit told him.

18   Snake fashion, Crotalus went forth, not knowing where he was going, for he had never been anywhere before. Hunger was probably his prime mover. In order to satisfy that hunger, he had to find something smaller than himself and kill it.

19   He came upon a baby lizard sitting in the sand. Eyes, nose, pit, and tongue told Crotalus it was there. Instinct told him what it was and what to do. Crotalus gave a tiny one-inch strike and bit the lizard. His poison killed it. He took it by the head and swallowed it. Thus was his first meal.

20   During his first two years Crotalus grew rapidly. He attained a length of two feet; his tail had five rattles on it and its button. He rarely bothered with lizards anymore, preferring baby rabbits, chipmunks, and round-tailed ground squirrels. Because of his slow locomotion he could not run down these agile little things. He had to contrive instead to be where they were when they would pass. Then he struck swiftly, injected his poison, and ate them after they died.

21   At two he was formidable. He had grown past the stage where a racer or a roadrunner could safely tackle him. He had grown to the size where other desert dwellers—coyotes, foxes, coatis, wildcats—knew it was better to leave him alone.

22   He found "her" on a rainy morning. Of that physical union six new rattlesnakes were born. Thus Crotalus, at two, had carried out his major primary function: he had reproduced his kind. In two years he had experienced everything that was reasonably possible for desert diamondback rattlesnakes to experience except death.

23   He had not experienced death for the simple reason that there had never been an opportunity for anything bigger and stronger than himself to kill him. Now, at two, because he was so formidable, that opportunity became more and more unlikely.

24   He grew more slowly in the years following his initial spurt. At the age of twelve he was five feet long. Few of the other rattlers in his den were older or larger than he.

25   He had a castanet of fourteen segments. It had been broken off occasionally in the past, but with each new molting a new segment appeared.

26   His first skin-shedding back in his babyhood had been a bewildering experience. He did not know what was happening. His eyes clouded over until he could not see. His skin thickened and dried until it cracked in places. His pit and his nostrils ceased to function. There was only one thing to do and that was to get out of that skin.

27   Crotalus managed it by nosing against the bark of a shrub until he forced the old skin down over his head, bunching it like the rolled top of a stocking around his neck. Then he pushed around among rocks and sticks and branches, literally crawling out of his skin by slow degrees. Wriggling free at last, he looked like a brand new snake. His skin was bright and satiny, his eyes and nostrils were clear, his pit sang with sensation.

28   For the rest of his life he was to molt three or four times a year. Each time he did it he felt as if he had been born again.

29   At twelve he was a magnificent reptile. Not a single scar defaced his rippling symmetry. He was diabolically beautiful and deadly poison.

30   His venom was his only weapon, for he had no power of constriction. Yellowish in color, his poison was odorless and tasteless. It was a highly complex mixture of proteids, each in itself direly toxic. His venom worked on the blood. The more poison he injected with a bite, the more dangerous the wound. The pain rendered by his bite was instantaneous, and the shock accompanying it was profound. Swelling began immediately, to be followed by a ghastly oozing. Injected directly into a large vein, his poison brought death quickly, for the victim died when it reached his heart.

31   At the age of twenty Crotalus was the oldest and largest rattler in his den. He was in the golden age of his viperhood.

32   He was six feet long and weighed thirteen pounds. His whole world was only about a mile in radius. He had fixed places where he avoided the sun when it was hot and he was away from his cave. He knew his hunting grounds thoroughly, every game trail, every animal burrow.

33   He was a fine old machine, perfectly adapted to his surroundings, accustomed to a life of leisure and comfort. He dominated his little world.

34   But men were approaching. Spilling out of their cities, men were settling in that part of the desert where Crotalus lived. They built roads and houses, set up fences, dug for water, planted crops.

35   They homesteaded the land. They brought new animals with them—cows, horses, dogs, cats, barnyard fowl.

36   The roads they built were death traps for the desert dwellers. Every morning new dead bodies lay on the roads, the bodies of the things the men had run over and crushed in their vehicles.

37   That summer Crotalus met his first dog. It was a German shepherd which had been reared on a farm in the Midwest and there had gained the reputation of being a snake-killer. Black snakes, garter snakes, pilots, water snakes; it delighted in killing them all. It would seize them by the middle, heedless of their tiny teeth, and shake them violently until they died.

38   This dog met Crotalus face to face in the desert at dusk. Crotalus had seen coyotes aplenty and feared them not. Neither did the dog fear Crotalus, although Crotalus then was six feet long, as thick in the middle as a motorcycle tire, and had a head the size of a man's clenched fist. Also this snake buzzed and buzzed and buzzed.

39   The dog was brave and a snake was a snake. The German shepherd snarled and attacked. Crotalus struck him in the underjaw; his fangs sank in almost half an inch and squirted big blobs of poison into the tissues of the dog's flesh.

40   The shepherd bellowed with pain, backed off, groveled with his jaws in the desert sand, and attacked again. He seized Crotalus somewhere by the middle of his body and tried to flip him in the air and shake him as, in the past, he had shaken slender black snakes to their death. In return, he received another poison-blurting stab in his flank and a third in the belly and a fourth in the eye as the terrible, writhing snake bit wherever it could sink his fangs.

41   The German shepherd had enough. He dropped the big snake and in sick, agonizing bewilderment crawled somehow back to his master's homestead and died.

42   The homesteader looked at his dead dog and became alarmed. If there was a snake around big enough to kill a dog that size, it could also kill a child and probably a man. It was something that had to be eliminated.

43   The homesteader told his fellow farmers, and they agreed to initiate a war of extermination against the snakes.

44   The campaign during the summer was sporadic. The snakes were scattered over the desert, and it was only by chance that the men came upon them. Even so, at summer's end, twenty-six of the vipers had been killed.

45   When autumn came the men decided to look for the rattler's den and execute mass slaughter. The homesteaders had become desert-wise and knew what to look for.

46   They found Crotalus's lair, without too much trouble—a rock outcropping on a slope that faced south. Cast-off skins were in evidence in the bushes. Bees flew idly in and out of the den's mouth. Convenient benches and shelves of rock were at hand where the snakes might lie for a final sunning in the autumn air.

47   They killed the three rattlers they found at the den when they first discovered it. They made plans to return in a few more days when more of the snakes had congregated. They decided to bring along dynamite with them and blow up the mouth of the den so that the snakes within would be sealed there forever and the snakes without would have no place to find refuge.

48   On the day the men chose to return nearly fifty desert diamondbacks were gathered at the portals of the cave. The men shot them, clubbed them, smashed them with rocks. Some of the rattlers escaped the attack and crawled into the den.

49   Crotalus had not yet arrived for the autumn rendezvous. He came that night. The den's mouth was a shattered mass of rock, for the men had done their dynamiting well. Dead members of his tribe lay everywhere. Crotalus nosed among them, tongue flicking as he slid slowly along.

50   There was no access to the cave anymore. He spent the night outside among the dead. The morning sun warmed him and awakened him. He lay there at full length. He had no place to go.

51   The sun grew hotter upon him and instinctively he began to slide toward some dark shade. Then his senses warned him of some animal presence near by; he stopped, half coiled, raised his head and began to rattle. He saw two upright figures. He did not know what they were because he had never seen men before.

52   "That's the granddaddy of them all," said one of the homesteaders. "It's a good thing we came back." He raised his shotgun.

From Charles Finney, "The Life and Death of a Western Gladiator."

Comprehension Checkup

Main Ideas, Supporting Details, and Purpose

Drawing on what you learned from the selection, answer the questions or fill in the blanks appropriately.

1. What is the author's main idea? _____

    _____

2. What was the author's purpose in writing the essay? _____

    _____

    _____

3. How does the author want the reader to feel about rattlesnakes at the end of the essay? _____

    _____

4. The rattlesnake "senses" the presence of other animals by using its _____.

5. The group of rattlesnakes described in the story lived in a _____.

Drawing Inferences from the Selection

Based on what you learned from the selection, indicate whether each statement is true or false by writing T or F in the blank provided.

1. _____ The rattlesnake's weapon is its virulent poison.

2. _____ Rattlesnakes work in concert to kill their prey.

3. _____ The baby rattlesnake is taught by older snakes how to fend for itself.

4. _____ The homesteaders waged a war of extermination against the rattlesnakes.

5. _____ Without the power of constriction, the rattlesnake would be among the most helpless creatures on earth.

6. _____ Crotalus was killed by the homesteaders.

Vocabulary in Context

Look through the paragraph indicated in parentheses to find a word that matches the definition below.

1. actively poisonous (paragraph 5)   _____

2. sleepy (13)   _____

3. to plan with ingenuity; devise (20)   _____

4. confusing or completely puzzling (26)   _____

5. fiendishly; wickedly (29)   _____

6. occurring at irregular intervals (44)   _____

7. assembled (47)   _____

8. shelter or protection from danger (47)   _____

Drawing Inferences from Cartoons

Study the cartoon by Gary Larson below and then write an appropriate caption or main idea sentence for it.

_____

THE FAR SIDE® By GARY LARSON

© 1983 FarWorks, Inc. All Rights Reserved/Dist. by Creators Syndicate

The Far Side® by Gary Larson © 1983 FarWorks, Inc. All Right Reserved. Used with Permission.

"Freeze, Earl! Freeze! … Something rattled!"

Internet Activity

There are many different kinds of rattlesnakes. To learn more about rattlesnakes, including one that is an albino, visit the website sponsored by the American International Rattlesnake Museum in Albuquerque, New Mexico:

www.rattlesnakes.com

First, read about two different kinds of rattlesnakes, and then make a list of their similarities and differences. What can you infer about the rattlesnake's ability to survive? Is it well-equipped to survive in the modern world or is it in danger of extinction?

The Wolf in Fables   _by Aesop_

Getting the Picture

While many people see the wolf as a symbol of untamed wilderness, others view the wolf as a vicious animal. Fables and fairy tales such as "Little Red Riding Hood" and "The Three Little Pigs" have emphasized the cunning and deceitfulness of the "Big Bad Wolf."

What inferences can you draw from these fables by Aesop about the characteristics of a wolf? List them after reading the selection.

THE WOLF AND THE CRANE

1   A wolf devoured his prey so ravenously that a bone got stuck in his throat, and in extreme agony, he ran and howled throughout the forest, beseeching every animal he met to pull out the bone. He even offered a generous reward to anyone who succeeded in pulling it out. Moved by his pleas as well as the prospect of the money, a crane ventured her long neck down the wolf's throat and drew out the bone. She then modestly asked for the promised reward, but the wolf just grinned and bared his teeth.

2   "Ungrateful creature!" he replied with seeming indignation. "How dare you ask for any other reward than your life? After all, you're among the very few who can say that you've put your head into the jaws of a wolf and were permitted to draw it out safely."

3   Moral: _Expect no reward when you serve the wicked, and be thankful if you escape injury for your pains._

THE SHEPHERD BOY AND THE WOLF

1   A shepherd boy, who tended his flock not far from a village, used to amuse himself at times by crying out "Wolf! Wolf!" His trick succeeded two or three times, and the whole village came running to his rescue. However, the villagers were simply rewarded with laughter for their pains.

2   One day the wolf really did come, and the boy cried out in earnest. But his neighbors thought that he was up to his old tricks and paid no attention to his cries. Consequently, the sheep were left at the mercy of the wolf.

3   Moral: _Even when liars tell the truth, they are never believed._

From _Aesop's Fables_, edited by Jack Zipes, pp. 17, 22. Copyright © 1992 by Jack Zipes. Used by permission of Dutton Signet, a division of Penguin Putnam Group (USA) Inc.

Drawing on what you learned from these two fables, list four characteristics of the wolf.

1. _____

2. _____

3. _____

4. _____

Based on what you already know and what you learned from these fables, explain the following sayings in your own words.

1. It's important to keep the wolf from one's door.

   _____

2. Beware a wolf in sheep's clothing.

   _____

3. He is as hungry as a wolf.

   _____

4. It's bad manners to wolf your food down.

   _____

5. He has many girlfriends and is such a wolf.

   _____

6. What inferences can you draw about the wolf from these sayings?

   _____

SELECTION

Excerpt from *Wolf Songs*   *by Farley Mowat*

"Once I had become aware of the strong feeling of property rights which existed amongst the wolves, I decided to use this knowledge to make them at least recognize my existence."

Getting the Picture

The following selection was written in the early 1960s by Farley Mowat, a noted conservationist. Mowat was hired by the Canadian government to investigate the claim that hordes of wolves were slaughtering arctic caribou. He was sent to live alone in the arctic tundra where he was supposed to establish contact with the wolves so he could better understand their behavior. This brief excerpt describes his initial contact with the wolf he came to call "George."

Bio-sketch

Farley Mowat, born and raised in Canada, considers himself to be a "Northern Man." He says that he likes to think he is a "reincarnation of the Norse saga men and, like them, [his] chief concern is with the tales of men, and other animals, living under conditions of natural adversity." The recipient of numerous awards, Mowat's two best-known works, *A Whale for the Killing* (1984) and *Never Cry Wolf* (1963), were made into popular movies.

Brushing Up on Vocabulary

cognizance   perception or knowledge. To take *cognizance* of something means to notice or recognize it. *Cognizance* comes from the Latin *cogni*, which means "to come to know."

baleful   harmful or threatening harm; ominous, deadly.

inviolate   kept sacred or unbroken, intact.

diurnal   done or happening in the daytime. The first part of the word does not come from *di* meaning "two," but from *dies* meaning "day."

nocturnal   the opposite of *diurnal*—means done or happening at night.

cache   a place in which stores of food are hidden.

austerely   very plainly or simply, with no ornamentation or luxury.

epitome   a good example that shows all the typical qualities.

George

1   Quite by accident I had pitched my tent within ten yards of one of the major paths used by the wolves when they were going to, or coming from their hunting grounds to the westward; and only a few hours after I had taken up residence one of the wolves came back from a trip and discovered me and my tent. He was at the end of a hard night's work and was clearly tired and anxious to go home to bed. He came over a small rise fifty yards from me with his head down, his eyes half-closed and a preoccupied air about him. Far from being the preternaturally alert and sus-picious beast of fiction, this wolf was so self-engrossed that he came straight on to within fifty yards of me, and might have gone right past the tent without seeing it at all, had I not banged my elbow against the teakettle, making a resounding clang. The wolf's head came up and his eyes opened wide, but he did not stop or falter in his pace. One brief, sidelong glance was all he vouchsafed to me as he contin-ued on his way.

2   It was true that I wanted to be inconspicuous, but I felt uncomfortable at being so totally ignored. Nevertheless, during the two weeks which followed, one or more wolves used the track past my tent almost every night—and never, except on one memorable occasion, did they evince the slightest interest in me.

3   By the time this happened I had learned a good deal about my wolfish neigh-bors, and one of the facts which had emerged was that they were not nomadic roamers, as is almost universally believed, but were settled beasts and the posses-sors of a large permanent estate with very definite boundaries.

4   The territory owned by my wolf family comprised more than a hundred square miles, bounded on one side by a river but otherwise not delimited by geograph-ical features. Nevertheless there *were* boundaries, clearly indicated in wolfish fashion.

5   Anyone who has observed a dog doing his neighborhood rounds and leaving his personal mark on each convenient post will have already guessed how the wolves marked out *their* property. Once a week, more or less, the clan made the rounds of the family lands and freshened up the boundary markers—a sort of lupine beating of the bounds. This careful attention to property rights was perhaps made neces-sary by the presence of two other wolf families whose lands abutted on ours, although I never discovered any evidence of bickering or disagreements between the owners of the various adjoining estates. I suspect, therefore, that it was more of a ritual activity.

6   In any event, once I had become aware of the strong feeling of property rights which existed amongst the wolves, I decided to use this knowledge to make them at least recognize my existence. One evening, after they had gone off for their reg-ular nightly hunt, I staked out a property claim of my own, embracing perhaps three acres, with the tent at the middle, and *including a hundred-yard-long section of the wolves' path.*

7   Staking the land turned out to be rather more difficult than I had anticipated. In order to ensure that my claim would not be overlooked, I felt obliged to make a property mark on stones, clumps of moss, and patches of vegetation at intervals of not more than fifteen feet around the circumference of my claim. This took most of the night and required frequent returns to the tent to consume copious quantities of tea; but before dawn brought the hunters home the task was done, and I retired, somewhat exhausted, to observe results.

8   I had not long to wait. At 0814 hours, according to my wolf log, the leading male of the clan appeared over the ridge behind me, padding homeward with his usual air of preoccupation. As usual he did not deign to glance at the tent; but when he reached the point where my property line intersected the trail, he stopped as abruptly as if he had run into an invisible wall. He was only fifty yards from me and with my binoculars I could see his expression very clearly.

9   His attitude of fatigue vanished and was replaced by a look of bewilderment. Cautiously he extended his nose and sniffed at one of my marked bushes. He did not seem to know what to make of it or what to do about it. After a minute of complete indecision he backed away a few yards and sat down. And then, finally, he looked directly at the tent and at me. It was a long, thoughtful, considering sort of look.

10   Having achieved my object—that of forcing at least one of the wolves to take cognizance of my existence—I now began to wonder if, in my ignorance, I had transgressed some unknown wolf law of major importance and would have to pay for my temerity. I found myself regretting the absence of a weapon as the look I was getting became longer, yet more thoughtful, and still more intent.

11   I began to grow decidedly fidgety, for I dislike staring matches, and in this particular case I was up against a master, whose yellow glare seemed to become more baleful as I attempted to stare him down.

12   The situation was becoming intolerable. In an effort to break the impasse I loudly cleared my throat and turned my back on the wolf (for a tenth of a second) to indicate as clearly as possible that I found his continued scrutiny impolite, if not actually offensive.

13   He appeared to take the hint. Getting to his feet he had another sniff at my marker, and then he seemed to make up his mind. Briskly, and with an air of decision, he turned his attention away from me and began a systematic tour of the area I had staked out as my own. As he came to each boundary marker he sniffed it once or twice, then carefully placed *his* mark on the outside of each clump of grass or stone. As I watched I saw where I, in my ignorance, had erred. He made his mark with such economy that he was able to complete the entire circuit without having to reload once, or to change the simile slightly, he did it all on one tank of fuel.

14   The task completed—and it had taken him no longer than fifteen minutes—he rejoined the path at the point where it left my property and trotted off towards his home—leaving me with a good deal to occupy my thoughts.

15   Once it had been formally established, and its existence ratified by the wolves themselves, my little enclave in that territory remained inviolate. Never again did a wolf trespass on my domain. Occasionally, one in passing would stop to freshen up some of the boundary marks on his side of the line, and, not to be outdone in ceremony, I followed suit to the best of my ability. Any lingering doubts I might have had as to my personal safety dissolved, and I was free to devote all my attention to a study of the beasts themselves.

16   Very early in my observations I discovered that they led a well-regulated life, although they were not slavish adherents to fixed schedules. Early in the evenings the males went off to work. They might depart at four o'clock or they might delay until six or seven, but sooner or later off they went on the nightly hunt. During this

hunt they ranged far afield, although always—as far as I could tell—staying within the limits of the family territory. I estimated that during a normal hunt they covered thirty or forty miles before dawn. When times were hard they probably covered even greater distances, since on some occasions they did not get home until the afternoon. During the balance of the daylight hours they slept—but in their own peculiarly wolfish way, which consisted of curling up for short wolf-naps of from five to ten minutes' duration; after each of which they would take a quick look about, and then turn round once or twice before dozing off again.

17   The females and the pups led a more diurnal life. Once the males had departed in the evening, the female usually went into the den and stayed there, emerging only occasionally for a breath of air, a drink, or sometimes for a visit to the meat cache for a snack.

18   This cache deserves special mention. No food was ever stored or left close to the den; and only enough was brought in at one time for immediate consumption. Any surplus from a hunt was carried to the cache, which was located in a jumble of boulders half-a-mile from the den, and stuffed into crevices, primarily for the use of the nursing female who, of course, could not join the male wolves on extended hunting trips.

19   The cache was also used surreptitiously by a pair of foxes who had their own den close by. The wolves must have known of the location of the foxes' home, and probably knew perfectly well that there was a certain amount of pilfering from their cache; but they did nothing about it even though it would have been a simple matter for them to dig out and destroy the litter of fox pups. The foxes, on their side, seemed to have no fear of the wolves, and several times I saw one flit like a shadow across the esker within a few yards of a wolf without eliciting any response.

20   Later I concluded that almost all the dens used by the Barren Land wolves were abandoned fox burrows which had been taken over and enlarged by the wolves. It is possible that the usefulness of the foxes as preliminary excavators may have guaranteed them immunity; but it seems more likely that the wolves' tolerance simply reflected their general amiability.

21   During the day, while the male wolves took it easy, the female would be reasonably active about her household chores. Emerging boisterously from the close confines of the den, the pups also became active—to the point of total exhaustion. Thus throughout the entire twenty-four-hour period there was usually something going on, or at least the expectation of something, to keep me glued to the telescope.

22   After the first two days and nights of nearly continuous observing I had about reached the limits of my endurance. It was a most frustrating situation. I did not dare to go to sleep for fear of missing something vital. On the other hand, I became so sleepy that I was seeing double, if not triple, on occasion; although this effect may have been associated with the quantities of wolf-juice which I consumed in an effort to stay awake.

23   I saw that something drastic would have to be done or my whole study program would founder. I could think of nothing adequate until, watching one of the males dozing comfortably on a hillock near the den, I recognized the solution to my problem. It was simple. I had only to learn to nap like a wolf.

24   It took some time to get the knack of it. I experimented by closing my eyes and trying to wake up again five minutes later, but it didn't work. After the first two or three naps I failed to wake up at all until several hours had passed.

25   The fault was mine, for I had failed to imitate *all* the actions of a dozing wolf, and, as I eventually discovered, the business of curling up to start with, and spinning about after each nap, was vital to success. I don't know why this is so. Perhaps

changing the position of the body helps to keep the circulation stimulated. I *do* know, however, that a series of properly conducted wolf-naps is infinitely more refreshing than the unconscious coma of seven or eight hours' duration which represents the human answer to the need for rest.

26   Unfortunately, the wolf-nap does not readily lend itself to adaptation into our society, as I discovered after my return to civilization when a young lady of whom I was enamored at the time parted company with me. She had rather, she told me vehemently, spend her life with a grasshopper who had rickets, than spend one more night in bed with me.

27   As I grew more completely attuned to their daily round of family life I found it increasingly difficult to maintain an impersonal attitude toward the wolves. No matter how hard I tried to regard them with scientific objectivity, I could not resist the impact of their individual personalities. Because he reminded me irresistibly of a Royal Gentleman for whom I worked as a simple soldier during the war, I found myself calling the father of the family George, even though in my notebooks, he was austerely identified only as Wolf "A."

28   George was a massive and eminently regal beast whose coat was silver-white. He was about a third larger than his mate, but he hardly needed this extra bulk to emphasize his air of masterful certainty. George had presence. His dignity was unassailable, yet he was by no means aloof. Conscientious to a fault, thoughtful of others, and affectionate within reasonable bounds, he was the kind of father whose idealized image appears in many wistful books of human family reminiscences, but whose real prototype has seldom paced the earth upon two legs. George was, in brief, the kind of father every son longs to acknowledge as his own.

29   His wife was equally memorable. A slim, almost pure-white wolf with a thick ruff around her face, and wide-spaced, slightly slanted eyes, she seemed the picture of a minx. Beautiful, ebullient, passionate to a degree, and devilish when the mood was on her, she hardly looked like the epitome of motherhood; yet there could have been no better mother anywhere. I found myself calling her Angeline, although I have never been able to trace the origin of her name in the murky depths of my own subconscious. I respected and liked George very much, but I became deeply fond of Angeline, and still live in hopes that I can somewhere find a human female who embodies all her virtues.

30   Angeline and George seemed as devoted a mated pair as one could hope to find. As far as I could tell they never quarreled, and the delight with which they greeted each other after even a short absence was obviously unfeigned. They were extremely affectionate with one another, but, alas, the many pages in my notebook which had been hopefully reserved for detailed comments on the sexual behavior and activities of wolves remained obstinately blank as far as George and Angeline were concerned.

31   Distressing as it was to my expectations, I discovered that physical lovemaking enters into the lives of a pair of mated wolves only during a period of two or three weeks early in the Spring, usually in March. Virgin females (and they are all virginal until their second year) then mate; but unlike dogs, who have adopted many of the habits of their human owners, wolf bitches mate with only a single male, and mate for life.

32   Whereas the phrase "till death us do part" is one of the more amusing mockeries in the nuptial arrangements of a large proportion of the human race, with wolves it is a simple fact. Wolves are also strict monogamists, and although I do not necessarily consider this an admirable trait, it does make the reputation for unbridled promiscuity which we have bestowed on the wolf somewhat hypocritical.

✔

Comprehension Checkup

Multiple Choice

Write the letter of the correct answer in the blank provided.

_____ 1. If the author were reading this selection out loud, he would most likely sound
   a. solemn
   b. admiring
   c. angry
   d. perplexed

_____ 2. From this article, you could conclude that the author
   a. has a genuine affection for animals
   b. considers hunting a favorite pastime
   c. is a rancher who is afraid that wolves will kill his cattle
   d. dislikes outdoor life

_____ 3. The word _offensive_ in the last line of paragraph 12 means
   a. illegal
   b. insulting
   c. damaging
   d. aggressive

_____ 4. From paragraph 22, you could infer that the "wolf-juice" the author consumed is most likely
   a. coffee
   b. beer
   c. tea
   d. milk

_____ 5. All of the following are examples of how male and female wolves behave _except_
   a. male and female wolves are promiscuous
   b. the males hunt for food while the females stay close to the den
   c. the males rest during the day while the females do household chores
   d. male and female wolves are likely to mate for life

_____ 6. The writer's main purpose in writing this selection is to
   a. relate humorous anecdotes about the wolf
   b. describe the wolf's behavior and habitat
   c. explain why wolves are disappearing from the wild
   d. persuade hunters to treat the wolf with more respect

_____ 7. The information presented in paragraphs 25–26 of the selection supports which of the following statements?
   a. Mowat discovered that a wolf-nap is far less refreshing than seven hours of sound sleep.
   b. Mowat discovered that all of the actions of a dozing wolf must be enacted to have a successful wolf-nap.
   c. Mowat discovered that by taking wolf-naps, he was not endearing himself to a particular lady friend.
   d. both (b) and (c)

_____ 8. Paragraphs 28 and 29 provide details that primarily
   a. describe the physical and personality characteristics of George and Angeline

b. demonstrate the superiority of wolf characteristics in contrast to
   humans
c. describe the paternal and maternal characteristics of the wolf
d. all of the above

_____ 9. Which of the following occurred first?
a. the lead wolf backed away and sat down
b. the author marked "his" property
c. the author turned his back on the wolf
d. the lead wolf made his mark and then trotted off toward home

_____ 10. Which of the following observations best support the author's contention that wolves led a well-regulated life?
a. while the males were gone, the females and pups retreated to
   the den
b. during the balance of daylight hours they slept
c. early in the evenings the wolves went off to hunt
d. all of the above

Vocabulary in Context

Each item below includes a sentence from the selection. Using the context clues provided, write a preliminary definition for the italicized word. Then look up the word in a dictionary and write the appropriate definition.

1. "Far from being the *preternaturally* alert and suspicious beast of fiction, this wolf was so self-engrossed that he came straight on to within fifty yards of me." (paragraph 1)

   Your definition: _____

   Dictionary definition: _____

2. "The wolf's head came up and his eyes opened wide, but he did not stop or *falter* in his pace." (1)

   Your definition: _____

   Dictionary definition: _____

3. "One brief, sidelong glance was all he *vouchsafed* to me as he continued on his way." (1)

   Your definition: _____

   Dictionary definition: _____

4. "It was true that I wanted to be *inconspicuous*, but I felt uncomfortable at being so totally ignored." (2)

   Your definition: _____

   Dictionary definition: _____

5. "Nevertheless, during the two weeks which followed, one or more wolves used the track past my tent almost every night—and never, except on one memorable occasion, did they *evince* the slightest interest in me." (2)

   Your definition: _____

   Dictionary definition: _____

6. "Once a week, more or less, the clan made the rounds of the family lands and freshened up the boundary markers—a sort of *lupine* beating of the bounds." (5)

   Your definition: _____

   Dictionary definition: _____

7. "In order to ensure that my claim would not be overlooked, I felt obliged to make a property mark on stones, clumps of moss, and patches of vegetation at intervals of not more than fifteen feet around the *circumference* of my claim." (7)

    Your definition: _____

    Dictionary definition: _____

8. "This took most of the night and required frequent returns to the tent to consume *copious* quantities of tea." (7)

    Your definition: _____

    Dictionary definition: _____

9. "As usual he did not *deign* to glance at the tent; but when he reached the point where my property line *intersected* the trail, he stopped as abruptly as if he had run into an invisible wall." (8)

    Your definition: _____

    Dictionary definition: _____

    Your definition: _____

    Dictionary definition: _____

In Your Own Words

1. Mowat discovered that in many instances the myths of wolf behavior are not the same as the reality. List as many discrepancies between the two as you can find.

2. Mowat asserted his property rights by "marking" the boundaries of his territory. How is the lead wolf's response contrary to what we might typically expect?

3. Mowat comes to admire the wolves in many respects and in some instances feels that their lifestyle is superior to ours. What specific aspects of wolf behavior does Mowat admire?

4. An artist could probably paint a picture using Mowat's descriptions of George and Angeline. Give a brief synopsis of each one, including character traits. What key details does Mowat use in order to portray the wolves in human terms?

5. Explain the symbiotic relationship between wolves and foxes.

The Art of Writing

In a brief essay, respond to one of the items below.

1. You have now read three selections on the wolf. Write a brief profile of the wolf.

2. In the United States, one of the most controversial conservation issues is the reintroduction of wolves into areas where they have long been extinct. One group feels that parks such as Yellowstone need wolves to preserve an ecological balance. These groups note that an overabundance of deer is currently overgrazing vast areas of the park. Because wolves are a natural predator of deer, they would help control the deer population. On the other hand, many feel that the wolf is detrimental to human beings, and the loudest opposition to reintroduction comes from the ranching community, which is fearful of massive livestock loss.

Come up with several suggestions for resolving the dispute between the two groups. If necessary, go to the library and do additional research.

Internet Activity

One of the best websites about wolves is sponsored by *Nova* of the Public Broadcasting System. Check out its website at

www.pbs.org/wgbh/nova/wolves

Then take a short quiz to see how much you know about the relationship between the domestic dog and the wolf. Finally, print an article of interest to you and list some inferences that can be drawn from it.

SELECTION

Excerpt from *Seabiscuit*   *by Laura Hillenbrand*

"As race day approached, the names War Admiral and Seabiscuit were on everyone's lips. Even President Roosevelt was swept up in the fervor."

Getting the Picture

In 1938, the racehorse Seabiscuit was a cultural icon. Then-president Franklin Delano Roosevelt was so caught up in the competition between Seabiscuit and War Admiral that he made several important advisors wait to see him while he listened to the race on the radio. When Laura Hillenbrand began her research for her book *Seabiscuit*, she was struck by how the assembled cast of characters—automobile magnate Charles Howard; Tom Smith, the original Horse Whisperer; and jockeys Red Pollard and George Woolf—all represented the pioneering spirit of the Old West. All were tough gamblers who were not afraid to take a chance. Hillenbrand was fascinated by the irony of Howard making his fortune by replacing horses with cars, yet achieving fulfillment by racing the horse many consider the greatest of all thoroughbreds.

Bio-sketch

Laura Hillenbrand has been writing about horse racing since 1988. She is a winner of the Eclipse Award, the highest journalistic award in thoroughbred racing. A long-time sufferer of Chronic Fatigue Syndrome, Hillenbrand's poor health made writing *Seabiscuit* truly a labor of love. Mostly housebound, she conducted phone interviews of more than 100 people for the book, which took over four years to write. Hillenbrand, who currently lives in Washington D.C., served as a consultant for the Universal Pictures movie featuring Tobey Maguire. *Seabiscuit* was named a *New York Times* Notable Book of the Year for 2001.

Brushing Up on Vocabulary

bush-league   an old baseball expression for minor and semiprofessional baseball leagues. Their games were usually played in uncomfortable and primitive conditions. Since many players in the "bush league" are either beginners or past their prime, the term means someone or something amateurish or incompetent.

Cinderella   a fairy tale recorded by Charles Perrault. In the story, a young girl is forced by her stepmother and stepsisters to wear rags and do manual labor. When a nearby prince holds a ball, Cinderella's fairy godmother transforms her into an elegant lady and sends her off to the royal palace. There she meets the prince, who falls in love with her. But at the stroke of midnight, she resumes her previous ragged state and flees, leaving her glass slipper behind. The prince discovers her despite her ragged appearance when the glass slipper fits on her foot. They are married and live "happily ever after." The name *Cinderella* is sometimes applied to a person, group, or animal who undergoes a sudden transformation and suddenly becomes a winner.

underdog   something or someone expected to lose in a contest or conflict.

shell-shocked   an early term for combat or battle fatigue.

The Race of the Century

1   In 1938, near the end of a decade of monumental turmoil, the year's number-one newsmaker was not Franklin Delano Roosevelt, Adolf Hitler, Lou Gehrig, or Clark Gable. It was an undersized, mud-colored, crooked-legged racehorse named Seabiscuit.

2   He came from nowhere. He spent nearly two seasons floundering in the lowest ranks of racing, misunderstood and mishandled. Then he attracted the attention of racehorse trainer Tom Smith, a mysterious, virtually mute refugee from the vanishing frontier who bore with him generations of lost wisdom about the secrets of horses. Smith recognized something in Seabiscuit.

3   His boss, California automobile magnate Charles Howard, agreed that the little horse had grit, and bought him cheap. "We had to rebuild him, both mentally and physically," Howard recalled later. "But you don't have to rebuild the heart when it's already there, big as all outdoors."

4   The third member of Seabiscuit's team of handlers, Red Pollard, was in his twelfth year of a failing career as a jockey and part-time prizefighter when Tom Smith hired him. His experience with horses at countless bush-league racetracks had given him insight into the minds of hard-used, nervous animals, and he quickly won Seabiscuit's trust.

5   One of the first things he did was tell Smith that the whip, used so liberally by the horse's former rider, had to be put away. "Treat him like a gentleman," said Pollard. "He'll run his heart out for you."

6   And run he did. Seabiscuit began winning races. His reputation spread, aided by radio, which enabled a vast number of citizens to experience his triumphs. Millions upon millions of people, torn loose by the Depression from their jobs, their savings, their homes, were desperate to lose themselves in anything that offered affirmation. Spectator sports were enjoying explosive growth, and none more than thoroughbred racing. When Seabiscuit, the Cinderella horse, burst onto the scene, something clicked.

7   Seabiscuit's growing legion of fans were eager for him to race against the era's other equine superstar, Triple Crown–winner War Admiral, son of the legendary Man o'War.

8   War Admiral had the same imperious, lordly way of his father. He was a hellion who spun and fought at the gate, tossed the starters aside, and lunged through false starts. Once under way, he had awesome, frightening speed. No horse in his age group could stay with him. The sleek blue blood awaited a horse who would take the true measure of his greatness. It would never have occurred to anyone in the East that this horse might be the stocky California contender, Seabiscuit.

9   In the fall of 1938 a contest between the two horses was finally arranged. Seabiscuit and War Admiral were set to race against each other at Maryland's Pimlico racetrack on November 1, in what was universally hailed as the race of the century.

10   Unfortunately, Red Pollard would not be riding Seabiscuit. Some five months earlier, on June 23, Red had been warming up a horse for a friend when the animal spooked and bolted; running at 30 m.p.h., the horse smashed Red's leg against the corner of a barn; nearly severing it below the knee.

11   His best friend, a jockey named George "Iceman" Woolf, took over as Seabiscuit's rider for the race. Woolf called Pollard, who was still in the hospital, to talk strategy.

"Fortune favors the 12   Like virtually everyone else, the Iceman believed that War Admiral simply had more *bold."* God-given ability than Seabiscuit. How, he asked Pollard, should he run this race?

—Terence   13   Pollard surprised him. He proceeded from the assumption, shared by almost no one else outside the Seabiscuit camp, that his horse had the speed to take the lead. He advised his friend to do something completely unexpected and perhaps unprecedented: When jockey Charley Kurtsinger launched War Admiral in his final drive for the wire, Woolf should let him catch up.

14   Pollard was sure that if Woolf let War Admiral challenge him, Seabiscuit would run faster and try harder than if Woolf attempted to hold the lead alone. "Maybe you would call it a kind of horse psychology," he explained. "Once a horse gives Seabiscuit the old look-in-the-eye, he begins to run to parts unknown. He might loaf sometimes when he's in front and think he's got a race in the bag. But he gets gamer and gamer the tougher it gets."

"But risks must be   15   It was an enormous risk. If Pollard was wrong about Seabiscuit, then his strat-
taken because the   egy would hand the victory to War Admiral. But Woolf recognized that his friend
greatest hazard in life   understood the horse better than he did. He came to view the race as Pollard did,
is to risk nothing."   as a test of toughness, and he had never seen a horse as tenacious as Seabiscuit.
                              "Seabiscuit's like a hunk of steel—Solid. Strong.," he once said. "Admiral has speed,
—Dear Abby   good speed . . . speed when unopposed. But he's not game." Of Seabiscuit he said,
                              "You could kill him before he'd quit."

16   Woolf agreed to do exactly what Pollard told him to do. He and Smith brought Seabiscuit to Pimlico and went to work.

17   As race day approached, the names War Admiral and Seabiscuit were on everyone's lips. Even President Roosevelt was swept up in the fervor. A rumor that he was going to "denounce one of the horses" during a Fireside Chat made the rounds, but he kept his allegiance secret. "The whole country is divided into two camps," wrote Dave Boone in the *San Francisco Chronicle*. "People who never saw a horse race in their lives are taking sides. If the issue were deferred another week, there would be a civil war between the War Admiral Americans and the Seabiscuit Americans."

18   In the track offices, horsemen gathered for the post-position draw. Both horses' handlers wanted the rail, which, if the horse could hold it, would ensure the shortest trip around the track. If Seabiscuit got the rail, the experts believed he might have a glimmer of a chance. If War Admiral got it, they believed the race would be over before it began.

19   War Admiral drew the rail.

20   On the day of the race, a Tuesday, a vast, agitated throng banged against Pimlico's fences six hours before the start. All morning long, automobiles and special trains disgorged thousands of passengers from every corner of the nation and the world.

21   By race time the grandstand and clubhouse were full to bursting, and the infield was packed with the overflow crowd. Fans stood upon every rooftop, fence, tree limb, and telephone pole as far as a mile from the start, hoping to catch a glimpse of the race.

22   Reporters massed by the railings in the press box. War Admiral was the toast of the newsmen; every single *Daily Racing Form* handicapper had picked him to win, as had some 95 percent of the other sportswriters. Only a small and militant sect

of California writers was siding with Seabiscuit. War Admiral was also the heavy favorite in the betting, but reporters mingling in the crowd found that most race-goers were rooting for the underdog.

23   At 4 p.m. the two horses and their riders stepped onto the track before a crowd, wrote sportswriter Grantland Rice, "keyed to the highest tension I have ever seen in sport, the type of tension that locks the human throat."

24   It took two tries to get the race started. First Woolf pulled Seabiscuit out of the walk-up because something felt wrong to him. Then War Admiral unraveled at the starting line, whirling in circles.

"No animal admires another animal."

—Blaise Pascal

25   They lined up for the third time. Seabiscuit and War Admiral walked up to the starting line together. The flagman's hand hovered high in the air, and then the flag flashed down as the strangely hushed track clanged with the sound of the bell. War Admiral and Seabiscuit burst off the line at precisely the same instant.

26   For thirty yards, the two horses hurtled down the track side by side, their strides settling into long, open lunges, their speed building and building.

27   A pulse of astonishment swept over the crowd. War Admiral, straining with all he had, was losing ground. First Seabiscuit's nose forged past him—then his throat, then his neck. War Admiral was kicking so hard that his hind legs appeared to be thumping into his girth, but he couldn't keep up.

28   An incredible realization sank into Charley Kurtsinger's mind: *Seabiscuit is faster.* Up in the press box, the California contingent roared.

29   After a sixteenth of a mile, Seabiscuit was half a length ahead and screaming along. He kept pouring it on, flicking his ears forward. The spectators were in a frenzy.

30   Kurtsinger was shell-shocked. His lips were pulled back and his teeth clenched. In a few seconds, Woolf and Seabiscuit had stolen the track from him, nullifying his post-position edge and his legendary early speed. Kurtsinger didn't panic. War Admiral, though outfooted, was running well, and he had a Triple Crown winner's staying power. Seabiscuit was going much, much too fast for so grueling a race. He couldn't possibly last.

31   As the two horses banked into the first turn, Woolf remembered Pollard's advice to reel Seabiscuit in. He eased back ever so slightly on the reins and felt the horse's stride shorten. With nothing but the long backstretch ahead of him, Woolf carried out Pollard's instructions. Edging Seabiscuit a few feet out from the rail, he tipped his head back and called back to Kurtsinger: "Hey, get on up here with me! We're supposed to have a horse race here! What are you doing lagging back there?"

32   Bounding forward in a gigantic rush, War Admiral slashed into Seabiscuit's lead. A shout rang out in the crowd, "Here he comes! Here he comes!" Woolf heard the wave of voices and knew what was happening. In a few strides, War Admiral swooped up alongside him. A few more, and he was even. Kurtsinger thought: *I'm going to win it.* The grandstand was shaking.

33   The horses stretched out over the track. Their strides, each twenty-one feet in length, fell in perfect sync. The speed was impossible; at the mile mark, a fifteen-year-old track record fell under them, broken by nearly a full second. The track rail hummed up under them and unwound behind.

34   The stands were boiling over. Spectators were fainting by the dozens. As 40,000 voices shouted them on, War Admiral found something more. He thrust his head in front.

35   Woolf glanced at War Admiral's beautiful head, sweeping through the air like a sickle. He could see the depth of the colt's effort in his large amber eye, rimmed in crimson and white. "His eye was rolling in its socket as if the horse was in agony," Woolf later recalled.

36   Woolf dropped low over the saddle and called into Seabiscuit's ear, asking him for everything he had. Seabiscuit gave it to him. War Admiral tried to answer, clinging

to Seabiscuit for a few strides, but it was no use. He slid from Seabiscuit's side as if gravity were pulling him backward. Seabiscuit's ears flipped up. Woolf made a small motion with his hand.

37   "So long, Charley." He had coined a phrase that jockeys would use for decades.

38   When he could no longer hear War Admiral's hooves beating the track, Woolf looked back. He saw the black form some thirty-five feet behind, still struggling to catch him. Woolf felt a stab of empathy. "I saw something in the Admiral's eyes that was pitiful," he would say later. "He looked all broken up. I don't think he will be good for another race. Horses, mister, can have crushed hearts just like humans."

39   The Iceman straightened out and rode for the wire, his face down. Seabiscuit sailed into history four lengths in front, running easy.

40   Up in the hospital, Red Pollard greeted reporters with a rhyme:

"The weather was clear, the track fast
War Admiral broke first and finished last."

"Well, what did you think of it?" one asked him.

"Seabiscuit did just what I'd thought he'd do," Pollard said. "He made a rear admiral out of War Admiral."

An envelope from Woolf arrived. Inside was $1,500, half the jockey's purse.

From Laura Hillenbrand, *Seabiscuit: An American Legend,* New York: Ballantine Books, 2001, pp. xvii–xix, 257, 259–260, 267–277. Copyright © 2001 by Laura Hillenbrand. Used by permission of Random House, Inc.

Comprehension Checkup

Multiple Choice

Write the letter of the correct answer in the blank provided.

_____ 1. The author suggests all of the following about drawing the rail position *except*
   a. If the horse can hold it, the rail position ensures the shortest trip around the track
   b. If War Admiral drew the rail, track experts believed the race could not be won by Seabiscuit
   c. Seabiscuit did not like to run along the inside rail
   d. The handlers of Seabiscuit and the handlers of War Admiral wanted the rail position

_____ 2. The author suggests all of the following *except*
   a. War Admiral was favored to win by those betting
   b. California writers remained loyal to Seabiscuit
   c. Most racegoers were rooting for War Admiral to win
   d. *Daily Racing Form* handicappers picked War Admiral to win

_____ 3. Jockey Charley Kurtsinger didn't panic when he realized that Seabiscuit was faster because he felt that
   a. War Admiral was running well
   b. Seabiscuit could not possibly maintain that pace throughout the race
   c. He could let Seabiscuit exhaust himself and then run him down
   d. all of the above

_____ 4. As described in paragraph 15, a *tenacious* horse is likely to be
   a. persistent
   b. stubborn

        c. obstinate

        d. all of the above

_____ 5. A *glimmer* of a chance in paragraph 18 refers to

        a. a slight chance

        b. a faint chance

        c. both (a) and (b)

        d. none of the above

True or False

Indicate whether the statement is true or false by writing T or F in the blank provided.

_____ 6. The race was so exciting that many fans watching the action unfold beneath them fainted.

_____ 7. At one point in the race, Charley Kurtsinger thought he was going to win.

_____ 8. A person who gives in easily is displaying a lot of *grit*.

_____ 9. A synonym for *sleek* is "rough."

_____ 10. Red Pollard and Charley Kurtsinger were best friends.

Sequence

Number the sentences in the order in which they occurred in the reading selection.

_____ An envelope from Woolf arrives with $1,500 inside.

_____ Woolf talks strategy with Pollard, who is still in the hospital recuperating.

_____ It took two tries to get the race started.

_____ War Admiral drew the rail.

_____ Seabiscuit sailed into history four lengths in front, running easy.

_____ Red Pollard injures his leg.

_____ After a sixteenth of a mile, Seabiscuit was half a length ahead and screaming along.

_____ War Admiral thrust his head in front.

_____ Charles Howard, automobile magnate, bought Seabiscuit cheap.

_____ War Admiral and Seabiscuit burst off the line at precisely the same instant.

_____ A crowd gathers six hours before the official start of the race.

Matching

Match the quotation with the speaker. Write the letter of the speaker in the appropriate blank. (Some speakers will be used more than once.)

        A. Charles Howard

        B. Red Pollard

        C. George Woolf

        D. Dave Boone

_____ 1. "If the issue were deferred another week, there would be a civil war between the War Admiral Americans and the Seabiscuit Americans."

_____ 2. "So long, Charley."

_____ 3. "Once a horse gives Seabiscuit the old look-in-the-eye, he begins to run to parts unknown."

_____ 4. "He made a rear admiral out of War Admiral."

_____ 5. "But you don't have to rebuild the heart when it's already there, big as all outdoors."

_____ 6. "His eye was rolling in its socket as if the horse was in agony."

_____ 7. "He'll run his heart out for you."

_____ 8. "You could kill him before he'd quit."

_____ 9. "The weather was clear, the track was fast, War Admiral broke first and finished last."

_____ 10. "Horses, mister, can have crushed hearts just like humans."

Vocabulary in Context

Look through the paragraph indicated in parentheses to find a word that matches the definition below.

1. a state of great confusion; agitation (paragraph 1)   _____

2. struggling helplessly (2)   _____

3. silent, refraining from speech (2)   _____

4. a person of great importance in a particular field (3)   _____

5. of or pertaining to a horse (7)   _____

6. domineering in a haughty manner (8)   _____

7. to idle away time (14)   _____

8. passion; zeal (17)   _____

Internet Activity

Racetracks make money from people betting on horse races, sometimes from gamblers who have become addicted to betting. To learn more about betting addictions, visit the website of Gamblers Anonymous at

www.gamblersanonymous.org

Take their twenty-question test to determine whether you have a gambling problem.
    To listen to radio broadcasts of some of Seabiscuit's races, check out the following PBS website:

www.pbs.org/wgbh/amex/seabiscuit

SELECTION

Excerpt from **_Living with Art_**   _by Rita Gilbert_

"Bonheur frequented the horse-trading fairs and slaughterhouses in order to gain intimate knowledge of animal anatomy."

Getting the Picture

Rosa Bonheur, the nineteenth century's leading painter of animals, is the most famous woman artist of her time. She realistically portrayed sheep, cows, tigers, wolves, and other animals. The underlying theme of Bonheur's work is "human-ity's union with nature." When someone criticized her by saying, "You are not fond of society," Bonheur replied, "That depends on what you mean by society. I am never tired of my brute friends." Bonheur, the daughter of an artist, began to study at the Louvre at 14 and soon eclipsed her father and her siblings, also artists. Throughout her lengthy career, she received many honors, including the Cross of the French Legion. Upon presenting this award to Bonheur, the Empress of France declared "genius has no sex." Bonheur, a nonconformist, was one of the first advo-cates of women's rights.

Brushing Up on Vocabulary

sidesaddle   a saddle for women. The rider sits facing forward with both feet on the left side of the horse.

puritanical   very strict in moral or religious matters; rigidly austere. The original Puritans were a group of Protestants who wanted to purify the Church of England in the sixteenth century by eliminating Roman Catholic trappings.

Buffalo Bill   William F. Cody was a frontier scout, soldier, and showman in the nineteenth century. Nicknamed *Buffalo Bill,* he began his successful Wild West Show in the 1880s. The show toured the United States, Canada, and Europe, presenting mock battles between Native Americans and the U.S. cavalry.

Rosa Bonheur (1822–1899)

1   For people who recognize her name, an automatic word-association is "horses." Schoolchildren often are shown reproductions of her monumental painting *The Horse Fair.* But a closer look at this artist, one of the most successful and deco-rated of her time, reveals there is much more to Rosa Bonheur than horses.

2   The name Bonheur means "happiness," and during most of her life the artist seems to have enjoyed a good deal of that. Born in 1822 and christened Rosalie, she was the eldest child of Raimond Bonheur, a painter and art teacher, and Sophie Marquis Bonheur, who had been his pupil. All four of the Bonheur children became artists, but Rosalie—who later changed her signature to Rosa—was the standout. She earned her first money as an artist at age twelve; at nineteen she exhibited at the Salon, the annual showing of professional artists in Paris. Over the next several years Bonheur would exhibit frequently, win increasingly prestigious awards, and gar-ner many commissions from buyers.

3   In her teens Bonheur formed a close friendship with Nathalie Micas, the daughter of one of her father's friends. The two women would eventually establish a home together, and they lived as companions until Micas's death in 1889. Meanwhile, Bonheur was beginning to attract considerable attention—part admiring, part scandalized—for her eccentric ways.

"The object of art is to give life a shape."

—Jean Anouilh

4   Bonheur frequented the horse-trading fairs and slaughterhouses in order to gain intimate knowledge of animal anatomy. On these excursions she dressed in male clothing—a practice so unusual for women in her day that she needed a special license from the police to avoid arrest. She rode horses astride, rather than in the "ladylike" sidesaddle, and smoked cigars or a pipe. Surprisingly, in view of her shock-ing conduct, Bonheur was welcomed and admired by the Empress Eugenie of France and even by that most puritanical of monarchs, Queen Victoria of England.

5   The house Bonheur and Micas shared was at Fontainebleau, near Paris. There they collected a menagerie that at various times included lions, an otter, sheep, goats, an ostrich, plus numerous horses and dogs. All the animals seem to have had the run of the place—even the lions, which would follow Bonheur around like pussycats.

The artist loved them and painted them; it was said that Micas could entrance the creatures with her gaze, so they would hold still for Bonheur to catch their likeness.

6   By 1887, at the age of sixty-five, Bonheur was financially and professionally secure. Her work was represented in many fine collections. Micas's death two years later was a severe blow. Only one event raised her spirits, and that was the arrival in Paris of the American showman Colonel William Cody, known as "Buffalo Bill," with his touring Wild West show. Long an admirer of America in general and the American West in particular, Bonheur was fascinated by Buffalo Bill's "cowboys and Indians" extravaganza. She made a great many sketches, entertained Buffalo Bill at her studio, and painted him on a prancing white horse.

7   When Bonheur was seventy-six, a young American painter, Anna Klumpke, arrived to make a portrait of the aging artist. Klumpke stayed on and soon earned her mentor's intense devotion. Just about a year later Rosa Bonheur died, quietly, of lung congestion. She was buried alongside Nathalie Micas, but she left her estate to Anna Klumpke.

8   Rosa Bonheur's life was one of passion, of great individuality—a life with art. Near the end, she described it this way: "Art is a tyrant. It demands heart, brain, soul, body. . . . I wed art. It is my husband, my world, my life dream, the air I breathe. I know nothing else, feel nothing else, think nothing else."

From Rita Gilbert, *Living with Art*, 5th ed., New York: McGraw-Hill, 1998, p. 455. Copyright © 1998 McGraw-Hill. Reprinted by permission of The McGraw-Hill Companies, Inc.

Comprehension Checkup

True or False

Indicate whether the statement is true or false by writing T or F in the blank provided.

_____   1.   The article suggests that Bonheur had a highly successful and lucrative career.

_____   2.   The author implies that the entire Bonheur family was involved in art.

_____   3.   Despite Bonheur's unconventional lifestyle, she was welcomed by royalty.

_____   4.   The animals at Fontainebleau were confined to the yard of Bonheur's property.

_____   5.   The author implies that the lions behaved tamely around Bonheur.

_____   6.   When Bonheur was sixty-nine, her long-time companion died.

_____   7.   Before her death, Bonheur served as a mentor to Anna Klumpke.

_____   8.   The author implies that Bonheur spent most of her life with one woman as her sole companion.

_____   9.   Art was an all-consuming passion for Bonheur.

_____   10.   The author believes that Bonheur's fame rests entirely on her ability to depict horses.

Vocabulary in Context

Indicate whether the words in italics are used correctly or incorrectly in the following sentences by writing C or I in the blanks provided.

_____   1.   Breathing is so *automatic* that most of us don't even think about it.

_____   2.   It was such a *monumental* work of art that nobody paid the slightest attention to it.

_____ 3. Elvis Presley was a *standout* in his live performances.

_____ 4. A university becomes *prestigious* when few people want to attend it.

_____ 5. Meryl Streep has *garnered* numerous awards for acting.

_____ 6. The art teacher received a *commission* to do a bronze sculpture of Justice Sandra Day O'Connor.

_____ 7. People will be *scandalized* if you follow the rules of polite behavior.

_____ 8. The *eccentric* gentleman behaved unconventionally.

_____ 9. Ashley's mother maintained a *menagerie* of animals in her house.

_____ 10. My boss is a real *tyrant*—she makes me stay at work later than everybody else.

In Your Own Words

1. The author mentions some of the difficulties that Bonheur needed to overcome to pursue her chosen career as an artist. Discuss some of these difficulties. How did Bonheur deal with them?

2. What can we infer about the character of Bonheur's father? What is his likely view of education?

3. Why were there so few women artists in the nineteenth century?

Internet Activity

You can view some of Rosa Bonheur's paintings on the following website.

www.artcyclopedia.com/artists/bonheur_rosa.html

After viewing the paintings, select a favorite. What is it about the painting that appeals to you? Can you infer anything about Bonheur's relationship to either nature or society from this particular work?

TEST-TAKING TIP

Creating Review Tools

Following are some tools you might use to improve your test scores:

To-Do lists—Make a list of the items you need to study for your test. Check each item off as you study it.

Flash Cards—Make 3 × 5 flash cards to test yourself. To learn vocabulary, for example, on one side of the card write the word you need to know, and on the other write the definition. Or, to study for a test, on one side write a review question, and on the other write the answer. Carry the cards with you. You will be surprised at the many opportunities you will have for studying them, such as when you are standing in line at the bank.

Summary Sheets—Create summary sheets by going through your lecture notes and text underlinings and jotting down the key points on a piece of paper. Quiz yourself on these key points by asking yourself to recall what is on the sheet.

Question-and-Answer Sheets—Create question-and-answer sheets by folding a piece of paper in half or using the front and the back of the paper to create tests for yourself. Then test yourself by trying to come up with the right answer to the question or even the right question for the answer.

Figurative Language

6

© Banco de Mexico Trust. Photo: Schalkwijk / Art Resource, NY

The Two Fridas
(1939)*
BY FRIDA KAHLO

*To see this work of art in
color, turn to the color
insert following page 260.

Frida Kahlo is known for her highly personal paintings. She often chose to represent her physical pain and her relationship with her husband, muralist Diego Rivera, using symbolic images. The painting above is meant to illustrate two contradictory sides of her personality.

1 How is the Frida on the left dressed? The Frida on the right? What is the difference in posture and in the way each is seated?

2 Why do you think the Frida on the left has a bleeding heart?

3 The Frida on the right is holding a locket showing Rivera as a small boy. The Frida on the left is holding a pair of scissors. What might these objects represent?

4 The two images of her are divided yet also united. In what ways are the two Fridas united?

218

Types of Figurative Language

Figurative language (or figures of speech) compares two or more unlike things directly or indirectly. Similes make the comparison directly, metaphors and personification—indirectly.

Similes use *like, as,* or *as if* to make the comparison. Look at the following example and see if you can identify the simile.

> "Silence fell while we both cooled down. I knew we would, we always did. Coming apart and coming together, like pigeons fussing on a street corner. It had been like this for as long as I could remember. He had raised me himself, in this shop."

Lisa Scottoline, *Running from the Law*, Harpertorch, 1996, p. 24. Copyright © 1996 by Lisa Scottoline. Reprinted by permission of HarperCollins Publishers, Inc.

In the example above, the settling of disagreements is compared to the actions of a flock of pigeons. The differences between the two things are readily apparent, but the similarities between the two enable the reader to come to a better understanding of the situation being described. Most of us have seen how pigeons interact. While they may separate momentarily, they soon come back together again. With a little imagination, the reader now better understands how the two individuals in the example respond to each other.

A **metaphor** compares two unlike things without using *like, as,* or *as if*. In a metaphor, one thing is spoken of as though it were something else. Now look at the following example of a metaphor:

> At 81, he is a prune—old, dried up, and wrinkly, but still sweet in the middle.

In this case, an old man is being directly compared to a prune.

Personification is figurative language that assigns human attributes or feelings to a nonhuman object. Authors use personification to make their writing clearer or more vivid. Look at the following example:

> In a hurry to get to California, Marcus set his speedometer at 85 and the car *gobbled* up the road before him.

A car is incapable of gobbling. This use of personification tells us that the car is moving very quickly.

Read the following example and locate the figures of speech:

> "[W]hen I spotted the Hamiltons, they struck me as the king, queen, and jack of diamonds. Satisfied and privileged, face cards all, nestled in a corner of this exclusive Main Line restaurant."

Scottoline, *Running from the Law*, p. 43

1. In the sentences above, what are the Hamiltons being compared to?

   _____

2. What are the similarities between the two things being compared?

   _____

3. What implications can be drawn about the Hamiltons from this comparison?

   _____

4. What are the author's likely feelings toward the Hamiltons?

   _____

Exercise 1: Identifying Similes, Metaphors, and Personification

Indicate whether the comparison being made uses a simile, metaphor, or personification by writing **S**, **M**, or **P** in the blank provided.

_____   1. My life is like a broken bowl. (Christina Rossetti)

_____   2. "Hope" is the thing with feathers that perches in the soul. (Emily Dickinson)

_____   3. I'm a riddle in nine syllables. (Sylvia Plath)

_____   4. A's had once come running. (William Goldman)

_____   5. To the north is the Gila River, small and timid most of the year. (Sandra Day O'Connor)

_____   6. The world is a glass overflowing with water. (Pablo Neruda)

_____   7. The sea awoke at midnight from its sleep. (Henry Wadsworth Longfellow)

_____   8. Oh my love is like the melody that's sweetly played in tune. (Robert Burns)

_____   9. The rain plays a little sleep-song on our roof at night. (Langston Hughes)

_____   10. The alarm clock meddling in somebody's sleep (Gwendolyn Brooks)

_____   11. Papa's hair is like a broom, all up in the air. (Sandra Cisneros)

_____   12. But when the trees bow down their heads, the wind is passing by. (Christina Rossetti)

_____   13. They don't walk like ordinary dogs, but leap and somersault like an apostrophe and comma. (Sandra Cisneros)

_____   14. As my mother taught me, life is a marathon. (Maria Shriver)

_____   15. The car as he drives, drifts from lane to lane like a raft on a river. (Joan Aleshire)

_____   16. When the stars threw down their spears and water'd heaven with their tears (William Blake)

Exercise 2: Interpreting Figurative Language

Read the passages below, and answer the questions that follow. (The simile and metaphor are set in italics.)

1   The fog spread over the forest *like a soft veil* shrouding everything. The air was *as dense as chocolate cake* and Mike's breathing sounded laborious to his ears. He had been walking the serpentine path for what seemed like hours caught *like a rat in a maze*. He prayed he was still headed in the right direction. Pictures of food filled his mind and he was as ravenous *as a bear awakening after the long winter's hibernation*. He knew he could sleep for a week.

2   In the fog, the trees loomed above him *as shadowy monsters ready to pounce*. Tree roots *like hidden traps* clutched and clawed at his feet as he stumbled along. *As frightening as a muffled scream*, a night owl's sudden cry pierced the air, causing

him to tremble uncontrollably. The forest *was a labyrinth* from which he might never escape.

3   Suddenly a light beckoned to him from afar. It shimmered in the distance *like the beams from a lighthouse on a dark sea*. The light flickered closer and closer until Monica emerged out of the blackness *like some ghostly apparition*. "Hi," she said. "When Monty came back alone I thought you might be in some sort of trouble."

1.   If the fog covering the forest is like a veil, how good is the visibility? _____

2.   What might the air have in common with chocolate cake? _____

3.   What does being caught *like a rat in a maze* indicate about his ability to escape? _____ Think of a more original comparison of your own. _____

_____

4.   In what way is the forest a labyrinth? Why is Mike afraid of parts of the forest? _____

5.   How do we know the beams of the flashlight were a welcome sight to Mike?

_____

6.   Monty is most probably a _____

Exercise 3: Identifying and Interpreting Figurative Comparisons

Each of the sentences below contains a figurative comparison. In the space provided, identify the real subject, indicate what it is being compared to, and explain the meaning of the sentence. Number 1 has been completed as an example.

1.   Flattery is like cologne water, to be smelt of, not swallowed.
     Subject: <u>flattery</u>

     Compared to: <u>cologne water</u>

     Meaning: <u>Flattery is not to be taken seriously.</u>

2.   In matters of style, swim with the current; in matters of principle, stand like a rock. (Thomas Jefferson)
     Subject: _____

     Compared to: _____

     Meaning: _____

     _____

3.   A good laugh is sunshine in a house.
     Subject: _____

     Compared to: _____

     Meaning: _____

4.   Wealth is like seawater; the more we drink, the thirstier we become. (Arthur Schopenhauer)
     Subject: _____

     Compared to: _____

     Meaning: _____

5. Life is a great big canvas, and you should throw all the paint on it you can. (Danny Kaye)

    Subject: _____

    Compared to: _____

    Meaning: _____

6. Some books are to be tasted; others to be swallowed; and some few to be chewed and digested. (Francis Bacon)

    Subject: _____

    Compared to: _____

    Meaning: _____

7. How sharper than a serpent's tooth it is to have a thankless child! (Shakespeare)

    Subject: _____

    Compared to: _____

    Meaning: _____

8. Success is a ladder which cannot be climbed with your hands in your pockets.

    Subject: _____

    Compared to: _____

    Meaning: _____

9. Marriage is like life in this—that it is a field of battle, and not a bed of roses. (Robert Louis Stevenson)

    Subject: _____

    Compared to: _____

    Meaning: _____

10. Friendship is like a bank account. You can't continue to draw on it without making deposits.

    Subject: _____

    Compared to: _____

    Meaning: _____

Analyzing Figurative Language in Poetry

Symposium   *by Paul Muldoon*

Bio-sketch

Paul Muldoon, winner of the 2003 Pulitzer Prize for Poetry, is an Irish poet known for his "puckish wit." He is currently a professor at Princeton University where he heads the creative writing program. The poem that follows is a "nonsense" poem that plays on proverbs.

> You can lead a horse to water but you can't make it hold
> its nose to the grindstone and hunt with the hounds.
> Every dog has a stitch in time. Two heads? You've been sold
> one good turn. One good turn deserves a bird in the hand.
>
> A bird in the hand is better than no bread.
> To have your cake is to pay Paul.

Make hay while you can still hit the nail on the head.
For want of a nail the sky might fall.

People in glass houses can't see the wood
for the new broom. Rome wasn't built between two stools.
Empty vessels wait for no man.

A hair of the dog is a friend indeed.
There's no fool like the fool
who's shot his bolt. There's no smoke after the horse is gone.

From Paul Muldoon, "Symposium," in *Poems 1968–1998*. Copyright © 2001 by Paul Muldoon. Reprinted by permission of Farrar, Straus & Giroux, Inc.

The proverbs Muldoon "fooled with" are listed below. Try to determine their meaning.

1. You can lead a horse to water but you can't make it drink. _____

   _____

2. Keep your nose to the grindstone. _____

3. You cannot run with the hare and hunt with the hounds. _____

   _____

4. A stitch in time saves nine. _____

5. Two heads are better than one. _____

6. One good turn deserves another. _____

7. A bird in the hand is better than two in the bush. _____

   _____

8. You can't have your cake and eat it too. _____

   _____

9. Make hay while the sun shines. _____

10. For want of a nail the shoe was lost. _____

11. People in glass houses shouldn't throw stones. _____

    _____

12. Rome wasn't built in a day. _____

13. Empty vessels make the most sound. _____

    _____

14. Time and tide wait for no man. _____

    _____

15. A friend in need is a friend indeed. _____

    _____

16. There's no fool like an old fool. _____

17. It's too late to shut the stable door after the horse has bolted. _____

    _____

18. There's no smoke without fire. _____

Internet Activity

As mentioned in his bio-sketch, Paul Muldoon won the Pulitzer Prize for poetry in 2003. The Pulitzer Prizes were founded by Joseph Pulitzer. At his death, Pulitzer left money to fund the prizes that bear his name. The first prizes were awarded in

1917. Go to the Pulitzer Prize website to find out who won the prize for poetry or literature in the year you were born. Can you draw any conclusions about the kinds of written materials that were considered exceptional for that year?

www.pulitzer.org

The First Book   *by Rita Dove*

Getting the Picture

The poem below was inspired by a visit Rita Dove made to her daughter's school. As she visited the classrooms, she realized that many of the children didn't enjoy reading because they were so afraid that they were going to fail. Dove, a voracious reader even as a child, found this very troubling. The poem is an extended metaphor because throughout it Dove compares reading to eating. As a child she said she "chewed" her way through many a book. To her, reading provides pleasure in the same way that delicious food does.

Bio-sketch

Rita Dove is the youngest person ever appointed to the position of poet laureate in the United States. *Thomas and Beulah,* her book of poetry celebrating the lives of her maternal grandparents, won the Pulitzer Prize in 1987. She is currently a professor at the University of Virginia.

> Open it.
>
> Go ahead, it won't bite.
> Well . . . maybe a little.
>
> More a nip, like. A tingle.
> It's pleasurable, really.
>
> You see it keeps on opening.
> You may fall in.
>
> Sure, it's hard to get started;
> remember learning to use
> knife and fork? dig in
> you'll never reach bottom.
>
> It's not like it's the end of the world—
> just the world as you think
>
> you know it.

From Rita Dove, "The First Book," in *On the Bus with Rosa Parks,* W.W. Norton & Company. Copyright © 1999 by Rita Dove. Reprinted by permission of the author.

Explain the meaning of the poem in your own words. How are reading and eating similar?

_____

_____

_____

Internet Activity

The Library of Congress website discusses recent poet laureates and gives a brief history of the award and its purposes. Find out who the current poet laureate is and what that person is doing to promote poetry. How have some of the past poet laureates, including Rita Dove, promoted poetry?

www.loc.gov./poetry/laureate.html

SELECTION

To Be of Use

by Marge Piercy

"I love people who harness themselves, an ox to a heavy cart, who pull like water buffalo."

Getting the Picture

As you are reading the poem, think about what work means to you.

Bio-sketch

Marge Piercy was born in Detroit, Michigan, to a family she characterizes as working class. She was the first member of her family to attend college. The poem "To Be of Use" is her way of expressing gratitude to those who do physical labor such as growing the food that we eat. Piercy has published 15 volumes of poetry, including *Colors Passing Through Us* in 2003. In addition, she has published several novels and a play.

Brushing Up on Vocabulary

amphora a large earthenware storage vessel of Greek and Roman antiquity, having an oval body with two handles extending from below the lip to the shoulder.

"If a man will not work, he will not eat."

—2 Thessalonians 3:10

The people I love the best
jump into work head first
without dallying in the shallows
and swim off with sure strokes almost out of sight.
They seem to become natives of that element,
the black sleek heads of seals
bouncing like half-submerged balls.
I love people who harness themselves, an ox to a heavy cart,
who pull like water buffalo, with massive patience,
who strain in the mud and the muck to move things forward,
who do what has to be done, again and again.

I want to be with people who submerge
in the task, who go into the fields to harvest
and work in a row and pass the bags along,
who are not parlor generals and field deserters
but move in a common rhythm
when the food must come in or the fire be put out.

The work of the world is common as mud.
Botched, it smears the hands, crumbles to dust.
But the thing worth doing well done
has a shape that satisfies, clean and evident.
Greek amphoras for wine or oil,

Hopi vases that held corn, are put in museums
but you know they were made to be used.
The pitcher cries for water to carry
and a person for work that is real.

From Marge Piercy, "To Be of Use," in *Circles on the Water: Selected Poems by Marge Piercy*.
Copyright © 1982 by Marge Piercy. Reprinted by permission of Alfred A. Knopf, Inc.

✔ Comprehension Checkup

Multiple Choice

Write the letter of the correct answer in the blank provided.

_____ 1. This poem implies that
    a. a life of leisure is better than a life of work
    b. work that is worth doing has its own intrinsic value
    c. strenuous labor should be avoided
    d. people should begin working when they are young

_____ 2. The speaker of the poem has little respect for people who
    a. direct others from the sidelines
    b. escape doing their fair share
    c. are above doing menial labor
    d. all of the above

_____ 3. A person who "jumps in head first"
    a. avoids difficult labor
    b. is ready and willing to go to work
    c. is reckless
    d. is a slow starter

_____ 4. The phrase "natives of that element" refers to people who
    a. are experiencing something foreign to them
    b. are in their natural environment
    c. make things seem easy
    d. both (b) and (c)

_____ 5. The phrase "dallying in the shallows" refers to people who are
    a. unable to swim
    b. prompt and courteous
    c. making only a half effort
    d. having fun

_____ 6. The ox image is used to describe
    a. people who avoid heavy labor
    b. people who need a lot of personal freedom
    c. people who are willing to exert themselves to accomplish some-
       thing
    d. people who are so slow they can't accomplish anything

_____ 7. The harvest image is used to describe
    a. people who hold back hoping someone else will do it
    b. people who are willing to work for others
    c. people who like to work by themselves
    d. people who are natural leaders

_____ 8. In "To Be of Use" the speaker is describing
    a. a philosophy about the importance of useful work
    b. a close friend

      c. an imaginary world

      d. the importance of taking it easy

_____ 9. The expression "common as mud" means

      a. rare

      b. everywhere

      c. disgusting

      d. lacking in value

_____ 10. The overall feeling of the poem is one of

      a. alarm

      b. high spirits

      c. seriousness

      d. sadness

In Your Own Words

1. In the poem, what do the references to Greek amphoras and Hopi vases tell us about work?

2. What is the meaning of the last two lines of the poem?

3. What does the author mean when she says, "The work of the world is common as mud"?

The Art of Writing

In a brief essay, respond to the item below.

What does this poem say about people and work? Describe a time when you were involved in work that you found very satisfying. When are you willing to do hard work?

Internet Activity

Do you have a career goal? Have you met with a career counselor to explore possible careers? Pull up your college's website and click on career services or counseling. Find out what services are available to you. Does the website contain an interest inventory? If so, take it to help you decide what sorts of careers match your interests and talents.

    Check out http://www.careerpath.com and print a want ad for a job that looks appealing to you.

Analyzing Figurative Language in Fiction

Excerpt from _Caramelo_   _by Sandra Cisneros_

"The ocean bottom is ridged like the roof of a mouth and disappears beneath your feet sometimes when you least expect it."

Getting the Picture

The following excerpt takes place in Acapulco, a tourist resort on the west coast of Mexico. The excerpt is from _Caramelo,_ a semiautobiographical story of an extended family whose life alternates between Mexico and the United States. As you read "Acapulco," note Cisneros's use of figurative language.

Bio-sketch

Sandra Cisneros was born and raised in Chicago, the daughter of a Mexican father and a Mexican American mother. Cisneros is the recipient of numerous awards for her critically acclaimed poetry and fiction. Her best-known work is *The House on Mango Street*, the story of a young girl growing up in a Hispanic neighborhood in Chicago. Before becoming a full-time writer, Cisneros was a teacher and counselor to high school dropouts.

Brushing Up on Vocabulary

palapas   small round tables with palm umbrellas usually located around a pool or on a beach. Tourists often like to sit at *palapas* and sip cold drinks.

Acapulco

1   Beyond la Caleta bay, the ring of green mountains dipping and rising like the ocean. And beyond that, sky bluer than water. Tourists yelling in Spanish, and yelling in English, and yelling in languages I don't understand. And the ocean yelling back in another language I don't know.

2   I don't like the ocean. The water frightens me, and the waves are rude. Back home, Lake Michigan is so cold it makes my ankles hurt, even in summer. Here the water's warm, but the waves wash sand inside my bathing suit and scratch my bottom raw. La Caleta is supposed to be the good beach, but I stay out of the water after the ocean tries to take me.

3   The froth of the waves churning and rolling and dragging everything in sight. I make sand houses where the sand is muddy and sucks at my feet, because the dry sand is so hot it burns. The ocean foam like the *babas* of a monkey, little bubbles that turn from green, to pink, and snap to nothing.

4   Candelaria, wearing a shell necklace, weaves a rose for me out of strips of braided palm fronds.

5   "Where did you learn how to do that?"

6   "This? I don't know. My hands taught me."

> *"Leisure is being allowed to do nothing."*
>
> —G.K. Chesterton

7   She puts the rose in my hat and runs into the ocean. When she moves into the deep water her skirt billows out around her like a lily pad. She doesn't wear a bathing suit. She wears her street clothes, an old blouse and a skirt gathered up and tucked in her waistband, but even like this, bobbing in the water, she looks pretty. Three tourists drinking coconut drinks in the shade of the palm-leaf *palapas* sing a loud Beatles song, "I Saw Her Standing There." Their laughter all across the beach like seagulls.

8   "Cande, watch for sharks!"

9   The ocean bottom is ridged like the roof of a mouth and disappears beneath your feet sometimes when you least expect it. That's why I have to shout to Candelaria to be careful when she wades out in the deeper water. The Acapulco water, salty and hot as soup, stings when it gets in your eyes.

10   "Lalita! Come on in."

11   "No, the water's mean."

12   "Don't be a silly-silly. Come on." Her voice against the roar of ocean, a small chirping.

13   "Noooo!"

14   "And if I throw you in, then what?"

15   We've been to la Roqueta island across the bay on a glass-bottom boat, and on the way there we've seen the underwater statue of la Virgen de Guadalupe all made of gold. We saw the donkey that drinks beer on la Roqueta beach. And we've seen the cliff divers at la Quebrada and the sunset at los Hornos where the ocean is out

16   Candelaria wearing her shell necklace and jumping with each wave, is brown as anybody born here, bobbing in the water. Sunlight spangling the skin of water and the drops she splashes. The water shimmering, making everything lighter. You could float away, like sea foam. Over there, just a little beyond reach. Candelaria sparkling like a shiny water bird. The sun so bright it makes her even darker. When she turns her head squinting that squint, it's then I know. Without knowing I know.

17   This all in one second.

18   Before the ocean opens its big mouth and swallows.

From Sandra Cisneros, "Un Recuerdo," in *Caramelo*, New York: Alfred A. Knopf, 2002, pp. 76–78. Copyright © 2002 by Sandra Cisneros. Published by Vintage Books in paperback in 2003 and originally in hardcover by Alfred A. Knopf, Inc. Reprinted by permission of Susan Bergholz Literary Services, New York, NY. All rights reserved.

Identify the figurative language that Cisnernos uses to describe the ocean. What is the overall effect of her description? What human attributes does Cisneros attribute to the ocean?

_____

_____

_____

_____

_____

_____

Analyzing Figurative Language In Nonfiction

SELECTION

Why Leaves Turn Color in the Fall   *by Diane Ackerman*

"Sunlight rules most living things with its golden edicts. When the days begin to shorten . . . a tree reconsiders its leaves."

Getting the Picture

A **literary allusion** is a reference to an event or person appearing in another literary work. Writers use allusions to quickly express complex thoughts or evoke images or reactions. In this sense, they are much like symbols. To fully understand a literary work containing allusions, you need to be able to recognize and understand the allusions that appear in it. Sometimes, research must be done to discover the meaning of an allusion. In the excerpt below, Diane Ackerman makes a literary allusion when she refers to Adam and Eve, the first man and woman on earth according to the Bible.

Bio-sketch

Ackerman's writing style is unique for its mixture of scientific concepts and poetic imagery. This style reflects her educational background. An English major as an undergraduate, she went on to complete an M.A. and a Ph.D. at Cornell University in science-related subjects. In 1991, she published *A Natural History of the Senses*. This was followed by the *Natural History of Love* in 1994, *A Slender Thread: Rediscovering Hope at the Heart of Crisis* in 1997, and *Cultivating Delight* in 2001. Ackerman is presently a professor of English at Cornell University.

Brushing Up on Vocabulary

stealth   secret, hidden; sly, sneaky.

macabre   gruesome and horrible. The *danse macabre* is an allegorical story in which Death leads humankind in a dance to the grave.

edict   a command or order.

petiole   the stalk that connects a leaf of a flowering plant to the plant stem.

photosynthesis   the process by which green plants (those containing chlorophyll) use the energy in sunlight to synthesize sugars and other organic molecules from carbon dioxide and water. Photosynthesis releases oxygen as a byproduct. *Photo* means "light" and *synthesis* means "put together or combine."

xylem   conducting tissue that transports water in plants.

carnal   of the flesh, natural; material or worldly.

mute   silent.

capricious   tending to change abruptly without apparent reason, unpredictable.

1   The stealth of autumn catches one unaware. Was that a goldfinch perching in the early September woods, or just the first turning leaf? A red-winged blackbird or a sugar maple closing up shop for the winter? Keen-eyed as leopards, we stand still and squint hard, looking for signs of movement. Early-morning frost sits heavily on the grass, and turns barbed wire into a string of stars. On a distant hill, a small square of yellow appears to be a lighted stage. At last the truth dawns on us: Fall is staggering in, right on schedule, with its baggage of chilly nights, macabre holidays, and spectacular, heart-stoppingly beautiful leaves. Soon the leaves will start cringing on the trees, and roll up in clenched fists before they actually fall off. Dry seed pods will rattle like tiny gourds. But first there will be weeks of gushing color so bright, so pastel, so confettilike, that people will travel up and down the East Coast just to stare at it—a whole season of leaves.

2   Where do the colors come from? Sunlight rules most living things with its golden edicts. When the days begin to shorten, soon after the summer solstice on June 21, a tree reconsiders its leaves. All summer it feeds them so they can process sunlight, but in the dog days of summer the tree begins pulling nutrients back into its trunk and roots, pares down, and gradually chokes off its leaves. A corky layer of cells forms at the leaves' slender petioles, then scars over. Undernourished, the leaves stop producing the pigment chlorophyll, and photosynthesis ceases. Animals can migrate, hibernate, or store food to prepare for winter. But where can a tree go? It survives by dropping its leaves, and by the end of autumn only a few fragile threads of fluid-carrying xylem hold leaves to their stems.

3   A turning leaf stays partly green at first, then reveals splotches of yellow and red as the chlorophyll gradually breaks down. Dark green seems to stay longest in the veins, outlining and defining them. During the summer, chlorophyll dissolves in the heat and light, but it is also being steadily replaced. In the fall, on the other hand, no new pigment is produced, and so we notice the other colors that were always there, right in the leaf, although chlorophyll's shocking green hid them from

view. With their camouflage gone, we see these colors for the first time all year, and marvel, but they were always there, hidden like a vivid secret beneath the hot glowing greens of summer.

4   An odd feature of the colors is that they don't seem to have any special purpose. Animals and flowers color for a reason—adaptation to their environment—but there is no adaptive reason for leaves to color so beautifully in the fall any more than there is for the sky or ocean to be blue. It's just one of the haphazard marvels the planet bestows every year. We find the sizzling colors thrilling, and in a sense they dupe us. Colored like living things, they signal death and disintegration. In time, they will become fragile and, like the body, return to dust. They are as we hope our own fate will be when we die: not to vanish, just to sublime from one beautiful state into another. Though leaves lose their green life, they bloom with urgent colors, as the woods grow mummified day by day, and Nature becomes more carnal, mute, and radiant.

5   We call this season "fall," from the Old English *feallan*, to fall, which leads back through time to the Indo-European *phol*, which also means to fall. So the word and the idea are both extremely ancient, and haven't really changed since the first of our kind needed a name for fall's leafy abundance. Fall is the time when leaves fall from the trees, just as spring is when flowers spring up, summer is when we simmer, and winter is when we whine from the cold.

6   Children love to play in piles of leaves, hurling them into the air like confetti, leaping into soft unruly mattresses of them. For children, leaf fall is just one of the odder figments of Nature, like hailstones or snowflakes. Walk down a lane overhung with trees in the never-never land of autumn, and you will forget about time and death, lost in the sheer delicious spill of color. Adam and Eve concealed their nakedness with leaves, remember? Leaves have always hidden our awkward secrets.

7   But how do the colored leaves fall? As a leaf ages, the growth hormone, auxin, fades, and cells at the base of the petiole divide. Two or three rows of small cells, lying at right angles to the axis of the petiole, react with water, then come apart, leaving the petioles hanging on by only a few threads of xylem. A light breeze, and the leaves are airborne. They glide and swoop, rocking in invisible cradles. They are all wing and may flutter from yard to yard on small whirlwinds or updrafts, swiveling as they go. Firmly tethered to earth, we love to see things rise up and fly— soap bubbles, balloons, birds, fall leaves. They remind us that the end of a season is capricious, as is the end of life.

Diane Ackerman, "Why Leaves Turn Color in the Fall", from *Natural History of the Senses* by Diane Ackerman. Copyright © 1990 by Diane Ackerman. Used by permission of Random House, Inc.

Comprehension Checkup

Drawing on what you learned in the chapter, answer the following questions.

1.   In the first paragraph, to what is barbed wire compared? _____

     To what is our vision compared? _____

     To what are dry seed pods compared? _____

2.   Throughout the first paragraph, Ackerman uses personification to describe the coming fall. List at least five examples. _____

     _____

     _____

3.   Look at Ackerman's use of personification in paragraph 2. Taken together, what do these images convey about nature? _____

     _____

4. To what is Ackerman referring when she speaks of a "vivid secret"?

    _____

    _____

5. How do the "sizzling" colors "dupe" us? What do the colors actually represent?

    _____

    _____

6. What figurative expressions does the author use to depict the falling leaves?

    _____

7. How can the end of a season and the end of life both be "capricious"?

    _____

Internet Activity

Fall colors provide us with one of nature's most beautiful displays. For information about the best time to see the colored leaves in your area, visit the USDA Forest Service website at

www.fs.fed.us/news/fallcolors/

The Use of Symbols

A **symbol** is a person, object, or event that stands for something beyond its literal meaning. A good symbol captures in a simple form a more complicated reality. For example, a white dove symbolizes peace, a skull symbolizes death, a flag symbolizes a country's values and aspirations, and a black cat crossing our path symbolizes bad luck. Writers use symbols to create a mood, to reinforce a theme, or to communicate an idea.

See if you can identify the following icons. What does each icon symbolize?

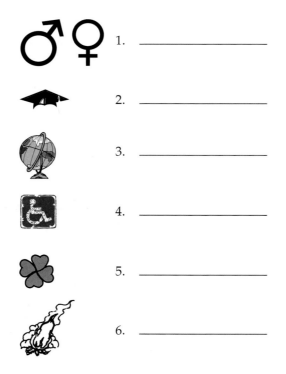

1. _____

2. _____

3. _____

4. _____

5. _____

6. _____

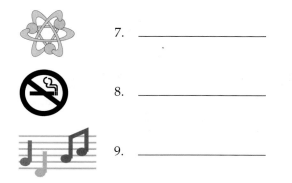

7. _____

8. _____

9. _____

Color Communication

"Languages are the pedigree of nations."

—Samuel Johnson

1   When you're in debt, you speak of being "in the red"; when you make a profit, you're "in the black." When you're sad, you're "blue"; when you're healthy, you're "in the pink"; and when you're jealous, you're "green with envy." To be a coward is to be "yellow" and to be inexperienced is to be "green." When you talk a great deal, you talk "a blue streak"; and when you are angry, you "see red." As revealed through these timeworn clichés, language abounds in color symbolism.

2   Colors vary greatly in their meanings from one culture to another. Think about the meanings your own culture gives to such colors as red, black, white, blue, yellow, and purple.

Color	Cultural Meanings and Comments
Red	In China red symbolizes prosperity and rebirth and is used for festive and joyous occasions; in France and the United Kingdom, masculinity; in many African countries, blasphemy or death; and in Japan, anger and danger. Red ink, especially among Korean Buddhists, is used only to write a person's name at the time of death or on the anniversary of the person's death, and so problems result when American teachers use red ink to mark the homework of Korean Buddhists.
Green	In the United States, green symbolizes capitalism, initiative, and envy; in Ireland, patriotism; among some Native Americans, femininity; to the Egyptians, fertility and strength; and to the Japanese, youth and energy.
Black	In Thailand, black symbolizes old age; in parts of Malaysia, courage; and in much of Europe and North America, death.
White	In Thailand, white symbolizes purity; in many Muslim and Hindu cultures, purity and peace; and in Japan and other Asian countries, death and mourning.
Blue	In Iran, blue symbolizes something negative; in Egypt, virtue and truth; in Ghana, joy; among the Cherokee, defeat.
Yellow	In China, yellow symbolizes wealth and authority; in the United States, caution and cowardice; in Egypt, happiness and prosperity, and in many countries throughout the world, femininity.
Purple	In Latin America, purple symbolizes death; in Europe, royalty; in Egypt, virtue and faith; in Japan, grace and nobility; and in China, barbarism.

3   There is some evidence that colors affect us physiologically. For example, respiratory movements increase in the presence of red light and decrease in the presence of blue light. Similarly, eye blinks increase in frequency when eyes are exposed

4

to red light and decrease when exposed to blue. This seems consistent with our intuitive feelings that blue is more soothing and red more provocative. After changing a school's walls from orange and white to blue, the students' blood pressures decreased and their academic performance improved.

Colors surely influence our perceptions and behaviors. People's acceptance of a product, for example, is largely determined by its package. For example, among consumers in the United States the very same coffee taken from a yellow can was described as weak, from a dark brown can it was described as too strong, from a red can it was described as rich, and from a blue can it was described as mild. Even our acceptance of a person may depend on the colors worn. Consider, for example, the comments of one color expert: "If you have to pick the wardrobe for your defense lawyer heading into court and choose anything but blue, you deserve to lose the case. . . ." Black is so powerful that it can work against the lawyer with the jury. Brown lacks sufficient authority. Green will probably elicit a negative response.

From Joseph A. DeVito, in *Essentials of Human Communication*, 3rd ed., New York: Addison Wesley Longman, 1999, pp. 131–133. Published by Allyn and Bacon, Boston, MA. Copyright © 1999 by Pearson Education. Reprinted by permission of the publisher.

See how many of the following phrases you can complete with the appropriate color word below. (Some color words will be used more than once.)

black	brown	gray	pink	rose
blue	gold	green	red	silver

1. He is in a _____ mood.
2. The little boy was good as _____.
3. Mike is true _____.
4. The movie star got the _____-carpet treatment.
5. Every cloud has a _____ lining.
6. People who drink too much are said to see _____ elephants.
7. He looks at the world through _____-colored glasses.
8. Nora is a good gardener. She has a _____ thumb.
9. Silence is _____en.
10. I'm going to _____-bag my lunch.
11. The police caught him _____-handed.
12. Jeff is the _____ sheep of the family.
13. He was beaten _____ and _____.
14. Play some more of those _____en oldies.
15. He's very smart. He has lots of _____ matter.
16. There's too much _____ tape involved.

Imagery

In addition to the figures of speech discussed earlier, writers also use **imagery** to create word pictures. Imagery is language that has a sensory quality. It can appeal to any of the five senses—sight, sound, taste, touch, and smell. A good reader must not only be able to recognize imagery, but also understand the author's intent in presenting it.

Analyzing Imagery

Excerpt from Pilgrim at Tinker Creek *by Annie Dillard*

"At the end of the island I noticed a small green frog. He was exactly half in and half out of the water, looking like a schematic diagram of an amphibian, and he didn't jump."

Getting the Picture

Identify the instances of imagery in the following paragraphs. What senses do they primarily appeal to? What overall effect does the imagery evoke? Also pay attention to Dillard's use of figurative language—what similes and metaphors does she use?

Bio-sketch

Annie Dillard was born in 1945 in Pittsburgh, Pennsylvania, and received her B. A. and M. A. degrees from Hollins College in Roanoke, Virginia. She has received numerous awards for her writings, which include essays, poetry, memoirs, literary criticism, and even a western novel. The following selection is taken from *Pilgrim at Tinker Creek,* for which she received the 1975 Pulitzer Prize for General Nonfiction. This book was the result of Dillard's stay on Tinker Creek in Virginia's Roanoke Valley, where she observed the natural world while exploring the subjects of theology, philosophy, and science. Many have compared this work to Thoreau's *Walden.*

Brushing Up on Vocabulary

ruck   fold, wrinkle, or crease.

enzymes   proteins originating from body cells that produce chemical changes such as paralysis.

Heaven and Earth in Jest

1   A couple of summers ago I was walking along the edge of the island to see what I could see in the water, and mainly to scare frogs. Frogs have an inelegant way of taking off from invisible positions on the bank just ahead of your feet, in dire panic, emitting a froggy "Yike!" and splashing into the water. Incredibly, this amused me, and, incredibly, it amuses me still. As I walked along the grassy edge of the island, I got better and better at seeing frogs both in and out of the water. I learned to recognize, slowing down, the difference in texture of the light reflected from mud-bank, water, grass, or frog. Frogs were flying all around me. At the end of the island I noticed a small green frog. He was exactly half in and half out of the water, looking like a schematic diagram of an amphibian, and he didn't jump.

2   He didn't jump; I crept closer. At last I knelt on the island's winterkilled grass, lost, dumbstruck, staring at the frog in the creek just four feet away. He was a very small frog with wide, dull eyes. And just as I looked at him, he slowly crumpled and began to sag. The spirit vanished from his eyes as if snuffed. His skin emptied and drooped; his very skull seemed to collapse and settle like a kicked tent. He was shrinking before my eyes like a deflating football. I watched the taut, glistening skin on his shoulders ruck, and rumple, and fall. Soon, part of his skin, formless as a pricked balloon, lay in floating folds like bright scum on top of the water:

it was a monstrous and terrifying thing. I gaped bewildered, appalled. An oval shadow hung in the water behind the drained frog; then the shadow glided away. The frog skin bag started to sink.

3

"The whole of nature is a conjugation of the verb to eat in the active and the passive."

—Dean William R. Inge

I had read about the giant water bug, but never seen one. "Giant water bug" is really the name of the creature, which is an enormous, heavy-bodied brown beetle. It eats insects, tadpoles, fish, and frogs. Its grasping forelegs are mighty and hooked inward. It seizes a victim with these legs, hugs it tight, and paralyzes it with enzymes injected during a vicious bite. That one bite is the only bite it ever takes. Through the puncture shoot the poisons that dissolve the victim's muscles and bones and organs—all but the skin—and through it the giant water bug sucks out the victim's body, reduced to a juice. This event is quite common in warm fresh water. The frog I saw was being sucked by a giant water bug. I had been kneeling on the island grass; when the unrecognizable flap of frog skin settled on the creek bottom, swaying. I stood up and brushed the knees of my pants. I couldn't catch my breath.

Annie Dillard, *Pilgrim at Tinker Creek*, New York: HarperCollins, 1974 pages 5–6 from "Heaven and Earth in Jest" by Annie Dillard. Copyright © 1974 by Annie Dillard. Reprinted by permission of HarperCollins Publishers Inc.

Comprehension Checkup

Drawing on what you learned from the selection, answer the following questions.

1. To what does Dillard compare the frog's collapse in the second paragraph?

    _____

    _____

2. What overall image is created by Dillard's figures of speech?

    _____

3. What does Dillard mean when she describes the frog as looking like "the schematic drawing of an amphibian"?

    _____

4. At the end of her encounter with the giant water bug, why was Dillard unable to catch her breath?

    _____

Vocabulary in Context

Look through the paragraph indicated in parentheses to find a word that matches the definition below.

1. terrible; desperate (paragraph 1) _____

2. uttering (1) _____

3. tightly drawn, not slack (2) _____

4. stared with open mouth as in wonder (2) _____

Internet Activity

Visit the site below to learn more about the giant water bug described above and see a picture of one.

www.insects.org/entophiles/hemiptera/hemi_005.html

In what culture are these bugs considered to be a delicacy?

Review Test 6 Main Ideas and Supporting Details, Transition Words, Vocabulary in Context, and Imagery

Excerpt from **Frida**   *by Hayden Herrera*

"But among the iron rods of the train, the handrail broke and went through Frida from one side to the other at the level of the pelvis."

Getting the Picture

This excerpt from Hayden Herrera's novel about the artist Frida Kahlo (see p. 218) gives both Kahlo's and her friend Alejandro Gomez Arias's accounts of the accident that changed her life. She spent over a month in the hospital and endured many operations. Doctors were amazed that she survived. As Kahlo told Arias, "death dances over my bed at night." Bedridden for over three months, she learned to paint when her mother attached a portable easel and a mirror to her bed so that she could be her own model.

Bio-sketch

Biographer/historian Hayden Herrera has lectured widely, curated several exhibitions of art, taught Latin American art at New York University, and was awarded a Guggenheim Fellowship. She is the author of numerous articles and reviews for such publications as *The New York Times*. In addition to *Frida*, her books include *Frida Kahlo: The Paintings, Mary Frank,* and *Matisse: A Portrait*. Frida Kahlo's life story is depicted in the movie *Frida*, starring Salma Hayek as the artist and Alfred Molina as her husband, the renowned Mexican muralist Diego Rivera. The movie, released in 2002, is based on Hayden Herrera's biography of Frida Kahlo.

Brushing Up on Vocabulary

toreador   a term for a bullfighter or matador; the term *toreador* (from the Spanish *torear,* to bait a bull) was first used by the French composer Georges Bizet in his opera *Carmen*.

lesion   an injury to the body tending to result in impairment or loss of function.

contusion   a bruise; an injury to the underlying tissue without the skin being broken.

Accident and Aftermath

1   It was one of those accidents that make a person, even one separated by years from the actual fact, wince with horror. It involved a trolley car that plowed into a flimsy wooden bus, and it transformed Frida Kahlo's life.

2   Far from being a unique piece of bad luck, such accidents were common enough in those days in Mexico City to be depicted in numerous *retablos* (small votive paintings offering thanks to a holy being, usually the Virgin, for misfortunes escaped). Buses were relatively new to the city, and because of their novelty they were jammed with people while trolley cars went empty. Then, as now, they were driven with toreador bravado, as if the image of the Virgin of Guadalupe dangling near the front

3

window made the driver invincible. The bus in which Frida was riding was new, and its fresh coat of paint made it look especially jaunty.

The accident occurred late in the afternoon on September 17, 1925, the day after Mexico had celebrated the anniversary of its independence from Spain. A light rain had just stopped; the grand gray government buildings that border the Zocalo looked even grayer and more severe than usual. The bus to Coyoacan was nearly full, but Alejandro and Frida found seats together in the back. When they reached the corner of Cuahutemotzin and 5 de Mayo and were about to turn onto Calzada de Tlalpan, a trolley from Xochimilco approached. It was moving slowly but kept coming as if it had no brakes, as if it were purposely aiming at a crash. Frida remembered:

4

A little while after we got on the bus the collision began. Before that we had taken another bus, but since I had lost a little parasol, we got off to look for it and that was how we happened to get on the bus that destroyed me. The accident took place on a corner in front of the San Juan market, exactly in front. The streetcar went slowly, but our bus driver was a very nervous young man. When the trolley went around the corner the bus was pushed against the wall.

5

I was an intelligent young girl, but impractical, in spite of all the freedom I had won. Perhaps for this reason, I did not assess the situation nor did I guess the kind of wounds I had. The first thing I thought of was a *ballero* [Mexican toy] with pretty colors that I had bought that day and that I was carrying with me. I tried to look for it, thinking that what had happened would not have major consequences.

6

It is a lie that one is aware of the crash, a lie that one cries. In me there were no tears. The crash bounced us forward and a handrail pierced me the way a sword pierces a bull. A man saw me having a tremendous hemorrhage. He carried me and put me on a billiard table until the Red Cross came for me.

7

When Alejandro Gomez Arias describes the accident, his voice constricts to an almost inaudible monotone, as if he could avoid reliving the memory by speaking of it quietly:

8

The electric train with two cars approached the bus slowly. It hit the bus in the middle. Slowly the train pushed the bus. The bus had a strange elasticity. It bent more and more, but for a time it did not break. It was a bus with long benches on either side. I remember that at one moment my knees touched the knees of the person sitting opposite me, I was sitting next to Frida. When the bus reached its maximal flexibility it burst into a thousand pieces, and the train kept moving. It ran over many people.

9

I remained under the train. Not Frida. But among the iron rods of the train, the handrail broke and went through Frida from one side to the other at the level of the pelvis. When I was able to stand up I got out from under the train. I had no lesions, only contusions. Naturally the first thing I did was to look for Frida.

10

Something strange had happened. Frida was totally nude. The collision had unfastened her clothes. Someone in the bus, probably a house painter, had been carrying a packet of powdered gold. This package broke, and the gold fell all over the bleeding body of Frida. When people saw her they cried, *'La bailarina, la bailarina!'* With the gold on her red, bloody body, they thought she was a dancer.

11   I picked her up—in those days I was a strong boy—and then I noticed with horror that Frida had a piece of iron in her body. A man said, 'We have to take it out!' He put his knee on Frida's body, and said 'Let's take it out.' When he pulled it out, Frida screamed so loud that when the ambulance from the Red Cross arrived, her screaming was louder than the siren. Before the ambulance came, I picked up Frida and put her in the display window of a billiard room. I took off my coat and put it over her. I thought she was going to die. Two or three people did die at the scene of the accident, others died later.

12   The ambulance came and took her to the Red Cross Hospital, which in those days was on San Jeronimo Street, a few blocks from where the accident took place. Frida's condition was so grave that the doctors did not think they could save her. They thought she would die on the operating table.

13   Frida was operated on for the first time. During the first month it was not certain that she would live.

14   The girl whose wild dash through school corridors resembled a bird's flight, who jumped on and off streetcars and buses, preferably when they were moving, was now immobilized and enclosed in a series of plaster casts and other contraptions. "It was a strange collision," Frida said. "It was not violent but rather silent, slow, and it harmed everybody. And me most of all."

15   Her spinal column was broken in three places in the lumbar region. Her collarbone was broken, and her third and fourth ribs. Her right leg had eleven fractures and her right foot was dislocated and crushed. Her left shoulder was out of joint, her pelvis broken in three places. The steel handrail had literally skewered her body at the level of the abdomen.

Hayden Herrera, *Frida: A Biography of Frida Kahlo,* New York: HarperCollins, 1983, pp. 47–48. Copyright © 1983 by Hayden Herrera. Reprinted by permission of HarperCollins Publishers Inc.

✔ Comprehension Checkup

Multiple Choice

Write the letter of the correct answer in the blank provided.

_____ 1. Which of the following statements best expresses the main idea of the selection?
a. Frida rode a bus.
b. A handrail broke and went through the pelvis of Frida.
c. Frida sustained severe injuries in a terrible bus accident, but survived.
d. Frida's spinal column was broken.

_____ 2. The author's main purpose is to
a. inform
b. entertain
c. persuade

_____ 3. The main pattern of organization of paragraph 3 is
a. example
b. listing
c. cause and effect
d. chronological order

_____ 4. All of the following statements about the bus are true *except*
　　a. The bus was new
　　b. The bus was fairly empty
　　c. The bus was made of wood
　　d. The bus was headed to Cayoacan

True or False

Indicate whether the statement is true or false by writing T or F in the blank provided.

_____ 5. Mexican Independence Day is September 17.

_____ 6. The bus driver was an anxious older man.

_____ 7. The trolley was electric with two cars.

_____ 8. The doctors were confident that they could save Frida's life.

_____ 9. Frida's right leg and right foot were injured in the accident.

_____ 10. The rods that pierced Frida were part of the bus.

Sequence of Events

Number the events in the order in which they occurred in the reading selection.

_____ a. Frida gets off a bus to look for her parasol.

_____ b. The trolley car plows into Frida's bus.

_____ c. Frida is operated on.

_____ d. Frida begins to hemorrhage.

_____ e. The ambulance comes and picks up Frida.

_____ f. The handrail pierces Frida.

_____ g. Frida is laid on the billiard table.

Vocabulary in Context

Each item below includes a sentence from the selection. Using the context clues provided, write a preliminary definition for the italicized word. Then look up the word in a dictionary and write the appropriate definition.

1. "It was one of those accidents that make a person, even one separated by years from the actual fact, *wince* with horror." (paragraph 1)

   Your definition: _____

   Dictionary definition: _____

2. "Far from being a *unique* piece of bad luck, such accidents were common enough in those days in Mexico City to be *depicted* in numerous retablos (small votive paintings offering thanks to a holy being, usually the Virgin, for misfortunes escaped)." (2)

   Your definition: _____

   Dictionary definition: _____

   Your definition: _____

   Dictionary definition: _____

3. "The bus in which Frida was riding was new, and its fresh coat of paint made it look especially *jaunty*." (2)

   Your definition: _____

   Dictionary definition: _____

4. "When Alejandro Gomez Arias describes the accident, his voice *constricts* to an almost *inaudible monotone,* as if he could avoid reliving the memory by speaking of it quietly:" (7)

   Your definition: _____

   Dictionary definition: _____

   Your definition: _____

   Dictionary definition: _____

5. "The bus had a strange *elasticity*." (8)

   Your definition: _____

   Dictionary definition: _____

6. "Frida's condition was so *grave* that the doctors did not think they could save her." (12)

   Your definition: _____

   Dictionary definition: _____

In Your Own Words

1. What is the overall impression created by this excerpt? What specific images contribute to this impression?

2. What details of the accident scene are clearly depicted? Why are these images particularly sharp or vivid?

Internet Activity

For additional information about Frida Kahlo, explore the following websites:

   www.sfmoma/artworks/3825.html

   www.fbuch.com.fridaby.htm

The first is an interactive website sponsored by the San Francisco Museum of Modern Art. The painting *Frieda and Diego Rivera,* 1931, is in the museum's permanent collection. Study the painting carefully. What do you think Kahlo was trying to express about the couple's relationship in the painting? Did she use any symbols?

   The second website shows many pictures and self-portraits by Kahlo, including a pencil sketch of her version of the accident. Summarize what you learn from the website about Kahlo.

SELECTION

From the Subway to the Streets _____ *by Nina Siegal*

"We all have an identity crisis or something. Why would we have a need to write our names everywhere? Everyone wants to be famous, and our generation is huge on that."

Getting the Picture

Can graffiti be art? Or is it always just vandalism? Why do you think people are willing to take the risk to "tag"? What problems has your city had with graffiti? Has your city recently allowed any graffiti to be painted as "art"?

Bio-sketch

Norma Siegal was born in Manhattan and grew up on Long Island. She received her B.A. from Cornell University in English literature and studied dramatic criticism and the techniques of dramatic composition at Yale University. Siegal began her career as a journalist for the *San Francisco Bay Guardian* and later wrote for various sections of *The New York Times*. Today she writes articles about international art, cultural institutions, and urban life styles for *Bloomberg News* and is an arts correspondent for Bloomberg Radio. She is also writing her first novel.

Brushing Up on Vocabulary

graffiti   markings as initials, slogans, or drawings, written or sketched on a sidewalk, wall, etc., also called "aerosol art." While graffiti, in the form of political or personal slurs, dates back to antiquity, graffiti as an art form began in the late 1960s in Philadelphia and New York City. It includes "wild style" colorful murals, and "scratchiti," a type of etching commonly found on the windows of subway trains.

tag   a graffiti signature, nickname.

tagging   the writing of a *tag* or nickname as often and as artistically as possible.

Tats Cru   a 1980s group of graffiti writers who became commercial artists. They now paint graffiti-style murals on walls for clients like Chivas Regal and Coca-Cola.

1   He swings open a small red gate at the end of the subway platform, ignoring the warning that reads "Do Not Enter or Cross Tracks," and enters the dark tunnel, just west of the Lafayette Avenue station in Clinton Hill, Brooklyn. A green light illuminates the youthful contours of his face as he saunters down the last narrow wedge of forbidden platform.

2   Before the C train has a chance to whip through the station again, he jumps down onto the tracks and crosses the hot rails to an abandoned stretch of line once used for cleaning trains. On a soot-covered wall he has claimed as his own subterranean gallery, he has painted "Made in Brooklyn" in bold silver block letters about three feet tall, next to his graffiti name, or tag, Ader—words meant to be seen from a moving train.

3   Ader, 19, is a member of a new generation carrying on a tradition started almost three decades ago in train yards across New York City. Their style is less ornate than the large, colorful, cartoon-inspired train murals that became a sign of street culture in the 1970s. And as the city has cracked down on graffiti, making it all but impossible to paint on subway cars, young graffiti writers have concentrated their energies on subway tunnels, storefront grates, billboards, the sides of buildings, even the streets themselves.

4   Their tools have changed, too. These days, many writers use rollers to apply buckets of acrylic paint onto walls. Some use small rocks to etch their signatures into train windows. Others write on stickers and post them on mailboxes and lampposts, or use masking tape and spray paint to write on the sidewalk.

5   And graffiti culture, like just about everything else, has entered the information age. Some graffiti writers say they are inspired by pictures of old and new work they find in graffiti magazines, with names like Stress, Submerge, and Third Degree,

or on the Internet. Some even use computer programs to plan their graffiti at home before they hit the streets.

6   Yet the motivations of today's graffiti writers are similar to those of previous generations. For many, the goal is to make a name for themselves in their neighborhoods. Nano, 24, who lives in Jackson Heights, Queens, said he started writing graffiti in 1989 because he wanted to stand out.

7   "We all have an identity crisis or something," he said. "Why would we have a need to write our names everywhere? Everyone wants to be famous, and our generation is huge on that."

8   Many graffiti writers also say they are making a social statement about corporate control of the city's visual landscape. "I think kids are really smart and know how to devour the corporate culture that is thrown at them," said Franklin Sirmans, an independent art curator.

9   Hugo Martinez, the owner of the Martinez Gallery in Chelsea, which has been exhibiting graffiti art since 1972, said: "These kids want to establish a new way of doing things, a new way of looking at identity and property. They want to redefine the world so that their name is on it."

10   They are also rebelling against what many say is authoritarian order. "I see myself as being a true quality-of-life offender," says Ader. "Instead of power to the government, it's power to us."

11   But Ader, who was born in Panama and lives in Fort Greene, Brooklyn, and is studying graphic design at the Pratt Institute, also knows that his hobby is a dangerous one. He said he was once jailed for five days after being arrested for writing graffiti. Like other young graffiti writers, he has honed his approach to suit the times.

12   "I try to do stuff that's more hidden, where it won't get cleaned up too quickly," he said. "A fire escape or a tunnel or a truck or trailer or van." He works only at night, and he works quickly, usually finishing his graffiti, done with house paint and a roller, in 10 or 15 minutes.

13   Though the art world embraced some graffiti writers in the 80s, and some art critics and gallery owners still keep an eye on the subculture, many graffiti writers do not want to be seen as artists. Ader's work has been exhibited in a gallery, yet he does not consider himself an artist. "I'm a graf writer," he said. "I'm just doing it."

14   To city officials, graffiti is vandalism, plain and simple. "I don't get into esthetic arguments," said Agostino Cangemi, chairman of the Mayor's Anti-Graffiti Task Force, which coordinates cleanup and prevention efforts citywide. "If you do any kind of etching or marking on someone else's property without their consent, it's graffiti."

15   Cracking down on graffiti was a priority for the Giuliani administration. Mr. Cangemi said the 10 main city agencies that deal with graffiti spent some $25 million on removal in 1998–99. Arrests of graffiti writers increased to 387 in 1998 from 32 in 1994.

16   Usually writers are charged with a misdemeanor, either making graffiti, possession of graffiti instruments, or criminal mischief. In cases where the act causes more than $250 worth of damage, they can be charged with a felony. Though graffiti writers are sometimes jailed, usually they are fined and required to do community service like cleaning subway cars, the police said.

17   A graffiti writer from Mexico City who calls himself Mosco and came to New York last year in the hopes of tagging subway trains, said the city's crackdown has had a grave impact on graffiti activity. "I've felt it," he said. "Every writer I talk to says, 'Be aware of this, be aware of that.' It's impossible to do large pieces in the city. There is no time and people call the cops."

18   Instead of doing large pieces, Mosco, 21, uses a roller to paint simple block letters on walls in the middle of the night. He said he chose his tag, which means

mosquito in Spanish, because it's "an irritating bug coming in at night and they sting, but it's hard to get them."

19 The death knell for New York's subway art movement, as some fans called it, came in 1989, when Mayor Ed Koch asked the Metropolitan Transportation Authority to pull all defaced trains out of service until they were cleaned. With the advent of stainless steel trains in the mid 1980s, cleanup became easier, and the primary showcase for graffiti writers' work was shut down.

20 Yet some who follow trends in graffiti say that as a result its writers have become more adventurous and innovative. Mr. Martinez, the gallery owner, said: "The streets have taken the place of the trains, and in a way it's more important than the trains. The work on the street is a battle between the privileged and the popular culture, whereas with the subway there was more of a feeling that this property belongs to all of us anyway." And today's graffiti writers, he said, are "more prolific on the streets than the kids in the 70s were on the subways."

21 Hector Nazario, a member of Tats Cru, a group of graffiti writers that opened a graphic arts business in the South Bronx in 1995, producing graffiti-style murals for companies like Coca-Cola and Reebok, agreed. "Once people stopped doing subway cars, it sort of opened up the floodgates and said the whole city's your canvas," he said.

22 Some graffiti writers, including scores of teenagers who come to New York from all over the world, still jump fences at train yards, toting backpacks filled with spray cans, to paint subway cars. Knowing their tags will never run, they snap photos. But many graffiti writers say they are not motivated to paint trains anymore because they know their work will not be seen.

"I want to do it because I want to do it."

—Amelia Earhart

23 Stephen J. Powers, 31, who came to New York in 1995 after a couple of years at art school in Philadelphia and has written a book about the history of graffiti— "The Art of Getting Over: Graffiti at the Millennium"—paints on storefront grates.

24 Powers sidles up to the grates in the light of day, with one to five gallons of oil-based enamel paint in hand, he said, wearing plain street clothes. Then he begins painting. He paints the entire grate, or sometimes several grates on a block, silver or white, covering over everything that has come before. Once the paint is dry, he paints the edges black, then paints black lines and curves into the white or silver backgrounds. Out of the pattern emerges his graffiti name, Espo, which he said stands for Exterior Painting Service Outreach.

25 If anyone stops to ask him what he is doing, Mr. Powers said, he explains, "I'm with Exterior Surface Painting Outreach, and I'm cleaning up this grate." Since it sounds like something official, he said, most people seem to be satisfied.

26 Because some of the grates look tidier when he is finished, Mr. Powers said, he considers his graffiti a kind of public service. (He takes before-and-after photographs to prove the point.) "The neighborhoods get the benefit of my cleaning it up, and I get my name up there," he said.

27 George L. Rodriguez, the chairman of Community Board 1 in the Bronx, said he was opposed to any form of graffiti that defaced public or private property. But some sanctioned graffiti can be positive for a community, he said. Though he has not seen the Espo grates, Mr. Rodriguez said, he did not have a problem with Mr. Powers's cleaning up eyesores. And while he could understand why some people might be upset about Mr. Powers's putting the name Espo on the grates, he said, "All artists put their signature on their work."

28 For Nato, who does most of his painting high up on the sides of buildings, working from rooftops, part of the thrill is getting into hard-to-reach places in the middle of the night. "It's like being a cat burglar, except you're not," he said. "It's a real high." And because he paints in remote spots, he said, his graffiti may be cleaned up less quickly. Indeed, Mr. Cangemi said he sometimes left writing on the

upper levels of buildings and on the sides of elevated subway stations. It is too risky to send city employees or private contractors into some of the dangerous places where graffiti writers go, he said.

29   Yet Nato also favors such locations because they offer esthetic complexity. "I'm into the placement, the scenery behind the wall, the fencing around it," he said.

30   Mr. Martinez, who calls Nato "the rooftop king," said his work represented a new movement in graffiti art, in which writers used surroundings to conceptualize their pieces. "It's an installation, and it's much more inclusionary," he said. "It takes into account the sky, the buildings and the signs and the enclave around his name."

31   For Angel L. Hueca, 20, billboards, walls, and train windows are where he makes his mark. Mr. Hueca, who uses the tag Grin (which he says stands for "getting rich is nada," or nothing), uses a marker or spray paint or scratches his tag into the windows of subway cars by using small rocks. Each etching takes about two minutes, he says, and he does them in empty cars late at night.

32   Some graffiti writers frown on scratching, saying it has little esthetic merit. It also bothers the public, Mr. Cangemi said, and the city is developing a way to cover train windows with plastic to stop scratchers.

33   Although graffiti has been recognized by some in the art world as a legitimate form of expression, it drives many New Yorkers to distraction. Private-property owners call it a scourge and spend millions of dollars each year removing scrawls from their buildings.

34   And the city offers young people places where they can make themselves known without vandalizing public or private property, Mr. Cangemi said. Young artists can submit work to the city for display in subway or advertising slots, for example. And in recent years, nonprofit groups have opened a number of so-called legal walls where graffiti writers can work without fearing arrest.

35   But Mr. Cangemi said legal walls did not work as well as some had hoped because they tended to draw to the neighborhood graffiti writers who then vandalized other property. And the adventurers among the young graffiti writers, like Ader and Nato, say legal walls and city-sponsored art programs are about as enticing as a trip to a suburban mall.

36   The thrill of being an outlaw still draws many young people to graffiti. "You go out on the street at night, and you feel like the city is singing your name," Nato said. "You're out there tagging your name, boom, boom, boom, and you get it, the fever. Everyone who does graffiti gets the fever at some point."

37   The fever keeps burning, despite the crackdown. To those who think that graffiti is dying, Ader has this to say: "I think they must be walking around drinking Nyquil all day. It's everywhere."

From Nina Siegal, "From the Subways to the Streets," *in New York Times,* August 22, 1999 p. CY1. Copyright © 1999 by The New York Times Co. Reprinted with permission.

"Don't let other people tell you what you want."

—Pat Riley

"There are only two stimulants to one's best efforts: the fear of punishment, and the hope of reward."

—John M. Wilson

 Comprehension Checkup

Multiple Choice

Write the letter of the correct answer in the blank provided.

_____ 1. The main idea of the selection is:
a. In the near future, graffiti is likely to be thought of as folk art.
b. Despite the city's crackdown on graffiti, a new generation of graffiti writers flourishes.

    c. The Mayor's Anti-Graffiti Task force has dealt a death blow to graffiti writers.

    d. Graffiti artists want to be known in their neighborhood.

_____ 2. The purpose of the article is to
   a. persuade the reader to report graffiti activity to the authorities
   b. defend the artistic merits of graffiti
   c. discuss the attitudes and values of typical graffiti artists
   d. inform the reader about graffiti as art

_____ 3. Paragraphs 3, 4, and 5 illustrate
   a. how etching has progressed to become a fine art
   b. how risky it is to paint graffiti
   c. how the style, tools, and location of graffiti have changed
   d. how graffiti is valued as an art form

_____ 4. Paragraphs 6 through 10
   a. describe local art galleries
   b. discuss the motivations of graffiti artists
   c. define the word *property*
   d. explain how graffiti artists choose their names

_____ 5. The statement "You feel like the city is singing your name . . ." is an example of
   a. cause and effect
   b. figurative language
   c. literary allusion
   d. inference

_____ 6. The "fever" that Nato speaks of in the last two paragraphs refers to
   a. the thrill of painting graffiti
   b. the tediousness of painting graffiti
   c. the desire to be respectable
   d. the desire to clean up eyesores

_____ 7. Graffiti art is
   a. likely to be of a permanent nature
   b. likely to be of a transitory nature
   c. valued by the public at large
   d. likely to be exhibited in fine establishments

_____ 8. For some graffiti artists who still paint subway cars, pictures of their work are
   a. worth the risk
   b. used by the police as evidence against them
   c. the only evidence they will have of their work
   d. both (a) and (c)

_____ 9. The Giuliani administration responded to the proliferation of graffiti by
   a. making more arrests and spending millions on removal
   b. having guards patrol the premises of key city structures
   c. launching a campaign to narrowly define the term *art*
   d. none of the above

_____ 10. New York City officials regard graffiti as
   a. a bonding activity for young people
   b. a cry of help
   c. a work of art
   d. vandalism

True or False

Indicate whether the statement is true or false by writing T or F in the blank provided.

_____ 1. According to the article, graffiti artists today are less likely to paint on subway cars.

_____ 2. Mosco says that large pieces are not feasible because people are likely to call the police.

_____ 3. Graffiti today is likely to be very ornate.

_____ 4. Graffiti arrests have plummeted since New York began its anti-graffiti campaign.

_____ 5. "Espo" considers his graffiti a kind of public service.

_____ 6. Ader works quickly at night to avoid detection.

_____ 7. Most graffiti offenses are misdemeanors.

_____ 8. Ader considers himself to be an artist in the true sense of the word.

_____ 9. Graffiti can more easily be removed from stainless steel trains.

_____ 10. Stephen J. Powers, an author, likes to paint on storefront grates during the day.

Vocabulary in Context

Indicate whether the words in italics are used correctly or incorrectly in the following sentences by writing C or I in the blanks provided.

_____ 1. Something *ornate* is simple and modest.

_____ 2. A man *defaced* the painting "Guernica" by throwing black paint on it.

_____ 3. The *advent* of summer means that hot weather is coming.

_____ 4. Harper Lee, a *prolific* writer, produced one book, *To Kill a Mockingbird*.

_____ 5. He is known for being an *innovative* artist because he likes to copy the work of others.

_____ 6. Kelly is tired of *toting* her heavy books to school each day.

_____ 7. The skating event was *sanctioned* by the Olympic Committee.

_____ 8. An attic is a *subterranean* room.

_____ 9. The boys *sidled* past the guards and entered the stadium.

_____ 10. The new lighting *illuminates* the room much better.

In Your Own Words

In Phoenix, Arizona, a law was passed banning the sale of spray paint to minors. In addition, the Phoenix Police department created a hotline for reporting graffiti activity, and community groups and blockwatchers painted over graffiti in their neighborhoods weekly. The measures appear to have worked. Of the original 100 "crews" of graffiti artists, it is estimated that only about 10 crews remain. What problems has your city had with graffiti? What has your community done to eradicate graffiti? Why do you think the public in general is so opposed to graffiti?

The Art of Writing

In a brief essay, respond to the item below.

Graffiti is considered by some experts to be an expression of pride, self-worth, and personal affirmation. Others consider it a form of language. What is your opinion? Taking into account your understanding of graffiti, how severe do you think the penalties should be for youthful offenders who tag?

Internet Activity

Want to check out graffiti "art"? Consult the following site, which features a collection of more than 3,000 examples of graffiti gathered from around the world. Be careful, though; some graffiti may contain offensive language or images.

www.graffiti.org

TEST-TAKING TIP

Taking Multiple-Choice Tests

On your next multiple-choice test, try applying these tips:

1. Pay close attention to oral and written directions.

2. Don't spend too much time on any one question. Leave a difficult question blank, put a mark beside it, and then come back to it if time permits.

3. For each question, read through all of the answers before choosing one.

4. Don't change an answer unless you are quite sure you have found a better one.

5. If one of your choices is a combination of two or more answers (such as *both A and B*), remember that both parts of the answer must be correct.

6. A longer answer is more likely to be correct than a shorter answer. It often takes more words to write a correct answer because it may need qualifying phrases to make it correct.

7. Avoid answers with all-inclusive words like *all*, *always*, *everyone*, *none*, and *nobody* because they are likely to be wrong. Any exception makes the answer wrong.

Tone

7

American Gothic,
(1930)*
BY GRANT WOOD

*To see this work of art in color, turn to the color insert following page 260.

1. Notice how the lines of the pitchfork are repeated in the man's shirt front and on the front of his overalls. What might the upright tines of the pitchfork symbolize?

2. The man looks the viewer straight in the eye, while the woman averts her eyes from the viewer and looks at something in the distance. Why might the artist have depicted the woman in this fashion?

3. The painting is frequently caricaturized. (Perhaps you have seen a likeness of it featuring the actor Paul Newman and his daughter Nell on the labels of Newman's Own Organics grocery products.) What qualities might make it a favorite subject of caricaturists?

4. What is the overall tone of the painting?

Inferring Tone

Tone refers to the emotional quality of an article. Just as a speaker's voice can convey a wide range of tones, so can a writer's voice. We infer a speaker's tone by paying attention to such things as word choice, voice volume, and facial expressions. The available clues are more limited when we are trying to infer the tone of a writer's voice. An essay does not speak loudly or softly, it can't frown or smile. If we want to identify the tone of a written work, we can only look at what the author has written. Word choice, phrasing, and subject matter all contribute to the tone of a piece of writing. When you're reading something, it's important for you to be aware of the author's tone. Is the author being humorous or argumentative or both? Is the author expressing outrage or giving praise? Is the author being ironic or earnest? Understanding the tone of a piece of writing is important to understanding its meaning.

A piece of writing can express one or more of a great variety of possible tones. You need to be familiar with some of the more common possibilities. We will begin by identifying the tones of particular statements taken from pieces of writing. These exercises will help you understand tone and will familiarize you with some of the many ways of describing tone. Then we will work on identifying and describing the overall tone of a piece of writing.

The words mentioned below are useful for describing tone. Words on the same line have the same or a similar meaning.

1. excited, stirred up, impassioned

2. loving, affectionate, fond

3. surprised, astonished, amazed, incredulous

4. mournful, sorrowful

5. cruel, brutal, vicious

6. angry, outraged, offended

7. bitter, resentful

8. formal, stiff

9. patronizing, condescending, supercilious

10. cheerful, glad, joyful, ecstatic, elated

11. humorous, funny, amusing, comical, entertaining

12. arrogant, haughty, contemptuous

13. cynical, negative, pessimistic

14. optimistic, positive, encouraging

15. whining, complaining, querulous

16. witty, clever

17. peevish, cross, irritable

18. charming, pleasing, attractive, delightful

19. flattering, fawning, obsequious

20. skeptical, doubtful, questioning

21. scolding, chiding

22. sad, glum

23. dictatorial, domineering, overbearing, tyrannical

24. rude, churlish, boorish
25. compassionate, caring, solicitous
26. self-pitying, self-indulgent
27. alarmed, fearful, anxious
28. critical, disapproving
29. depressed, gloomy, discouraged
30. solemn, grave, somber
31. informal, casual, relaxed
32. objective, neutral, matter-of-fact
33. evasive, secretive, furtive
34. remorseful, regretful
35. scornful, derisive, contemptuous
36. vindictive, vengeful
37. serious, earnest, sober
38. befuddled, confused
39. sarcastic, mocking, sneering
40. admiring, appreciative
41. playful, lively
42. irreverent, disrespectful, impertinent
43. disgusted, offended
44. appreciative, thankful, grateful
45. nostalgic, sentimental, wistful
46. perplexed, puzzled, bewildered
47. contemptuous, disdainful, scornful
48. ambivalent, conflicted, wavering
49. informative, instructive
50. sincere, honest, frank
51. satiric, mocking
52. ironic, tongue-in-cheek

Exercise 1: Identifying Tone

Read the following dialog between a police officer and a speeding motorist. After reading each statement, indicate which word best describes the speaker's tone by writing the appropriate letter in the blank provided.

The Traffic Ticket

_____ 1. Officer: "Lady, what's the matter with you? What took you so long to stop?"
a. casual
b. cross
c. pessimistic

_____ 2. Driver: "Officer, I didn't hear the siren. What's your problem? I know I didn't do anything wrong."
a. sincere
b. vicious
c. disdainful

_____ 3. Officer: "You were speeding."
a. clever
b. matter-of-fact
c. appreciative

_____ 4. Driver: "Me? Speeding? Are you sure?"
a. chiding
b. charming
c. doubting

_____ 5. Officer: "Ma'am, what's wrong with you? Do you have any idea at all how fast you were going?"
a. annoyed
b. vicious
c. appreciative

_____ 6. Driver: "Oh my goodness! How fast *was* I going?"
a. ambivalent
b. alarmed
c. vengeful

_____ 7. Officer: "I have you on the radar gun going 50 miles an hour in a 15-mile-an-hour school zone."
a. admiring
b. playful
c. informative

_____ 8. Driver: "Are you sure Officer? How can that be? I was watching my speedometer."
a. thankful
b. perplexed
c. sneering

_____ 9. Officer: "No doubt about it, lady! Our radar is very accurate."
a. assertive
b. sentimental
c. wavering

_____ 10. Driver: "I'm so sorry, Officer I'm really sorry. I'll be more careful next time."
a. wistful
b. contemptuous
c. remorseful

_____ 11. Officer: "Hand me your driver's license and your registration."
a. ambivalent
b. demanding
c. fawning

_____ 12. Driver: "Yes. Oh my! I can't believe it. I can't find them. I was in such a hurry I must have left them at home."
a. bored
b. cruel
c. bewildered

Traffic School: Some random comments by the officer teaching traffic school two weeks later.

_____ 1. Officer: "Good morning class. Apparently you all couldn't think of anything else to do today, right?"
a. angry
b. humorous
c. elated

_____ 2. Officer: "I want to give you some sobering statistics. Every year traffic accidents kill 43,000 people, injure 2.6 million, and cause 130 billion dollars in damage."
a. self-indulgent
b. grave
c. churlish

_____ 3. Officer: "We *can't* control other drivers, but we *can* control our own behavior."
a. impassioned
b. witty
c. haughty

_____ 4. Officer: "For your safety and the safety of other motorists, *please* think about the consequences of your actions."
a. boorish
b. disapproving
c. imploring

Exercise 2: Identifying Tone in Textbook Material

Read the passages below and choose the word that best describes the speaker's tone by writing the appropriate letter in the blank provided.

_____ 1. Our impact on the health of the oceans is much more profound than we often assume. You can do a lot to help save the oceans. First of all, take care of the environment. If you go to the seashore or go snorkeling or diving, do not disturb in any way the environment. Return any overturned rocks to their original positions. Leave all forms of life where they are. If you go fishing, know the regulations and take only what you really need for food. Return undersized fish. Corals and shells should be left alone, and alive, in their natural home. Be sure to tell merchants you object to their sale of shells, corals, sand dollars, and other marine life, which were most probably collected alive and killed for sale. Don't buy the yellowfin tuna that is caught in nets that trap dolphins. Look for the "dolphin-safe" seal on the label.

From Peter Castro, *Marine Biology*, 3rd ed., New York: McGraw-Hill, 2003, p. 397. Copyright © 2003 McGraw-Hill. Reprinted by permission of The McGraw-Hill Companies, Inc.

a. cynical
b. serious
c. arrogant
d. outraged

_____ 2. Remember the *Leave It to Beaver* reruns on television? Mother would spend the day whisking around the house in a stylish outfit

"Hurt not the earth, neither the sea, nor the trees."

—Revelations 7.3

"The battle for women's rights has been largely won."

—Margaret Thatcher

protected by an apron, tidying and scrubbing and fixing a delicious dinner, and greet Father warmly when he returned from his day at work. Well, times have changed. Or have they? More than 61 percent of married American women are part of the workforce today. But guess who is still tidying and scrubbing and fixing delicious dinners in American homes? Women. And—here's the kicker—*most women seem to think this is fair!*

From Michael Hughes in *Sociology: The Core*, 6th ed., New York: McGraw-Hill, 2002, p. 252. Copyright © 2002 McGraw-Hill. Reprinted by permission of The McGraw-Hill Companies, Inc.

    a. rueful

    b. nostalgic

    c. amazed

    d. scolding

_____ 3. We have seen that anorexia is a serious disease with deep-seated causes and devastating, potentially fatal effects. Julie was one of those who couldn't beat anorexia. She died when she was only 17. We will never go to college together and share a dorm room. She will never fulfill her dream of becoming a nurse. And we will never grow old living beside each other and watching our kids grow up together. Anorexia killed my beautiful vibrant friend.

From Stephen E. Lucas in *The Art of Public Speaking*, 7th ed., New York: McGraw-Hill, 2001, p. 358. Copyright © 2001 McGraw-Hill. Reprinted by permission of The McGraw-Hill Companies, Inc.

    a. sorrowful

    b. angry

    c. loving

    d. whining

_____ 4. Our math classroom is on the third floor of a building that overlooks the top floor of a parking ramp. At most three or four cars are parked up there, although it contains enough space for at least fifty cars. The lower levels of the ramp are also fairly empty. The ramp is only for the use of faculty. We students have to park some distance from campus and even then we have to get to school by 7:30 in the morning if we are to find a parking space. . . . I think the current situation is disgusting. The faculty already enjoy many privileges, including "faculty restrooms," which are distinctive from those simply labeled "restroom." Enough is enough!

From Michael Hughes in *Sociology: The Core*, 6th ed., New York: McGraw-Hill, 2002, p. 171. Copyright © 2002 McGraw-Hill. Reprinted by permission of The McGraw-Hill Companies, Inc.

    a. outraged

    b. vindictive

    c. pessimistic

    d. alarmed

_____ 5. If you are beginning to think that being computer illiterate may be occupational suicide, you are getting the point. Workers in every industry come in contact with computers to some degree. Even burger flippers in fast-food chains read orders on computer screens. Nearly 80 percent of the respondents to a 1999 survey said that they believe it is impossible to succeed in the job market without a working knowledge of technology. Respondents who earned $45,000 a year or more were three times more likely to use a computer than those who earned less. As information technology eliminates old jobs while creating new ones, it is up to you to learn the skills you need to be certain you aren't left behind.

    a. excited

    b. bitter

    c. cautious

    d. serious

_____ 6. I honestly feel Robert can contribute more than I can. He's better educated. He's just plain smarter. He's genuinely gifted, and when he's able to apply himself, he can really accomplish something, can make a name for himself.

    a. critical

    b. sympathetic

    c. candid

    d. sentimental

_____ 7. "Anna, I told you to stop talking. If I've told you once, I've told you 100 times. I told you yesterday and the day before that. The way things are going, I'll be telling it to you all year, and, believe me, I'm getting pretty tired of it. And another thing, young lady. . ."

    a. ironic

    b. sorrowful

    c. scolding

    d. playful

_____ 8. Ever wonder how schools get their names—and which names are the most popular? The National Education Resource Center researched the most popular proper names for U.S. high schools: Washington, Lincoln, Kennedy, Jefferson, Roosevelt (both Franklin and Teddy), and Wilson. (Presidents do well.) (To date, no school has chosen Richard M. Nixon as a namesake.) But proper names are not the most common high school names. Directions dominate: Northeastern, South, and Central High School are right up there. While creativity obviously is not a criterion, politics is. Citizens fight over whether schools should be named after George Washington—who, after all, was a slaveholder. And, considering how many women are educators, it is amazing that so few schools are named to honor women. Some schools have honored writers or reflect local leaders and culture. In Las Vegas, you will find schools named Durango, Silverado, and Bonanza, which some complain sound more like casinos than western culture.

    a. affectionate

    b. flippant

    c. optimistic

    d. outraged

_____ 9. It's Saturday morning, and you are helping clean out your grandmother's attic. After working a while, you stumble upon a trunk, open it, and discover inside hundreds of old postcards. Thinking about getting to the football game on time, you start tossing the cards into the trash can. Congratulations! You have just thrown away a year's tuition.

From Stephen E. Lucas, *The Art of Public Speaking*, 7th ed., New York: McGraw-Hill, 2001, p. 215.

    a. elated
    b. regretful
    c. sarcastic
    d. demanding

_____ 10. When the expectant mother drinks, alcohol is absorbed into her bloodstream and distributed throughout her entire body. . . The fetus is surrounded by the same alcoholic content as its mother had. After being drowned in alcohol, the fetus begins to feel the effect. But it can't sober up. It can't grab a cup of coffee. It can't grab a couple of aspirin. For the fetus's liver, the key organ in removing alcohol from the blood, is just not developed. The fetus is literally pickled in alcohol.

From Stephen E. Lucas, *The Art of Public Speaking*, 7th ed., New York: McGraw-Hill, 2001, p. 263. Copyright © 2001 McGraw-Hill. Reprinted by permission of The McGraw-Hill Companies, Inc.

    a. carefree
    b. aghast
    c. casual
    d. congratulatory

Exercise 3: Determining Tone in Literature

Read the following excerpts and indicate the tone of the passage. (You may refer to the list of words at the beginning of the chapter.)

1. I could've been somebody, you know? my mother says and sighs. She has lived in this city her whole life. She can speak two languages. She can sing an opera. She knows how to fix a TV. But she doesn't know which subway train to take to get downtown. I hold her hand very tight while we wait for the right train to arrive.

    She used to draw when she had time. Now she draws with a needle and thread, little knotted rosebuds, tulips made of silk thread. Someday she would like to go to the ballet. Someday she would like to see a play. She borrows opera records from the public library and sings with velvety lungs powerful as morning glories.

    Today while cooking oatmeal she is Madame Butterfly until she sighs and points the wooden spoon at me. I could've been somebody, you know? Esperanza, you go to school. Study hard. That Madame Butterfly was a fool. She stirs the oatmeal. Look at my *comadres*. She means Izaura, whose husband left, and Yolanda, whose husband is dead. Got to take care all your own, she says shaking her head.

    Then out of nowhere:

    Shame is a bad thing, you know. It keeps you down. You want to know why I quit school? Because I didn't have nice clothes. No clothes, but I had brains.

Yup, she says disgusted, stirring again. I was a smart cookie then.

The tone is _____

What clues did you use to determine the tone? _____

_____

2.   My Rules

If you want to marry me, here's what you'll have to do
You must learn how to make a perfect chicken dumpling stew
And you must sew my holey socks and you must soothe my
troubled mind
And develop the knack for scratching my back
And keep my shoes spotlessly shined
And while I rest you must rake up the leaves
And when it is hailing and snowing
You must shovel the walk, and be still when I talk
And—hey, where are you going??

Shel Silverstein from *Where the Sidewalk Ends*

The tone is _____

What clues did you use to determine the tone? _____

_____

3.   I was glad enough when I reached my room and locked out the mold and the darkness. A cheery fire was burning in the grate, and I sat down before it with a comforting sense of relief. For two hours I sat there, thinking of bygone times; recalling old scenes, and summoning half-forgotten faces out of the mists of the past; listening, in fancy, to voices that long ago grew silent for all time, and to once familiar songs that nobody sings now.

I slept profoundly, but how long I do not know. All at once I found myself awake, and filled with a shuddering expectancy. All was still. All but my own heart—I could hear it beat. Presently the bedclothes began to slip away slowly toward the foot of the bed, as if someone were pulling them! I could not stir; I could not speak.

The tone is _____

What clues did you use to determine the tone? _____

4.   Attention, techno-weenies. Stop littering the info highway. Don't call a grammatical time-out when you log on. English is English, whether it comes over the phone, via the Postal Service (excuse me, "snail mail"), or on the Internet.

Let's clean up cyberspace, gang. You wouldn't use *pls* for *please*, *yr* for *your*, or *thnx* for *thanks* in a courteous letter. So why do it on the Net? You don't shout or whisper on the telephone. So why use ALL CAPITAL or all lowercase letters in your e-mail? Making yourself hard to read is bad "netiquette."

And another thing. IMHO (in my humble opinion), those abbreviations like CUL (see you later) and BTW (by the way) are overused. You're too busy for full sentences? So what are you doing with the time you're saving by using cute shortcuts? Volunteering at your local hospital? Sure. I'm ROFL (rolling on floor laughing).

You digerati can speak E-lingo among yourselves, but try real English if you want the cyber-impaired to get it. Next time you log on, remember there's a person at the other end, not a motherboard. Use appropriate grammar and punctuation. Be clear and to the point. And consider phoning once in a while.

From Patricia T. O'Conner, *Woe Is I*, New York: Riverhead Books, 1996, p. 126.

The tone is _____

What clues did you use to determine the tone? _____

_____

5. At precisely 5:30 in the morning, a bearded man in khaki trousers, a flannel shirt, and a string tie strode to the end of the dock and announced through a megaphone: "Bass anglers, prepare for the blast-off!" In unison, the fishermen turned their ignitions, and Lake Maurepas boiled and rumbled and swelled. Blue smoke from the big outboards curled skyward and collected in an acrid foreign cloud over the marsh. The boats inched away from the crowded ramp and crept out toward where the pass opened its mouth to the lake. The procession came to a stop at a lighted buoy.

"Now the fun starts," said a young woman standing next to R.J. Decker. She was holding two sleeping babies.

The starter raised a pistol and fired into the air. Instantly a wall of noise rose off Maurepas: the race was on. The bass boats hiccuped and growled and then whined, pushing for more speed. With the throttles hammered down, the sterns dug ferociously and the bows popped up at such alarming angles that Decker was certain some of the boats would flip over in midair. Yet somehow they planed off perfectly, gliding flat and barely creasing the crystal texture of the lake. The song of the big engines was that of a million furious bees; it tore the dawn all to hell.

It was one of the most remarkable moments Decker had ever seen, almost military in its high-tech absurdity: forty boats rocketing the same direction at sixty miles per hour. In darkness.

Most of the spectators applauded heartily.

"Doesn't anyone ever get hurt?" Decker asked the woman with the two babies, who were now yowling.

"Hurt?" she said. "No, sir. At that speed you just flat-out die."

From Carl Hiaasen, *Double Whammy*, p. 129. Copyright © 1988 by Carl Hiaasen. Used by permission of Penguin Putnam Group (USA) Inc.

In the passage above, the term *blast-off* is used to convey the seriousness of this sport. Normally, the term is associated with what Florida activity? _____

_____

What kind of figurative language is the author using when he says the boats "hiccuped, growled, and whined"? _____

What kind of figurative language is the author using when he likens the sound of the boats to bees? _____

Why does the start of the race seem like a military operation? _____

_____

What can you infer about the author's feelings toward this sport? _____

_____

Exercise: Detecting Tone

Daughter's Friend Is a Boy   *by Art Buchwald*

Getting the Picture

In this particular article, Art Buchwald writes about an issue of propriety or morality that sometimes arises between parents and their college-age children.

Bio-sketch

Buchwald is one of the foremost humorists in the United States today. His job, as he sees it, is to expose us to our failings as human beings and members of society. Buchwald has written numerous books and is also a regular contributor to a syndicated newspaper column. He is also the recipient of the Pulitzer Prize. Currently residing in Washington, D.C., he frequently pokes fun at the activities on Capitol Hill.

Brushing Up on Vocabulary

separate but equal   refers to keeping one group apart from another but giving both groups equal opportunities or resources. In 1954, in the famous case of *Brown* v. *Board of Education,* the U.S. Supreme Court declared that states may not maintain a system of separate but equal schools for whites and African Americans.

Read each item and then choose the word that best describes the tone of each speaker.

In the good old days, when your daughter said she was bringing home a friend for the weekend, it meant she was bringing home a girlfriend—and when your son said he was bringing home a friend for the weekend, it was a boy. This is not the case anymore, and it is causing houseguest problems throughout the country.

I was over at Ripley's house the other evening, when his daughter, Joan, arrived home for the weekend with her "friend," a tall strapping fellow named Mickey.

_____ 1. "Oh, my goodness! Oh, my goodness! said Mrs. Ripley. "Well, Mickey, I guess you want to put your things away."
   a. detached
   b. flustered
   c. pessimistic

_____ 2. Joan, pointing down the hallway, instructed, "Put them in my room."
   a. evasive
   b. diplomatic
   c. dictatorial

_____ 3. "M-m-m-Mickey can s-s-sleep in the attic," said Mrs. Ripley.
   a. distressed
   b. prayerful
   c. sentimental

_____ 4. Joan's mouth fell open. "Why can't he sleep in my room?"
a. cheerful
b. loving
c. astonished

_____ 5. Mr. Ripley blew up. "Because I know he'd rather sleep in the attic."
a. joyful
b. angry
c. evasive

_____ 6. Mickey: "Thank you very much. That's really very nice of you, but Joan's room is fine with me."
a. elated
b. polite
c. alarmed

_____ 7. Mr. Ripley snarled, "Well, it isn't fine with me! Listen here Mickey. We need to talk to Joan alone."
a. gentle
b. conciliatory
c. harsh

_____ 8. Joan began crying. "How could you humiliate me in front of my friend?"
a. sorrowful
b. resigned
c. apathetic

_____ 9. Mrs. Ripley said solicitously, "How did we humiliate you, honey?"
a. excited
b. bored
c. concerned

_____ 10. Joan: "By asking Mickey to sleep in the attic when you know perfectly well there are two beds in my room."
a. cheerful
b. evasive
c. matter-of-fact

_____ 11. "My dear girl," Mr. Ripley huffed, "it's not a question of the number of beds. Perhaps you don't realize, but there's a certain propriety about people sharing rooms when they're not married."
a. outraged
b. amused
c. wry

_____ 12. Joan looked blankly at them and said, "What propriety could there possibly be?"
a. baffled
b. puzzled
c. both (a) and (b)

_____ 13. Mrs. Ripley: "Sweetheart, calm down. I know we're old-fashioned and out-of-date, but your father and I get very nervous when we know two unmarried people of the opposite sex are in the same room under our roof."
a. mocking
b. placating
c. accusatory

Bicolored Rooster with the cross of Lorraine (1945)

PABLO PICASSO

"Every child is an artist. The problem is how to remain an artist once he grows up."
—Pablo Picasso

View and Reflect

In your journal, consider why most children do not grow up to be artists.

The Scholar (1926)

Norman Rockwell

"Education is not the filling of a pail, but the lighting of a fire."—William Butler Yeats

View and Reflect

Based on both the quotation and the painting here, write a journal entry in which you consider what makes a student successful.

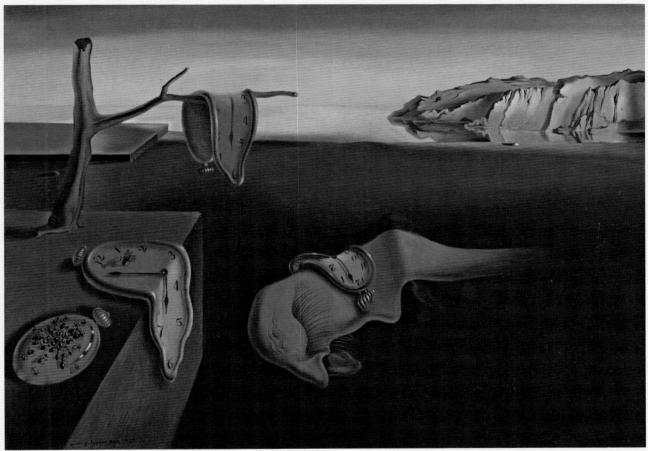

The Persistence of Memory (1931)

SALVADOR DALI

"Nothing really belongs to us but time, which even he has who has nothing else."
—Baltasar Gracian

View and Reflect

In your journal, consider how both the quotation and the painting here emphasize
the importance of time.

The Oath of the Horatii (1784)

JACQUES-LOUIS DAVID

"Every artist dips his brush into his own soul, and paints his own nature into his pictures."—Henry Ward Beecher

View and Reflect

Write a journal entry in which you consider the author's purpose in painting this picture.

La carte postale (The Postcard, 1960)

RENÉ MAGRITTE

"Imagination is the eye of the soul."—Joseph Joubert

View and Reflect

This painting has been interpreted in a variety of ways. After considering both the quotation and the painting, write a journal entry in which you interpret the painting from your own perspective.

The Cardsharps (1594)

MICHELANGELO MERISI DA CARAVAGGIO

"The darkest hour of any man's life is when he sits down to plan how to get money without earning it."—Horace Greeley

View and Reflect

In your journal, consider what the card players in the painting gain and what they lose by cheating.

The Horse Fair (1853)

ROSA BONHEUR

"Art at its most significant is a Distant Early Warning System that can always be relied on to tell the old culture what is beginning to happen to it."—Marshall McLuhan

View and Reflect

In your journal, consider what you can infer about the society in which this painting was created.

The Two Fridas (1939)

FRIDA KAHLO

"I never painted dreams. . . . I painted my own reality."—Frida Kahlo

View and Reflect

In your journal, consider the sense in which this painting reflects Kahlo's "own reality."

American Gothic (1930)

GRANT WOOD

"The art of a people is a true mirror to their minds."—Jawaharlal Nehru

View and Reflect

Write a journal entry in which you describe the attitude of the painter toward the people he depicted in the painting.

Mona Lisa (1503)

LEONARDO DA VINCI

"When I look at a painting, it isn't only the painting I see but the thing that I am. If there is more in the painting than I am, then I won't see it."—Ivan Eyre

View and Reflect

In a journal entry, express your opinion about what has made the *Mona Lisa* so fascinating—the image itself or what viewers see of themselves in the painting.

The Uprising (1848)

HONORÉ DAUMIER

"One should never put on one's best trousers to go to battle for freedom and truth."
—Henrik Ibsen

View and Reflect

In your journal, consider whether Honoré Daumier was a supporter of the status quo or the revolution.

Trial by Jury (1964)

THOMAS HART BENTON

"A jury consists of twelve persons chosen to decide who has the better lawyer."
—Robert Frost

View and Reflect

In your journal, analyze the quotation from Robert Frost and consider whether Benton's painting supports or undermines Frost's contention.

The Declaration of Independence (1818)

JOHN TRUMBULL

"To be truly free, it takes more determination, courage, introspection, and restraint than to be in shackles."—Pietro Belluschi

View and Reflect

Reflect in your journal on how the quotation above can be applied to the signers of the Declaration of Independence and how it applies to us today.

The Tragedy (1903)

PABLO PICASSO

"A man's dying is more the survivors' affair than his own."—Thomas Mann

View and Reflect

Write a journal entry in which you reflect on the feelings of the people in the picture, the quotation, and your own experiences.

The Peaceable Kingdom (1834)

EDWARD HICKS

"All animals are equal, but some animals are more equal than others."—George Orwell

View and Reflect

Write a journal entry in which you reflect on the contrasting points of view expressed by Edward Hicks in this painting and George Orwell in the quotation above.

The Great Figure

Among the rain
and lights
I saw the figure 5
in gold
on a red
firetruck
moving
tense
unheeded
to gong clangs
siren howls
and wheels rumbling
through the dark city

The Metropolitan Museum of Art, Alfred Stieglitz Collection, 1949. (49.59.1)

I Saw the Figure 5 in Gold (1928)
CHARLES DEMUTH

View and Reflect

Write a journal entry in which you consider the relationship between this painting and William Carlos Williams's poem "The Great Figure."

_____ 14. "This is ridiculous! Mickey and I aren't strangers," Joan said scornfully. "Where do you think we live in Cambridge?"
a. light-hearted
b. bantering
c. derisive

_____ 15. "I don't want to know where you live in Cambridge! You're not in Cambridge this weekend! You're in our house!" Mr. Ripley yelled.
a. indignant
b. embarrassed
c. patient

_____ 16. Joan: "Well, excuse me. I guess I was mistaken. I thought it was my house, too."
a. diplomatic
b. sarcastic
c. pleading

_____ 17. Mrs. Ripley: "Sweetie, please listen to reason. It is your house—but it's not Mickey's house. After all it would seem to me you would enjoy one weekend sleeping alone in your own room."
a. imploring
b. resigned
c. furious

_____ 18. "If I'd known this was going to be such a big deal, I wouldn't have come home," Joan pouted.
a. forgiving
b. sulking
c. apathetic

_____ 19. "It's not a big deal," said Mr. Ripley seriously. "It's a simple question of moral standards. Ours seem to be different from yours. They may not be better but they are different."
a. belligerent
b. earnest
c. accusatory

_____ 20. Joan's mouth hung open, "And that's why you want to ruin our weekend?"
a. incredulous
b. amused
c. pleased

_____ 21. Mrs. Ripley chuckled: "We're not trying to ruin your weekend, dear. What we're offering you are separate but equal accommodations. . . ."
a. demanding
b. scolding
c. humorous

_____ 22. "That's very funny, Mom," said Joan caustically. "But all the way down in the car Mickey was counting on sleeping in my room. He wouldn't have come if he had known he had to sleep in the attic."
a. satisfied
b. bitter
c. sympathetic

_____ 23. "He'll sleep in your room over my dead body," screeched Mr. Ripley.
   a. detached
   b. incensed
   c. resigned

I decided to intercede. "I have a suggestion. Since Mickey was counting on sleeping in Joan's room, why don't you let him sleep there and have Joan sleep in the attic?"

All three looked at me.

Then Mr. Ripley said, "Wait a minute. Suppose Joan decides to come down from the attic in the middle of the night?"

"It's simple," I said. "Make Mickey promise to lock his door."

Question: What is humorous about Buchwald's solution to the problem? What is the solution meant to illustrate?

From Art Buchwald, "Daughter's 'Friend' Is a Boy." Copyright © 1977 Tribune Media Services, Inc. Reprinted with permission.

Internet Activity

You can find Art Buchwald's newspaper column at

   www.washingtonpost.com

Type in Buchwald's name and select a column that interests you. What is the overall tone of the column? (You can refer to the list at the beginning of the chapter.) List specific statements from the column that support your choice.

Irony and Satire

Irony refers to a contrast between what people say and what they actually mean. An ironic comment intends a meaning that is contrary to its stated meaning. The intended meaning is often the opposite of the stated meaning. For instance, if someone backs into your car, you might say, "That's just great!" Your intended meaning is that something bad just happened, but your words say that something good just happened. Since the meaning of an ironic statement is often expressed indirectly, you must use inference to discover it.

Satire refers to comments that exaggerate flaws or failings for the purpose of making them seem ridiculous. Because satire relies on distortion, it is often humorous. Almost anything can be satirized, including people, institutions, and ideas.

Exercise: Identifying Irony and Satire

Bodybuilders' Contest   *by Wislawa Szymborska*

Getting the Picture

In the following poem, Wislawa Szymborska pokes fun at bodybuilders.

Bio-sketch

The Polish poet Wislawa Szymborska (1923–   ) won the Nobel Prize for Literature in 1996. The Nobel committee praised her for the "ironic precision" of her poetry.

> From scalp to sole, all muscles in slow motion.
> The ocean of his torso drips with lotion.
> The king of all is he who preens and wrestles
> with sinews twisted into monstrous pretzels.
>
> Onstage he grapples with a grizzly bear
> the deadlier for not really being there.
> Three unseen panthers are in turn laid low,
> each with one smoothly choreographed blow.
>
> He grunts while showing his poses and paces.
> His back alone has twenty different faces.
> The mammoth fist he raises as he wins
> is tribute to the force of vitamins.

From Wislawa Szymborska, "Bodybuilders' content" in *View With a Grain of Sand*, p. 25. Copyright © 1993 by Wislawa Szymborska, English translation by Stainskew Baranczak and Clare Cavanagh. Copyright © 1995 by Harcourt Brace, Inc., reprinted by permission of the publisher.

In Your Own Words

1. What is the tone of this poem?

2. How can we tell that the poet is making fun of bodybuilders? Exactly what in the poem makes her feelings clear?

3. How many of the senses are represented in this poem? What is the overall image of the bodybuilder?

4. What metaphors does Szymborska use? What is she trying to convey with each of these metaphors?

The Art of Writing

Write a paraphrase of the poem being careful to include the implied main idea.

SELECTION

Waiting in Life's Long Lines   *by Tom Mather*

"Standing in line is so important, it's the first thing they teach you how to do at school."

Getting the Picture

In the following satire, Tom Mather humorously talks about standing in line.

Bio-sketch

Tom Mather is a former humor columnist for the *BGNews* at Bowling Green State University in Bowling Green, Ohio. He published his first book, *The Cheeseburger*

Philosophy, at the age of 21. Below is an excerpt from his second book, *Voyages in the Toilet Dimension,* which was published in 1999.

Brushing Up on Vocabulary

admonish   to reprove or scold in a mild-mannered way. The word *admonish* derives from the Latin *ad,* meaning "to" and *monere,* meaning "advise or warn."

out of line   behaving improperly.

"When you sit with a nice girl for two hours, you think it's only a minute. But when you sit on a hot stove for a minute, you think it's two hours."

—Albert Einstein

"The passing minute is every man's possession, but what has once gone by is not ours."

—Marcus Aurelius

1   It's time to discuss the Great American Pastime. And I'm not talking about baseball.

2   No, America's new pastime is standing in line.

3   Standing in line is so important, it's the first thing they teach you how to do at school:

4   "As soon as you're finished, everyone get in line."

5   "We're not leaving until everyone gets in line."

6   They continually admonish bad kids by telling them that they are "out of line."

7   It seems that for practically everything we do today, we have to wait in line. Whether it's to see the new baby, or pay our respects to the dead, we wait in line.

8   We stand in line so much, we even wait when we're not working. What happens when you get fired? You go wait in the unemployment line. The government figures, "They don't have anything else to do. They might as well stand in line."

9   To be fair, people in other countries stand in line too. It's just a little different when they do it. For example, you probably have heard how in many countries the people wait hours in long lines for food. You might not realize that Americans wait hours in long lines for fun.

10   Yes, that's right. It's gotten so bad there are even parks designed specifically for standing in line. Some of the more famous ones are Disneyland, Disney World, and Six Flags. Have you been to any of these? Whoever said, "The shortest distance between two points is a line," never went to an amusement park. They have designed rides that allow you to stand in line for up to three hours, so that you can go down hills and through turns at 70 miles per hour. Never mind that most people did that on the trip there, because they wanted to get there as early as possible, to avoid the lines.

11   So if being in a line can be so much "fun," then how come we hate it so much? I think it's not so much the actual standing in line that we hate. The problem is that one line always moves faster than the other. And it's always the line you're not in. If you get in the short line, there is inevitably some crazy event that holds up the line. You know you're going to be in trouble when you hear one of the following:

"Price check on lane fourteen, price check on lane fourteen."
"What do you mean you don't take VISA?" or
"I could've *sworn* I brought my checkbook."

12   And no place is more annoying about lines than banks. There will be 30 people in line, and one teller. But that kind of thing you're used to. What the banks like to do, in addition, are to have five other tellers working at the same time on other projects. They each sit at their own window, watching to see how long the line can get, counting pennies. This in turn leads to a lot of bank robberies, because some people get so mad at those holding up the line, they decide it's just easier and quicker to hold up the line.

13   Lines aren't simply long, they can be confusing too. There's the line to get tickets, the line to get food, the line to get in, and the line to get out. Half of the problem is figuring out which line is the one you want to be in.

14 "Is this the line to buy tickets?"

15 "Tickets? I thought this was the line for the women's bathroom."

From Tom Mather, *The BG News*, Bowling Green State University August 6, 1997. Reprinted with permission.

Comprehension Checkup

Write the letter of the correct answer in the blank provided.

_____ 1. The topic of this article is
   a. baseball
   b. standing in line at banks
   c. standing in line
   d. waiting in line at theme parks

_____ 2. The author mentions that Americans stand in line for all of the following *except*
   a. to visit a new baby
   b. to pay our respects to the dead
   c. to see a teller at a bank
   d. to visit Santa Claus and his elves

_____ 3. The author's purpose in writing this selection is to
   a. inform us of ways to foil bank robberies
   b. entertain us with examples of where and when Americans stand in line
   c. persuade us to abandon the time-wasting custom of standing in line
   d. explain how the custom of standing in line differs in the U.S. from other countries

_____ 4. The tone of this article could best be described as
   a. sentimental and sad
   b. humorous and ironic
   c. angry and vindictive
   d. cautious and logical

_____ 5. You can infer from the article that the author believes that
   a. standing in line has gotten out of hand
   b. people better learn to cope with the irritation of standing in line
   c. standing in line is fun
   d. people should learn to talk to each other while standing in line to relieve the boredom

_____ 6. The statement "because some people get so mad at those holding up the line, they decide it's just easier and quicker to hold up the line" is an example of
   a. a play on words
   b. a literary allusion
   c. an ironic exaggeration
   d. both (a) and (c)

_____ 7. The main intention of the writer is to
   a. describe rude persons who hold up lines
   b. expose the rudeness of bank tellers
   c. comment on the problems inherent in standing in lines
   d. extol the virtues of a system where lines don't exist and it's every man for himself

_____   8.   The author of this selection says that schools
a. encourage students to stand in line
b. disparage students by telling them that they are out of line
c. both (a) and (b)
d. none of the above

_____   9.   The author would agree that
a. Americans wait hours in lines for food
b. children should not be forced to stand in line
c. lines are lots of fun if you have the right attitude
d. lines can be confusing at times

_____   10.   The author ends the selection with an illustration of
a. the difficulty in figuring out the correct line to stand in
b. the irritation people feel when standing in a lengthy line
c. the differences between the employed and the unemployed
d. the differences between U.S. citizens and Europeans

SELECTION

The Art Breakers   *by Patrick Rogers and Peter Mikelbank*

"[Stephane Breitwieser] simply grabbed the goods and stashed them under his coat while guards weren't looking."

Getting the Picture

The selection below describes the destruction of some irreplaceable works of art. The Flemish painter Pieter Bruegel the Elder (1525–1569) painted scenes of peasant life. Jean-Antoine Watteau (1684–1721) and François Boucher (1703–1770) were both French painters who used an elaborate decorative style of painting called Rococo. The thefts discussed in the reading selection occurred throughout Western Europe, from Belgium to Austria.

Bio-sketch

Peter Mikelbank and Patrick Rogers are presently writers for *People* magazine. Mikelbank is a special correspondent in Paris, and Rogers is an associate editor.

Brushing Up on Vocabulary

objet d' art   an object of artistic worth or interest.

nefarious   extremely wicked. The word is made up of the Latin word parts *ne*, meaning "not," *fari*, meaning "speak," and *osus*, meaning "full of." The literal meaning is "full of what should not be spoken." If our actions are *nefarious*, we are "speaking" against the pronouncements of the gods and are therefore unpious and wicked.

rip off   a slang expression dating from the 1900s meaning "steal," "cheat," or "plagiarize."

MO (modus operandi), a way of acting or doing. In criminal justice, *MO* is the means or method by which a crime is committed.

sacrilegious desecration or disrespectful treatment of something held sacred or dedicated to a religious purpose. It comes from the Latin *sacer*, meaning "sacred," and *legere*, meaning "to gather up or take away."

1   It's hard to imagine an art lover more ardent than Frenchman Stephane Breitwieser, who spent seven years amassing paintings and objets d'art worth up to $1.9 billion. It's harder still to imagine a collector more nefarious. Caught in November after he stole a 17th-century bugle in Lucerne, Switzerland, the 31-year-old waiter has since confessed to ripping off more than 170 small museums in six European countries, making him the most prolific art thief in history. His MO: He simply grabbed the goods and stashed them under his coat while guards weren't looking. His private gallery was a bedroom in his mother's home.

2   Still, Stephane's audacity was soon surpassed—by that of his mother, Mireille, 51, who was arrested on May 14. Authorities say that Mme. Breitwieser, a nurse, admitted to chopping up 60 paintings—including masterpieces by Brueghel, Boucher, and Watteau—and putting them out with the trash. In addition searchers have recovered 110 statues and musical instruments that Mireille dumped in the Rhine-Rhone Canal 70 miles from the pair's home in the town of Eschentzwiller, near the German and Swiss borders. "Mireille heard her son had been arrested and just believed she had to get rid of everything," says Alain Miribel, police spokesman for nearby Strasbourg.

3   While some of the soggy sculptures have already been refurbished, the paintings are gone for good. Indeed, connoisseurs are calling this the worst blow to Western cultural heritage in decades. "The willful destruction of works representing 60 top European masters is simply without comparison," says Alexandra Smith, a London representative of the Art Loss Register, an international organization that tracks stolen art. "To find anything like this, you'd have to look at something like what the Nazis did during World War II."

4   Details are scarce about the Breitwiesers, who remain behind bars while awaiting formal charges, but one acquaintance is unsurprised to find the odd couple under arrest. Retired sales director Roland LeGoff, 66, a former next-door neighbor in the Alsatian village of Ensisheim, describes them as "two sick people" who fought constantly and bombarded his family with harassing phone calls. "They made our lives a living hell," recalls Le Goff, who says he reported the Breitwiesers to the police at least a dozen times between 1994 and 1996, when the pair moved to nearby Eschentzwiller.

5   By then investigators say, Stephane had already launched his crime spree, beginning with heists from local art galleries and moving on to museums elsewhere in France, as well as in Germany, Holland, Switzerland, Austria, and Belgium. Breitwieser—who claimed to be the grandson of a famous Alsatian painter, Robert Breitwieser (actually a great-uncle)—told police he usually went to each museum only once. But on November 19, a guard called the cops after spotting him on a return trip to Lucerne's Richard Wagner Museum, where a 17th-century bugle worth $6,000 had gone missing after Stephane's visit a week earlier. During the commotion, authorities say, Breitwieser's girlfriend, nurse Anne-Catherine Kleinklauss, 31 (later arrested as an accomplice), slipped away and alerted Mireille, who promptly began shredding canvases and stuffing the confetti-size remnants into used vegetable cans.

6   Mireille reportedly told prosecutors that she thought it would be sacrilegious to destroy at least one of her son's stolen treasures—a wooden figure of Mary and Jesus—so she placed it in a quiet country chapel, although she can no longer remember the

location. Based on that and other information gathered while interrogating the Breitwiesers, investigators hope to recover more artwork. But for now, curators across Europe are still counting their losses—and mourning. "It's such a pretty thing and now destroyed," says a spokesman for the Chateau de Blois in France's Loire Valley, of a 1536 oil-on-wood portrait of Mary, Queen of Scots, that Stephane pinched. As for the Breitwiesers, they are one mother and child that museum officials hope never to see again.

From Patrick Rogers and Peter Mikelbank, "The Art Breakers," in *People*, 6/3/02, pp. 97–98. Reprinted with permission.

Comprehension Checkup

True or False

Indicate whether the statement is true or false by writing T or F in the blank provided.

_____   1. While statues and musical instruments were recovered, the paintings were destroyed.

_____   2. Both Breitwiesers were arrested.

_____   3. The Breitwiesers' arrest was not the first time they had come to the attention of the police.

_____   4. Stephane Breitwieser executed complicated heists that required great planning to pull off.

_____   5. Stephane Breitwieser began his thievery with the theft of a 17th-century bugle in Lucerne, Switzerland.

_____   6. Stephane Breitwieser is the great-nephew of a famous Alsatian painter.

_____   7. Stephane Breitwieser's girlfriend was also implicated in the thefts.

_____   8. A wooden figure of Mary and Jesus is likely to have survived.

_____   9. Police hope to recover a portrait of Mary, Queen of Scots, in the near future.

_____   10. The harm done by the Breitwiesers to museum collections was insignificant.

Vocabulary in Context

Each question below has a sentence from the selection and another sentence. A word is italicized in both sentences. Use the context clues in the two sentences to determine the meaning of the word.

1. "Caught in November after he stole a 17th-century bugle in Lucerne, Switzerland, the 31-year-old waiter has since confessed to ripping off more than 170 small museums in six European countries, making him the most *prolific* art thief in history."

    Janet Evanovich, a *prolific* writer, completes a new mystery every year.

    prolific means _____

2. "While some of the *soggy* sculptures have already been *refurbished*, the paintings are gone for good."

    She took the *soggy* clothes out of the washer and put them in the dryer.

Her home was completely *refurbished* after the fire gutted the inside.

soggy means _____

refurbished means _____

3. "Retired sales director Roland LeGoff, 66, a former next-door neighbor in the Alsatian village of Ensisheim, describes them as 'two sick people' who fought constantly and *bombarded* his family with *harassing* phone calls."

   Tom Cruise is always *bombarded* with requests for his autograph by admiring female fans.

   After the fourth *harassing* note, Mark was forced to seriously consider going to the police.

   bombarded means _____

   harassing means _____

4. "It's hard to imagine an art lover more *ardent* than Frenchman Stephane Breitwieser, who spent seven years *amassing* paintings and objets d' art worth up to $1.9 billion."

   Most professional football players have an *ardent* desire to win the Super Bowl.

   The pirate set about *amassing* a fortune in gold doubloons.

   ardent means _____

   amassing means _____

5. "Still, Stephane's *audacity* was soon surpassed—by that of his mother, Mireille, 51, who was arrested on May 14."

   She has the *audacity* to pretend to be my friend after attempting to steal my boyfriend.

   audacity means _____

6. "During the commotion, authorities say, Breitwieser's girlfriend, nurse Anne-Catherine Kleinklauss, 31 (later arrested as an *accomplice*), slipped away and alerted Mireille. . . ."

   Sometimes pickpockets work alone, and sometimes they have *accomplices*.

   accomplice means _____

Internet Activity

Art theft continues to be a worldwide problem. In 1986, a gang of Irish thieves broke into an estate in Ireland and made off with 11 paintings, including works by Goya, Rubens, Gainsborough, and Vermeer. So far none have been recovered. In 2002, two priceless paintings by Vincent Van Gogh were stolen from a museum. To find out about works of art stolen recently, go to the following website and click on "Update."

www.saztv.com

Find an article about a recent art theft and write a description of a stolen painting. What is the overall tone of the painting that was stolen?

TEST-TAKING TIP

Taking Multiple-Choice Tests (continued)

Here are some more tips for taking multiple-choice tests:

1. When the question asks you to pick a missing word, look for grammatical clues such as *a* and *an*. *A* goes before words beginning with consonants and *an* goes before words beginning with vowels.

2. Sometimes one of the answers will be *all of the above*. If you are pretty sure that two of the three answers are correct, but are unsure about the third answer, go with *all of the above*.

3. Two questions on the test may be similar. Use the correct answer for one question to help you find the correct answer for the other.

4. If there is no penalty for guessing, make an educated guess rather than leaving a question blank.

5. If you are using a computerized scoring sheet, be sure to eliminate any stray marks.

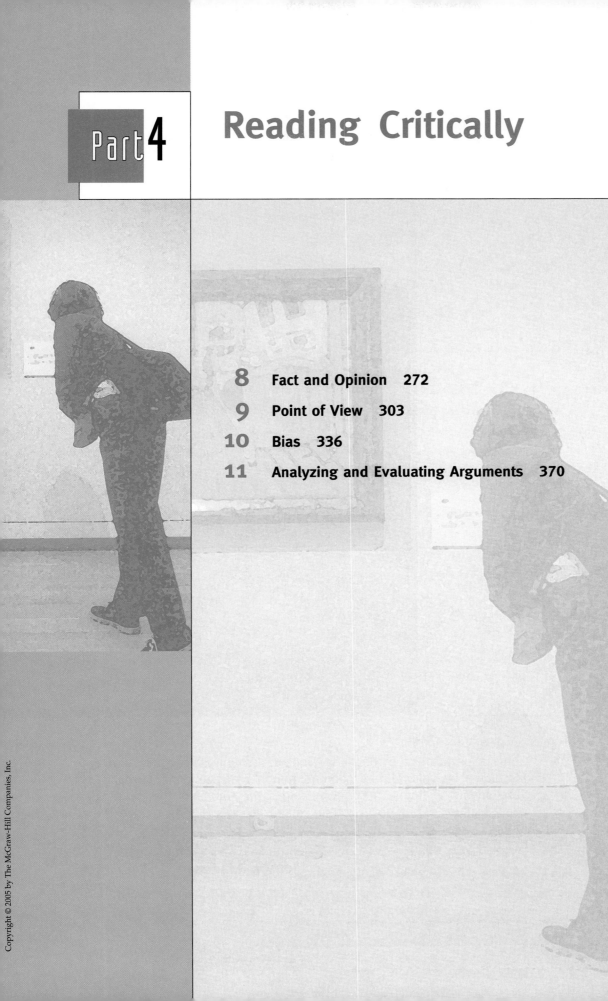

Part 4

Reading Critically

Fact and Opinion

8

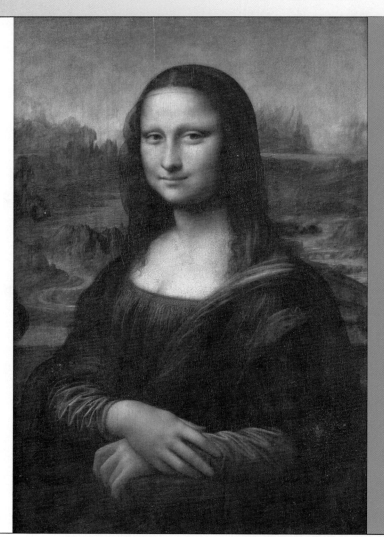

Mona Lisa, (1503)*
BY LEONARDO DA
VINCI

*To see this work of art in
color, turn to the color
insert following page 260.

Photo: R.G. Ojeda. Louvre, Paris. Inv.: 779. Réunion des Musées Nationaux/Art Resource, NY.

1 Some experts believe that it is Mona Lisa's enigmatic smile that
fascinates viewers. Others contend that her amazing eye contact—her
gaze seems to follow the viewer across the room—is the painting's
special allure. What do you think makes so many long to see the
Mona Lisa?

2 Why do you think da Vinci was so attached to this painting?

3 What is your opinion of this famous work of art?

Introduction to Fact and Opinion

In order to be a critical reader, you must be able to tell the difference between **fact and opinion.** Writers sometimes present opinions as though they were facts. You need to be able to know when this is happening.

A **fact** is a statement whose truth or falsity can be proved in some objective way. Statements of fact can be verified or disproved by records, tests, historical or scientific documents, or personal experience. A statement of fact offers neither judgment nor evaluation. Factual statements present information without interpreting it. Statements of fact often rely on concrete data or measurements. Here are some examples of statements of fact and how they can be proved.

Statement	Type of Proof
George Washington was our first president.	Historical records
I have seven french fries left on my plate.	Counting
It's sunny outside.	Observation
He's six feet tall.	Measurement

An **opinion** expresses a personal preference or value judgment. Statements of opinion cannot be proved to be true or false. Here are some examples of opinions. The words that express a preference or value judgment are underlined.

George Washington was a <u>great</u> president.

These french fries are <u>delicious</u>.

It is a <u>lovely</u>, sunny day.

He is <u>very</u> tall.

Statements of future events or probabilities are often opinions no matter how reasonable or likely they seem.

By the year 2012, 90 percent of Americans will be online.

In 2010, water will be rationed.

Statements of fact can sometimes be false. Both of the following statements are factual, but only one of them is correct.

George Washington was 67 years old when he died.

George Washington was 66 years old when he died.

Exercise 1: Identifying Facts and Opinions

Study the painting of the *Mona Lisa* on page 272. Indicate whether each statement below contains a fact or an opinion by writing F or O in the space provided. (Note that not all factual statements will be true.)

_____ 1. The *Mona Lisa* measures 30 × 21 inches (or approximately 77 × 53 centimeters).

_____ 2. The *Mona Lisa* has been a part of France's royal collection since the early sixteenth century.

_____ 3. The painting of the polite lady with the self-satisfied expression is perhaps the most recognized work of art in the world.

_____ 4. The otherworldly landscape in the background seems at odds with *Mona Lisa's* maternal image in the foreground.

_____ 5. Leonardo painted the *Mona Lisa* with oils on a poplar wooden panel.

_____ 6. The *Mona Lisa* is encased in a 157×98-inch box of triplex glass, a gift from the Japanese on the occasion of the painting's 1974 trip to Japan—the last time it left the Louvre.

_____ 7. This bullet-proof box is kept at a constant 68 degrees Fahrenheit and 55 percent humidity, which is maintained by a built-in air conditioner and nine pounds of silica gel.

_____ 8. Mona Lisa seems like a goddess or a saint.

_____ 9. The painting's magic might derive from our desire to know whether the lady is smiling, and if she is, why?

_____ 10. In 2003, the *Mona Lisa* received a checkup in which the box surrounding it was opened and the climatic conditions as well as the painting's condition were examined.

Exercise 2: Identifying Facts and Opinions

First, study the illustration on the following page. Then indicate whether each statement contains a fact or opinion by writing F or O in the space provided. (Remember that a statement may state a fact, even if it is false.)

_____ 1. Your future life depends on the position of the stars and planets on the date of your birth.

_____ 2. The Western system of astrology is based on month and day of birth.

_____ 3. The Eastern system of astrology is based on year of birth.

_____ 4. A child born on March 15, 2003, is a "Pisces" in Western astrology.

_____ 5. In the Eastern system, a child born in 2003 is a "goat."

_____ 6. In the Western system of astrology, the symbol for Capricorn is a goat.

_____ 7. In the Eastern system, a "rabbit" seeks tranquility.

_____ 8. Except for the scales of Libra, the twelve signs of the zodiac are symbolized by living creatures.

_____ 9. The symbols of the Eastern zodiac are all animals.

_____ 10. The zodiac has an amazing influence on our lives.

_____ 11. According to the Western zodiac, a Libra is compassionate, diplomatic, and pleasant.

_____ 12. Virgo is the only female in the Western zodiac; the other three human signs are all male.

Eastern (Chinese)

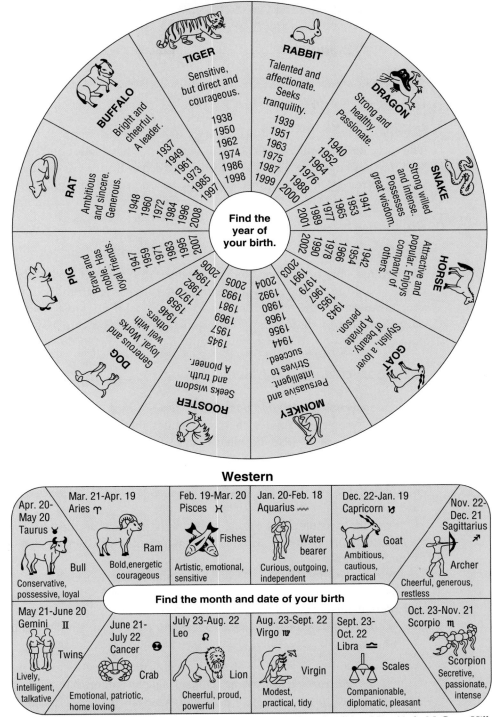

Western

From Jon Peterson and Stacey A. Hagen in *Better Writing Through Editing*, New York: McGraw-Hill, 1999, p. 56. Copyright © 1999 McGraw-Hill. Reprinted by permission of The McGraw-Hill Companies, Inc.

Excerpt from *Introduction to Psychology*   *by Dennis Coon*

"Astrology's popularity shows the difficulty many people have separating valid psychology from systems that seem valid but are not."

Getting the Picture

The topic of the next two selections is astrology. These selections continue our work with fact and opinion. The first selection, which is from a psychology textbook, discusses astrology as a pseudoscience. The second selection, which is from the popular *Don't Know Much About* series, compares astrology to astronomy.

Brushing Up on Vocabulary

nitpicking   being critical of inconsequential information or data.

horoscopes   predictions or advice based on the position of the planets and signs of the zodiac at the time of your birth. *Horoscope* comes from the Greek word parts *hora* meaning "hour" and *skopos* meaning "watching." Most newspapers publish daily horoscopes that attempt to predict what is going to happen to you on a particular day and to advise you how to act according to those predictions.

Pseudopsychology—Astrology

1   A **pseudopsychology** *is any unfounded system that resembles psychology.* Many pseudopsychologies offer elaborate schemes that give the appearance of science, but are actually false. (*Pseudo* means "false.") Pseudopsychologies change little over time because their followers do not seek new data. In fact, pseudopsychologists often go to great lengths to avoid evidence that contradicts their beliefs. Scientists, in contrast, actively look for contradictions as a way to advance knowledge. They must be skeptical critics of their own theories.

2   If pseudopsychologies have no scientific basis, how do they survive and why are they so popular? There are several reasons, all of which can be demonstrated by a critique of astrology.

3   **Problems in the Stars**   Astrology is probably the most popular pseudopsychology. Astrology *holds that the position of the stars and planets at the time of one's birth determines personality traits and affect behavior.* Like other pseudopsychologies, astrology has repeatedly been shown to have no scientific validity.

4   The objections to astrology are numerous and devastating:

5   1.   The zodiac has shifted by one full constellation since astrology was first set up. However, most astrologers simply ignore this shift. (In other words, if astrology calls you a Scorpio you are really a Libra and so forth.)

6   2.   There is no connection between the "compatibility" of couples' astrological signs and their marriage and divorce rates.

7   3.   Studies have found no connection between astrological signs and leadership, physical characteristics, career choices, or personality traits.

8   4.   The force of gravity exerted by the physician's body at the moment of birth is greater than that exerted by the stars. Also, astrologers have failed to explain why the moment of birth should be more important than the moment of conception.

9   5. A study of over 3,000 predictions by famous astrologers found that only a small percentage were fulfilled. These "successful" predictions tended to be vague ("There will be a tragedy somewhere in the east in the spring.") or easily guessed from current events.

10   In short, astrology doesn't work.

11   *Then why does astrology often seem to work?*

12   The following discussion tells why.

13   **Uncritical Acceptance** If you have ever had your astrological chart done, you may have been impressed with its apparent accuracy. However, such perceptions are typically based on **uncritical acceptance** (*the tendency to believe positive or flattering descriptions of yourself*). Many astrological charts are made up of mostly flattering traits. Naturally, when your personality is described in *desirable* terms, it is hard to deny that the description has the "ring of truth." How much acceptance would astrology receive if the characteristics of a birth sign read like this:

14   **Virgo:** You are the logical type and hate disorder. Your nitpicking is unbearable to your friends. You are cold, unemotional, and usually fall asleep while making love. Virgos make good doorstops.

15   **Positive Instances** Even when an astrological description contains a mixture of good and bad traits, it may seem accurate. To find out why, read the following personality description.

YOUR PERSONALITY PROFILE

16   You have a strong need for other people to like you and for them to admire you. You have a tendency to be critical of yourself. You have a great deal of unused energy which you have not turned to your advantage. While you have some personality weaknesses, you are generally able to compensate for them. Your sexual adjustment has presented some problems for you. Disciplined and controlled on the outside, you tend to be worrisome and insecure inside. At times you have serious doubts as to whether you have made the right decision or done the right thing. You prefer a certain amount of change and variety and become dissatisfied when hemmed in by restrictions and limitations. You pride yourself on being an independent thinker and do not accept other opinions without satisfactory proof. You have found it unwise to be too frank in revealing yourself to others. At times you are extroverted, affable, sociable, while at other times you are introverted, wary, and reserved. Some of your aspirations tend to be pretty unrealistic.

17   Does this describe your personality? A psychologist read this summary individually to college students who had taken a personality test. Only 5 students out of 79 felt that the description failed to capture their personalities. Another study found that people rated this "personality profile" as more accurate than their actual horoscopes.

18   Reread the description and you will see that it contains both sides of several personality dimensions ("At times you are extroverted . . . while at other times you are introverted . . ."). Its apparent accuracy is an illusion based on the **fallacy of positive instances,** *in which we remember or notice things that confirm our expectations and forget the rest.* The pseudopsychologies thrive on this effect. For example, you can always find "Leo characteristics" in a Leo. If you looked, however, you could also find "Gemini characteristics," "Scorpio characteristics," or whatever.

19   **The Barnum Effect**   Pseudopsychologies also take advantage of the **Barnum effect,** *which is a tendency to consider personal descriptions accurate if they are stated in very general terms.* P. T. Barnum, the famed circus showman, had a formula for success: "Always have a little something for everybody." Like the all-purpose personality profile, palm readings, fortunes, horoscopes, and other products of pseudopsychology are stated in such general terms that they can hardly miss. There is always "a little something for everybody." To observe the Barnum effect, read *all* 12 of the daily horoscopes found in newspapers for several days. You will find that predictions for other signs fit events as well as those for your own sign do.

20   Astrology's popularity shows the difficulty many people have separating valid psychology from systems that seem valid but are not. The goal of this discussion, then, has been to make you a more critical observer of human behavior and to clarify what is, and what is not, psychology. In the meantime, here is what the "stars" say about your future:

21   Emphasis now on education and personal improvement. A learning experience of lasting value awaits you. Take care of scholastic responsibilities before engaging in recreation. The word *reading* figures prominently in your future.

From Dennis Coon, *Introduction to Psychology: Gateways to Mind and Behavior,* 9th ed., pp. 21–22. Copyright © 2001 Thomson Learning. Reprinted with permission of Wadsworth, a division of Thomson Learning: **www.thomsonrights.com**. Fax 800-730-2215.

Comprehension Checkup

True or False

Indicate whether the statement is true or false by writing T or F in the blank provided.

_____   1. Pseudopsychologists look for examples that contradict their beliefs.

_____   2. Pseudopsychologies are always changing and improving.

_____   3. Astrology has been shown to have scientific validity.

_____   4. A person who *aspires* to be a doctor seeks to become one.

_____   5. Scorpios always display Scorpio characteristics.

Multiple Choice

Write the letter of the correct answer in the blank provided.

_____   6. A pseudopsychology is a _____ system that purports to be a valid psychology.
             a. valid
             b. current
             c. false
             d. common sense

_____   7. Pseudopsychologies state personality descriptions in general terms and so provide "a little something for everybody." They do this to take advantage of
             a. the force of gravity
             b. uncritical acceptance
             c. the fallacy of positive instances
             d. the Barnum effect

———— 8. So called "psychic hotlines" typically dispense lots of flattering information to callers. The "psychics" are relying on _____ to create an illusion of accuracy.
   a. analysis of the zodiac
   b. uncritical acceptance
   c. the Barnum effect
   d. the fallacy of positive instances

———— 9. Each New Year's Day, "psychics" make predictions about events that will occur during the coming year. The vast majority of these predictions are wrong, but the practice continues each year. The _____ helps to explain why people only remember predictions that seemed to come true and forget all of the errors.
   a. pattern of uncritical acceptance
   b. fallacy of positive instances
   c. Barnum effect
   d. Virgo effect

———— 10. Other kinds of pseudopsychology mentioned in the essay are
   a. palm readings
   b. personality profiles
   c. fortunes
   d. all of the above

Fact and Opinion

Indicate whether the statement is a fact or an opinion by writing F or O in the blank provided.

———— 1. The zodiac has shifted by one full constellation since astrology was first set up.

———— 2. Many astrological charts are made up of mostly flattering traits.

———— 3. Only 5 students out of 79 felt that the description failed to capture their personalities.

———— 4. Studies have found no connection between astrological signs and leadership. . . .

———— 5. *Pseudo* means "false."

SELECTION

Excerpt from *Don't Know Much About the Universe*   *by Kenneth C. Davis*

"Copernicus, Tycho Brahe, Kepler, and Galileo provided clients with astrological charts."

Getting the Picture

Many newspapers and magazines around the country carry daily horoscopes. And millions of readers consult them. Some consult their horoscopes just "for the fun of it." Others, however, take horoscopes very seriously, using them to guide their daily activities and plan their futures. How do you feel about horoscopes? If you still take them seriously after the previous selection, perhaps the selection below will change your mind.

Bio-sketch

Kenneth C. Davis is the author of the bestselling *Don't Know Much About . . .* series. Using a question-and-answer approach, Davis's goal is to make learning fun. To that end, he provides the reader with a vast amount of information in a highly entertaining format. Previous books have given instruction on history, geography, the Civil War, and the Bible. Davis currently is a contributing editor to *USA Weekend*.

Brushing Up on Vocabulary

lore   a body of knowledge about a particular subject.

Nero   an ancient Roman emperor who is associated with great cruelty. He is believed to have started a fire that consumed Rome and then played his fiddle while watching the city burn.

pagan   a person who is not a Christian, Jew, or Muslim; a person who believes in many deities associated with nature.

What Does Astrology Have to Do with Astronomy?

1   The belief that the positions of the Sun, Moon, and planets influence the course of human affairs and earthly occurrences is as old as the fascination with the skies. From the earliest days of studying the skies, astrology and astronomy were closely linked. As a "science," astrology was utilized to predict or affect the destinies of individuals, groups, and even nations. The Greeks built upon existing Mesopotamian and Egyptian lore while applying the new rules of geometry to describe the orbits of the planets. They also fully developed the idea of the twelve constellations of the zodiac and the concept that the positions of the planets, Sun, and Moon at the time of birth determine a person's fate, which gradually became an accepted idea. It grew to include the notion that the heavens also governed wealth, marriage, and death. Even Greek medicine, which made tremendous scientific strides, saw various functions of the body and different organs as being ruled by different combinations of planets and constellations.

2   The Romans, who later adopted or adapted many Greek ideas, preferred their own ancient means of divining the future, but Greek astrology eventually became accepted in Roman times as well. Emperor Augustus elevated astrology to a royal art. And the Roman writer Seneca, who was born around the time of Jesus and later tutored the Emperor Nero, once said, "Think you so many thousand stars shine on in vain? . . . Even those stars that are motionless, or because of their speed keep equal pace with the rest of the universe and seem not to move, are not without rule or dominion over us."

3   In the Christian era, astrology started to take some lumps. The most influential church thinker of the Middle Ages, St. Augustine (354–430), summed up the Christian objections to astrology. In his *Confessions*, Augustine recalled that before he renounced his pagan upbringing, he had consulted astrologers. But he was convinced otherwise and, to him, "the lying divinations and impious dotages" of astrologers were the Devil's work. In *City of God*, he said that the world is ruled by divine providence, not by chance or fate. The proof for Augustine came in a story told by a friend. Two children were born at the same moment, in the same household. Surely their fates would be the same. But one of the infants was the child of the master of the house. The other was the child of a slave. The position of the stars, exactly the same at the moment of their births, did not change their fates. The same logic would apply to the birth of twins, and Augustine pointed to the biblical brothers Esau and Jacob, born instants apart yet so completely different in temperament and fate.

4   In spite of Augustine's objections, astrology continued to flourish through Christian times, and many popes over the centuries called upon astrologers in making

"A man only understands what is akin to something already existing in himself."

—Henri Frederic Amiel

decisions. Even the arrival of the Renaissance and Enlightenment did not weaken its pull. In fact, throughout the early history of astronomy, many of the greatest names in the field, responsible for some of its greatest discoveries, turned to astrology to pay the bills. Copernicus, Tycho Brahe, Kepler, and Galileo provided clients with astrological charts. Even the mighty Newton is said to have first become interested in astronomy after looking at an astrological book. They had been preceded by great scholars of the Middle Ages, such as Albert Magnus, and St. Thomas Aquinas, the influential church thinker, who both admitted that the stars had a strong governing influence. But they argued that man's free will allowed him to resist these powers.

5   As a "pseudoscience," astrology must be viewed as diametrically opposed to the findings and theories of modern Western science. As the medieval Jewish philosopher Maimonides (1135–1204) once put it even more strongly, "Astrology is a disease, not a science."

6   In spite of science, astrology still holds a particular fascination for many people who see their lives linked to the constant motion of the stars. The late Carl Sagan pointed out in his popular book *Cosmos* that modern language retains a sense of the influence of astrology. As Sagan noted, "*Disaster*, which is Greek for 'bad star,' *influenza*, Italian for [astral] 'influence,' *mazeltov*, Hebrew—and, ultimately, Babylonian—for 'good constellation.'"

7   Well documented is Hitler's preoccupation with astrology. It has been said that on the basis of what his astrologers saw in his star charts, Hitler squandered several opportunities to attack England at a time when such an invasion might have succeeded. In fact, during World War II, the British government used astrologers to attempt to figure out what Hitler's astrologers were telling him!

"The first problem for all of us, men and women, is not to learn, but to unlearn."

—Gloria Steinem

8   The basic principle of astrology is that the heavenly bodies somehow influence what happens on Earth. Astrologers demonstrate this influence by means of a chart called a *horoscope* (from ancient Greek for "hour" and "observer"), which shows the positions of the planets in relation to both Earth and stars at a certain time. When seeking actual evidence of planetary influence, proponents of astrology point to the fact that the Sun and Moon do influence the tides on Earth. They argue that if that is true, why can't they influence human life as well, since water is so crucial to life, and humans are largely composed of water. Powerful logic is not astrology's strong suit.

9   Horoscopes traditionally place the Earth at the center of the solar system—or even the universe—because that is what was thought to be true when the basic rules of astrology were set down. In astrology, the Sun and Moon are considered "planets" along with the other eight known planets (although there were only five planets known in ancient Babylon and Greece). Astrology contends that the planets hold more influence than other heavenly bodies. Another key element of the astrological scheme is the zodiac, a band of stars that circles the earth and is divided into twelve equal parts—or the familiar *signs*.

From Kenneth C. Davis, *Don't Know Much About the Universe*, New York: HarperCollins, 2001, pp. 29–32. Copyright © 2001 by Kenneth C. Davis. Reprinted by permission of HarperCollins Publisher, Inc.

Comprehension Checkup

Fact and Opinion

Indicate whether the statement is a fact or an opinion by writing F or O in the blank provided.

_____   1.   The Greeks built upon existing Mesopotamian and Egyptian lore while applying the new rules of geometry to describe the orbits of the planets.

_____ 2. And the Roman writer Seneca, who was born around the time of Jesus and later tutored the Emperor Nero, once said, "Think you so many thousand stars shine on in vain? . . ."

_____ 3. In his *Confessions,* Augustine recalled that before he renounced his pagan upbringing, he had consulted astrologers.

_____ 4. Surely their fates would be the same.

_____ 5. Copernicus, Tycho Brahe, Kepler, and Galileo provided clients with astrological charts.

_____ 6. "Astrology is a disease, not a science."

_____ 7. During World War II, the British government used astrologers to attempt to figure out what Hitler's astrologers were telling him!

_____ 8. Powerful logic is not astrology's strong suit.

_____ 9. In astrology, the Sun and Moon are considered planets along with the other eight known planets (although there were only five planets known in ancient Babylon and Greece).

_____ 10. Astrology contends that the planets hold more influence than other heavenly bodies.

In Your Own Words

Read the daily horoscope in your local newspaper. Does the horoscope for your astrological sign seem to apply to you? Read what is written for people with other astrological signs. Does that information seem to apply equally as well to you? Does this lead you to any conclusions about astrological forecasts?

SELECTION

A Review of *The Sixth Sense*   *by Roger Ebert*

"Bruce Willis often finds himself in fantasies and science-fiction films. Perhaps he fits easily into them because he is so down-to earth."

Bio-sketch

Roger Ebert, the cohost of the popular TV program *Ebert & Roeper*, has won a Pulitzer Prize for his work as a film critic for the *Chicago Sun-Times*. His website was recently named the best online movie review site by the Online Film Critics Society.

1   *The Sixth Sense* isn't a thriller in the modern sense, but more of a ghost story of the sort that flourished years ago, when ordinary people glimpsed hidden dimensions. It has long been believed that children are better than adults at seeing ghosts; the barriers of skepticism and disbelief are not yet in place. In this film, a small boy solemnly tells his psychologist: "I see dead people. They want me to do things for them." He seems to be correct.

2   The psychologist is Malcolm Crowe (Bruce Willis), who is shot by an intruder one night in his home—a man who had been his patient years earlier and believes he was wrongly treated. The man then turns the gun on himself. "The next fall," as the subtitles tell us, we see Crowe mended in body but perhaps not in spirit, as he takes on a new case, a boy named Cole Sear (Haley Joel Osment) who exhibits some of the same problems as the patient who shot him. Maybe this time he can get it right.

3   The film shows us things adults do not see. When Cole's mother (Toni Collette) leaves the kitchen for just a second and comes back in the room, all of the doors and drawers are open. At school, he tells his teacher, "They used to hang people here." When the teacher wonders how Cole could possibly know things like that, he helpfully tells him, "When you were a boy they called you Stuttering Stanley."

4   It is Crowe's task to reach this boy and heal him, if healing is indeed what he needs. Perhaps he is calling for help; he knows the Latin for, "From out of the depths I cry unto you, oh Lord!" Crowe doesn't necessarily believe the boy's stories, but Crowe himself is suffering, in part because his wife, once so close, now seems to be drifting into an affair and doesn't seem to hear him when he talks to her. The boy tells him, "Talk to her when she's asleep. That's when she'll hear you."

5   Using an "as if" approach to therapy, Crowe asks Cole, "What do you think the dead people are trying to tell you?" This is an excellent question, seldom asked in ghost stories, where the heroes are usually so egocentric they think the ghosts have gone to all the trouble of appearing simply so the heroes can see them. Cole has some ideas. Crowe wonders whether the ideas aren't sound even if there aren't really ghosts.

6   Bruce Willis often finds himself in fantasies and science-fiction films. Perhaps he fits easily into them because he is so down-to-earth. He rarely seems ridiculous, even when everything else on the screen is absurd because he never overreaches; he usually plays his characters flat and matter-of-fact. Here there is a poignancy in his bewilderment. The film opened with the mayor presenting him with a citation, and that moment precisely marks the beginning of his professional decline. He goes down with a sort of doomed dignity.

7   Haley Joel Osment, his young costar, is a very good actor in a film where his character possibly has more lines than anyone else. He's in most of the scenes, and he has to *act* in them—this isn't a role for a cute kid who can stand there and look solemn in reaction shots. There are fairly involved dialogue passages between Willis and Osment that require good timing, reactions, and the ability to listen. Osment is more than equal to them. And although the tendency is to notice how good he is, not every adult actor can play heavy dramatic scenes with a kid and not seem to condescend (or, even worse, to be subtly coaching and leading him), Willis can. Those scenes give the movie its weight and make it as convincing as, under the circumstances, it can possibly be.

8   I have to admit I was blindsided by the ending. The solution to many of the film's puzzlements is right there in plain view, and the movie hasn't cheated, but the very boldness of the storytelling carried me right past the crucial hints and right through to the end of the film, where everything takes on an intriguing new dimension. The film was written and directed by M. Night Shyamalan, whose previous film *Wide Awake*, was also about a little boy with a supernatural touch; I didn't think that one worked. *The Sixth Sense* has a kind of calm, sneaky self-confidence that allows it to take us down a strange path intriguingly.

From Roger Ebert in *Roger Ebert's Movie Yearbook 2002*, pp. 521–522, 2001. Andrews McMeel Publishing. Reprinted with permission.

Comprehension Checkup

Fact and Opinion

Indicate whether the statement is a fact, an opinion, or both by writing F, O, or B in the blank provided.

_____ 1. *The Sixth Sense* isn't a thriller in the modern sense, but more of a ghost story of the sort that flourished years ago, when ordinary people glimpsed hidden dimensions.

_____ 2. In this film, Cole Sear tells his psychologist: "I see dead people. They want me to do things for them."

_____ 3. The psychologist is Malcolm Crowe (Bruce Willis), who is shot by an intruder one night in his home—a man who had been his patient years earlier and believes he was wrongly treated.

_____ 4. The man then turns the gun on himself.

_____ 5. When Cole's mother (Toni Collette) leaves the kitchen for just a second and comes back in the room, all of the doors and drawers are open.

_____ 6. At school he tells his teacher, "They used to hang people here."

_____ 7. Perhaps he is calling for help; he knows the Latin for, "From out of the depths I cry unto you, oh Lord!"

_____ 8. Perhaps he fits easily into them because he is so down-to-earth.

_____ 9. Haley Joel Osment, his young costar, is a very good actor in a film where his character possibly has more lines than anyone else.

_____ 10. Osment is more than equal to them.

_____ 11. I have to admit I was blindsided by the ending.

_____ 12. The film was written and directed by M. Night Shyamalan, whose previous film *Wide Awake* was also about a little boy with a supernatural touch; I didn't think that one worked.

_____ 13. *The Sixth Sense* has a kind of calm, sneaky self-confidence that allows it to take us down a strange path intriguingly.

Internet Activity

You can find movie reviews by Roger Ebert at

http://www.suntimes.com/index/ebert.html

Select a review of a movie that you have recently seen. Print it and underline five opinion statements and five factual statements in it.

Distinguishing Between Fact and Opinion

This last section on fact and opinion contains an excerpt from a popular health textbook describing herbal remedies, an essay by Dr. Benjamin Ansell, director of U.C.L.A.'s Center for Primary Care-Based Cardiovascular Disease Prevention, and an article by Mary Carmichael of *Newsweek*.

SELECTION

Excerpt from *Core Concepts in Health*   *by Paul M. Insel and Walton Roth*

"As in the case of St. John's Wort, the chemicals in botanical supplements can interact dangerously with prescription and over-the-counter drugs."

Getting the Picture

"The desire to take medicine is perhaps the greatest feature which distinguishes man from animals."

—William Osler

According to Wayne Payne, author of *Understanding Your Health,* some 60 million Americans today are using an almost endless variety of vitamins, minerals and other supplements in a quest for improved health. These products are being consumed in record quantities, despite the fact that they are not subject to Food and Drug Administration (FDA) requirements for safety and effectiveness. Thus, consumers may not only be wasting billions of dollars on unproven, even useless health care products; they may also be causing themselves serious harm.

Information from Wayne A. Payne, *Understanding Your Health,* 6th ed., New York: McGraw-Hill, 2000, p. 547.

Brushing Up on Vocabulary

St. John's wort   (*Hypericum perforatum*) a flowering plant from which an over-the-counter herbal supplement is derived, used to treat depression. As a dietary supplement, it is not subject to the same type of testing and regulation as prescription medications. St. John's wort has been thought to have curative properties since the time of Hippocrates in ancient Greece. Although the herb appears to benefit some people who suffer from mild to moderate depression, it may interact with or reduce the effectiveness of many medications used to treat heart disease, seizures, and HIV. There are approximately 7.5 million users of St. John's wort.

aristolochic acid   a powerful carcinogen and nephrotoxin (a substance that causes damage to the kidneys). Many herbal products contain this ingredient, including popular weight-loss pills.

Herbal Remedies: Are They Safe?

1   In February 2000, the FDA issued a Public Health Advisory warning of drug interactions between St. John's wort and drugs used to treat HIV infection, heart disease, and several other conditions. Because St. John's wort uses the same metabolic pathway as these drugs, it reduces their concentration in the blood and thus their effectiveness.

2   In May of the same year, the FDA issued a warning about botanical products that contain aristolochic acid. In 1990–1992, Chinese herbs containing aristolochic acid caused severe kidney damage, renal failure, and bladder cancer in patients at a weight-loss clinic in Belgium; due to a manufacturing error, aristolochia had been inadvertently substituted for another ingredient in weight-loss pills. Several European countries have banned the use of herbal products containing aristolochic acid, but such products are still obtainable in the United States, as are products believed to be contaminated with aristolochic acid.

"Primum non nocere—'First do no harm.'"

—Plaque on the wall of the University of Chicago Hospital

3   These FDA warnings reflect growing safety concerns about herbal remedies, botanicals, and dietary supplements, which now represent a more than $15-billion-a-year industry in the United States. Some problems result from lack of regulation, standardization, and quality control in both the United States and other countries, and other problems result from attempts to apply Western manufacturing methods to traditional herbal remedies. Safety concerns include drug interactions, lack of standardization, contamination, and toxicity.

DRUG INTERACTIONS

4   As in the case of St. John's wort, the chemicals in botanical supplements can interact dangerously with prescription and over-the-counter drugs. Heart and kidney transplant patients who were taking St. John's wort experienced symptoms of acute transplant rejection. These patients' lives were probably saved because they told their physicians that they were taking St. John's wort. Alarmingly, a high percentage of patients fail to tell their physicians about their use of herbal substances. Botanicals may decrease the effects of drugs, making them ineffective, or increase their effects, in some instances making them toxic. Botanicals can also interact with alcohol, usually heightening alcohol's effects.

LACK OF STANDARDIZATION

5   There is also a lack of standardization in the manufacturing of herbal products in the United States. The Dietary Supplement Health and Education Act of 1994 requires that dietary supplement labels list the name and quantity of each ingredient. If a product contains botanical ingredients, the label must also specify the part of the plant from which the ingredient is derived.

6   In listing the names of ingredients, manufacturers can use either common names or Latin names. Latin names are the same throughout the world, but common names differ. Sometimes different plant species have the same common name, as in the case of ginseng, which may be Chinese ginseng (*Panax ginseng*), American ginseng (*Panax quinquefolium*), or Siberian ginseng (*Eleutherococcus senticosus*). Even Latin names may refer to different species, as in the case of the cornflower, echinacea. At least three different species of echinacea are found in commercial preparations. Although the plants look similar, they have quite distinct chemical compositions and, as a result, different biological activities.

7   The content of herbal preparations is also variable. A *Consumer Reports* study found that the amount of the active ingredient in ten widely sold ginseng products varied widely, with some pills containing twenty times as much as others. Even those with the same labeled milligram dosage had tenfold differences in concentration.

8   Part of the reason for such variation is the difficulty of isolating individual ingredients. Manufacturers are trying to standardize the process of preparing plant extracts so that every pill, tablet, capsule, or bottle of liquid contains the same amount of the active ingredient. First, though, they have to determine which of the hundreds of chemicals in a plant extract are responsible for its medicinal effects. This is a difficult task; scientists are far from having a complete list of all the chemical constituents of even a single plant. The types and amounts of chemicals present in an extract are also affected by the growing, harvesting, processing, and storage conditions of plants.

CONTAMINATION, ADULTERATION, AND TOXICITY

9   A variety of traditional Chinese remedies contain heavy metals, such as lead, mercury, and arsenic, as part of the formula, all of which can be highly toxic and can cause irreversible damage. Some Chinese herbal remedies have been found to con-

tain pharmaceutical drugs, including tranquilizers and steroids. Others contain herbs not listed on the label, and sometimes substitute herbs that have toxic effects.

10   Furthermore, many plants are poisonous. Many medical systems that rely on herbal remedies use poisonous plants because of their beneficial effects in very low dosages. (Even conventional medicine uses such drugs—for example, digitalis, derived from the foxglove plant, for heart disease.) Adverse events can occur if the safe dosage is exceeded; the problem is that for many botanicals, the safe dosage is not known.

11   Some botanicals are not poisonous but can cause damage to the liver or kidney if taken over long periods of time; for many others it is not known if their regular long-term use is safe.

THE ROLE OF GOVERNMENT IN SAFETY ISSUES

12   In the United States, because herbs are considered supplements rather than food or drug products, they do not have to meet FDA food and drug standards for safety or effectiveness, nor do they currently have to meet any manufacturing standards. The manufacturer is responsible for ensuring that a supplement is safe before it is marketed. The FDA has the power to restrict a substance if it is found to pose a health risk after it is on the market, usually on the basis of voluntary reporting of adverse events by the manufacturer. Under U.S. law, if a supplement is suspected of causing harm, the burden of proof lies with the FDA. Because U.S. manufacturers can put almost anything into an herbal supplement, American consumers are at risk for buying and using products that may be not just useless but harmful as well. Part of the reasoning behind this situation is that "natural" products are considered safer than conventional medicines. As recent incidents with St. John's wort and aristolochic acid demonstrate, this is not always the case.

AVOIDING HEALTH FRAUD AND QUACKERY

"Promise, large promise, is the soul of advertising."

—Samuel Johnson

13   The first rule of thumb for evaluating any health claim is this—if it sounds too good to be true, it probably is. Also, be on the lookout for the typical phrases and marketing techniques fraudulent promoters use to deceive consumers.

14   "Duck" when you encounter these!

- The product is advertised as a quick and effective cure-all for a wide range of ailments.
- The promoters use words like *scientific breakthrough, miraculous cure, exclusive product, secret ingredient,* or *ancient remedy.* Also remember that just because a product is described as "natural" or unprocessed does not necessarily mean it's safe.
- The text is written in "medicalese"—impressive-sounding terminology to disguise a lack of good science.
- The promoter claims the government, the medical profession, or research scientists have conspired to suppress the product.
- The advertisement includes undocumented case-histories claiming amazing results.
- The product is advertised as available from only one source, and payment is required in advance.
- The promoter promises a no-risk "money-back guarantee." Be aware that many fly-by-night operators are not around to respond to your request for a refund.

✔ Comprehension Checkup

Fact and Opinion

Indicate whether the statement is a fact or an opinion by writing F or O in the blank provided.

_____ 1. In February 2000, the FDA issued a Public Health Advisory warning of drug interactions between St. John's wort and drugs used to treat HIV infection, heart disease, and several other conditions.

_____ 2. In May of the same year, the FDA issued a warning about botanical products that contain aristolochic acid.

_____ 3. In listing the names of ingredients, manufacturers can use either common names or Latin names.

_____ 4. Some botanicals are not poisonous but can cause damage to the liver or kidney if taken over long periods of time; for many others it is not known if their regular long-term use is safe.

_____ 5. In the United States, because herbs are considered supplements rather than food or drug products, they do not have to meet FDA food and drug standards for safety and effectiveness, nor do they currently have to meet any manufacturing standards.

_____ 6. Under U.S. law, if a supplement is suspected of causing harm, the burden of proof lies with the FDA.

_____ 7. The first rule of thumb for evaluating any health claim is this—if it sounds too good to be true, it probably is.

_____ 8. "Duck" when you encounter these!

Indicate whether the paragraphs indicated contain material that is primarily fact or primarily opinion.

Paragraph 1 _____

Paragraph 2 _____

Paragraph 6 _____

Paragraph 9 _____

SELECTION

When Health Supplements May Do Harm   _by Benjamin J. Ansell, M.D._

"The absence of a prospective review process may very well have contributed to the late discovery of harm associated with supplements like ephedra..."

Getting the Picture

The following selection presents a synopsis of possible problems with health supplements, most of which do not fall under the jurisdiction of the federal Food and Drug Administration (FDA). While prescription drugs must go through a systematic approval process before they can be sold, the FDA has little control over the sale of dietary and herbal supplements. Only recently, the FDA has outlawed the sale of supplements containing ephedra.

Bio-sketch

Benjamin J. Ansell received a dual undergraduate degree in both Biology and Music from Cornell University and his MD from UCLA. He subsequently performed his internship and residency at the UCLA Medical Center. Ansell is currently the director of the UCLA comprehensive health program. His publications have focused on cholesterol management, stroke reduction, and cardiovascular risk reduction in women.

Brushing Up on Vocabulary

cardiovascular   pertaining to the heart and blood vessels.

placebos   substances having little or no medical effects.

ephedra   an herbal supplement often taken to lose weight, but recently blamed for several deaths, especially of athletes.

1   Recently, I entered a store specializing in dietary supplements, curious about the information I would receive when I explained to the teenage clerk that I was particularly interested in preventing a heart attack.

2   I did not mention that I was a physician specializing in the prevention of heart disease, or that there were relatively few measures proven to reduce heart disease risk. But so many patients had brought in bags of supplements and "vitamins," convinced of their cardiovascular benefit that I wanted to see how these products were being marketed.

3   In the self-described "health" store, the salesclerk asked a few questions about my cholesterol, blood pressure, exercise habits, etc. Then she showed me over half a dozen products, from $8 to $36 apiece, and assured me that they would address a variety of health risks.

4   These products included a pill that was supposed to improve my circulation and another that would supposedly boost my "metabolism." Another was listed as an herbal "vascular health" pill, with a long list of plant species names, none of them familiar.

5   Most products had labels containing descriptions of vague medical benefits, like "for cardiovascular health," with a notation that the Food and Drug Administration had not evaluated these claims.

6   I asked the clerk about proof that these pills worked and about risks when taking these various agents together. She assured me that they were "all completely natural and very extensively tested." After all, she went on, "they are mostly vitamins."

7   In truth, only half of the bottles she recommended contained any vitamins at all. One of these was a combination of vitamins B6 and B12 and folic acid to lower blood levels of homocysteine, an amino acid byproduct associated with increased cardiovascular risk when it is elevated.

8   The remaining products were neither vitamins nor minerals—some were pulverized plant leaves or seeds. Others were from crushed bacteria. I thanked the clerk for spending the time to educate me.

9   Conventional medical education and treatment guidelines discourage the use of vitamins and supplements as therapeutics for heart disease, largely because they have not been shown to have any benefit. Interestingly, while diets emphasizing foods rich in certain vitamins correlate with improved cardiovascular and cancer risks, the pill forms of these same nutrients have proved to be no more effective than placebos.

10   In some studies, the vitamins have proved to be worse than placebos, while in other trials, combinations of vitamins have actually reduced the benefits of proven treatments.

11   Nonetheless, the appeal of supplement medications is understandable, especially when the costs, complexity, and publicized risks of prescription medications are all on the rise.

12   In promoting a product as a "supplement," manufacturers often rely on a combination of factors: vague claims made by sellers, word of mouth, and the distrust by many of organized medicine and the pharmaceutical industry. Supplement manufacturers are permitted to use advertisements and testimonials claiming that their products are "all natural" and "completely safe, without side effects."

13   The manufacturers of prescription drugs are allowed to make claims only about efficacy and safety that are based on results from controlled clinical trials approved by the FDA.

14   When Congress passed the Dietary Supplement and Health Education Act of 1994, it created this inequity between the marketing of medicines and supplements. This legislation placed the burden on the FDA to prove that a "supplement" is harmful before it can be removed from the market. In stark contrast, medicine approved by the agency must satisfy many safety and efficacy requirements before it can be sold.

15   The absence of a prospective review process may very well have contributed to the late discovery of harm associated with supplements like ephedra, the contamination of another supplement with a prescription blood thinner warfarin and an anxiety medication, and the fatal effects of an amino acid product.

16   Even when the offending supplement manufacturer is forced to withdraw a product, little can be done to prevent the fresh marketing of the product under a new brand name.

17   In August, 2002, the Justice Department began a criminal investigation of Metabolife International Inc., which makes a popular brand of ephedra that has been linked to dozens of deaths, strokes, and seizures in recent years and which has refused to report patient complaints to the FDA.

18   A spokeswoman for Metabolife said that the safety of the company's ephedra-based dietary supplements had been supported by studies carried out over 20 years.

19   Still, the presumption of safety until harm is proved represents a flawed approach.

20   Many of my patients who readily take supplements or high doses of vitamins assuming that "they can't hurt" are reluctant to accept prescribed therapies whose risks are clearly defined on the label.

21   From my health store experience, I can understand why vague claims are implied without any reference to safety or efficacy.

22   Clearly, the time has come to demand that the burdens of proof and disclosure regarding the marketing of supplements be made similar to those required for prescription medications.

23   In the meantime, a healthy dose of skepticism seems to be the best supplement of all.

Comprehension Checkup

Multiple Choice

Write the letter of the correct answer in the blank provided.

_____ 1. Why does Dr. Ansell put the word *health* in quotation marks in paragraph 3?
   a. He is quoting from the salesclerk.
   b. He is announcing his approval of health food stores.

    c. He means to imply doubt that the store is really selling products that are good for health.

    d. He means to imply that the vitamins are cheap and readily available to all those who want to live a healthy life.

_____ 2. Dr. Ansell implies that the lack of extensive testing and an adequate review process contribute to
    a. the high cost of dietary supplements
    b. the marketing of products that can cause considerable harm
    c. the employment of teenage health-food clerks
    d. the safety and effectiveness of dietary supplements

_____ 3. When Dr. Ansell describes the "inequity" between prescription drugs and supplements he means that
    a. drug companies are only allowed to make claims about their products that are validated by clinical trials
    b. food supplement companies are allowed to make claims about their products based on word-of-mouth and testimonials
    c. both (a) and (b)
    d. none of the above

_____ 4. Dr. Ansell suggests that
    a. health supplements have an unfair advantage over prescription medications
    b. if a product is withdrawn from the market it will be prevented from reappearing under a new name
    c. Metabolife reported all patient complaints to the FDA in accordance with the directives of the Justice Department
    d. ephedra was amply researched in clinical trials

_____ 5. Dr. Ansell would like to see
    a. prescription drugs on an unequal footing with supplements
    b. prescription drugs on an equal footing with supplements
    c. supplements banned from the marketplace
    d. patients take more vitamins and less of their prescription medicine

True or False

Indicate whether the statement is true or false by writing T or F in the blank provided.

_____ 6. The author believes that all of the products sold in health stores are good for your health.

_____ 7. The pills that Dr. Ansell was shown were primarily vitamins.

_____ 8. Conventional medical research has demonstrated that vitamin pills have considerable cardiovascular benefit.

_____ 9. While a diet rich in certain vitamins may decrease a person's risk of getting cancer or heart disease, the same cannot be said about vitamins in pill form.

_____ 10. With regard to supplements, a product is assumed to be safe until it is demonstrated to be dangerous.

In Your Own Words

Have you ever sought alternative forms of treatment for a health condition? Do you know someone who has? Would you consider using a nutritional supplement as a treatment? Would you tell your regular physician you were taking a dietary supplement? Why or why not?

The Art of Writing

In a brief essay, respond to one of the items below.

1. Elderly people are particularly susceptible to fraudulent claims for products promising new, quick, or easy ways to stay thin, strong, or attractive. How can we protect this group in particular from falling under the spell of quacks?

2. In 2001, the Federal Trade Commission reviewed 300 weight-loss ads for 218 dietary supplements: 40 percent of the ads were found to have made at least one statement that was absolutely false, and 55 percent of the ads made a claim that was very likely to be false or at the least lacked adequate substantiation. A comparison with ads that had run in 1992 revealed that deceptive advertising has significantly increased. Since 1990, the Federal Trade Commission (FTC) has filed 93 cases against false weight-loss claims. Despite their efforts, FTC chairman Timothy Muris says, "The problem is getting worse, not better." What do you think should be done to improve the current situation?

3. Recently supplement use by minors has come under scrutiny. It is estimated that more than one million minors nationwide have used nutritional supplements. In addition to weight-loss products, supplements such as creatine and androstenedione are particularly popular with high school, college, and professional athletes. In the last ten years, sales of creatine, a product designed to increase muscle mass, grew by more than 900 percent. "People think if they can buy these products at a so-called health food store, it can be good for them," said Iris Shaffer, executive director of Healthy Competition Foundation in Chicago, which has been studying the use of supplements and youth since 1999. During the last decade, the dietary supplement industry has doubled its annual revenues. A large part of that increased revenue has been sales to teenagers. Supplement use by young people is of particular concern to the FDA because the long-term effects are unknown. Right now supplements are "affordable, available, and legal." What can be done to keep supplements out of the hands of the young? Should we try to restrict their use by young people? Or will young people just turn to the black market?

Vocabulary Practice

The vocabulary words listed in column A come from the two essays you have just read.

   Match the words in column A with their definitions in column B, and write the appropriate answer letter in the space provided.

Column A	Column B
_____ 1. inadvertently	a. the branch of medicine concerned with the use of remedies to treat disease
_____ 2. contaminated	b. the obligation to offer credible evidence in a court of law—in support of a contention
_____ 3. banned	c. dishonest
_____ 4. toxicity	d. crushed completely
_____ 5. extract	e. informal oral communication by speech

_____	6.	burden of proof	f.	unfairness
_____	7.	rule of thumb	g.	not lasting; transitory
_____	8.	fraudulent	h.	a strong substance
_____	9.	fly-by-night	i.	unintentionally
_____	10.	pulverized	j.	polluted; tainted
_____	11.	therapeutics	k.	quality of being poisonous
_____	12.	word of mouth	l.	doubt
_____	13.	inequity	m.	prohibited; forbidden
_____	14.	skepticism	n.	a rough practical method or procedure

SELECTION

Are We Dying to Be Thin?   *by Mary Carmichael*

"[Ephedra] is definitely a hit with athletes, particularly bodybuilders, despite being banned by many sports leagues (but not Major League Baseball)."

Getting the Picture

According to FDA Commissioner Mark McClellan, the supplement industry is a "buyer-beware market." There are currently more than 1,000 manufacturers of dietary supplements, and all are exempt from most safety oversight. While ephedra-based products such as Metabolife and Ripped Fuel account for less than 1 percent of all dietary supplement sales, they are linked to more than 60 percent of adverse effects associated with supplements.

Bio-sketch

Mary Carmichael is currently an assistant editor for *Newsweek* magazine and contributes to the Society, Tipsheet, and Enterprise sections of the magazine. She graduated from Duke University with a B.A. in biological anthropology/public policy. After being a reporter for two newspapers, she came to *Newsweek* as an intern for the Periscope section and now covers science for the magazine.

Brushing Up on Vocabulary

watchdog   a guardian; to scrutinize behavior in order to detect illegal or unethical conduct.

hype   to promote or publicize in a showy fashion.

skyrocketing   rising or increasing rapidly or suddenly, especially to unprecedented levels.

1   The makers of the wildly popular rapid weight-loss supplement Xenadrine RFA-1 like to brag in ads that their product "makes national news." The death of Baltimore Orioles pitcher Steve Bechler, after heatstroke drove his temperature to 108 degrees, can't have been what they had in mind. Struggling to lose weight, the 23-year-old had been taking Xenadrine RFA-1, according to Orioles officials. Broward County medical examiner Joshua Perper put the ephedra pill at the top of his list of possible factors in Bechler's death.

*"Nothing is more
fatal to health than
the overcare of it."*

—Benjamin Franklin

2   Shane Freedman, general counsel for Xenadrine's manufacturer, Cytodyne Technologies, calls the link "extremely premature and bordering on reckless." But for years, watchdog groups and physicians have been saying the same thing about the hype surrounding ephedra. Bechler's death has reignited an intense debate about the safety of the herb, one that began almost as soon as its popularity mushroomed thanks to aggressive advertising in 1994—the same year that the FDA lost power to regulate dietary supplements. Since then, more than 1,400 adverse reactions and 100 deaths have been blamed on ephedra-based supplements—and some 12 million dieters and athletes want to know if they are at risk.

3   There's little doubt about ephedra's popularity. The herb is found in all four of America's best-selling weight-loss products, which together generate more than $161 million in annual sales. It is definitely a hit with athletes, particularly bodybuilders, despite being banned by many sports leagues (but not Major League Baseball). Athletes are especially prone to ephedra abuse, notes nutritionist Rehan Jalali, head of the Supplement Research Foundation, a fitness-information center. Teens are more likely to ignore guidelines and overuse the products, too. Since most ephedra pills aren't meant for kids under 18, health stores like GNC have recently started carding potential buyers. Minors can still get their hands on ephedra, though. The cheap Yellow Jackets brand was a favorite of 16-year-old Illinois football player Sean Riggins. He died in 2002; the coroner blamed an ephedra-induced heart attack. The brand is now banned, but others still crowd shelves.

4   Athletes and teens aren't the only ones taking chances. Though healthy users who take recommended doses are probably safe, many doctors say the herb poses a serious risk for patients with hypertension, heart disease, overactive thyroids, or diabetes. Bechler belonged to the first group. His high blood pressure, combined with rapid weight loss, may have weakened his body—already strained by ephedra and workouts in the Florida heat.

5   Ephedra's potential danger is a function of its active ingredient, ephedrine, which stimulates beta receptors on fat cells. This increases metabolism, causing the body to burn more fat. Heart cells also carry beta receptors. When combined with caffeine—as it almost always is in supplements—ephedrine stimulates those cells too, raising the heart rate and blood pressure, and sometimes causing insomnia, an irregular heartbeat, or even a heart attack or stroke.

6   Bad publicity, skyrocketing insurance rates, and GNC's carding policy have convinced many makers to pull their ephedra products and introduce new alternatives. All of the new products are heavy on caffeine; some also contain substances similar to ephedra, like bitter orange and octopamine. These products may be safer than ephedra, and anyone can buy them, but they're largely untested and their huge caffeine loads aren't heart-healthy. Jalali, who sometimes uses ephedra, is switching to several new substitutes. But there's only one sure way to avoid risk; don't take weight-loss supplements at all.

 Comprehension Checkup

Fact and Opinion

Indicate whether the statement is a fact, an opinion, or both by writing F, O, or B in the blank provided.

_____ 1. All of the new products are heavy on caffeine; some also contain substances similar to ephedra like bitter orange and octopamine.

_____ 2. Broward County medical examiner Joshua Perper put the ephedra pill at the top of his list of possible factors in Bechler's death.

_____ 3. But there's only one sure way to avoid risk; don't take weight-loss supplements at all.

_____ 4. There's little doubt about ephedra's popularity.

_____ 5. The herb is found in all four of America's best-selling weight-loss products, which together generate more than $161 million in annual sales.

_____ 6. Jalali, who sometimes uses ephedra, is switching to several new substitutes.

_____ 7. Heart cells also carry beta receptors.

Evaluating Health News

Health-related research is now described in popular newspapers and magazines instead of only medical journals, and so more and more people have access to the information. Greater access is certainly a plus, but news reports of research studies may oversimplify both the results and what those results mean to the average person. Researchers do not set out to mislead people, but they must often strike a balance between reporting promising preliminary findings to the public, thereby allowing people to act on them, and waiting 10 to 20 years until long-term studies confirm or disprove a particular theory.

All of this can leave you in a difficult position. You cannot become an expert on all subjects, capable of effectively evaluating all the available health news. However, the following questions should help you better assess health advice appearing in the popular media:

1. _Is the report based on research or on an anecdote?_ Advice based on carefully designed research studies has more validity than advice that relies on testimonials or stories.

2. _What is the source of the information?_ A study published in a respected peer-reviewed journal has been examined by editors and other researchers in the field, people who are in a position to evaluate the merits of a study and its results. Research presented at medical meetings should be considered very preliminary because the results have not yet undergone a thorough prepublication review. It is also wise to ask who funded a study to determine whether there is any potential for bias. Information from government agencies and national research organizations is usually considered fairly reliable.

3. _How big was the study?_ A study that involves many subjects is more likely to yield reliable results than a study involving only a few people. Another important indication that a finding is meaningful is if several different studies yield the same results.

4. _Who were the participants involved in the study?_ Research findings are more likely to apply to you if you share important characteristics with the participants of the study. For example, the results of a study on men over 50 who smoke may not be particularly meaningful for a 30-year-old nonsmoking woman. Even less applicable are studies done in test tubes or on animals. Such research should be considered very preliminary in terms of its applicability to humans. Promising results from laboratory or animal research frequently cannot be replicated in human study subjects.

*"The placebo cures
30 percent of the
patients—no matter
what they have."*

—David Kline

5. *What kind of study was it?* Epidemiological studies rely on observation or interviews to trace the relationship among lifestyle, physical characteristics, and diseases. While epidemiological studies can suggest links, they cannot establish cause-and-effect relationships. Clinical or interventional studies or trials involve testing the effects of different treatments on groups of people who have similar lifestyles and characteristics. They are more likely to provide conclusive evidence of a cause-and-effect relationship. The best interventional studies share the following characteristics:

    * *Controlled.* A group of people who receive the treatment is compared with a matched group who does not receive the treatment.
    * *Randomized.* The treatment and control groups are selected randomly.
    * *Double-blind.* Researchers and participants are unaware of who is receiving the treatment.
    * *Multicentered.* The experiment is performed at more than one institution.

6. *What do statistics really say?* First, are the results described as "statistically significant"? If a study is large and well designed, its results can be deemed statistically significant, meaning there is less than a 5 percent chance that the findings resulted from chance.

*"Common sense is in
medicine the master
workman."*

—Peter Latham

7. *Is new health advice being offered?* If the media report new guidelines for health behavior or medical treatment, examine the source. Government agencies and national research foundations usually consider a great deal of evidence before offering health advice. Above all, use common sense, and check with your physician before making a major change in your health habits based on news reports.

The Facts About Health Information on the Internet

The development of the Internet (World Wide Web) has made information more and more accessible to the masses including an almost unlimited amount of health information. However, all Internet websites do not provide scientifically sound, accurate, and reliable information. The Internet is also a source of much misinformation and even fraud.

The Federal Trade Commission (FTC) is a federal government agency charged with making sure that advertising claims for products are not false or misleading. In an effort to clean up websites, the FTC initiated "Operation Cure-All." As part of this operation, the FTC conducted two "Health Claim Surf Days" during which they identified 800 websites and usenet newsgroups with questionable content. The FTC sent mailers to these sites and 28 percent either removed the claims or the website completely. In spite of the FTC's efforts, there is still much health misinformation on the Web, leading one FTC official to suggest that ". . . miracle cures, once thought to have been laughed out of existence, have now found a new medium . . . on the Internet."

Another research study randomly selected 400 websites from 27,000 available on four different search engines for a study of cancer. Nearly half had unverified information and 6 percent had major inaccuracies. Clearly, Internet users must be careful in selecting websites for obtaining fitness, health, and wellness information.

There are some general rules that can be followed to help you when you use the Web to obtain health information. In general, government websites are good sources that contain sound information prepared by experts and based on scientific research. Government sites will typically include "gov" as part of the address. Professional organizations and universities can also be good sources of information. Organizations will typically have "org" and universities will typically have "edu" as part of their addresses. However, caution should still be used with organizations because it is easy to start an organization and obtain an "org" web address. Your greatest trust can be placed in the sites of stable organizations of long standing such as the AMA, the American Cancer Society, the American Heart Association, the American College of Sports Medicine, the National Council Against Health Fraud, and the American Alliance for Health, Physical Education, Recreation, and Dance. The great majority of websites promoting health products have "com" in the title because these are commercial sites that are in business to make a profit. Thus, they are more inclined to contain information that is suspect or even incorrect. It is important to evaluate with special care information found at "com" sites. The Tufts University School of Nutrition Science and Policy has developed a website that rates diet and health sites on the Internet. You may want to consult this website (http://navigator.tufts.edu).

With time and effort, you can gain the information you need to make good decisions about products and services that you purchase. Taking the time to investigate a product will help you save money and avoid making poor decisions that affect your health, fitness, and wellness. When you are making decisions about products or services, it is a good idea to begin your investigation well in advance of the day when a decision is to be made. Salespeople often suggest that "this offer is only good today." They know that people often make poor decisions when under time pressure, and they want you to make a decision today so that they won't lose a sale.

Information from Charles B. Corbin, *Concepts in Fitness and Wellness*, 4th ed., New York: McGraw-Hill, 2002, pp. 453, 455, 458.

Comprehension Checkup

Fact and Opinion

Indicate whether the statement is a fact or an opinion by writing F or O in the blank provided.

_____ 1. The FTC sent mailers to these sites and 28 percent either removed the claims or the website completely.

_____ 2. Another research study randomly selected 400 websites from 27,000 available on four different search engines for a study of cancer.

_____ 3. Clearly, Internet users must be careful in selecting websites for obtaining fitness, health, and wellness information.

_____ 4. Professional organizations and universities can also be good sources of information.

_____ 5. However, caution should still be used with organizations because it is easy to start an organization and obtain an "org" web address.

_____ 6. The Tufts University School of Nutrition Science and Policy has developed a website that rates diet and health sites on the Internet.

Internet Activity

The importance of evaluating health care supplements and health-related research carefully cannot be overstated, especially if this information comes to you over the Internet. Using any search engine, type in "health supplements," and select a website to evaluate. After answering the questions below, write a paragraph summarizing your conclusions about the website.

Name of Internet site:

_____

Web address:

_____

Type of information provided:

_____

_____

Organization or person responsible for information:

_____

_____

Place an X on the line if the statement is true for the site you are evaluating. Total the number of Xs. The more Xs, the more likely the site is reputable.

_____ 1. The site does not sell products associated with the information provided.

_____ 2. The provider is a person, an organization (org), or a governmental agency (gov) with a sound reputation.

_____ 3. The site does not try to discredit well-established organizations or government agencies.

_____ 4. The site does not rely on testimonials, celebrities, or people with unknown credentials.

_____ 5. The site is well-regarded by experts, and has a high rating at http://navigator.tufts.edu.

_____ 6. The site has a history of providing good information.

_____ 7. The site provides complete information that is documented by research.

_____ 8. No claims of quick cures or miracle results are made.

_____ 9. The site provides information consistent with health textbooks or medical encyclopedias.

Information from Charles B. Corbin, *Concepts of Fitness and Wellness*, 4th ed., New York: McGraw-Hill, 2002, pp. 453–458.

© LeMieux. Reprinted with special permission of King Features Syndicate.

What main idea from the previous selections does this cartoon reinforce?

Review Test 7: Supporting Details and Inference

Excerpt from Gilbert's *Living with Art*   *by Mark Getlein*

"All clues, however far-fetched, were followed up, but no trace of Mona Lisa could be found."

Getting the Picture

The article below describes the theft of Leonardo Da Vinci's *Mona Lisa*, one of the most famous paintings in the world. Da Vinci (1452–1519) was an Italian artist, scientist, and inventor. Because of his widely varied interests, he created few paintings in his lifetime. The *Mona Lisa* was probably commissioned by a local merchant who wanted a portrait of his young wife. By portraying the young woman in a relaxed, informal way, the painting broke many of the stylistic barriers of the time. Da Vinci, who studied anatomy, created especially lifelike hands. But, the eyes of the *Mona Lisa* and the enigmatic half-smile are the painting's best-known features. The *Mona Lisa* hung in Napoleon's bedroom until it was transferred to the Louvre in 1804.

Brushing Up on Vocabulary

enigmatic   perplexing or mysterious. It is derived from the Greek words *ainigma* and *ainissesthai*, meaning to speak in riddles. To the ancient Greeks, riddles were a serious business: If you were unable to answer one correctly, you might be handed over to the poser of the riddle for a lifetime of servitude.

patriotism   devoted love, support, and defense of one's country. This word comes from the Greek words *pater*, meaning "father," and *patrios*, meaning "founded by the forefathers." The word *patriotism* referred to someone who was so devoted to his family that he would defend them and the land that his "fathers" founded at great cost.

Vincenzo Perugia

1   At 7:20 on the morning of August 21, 1911, three members of the maintenance staff at the Louvre paused briefly in front of the *Mona Lisa*. The chief of maintenance remarked to his workers, "This is the most valuable picture in the world." Just over an hour later the three men again passed through the Salon Carré, where Leonardo's masterpiece hung, and saw that the painting was no longer in its place. The maintenance chief joked that museum officials had removed the picture for fear he and his crew would steal it. The joke soon proved to be an uncomfortably hollow one. *Mona Lisa* was gone.

2   Thus begins the story of the most famous art theft in history, of the most famous painting in the world, and of the man who would inevitably become the most famous art thief of all time: Vincenzo Perugia.

3   French newspapers announced the catastrophe under the banner headline "Unimaginable!" All during the weeks that followed, rumors abounded. A man carrying a blanket-covered parcel had been seen jumping onto the train for Bordeaux. A mysterious draped package had been spotted on a ship to New York, a ship to

South America, a ship to Italy. The painting had been scarred with acid, had been dumped in the sea. All clues, however far-fetched, were followed up, but no trace of the *Mona Lisa* could be found.

4   More than two years would pass before the thief surfaced. Then, in November of 1913, an art dealer in Italy received a letter from a man who signed himself "Leonard." Would the dealer like to have the *Mona Lisa?* Would he. Of course it was a joke. But was it? The dealer arranged to meet "Leonard" in a hotel room in Florence. "Leonard" produced a wooden box filled with junk. The junk was removed, a false bottom came out of the box, and there, wrapped in red silk and perfectly preserved, was the smiling face of *Mona Lisa*. The dealer swallowed his shock and phoned for the police.

5   "Leonard" was actually an Italian named Vincenzo Perugia—a house painter who had once done some contract work in the Louvre. As he told the story of the theft, it was amazingly simple. On the morning in question Perugia, dressed in a workman's smock, walked into the museum, nodded to several of the other workers, and chose a moment when no one else was in the Salon Carré to unhook the painting from the wall. Then he slipped into a stairwell, removed the picture from its frame, stuck it under his smock, and walked out. Stories that Perugia had accomplices have never been proved.

6   What were the thief's motives? And why, after pulling off what can only be described as the heist of the century, did he so naively offer the painting to the Italian dealer? Perugia claimed he was motivated by patriotism. *Mona Lisa* was an Italian painting by an Italian artist. Believing (mistakenly) that it had been stolen by Napoleon to hang in France, he wanted to restore it to its rightful home. At the same time, however, he expected to be "rewarded" by the Italian government for his heroic act and thought $100,000 would be a good amount. No one shared this point of view.

7   Perugia was tried, convicted, and sentenced to a year in prison. After his release he served in the army, married, settled in Paris, and operated a paint store. Soon Perugia, who had so briefly captured the world's headlines, settled back into the obscurity from which he had emerged.

8   And *Mona Lisa*. After a triumphal tour of several Italian museums, she was returned to France. She hangs—at least as of this writing—safely in the Louvre. Romantics say her smile is even more enigmatic than before.

Comprehension Checkup

True or False

Indicate whether the statement is true or false by writing T or F in the blank provided.

_____   1.   The man calling himself "Leonard" was actually Vincenzo Perugia.

_____   2.   The author implies that Perugia was not motivated solely by patriotism.

_____   3.   A *naive* individual is sophisticated and worldly.

_____   4.   The French police immediately settled on Perugia as the most likely culprit.

_____   5.   The painting was finally recovered in Rome, Italy.

Multiple Choice

Write the letter of the correct answer in the blank provided.

_____ 6. Perugia was able to steal the *Mona Lisa* successfully because
    a. he had previously worked at the Louvre and thus did not seem out of place
    b. he was wearing clothing that was loose enough to conceal a painting
    c. he was able to steal the painting when no one was looking
    d. all of the above

_____ 7. Perugia was under the impression that
    a. he was engaging in a patriotic gesture
    b. he would be richly rewarded for his services by the Italian government
    c. he would easily be able to sell the painting for millions of dollars
    d. both (a) and (b)

_____ 8. We can assume that
    a. Perugia was no longer welcome in his native Italy
    b. the government of France forgave Perugia once his debt to society had been paid
    c. Perugia continued to enjoy his status as a celebrity
    d. the *Mona Lisa* is back in Italy where it belongs

_____ 9. The reader can conclude that
    a. the *Mona Lisa* was seriously damaged by Perugia's theft
    b. Perugia had thought about how to conceal the *Mona Lisa*
    c. Perugia had no intention of parting with the *Mona Lisa*
    d. the chief of maintenance was behind the scheme to steal the painting

_____ 10. The reader can conclude that
    a. the *Mona Lisa* is more carefully protected today
    b. the Italian government determined that the *Mona Lisa* belongs in Italy
    c. the rumors that the painting had been defaced proved to be correct
    d. many hours went by before the painting was discovered to be missing

Internet Activity

To learn more about the *Mona Lisa* and the measures the Louvre has taken to protect it, visit the following website sponsored by the University of Florida College of Fine Arts.

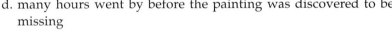

www.arts.ufl.edu/art/rt_room/mona/mona2.html

Make a brief outline of your findings and underline the opinions in your outline.

TEST-TAKING TIP

Improving Your Performance on Essay Tests (1)

Before the test

There is no substitute for simply knowing the course material well. But that can be a big task, and realistically, some parts of the material are probably more important, and more likely to appear on an essay test, than others.

One way to give your preparation some focus is to try to think of questions that might appear on the test:

- Ask yourself what questions you think your teacher might ask.

- Look at your returned test papers. You can learn a lot by reading the instructor's comments and correcting the answers.

- Review your class notes and any handouts to see what the teacher emphasized in the course. What topics did the teacher spend the most time on? What topics did the teacher seem to care the most about?

Keep in mind that an essay question may ask for information on a specific topic or it may be directed at a general understanding of the course material. You need to prepare yourself for both kinds of questions.

General or "big picture" essay questions often deal with relationships among topics or concepts. A good way to prepare for these questions is to:

- Make an outline or map of the course material.

- Look at your class notes, handouts, and your textbook, and organize this material into an outline. If your teacher has closely followed a textbook, the book's table of contents should give you a good start on making your outline.

- Prepare answers to your possible questions. You may even want to practice writing out answers.

Point of View

9

Vietnam Veterans Memorial
(1981–1983)
BY MAYA YING LIN

"It is the name of the deceased, rather than the image or likeness, that conveys immortality."

1 What do you think this quote means?

2 What is your point of view about war? About the war in Vietnam?

Introduction to Point of View

Point of view is defined as a mental attitude from which a person views or judges something. Other terms for point of view are *perspective* and *standpoint*. A point of view can be favorable, unfavorable, or neutral. A writer's point of view leads to opinions and beliefs.

View I   View II   View III

In the best-selling book *The 7 Habits of Highly Effective People*, Stephen R. Covey describes an experiment that took place at Harvard University. Professors showed one group of students the drawing at top left of a toothless old woman with a large nose and chin buried in her dark collar. Another group of students was shown the drawing at upper right of a profile of a young woman. Each group studied their assigned drawing for about ten seconds. When ten seconds had elapsed, both groups were shown the third picture at top center. When the groups were asked to describe what they now saw, each group strongly tended to describe the picture it had previously studied for 10 seconds. But when particular features of either the old woman or the young lady were pointed out to the group as a whole, the students momentarily saw the other point of view expressed in the other picture. However, when they looked away for a brief interval, they again immediately saw the picture they had been conditioned to see.

All of us have points of view on many topics. Our particular backgrounds and experiences shape our points of view. It took the Harvard students only ten seconds to become conditioned to see only one image. Our family, friends, school experiences, religion, and the media among other influences have conditioned us over a lifetime to have particular points of view and to see things in certain ways.

The cartoon on the next page illustrates how point of view is relative to our experiences.

A critical reader must be able to recognize and understand an author's point of view. While you may not agree with the author on a particular subject, it is important to maintain an open and questioning attitude.

"It's all according to your point of view. To me, you're a monster."

© 2004 J.B. Handelsman from cartoonbank.com. All Rights Reserved.

Exercise 1: Identifying Point of View

To better understand point of view, select one of the following fairy tales and retell it from the point of view of the character mentioned.

1. *Cinderella* from the point of view of one of her stepsisters.
2. *Little Red Riding Hood* from the point of view of the wolf.
3. *Snow White and the Seven Dwarfs* from the point of view of the Queen.

Exercise 2: Identifying an Author's Point of View in Textbook Material

Read each of the following selections from textbooks, and indicate the author's point of view in your own words.

Example:

Many people are concerned that art be "pretty." These people often remark, for example, "I only want to look at pleasant things" or "There's already too much ugliness in this world" or "Isn't that cute! It's darling!" They want only happy endings at the movies; they want only to be entertained. The problem with insisting that all art be pretty is that doing so limits art to one kind of expression. Because human experience is much richer than the cute and pleasant, art should be free to reflect life in all its richness. It would be nice if everything in life were pleasing, but some of the most important things are not so nice. Birth and death can be rather painful; so can falling in or out of love.

Who is to stop an artist from saying something truthful about these or any other aspects of life that she or he finds meaningful?

From Thomas Buser, *Experiencing Art Around Us*, St. Paul, MN: West Publishing, 1995, p. 18.

Author's Point of View: <u>Art should be free to reflect all facets of life.</u>

1. Stress is not always harmful. In fact, a lack of stress, sometimes called "rust out," can lead to boredom, apathy, and less than optimal health. Moderate stress may enhance behavioral adaptation and is necessary for maturation and health. Stress stimulates psychological growth. It has been said that "freedom from stress is death" and "stress is the spice of life."

From Charles B. Corbin, *Concepts of Fitness and Wellness*, 4th ed., New York: McGraw-Hill, 2002, p. 348.

Author's Point of View: _____

_____

2. If you want to get ahead in an organization, it is important to do a good job. But it is also important that people like you. If people like you, they will forgive just about anything you do wrong. If they don't like you, you can do everything right and it will not matter. Many hardworking talented people have been bypassed for promotion and fired simply because their boss or some other high-level manager didn't like them. In fact, when Henry Ford fired Lee Iacocca, he used only four words to explain his decision: "I don't like you."

From Robert N. Lussier, *Human Relations in Organizations*, 4th ed., New York: McGraw-Hill, 1999, p. 16.

Author's Point of View: _____

_____

3. Smoking interferes with your studying and your concentration: It's a disaster for your lungs, all of your body systems, your skin and your other organs, your immune system, and your brain. It's an insult you commit against yourself. (You already know the specific health risks, so I won't bore you with those. And I won't even mention chewing tobacco and its carcinogenic effects on the mouth, the throat, and the rest of the body.) If you don't smoke, that's terrific. Keep on *not* smoking. If you do smoke, make the decision to quit. I know it's a tough habit to break. Cigarette smoking is considered more addictive than cocaine, but if you want to quit, you can. Do you really want to go through life with cigarettes controlling you?

From Janet Elder, *Exercise Your College Reading Skills*, 1st ed., New York: McGraw-Hill, 2004, p. S–12.

Author's Point of View: _____

_____

4. The educational practice known as *tracking*, or grouping students by abilities, may contribute to failure. Students placed in low-track classes lack the stimulation of higher-ability peers and often get poorer teaching. They rarely move up to higher tracks, and many lose interest in trying to do better. Furthermore, since school failure and contact with antisocial peers are often related to antisocial behavior, grouping poor achievers together may solidify problem behaviors.

From Diane E. Papalia, *Human Development*, 8th ed., New York: McGraw-Hill, 2001, p. 439.

Author's Point of View: _____

_____

5. Jennifer unlocked her door quickly, raced inside, and shut it loudly behind her. She fastened the lock, threw the bolt, dropped her books on the floor, and made her way to the kitchen for her usual snack. Within a few minutes Jennifer was ensconced on the sofa, the television on and her stuffed animals clutched firmly in her hand. She decided to do her homework later. Her parents would be home then, and she tried not to spend too much time thinking about being lonely. She turned her attention to the television, to spend the next few hours watching talk shows. Jennifer is a latchkey kid. More than 3 million children between 5 and 13, like Jennifer, are left to care for themselves after school. Although the average latchkey child is left alone two and a half hours per day, a significant number are alone much longer, more than thirty-six hours per week. Some latchkey children adjust to their situations. But, for others, problems do develop, and sad to say there are few educational or social agencies to respond to their needs.

From Diane E. Papalia, *Human Development*, 8th ed., New York: McGraw-Hill, 2001, p. 439.

Author's Point of View: _____

_____

6. Lamar was finishing junior high school with resignation and despair. He had just managed to squeak through Beaton Junior High with poor grades and no understanding of how this frustrating experience would help him. He wasn't good at schoolwork and felt that the classes he had to sit through were a waste of time. Lamar's father had left school after eighth grade to go to work. Although he did not make much money, he had a car and seemed to be getting along okay. Lamar's mother had left high school when she became pregnant and had never returned. Neither of Lamar's parents thought school was critical, although both wanted Lamar to finish. But Lamar's patience was wearing thin. He wanted to end these long, boring days, get a job, and get a car. He'd had enough of school. Unfortunately, Lamar is a good candidate to join the nation's dropouts. Today, roughly one out of every nine students does not graduate from high school. This represents not only a loss of human potential but also increased costs in welfare, unemployment benefits, and potential criminal activity. And that is a national tragedy.

From Myra Pollack Sadker and David Miller Sadker in *Teachers, Schools, and Society*, 5th ed., New York: McGraw-Hill, 2000, p. 58. Copyright © 2000 McGraw-Hill. Reprinted by permission of The McGraw-Hill Companies, Inc.

Author's Point of View: _____

_____

7. The first step to improvement is always self-awareness. Analyze your shortcomings as a listener and commit yourself to overcoming them. Good listeners are not born that way. They have *worked* at learning how to listen effectively. Good listening does not go hand in hand with intelligence, education, or social standing. Like any other skill, it comes from practice and self-discipline. Begin to think of listening as an active process. So many aspects of modern life encourage us to listen passively. We "listen" to the radio while studying or "listen" to the television while moving about from room to room. This type of passive listening is a habit—but so is active listening. We can learn to identify those situations in which active listening is important. If you work seriously at becoming a more efficient listener, you

will reap rewards in your schoolwork, in your personal and family relations, and in your career.

Author's Point of View: _____

_____

8. Littleton, Colorado; Jonesboro, Arkansas; West Paducah, Kentucky; Peal, Mississippi; Edinboro, Pennsylvania; Springfield, Oregon—these are now more than just names of small and medium-size cities. They resonate with the sound of gunshots of kids killing other kids on school grounds. Each town was the scene of schoolhouse murders. As a result, people no longer perceive schools as safe havens but as another extension of the harsh reality of violence in society. But how accurate is that impression? Statistics demonstrate that a child has a one in a million chance of being killed at school. According to the Center for Disease Control, 99 percent of violent deaths of school-aged children occurred *outside* school grounds. Twenty-three times more children are killed in gun *accidents* than in school killings. Schools, then, are *safer* than their neighborhoods, but people still are unnerved by a perception of an alarming rise in schoolyard violence, perhaps generated by heavy media coverage of the recent incidents.

Author's Point of View: _____

SELECTION

Popular Mechanics   *by Raymond Carver*

"He crowded her into the wall then, trying to break her grip. He held on to the baby and pushed with all his weight."

Getting the Picture

As you are reading "Popular Mechanics" by Raymond Carver, think about the point of view of each character. Where should your sympathies lie, with the wife, the husband, or the baby?

Bio-sketch

Raymond Carver is considered by many to be one of the great short story writers of the twentieth century. The language of his stories is deceptively simple, and, as in this short story, is meant to mirror the language used by the working poor. Carver based his realistic portrayals on what he knew best. Married at nineteen, and a father soon afterward, Carver, with no marketable skills, was forced to work at a series of odd jobs to support his family. Unfortunately, the strains proved to be too much, and his first marriage ended in divorce. Eventually, he received his B.A. from what is now California State University—Humboldt and began a career as an English and creative writing instructor.

Throughout his twenty-year career, his writings have received many honors, including nominations for a Pulitzer Prize, three O' Henry awards, two grants from the National Endowment for the Arts, and a Guggenheim Fellowship. Mr. Carver died in 1988 of lung cancer, and his second wife, the poet Tess Gallagher, collaborated with director Robert Altman to create the critically acclaimed movie *Short Cuts*, based on a collection of Carver short stories. Interestingly, the short story below has also been published under the title "Little Things." What do you suppose, given Carver's personal history, he meant to imply by the change in the title?

1   Early that day the weather turned and the snow was melting into dirty water. Streaks of it ran down from the little shoulder-high window that faced the backyard. Cars slushed by on the street outside, where it was getting dark. But it was getting dark on the inside too.

2   He was in the bedroom pushing clothes into a suitcase when she came to the door.

3   "I'm glad you're leaving! I'm glad you're leaving!" she said. "Do you hear?"

4   He kept on putting his things into the suitcase.

5   "I'm so glad you're leaving!" She began to cry. "You can't even look me in the face, can you?"

6   Then she noticed the baby's picture on the bed and picked it up.

7   He looked at her and she wiped her eyes and stared at him before turning and going back to the living room.

8   "Bring that back," he said.

9   "Just get your things and get out," she said.

10   He did not answer. He fastened the suitcase, put on his coat, looked around the bedroom before turning off the light. Then he went out to the living room.

11   She stood in the doorway of the little kitchen, holding the baby.

12   "I want the baby," he said.

13   "Are you crazy?"

14   "No, but I want the baby. I'll get someone to come by for his things."

15   "You're not touching this baby," she said.

16   The baby had begun to cry and she uncovered the blanket from around his head.

17   "Oh, oh," she said, looking at the baby.

18   He moved toward her.

19   "For God's sake!" she said. She took a step back into the kitchen.

20   "I want the baby."

21   "Get out of here!"

22   She turned and tried to hold the baby over in a corner behind the stove.

23   But he came up. He reached across the stove and tightened his hands on the baby.

24   "Let go of him," he said.

25   "Get away, get away!" she cried.

26   The baby was red-faced and screaming. In the scuffle they knocked down a flowerpot that hung behind the stove.

27   He crowded her into the wall then, trying to break her grip. He held on to the baby and pushed with all his weight.

28   "Let go of him," he said.

29   "Don't," she said. "You're hurting the baby," she said.

30   "I'm not hurting the baby," he said.

31   The kitchen window gave no light. In the near-dark he worked on her fisted fingers with one hand and with the other hand he gripped the screaming baby up under an arm near the shoulder.

32   She felt her fingers being forced open. She felt the baby going from her.

33   "No!" she screamed just as her hands came loose.

34   She would have it, this baby. She grabbed for the baby's other arm. She caught the baby around the wrist and leaned back.

35   But he would not let go. He felt the baby slipping out of his hands and he pulled back very hard.

36   In this manner, the issue was decided.

In Your Own Words

1. In paragraph one of Carver's story, the descriptive details are meant to convey a feeling of _____

2. When did the man decide he wanted the baby?

3. What is the man's likely reason for wanting the baby?

4. Is the baby in any actual physical danger?

5. What is meant by the last line of the story? What has been decided? What has happened to the baby?

SELECTION

The Lady or the Tiger?   *by Frank R. Stockton*

"Now the point of the story is this: Did the tiger come out of the door, or did the lady?"

Getting the Picture

Ralph Waldo Emerson once wrote: "As a man thinketh so is he, and as a man chooseth so is he." The princess described in this classic short story faces a clear dilemma. She must choose the fate of her lover and in the process reveal what sort of person she is. As you are reading the story, keep the quotation in mind. When you finish, explain the meaning of the quotation as it applies to the princess.

Bio-sketch

Frank Stockton (1834–1902) was born in Philadelphia. He became a wood engraver by trade, but he spent much of his time writing stories. His earliest stories were for children, but later he began writing for adults. Stockton's most famous story, "The Lady or the Tiger?" appeared in 1882 in the *Century Magazine*. It caused a great outcry and debates were held all over the country to decide the ending.

Brushing Up on Vocabulary

epithalamic measure   marriage dance.

barbaric   lacking civilizing influences; primitive. It comes from the Latin word *barbaricus*, meaning "foreign or rude." It is often used to describe someone who is uncultured and ignorant.

1   In the very olden time, there lived a semibarbaric king, whose ideas, though somewhat polished and sharpened by the progressiveness of distant Latin neighbors, were still large, florid, and untrammeled, as became the half of him which was barbaric. He was a man of exuberant fancy, and, withal, of an authority so irresistible that, at his will, he turned his varied fancies into facts. He was greatly given to self-communing; and when he and himself agreed upon any thing, the thing was done.

When every member of his domestic and political systems moved smoothly in its appointed course, his nature was bland and genial; but whenever there was a little hitch, and some of his orbs got out of their orbits, he was blander and more genial still, for nothing pleased him so much as to make the crooked straight and crush down uneven places.

2   Among the borrowed notions by which his barbarism had become semified was that of the public arena, in which, by exhibitions of manly and beastly valor, the minds of his subjects were refined and cultured.

3   But even here the exuberant and barbaric fancy exerted itself. The arena of the king was built, not to give the people an opportunity of hearing the rhapsodies of dying gladiators, nor to enable them to view the inevitable conclusion of a conflict between religious opinions and hungry jaws, but for purposes far better adapted to widen and develop the mental energies of the people. This vast amphitheater, with its encircling galleries, its mysterious vaults, and its unseen passages, was an agent of poetic justice, in which crime was punished, or virtue rewarded, by the decrees of an impartial and incorruptible chance.

4   When a subject was accused of a crime of sufficient importance to interest the king, public notice was given that on an appointed day the fate of the accused person would be decided in the king's arena—a structure which well deserved its name; for although its form and plan were borrowed from afar, its purpose emanated solely from the brain of this man, who, every barleycorn a king, knew no tradition to which he owed more allegiance than pleased his fancy, and who ingrafted on every adopted form of human thought and action the rich growth of his barbaric idealism.

5   When all the people had assembled in the galleries, and the king, surrounded by his court, sat high up on his throne of royal state on one side of the arena, he gave a signal, a door beneath him opened, and the accused subject stepped out into the amphitheater. Directly opposite him, on the other side of the enclosed space, were two doors, exactly alike and side by side. It was the duty and the privilege of the person on trial to walk directly to these doors and open one of them. He could open either door he pleased. He was subject to no guidance or influence but that of the aforementioned impartial and incorruptible chance. If he opened the one, there came out of it a hungry tiger, the fiercest and most cruel that could be procured, which immediately sprang upon him and tore him to pieces as a punishment for his guilt. The moment that the case of the criminal was thus decided, doleful iron bells were clanged, great wails went up from the hired mourners posted on the outer rim of the arena, and the vast audience, with bowed heads and downcast hearts, wended slowly their homeward way, mourning greatly that one so young and fair, or so old and respected, should have merited so dire a fate.

6   But if the accused person opened the other door, there came forth from it a lady, the most suitable to his years and station that his majesty could select among his fair subjects, and to this lady he was immediately married as a reward of his innocence. It mattered not that he might already possess a wife and family, or that his affections might be engaged upon an object of his own selection. The king allowed no such subordinate arrangements to interfere with his great scheme of retribution and reward. The exercises, as in the other instance, took place immediately, and in the arena. Another door opened beneath the king, and a priest, followed by a band of choristers and dancing maidens blowing joyous airs on golden horns and treading an epithalamic measure, advanced to where the pair stood, side by side; and the wedding was promptly and cheerily solemnized. Then the brass bells rang forth their merry peals, the people shouted glad hurrahs, and the innocent man, preceded by children strewing flowers on his path, led his bride to his home.

7   This was the king's semibarbaric method of administering justice. Its perfect fairness is obvious. The criminal could not know out of which door would come the lady. He opened either he pleased, without having the slightest idea whether, in the next instant, he was to be devoured or married. On some occasions the tiger came out of one door, and on some out of the other. The decisions of this tribunal were not only fair, they were positively determinate. The accused person was instantly punished if he found himself guilty; and if innocent, he was rewarded on the spot, whether he liked it or not. There was no escape from the judgments of the king's arena.

8   The institution was a very popular one. When the people gathered together on one of the great trial days, they never knew whether they were to witness a bloody slaughter or a hilarious wedding. This element of uncertainty lent an interest to the occasion which it could not otherwise have attained. Thus, the masses were entertained and pleased, and the thinking part of the community could bring no charge of unfairness against this plan; for did not the accused person have the whole matter in his own hands?

9   This semibarbaric king had a daughter as blooming as his most florid fancies and with a soul as fervent and imperious as his own. As is usual in such cases, she was the apple of his eye and was loved by him above all humanity. Among his courtiers was a young man of that fineness of blood and lowness of station common to the conventional heroes of romance who love royal maidens. This royal maiden was well satisfied with her lover, for he was handsome and brave to a degree unsurpassed in all this kingdom; and she loved him with an ardor that had enough of barbarism in it to make it exceedingly warm and strong. This love affair moved on happily for many months until one day the king happened to discover its existence. He did not hesitate nor waver in regard to his duty in the premises. The youth was immediately cast into prison, and a day was appointed for his trial in the king's arena. This, of course, was an especially important occasion; and his majesty, as well as all the people, was greatly interested in the workings and development of this trial. Never before had such a case occurred; never before had a subject dared to love the daughter of a king. In after-years such things became commonplace enough; but then they were, in no slight degree, novel and startling.

10   The tiger cages of the kingdom were searched for the most savage and relentless beasts, from which the fiercest monster might be selected for the arena; and the ranks of maiden youth and beauty throughout the land were carefully surveyed by competent judges in order that the young man might have a fitting bride in case fate did not determine for him a different destiny. Of course, everybody knew that the deed with which the accused was charged had been done. He had loved the princess, and neither he, nor she, nor anyone else thought of denying the fact; but the king would not think of allowing any fact of this kind to interfere with the workings of the tribunal, in which he took such delight and satisfaction. No matter how the affair turned out, the youth would be disposed of; and the king would take an aesthetic pleasure in watching the course of events which would determine whether or not the young man had done wrong in allowing himself to love the princess.

11   The appointed day arrived. From far and near the people gathered and thronged the great galleries of the arena; and crowds, unable to gain admittance, massed themselves against its outside walls. The king and his court were in their places, opposite the twin doors—those fateful portals, so terrible in their similarity!

12   All was ready. The signal was given. A door beneath the royal party opened, and the lover of the princess walked into the arena. Tall, beautiful, fair, his appearance was greeted with a low hum of admiration and anxiety. Half the audience had not

known so grand a youth had lived among them. No wonder the princess loved him! What a terrible thing for him to be there!

13   As the youth advanced into the arena, he turned, as the custom was, to bow to the king. But he did not think at all of that royal personage; his eyes were fixed upon the princess, who sat to the right of her father. Had it not been for the moiety of barbarism in her nature, it is probable that lady would not have been there; but her intense and fervid soul would not allow her to be absent on an occasion in which she was so terribly interested. From the moment that the decree had gone forth that her lover should decide his fate in the king's arena, she had thought of nothing, night or day, but this great event and the various subjects connected with it. Possessed of more power, influence, and force of character than anyone who had ever before been interested in such a case, she had done what no other person had done—she had possessed herself of the secret of the doors. She knew in which of the two rooms that lay behind those doors stood the cage of the tiger, with its open front, and in which waited the lady. Through these thick doors, heavily curtained with skins on the inside, it was impossible that any noise or suggestion should come from within to the person who should approach to raise the latch of one of them. But gold—and the power of a woman's will—had brought the secret to the princess.

14   And not only did she know in which room stood the lady ready to emerge, all blushing and radiant, should her door be opened, but she knew who the lady was. It was one of the fairest and loveliest of the damsels of the court who had been selected as the reward of the accused youth, should he be proved innocent of the crime of aspiring to one so far above him; and the princess hated her. Often had she seen, or imagined that she had seen, this fair creature throwing glances of admiration upon the person of her lover, and sometimes she thought these glances were perceived and even returned. Now and then she had seen them talking together; it was but for a moment or two, but much can be said in a brief space. It may have been on most unimportant topics, but how could she know that? The girl was lovely, but she had dared to raise her eyes to the loved one of the princess; and with all the intensity of the savage blood transmitted to her through long lines of wholly barbaric ancestors, she hated the woman who blushed and trembled behind that silent door.

15   When her lover turned and looked at her, and his eye met hers as she sat there paler and whiter than anyone in the vast ocean of anxious faces about her, he saw, by the power of quick perception which is given to those whose souls are one, that she knew behind which door crouched the tiger, and behind which stood the lady. He had expected her to know it. He understood her nature, and his soul was assured that she would never rest until she had made plain to herself this thing, hidden to all other lookers-on, even to the king. The only hope for the youth in which there was any element of certainty was based upon the success of the princess in discovering this mystery; and the moment he looked upon her, he saw she had succeeded, as in his soul he knew she would succeed.

16   Then it was that his quick and anxious glance asked the question: "Which?" It was as plain to her as if he shouted it from where he stood. There was not an instant to be lost. The question was asked in a flash; it must be answered in another.

17   Her right arm lay on the cushioned parapet before her. She raised her hand and made a slight, quick movement toward the right. No one but her lover saw her. Every eye but his was fixed on the man in the arena.

18   He turned, and with a firm and rapid step he walked across the empty space. Every heart stopped beating, every breath was held, every eye was fixed immovably upon that man. Without the slightest hesitation he went to the door on the right and opened it.

* * * *

"He who reflects too much will achieve little."

—J.C.F. von Schiller

19   Now, the point of the story is this: Did the tiger come out of the door, or did the lady?

20   The more we reflect upon this question, the harder it is to answer. It involves a study of the human heart which leads us through devious mazes of passion, out of which it is difficult to find our way. Think of it, fair reader, not as if the decision of the question depended upon yourself, but upon that hot-blooded semibarbaric princess, her soul at white heat beneath the combined fires of despair and jealousy. She had lost him, but who should have him?

21   How often, in her waking hours and in her dreams, had she started in wild horror and covered her face with her hands as she thought of her lover opening the door on the other side of which waited the cruel fangs of the tiger!

22   But how much oftener had she seen him at the other door! How in her grievous reveries had she gnashed her teeth and torn her hair when she saw his start of rapturous delight as he opened the door of the lady! How her soul had burned in agony when she had seen him rush to meet that woman, with her flushing cheek and sparkling eye of triumph; when she had seen him lead her forth, his whole frame kindled with the joy of recovered life; when she had heard the glad shouts from the multitude and the wild ringing of the happy bells; when she had seen the priest, with his joyous followers, advance to the couple and make them man and wife before her very eyes; and when she had seen them walk away together upon their path of flowers, followed by the tremendous shouts of the hilarious multitude, in which her one despairing shriek was lost and drowned!

23   Would it not be better for him to die at once and go to wait for her in the blessed regions of semibarbaric futurity?

24   And yet, that awful tiger, those shrieks, that blood!

25   Her decision had been indicated in an instant, but it had been made after days and nights of anguished deliberation. She had known she would be asked, she had decided what she would answer, and without the slightest hesitation she had moved her hand to the right.

26   The question of her decision is one not to be lightly considered, and it is not for me to presume to set myself up as the one person able to answer it. And so I leave it with all of you: Which came out of the opened door—the lady or the tiger?

From Frank R. Stockton, "The Lady or the Tiger", first published 1882.

✔ Comprehension Checkup

Multiple Choice

Write the letter of the correct answer in the blank provided.

_____   1.   The king is described as possessing all of the following character traits except
a. semibarbaric
b. tyrannical
c. generous and forgiving
d. self-absorbed

_____   2.   Given the similarity of the princess to her father, we can assume that she was
a. timid
b. semibarbaric
c. fervid
d. both (b) and (c)

_____ 3. The narrator calls the king's system of deciding the fate of the accused "poetic justice." This is an example of
a. literary allusion
b. irony
c. patterns of organization
d. summary

_____ 4. The princess's lover was lacking
a. good looks
b. high social standing
c. bravery
d. height

_____ 5. The tiger chosen for the trial of the princess's lover was all of the following _except_
a. savage
b. relentless
c. meek
d. fierce

_____ 6. The maiden chosen for the princess's lover was
a. fair and lovely
b. blushing and radiant
c. rich and powerful
d. both (a) and (b)

_____ 7. The guilt or innocence of the accused is determined by
a. a confession
b. a court of law
c. the appearance of a tiger or a lady
d. the king's subjects

_____ 8. "... she was the apple of his eye ..." is a figurative expression meaning that
a. the king considered the princess to be expendable
b. the king was very fond of the princess
c. the princess was the king's favorite person
d. (b) and (c)

_____ 9. The king's system of dispensing justice is
a. arbitrary and capricious
b. fair to all concerned
c. unpopular with his subjects
d. civilized

_____ 10. The author states that the reader must look to the character of the princess to determine
a. whether the princess's lover will live or die
b. whether love or jealousy will win out
c. how the story will end
d. all of the above

True or False

Indicate whether the statement is true or false by writing T or F in the blank provided.

_____ 1. The king's daughter has a fervent soul.

_____ 2. The king places a high value on human life.

_____   3.   The king approves of his daughter's love affair.

_____   4.   Both the king and the princess are present at the arena.

_____   5.   The princess is fond of the maiden behind the door.

_____   6.   The princess points to the door on the left.

_____   7.   The princess's lover unhesitatingly follows the princess's signal to go to the right.

_____   8.   The princess's lover expected the princess to know the secret of the doors.

_____   9.   When the princess's lover turned toward the king, his attention was focused on the princess.

_____ 10.   Of all the onlookers, the king alone knew the secret of what was behind each door.

Vocabulary in Context Practice

Using the context clues below, write a definition for the italicized word.

1.   ". . . by the decrees of an *impartial* and incorruptible chance."

     Definition: _____

2.   ". . . with bowed heads and *downcast* hearts . . ."

     Definition: _____

3.   "He did not hesitate nor *waver* in regard to his duty in the premises."

     Definition: _____

4.   ". . . opposite the twin doors—those fateful *portals* . . ."

     Definition: _____

5.   ". . . but her intense and *fervid* soul would not allow her to be absent . . ."

     Definition: _____

6.   ". . . which leads us through devious *mazes* of passion, out of which it is difficult to find our way."

     Definition: _____

Look through the paragraph indicated in parentheses to find a word that matches the definition below.

1.   pleasantly gentle or agreeable (1) _____

2.   ecstatic expression of feeling or enthusiasm (3) _____

3.   issued forth; originated (4) _____

4.   proceeded or went; traveled (5) _____

5.   pertaining to a sense of beauty (10) _____

6.   an indefinite portion, part or share (13) _____

7.   daydreams (22) _____

In Your Own Words

1.   Describe the nature of the princess in your own words. How might these qualities influence her decision?

2. From what you know of the princess, which door do you think she pointed to: the one hiding the lady or the one hiding the tiger? State your reasons.

3. The princess's lover went to the door on the right "without the slightest hesitation." If you were the young man, would you follow the princess's direction? Explain your answer.

The Art of Writing

In a brief essay, respond to the item below.

Write your own ending, telling what happens when the young man opens the door. Describe the princess's reaction as the door opens. Describe the young man's reaction to what he finds.

Internet Activity

In the short story "The Lady or the Tiger?", the princess must choose between two unpleasant alternatives. The Institute for Global Ethics addresses ethical dilemmas. In particular, the website focuses on "tough choices" or those that "pit one right value against another." Visit their website at: www.globalethics.org/pub/toughchoices.html. The website includes the first chapter of Rushworth Kidder's book *How Good People Make Tough Choices*. Skim the introductory material and then carefully read the ethical dilemma that a librarian working at the reference desk at a public library recently faced. What do you think the librarian decided to do? If you were in a similar situation, what would you do?

SELECTION

Excerpt from *America Past and Present*   *by Robert A. Divine*

"By mid-1967, in fact, more than 400,000 Americans were fighting in Vietnam. As many as 300 died each week."

Getting the Picture

The following selection from the history textbook *America Past and Present* discusses the Vietnam War. Fought in the 1960s and 1970s, the war was highly divisive within the United States. Throughout the 1960s, the war became increasingly controversial. Initially, Presidents Eisenhower and Kennedy sent military advisers to aid the noncommunist South Vietnamese in resisting the communist North Vietnamese. Under President Johnson, the U.S. involvement deepened to the point where half a million U.S. troops became involved in the conflict. In 1973, President Nixon negotiated a cease-fire with North Vietnam, and soon all U.S. troops returned home. In 1982, a Vietnam War Memorial was dedicated to American soldiers who were killed or missing in action in Vietnam.

Bio-sketch

Robert A. Divine is the George W. Littlefield Professor (Emeritus) at the University of Texas at Austin. An award-winning teacher, he taught diplomatic history for 42 years. His primary interest is recent political and diplomatic history with an emphasis on presidents from Franklin Roosevelt to George Bush. His book, *Perpetual War for Perpetual Peace* (2000), is an analysis of U.S. involvement in the wars of the twentieth century.

Brushing Up on Vocabulary

Tet   the first day of the Vietnamese New Year. On January 30, 1968, Communist forces struck civilian and military sites without warning throughout South Vietnam, including the U.S. embassy in Saigon.

Surviving Vietnam

"Above all, Vietnam was a war that asked everything of a few and nothing of most of America."

—Myron McPherson

1   Vietnam ranks after World War II as America's second most expensive war. Between 1950 and 1975, the United States spent $123 billion on combat in Southeast Asia. More importantly, Vietnam ranks—after our Civil War and World Wars I and II—as the nation's fourth deadliest war, with 57,661 Americans killed in action.

2   Yet, when the last U.S. helicopter left Saigon, Americans suffered what historian George Herring terms "collective amnesia." Everyone, even those who had fought in 'Nam, seemed to want to forget Southeast Asia. It took nearly ten years for the nation to erect a national monument to honor those who died in Vietnam. The Vietnam Veterans Memorial in Washington, D.C., was dedicated in November 1982; on its polished black granite walls are carved the names of the dead and missing in action. And only in 1981 did collections of oral histories of some of those who served in Vietnam begin to appear: Al Santoli's well-documented *Everything We Had: An Oral History of the Vietnam War by Thirty-three American Soldiers Who Fought It* and Mark Baker's *Nam: The Vietnam War in the Words of the Men and Women Who Fought There.* Both books demonstrate that in the steaming jungles of Vietnam one thing mattered most: survival.

3   One Vietnam veteran expressed the general feeling of men in combat: "War is not killing. Killing is the easiest part. . . . Sweating twenty-four hours a day, seeing guys drop all around you from heatstroke, not having food, not having water, sleeping only three hours a night for weeks at a time, that's what war is. Survival."

4   During his term President Kennedy ordered a more than tenfold increase in the number of U.S. advisers in Vietnam. Yet, for the ten to twelve thousand predominantly career soldiers there by December of 1962, Vietnam seemed a nice little nine-to-five war. Recalls radio technician Jan Barry of the army's 18th Aviation Company, "If we wanted to go out and chase people around and shoot at them . . . we had a war going. If we didn't . . . they left us alone." In those early days, even the Special Forces Green Berets "used to stop at four-thirty and have a happy hour and get drunk," says Barry, adding that "there was no war after four-thirty. On Saturdays, no war. On Sundays, no war. On holidays, no war. That's right, a nine-to-five war."

5   Within two years, however, the Joint Chiefs of Staff and President Johnson committed 50,000 American troops to combat in Vietnam, and the nice little war turned grim. By mid-1967, in fact, more than 400,000 Americans were fighting in Vietnam. As many as 300 died each week. Combat, recalls 26th Marine division scout-sniper James Hebron, turned out "totally different" from what he had expected when he had joined the corps at age seventeen early in 1967. "There was no romance at all," says Hebron. During one combat period, Hebron's Bravo Company went without a hot meal for seven months. During that same operation, he notes, "I didn't brush my teeth for two months," explaining that "they sent toothbrushes . . . we had to use them to clean our rifles."

"The object of war is to survive it."

—John Irving

6   The Screaming Eagles of the elite 101st Airborne Division arrived in Vietnam shortly before the Tet offensive of January 1968. Lieutenant Robert Santos, destined to become one of the division's most decorated men, told his platoon, "Two things

can happen to you. You can get wounded and go home early. Or you can die." He added that the "best way to go home is whole. If you stick with me . . . and learn from the [more experienced men] you won't get wounded. You won't die." Santos and his men earned a basketful of medals for valor in combat. Lieutenant Santos explains those medals in grim terms: "My responsibility was to kill and in the process of killing to be so good at it that I indirectly saved my men's lives." So, notes Santos, "You come home with the high body count, high kill ratio," but, he concludes, "there's nothing, nothing, that's very satisfying about that."

7   Few who served in Vietnam survived unscathed, whether psychologically or physically. One of the 303,600 Americans wounded during the long war was 101st Airborne platoon leader James Bombard, first shot and then blown up by a mortar round during the bitter Tet fighting at Hue in February 1968. He describes his traumatic experience as

8   feeling the bullet rip into your flesh, the shrapnel tear the flesh from your bones and the blood run down your leg. . . . To put your hand on your chest and to come away with your hand red with your own blood, and to feel it running out of your eyes and out of your mouth, and seeing it spurt out of your guts, realizing you were dying. . . . I was ripped open from the top of my head to the tip of my toes. I had forty-five holes in me.

9   Somehow Bombard survived Vietnam.

10   The fighting continued for four years after President Nixon took office. Robert Rawls served as a rifleman with the 1st Cavalry Division from early 1969 to 1970. He recalls:

11   We got fire fights after fire fights. My first taste of death. After fire fights you could smell it. They brought the [dead men] back wrapped in ponchos. . . . [T]hey just threw them up on the helicopter and [piled empty, reusable supply cases] on top of them. You could see the guys' feet hanging out. . . . I had nightmares. . . . I can still see those guys.

12   As the war dragged on, pacifist frustration at home paralleled the bitterness of those who had fought in Vietnam. John Muir's experience is typical. Early in the war, Muir had served as a rifleman with the 1st Marine Division during the battle of Dong Ha. Muir's single company fought continuously for four days and four nights, frequently in hand-to-hand combat, against two divisions of the North Vietnamese Army. When the marines were relieved, only ninety-one men—all wounded—were still able to fight at all. Muir's squad, however, had been wiped out: He had ended up throwing rocks at his attackers.

13   "It was a major battle," recalls Muir. "We did a fine job there. If it had happened in World War II, they still would be telling stories about it. But it happened in Vietnam, so nobody knows about it."

14   Withdrawing U.S. forces from Vietnam ended only the combat. Returning veterans fought government disclaimers concerning the toxicity of the defoliant Agent Orange. VA hospitals across the nation still contain thousands of para- and quadriplegic Vietnam veterans, as well as the maimed from earlier wars. Throughout America the "walking wounded" find themselves still embroiled in the psychological aftermath of Vietnam. To this day, says former 1st Infantry Division combat medic David Ross, "If I'm walking someplace and there's grass, I find myself sometimes doing a shuffle and looking down at the ground. . . . I'm looking for a wire or a piece of vine that looks too straight, might be a [land mine] trip wire. Some of the survival habits you pick up stay residual for a long time."

From Robert A. Divine et al., *America Past and Present,* 5th ed., pp. 954–955. Copyright © 1999 by Addison Wesley Educational Publishers, Inc. Reprinted by permission of Pearson Education, Inc.

✔

Comprehension Checkup

True or False

Indicate whether the statement is true or false by writing T or F in the blank provided.

_____ 1. The Vietnam War was the deadliest war in U.S. history.

_____ 2. Collections of oral histories of Vietnam veterans did not begin appearing until after the conflict was over.

_____ 3. Many U.S. soldiers in Vietnam made surviving their foremost goal.

_____ 4. President Kennedy reduced the number of Americans serving as military advisers to the South Vietnamese.

_____ 5. Under President Kennedy, soldiers stationed in Vietnam were mostly persons who had chosen to make the military their careers.

_____ 6. Some soldiers who arrived in Vietnam were disillusioned to discover that the war did not have a romantic side.

_____ 7. Once the conflict escalated in the early 1960s, U.S. soldiers faced many hardships.

_____ 8. The Tet offensive occurred in 1978.

_____ 9. Robert Santos and his division earned many medals.

_____ 10. James Bombard was lucky to be able to return home unscathed by his Vietnam experience.

Multiple Choice

Write the letter of the correct answer in the blank provided.

_____ 1. "Collective amnesia" refers to
a. a desire to remember and celebrate an event
b. a desire to forget an event or put it out of mind
c. a desire to reminisce about the past
d. a desire to commiserate over past sorrows

_____ 2. Jan Barry's reference to a "nine-to-five" war implies that
a. soldiers fought around-the-clock in stressful circumstances
b. soldiers could fight when they wanted to
c. soldiers were unlikely to be waging war on the weekends
d. both (b) and (c)

_____ 3. Lieutenant Robert Santos was
a. unsuccessful at killing the enemy
b. not recognized by his superiors for bravery
c. conflicted about achieving a high kill ratio
d. a member of the Screaming Hawks

_____ 4. A _traumatic_ experience is one that has
a. no effect on a person
b. a slight effect on a person
c. a great effect on a person
d. a relaxing effect on a person

_____ 5. After President Nixon was elected to office,
a. the fighting in Vietnam ceased immediately
b. the fighting continued for two more years

c. an immediate cease-fire was negotiated

d. the fighting continued for an additional four years

———— 6. In Vietnam, the dead American soldiers were
a. handled with dignity and respect
b. wrapped in ponchos
c. evacuated by helicopter
d. both (b) and (c)

———— 7. A *pacifist* is someone who
a. subjugates others
b. advocates going to war
c. opposes war or violence to settle disputes
d. has a calm disposition

———— 8. *Hand-to-hand* combat implies
a. direct physical contact with the enemy
b. dropping bombs from a great distance
c. overwhelming the enemy with tanks and mobile units
d. none of the above

———— 9. When the author says that the squad was *wiped out*, he means that its members
a. were completely exhausted
b. were nearly all killed
c. were intoxicated
d. were discharged from the armed services

———— 10. Soldiers who returned home after the war
a. were treated as heroes
b. suffered few ill effects of their experiences
c. had to contend with the aftereffects of exposure to Agent Orange
d. made an easy transition to civilian life

Vocabulary Practice

Fill in the blanks with a word from the list below. Not all of the words will be used.

amnesia	disclaimer	maimed	predominantly	toxicity
combat	elite	offensive	residual	traumatic
dedicated	embroiled	paralleled	shuffled	unscathed
destined	grim	paraplegic	spurt	valor

1. Mara ————————— her book to a very close personal friend.

2. Luckily, we came out of the accident completely —————————.

3. The soldier received a medal for courage and ————————— beyond the call of duty.

4. The ————————— of many new drugs has not yet been determined.

5. Bill Gates's teachers recognized at an early age that Bill Gates was ————————— for greatness.

6. For many young boys, a growth ————————— occurs around age twelve.

7. Persons attending the politician's $500-a-plate dinner were ————————— wealthy.

8.   Michael and Jennie are _____ in a very nasty divorce.

9.   I felt a special closeness to him because his situation at school so closely _____ mine.

10. Sarah pulled herself out of bed and with the aid of a walker _____ off to get breakfast.

In Your Own Words

1.   What is the main idea of this selection?

2.   What do you think the author's point of view is toward the Vietnam War? Does he give us any clues to his point of view? In general, are the quotations he provides throughout the selection positive or negative about the war?

3.   If you had been a young person growing up in the 1960s, what do you think your response would have been to the Vietnam conflict? Would you have supported it or opposed it?

4.   Do you think that people who protested against the war at home showed a lack of respect for the soldiers doing the fighting? Do you think that the protestors were patriotic or unpatriotic?

The Art of Writing

In a brief essay, respond to the item below.

In 1967, naval aviator John McCain was shot down over Hanoi. Severely injured, he was held as a prisoner-of-war (POW) for five-and-a-half years. At times, he was tortured and held in solitary confinement. Despite such harsh treatment, he not only survived, but returned to serve in first the House of Representatives and then the Senate. What qualities do you think an individual must possess to be able to survive and overcome such an ordeal?

Vietnam War Memorial: Multiple Points of View

Getting the Picture

The Vietnam Veterans Memorial, located on the mall in Washington, D.C., receives about 3.5 million visitors annually. Designed to help promote national reconciliation, it has become America's best-known public art. Although initial reaction to the memorial design was positive, many veterans came to feel that it had a tone of "defeat." As a result, a flag and *The Face of Honor* sculpture were added.

Presented below is a sample of different points of view about the memorial from a variety of sources. These viewpoints are given in chronological order starting from 1982 and ending in 2000.

"What's In A Name"

1   The Vietnam War Memorial is on hallowed ground—two acres of land near the Lincoln Memorial and the Washington Monument. The controversial design follows a controversial war that cost almost 58,000 lives. The war was a 25-year struggle to contain

communism, a war that U.S. presidents could not afford to lose and were afraid to win. It ended in the final eerie days of spring 1975, when South Vietnam slowly collapsed like a building going down under demolition charges and the last of the besieged Americans lifted off a rooftop in a helicopter.

2   How do you have a memorial for this sort of thing? Seven-million dollars were raised for it and the winning design was that of Maya Ying Lin, a young Yale architecture student. The contestants were instructed only that their entries display the names of the fallen "without political or military content." I think it is one of the most impressive memorials I ever saw.

3   It is an outdoor affair. As you approach the monument, you come up a walk bent to make a long V, each side of which is two hundred and fifty feet long. The meadow is on one side, and the polished granite slabs on the other. The slabs have names on them; they are sunk into a gentle hill. It is the names that do it. They are not listed by rank or alphabet, but in the order of their deaths. These were eager young men fighting in the jungles. Sometimes they thought they knew what they were doing; often they were confused. Now the names are there—Leland G. Deeds, Imlay S. Swiddeson, Richard M. Seng—but take your eye off the cluster and you can't find the place again. It's just names, people, you and me and our sons. There are no inscriptions to tell you what to think; there are no heroic utterances. It is stark. Each name is a special boy who never came home. It is all left to the observer. The dark, shining slabs of granite are as hard and polished as a mirror, and you can see your image reflected over the names as you lean forward. My eyes moistened. In the crowd we looked at each other, deeply moved.

4   The austere jumble is extraordinarily personal, it appears, judging by the first week's experience. In a bold, slow tone, the individual names were read in a chapel in Washington's National Cathedral, one of the ceremonies that took place to honor those who served in Vietnam. It took three days, one thousand names an hour, with only a few hours off each morning. At the memorial itself, volunteers have books telling where individual names can be located. Small flags flutter at the base; at some spots a family has placed a wreath. One reads, "SP/4 Peter Lopez, A True American Hero, Eddie, Danny, Rosie, Lizbel, Mable, Mom and Dad: We miss you."

5   One man points at the name of Jose P. Ramos and his friend takes the picture. There is a search for names, and it will be hard to keep the place clear of trivia all saying the same thing: This is not a name, it is a person.

6   Some have said they think the memorial is too negative; perhaps they have spoken before seeing its powerful effect on visitors. Crowds increased each day at the memorial ceremonies. Officials agreed to add a conventional sculpture of three soldiers next year. They can do nothing, I think, to increase its impressiveness.

Comprehension Checkup

Multiple Choice

Write the letter of the correct answer in the blank provided.

_____ 1. ". . . South Vietnam slowly collapsed like a building going down under demolition charges . . ." is an example of a
a. simile
b. metaphor
c. personification
d. literary allusion

_____ 2. Which of the following statements is an opinion?
a. At the memorial itself, volunteers have books telling where individual names can be located.
b. They can do nothing, I think, to increase its impressiveness.
c. They are not listed by rank or alphabet, but in the order of their deaths.
d. One man points at the name of Jose P. Ramos, and his friend takes the picture.

_____ 3. The writer states that the Vietnam War was
a. controversial
b. fought to contain communism
c. too long
d. both (a) and (b)

_____ 4. We can assume that the writer feels that
a. seven million dollars was too much money to spend for a memorial
b. the memorial is too stark without the addition of a conventional piece of sculpture
c. the memorial needs no further embellishment
d. the memorial would be more effective if no names were inscribed on the granite slabs

Vietnam Memorial War

1   Maya Ying Lin was 13 in January 1973, when the cease-fire between the United States and North Vietnam was declared. In 1981, the Ohio-born Lin—by then a 21-year-old senior majoring in architecture at Yale University—produced the winning proposal in the design competition for a memorial to Vietnam veterans to be located on the mall in Washington, D.C. It called for two 200-foot-long walls (later expanded to 250 feet) of polished black granite to be set into a gradual rise in the landscape of Constitution Gardens, meeting at a 136-degree angle at the point where the walls and slope would be at their highest (10 feet). The names of the war dead, chronologically arranged in the order in which the servicemen fell, were to be incised in the stone, with only the dates of the first and last deaths, 1959 and 1975, to be recorded.

2   A year and a half later, the memorial was dedicated during Veterans' Day celebrations last November. Sometime later this year, the memorial's "modifications"—a flagpole and a realistic sculpture of three infantrymen, which were not in the original design—will be added near the memorial's entrance. Like so much about the Vietnam War, the memorial and its additions became the source of controversy—and finally of a compromise that would not have been as likely in the days during the war.

3   What had happened? Lin's proposal followed the guidelines set forth by the Vietnam Veterans Memorial committee, which included the stipulations that "the emphasis is to be on those who died," that the memorial be "without political or military content," and that it include the "suitable display of the names of the 57,692 Americans who died in Vietnam." The jury that chose Lin was made up primarily of architects, landscape designers, and artists. Charles Atherton, an architect and secretary of the Federal Fine Arts Commission, which rules on the building of new structures on federal land, says that the commission was particularly pleased with the jury's choice of a design that had "great respect for the environment." Lin used no vertical

lines, nothing to "disturb" the integrity of the location, an area roughly between the Lincoln and Washington monuments.

4   The designer—now in her first year of the graduate architecture program at the Harvard School of Design—sees her age as having been a boon, since she was too young to be involved in the politics of the Vietnam era. "It's a memorial to other human beings; to the people who served, to those who died, and to those who lost people," she says. She cites as primary models European memorials constructed after the First World War, especially one in France designed by the British architect Edwin Lutyens, where the experience of walking into or through the memorial provides the stimulus for reflection.

5   Not everyone thought this was enough, it turned out. Atherton recalls no opposition to the design during the first meeting on implementation. At the second one, though, a statement was made on behalf of surviving veterans to the effect that they were neither represented nor honored by the monument. Various veterans groups, which have provided much of the approximately $7 million funding for the monument and which originally supported the Lin design, got behind the movement to propose changes. The memorial fund proceeded to create a second jury made up of Vietnam veterans to decide on an appropriate additional memorial. The jury chose sculptor Frederick Hart, who had been on the third-place design team in the original competition. His eight-foot sculpture of the three soldiers was to be featured prominently toward the apex of Lin's design, with the 59-foot flagpole in the near distance.

6   In March 1982, Secretary of the Interior James Watt proposed this change, and the Fine Arts Commission voiced opposition, suggesting a compromise that would separate the sculpture from the memorial structure. By that time, the American Institute of Architects had entered the fray, objecting to the undercutting of the original competition process. As the final granite slabs were being put in place on the monument, the Fine Arts Commission set an open hearing in October on the fate of the Hart sculpture. It was an emotional hearing, especially on the part of various veterans, who pleaded in favor of the statue as a literal representation to which the survivors could relate. Says Atherton, "You had to recognize the enormously strong feelings aroused, the compelling evidence by those in support of the flag and the statue. That couldn't be ignored on purely esthetic grounds." Lin appealed to the commission to protect the integrity of the design, voicing fears that the additions, if placed centrally, would turn it into "no more than an architectural backdrop."

7   At the end of the hearing, J. Carter Brown, chairman of the Fine Arts Commission and director of the National Gallery of Art, announced the commission's approval of the flagpole and statue, and its intention to see that these elements be placed near one another at the entrance to the memorial area. There the sculpture could strike "a chord of recognition" for many, while preserving the feeling of the original design, about which he said: "I think the litany of those names is enough to bring enormous emotions to everyone's heart." Brown referred his listeners to the abstract nature of the Washington monument, which has no statues of "George crossing the Delaware." As for the sculpture, Brown says it is a credit to Hart. "The three soldiers act as a kind of Greek chorus, facing the monument, commenting on its meaning. We were lucky with the statue; it could have been kitschy, but it isn't."

8   The commission's compromise decision was hailed by the American Institute of Architects, the Vietnam Veterans Memorial Committee, the Interior Department, and designer Lin. "I feel relief," she says, at the decision "not to let the sculpture destroy the quiet and simplicity" of the original design. The finished memorial is, she says,

"so close to what I had envisioned that it's scary. Now that it's completed, it's got a life of its own. I feel like just another visitor."

Comprehension Checkup

Multiple Choice

Write the letter of the correct answer in the blank provided.

_____ 1. The writer encloses the word *modifications* in quotes to indicate
  a. that in a sense the flagpole and the sculpture of the three infantrymen did not modify the original design
  b. Lin's design failed to maintain the integrity of the location
  c. Lin failed to follow the rules of the competition
  d. acceptance of Lin's original design

_____ 2. As the designer of the memorial, Maya Ying Lin viewed her age at the time of the cease-fire as
  a. a handicap
  b. a benefit
  c. of no great importance
  d. a slight consideration

_____ 3. When Brown refers to Hart's sculpture "as a kind of Greek chorus," he is using a
  a. literary allusion
  b. caricature
  c. euphemism
  d. satire

_____ 4. The commission's compromise entailed
  a. abandoning the idea of a sculpture and a flagpole
  b. moving the Hart sculpture from the highest point of the Wall to the entrance of the memorial
  c. asking Lin to redesign the memorial to accommodate the additions
  d. relinquishing control of the memorial to the Vietnam veterans

What Happens When a Woman Designs a War Monument?

1 A few days before the official dedication, I went to have a look at the Vietnam Memorial. I was prepared for an ambivalent experience. Like all monuments, it proposes a place in history for its subject. In this case, though, the task of interpretation was full of risk: memories of Vietnam are divided, in conflict. Even the idea of remembrance is charged. Until a group of veterans organized this project, America's official preference had been amnesia.

2 The design for a memorial was selected in a national competition won unanimously by Maya Ying Lin, an architectural student at Yale University. From the outburst of vituperation that greeted Maya Lin's project one might have thought she proposed to erect a statue of Ho Chi Minh. Judgments ranged from "a tribute to Jane Fonda" to "a black hole" to "a wailing wall for Draft Dodgers and New Lefters of the future."

3 The object of this vehemence—I discovered on my visit—is a serene and beautiful place. It's a place with a rare capacity to move. On the day I was there, I saw flowers and personal mementos leaning against the sides of the walls, messages

taped to them. Instinctively, visitors reached out to touch the names of relations and comrades, their hands reflected in the polished surface so that another hand appeared to be reaching out from within.

4   At about the same time I was observing all of this, the Washington Fine Arts Commission was voting to make certain modifications to the memorial. These will include a large flagpole with the emblems of the five military services carved into its base and a realistic statue of three soldiers (two white and one black) in full battle regalia. But why should this be necessary? Where does Maya Lin's compelling work "fail"?

5   It seems to me that Maya Lin's monument is being assaulted because it is out of character. It is not the kind of war memorial that is a memorial to war—no charging GIs with bayonets fixed here. Vietnam veterans wanted to build a memorial precisely to establish a connection with veterans of other wars whose monuments abound. Most people can scarcely imagine a monument without statues and classical decor. To build one outside this area of convention seems a provocation. Many Vietnam veterans were especially sensitive to the fact that the memorial is an exception. What is being said, in essence, is that abstract art cannot evoke abstract ideas like "courage," "honor," or "sacrifice."

6   The final reason that had Maya Lin's (male) critics in such a dither was that the source of this seditious modernism was not simply a student, not simply an Asian, but worst of all a woman. That a woman should have won the commission was the final affront, absolute confirmation that the war was to be remembered differently, a monument emasculated.

From Michael Sorkin, "What Happens when a woman designs a war monument?" in *Vogue*, May 1983, p. 120, 122. Reprinted by permission of the author.

Comprehension Checkup

Multiple Choice

Write the letter of the correct answer in the blank provided.

_____   1. We can assume that the writer thinks Maya Lin's monument
              a. glorifies war
              b. will not be complete even with modifications
              c. has a rare capacity to move individuals
              d. insults veterans

_____   2. The writer feels that the memorial has been criticized for all of the following reasons *except*
              a. it was designed by a woman
              b. it represents an abstract architectural design
              c. it is unlike other war memorials
              d. it touches people emotionally

_____   3. When the writer describes the memorial as a "serene and beautiful place" we can assume
              a. the writer's point of view is positive
              b. the writer's point of view is negative

_____   4. The words *outburst of vituperation* imply
              a. condemnation
              b. castigation
              c. denunciation
              d. all of the above

Vietnam Memorial

1   In 1982, a group of Vietnam veterans had just obtained Congressional approval for a memorial that would pay long-delayed tribute to those who had fought in Vietnam with honor and courage in a lost and highly unpopular cause. They had chosen a jury of architects and art worldlings to make a blind selection in an open competition; that is, anyone could enter, and no one could put his name on his entry. Every proposal had to include something—a wall, a column—on which a hired engraver could inscribe the names of all 57,000-plus members of the American military who had died in Vietnam. Nine of the top 10 choices were abstract designs that could be executed without resorting to that devious and accursed bit of trickery: skill. Only the No. 3 choice was representational. Up on one end of a semicircular wall bearing the 57,000 names was an infantryman on his knees beside a fallen comrade, looking about for help. At the other end, a third infantryman had begun to run along the top of the wall toward them. The sculptor was Frederick Hart.

2   The winning entry was by a young Yale undergraduate architectural student named Maya Lin. Her proposal was a V-shaped wall, period, a wall of polished black granite inscribed only with the names; no mention of honor, courage, or gratitude; not even a flag. Absolutely skillproof, it was.

3   Many veterans were furious. They regarded her wall as a gigantic pitiless tombstone that said, "Your so-called service was an absolutely pointless disaster." They made so much noise that a compromise was struck. An American flag and statue would be added to the site. Hart was chosen to do the statue. He came up with a group of three soldiers, realistic down to the aglets of their boot strings, who appear to have just emerged from the jungle into a clearing, where they are startled to see Lin's V-shaped black wall bearing the names of their dead comrades.

4   Naturally enough, Lin was miffed at the intrusion, and so a make-peace get-together was arranged in Plainview, New York, where the foundry had just completed casting the soldiers. Doing her best to play the part, Lin asked Hart—as Hart recounted it—if the young men used as models for the three soldiers had complained of any pain when the plaster casts were removed from their faces and arms. Hart couldn't imagine what she was talking about. Then it dawned on him. She assumed that he had covered the model's body in wet plaster and removed it when it began to harden. No artist of her generation (she was 21) could even conceive of a sculptor starting out solely with a picture in his head, a stylus, a brick of moist clay, and some armature wire. No artist of her generation dared even speculate about . . . skill.

From Tom Wolfe, "The Invisible Artist" in *Hooking Up*. Copyright © 2000 by Tom Wolfe. Reprinted by permission of Farrar, Straus and Giroux, LLC.

Comprehension Checkup

Multiple Choice

Write the letter of the correct answer in the blank provided.

_____ 1. We can assume that a blind selection was used to
   a. allow those who were well known in the art world to have a better chance of being chosen
   b. give each entry an equal chance to be chosen
   c. keep the press from knowing the results too early in the process
   d. keep the public from voicing opinions prematurely

_____ 2. Which of the following value assumptions does the writer seem to make?
    a. A person as young as Lin could not possibly understand the concept of skill.
    b. A representational design embodying skill is superior to a design that is abstract.
    c. The veterans were justifiably angry about Lin's design.
    d. all of the above.

_____ 3. The expression "miffed at the intrusion" implies
    a. acceptance
    b. displeasure
    c. annoyance
    d. both (b) and (c)

_____ 4. The tone of the writer toward Maya Lin is
    a. indifferent
    b. sympathetic
    c. contemptuous
    d. neutral

Boundaries

1 I wanted to create a memorial that everyone would be able to respond to, regardless of whether one thought our country should or should not have participated in the war. On a personal level, I wanted to focus on the nature of accepting and coming to terms with a loved one's death. Simple as it may seem, I remember feeling that accepting a person's death is the first step in being able to overcome that loss.

2 I felt that as a culture we were extremely youth-oriented and not willing or able to accept death or dying as a part of life. The rites of mourning, which in more primitive and older cultures were very much a part of life, have been suppressed in our modern times. In the design of the memorial, a fundamental goal was to be honest about death, since we must accept that loss in order to begin to overcome it. The pain of the loss will always be there, it will always hurt, but we must acknowledge the death in order to move on.

3 What then would bring back the memory of a person? A specific object or image would be limiting. A realistic sculpture would be only one interpretation of that time. I wanted something that all people could relate to on a personal level. At this time I had as yet no form, no specific artistic image.

4 Then someone in my class received the design program, which stated the basic philosophy of the memorial's design and also its requirements: all the names of those missing and killed (57,000) must be a part of the memorial; the design must be apolitical, harmonious with the site, and conciliatory.

5 These were all the thoughts that were in my mind before I went to see the site.

6 Without having seen it, I couldn't design the memorial, so a few of us traveled to Washington, D.C., and it was at the site that the idea for the design took shape. The site was a beautiful park surrounded by trees, with traffic and noise coming from one side—Constitution Avenue.

7 I had a sudden impulse to cut into the earth.

8 I imagined taking a knife and cutting into the earth, opening it up, an initial violence and pain that in time would heal. The grass would grow back, but the initial cut would remain a pure flat surface in the earth with a polished, mirrored

surface, much like the surface on a geode when you cut it and polish the edge. The need for the names to be on the memorial would be the memorial; there was no need to embellish the design further. The people and their names would allow everyone to respond and remember.

9   It would be an interface, between our world and the quieter, darker, more peaceful world beyond. I chose black granite in order to make the surface reflective and peaceful. I never looked at the memorial as a wall, an object, but as an edge to the earth, an opened side. The mirrored effect would double the size of the park, creating two worlds, one we are a part of and one we cannot enter. The two walls were positioned so that one pointed to the Lincoln Memorial and the other pointed to the Washington Monument. By linking these two strong symbols for the country, I wanted to create a unity between the nation's past and present.

10   On our return to Yale, I quickly sketched my idea up, and it almost seemed too simple, too little. But the image was so simple that anything added to it began to detract from it.

11   I always wanted the names to be chronological, to make it so that those who served and returned from the war could find their place in the memorial.

12   As far as all the controversy, I really never wanted to go into it too much. The memorial's starkness, its being below grade, being black, and how my age, gender, and race played a part in the controversy, we'll never quite know. I think it is actually a miracle that the piece ever got built. From the beginning I often wondered, if it had not been an anonymous entry 1026 but rather an entry by Maya Lin, would I have been selected?

From Maya Lin, *Boundaries,* pp. 4:10–4:11. Copyright © 2000 by Maya Lin Studio, Inc. Reprinted with permission of Simon & Schuster Adult Publishing Group.

 ## Comprehension Checkup

Multiple Choice

Write the letter of the correct answer in the blank provided.

_____ 1. Which one of the following statements best reveals the writer's attitude toward the memorial?
a. A memorial is not the place for personal reflection.
b. A war memorial must include a heroic statue.
c. A realistic sculpture would have been too limiting.
d. A black memorial is more appropriate for a losing war effort.

_____ 2. A key point the writer makes is
a. in light of the many controversies, it's surprising that the memorial was ever built
b. the site did not influence the design
c. the reflective properties of black granite was an unexpected dividend
d. it was important that the names of those who died be listed on the memorial in alphabetical order

_____ 3. The writer would agree with which of the following statements?
a. Black granite was chosen to indicate deep sadness and shame.
b. The names are the memorial; no further embellishment is required.

    c. It was important to link the Vietnam Memorial to the Washington Monument and the Jefferson Memorial.

    d. A memorial should make a political statement.

_____ 4. What can we infer about the values of the writer?

    a. She feels that the first step toward overcoming a loved one's death is acceptance of the loss.

    b. She believes that American culture focuses too much on the problems of the elderly.

    c. She feels that death and dying should be a part of life.

    d. both (a) and (c)

A Quiet Place for Personal Reflection

1   Snow and ice carpet the ground, making walking especially hazardous. Yet thousands have come on this cold January day to see the Vietnam Veterans Memorial.

2   Each year, more than 2.5 million people visit the site, located just north of the Lincoln Memorial, ranking it among the most popular tourist attractions in Washington.

3   For many, the monument's shimmering black panels—containing the names of the more than 58,000 American men and women who died in Vietnam—symbolize the nation's effort to come to grips with one of the most divisive chapters in its history.

4   "This place is an important national symbol, like the Statue of Liberty," says John R. Gifford, 43, a Westport, Massachusetts, police officer who was making his second visit to the memorial.

5   But, Gifford says, the "Wall" is more than just a symbol. It has deep personal meaning for those who lived during the Vietnam era—especially those who fought or lost a loved one in the war. "You can see how hard it is when folks who have lost someone near and dear to them in Vietnam come here," he says.

6   The monument contains 140 slabs of black granite quarried in India. The names are inscribed in chronological order, beginning with the first American casualty in 1959 and ending with those who died in 1975, the year South Vietnam fell.

7   The Wall consists of two sections, each 246 feet long, that meet at a 125-degree angle, forming a wide V. The height of the wall rises from just a foot, at each end, to about 10 feet at the point where the sections meet.

8   The design by Maya Lin, a young architecture student, was controversial when she proposed it almost two decades ago. Many veterans wanted a more traditional war monument—with statues of soldiers. But Lin wanted the memorial to be "a quiet place, meant for personal reflection and private reckoning." When submitting her design in 1981, she wrote, "The actual area is wide and shallow, allowing for a sense of privacy, and the sunlight from the memorial's southern exposure, along with the grassy park surrounding and within its walls, contribute to the serenity of the area. Thus, the memorial is for those who have died, and for us to remember them."

9   To mollify the critics, the Vietnam Veterans Memorial Fund (VVMF) in 1982 commissioned the late Frederick Hart, a noted Washington, D.C., sculptor, to create a traditional statue to accompany Lin's design. Sited just a few feet from the Wall, it depicts three rifle-carrying infantryman—a white, a black, and a Hispanic.

10   Judging by the streams of visitors to the Wall, and the solemnity that envelops it, Lin's concept was sound. "This is such a solemn place," says Mark Yanick, a 37-year-old human resources trainer from Washington, D.C., who had brought an out-of-town friend to see the Wall. "This is the only monument I've ever been to where there is total silence, even when it's crowded."

11   The memorial is the brainchild of Jan C. Scruggs, an infantryman who was wounded in Vietnam. Scruggs conceived of the idea for a memorial after watching Michael Chamino's *The Deer Hunter,* a troubling 1979 film about the tortured lives of a group of returning Vietnam vets. "After I made the decision that we needed something like this, I became obsessed with it," he says.

12   Along with other veterans from "Nam," Scruggs formed the VVMF in 1979 to raise money and find a location and design for the memorial. The project came together with remarkable speed. Within a few years, they had raised more than $8 million from private sources, including more than 275,000 individuals. In 1980, Congress provided two acres on the Mall for the memorial.

13   That year, the VVMF held a design competition. Lin, then a 21-year-old student at Yale University, bested the 1,421 entries submitted, many by some of the world's leading architects. Construction began in March 1982, and in November the memorial was dedicated.

14   "We figured that a lot of people would come the first year because it would be a novelty, but after that it would just be something for the vets," Scruggs says. "Now it's a symbol to the nation, much like the Eiffel Tower is the symbol of France."

Comprehension Checkup

Multiple Choice

Write the letter of the correct answer in the blank provided.

_____   1. The phrase *to mollify* as used in paragraph 9 means
                a. to annoy
                b. to appease
                c. to embroil
                d. to mislead

_____   2. It is amazing that
                a. it took so long to raise enough money to build the monument
                b. visitors to the memorial become so loud and excited
                c. the memorial grounds remain quiet even when they are crowded
                d. such a small number of people submitted design proposals

_____   3. We can assume that
                a. the Wall has become a national symbol that has little personal meaning for people who visit it
                b. the memorial depicts the passing of time from the first fatality to the last
                c. Lin's design proposal was popular right from the start
                d. the memorial is located far from other monuments in Washington, D.C.

_____   4. It is ironic that
                a. a wall has come to symbolize a nation's coming to terms with a difficult chapter in its history
                b. the controversial memorial has endured as a popular tourist attraction
                c. the design submitted by a young architecture student was chosen over designs submitted by world famous architects
                d. all of the above

Some Facts About the Vietnam Wall

Drawing on what you learned from the previous selections, insert the missing information in the blanks.

1. The Vietnam Memorial was designed by _____, an architecture student at _____ University.

2. Out of _____ entries submitted in the competition to design the Vietnam Memorial, the winning entry was number _____.

3. The Vietnam Memorial is located near the _____ Monument and the _____ Memorial.

4. The names of more than _____ soldiers missing or killed in action are carved into the memorial. (Use the most recent count.)

5. The memorial is made of _____ (number) polished black _____ slabs.

6. The first American casualty in the Vietnam War occurred in _____.

7. In 1982, a sculpture of three infantrymen by _____ was commissioned.

8. The Vietnam Memorial was the idea of _____, an infantryman wounded in Vietnam.

9. The memorial was dedicated on _____ Day.

Who Said It?

Match the quotation with the speaker. Write the letter of the speaker in the appropriate blank.

A. Charles Atherton   E. Jan C. Scruggs

B. J. Carter Brown   F. Tom Wolfe

C. John R. Gifford   G. Mark Yanick

D. Maya Lin

_____ 1. "I think the litany of those names is enough to bring enormous emotions to everyone's heart."

_____ 2. "Thus the memorial is for those who have died, and for us to remember them."

_____ 3. "Now it's a symbol to the nation, much like the Eiffel Tower is the symbol of France."

_____ 4. "You had to recognize the enormously strong feelings aroused, the compelling evidence by those in support of the flag and the statue."

_____ 5. "No artist of her generation dared even speculate about . . . skill."

_____ 6. "This place is an important national symbol, like the Statue of Liberty."

_____ 7. "This is the only monument I've ever been to where there is total silence, even when it's crowded."

Determining Point of View

Below is a list of the selections you have just read. For each one, indicate whether the author's point of view about the Vietnam Memorial is primarily positive, negative, or neutral.

1. "What's in a Name" _____

2. "Vietnam Memorial War" _____

3. "What Happens When a Woman Designs a War Monument?" _____

4. "Vietnam Memorial" _____

5. "Boundaries" _____

6. "A Quiet Place for Personal Reflection" _____

In Your Own Words

1. Over the last twenty years, the National Park Service has collected more than 65,000 objects left at the Vietnam Memorial by visitors, including service medals, combat boots, flowers, poems, and photographs. Some visitors to the memorial place a piece of paper over a name and then draw back and forth with a pencil to make a "rubbing" of it. Why do you think many visitors are so expressive when they visit the memorial?

2. Paul Spreiregen, a Washington-based architect who organized the competition and helped select the judging panel, views Lin's design as an effective symbol: "It's a rift in the earth, as the war was a tear in the fabric of the American experience." Stanley Karrow, author of *Vietnam: A History*, says that the monument "stands as a vivid symbol of both unity and redemption." What do you think the memorial symbolizes?

The Art of Writing

In a brief essay, respond to one of the items below.

1. The Vietnam Memorial is often referred to as "the Wall." There are many idiomatic expressions that have the word *wall* in them, such as: the walls have ears, one's back to the wall, beat one's head against the wall, climb the walls, drive someone up the wall, fly on the wall, go to the wall, handwriting on the wall, hole in the wall, off the wall, run into a stone wall. Choose one of these expressions and explain its meaning.

2. Read the poem "Mending Wall" by Robert Frost. What does Frost think should be done with walls? Do you think that "good fences make good neighbors"?

3. Compare and contrast Tom Wolfe's view of the Vietnam Memorial with that of *The New Republic*'s editor. Explain which view you find closest to your own and explain why.

Internet Activity

1. Investigate the Virtual Wall at

   www.thevirtualwall.org.

Write a summary of your findings.

2. Using the World Wide Web, investigate one of the following "walls" and write a summary of your findings.

Wall Street

Hadrian's Wall

Berlin Wall

Wailing Wall

Great Wall of China

Making Connections

A documentary about Maya Ying Lin entitled *Maya Lin: A Strong Clear Vision* (produced by Freida Lee Mock and Terry Sanders, 82 min) won an Academy Award in 1995. A brief clip from this film can be seen at

www.americanfilmfoundation.com/order/maya_lin.html

TEST-TAKING TIP

Improving Your Performance on Essay Tests (2)

During the Test

- **Read the question carefully!** You might write a wonderful essay, but if it doesn't answer the question, it will not do you much good. Make sure you know what the question is asking, and make sure you consider all parts of the question.

- **Think about how best to answer the question before you start writing!** What material from the course will the answer involve? What do you remember about this material. Think of specific examples that will illustrate your points. Make sure you can answer the six question words: who, what, where, when, why, and how. If you are prepared well for the test, the more you think about this material, the more of it you will remember.

- **Start writing!** Remember to write carefully and legibly. Try to avoid erasures, crossed out words, and words written between lines and in the margins. You might want to consider using a pen with erasable ink. And make sure you answer in complete sentences.

- **Finally, proofread your essay before turning it in!** Correct as many grammar, spelling, and punctuation errors as you can. Sloppy writing is likely to produce a bad impression.

If you find you do not have time to answer the questions at the end of the test, write some notes in summary form. These will often earn you at least partial credit.

10 Bias

The Uprising
(1848)*

BY HONORÉ DAUMIER

*To see this work of art in color, turn to the color insert following page 260.

The Phillips Collection, Washington, D.C.

This painting depicts a scene from a revolution. According to Duncan Phillips who purchased the painting in 1931, *Uprising* stands as a "symbol for all pent-up human indignation."

1 What emotion is the man with the raised fist expressing? What is the significance of his casual dress?

2 Is the crowd standing still or advancing? How can you tell?

3 Is there anything in this painting that could relate to the war for American independence?

Introduction to Bias

A **bias** is a strong leaning in either a positive or negative direction. A bias is very similar to a prejudice. Good critical readers must be aware of their own biases and the biases of others.

Sometimes writers simply state their biases; however, most biases are implied by the writer. Subjective material generally places more emphasis on opinions than facts, and it is more likely to display a strong bias.

A critical reader will study the author's line of reasoning, notice whether opinions are supported by facts and reasons, and then decide if the author's bias has hindered the making of a good argument.

Look at the following cartoon. Does the person in the first frame express a bias?

As you are reading textbook material, keep in mind that the authors also have biases. Their biases will influence the way they present the material. Although textbooks primarily deal with factual material, authors must decide what facts to include, omit, and emphasize. Pay attention to the author's tone and choice of words to determine whether he or she is biased. Such caution is especially important when the material deals with a controversial issue.

Two interesting and important personalities in the early history of the United States were John Adams and Alexander Hamilton. In 1789, George Washington was unanimously elected our first president, Adams became our first vice-president, and Hamilton became our first secretary of the treasury. Hamilton resigned from the cabinet in 1795, during Washington's second term. Adams was elected the second president in 1797 and served one term. Adams and Hamilton, both instrumental in the founding of the United States, came to have an increasing dislike for each other. Read the following two quotes from two different history textbooks and decide which example gives the reader a more negative view of Alexander Hamilton.

Example 1

Hamilton even secretly plotted with certain members of the cabinet against President Adams, who had a conspiracy rather than a cabinet on his hands.

From Thomas A. Bailey, et al., *American Pageant*, Vol. I: To 1877, 11th ed., Boston: Houghton Mifflin, 1998, p. 201.

Example 2

Although Hamilton had resigned from the Treasury Department in 1795, key members of Adams's cabinet turned to the former secretary for advice.

From James West Davidson, et al., *Nation of Nations*, Vol. 1: To 1877, 4th ed., New York: McGraw-Hill, 2001, p. 248.

The first quote appears to portray Hamilton in a far more sinister way. The words *plotted* and *conspiracy* are examples of words with strong negative feelings.

Denotative and Connotative Language

"Thanks to words we have been able to rise above the brutes; and thanks to words we have often sunk to the level of demons."

—Aldous Huxley

When you look a word up in the dictionary, you are determining its exact meaning without the suggestions or implications that it may have taken on. This is called the **denotative** meaning of a word. In contrast, the **connotative** meaning of a word refers to the ideas or feelings suggested by the word.

Words that have the same denotative meaning can have much different connotative meanings. The words *cautious* and *timorous*, for example, have similar denotative meanings, but their connotative meanings are very different. *Cautious* has a positive ring. It's good to be "cautious," isn't it? The word *timorous*, however, has a more negative connotative meaning. It suggests fearfulness or reluctance. The words *firm*, *resolute*, and *obstinate* all have similar denotative meanings. Which of these words has the more negative connotation?

Not all words have connotative meanings. The words pen or pencil, for example, do not call up strong emotional feelings. Words that are heavily connotative are often referred to as "loaded" or "emotionally charged." Writers who have a particular point of view and want to persuade you to accept that view often make use of loaded words or phrases. Thus, subjective material is more likely to rely on heavily connotative language, and it is more likely to display a strong bias. If a writer approves of a city's monetary policy toward libraries, the word *thrifty* might be used. If the writer disagrees with the policy, the word *cheap*, which calls up negative feelings, might be used instead. The connotation of the words used can tell you a lot about the speaker or writer's opinion.

Exercise 1: Recognizing Connotative Meaning

Which of the following words in each group is the most positive?

1. _____ resolute, stubborn, unyielding
2. _____ timid, wary, cautious
3. _____ bizarre, eccentric, nutty
4. _____ old-fashioned, traditional, out-of-date

5. _____ obnoxious, abrasive, self-assertive

6. _____ thin, slim, scrawny

7. _____ miserly, cheap, thrifty

8. _____ foolhardy, courageous, vainglorious

9. _____ curious, nosy, officious

10. _____ solemn, dignified, glum

Exercise 2: Identifying Connotative Language

What are the three connotative words in the following cartoon? Put these three connotative words in order from the most positive to the most negative.

1. _____

2. _____

3. _____

PEANUTS reprinted by permission of United Feature Syndicate, Inc.

Exercise 3: Using Connotative Language

Well-known linguist S. I. Hayakawa developed the idea of "conjugating irregular verbs" to demonstrate how connotative language works. With Hayakawa's method, an action or a personality trait is "conjugated" to show how it can be viewed either favorably or unfavorably depending on the "spin" we put on it.

For example:

> I'm casual.
> You're a little careless.
> He's a slob.

Or:

> I'm thrifty.
> You're money conscious.
> She's a cheapskate.

Try a few of these conjugations yourself.

1. I'm tactful.
2. I'm conservative.
3. I'm relaxed
4. I'm quiet.
5. I'm proud.

Euphemism

The word *euphemism* is derived from the Greek word *euphemos*, meaning "to use a good word for an evil or unfavorable word." The Greek prefix *eu* means "good," and *phemi* means "speak."

When someone substitutes an inoffensive word or phrase for one that could be offensive to someone, they are using a euphemism. Most of the time euphemisms are used to be polite or to avoid controversy. The result is often a more positive connotation, such as when a garbage collector is referred to as a "sanitation engineer" or a clerk is referred to as a "junior executive."

Euphemisms can also be used to mislead or obscure the truth. For example, workers are sometimes fired or dismissed or terminated. A number of euphemisms are available for referring to this process that removes responsibility from employer or employee, and places it, instead, on economic or market forces, such as having a "reduction in force" or "releasing resources." The cartoon below illustrates this point.

STONE SOUP © 2003 Jan Eliot. Reprinted by permission of Universal Press Syndicate. All rights reserved.

Exercise: Identifying Euphemisms

Rewrite the paragraph below by substituting more direct and frank language for the italicized euphemisms.

I was driving down the street in my *preowned vehicle* when I came upon a *pavement deficiency*. As a result I *made contact with* the car in front of me. The other car was being driven by a *senior citizen* who yelled at me angrily. I immediately started to *perspire* because I was afraid I would be late getting to the *memorial park*. When I spoke to the policeman who arrived shortly I *stretched the truth* a little about the speed I was going, but he issued me a ticket anyway. I don't know how I'm going to be able to pay the ticket, because I was *recently terminated* from my job and I am currently *financially embarrassed*. I did, however, arrive in time to see the *deceased*, my pet cat, *laid to rest*. He had *passed on* because a *mixed breed dog* not on a leash had attacked him. I noticed that the *animal control warden* had come to pay his respects. It had been a hard day and so I headed to a *cocktail lounge* to meet friends.

SELECTION

Excerpt from *Teachers, Schools, and Society*   *by Myra and David Sadker*

"Perhaps the most fundamental form of bias in instructional materials is the complete or relative exclusion of a particular group or groups . . ."

Getting the Picture

In the United States, the question of bias in textbooks is increasingly becoming a topic of discussion and controversy. The excerpt below by Myra and David Sadker describes various forms of bias that can appear in textbooks.

Bio-sketch

Dr. Myra Sadker was professor of education and dean of the school of education at American University (Washington, D.C.) until her death in 1995 from breast cancer. Myra and her husband, Dr. David Sadker, also a professor at American University, gained a national reputation for their work in confronting gender bias and sexual harassment. The Sadkers' work has been reported in hundreds of newspapers and magazines.

Brushing Up on Vocabulary

suffrage   the right to vote. Originally *suffrage* meant "intercessory prayers." The term evolved to mean a vote given to support a proposal or in favor of the election of a particular person. The Constitution of the United States declares, "No state shall be deprived of its equal *suffrage* in the Senate."

suffragette   a woman seeking the right to vote through organized protest. The *suffragettes* were members of the Women's Suffrage Movement, an organization that combined demonstrations and militant action to campaign for the right to vote in the late nineteenth and early twentieth centuries.

bootlegger   a smuggler of liquor. The term, which arose in the late nineteenth century, refers to the smugglers' habit of concealing bottles of liquor in their boots.

Seven Forms of Bias

1   Many Americans are passionate about how various groups are portrayed in textbooks. In the 1970s and 1980s, textbook companies and professional associations, such as the American Psychological Association, issued guidelines for nonracist and nonsexist books; as a result, textbooks became more balanced in their description of underrepresented groups. Today, educators work to detect underrepresentation of those groups.

2   Following is a description of seven forms of bias, which can be used to assess instructional materials. Although this approach has been used to identify bias against females and various racial and ethnic groups, it can also help identify bias against the elderly, people with disabilities, non-English speakers, gays and lesbians, limited English speakers, and other groups.

INVISIBILITY

3   Perhaps the most fundamental form of bias in instructional materials is the complete or relative exclusion of a particular group or groups from representation in text narrative or illustrations. Research suggests, for example, that textbooks published prior to the 1960s largely omitted any consideration of African-Americans within contemporary society and, indeed, rendered them relatively invisible in accounts of or references to the United States after Reconstruction. Latinos, Asian-Americans, and Native Americans were largely absent from most resources as well. Many studies indicate that women, who constitute more than 51 percent of the U.S. population, represented approximately 30 percent of the persons or characters referred to throughout the textbooks in most subject areas.

STEREOTYPING

4   By assigning rigid roles or characteristics to all members of a group, individual attributes and differences are denied. While stereotypes can be positive, they are more often negative. Some typical stereotypes include

5   • African-Americans as servants, manual workers, professional athletes, troublemakers
     • Asian-Americans as laundry workers, cooks, or scientists
     • Mexican-Americans as non-English speakers or migrant workers
     • Middle-class Americans in the dominant culture as successful in their professional and personal lives
     • Native Americans as "blood-thirsty savages" or "noble sons and daughters of the earth"
     • Men in traditional occupational roles and as strong and assertive

- Women as passive and dependent and defined in terms of their home and family roles

IMBALANCE AND SELECTIVITY

6   Curriculum may perpetuate bias by presenting only one interpretation of an issue, a situation, or a group of people. These imbalanced accounts simplify and distort complex issues by omitting different perspectives. Examples include

7   - The origins of European settlers in the New World are emphasized, while the origins and heritage of other racial and ethnic groups are omitted.
    - The history of the relations between Native Americans and the federal government is described in terms of treaties and "protection," omitting broken treaties and progressive government appropriation of Native American lands.
    - Sources refer to the fact that women were "given" the vote but omit the physical abuse and sacrifices suffered by the leaders of the suffrage movement that "won" the vote.
    - Literature is drawn primarily from Western male authors.
    - Math and science courses reference only European discoveries and formulas.

UNREALITY

8   Many researchers have noted the tendency of instructional materials to ignore facts that are unpleasant or that indicate negative positions or actions by individual leaders or the nation as a whole. By ignoring the existence of prejudice, racism, discrimination, exploitation, oppression, sexism, and intergroup conflict and bias, we deny children the information they need to recognize, understand, and perhaps some day conquer the problems that plague society. Examples of unreality may be found in programs that portray

9   - People of color and women as having economic and political equality with white males.
    - Technology as the resolution of all our persistent social problems.

FRAGMENTATION AND ISOLATION

10   Bias through fragmentation or isolation primarily takes two forms. First, content regarding certain groups may be physically or visually fragmented and delivered separately (for example, a chapter on "Bootleggers, Suffragettes, and Other Diversions"). Second, racial and ethnic group members may be depicted as interacting only with persons like themselves, isolated from other cultural communities. Fragmentation and isolation ignore dynamic group relationships and suggest that nondominant groups are peripheral members of society.

LINGUISTIC BIAS

11   Language is a powerful conveyor of bias in instructional materials, in both blatant and subtle forms. Written and verbal communication reflects the discriminatory nature of the dominant language. Linguistic bias issues include race or ethnicity, gender, accents, age disability, and sexual orientation—for example,

12   - Native Americans are frequently referred to as "roaming," "wandering," or "roving" across the land. These terms might be used to apply to buffalo or wolves; they suggest a merely physical relationship to the land, rather than a social or purposeful relation. Such language implicitly justifies the seizure of native lands by "more goal-directed" white Americans who "traveled" or "settled" their way westward.

- Such words as *forefathers, mankind,* and *businessman* deny the contribution and existence of females.

13   The insistence that we live in an English only, monolingual society creates bias against non-English speakers in this country and abroad. An imbalance of word order ("boys and girls") and a lack of parallel terms ("girls and young men") are also forms of linguistic bias.

COSMETIC BIAS

14   Cosmetic bias offers the appearance of an up-to-date, well-balanced curriculum. The problem is that, beyond the superficial appearance, bias persists. Cosmetic bias emerges in a science textbook that features a glossy pullout of female scientists but includes precious little narrative of the scientific contributions of women. A music book with an eye-catching, multiethnic cover that projects a world of diverse songs and symphonies belies the traditional white male composers lurking behind the cover. This "illusion of equity" is really a marketing strategy directed at potential purchasers who *flip* the pages and might be lured into purchasing books that appear to be current, diverse, and balanced.

From Myra Pollack Sadker and David Miller Sadker in *Teachers, School, and Society,* 6th ed., New York: McGraw-Hill, 2003, pp. 276–279. Copyright © 2003 McGraw-Hill. Reprinted by permission of The McGraw-Hill Companies, Inc.

 ## Comprehension Checkup

Multiple Choice

Write the letter of the correct answer in the blank provided.

_____ 1. The authors' primary purpose is to
    a. argue that bias against nondominant groups should be eliminated from textbook material
    b. describe the destructive effects of stereotyping
    c. describe seven forms of group bias that often appear in textbooks
    d. explain the history of group bias in textbooks

_____ 2. You could infer from this excerpt that the authors favor
    a. exposing students to multiple viewpoints about particular issues
    b. presenting historical facts regardless of their unpleasantness
    c. minimizing the contributions of nondominant groups in textbook material
    d. both (a) and (b)

_____ 3. The last sentence of paragraph 3 ("Many studies indicate that women . . .") is a statement of
    a. fact
    b. opinion

_____ 4. Which of the following best expresses the main idea of paragraph 3?
    a. the first sentence
    b. the second sentence
    c. the last sentence
    d. There is no main idea.

_____ 5. In the last paragraph, the authors express a bias against textbooks that
    a. include the contributions of nondominant groups
    b. devalue Western culture

c. emphasize female accomplishments over male ones

d. only purport to take into account the contributions of non-dominant groups

_____ 6. A synonym for the word *blatant* as used in the paragraph on linguistic bias is
a. dominant
b. obvious
c. offensive
d. tasteless

_____ 7. The authors probably feel that stereotyping
a. cannot be avoided
b. obscures individual differences

_____ 8. The word *peripheral* as used in "peripheral members of society" most likely means
a. dominant
b. superficial
c. marginal
d. essential

_____ 9. As used in the last paragraph, the word *lurking* has a
a. negative connotation
b. positive connotation

_____ 10. In the last paragraph the phrase *illusion of equity* implies that
a. the material is balanced and diverse
b. bias still persists in the material
c. the material presented is comprehensive and fair
d. none of the above

SELECTION

Textbook Bias Cops Ban Ideas   *by Diane Ravitch*

"Every textbook, every reading passage used on a standardized test, is scrutinized by . . . reviewers for words and topics that might possibly offend someone."

Getting the Picture

In the following selection, Diane Ravitch argues against the use of "bias cops" who "sanitize" textbooks in order to insulate students from material that might disturb them. She argues that while students are protected from reading material deemed offensive, they are also given boring material that provides slight opportunities for critical thinking. Ravitch asserts that this censorship is widespread and is harming children and "diminishing our culture." Moreover, it is creating a powerful schism between the unedited material that children see and hear every day in the media and the sanitized stories that are currently found in their textbooks.

Bio-sketch

Diane Ravitch is a historian of education and Research Professor of Education at New York University. She served as an assistant secretary in the U.S. Department of Education under President George H. W. Bush. President Bill Clinton appointed her to the National Assessment Governing Board, which supervises national testing. In 2003 Ravitch published *The Language Police* which illustrates guidelines used by major educational publishers and state agencies. The guidelines are used by writ-ers, editors, and illustrators when preparing textbooks and tests for K–12 students.

Brushing Up on Vocabulary

taboo   The word *taboo,* originally borrowed from Polynesian languages, means "forbidden" or "not acceptable."

busybody   a person who pries into or meddles in the affairs of others.

right- and left-wingers   *Right-wingers* are considered politically or economically conservative or reactionary, thus not wanting change, while *left-wingers* are considered liberal or radical, thus desiring change. Interestingly enough, the word *right* originally meant "strength." We use the term *right hand* because a person's right hand is usually stronger than the left hand. The word *left* then originally meant "weakness."

Kids' Free Thought Loses to Sensitivity

1   A few years ago, while serving on a federal testing board, I became aware of wide-spread censorship in the educational publishing industry. I learned that a "bias and sensitivity committee" reviews every word that appears on standardized tests and in mass-market textbooks.

2   The new idea of bias is nothing like what most of us think of as bias. I observed a bias and sensitivity committee reject reading passages for a fourth-grade test that were potentially objectionable to very small numbers of people.

3   For example, a story about how owls locate their prey at night was turned down because the owl is taboo for certain Native American tribes. A story about the history of peanuts was ruled out because some children are allergic to peanuts. In another case, a story about how women and their daughters in the 19th century sewed quilts was condemned as sexist, even though it was historically accurate.

4   The practice of banning certain words and topics in textbooks and tests is not called "censorship," even though it is. Every textbook, every reading passage used on a standardized test, is scrutinized by these reviewers for words and topics that might possibly offend someone.

5   Bias and sensitivity review began with the best of intentions in the 1970s as a way to eliminate racist and sexist language, but over the years it has evolved into a process that allows anonymous committees to censor commonplace words, topics and images. During my research for my book *The Language Police,* I gathered bias and sensitivity guidelines from every major publisher of textbooks and tests. Each of them contains list of words to be avoided or changed or deleted. I collated all of these lists, and came up with more than 500 words and dozens of topics that have been banned from school materials.

6   Among the hundreds of words that America's schoolchildren must be protected from are: "brotherhood" (alternative: amity), "Founding Fathers" (alternative: the founders), "fat" (alternative: heavy), "extremist" (alternative: believer), the "elderly" (alternative: older persons), "craftsmanship" (no alternative), "cowgirl" or "cowboy" (alternative: cowhand), and "snow cone" (alternative: flavored ice).

7   Some words are banned with no alternative, like "busybody" (offensive to older women), "senior citizens" (offensive to older people), "yacht" (elitist), "God" (offen-sive to certain religious groups) and "Satan" (offensive to certain religious groups).

8   The topics that are similarly excluded from tests or textbooks (or both) are those that offend right-wingers, left-wingers, or any other advocacy group, including: junk foods (like birthday cake), divorce, drinking, unpunished crimes, religious holidays, Thanksgiving, controversial people, disobedient children, disrespect for authority,

poverty, witches, sorcery, Halloween, evolution (but also dinosaurs and fossils because they imply evolution).

9 Children taking tests are supposed to be so sensitive that their scores will plummet if they read about a child who got an expensive bicycle or went on a vacation or lives in a luxurious home. Nor should tests have any reference to such "scary" creatures as snakes, rats, mice, roaches, or lice. Bias and sensitivity reviewers believe students will be so distracted by reading about certain topics that they will not be able to finish the test.

10 For the past 30 years or so, advocacy groups found that they could intimidate textbook publishers by threatening to make their products controversial at public hearings. The easier it was to do so, the more pressure groups added to their demands.

11 To avoid controversy, the publishers have assumed responsibility for censoring themselves. They conduct their own bias and sensitivity reviews. This enables them to bring their products to state board of education meetings free of any potentially offensive words or topics or images. They police their writers, editors, and illustrators. The testing companies are even more vigilant than the textbook companies in removing anything that might give offense to feminists, religious conservatives, multiculturalists, the elderly, the handicapped, or any other organized group.

12 This activity has been going on for years unnoticed. It came into public view a year ago when the public learned that the New York State Education Department had been rewriting literary passages by famous writers like Franz Kafka, Isaac Bashevis Singer, and Elie Wiesel for use on the state examinations. Bureaucrats were deleting sentences and words that might offend someone or some group, not thinking of themselves as censors. They were acting in conformity with the industry standard in testing.

13 What can we do?

14 • Get angry. The public should not tolerate this censorship that dumbs down what students read.

• Teachers—not state committees—should decide which textbooks they want to use.

• The public should insist that publishers and state education departments make full disclosure of the words, topics, and images that they routinely eliminate from tests and textbooks.

15 These agencies should be expected to reveal their "bias guidelines" on their website and post the names and qualifications of those who are given the power to censor.

16 The main effect of the censorship is to make school boring, trivial, and unreal. We should encourage teachers, students, and writers to use judgment and common sense. We aren't doing that when the censors are free to remove anything that is controversial or offensive to anyone.

Diane Ravitch, "Textbook Bias Cops Ban Ideas," *The Arizona Republic*, 5/18/03, Section V, pp. 1, 3. Copyright © 2003 by Diane Ravitch, all rights reserved. Grateful acknowledgement is made for permission to publish "Textbook Bias Cops Ban Ideas", which was first published in *The Arizona Republic*, 5/18/03, Section V, pp. 1, 3, to Writers Representatives LLC, New York, NY, to whom all rights inquiries regarding this material should be directed.

Comprehension Checkup

Multiple Choice

Write the letter of the correct answer in the blank provided.

_____ 1. The main idea of this selection is
        a. racial, sexual, and cultural insensitivity should not be tolerated in textbooks

         b. educators and editors apply bias and sensitivity guidelines to censor textbooks and exams to the detriment of the student reader

         c. all publishers should be required to reveal their bias guidelines

_____ 2. The author's primary purpose is to point out the dangers inherent in
         a. anonymous committees
         b. advocacy groups
         c. censorship

_____ 3. The words *brotherhood, founding fathers,* and *cowboy* are likely to be banned from textbooks because they are deemed to be
         a. racist
         b. sexist
         c. offensive to "older persons"

_____ 4. The dominant tone throughout this selection is
         a. playful
         b. alarmed
         c. nostalgic

_____ 5. The author's point of view toward self-censorship on the part of textbook publishers is
         a. favorable
         b. unfavorable
         c. neutral

_____ 6. We can infer that Ravitch is not fond of the practice of
         a. putting literary passages by well-known authors in state examinations
         b. allowing teachers from local school districts to determine suitable curricula rather than state committees
         c. deleting from textbooks topics that could be offensive to some children

_____ 7. As used in paragraph 9, *plummet* most nearly means
         a. rush
         b. force
         c. plunge

_____ 8. The word *bureaucrats* in paragraph 12 has a
         a. positive connotation
         b. negative connotation
         c. neutral meaning

_____ 9. If we were to retitle Arthur Miller's *Death of a Salesman* as *Death of a Sales Representative* we would be using a(n)
         a. literary allusion
         b. analogy
         c. euphemism

_____ 10. Which of the following statements from the selection represents an opinion rather than a fact?
         a. "I collated all of these lists, and came up with more than 500 words and dozens of topics that have been banned from school materials."
         b. "The public should not tolerate this censorship that dumbs down what students read."
         c. "A story about the history of peanuts was ruled out because some children are allergic to peanuts."

_____ 11. "The new idea of bias is nothing like what most of us think of as bias." This statement represents
   a. fact
   b. opinion

In Your Own Words

Compare and contrast the viewpoints on censorship as expressed by Myra and David Sadker and Diane Ravitch. The Sadkers provide a justification or rationale for the bias and sensitivity committees. What justifications do they provide? Do you agree with their views? Ravitch appears to want to wrest control of the decision-making process about appropriate materials in textbooks away from publishers and bias and sensitivity committees. She wants to entrust teachers at the local level with this power. Is this a good idea? Why or why not?

The Art of Writing

In a brief essay, respond to the items below.

When do you think it is appropriate to censor textbooks for material that could be objectionable to some group? Is it important for children to read textbooks that contain controversial or objectionable thoughts or expressions? When children are exposed to so much objectionable and offensive material by the mass media, does it make sense to censor textbooks?

Internet Activity

Go to the American Library Association's website at

www.ala.org

Type in "banned books" to locate a list of the 100 most frequently challenged books. Print a copy of the list and see which books you recognize. How many have you read? Do you think these books should be banned? Are there other ways to respond to objectionable books than banning them?

Judy Blume, author of numerous children's books, many of which are on this list, had this to say: "It's not just the books under fire now that worry me. It is the books that will never be written. The books that will never be read. And all due to the fear of censorship. As always, young readers will be the real losers." Do you think that Judy Blume makes a good point? Are there good reasons for banning books?

Excerpt from _Teachers, Schools, and Society_   _by Myra and David Sadker_

Where Do You Stand?

Over the years, you probably have had ideas about the purpose of schools. To help you clarify your thoughts—and raise options you may have not yet explored—look at the following list of school goals. These goals come from a variety of sources and are sometimes contradictory. But they have been advocated singly and in combination by different groups at different times and have been adopted by different schools. In each case, register your own judgment on the values and worth of each goal.

Using the scale below, circle the number that best reflects how important you think each school goal is.

1   Very unimportant

2   Unimportant

3   Moderately important

4   Important

5   Very Important

	Very Unimportant				Very Important
1. To prepare workers to compete successfully in a technological world economy	1	2	3	4	5
2. To transmit the nation's cultural heritage, preserving past accomplishments and insights	1	2	3	4	5
3. To encourage students to question current practices and institutions; to promote social change	1	2	3	4	5
4. To develop healthy citizens aware of nutrition, exercise, and good health habits	1	2	3	4	5
5. To lead the world in creating a peaceful global society, including an understanding of other cultures and languages	1	2	3	4	5
6. To provide a challenging education for America's brightest students	1	2	3	4	5
7. To develop strong self-concept and self-esteem in students	1	2	3	4	5
8. To nurture creative students in developing art, music, and writing	1	2	3	4	5
9. To educate students in avoiding social pitfalls: unwanted pregnancy, drugs, alcohol, and AIDS	1	2	3	4	5
10. To unite citizens from diverse backgrounds (national origin, race, ethnicity) as a single nation with a unified culture	1	2	3	4	5
11. To provide support to families through after-school child care, nutritional supplements	1	2	3	4	5
12. To instill patriotism	1	2	3	4	5
13. To teach students our nation's work ethic: punctuality, responsibility, and cooperation	1	2	3	4	5
14. To develop academic skills in reading, writing, mathematics, and science	1	2	3	4	5
15. To provide a dynamic vehicle for social and economic mobility	1	2	3	4	5
16. To prepare educated citizens who can undertake actions that spark change	1	2	3	4	5
17. To ensure the cultural richness and diversity of the United States	1	2	3	4	5
18. To help eliminate racism, sexism, anti-Semitism, and other forms of discrimination	1	2	3	4	5
19. To prepare as many students as possible for college and/or well-paid careers	1	2	3	4	5
20. To provide child care for the nation's children and to free parents to work and/or pursue their interests and activities	1	2	3	4	5

Let's investigate how your choices reflect your values. If you scored high on item 17, you likely respond favorably to our nation's cultural diversity and are probably a proponent of **multiculturalism.** If you scored high on items 2 and 10, you likely value the role schools serve in teaching a common set of principles and values and are probably a proponent of a **core curriculum.**

From Myra Pollack Sadker and David Miller Sadker in *Teachers, Schools, and Society,* 5th ed., New York: McGraw-Hill, 2000, pp. 145–146. Copyright © 2000 McGraw-Hill. Reprinted by permission of The McGraw-Hill Companies, Inc.

Multiculturalism versus Core Curriculum

The following selections continue to explore the question of multiculturalism versus core curriculum.

SELECTION

Excerpt from *Teachers, Schools and Society*   *by Myra and David Sadker*

"What some call cultural literacy others see as cultural imperialism. 'Whose knowledge is of most worth?' is the question of the day."

Getting the Picture

"What balance should schools seek between teaching a common core curriculum that binds all Americans together and teaching a curriculum that celebrates the many cultures that have been brought to the United States?" —(*Myra and David Sadker*)

Brushing Up on Vocabulary

George Orwell   the pseudonym of the English author Eric Blair (1903–1950). His most famous novels are *Animal Farm* and *Nineteen Eighty-four.*

Aldous Huxley   an English author of the twentieth century (1894–1963). His best-known work is *Brave New World.*

Cultural Literacy or Cultural Imperialism?

"One could get a first-class education from a shelf of books five feet long."
—Charles William Eliot (when president of Harvard)

1   Both George Orwell and Aldous Huxley were pessimists about the future. "What Orwell feared were those who would ban books," writes author Neil Postman. "What Huxley feared was that there would be no one who wanted to read one." Perhaps neither of them imagined that the great debate would revolve around neither fear nor apathy but, rather, deciding which books are most worth reading.

2   Proponents of core knowledge, also called cultural literacy, argue for a common course of study for all students, one that ensures that an educated person knows the basics of our society. Novelist and teacher John Barth laments what ensues without core knowledge:

3   In the same way you can't take for granted that a high school senior or a freshman in college really understands that the Vietnam War came after World War II, you can't take for granted that any one book is common knowledge even among a group of liberal arts or writing majors at a pretty good university.

4   Allan Bloom's *The Closing of the American Mind* was one of several books that sounded the call for a curriculum canon. A canon is a term with religious roots, referring to a list of books officially accepted by the church or a religious hierarchy. A curriculum canon applies this notion to schools by defining the most useful and valued books in our culture. Those who support a curricular canon believe that all students should share a common knowledge of our history and the central figures of our culture, an appreciation of the great works of art and music and, particularly, the great works of literature. A shared understanding of our civilization is a way to bind our diverse people.

5   Allan Bloom, professor of social thought at the University of Chicago, took aim at the university curriculum as a series of often unrelated courses lacking a vision of what an educated individual should know, a canonless curriculum. He claimed that his university students were ignorant of music and literature, believing that too many students graduate with a degree but without an education. One of the criticisms of Bloom's vision was that his canon consisted almost exclusively of white, male European culture. Critics charged that the canons were loaded with "dead white males."

6   E. D. Hirsch, Jr., in his book *Cultural Literacy,* was more successful than Bloom in including the contributions of various ethnic and racial groups, as well as women. This is a rarity among core curriculum proponents. In fact, Hirsch believes that it is the poorer children and children of color who will most benefit from a cultural literacy curriculum. He points out that children from impoverished homes are less likely to become culturally literate. A core curriculum will teach them the names, dates, places, events, and quotes that every literate American needs to know in order to succeed. In 1991, Hirsch published the first volume of the core knowledge series, *What Your First Grader Needs to Know.* Other grades followed in these mass-marketed books directed not only at educators but at parents as well. Try your hand at identifying some of Hirsch's core curriculum concepts:

7   Achilles

       Homer

       Uriah Heep

       John Bull

       je ne sais quoi

       Pike's Peak

       phylum

       ukelele

       Uncle Tom

       Emile Zola

8   Not everyone is enamored with the core curriculum idea. A number of educators wonder who gets included in this core, and, just as interesting, who gets to choose? Are Hirsch, Bloom, and others to be members of a very select committee, perhaps a blue-ribbon committee of "Very Smart People"? Why are so many of these curriculum canons so white, so male, so Eurocentric, and so exclusionary?

9   It is not surprising that many call for a more inclusive telling of the American story, one that weaves the contributions of many groups and of women as well as of white males into the textbook tapestry of the American experience. Those who support multicultural education say that students of color and females will achieve more, will like learning better, and will have higher self-esteem if they are reflected in the pages of their textbooks. And let's not forget white male students. When they read about people other than themselves in the curriculum, they are more likely to

honor and appreciate their diverse peers. Educator and author James Banks calls for increased cultural pluralism:

10   People of color, women, other marginalized groups are demanding that their voices, visions, and perspectives be included in the curriculum. They ask that the debt Western civilization owes to Africa, Asia, and indigenous America be acknowledged. . . . However, these groups must acknowledge that they do not want to eliminate Aristotle and Shakespeare, or Western civilization, from the school curriculum. To reject the West would be to reject important aspects of their own cultural heritages, experiences, and identities.

11   Advocates of a core curriculum claim that it will empower the poor and the disadvantaged. Opponents say it will rob them of the chance to see their experiences reflected in history and literature. What some call cultural literacy others see as cultural imperialism. "Whose knowledge is of most worth?" is the question of the day. And, as America becomes a nation of growing diversity, the argument will continue to drive the debate about what is core, what is fair, and what should be in the curriculum.

"A nation is a body of people who have done great things together in the past and hope to do great things together in the future."

—Frank Underhill

From Myra Pollack Sadker and David Miller Sadker in *Teachers, Schools, and Society*, 6th ed., New York: McGraw-Hill, 2003, pp. 284–286. Copyright © 2003 McGraw-Hill. Reprinted by permission of The McGraw-Hill Companies, Inc.

Comprehension Checkup

Core or Multicultural

Indicate whether the statement is representative of the core curriculum or multicultural philosophy of education by writing C or M in the blank provided.

_____   1. "Non-Western cultures have rich traditions that any student could and should benefit from. In fact, people steeped only in the art and ideas of Europe cannot consider themselves well educated."

_____   2. "We need to prepare students for living in a diverse democracy. Focusing only on the West won't accomplish that."

_____   3. "It is important for all Americans to have common cultural connections to preserve national unity and cohesiveness."

_____   4. "Students, regardless of their color or ethnicity, cannot properly prepare to live in an increasingly global society without having at least some understanding of a broad range of cultures."

_____   5. "Americans, regardless of their heritage, live in the West, with Western traditions, institutions, and culture. Students in the U.S. need a grounding in the Western tradition in order to understand their own society. Notions like equality before the law and democratic institutions come out of the Western tradition."

_____   6. "It is undemocratic and just plain narrow-minded to expose students solely or largely to Western culture and a Western point of view."

_____   7. "Almost all scientific and political advances have taken place in the West. Even in less quantifiable disciplines, like literature or philosophy, the size and historical impact of the Western canon far outweigh those of, say, Asia or Africa."

_____   8. "The notion that the West did it all alone is a fallacy. Take the Greeks, for instance. They were influenced by the rich cultures of the Mediterranean and Africa."

True or False

Indicate whether the statement is true or false by writing T or F in the blank provided.

_____   1. John Barth favors a multicultural curriculum.

_____   2. Alan Bloom was criticized for excluding ethnic and racial groups
              from his curriculum canon.

_____   3. E. D. Hirsch, Jr., believes that teaching a core curriculum will enable
              minority students to become more successful.

_____   4. Proponents of multicultural education believe that a more inclusive
              curriculum will boost the self-esteem of females.

_____   5. James Banks, a proponent of cultural pluralism, is in favor of elimi-
              nating the study of Western civilization from the school curriculum.

_____   6. A synonym for *empower* is weaken.

_____   7. A plant that is *indigenous* to the United States was brought here
              from somewhere else.

_____   8. If someone *laments* the loss of something, they are filled with
              sorrow or regret.

In Your Own Words

1. Should traditional heroes, sometimes called "DWM" (dead white males)—
    such as Washington, Jefferson, and other revered Americans—be the focus of
    the curriculum, or should the experiences and contributions of other groups,
    women, and people of color be included?

2. Should history continue to emphasize European roots, or should Afrocentric
    issues be included? What about the views of other groups? For instance,
    should a penetrating view of European settlement of the Americas as seen
    through the eyes of Native Americans and Mexican-Americans be taught to
    school children?

3. Should U.S. history tell only a story of victors and triumphs, or should it also
    relate varied views of social, cultural, and economic issues? (*Sadker, p. 243*)

SELECTION

Excerpt from *The Death of the West*   *by Patrick J. Buchanan*

*"What will America's future be when it is decided by a generation oblivious to American
history . . ."?*

Getting the Picture

In his book *The Death of the West*, Patrick J. Buchanan discusses how "uncontrolled
immigration is threatening to convert America into a conglomeration of peoples
with almost nothing in common—not history, heroes, language, culture, faith, or
ancestors." In the excerpt below, Buchanan talks about how revisions in history
textbooks undermine our sense of solidarity.

Bio-sketch

Patrick J. Buchanan was the Reform Party's Presidential candidate in 2000. He frequently expresses his opinions on CNN's *The Capitol Gang* and *Crossfire.*

Brushing Up on Vocabulary

Noah Webster (1758–1843)   a United States essayist who was also interested in writing and compiling dictionaries.

Aleksandr Solzhenitzyn (1918–1994)   a Russian novelist who moved to the United States in 1974.

The New History

"Those who cannot remember the past are condemned to repeat it."

—George Santayana

1   "Every child in America should be acquainted with his own country. As soon as he opens his lips, he should rehearse the history of his own country; he should lisp the praise of liberty, and of those illustrious heroes and statesmen, who have wrought a revolution in her favor." So said Noah Webster. So we once believed. But the cultural revolution is purging the history "of those illustrious heroes and statesmen" from public schools to prepare a new curriculum, to separate children from parents in their beliefs, and to cut children off from their heritage. Said Aleksandr Solzhenitzyn: "To destroy a people you must first sever their roots." To create a "new people," the agents of our cultural revolution must first create a new history; and that project is well advanced.

2   In 1992, UCLA was awarded two million dollars by the National Endowment for the Humanities and the U.S. Department of Education to develop new National History Standards for the textbooks for children from the fifth through twelfth grades. In 1997, UCLA completed its assignment. In the history texts to be studied by American children in the public schools of the future:

3
- No mention was made of Samuel Adams, Paul Revere, Thomas Edison, Alexander Graham Bell, or the Wright Brothers.
- Harriet Tubman was referenced six times, while Robert E. Lee was ignored.
- The founding dates of the Sierra Club and the National Organization for Women were recommended for special notice.
- Instructions for teaching students about the traitor Alger Hiss and executed Soviet spies Julius and Ethel Rosenberg, who gave the atom bomb secrets to Stalin, urged "leeway for teachers to teach it either way."
- The Constitutional Convention was never mentioned.
- The presidency of George Washington was unmentioned, as was his Farewell Address. Instead, students were "invited to construct a dialogue between an Indian leader and George Washington at the end of the Revolutionary War."
- America's 1969 moon landing did not appear, but the Soviet Union was commended for its great "advances" in space exploration.
- Teachers were urged to have their pupils conduct a mock trial of John D. Rockefeller of Standard Oil.
- Students were instructed to "analyze the achievements of and grandeur of Mansa Musa's court, and the social customs and wealth of the kingdom of Mali," and to study Aztec "skills, labor system, and architecture." No mention of the quaint old Aztec custom of human sacrifice.

4   In December 2000, the *Washington Times* reported on the new Virginia State Standards for Learning History. First graders will find Pocahontas gets equal time with Capt.
John Smith. In introducing younger children to the Civil War, teachers have dropped Lee
and "Stonewall" Jackson. Third graders will study the "highly developed West African
kingdom of Mali" of our old friend Mansa Musa. A new emphasis is to be placed on
Confucianism and Indus Valley civilization. Who and what were dropped to make room
for Confucius? Paul Revere, Davy Crockett, Booker T. Washington, John Paul Jones,
Thanksgiving, the Pilgrims, Independence Day, and Virginia statesman Harry F. Byrd, Sr.

5   The war on America's past and the dumbing down of American children—to
make their minds empty vessels into which the New History may be poured—is succeeding. In a recent student survey, 556 seniors, from 55 of the nation's top-rated
colleges and universities, were asked 34 questions from a high school course on
U.S. history. Four out of five flunked. Only one-third of the college seniors could
name the American general at Yorktown. Only 23 percent named Madison as the
principal author of the Constitution. Only 22 percent linked the words "government
of the people, by the people, and for the people" to Lincoln's Gettysburg Address.
The good news—98 percent knew the rapper Snoop Doggy Dog, and 99 percent
identified Beavis and Butthead.

6   "We cannot escape history," said Lincoln. But thanks to our cultural revolution,
the Gen-Xers may have just done it. Today, not one of the 55 elite colleges and universities as rated by *U.S. News & World Report* requires a course in American history to graduate.

7   "The debate about curriculum," writes Dr. Arthur Schlesinger, Jr., "is a debate
about what it means to be an American. What is ultimately at stake is the American future. But what will America's future be when it is decided by a generation
oblivious to American history and suffering from cultural Alzheimer's?

From Patrick J. Buchanan in *The Death of the West*, New York: St. Martin's Press, 2002, pp. 172–175.
Copyright © 2002 by Patrick J. Buchanan. Reprinted by permission of St. Martin's Press, LLC.

In Your Own Words

1.   What bias does Buchanan express about changes in the way history is taught?

2.   Describe the tone of this excerpt.

3.   Indicate a place in this excerpt where Buchanan expresses sarcasm.

4.   Name some authorities cited by Buchanan to bolster his opinion.

5.   Study the following cartoon. What is the cartoon's main idea? What main
     ideas from the previous selections does the cartoon highlight?

NON SEQUITUR © 1992 Wiley Miller. Dist. by Universal Press Syndicate. All rights reserved.
Reprinted with permission.

Internet Activity

In 1993, Pat Buchanan helped found the American Cause, an organization dedicated to conservative beliefs. Go to its website to find out more about the organization:

www.theamericancause.org

Click on "About the Cause" from the menu on the left for information about the organization's fundamental beliefs; click on "On the Issues" and then "Education" to find out more about the organization's positions on education. Are there any examples of biased statements in the material on the website? Does the information presented in these web pages further your understanding of Buchanan's point of view as presented in the selection you just read?

Is the United States Going Test Crazy?

Those who support cultural literacy not only have a specific curricular content in mind but also have a clear idea of what a test for cultural literacy would look like. How well would you do on such a test? Assume that you have just applied to Cabin Cove Schools—a place where you have always wanted to teach. To ensure that teachers are "culturally literate," the school board requires that all teacher candidates take a test. Try your hand at the following questions and get a first-hand "feel" for the testing controversy.

HISTORY

_____ 1. Thomas Jefferson authored
    a. The Bill of Rights.
    b. The Declaration of Independence.
    c. The U.S. Constitution.
    d. The Emancipation Proclamation.

_____ 2. The _Federalist Papers_ were designed to
    a. win popular support for the American Revolution.
    b. establish freedom of speech.
    c. win support for the U.S. Constitution.
    d. free and enfranchise slaves.

_____ 3. Senator Joseph McCarthy was associated with
    a. government corruption.
    b. civil rights.
    c. education funding.
    d. Communist hunting.

_____ 4. The Cherokee syllabary was developed by
    a. Sitting Bull.
    b. Maria Tallchief.
    c. Geronimo.
    d. Sequoyah.

LITERATURE

_____ 5. The novel _1984_ concerns
    a. time travel.
    b. government-imposed conformity.
    c. a hoax about an invasion from Mars.
    d. World War III.

_____ 6. Stratford-on-Avon is associated with
a. Shakespeare.
b. Wollstonecraft.
c. Chaucer.
d. Shelley.

_____ 7. Jane Austen wrote about the Bennett family's five daughters in
a. 10 Downing Street.
b. Pride and Prejudice.
c. Midliothian Tales.
d. Clarissa.

GEOGRAPHY

8. List the states that touch on the Pacific Ocean. _____

_____

9. List as many countries as you can that border the former Soviet Union.

_____

10. Where is Mount St. Helens? _____

SCIENCE

_____ 11. Coal, gas, and oil shortages may result in an increased dependence
on electricity. What is your evaluation of this idea?
a. The economy cannot be changed that quickly.
b. Electric automotive technology will simply not match gasoline
engines.
c. Electricity is generally produced from coal, gas, and oil, so it
cannot replace them.
d. The current cost of electricity is much higher than that of coal or
gas and somewhat higher than that of gasoline, so it is a very
expensive and unlikely eventuality.

_____ 12. What is the approximate distance between the earth and the sun?
a. 90,000 miles
c. 900,000 miles
c. 9,000,000 miles
d. 90,000,000 miles

_____ 13. What is the major cause of urban pollution?
a. automobiles
b. factories
c. open incineration of garbage
d. heat inversion causing smog

The following are the answers to the quiz. Take a moment and see how you did:

1. b; 2. c; 3. d; 4. d; 5. b; 6. a; 7. b, 8. Hawaii, Alaska, Oregon, Washington,
and California; 9. Afghanistan, China, Czechoslovakia, Finland, Hungary,
Iran, Mongolia, North Korea, Norway, Rumania, and Turkey (if you
identified at least seven of these countries, give yourself full credit);
10. Washington State; 11. c; 12. d; 13. a.

Add up your correct responses and compare your results with the following score card:

9–13 correct: You have demonstrated an adequate level of general knowledge.
You are culturally literate. Welcome to the Cabin Cove School district.

6–8 correct: You have qualified for probationary status. If you agree to enroll in a number of courses at Cabin Cove College, you will be allowed to teach in the public schools.

Fewer than 6 correct: You have failed the teacher assessment test and will not be offered a position in this community.

How do you feel about the use of such a test to determine your future? Do you think that it is unfair to measure your teaching skills and abilities according to this single dimension, or do you feel that it is reasonable to assume all teachers should be expected to demonstrate a minimal level of general knowledge and cultural literacy? These questions and more have emerged in the past few years as the U.S. public has become concerned—some say obsessed—with testing.

Standardized testing is also charged with bias against females and students of color. Researcher Phyllis Rosser found that girls receive lower scores than boys, in part because of bias in test construction. For example, 15 percent more males than females respond correctly to the following analogy item (and, as you might suspect, such a question may also be particularly challenging to less affluent students):

Dividends: Stockholders:

a. investments: corporations

b. purchase: customers

c. royalties: authors

d. tapes: workers

e. mortgages: homeowners

If you are curious, the correct answer is (c).

From Myra Pollack Sadker and David Miller Sadker, "Cabin Cove Teacher Assessment Scale for Teachers," in *Teachers, Schools, and Society*, 5th ed., New York: McGraw-Hill, 2000, pp. 258–262. Copyright © 2000 McGraw-Hill. Reprinted by permission of The McGraw-Hill Companies, Inc.

The Art of Writing

In a brief essay, respond to the items below.

According to the biology department of Utah State University, medical and dental schools (such as the University of Buffalo Dental School) are increasingly taking into account an applicant's cultural literacy when assessing candidates. Do you think that medical and dental schools should consider an applicant's cultural literacy as part of the admissions process? If so, how should an admission's committee characterize cultural literacy? How should the committee test an applicant's cultural literacy?

Exercise: Identifying Bias in Textbook Material

Read each paragraph. Then choose the best answer for each item.

A. Elephants, like humans, grieve, cry from frustration and sadness, and help one another. They have a long childhood and remain with their mothers for fifteen years. They are sensitive, intelligent, and affectionate, and they long for social relationships. Now try to imagine one of these magnificent creatures in complete isolation, spending its entire life in either a small cage or the back of a truck, being moved from city to city. Confined, chained, and caged, the elephant quickly learns the futility and brutal repercussion of protesting. Picture this dignified and social animal responding to this isolation and lack of space. Pacing, weaving, rocking, sucking, or chewing on the steel bars of the cage are the animals' response to monotony and loneliness. Many, of course, simply go mad.

From Larry A. Samovar in *Oral Communication: Speaking Across Cultures*, 10th ed., New York: McGraw-Hill, 1998, p. 268. Copyright © 1998 McGraw-Hill. Reprinted by permission of The McGraw-Hill Companies, Inc.

_____ 1. The author is most opposed to which of the following?
   a. depriving an elephant of its mother
   b. moving elephants from city to city
   c. depriving an elephant of companionship and space
   d. depriving an elephant of peanuts

_____ 2. The choice of the words "futility and brutal repercussion of protesting" suggest that
   a. the elephant will be sent to a zoo if it causes trouble
   b. the elephant will be dealt with harshly if it protests
   c. the elephant will not be allowed to socialize with other elephants if it does not behave
   d. elephants will not receive treats if they cause trouble

B. There it was—the ship from New York bobbing down the Atlantic Coast and through the Caribbean. It was a 3,100-ton barge loaded with unwanted trash. After 41 days and more than 2,000 smelly miles at sea, the barge was still searching for a home. With an end to its odious odyssey nowhere in sight, the scow raised once again the dilemma of a throwaway society, quickly running out of room for all its solid waste.

From Larry A. Samovar in *Oral Communication: Speaking Across Cultures*, 10th ed., New York: McGraw-Hill, 1998, p. 130. Copyright © 1998 McGraw-Hill. Reprinted by permission of The McGraw-Hill Companies, Inc.

_____ 1. In this paragraph, the author expresses disgust for
   a. large barges
   b. a society that does not reuse and recycle materials
   c. smelly trash
   d. New Yorkers

_____ 2. Which phrase best expresses the author's disapproval?
   a. "bobbing down the Atlantic Coast"
   b. "throwaway society, quickly running out of room"
   c. "2,000 smelly miles at sea"
   d. "solid waste"

C. One of history's most tragic figures, Wolfgang Amadeus Mozart began his performing career as a child prodigy. He played the piano (still something of a novelty in his day), harpsichord, organ, and violin beautifully, and was taken by his father on a number of concert tours through several European countries. The young performer delighted his noble audiences, but was rewarded with flattery and pretty gifts rather than fees. Mercilessly prodded by his self-seeking father, upon whom he remained emotionally dependent most of his life, Mozart constantly sought to please his parent (who was never satisfied), his wife (demanding and ungrateful), his public (appreciative but ungenerous), and finally himself (who never doubted his own genius). Though fun-loving, sociable, and generous to a fault, Mozart never learned the art of getting along with people. He could not refrain from offering honest but unsolicited criticism; nor could he bring himself to flatter a potential patron. Fiercely independent, he insisted upon managing his own affairs, although he was quite incapable of doing so. Few besides Mozart's great contemporary Haydn appreciated the true worth of this man who wrote such quantities of beautiful music in such a short time. Mozart lived a short and difficult life, and now lies buried in an unmarked grave.

_____ 1. Which statement best expresses the main point the author is trying to convey about Mozart's life?
   a. "[Mozart] was rewarded with flattery and pretty gifts rather than fees."
   b. "Mozart lived a short and difficult life. . . ."
   c. "[Mozart] began his performing career as a child prodigy."
   d. "Mozart constantly sought to please his parent. . . ."

_____ 2. In this paragraph, the author expresses disapproval of all the following *except*
   a. Mozart's father
   b. Mozart's wife
   c. Mozart's mother
   d. Mozart's public

D. There are hundreds of fad diets and diet books, but such diets are usually unbalanced and may result in serious illness or even death. Fad diets cannot be maintained for long periods; therefore, the individual usually regains any lost weight. Less than 5 percent of people who lose weight maintain the loss for more than a year. Constant losing and gaining, known as the "yo-yo syndrome," may be as harmful as the original overweight condition.

_____ 1. The author is opposed to
   a. fruits and vegetables
   b. fad diets
   c. constant losing and gaining of weight
   d. both (b) and (c)

_____ 2. The author would agree that
   a. fad diets are often popularized by celebrities
   b. fad diets are a good way to maintain a healthy weight
   c. fad diets are likely to be unhealthy
   d. if persons lose weight by means of a fad diet, it is likely they will maintain the weight loss for at least several years

E. You should know that the gap between the earnings of high school graduates and college graduates, which is growing every year, now ranges from 60 to 70 percent. According to the U.S. Census Bureau, the holders of bachelor's degrees will make an average of $50,623 per year as opposed to just $26,795 for high school graduates. That's a whopping additional $23,828 a year. Thus, what you invest in a college education is likely to pay you back many times. That doesn't mean there aren't good careers available to non-college graduates. It just means that those with an education are more likely to have higher earnings over their lifetime. But the value of a college education is more than just a larger paycheck. Other benefits include increasing your ability to think critically and communicate your ideas to others, improving your ability to use technology, and preparing yourself to live in a diverse world. Knowing you've met your goals and earned a college degree also gives you the self-confidence to continue to strive to meet your future goals.

From William G. Nickels et. al., in *Understanding Business*, 6th ed., New York: McGraw-Hill, 2002, p. GR-3. Copyright © 2002 McGraw-Hill. Reprinted by permission of The McGraw-Hill Companies, Inc. [revised figures from 2001 US Census]

_____ 1. The author would agree that
- a. college is a waste of time for many people
- b. college is a good investment
- c. it is unlikely that in the future there will be an earnings gap between those who choose to attend college and those who do not
- d. students are unlikely to recover their original investment in a college education

_____ 2. The author would disagree with which of the following statements?
- a. A college education is unlikely to develop critical thinking skills.
- b. A college degree is unlikely to contribute to a feeling of self-confidence.
- c. A college education is unlikely to prepare a student to live in a diverse, technical world.
- d. all of the above

F. Let us imagine that you are feeling good as you take a long, deep puff on your cigarette. But let us add a touch of realism to this scene by asking you to also picture what your body is doing with this invisible and sinister chemical as it invades your body. Your gums and teeth are the first recipients of the poisonous chemical. While the smoke pays but a short visit to your mouth it is leaving enough pollution to increase the risk of painful gum diseases and the agony of mouth and throat cancer. But this is just the beginning. As the smoke continues its journey into your unsuspecting lungs, you will soon find that your breathing is shallow and impaired, for now the smoke deposits insidious toxins that, after a period of time, will increase your chances of crippling and deadly cancer. Your stomach too will experience the effects of this corrupt and silent killer. While you cannot see them, small bits of acid are coating your stomach, adding to the chances that you will develop lacerated ulcers. Think about all this the next time you decide that it is okay to take one little puff of this cleverly concealed stick of dynamite.

From Larry A. Samovar in *Oral Communication: Speaking Across Cultures*, 10th ed., New York: McGraw-Hill, 1998, p. 268. Copyright © 1998 McGraw-Hill. Reprinted by permission of The McGraw-Hill Companies, Inc.

_____ 1. Which phrase expresses the author's bias against smoking?
- a. "invisible and sinister chemical"
- b. "agony of mouth and throat cancer"
- c. "corrupt and silent killer"
- d. all of the above

_____ 2. The author would agree that
- a. smoking is on the rise with young teens
- b. young girls smoke to keep from gaining weight
- c. smoking is not a healthful activity
- d. smoking is such a pleasurable activity that it is worth the risk of cancer and other diseases

Exercise: Identifying Bias

Read the following accounts of a confrontation between women faculty members and the administration of a local college. Circle the biased or loaded words in both accounts and then write an objective or unbiased account of the event.

1. This past week, 25 female faculty members struck a blow against male dominance and caught the attention of Wellstone College's sexist administration for three hours. The well-justified protest was organized by those hard-working female teachers in the trenches who are forced to cope with degrading working conditions, unfair salary scales, and lack of promotional opportunities. Embarrassed administrators watched in disgrace as the teachers organized a peaceful, orderly picket line in front of the administration building. The teachers carried placards and talked calmly and earnestly to passersby. Many passersby voiced support of the protest. When the media arrived, an apologetic college vice president rushed forward to agree to form a committee to study the group's modest demands and to immediately curtail discriminatory policies. The group's success serves as an inspiration to oppressed female employees everywhere.

2. An outlandish protest was lodged against the administration of Wellstone College on November 15. A group of irate female faculty disgraced themselves by milling about in front of the administration building. They thrust placards in the faces of passersby and railed against supposed inequities in hiring, wages, working conditions, and promotion of female faculty. It required a great deal of patience and diplomacy on the part of the college vice president to maintain control of the disturbance and to soothe the group's hurt feelings. Speaking in a dignified manner, the vice president promised to evaluate the teachers' claims in a calmer, more appropriate setting. Judging from the chorus of boos that were heard, it appears that the ladies have done a grave disservice to themselves and to the college with their immoderate demands and juvenile, attention-seeking behavior.

Neutral Version

_____

_____

_____

_____

_____

_____

_____

SELECTION

Excerpt from *Mass Media Mass Culture*   by James R. Wilson and Stan LeRoy Wilson

"Even though the goals of propaganda may not be evil, some of the techniques used are questionable because they appeal primarily to our emotions rather than to our intellect."

Getting the Picture

"Propaganda is a daily feature of our popular culture. It is a prime ingredient in political rhetoric and is used extensively in advertising campaigns. For these reasons, it is important for all of us to be familiar with the basic propaganda devices so that we can detect them, ward off their emotional appeal, and analyze the messages intellectually." (*James R. Wilson*)

Bio-sketch

James Ross Wilson is a professor of mass communication and journalism at California State University, Fresno. In addition to teaching classes in mass communications, Wilson serves as general manager of the student-run radio station. He has also trained military personnel for work in the Armed Forces Radio and Television Service.

   Stan LeRoy Wilson is professor emeritus of mass communication at the College of the Desert in Palm Desert, California. He has had a 34-year teaching career at California state universities and community colleges. In addition to his teaching career, he served 17 years on the Palm Desert City Council, including four terms as mayor, and presently serves on the Riverside County Board of Supervisors.

Brushing Up on Vocabulary

egghead This term means "intellectual" but the word is usually used in a derogatory manner.

Propaganda

1   Webster's dictionary defines **propaganda** as "a systematic effort to promote a particular cause or point of view."

2   Thus by definition, propaganda is not evil or deceptive. However, ever since the British used propaganda to solicit U.S. support for the Allies' war effort against Germany in World War I, the word has taken on undesirable connotations. But even though the goals of propaganda may not be evil, some of the techniques used are questionable because they appeal primarily to our emotions rather than to our intellect.

3   Propaganda was probably used most destructively in the 1930s, when Adolf Hitler used it to take control of Germany and neighboring lands. One of Hitler's first acts when he came to power was to name Joseph Goebbels minister of propaganda. Goebbels immediately took over the German mass media and turned them into propaganda outlets that endorsed Hitler and his reign of terror. While Hitler waged his propaganda campaign, the rest of the world sat back and watched. Yet years earlier, in his 1925 book, *Mein Kampf*, which he wrote in prison, Hitler had spelled out the importance of propaganda and how he planned to use it:

4   The great masses' receptive ability is only very limited, their understanding is small, but their forgetfulness is great. As a consequence of these facts, all effective propaganda has to limit itself only to a very few points and to use them like slogans until even the very last man is able to imagine what is intended by such a word. As soon as one sacrifices this basic principle and tries to become versatile, the effect will fritter away, as the masses are neither able to digest the material offered nor to retain it. Thus the result is weakened and finally eliminated.

5   If this philosophy sounds as if it is alive and well in American advertising today, it is because propaganda techniques are still very much in use. But fortunately the

American advertising industry aims only to sell us consumer goods and political candidates, not the bigotry and totalitarianism of Adolf Hitler. Following are some of the more common forms of propaganda devices used today.

SLOGANS

6   The slogan is equally effective in advertising and political campaigns. In the latter, it usually takes the form of a chant that can unite large crowds into one common emotion. An example of a political slogan is "Four More Years," chanted by delegates to the 1996 Democratic National convention. Product slogans include Nike's "Just Do It," "Always Coca-Cola," "It's Miller Time," the U.S. Army's "Be All That You Can Be," and Hallmark's "When You Care Enough to Send the Very Best."

NAME-CALLING

7   Name-calling is a device used widely in political and ideological battles as well as in commercial advertising campaigns. It tries to make us form a judgment without examining the evidence on which it should be based. Propagandists appeal to our instincts of hate and fear. They do this by giving bad names to those individuals, groups, nations, races, or consumer products that they would like us to condemn or reject. Such names as *communist, capitalist, imperialist, pervert,* and *egghead* are just a few that have been used to discredit the opposition.

8   Not all name-calling is so blatant. Often it can work by inference or association. Presidential candidate Al Smith once used indirect name-calling against President Franklin D. Roosevelt by stating, "There can be only one capital, Washington or Moscow." He was indirectly calling the incumbent president a communist.

9   Most name-calling in advertising uses this indirect approach: "Our painkiller doesn't give you an upset stomach"—implying, of course, that the competition does. Some advertisers actually name a competing brand and charge it with being inferior.

GLITTERING GENERALITIES

10   Glittering generalities are broad, widely accepted ideals and virtuous words that are used to sell a point of view. Like name-calling, glittering generalities urge us to accept and approve something without examination. Many ads declare the product to be "the best," or "the greatest," or "preferred by more people." Such expressions as "the American way," "it's in the public interest," and "taste America's favorite bran flake cereal" are examples. Words such as *America, truth, freedom, honor, liberty, justice, loyalty, progress, democracy,* and *America's favorite* are all common glittering generalities.

TRANSFER

11   Some advertisements use symbols of authority, prestige, and respect that arouse emotions to sell a cause, a candidate, or a consumer product through the process of subconscious transfer or association. Typical examples are a political candidate photographed next to the American flag ("She's a good American") and a cigarette smoker by a peaceful lake ("Enjoy the natural taste of this brand of cigarette and you too will feel healthy and calm").

12   Many ads for automobiles feature a physically attractive person in the passenger seat or at the wheel. The point, of course, is to transfer the sexuality of the person to the brand of vehicle. Designer jeans and perfume ads are also effective in transferring sexuality to their products.

13   And who can forget the cough syrup television commercial in which a soap opera actor established his authority as an official spokesperson for the product by looking directly into the camera and declaring "I'm not a doctor, but I play one on TV"?

TESTIMONIAL

14   A testimonial is an endorsement of a product or an individual by celebrities or other well-respected persons. When a movie star endorses a particular savings and loan institution, for example, thousands of people may invest there solely on the rationale that if it is good enough for their idol, it's good enough for them. How many sports fans have selected a certain brand of athletic shoe, shaving cream, or deodorant because their favorite professional athlete endorsed it?

PLAIN FOLKS

15   The plain-folks device creates the impression that the advertisers or political candidates are just ordinary folks like you and me. In every presidential election, we see candidates doing things such as visiting a coal mine wearing hard hats. They don't actually go down into the coal mine, so obviously they don't wear the hard hats for protection. Instead, the hats are used to give the impression that they are just ordinary folks like the rest of the workers. Similarly, many laundry detergent ads show "ordinary housewives" rather than attractive models promoting the product.

CARD STACKING

16   Card stacking is the technique by which facts, illustrations, and statements are carefully selected to make the maximum impact and sometimes give misleading impressions. The cliché that "statistics don't lie, but you can lie with statistics" applies to this technique. For example, a politician may tell his constituents that he votes only for bills that help his district, while neglecting to mention that when special-interest groups have opposed such a bill, he has ducked the issue by not showing up for the vote.

17   An advertisement claiming that "Four out of five dentists surveyed recommend Chewy chewing gum" may certainly be true, but it may also omit the fact that only five dentists were contacted and four of them were paid to give an anonymous endorsement.

BANDWAGON

18   The bandwagon device is based on the idea that "if everybody else is doing it, so should you." "Jump on the bandwagon," "follow the crowd," "be the first in your neighborhood," and "don't throw your vote away by voting for a loser" are clichés associated with this device. The psychology behind this technique makes political polling important at election time. The fact that each candidate needs to project the image that he or she is a winner often leads to some conflicting polling results. (Pollsters can skew their results by carefully selecting their samples or using loaded wording in their questions.) Advertisements telling you to join the Pepsi generation ("Generation X") or to have a good time with the crowd when it's "Miller time" are examples of bandwagon.

SEX APPEAL

19   We don't ordinarily think of sex as a propaganda device, but it sells products in many ways. In recent years, emotional appeals based on sex have been used more and more in product advertising. How about beer commercials or the aftershave lotion ad that features a sexy female voice crooning, "My men wear English Leather or they wear nothing at all"? Or the billboard for Canadian Black Velvet whiskey showing a sexy blond in a black velvet dress with the words "Feel the Velvet Canadian?" And don't forget the Calvin Klein ads that feature partially clad and sometimes nude men and women.

When it comes to beer commercials, many people believe that you can only drink the product while playing volleyball on the beach with beautiful, bikini-clad women. Sex appeal is used to stimulate emotions and sell consumer products to both sexes.

MUSIC

20   The last device in our list is also seldom thought of as a propaganda device, yet it is one of the most effective techniques in radio and television commercials. Music is an excellent tool for creating specific moods, and it can be used effectively for product identification. Often people will think of a certain product when they hear a tune that has been associated with the product in ads. In past years, songs used in commercials have gone on to become popular songs on the radio and in record sales (e.g., Coca-Cola's "I'd Like to Teach the World to Sing"), and popular songs have been used in commercials (e.g., the Beatles's "Revolution," used in Nike commercials). Other songs have been catchy enough to just run through your mind ("Give Me a Break, Give Me a Break, Break Me Off a Piece of That Kit-Kat Bar").

21   In politics, music is used to stir the crowds, and the president of the United States uses it effectively to generate a mood of respect when making a grand entrance to the strains of "Hail to the Chief," "Happy Days Are Here Again," or catchy political campaign theme songs.

From James R. Wilson in *Mass Media Mass Culture*, 5th ed., New York: McGraw-Hill, 2001, pp. 352–357. Copyright © 2001 McGraw-Hill. Reprinted by permission of The McGraw-Hill Companies, Inc.

Internet Activity

We often think of propaganda just in negative terms, but propaganda can also be put to positive uses. One such example was the concerted effort by the U.S. government during World War II to get Americans involved in the war effort. The following website shows a variety of government posters designed to encourage Americans to become involved:

www.library.northwestern.edu/govpub/collections/wwii–posters/

Go to this website, print out three posters, identify any words showing bias, and then discuss the propaganda devices used.

Exercise: Identifying Propaganda Devices

For each passage, identify the propaganda device being used. Use each device only once.

bandwagon	name-calling	testimonial
card stacking	plain folks	transfer
glittering generalities	sex appeal	
music	slogans	

1. Smartnet—the Internet broker with great information, great service, and great people to help you invest your money wisely. _____

2. "I wouldn't think about banking anywhere else than Dollar Bank." —Sarah Brooks, CEO of True Blue Corporation _____

3. Satin Hand Cream is available without a prescription. For pennies a day, it can make your hands beautiful again. Effectively eliminates dryness, scaliness, and embarrassing age spots. _____

4. Janet Hardworker for Governor—just a small-town gal with a big heart

   _____

5. A commercial: A driver zooms away in a black Jaguar accompanied by the music "Born to be Wild." _____

6. The president running for reelection: "Don't switch horses in midstream."

   _____

7. My opponent is misguided in his support of vouchers for private schools. His foolish, reckless scheme will bankrupt the public schools. Think again before giving him your vote in November. _____

8. A picture of the Statue of Liberty with the following statement below it: Freedom Insurance will protect your family when they need it the most.

   _____

9. "All trucks on our lot have to go. We need room for the new inventory. Hurry on down. Don't be left out of this once-in-a-lifetime deal. If you don't try us, we both lose." _____

10. Sexy model purrs, "Nothing comes between me and my blue velvet jeans."

    _____

What propaganda device does the following cartoon illustrate? _____

STEVE BENSON reprinted by permission of Newspaper Enterprise Association, Inc.

TEST-TAKING TIP

Improving Your Performance on Essay Tests (3)

Organizing Your Answer

Once you have considered the question and recalled the material you need to answer it, you are ready to think about organizing your answer. Organizing your answer clearly—especially for "big picture" essay questions—will show the teacher how well you understand the relationships among ideas and concepts.

A good answer to an essay question typically includes:

- An introduction, with a clear introductory statement (or thesis).
- Three paragraphs of development, including supporting examples, developed in the same order in which the main ideas are mentioned in the introductory statement (each paragraph should develop only one main idea).
- A conclusion.

The introductory statement plays a crucial role in organizing an answer on an essay exam, since it drives the development of the body paragraphs. How can you write an effective introductory statement? One way is to turn the essay question itself into your introductory statement. Imagine you encounter the following item on an exam:

> Discuss whether *an increase in state financial aid for public education will raise student scores on standardized tests.*

You can use this question as the basis of your introductory statement by turning it into a statement and adding reasons. For example, your introductory statement might start:

- *An increase in state financial aid for public education will raise student scores on standardized tests because . . . .* [list three reasons]

Or

- An increase in state financial aid for public education will not raise student scores on standardized tests because . . . . [list three reasons]

Once you've devised your introductory statement, you have the outline of your body paragraphs.

Sample Introductory Statement

An increase in state financial aid for public education will raise student scores on standardized tests because *teacher salaries can be increased,* which will attract more talented people into teaching; *more teachers can be hired,* which will reduce class size; and school districts will have *more money available for learning resources and activities.*

Each body paragraph would develop one of the ideas included in the introductory statement:

- Paragraph 1 the role more talented teachers would play in increasing test scores.
- Paragraph 2 the role smaller classes would play in increasing test scores.
- Paragraph 3 the role more learning resources would play in increasing test scores.

11

Analyzing and Evaluating Arguments

The Nelson-Atkins Museum of Art, Kansas City, Missouri. Bequest of the artist F/75-21/11. Photo by Mel McLean. © T.H. Benton and R.P. Benton Testamentary Trusts/Licensed by VAGA, New York, NY. © T.H. Benton and R.P. Benton Testamentary Trusts/UMB Bank.

Trial by Jury (1964)*

BY THOMAS HART
BENTON

*To see this work of art in color, turn to the color insert following page 260.

This painting introduces the chapter on argument.

1   Which figure in the painting is making an argument? Do you think this person is the prosecutor or the defense attorney?

2   How many jurors appear in the painting? What is the composition of the jury in terms of sex and ethnicity?

3   Who do you think the defendant is?

4   Does this scene accurately depict how a courtroom looks? In what ways does it differ? Have you ever served on a jury?

Identifying Arguments

The critical reader must be able to **evaluate arguments.** When you evaluate an argument (a claim supported by reasons or evidence), you determine its value or persuasiveness. When an author tries to persuade the reader that something is true or correct by presenting supporting reasons or evidence, an argument is being made.

This means that an argument is different from an assertion. If an author says "Toughguy makes better trucks than Strongman," that's an assertion, not an argument, because no reasons or evidence is given. But if an author says, "Toughguy makes better trucks than Strongman because Toughguy trucks are more reliable and last longer," then an argument is being made. The author is stating a claim (Toughguy trucks are better than Strongman trucks) and is backing up this claim with reasons (Toughguy trucks last longer and hold up better).

Arguments can be broken down into their parts. Argument are made up of **assumptions, premises,** and a **conclusion.**

The **assumptions** of an argument support the conclusion but are not stated in the argument. Assumptions tie the premises to the conclusions. They are claims that lie in the background of the argument that make the argument work. Our sample argument assumes that trucks that are more reliable and last longer are better than trucks that are less reliable and do not last as long. That's an assumption that many would agree with. But what about someone who cares more about the appearance or style of a truck than how reliable it is or how long it lasts? Our argument assumes that appearance is not all that important. Our argument only works if its assumptions are true. To find the assumptions underlying an argument, ask yourself what is left unstated in the argument that must be true for it to work.

The **premises** of an argument are the reasons or evidence that the author presents to support the conclusion. Our example has two premises: Toughguy trucks are more reliable, and Toughguy trucks last longer. The premises of an argument are often introduced by words such as "since" or "because."

The **conclusion** of an argument is the claim that is the point of the argument. When an author makes an argument, it's the conclusion that the author is trying to persuade the reader to accept as true. The premises and assumptions in an argument are there to support the conclusion. Going back to our example, the conclusion of our argument is that, "Toughguy makes better trucks than Strongman." The conclusion of an argument is often introduced by words such as *accordingly, consequently,* or *thus.*

Evaluating Arguments

Now that we know what an argument is and how it is put together, let's talk about how to evaluate an argument. To evaluate an argument, you need to analyze it. When you *analyze* an argument, you break it down into its parts and examine them by themselves and in relation to the other parts of the argument. Here are the steps for analyzing an argument.

First, identify the argument's conclusion (claim). What is the conclusion the author is trying to persuade the reader to accept as true? What is the point of the argument?

Second, identify the assumptions that the argument makes.

Third, identify the premises (reasons or evidence) that the author puts forth in support of the conclusion.

Fourth, think critically and skeptically about the premises (reasons or evidence) that the argument presents and the assumptions that the argument makes. Are the premises true? Do the assumptions defeat or weaken the argument? Take our example. Is it true that Toughguy trucks are more reliable than Strongman trucks? Is it true that Toughguy trucks last longer than Strongman trucks? How important is appearance? If toughguy trucks are more reliable and last longer than Strongman trucks, but Strongman trucks are better looking, are Toughguy trucks really superior to Strongman trucks?

Fifth, ask yourself how well the premises and assumptions support the conclusion. If the assumptions are not shared by the reader or if the premises are weak or false, then the argument will be unpersuasive or even unsound.

The next section will introduce you to **logical fallacies** commonly found in argumentative material. Logical fallacies are ways of arguing or reasoning that may seem to make sense but actually have a fatal flow. They often seek to manipulate by appealing to emotion. The name of each fallacy indicates the particular error in reasoning that has occurred. Propaganda, which we discussed in Chapter 10, often makes use of logical fallacies.

An Introduction to Logical Fallacies

Faulty cause and effect (*post hoc, ergo propter hoc*)

The Latin meaning, "after this, therefore because of this," suggests that because B follows A, A must *cause* B. But just because two events or two sets of data are sequential does not necessarily mean that one caused the other. In the following cartoon, Fred Bassett is guilty of faulty cause and effect reasoning. He thinks that because the car washing happened before the rain, the car washing caused the rain.

Copyright © 2002, Tribune Media Services, Inc. Reprinted with permission.

Non sequitur ("it does not follow")

A non sequitur applies to any argument in which the conclusion does not follow from the evidence. "She will make a fine governor because she was an excellent attorney" is an example of a non sequitur. There is not a lot of reason to believe that because she was an excellent attorney she will make a fine governor.

Begging the question

This fallacy occurs when you assume as true what you are trying to prove. This sort of faulty reasoning could occur when a person says "stores should be required to carry organic vegetables because organic vegetables are superior to nonorganic vegetables." It may or may not be true that organic vegetables are superior to nonorganic. It is something that reasonable people disagree about.

Circular logic

In this type of fallacy, the conclusion restates the information presented as evidence. Here's an example: "Al Gore lost Tennessee because he didn't get enough votes." That Al Gore lost Tennessee and that he didn't get enough votes there say the same thing. Here's another example. "The team is in last place because they have lost more games than the other teams."

Hasty generalization

In this fallacy, the conclusion is based on too little evidence. "Jane had a very hard time with her first husband and concluded that all men are no good."

Either/or fallacy (or false dilemma)

This is a fallacy of "black-and-white thinking": Only two choices are given; there are no shades of gray. People who exhibit this type of thinking have a "bumper sticker" mentality. They say things like "America—love it or leave it." When we polarize issues, we make it more difficult to find a common ground. In the following cartoon, Hagar's wife is offering only two viewpoints to an issue.

© Hagar the Horrible. Reprinted with special permission of King Features Syndicate.

False analogy

In this fallacy, two things that may not really be similar are portrayed as being alike. The store brand of coffee may be packaged to look like the name brand, but are the two the same? We have to ask some questions to determine the answer. Is the coffee of the same quality? Is there as much coffee in the can? In most false analogies, there is simply not enough evidence available to support the comparison.

Ad hominem argument (argument against the man)

This fallacy involves an attempt to discredit an argument by attacking the person making it. Saying that Jill is a liar does not disprove Jill's argument that free speech is critical in a democracy.

Ad populum argument (argument to the people)

This kind of argument seeks to win agreement by making an appeal to common prejudices, values, and emotions. It does not rely on facts or reasoning. Take the following example: "Americans are strong, independent, and free, so we need to privatize Social Security." Americans like to think of themselves as being strong, independent, and free. If these values are secured by privatizing Social Security, then many Americans may want to do this. The question to be asked is whether these values have anything to do with privatizing Social Security. A common form of an *ad populum* argument is an appeal to patriotism, as in the following example. "Support America. Buy American cars." Of course, what is not stated is that many parts of American cars are made outside the United States, and many "foreign" cars are assembled in the United States. At its extreme, *ad populum* arguments rely on "mob appeal."

Red herring

This fallacy involves directing attention away from a debatable point to one that most people will quickly agree with. An uncooked herring has a very strong odor. If a herring is dragged across the trail of an animal (or person) that dogs are tracking, the dogs will abandon the original scent and follow the scent of the herring. A red herring argument is meant to distract the listener from the issue at hand. "It is pointless to worry about too much violence on television when thousands are killed by drunk drivers every year."

Slippery slope

This fallacy assumes that taking a first step down a path will necessarily lead to later steps. If we let X happen, the next thing you know Y will happen. The image is one of a boulder rolling uncontrollably down a steep hill. The boulder can't be stopped until it reaches the very bottom. "Requiring ratings on record labels will lead to censorship and government control of free speech." When we assume that the first step will inevitably lead to disaster without providing evidence, we are committing the slippery slope fallacy. The following cartoon illustrates slippery slope thinking.

© Piccolo. Reprinted with special permission of King Features Syndicate.

Exercise: Identifying Logical Fallacies

Indicate the logical fallacies being used in each of the following items.

_____ 1. Central State University has won its first two basketball games, and therefore it's going to win all of its games.
   a. slippery slope
   b. either/or
   c. hasty generalization

_____ 2. I just washed my car, so I know it's going to rain.
   a. begging the question
   b. faulty cause and effect
   c. ad hominem

_____ 3. The Wildcats are in last place in the league because they lost more games than any other team.
   a. ad populum
   b. ad hominem
   c. circular logic

_____ 4. Senator Wealthy wants to change the inheritance tax laws. But he's a notorious womanizer who has a profligate lifestyle. So let's not waste our time with his proposals.
   a. hasty generalization
   b. ad hominem
   c. non sequitur

_____ 5. Either the Democrats quickly unite behind Gary Goodfellow, or the Republicans are going to roll to victory.
   a. faulty cause and effect
   b. red herring
   c. either/or

_____ 6. Don't ever let children have second helpings of dinner. If you do, pretty soon they will be gorging themselves.
   a. red herring
   b. slippery slope
   c. begging the question

_____ 7. Americans are honest, hardworking, and caring. That's why we need to lower taxes.
   a. ad populum
   b. either/or
   c. slippery slope

_____ 8. Phil likes chocolate because he's a caring person.
   a. either/or
   b. non sequitur
   c. ad populum

_____ 9. Araceli did poorly in a bilingual school. Bilingual education must be a failure.
   a. ad hominem
   b. red herring
   c. hasty generalization

_____ 10. To improve education, we can either hire more teachers or build more schools.
   a. either/or
   b. false analogy
   c. slippery slope

_____ 11. All of the following contain fallacies *except:*
   a. We can't adopt Laurie Legislator's proposal. She comes from a long line of chiselers.
   b. The school rules state that after three absences you can be dropped from a class.
   c. I'm going to have bad luck for the rest of the year because a black cat crossed my path on New Year's Day.

_____ 12. All of the following contain fallacies *except:*
   a. Two of my son's friends got in accidents the day after they got their licenses at sixteen. Sixteen-year-olds should not be allowed to drive.
   b. An Infiniti is a good car because it costs a lot of money.
   c. I didn't study for the final exam, and I failed it.

13. Look at the illustration below and consider the strategies it uses to get its message across. Can you identify any propaganda techniques or logical fallacies in the work? Explain your thinking.

We will roll up our sleeves.
We will move forward together.
We will overcome.
We will never forget.

A message from

Courtesy of the General Electric Company.

_____

_____

_____

_____

Exercise: Identifying Arguments

Identify the conclusion (or central issue) and the supporting reasons in each of the following excerpts. Where indicated, also list the logical fallacies used.

A. A Fair Share of Resources?

The affluent lifestyle that many of us in the richer countries enjoy consumes an inordinate share of the world's natural resources and produces a shockingly high proportion of pollutants and wastes. The United States, for instance, with less than 5 percent of the total population, consumes about one-quarter of most commercially traded commodities and produces a quarter to half of most industrial wastes.

To get an average American through the day takes about 450 kg (nearly 1,000 lbs) of raw materials, including 18 kg (40 lbs) of fossil fuels, 13 kg (29 lbs) of other minerals, 12 kg (26 lbs) of farm products, 10 kg (22 lbs) of wood and paper, and 450 liters (119 gal) of water. Every year we throw away some 160 million tons of garbage, including 50 million tons of paper, 67 billion cans and bottles, 25 billion styrofoam cups, 18 billion disposable diapers, and 2 billion disposable razors.

This profligate resource consumption and waste disposal strains the life-support system of the Earth on which we depend. If everyone in the world tried to live at consumption levels approaching ours, the results would be disastrous. Unless we find ways to curb our desires and produce the things we truly need in less destructive ways, the sustainability of human life on our planet is questionable.

From William Cunningham & Barbara Saigo in *Environmental Science*, 6th ed., New York: McGraw-Hill, 2001, p. 27. Copyright © 2001 McGraw-Hill. Reprinted by permission of The McGraw-Hill Companies, Inc.

1. What is the central issue that is being argued? _____

   _____

   _____

2. List the author's support for the argument.

   a. _____
   b. _____
   c. _____

B. Inside Job

Roughly four or five fast-food workers are now murdered on the job every month, usually during the course of a robbery. Although most fast-food robberies end without bloodshed, the level of violent crime in the industry is surprisingly high. In 1998, more restaurant workers were murdered on the job in the United States than police officers.

America's-fast food restaurants are now more attractive to armed robbers than convenience stores, gas stations, or banks. Other retail businesses increasingly rely upon credit card transactions, but fast-food restaurants still do almost all of their business in cash. While convenience store chains have worked hard to reduce the amount of money in the till (at 7-Eleven stores the average robbery results in a loss of about thirty-seven dollars), fast-food restaurants often have thousands of dollars on the premises. Gas stations and banks now routinely shield employees behind bullet-resistant barriers, a security measure that would be impractical at most fast-food restaurants. And the same features that make these restaurants so convenient—their location near intersections and highway off-ramps, even their drive-through windows—facilitate a speedy getaway.

The same demographic groups widely employed at fast-food restaurants—the young and the poor—are also responsible for much of the nation's violent crime. According to industry studies, about two-thirds of the robberies at fast-food restaurants involve current or former employees. The combination of low pay, high turnover, and ample cash in the restaurant often leads to crime. A 1999 survey by the National Food Service Security Council, a group funded by the large chains, found that about half of all restaurant workers engaged in some form of cash or property theft—not including the theft of food. The typical employee stole about $218 a year; new employees stole almost $100 more.

Studies conducted by Jerald Greenberg, a professor of management at the University of Ohio and an expert on workplace crime, have found that when people are treated with dignity and respect, they're less likely to steal from their employer. "It may be common sense," Greenberg says, "but it's obviously not common practice." The same anger that causes most petty theft, the same desire to strike back at an employer perceived as unfair, can escalate to armed robbery. Restaurant managers are usually, but not always, the victims of fast-food crimes. Not long ago, the day manager of a McDonald's in Moorpark, California, recognized the masked gunman emptying the safe. It was the night manager.

The leading fast-food chains have tried to reduce violent crime by spending millions on new security measures—video cameras, panic buttons, burglar alarms, additional lighting. But even the most heavily guarded fast-food restaurants remain vulnerable. In April of 2000, a Burger King on the grounds of Offut Air Force Base in Nebraska was robbed by two men in ski masks carrying shotguns. They were wearing purple Burger King shirts and got away with more than $7,000. Joseph A. Kinney, the president of the National Safe Workplace Institute, argues that the fast-food industry needs to make fundamental changes in its labor relations. Raising wages and making a real commitment to workers will do more to cut crime than investing in hidden cameras. "No other American industry," Kinney notes, "is robbed so frequently by its own employees."

From Eric Schlosser, *Fast-Food Nation: The Dark Side of the All-American Meal*, New York: Houghton Mifflin, 2001, pp. 83–85. Copyright © 2001 by Eric Schlosser. Reprinted by permission of Houghton Mifflin Company. All rights reserved.

1. What is the central issue that is being argued? _____

   _____

   _____

   _____

   _____

2. List the author's support for the argument.

   a. _____

b. _____

c. _____

C. Come Together . . . Right Now!

Small children play with cyberpets while old women stare out their windows at empty streets. Grandparents feel lonely and useless while, a thousand miles away, their grandchildren do not get the love and attention they desperately need. What's wrong with this picture? A lot.

In our society today, we practice a particularly virulent form of segregation—we separate people by age. We put our 3-year-olds together in preschools or day care centers, our 14-year-olds together in high schools, and our 80-year-olds in nursing homes—institutions that Betty Friedan, in *The Fountain of Age*, vividly labels "playpens for adults."

Segregating the generations in this way means that people of all ages lose out: Older people are deprived of the energy and joy of children, and our kids end up learning their ideas about the world from each other or from television instead of through that most time-honored of traditions: being socialized by their elders.

But age segregation is more than just one of those regrettable casualties of changing times. It is a dangerous pattern that leads to all sorts of other social breakdowns. When our elders have no regular, everyday contact with young people, they rarely have the same emotional stake in the fate of their communities. They are less likely to care about the environment and to invest in green spaces and playgrounds. An older person who never mingles with children and no longer feels a sense of common cause with the young may not vote in favor of school referendums, child-health laws, or funding for teen programs. To put it bluntly, he may simply fail to see what a good school system has to do with him and his well-being. By the same token, a child who has no contact with old people is more likely to look the other way when one of them needs assistance or to become impatient when they share a joke or story. Age segregation fosters short-term selfish planning by the old and less empathy and respect from the young.

Because they don't get to know each other as people, old and young alike tend to think in negative stereotypes (often, alas, generated by the media). This breeds misunderstanding and fear. How many times do older people freeze up when they see a rambunctious group of young people approaching? Or hold back from nurturing or correcting other people's kids for fear of being misinterpreted? For their part, children often see older people as hopelessly out of it, if not downright weird, with nothing to contribute to their lives.

Yet society cannot hold together when old people are afraid of children and children are afraid of old people. Every culture is just one generation away from anarchy: It is the socialization of the young by the elders that allows the next generation to come of age civilized. A society in which this torch no longer gets passed is a society in trouble.

Each generation has its own wisdom and ways of loving. When we bring them together, we create a kind of social wealth that enriches us all.

1. What is the central issue that is being argued? _____

   _____

   _____

2. List the author's support for the argument.

   a. _____

   _____

   b. _____

   c. _____

D. Yes, Let's Pay for Organs

Pennsylvania plans to begin paying the relatives of organ donors $300 toward funeral expenses. Already there are voices opposing the very idea of pricing a kidney.

It is odd that with 62,000 Americans desperately awaiting organ transplantation to save their life, no authority had yet dared to offer money for the organs of the dead in order to increase the supply for the living. If we can do anything to alleviate the catastrophic shortage of donated organs, should we not?

One objection is that Pennsylvania's idea will disproportionately affect the poor. The rich, it is argued, will not be moved by a $300 reward; it will be the poor who will succumb to the incentive and provide organs.

So what? Where is the harm? What is wrong with rewarding people, poor or not, for a dead relative's organ? True, auctioning off organs in the market so that the poor could not afford to get them would be offensive. But this program does not restrict supply to the rich. It seeks to increase supply for all.

Moreover, everything in life that is dangerous, risky, or bad disproportionately affects the poor: slum housing, street crime, small cars, hazardous jobs. By this logic, coal mining should be outlawed because the misery and risk and diseases of coal mining disproportionately fall on people who need the money.

No, the real objection to the Pennsylvania program is this: It crosses a fateful ethical line regarding human beings and their parts. Until now we have upheld the principle that one must not pay for human organs because doing so turns the human body—and human life—into a commodity. Violating this principle, it is said, puts us on the slippery slope to establishing a market for body parts. Auto parts, yes. Body parts, no. Start by paying people for their dead parents' kidneys, and soon we will be paying people for the spare kidneys of the living.

Well, what's wrong with that? the libertarians ask. Why should a destitute person not be allowed to give away a kidney that he may never need so he can live a better life? Why can't a struggling mother give her kidney so her kids can go to college?

The answer is that little thing called human dignity. We have a free society, but freedom stops at the point where you violate the very integrity of the self. We cannot allow live kidneys to be sold at market. It would produce a society in which the lower orders are literally cut up to serve as spare parts for the upper. No decent society can permit that.

But kidneys from the dead are another matter entirely. To be crude about it, whereas a person is not a commodity, a dead body can be. Yes, it is treated with respect. But it is not inviolable. It does not warrant the same reverence as that accorded a living soul.

The Pennsylvania program is not just justified, it is too timid. It seeks clean hands by paying third parties—the funeral homes—rather than giving cash directly to the relatives. Why not pay them directly? And why not $3,000 instead of $300? That might even address the rich/poor concern: after all, $3,000 is real money, even for bankers and lawyers.

The Pennsylvania program does cross a line. But not all slopes are slippery. There is a new line to be drawn, a very logical one: rewards for organs, yes—but not from the living.

The Talmud speaks of establishing a "fence" around the law, making restrictions that may not make sense in and of themselves but that serve to keep one away from more serious violations. The prohibition we have today—no selling of *any* organs, from the living or the dead—is a fence against the commoditization of human parts. Laudable, but a fence too far. We need to move the fence in and permit incentive payments for organs from the dead.

Why? Because there are 62,000 people desperately clinging to life, some of whom will die if we don't have the courage to move the moral line—and hold it.

From Charles Krauthammerm, "Yes, Let's Pay for Organs," *Time*, 5/17/99, p. 100. © 1999 TIME, Inc. Reprinted by permission.

1. What is the central issue that is being argued? _____

    _____

    _____

2. List the author's support for the argument.

    a. _____

    b. _____

    c. _____

    _____

3. What logical fallacies or propaganda devices can you identify?

    _____

    _____

    _____

    _____

    _____

4. How does the author respond to the opposing point of view?

    _____

    _____

5. What is your overall evaluation of this argument?

    _____

    _____

    _____

    _____

    _____

Our Heritage: Legal and Political

The last section of this chapter, on our legal and political heritage, has excerpts from *John Adams* by David McCullough, *Benjamin Franklin* by Walter Isaacson, and *The Majesty of the Law* by Sandra Day O'Connor. It also includes the Declaration of Independence and The Bill of Rights.

SELECTION

Excerpt from *John Adams*   *by David McCullough*

"There was no member of the Virginia delegation who did not own slaves, and of all members of Congress at least a third owned or had owned slaves."

Getting the Picture

Both John Adams, the second president, and Thomas Jefferson, the third president, died on the same day—the Fourth of July, 1826. Although both had wished to attend the fiftieth anniversary celebration of the Declaration of Independence, neither was able to. Congress nevertheless paid tribute to both men, forever linking the two old "patriots"—Adams, the chief advocate of the Declaration, and Jefferson, its author. In his epitaph, Adams chose to say nothing of his political accomplishments, instead extolling the virtues of piety, humility, and industry. Jefferson wished to be remembered for his creative work. The inscription on his tombstone reads as follows:

Here Was Buried

THOMAS JEFFERSON

Author of the Declaration of American Independence,

Of the Statute of Virginia for Religious Freedom,

And Father of the University of Virginia

Bio-sketch

Historian David McCullough won the Pulitzer Prize for a biography of President Truman in 1993 and again in 2001 for a biography of John Adams, our second president. He has said that the six years that it took him to write *John Adams* were the best years of his writing career.

Brushing Up on Vocabulary

redundant   wordy or unnecessarily repetitious. Derived from Latin *unda*, meaning "wave." When speakers or writers are wordy, they are said to have a *redundant* style because their "waves" of words go on and on and repeat themselves.

preamble   an introductory statement; preface. In Latin, *pre* means "before," and *ambular* means "to walk." The introductory portion of an essay or a speech is called a *preamble* because it comes first or "walks before."

mercenary   a professional soldier hired to serve in a foreign army. The word can be traced back to the Latin *mercenarius,* meaning one who works for wages. When Jefferson mentions "mercenaries" in the Declaration of Independence, he is referring to the Hessians who fought under the British flag in the Revolutionary War.

Jefferson, Adams, and the Declaration of Independence

1   Jefferson was to draft the declaration. But how this was agreed to was never made altogether clear. He and Adams would have differing explanations, each writing long after the fact.

2   According to Adams, Jefferson proposed that he, Adams, do the writing, but that he declined, telling Jefferson he must do it.

3   "Why?" Jefferson asked, as Adams would recount.

4   "Reasons enough," Adams said.

5   "What can be your reasons?"

6   "Reason first: you are a Virginian and a Virginian ought to appear at the head of this business. Reason two: I am obnoxious, suspected and unpopular. You are very much otherwise. Reason third: You can write ten times better than I can."

7   Jefferson would recall no such exchange. As Jefferson remembered, the committee simply met and unanimously chose him to undertake the draft. "I consented: I drew it [up]."

. . .

8   Congress had to review and approve the language of the drafted declaration before it could be made official. Deliberations commenced at once, continuing through the next morning, July 3, when mercifully the temperature had dropped ten degrees, broken by the storm of the previous day.

9   For Thomas Jefferson it became a painful ordeal, as change after change was called for and approximately a quarter of what he had written was cut entirely. Seated beside Benjamin Franklin, the young Virginian looked on in silence. He is not known to have uttered a word in protest, or in defense of what he had written. Later he would describe the opposition to his draft as being like "the ceaseless action of gravity weighing upon us night and day." At one point Franklin leaned over to tell him a story that, as a printer and publisher over so many years, he must have offered before as comfort to a wounded author. He had once known a hatter who wished to have a sign made saying, JOHN THOMPSON, HATTER, MAKES AND SELLS HATS FOR READY MONEY, this to be accompanied by a picture of a hat. But the man had chosen first to ask the opinion of friends, with the result that one word after another was removed as superfluous or redundant, until at last the sign was reduced to Thompson's name and the picture of the hat.

10   Beyond its stirring preamble, most of the document before Congress was taken up with a list of grievances, specific charges against the King— "He has plundered our seas, ravaged our coasts, burnt our towns. He is at this time transporting large armies of foreign mercenaries to complete the works of death, desolation and Tyranny. . . ." And it was the King, "the Christian King of Great Britain," Jefferson had emphasized, who was responsible for the horrors of the slave trade. As emphatic a passage as any, this on the slave trade was to have been the ringing climax of all the charges. Now it was removed in its entirety because, said Jefferson later, South Carolina and Georgia objected. Some northern delegates, too, were a "little tender" on the subject, "for though their people have very few slaves themselves yet they had been pretty considerable carriers."

11   In truth black slavery had long since become an accepted part of life in all of the thirteen colonies. Of a total population in the colonies of nearly 2,500,000 people in 1776, approximately one in five were slaves, some 500,000 men, women, and children. In Virginia alone, which had the most slaves by far, they numbered more than 200,000. There was no member of the Virginia delegation who did not own slaves, and of all members of Congress at least a third owned or had owned slaves. The total of Thomas Jefferson's slaves in 1776, as near as can be determined from his personal records, was about 200, which was also the approximate number owned by George Washington.

. . .

12   In time Jefferson and Adams would each denounce slavery. Jefferson was to write of the degrading effects of the institution on both slave and master. Adams would call slavery a "foul contagion in the human character." But neither [they] nor any other delegate in Congress would have let the issue jeopardize a declaration of independence, however strong their feelings. If Adams was disappointed or downcast over the removal of Jefferson's indictment of the slave trade, he seems to have said nothing at the time. Nor is it possible to know the extent of Jefferson's disappointment or if the opposition of South Carolina and Georgia was truly as decisive as he later claimed. Very possibly there were many delegates, from North and South, happy to see the passage omitted for the reason that it was patently absurd to hold the King responsible for horrors that, everyone knew, Americans—and Christians no less than the King—had brought on themselves. Slavery and the slave trade were hardly the fault of George III, however ardently Jefferson wished to fix the blame on the distant monarch.

13   Of more than eighty changes made in Jefferson's draft during the time Congress deliberated, most were minor and served to improve it. But one final cut toward the conclusion was as substantial nearly as the excise of the passage on the slave trade, and it appears to have wounded Jefferson deeply.

14   To the long list of indictments against the King, he had added one assailing the English people, "our British brethren," as a further oppressor, for allowing their Parliament and their King "to send over not only soldiers of our common blood, but Scotch and foreign mercenaries to invade and destroy us." And therein, Jefferson charged, was the heart of the tragedy, the feeling of betrayal, the "common blood" cause of American outrage. "These facts have given the last stab to agonizing affection, and manly spirit bids us renounce forever these unfeeling brethren," he had written. "We must endeavor to forget our former love for them."

15   This most emotional passage of all was too much for many in Congress, and to it Jefferson had added a final poignant note: "We might have been a free and great people together." Nearly all of this was removed. There was to be no mention of a "last stab," or "love," or of the "free and great people" that might have been.

16   Finally, to Jefferson's concluding line was added the phrase "with a firm reliance on the protection of divine Providence," an addition that John Adams assuredly welcomed. Thus it would read:

17   And for the support of this Declaration, with a firm reliance on the protection of divine Providence, we mutually pledge to each other our lives, our fortunes, and our sacred honor.

18   But it was to be the eloquent lines of the second paragraph of the Declaration that would stand down the years, affecting the human spirit as neither Jefferson nor anyone could have foreseen. And however much was owed to the writings of others, as Jefferson acknowledged, or to such editorial refinements as those contributed by Franklin or Adams, they were, when all was said and done, his lines. It was Jefferson who had written them for all time:

19   We hold these truths to be self-evident, that all men are created equal, that they are endowed by their Creator with certain unalienable rights, that among these are life, liberty, and the pursuit of happiness. That to secure these rights, governments are instituted among men, deriving their just powers from the consent of the governed.

. . .

20   In old age, trying to reconstruct events of that crowded summer, both Thomas Jefferson and John Adams would incorrectly insist that the signing took place July 4.

21   Apparently there was no fuss or ceremony on August 2. The delegates simply came forward in turn and fixed their signatures. The fact that a signed document now existed, as well as the names of the signatories, was kept secret for the time being, as all were acutely aware that by taking up the pen and writing their names, they had committed treason. Whether Benjamin Franklin quipped "We must all hang together, or most assuredly we shall hang separately" is impossible to know, just as there is no way to confirm the much-repeated story that the diminutive John Hancock wrote his name large so the King might read it without his spectacles. But the stories endured because they were in character, like the remark attributed to Stephen Hopkins of Rhode Island. Hopkins, who suffered from palsy, is said to have observed, on completing his spidery signature, "My hand trembles, but my heart does not."

From David McCullough, *John Adams*, pp. 119, 130–131, 134–136, 138. Copyright © 2001 by David McCullough. Reprinted with permission of Simon & Schuster Adult Publishing Group.

Comprehension Checkup

Multiple Choice

Write the letter of the correct answer in the blank provided; you may refer to the reading selection, or other sections of this book if necessary.

_____ 1. The mode of rhetoric in this selection is primarily
    a. narration
    b. description
    c. exposition
    d. persuasion

_____ 2. The overall pattern of organization is primarily
    a. cause and effect
    b. comparison contrast
    c. example
    d. chronological order

_____ 3. In paragraph 1, Adams portrays himself as
    a. self-congratulatory
    b. defeated
    c. self-deprecatory
    d. gleeful

_____ 4. In the debate over the wording of the Declaration, Jefferson
    a. became angry when changes were suggested
    b. was actively engaged in debating corrections
    c. remained silent
    d. fought vigorously for every word

_____ 5. Jefferson was a proud representative of
    a. Delaware
    b. Virginia

          c. Massachusetts

          d. New York

_____ 6. On his plantation, Jefferson
   a. hired only free men
   b. had only a few slaves
   c. had many slaves
   d. farmed with the aid of family members only

_____ 7. The actual signing of the Declaration of Independence occurred on
   a. July 2
   b. July 4
   c. August 2
   d. December 26

_____ 8. The state with the most recorded slaves was
   a. South Carolina
   b. Georgia
   c. Kentucky
   d. Virginia

_____ 9. Jefferson's Declaration
   a. listed grievances against the king
   b. defended the practice of slavery
   c. criticized the use of foreign mercenaries
   d. both (a) and (c)

_____ 10. In his original draft of the Declaration, in addition to his indictment of the king, Jefferson also assailed
   a. the British people
   b. John Locke
   c. the Virginia delegation
   d. France

True or False

Indicate whether the statement is true or false by writing T or F in the blank provided.

_____ 1. Washington and Jefferson owned a comparable number of slaves.

_____ 2. By affixing their signatures to the Declaration, the delegates were committing an act of treason.

_____ 3. John Hancock was large in stature.

_____ 4. Approximately 40 changes were made to Jefferson's Declaration.

_____ 5. The most memorable lines in Jefferson's Declaration are contained in the second paragraph.

Vocabulary in Context

Cross out the incorrect word in each sentence and write the correct word from the following list in the blank provided. (Use each word only once.)

ardent	desolate	eloquent	plundered
commence	diminutive	emphatic	poignant
denounced	downcast	excise	superfluous

_____ 1. Once children turn five in the United States they usually   their formal schooling.

_____ 2. Santa's elves are known for their   size.

_____ 3. The audience applauded enthusiastically after the president delivered a stirring and   speech.

_____ 4. He already had accumulated sufficient credits to graduate; any further credits were purely

_____ 5. After Carolyn failed her final exams, she was especially

_____ 6. In his closing argument, the prosecutor   the defendant's heinous crime.

_____ 7. Mike professed his love to his sweetheart in a warm, loving,   manner.

_____ 8. When asked whether she wanted to be given a Lexus as her award, Carmen gave a very   nod "yes."

_____ 9. The grave-robbers   the valuables in the tombs.

_____ 10. Conditions in the country were   after the drought destroyed the land.

_____ 11. The movie *Selena*, about the life of the late singer, was heartbreaking and   in places.

_____ 12. The surgeon's only recourse was to   the infected flesh after gangrene had set in.

In Your Own Words

1. The pursuit of happiness is one of the "unalienable rights" written into the Declaration. What do you think Jefferson meant by "the pursuit of happiness"? What do you think most Americans today require for a "happy life"?

2. Oscar Wilde once said, "In this world there are only two tragedies. One is not getting what one wants, and the other is getting it." What do you think he meant? Do you agree or disagree with him?

The Art of Writing

In a brief essay, respond to the item below.

Rabbi Harold Kushner says that an individual doesn't become happy by pursuing happiness. Instead, he says that "happiness is like a butterfly—the more you chase it, the more it flies away from you and hides. But stop chasing it, put away your net and busy yourself with other, more productive things than the pursuit of personal happiness, and it will sneak up on you from behind and perch on your shoulder." Explain Kushner's concept using examples from your own life.

STUDY TECHNIQUE 9

Venn Diagram

A Venn diagram is an illustration that shows similarities and differences between topics using a graphic of two overlapping circles. Notice the diagram below. In the circle on the left, characteristics specific only to Jefferson are listed; in the circle on the right, characteristics specific only to Adams are listed; in the overlapping area, characteristics shared by both Adams and Jefferson are listed.

Complete the Venn diagram comparing and contrasting Jefferson and Adams by listing more traits unique to each of these men and more traits they shared. Then write a paragraph comparing and contrasting the two men. You will find that it is much easier to write a comparison-contrast assignment after creating such a Venn diagram.

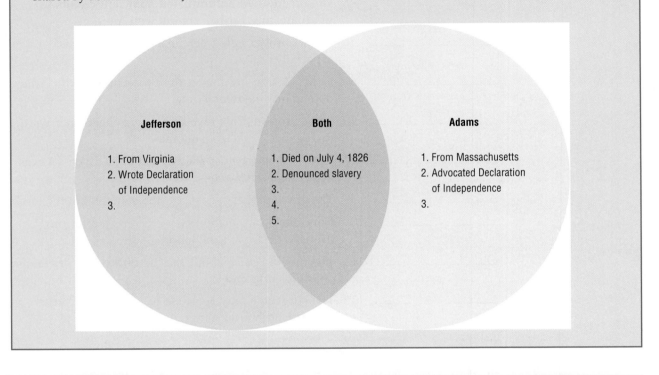

Jefferson	Both	Adams
1. From Virginia	1. Died on July 4, 1826	1. From Massachusetts
2. Wrote Declaration of Independence	2. Denounced slavery	2. Advocated Declaration of Independence
3.	3.	3.
	4.	
	5.	

SELECTION

Excerpt from *Benjamin Franklin: An American Life*   *by Walter Isaacson*

"The document Jefferson drafted was in some ways similar to what Franklin would have written."

Getting the Picture

Today, we remember Benjamin Franklin primarily for his inventions, such as bifocals and the lightning rod, and for his humorous sayings, such as "Early to bed, early to rise, makes a man healthy, wealthy, and wise." But in the course of American history he was much more than that, often providing the voice of reason to the "young hotheads." At the time of the writing of the Declaration of Independence, despite Franklin's being in poor health, his counsel proved invaluable.

Bio-sketch

Walter Isaacson, president of the Aspen Institute, has been the chairman of CNN and managing editor of *Time* magazine. He is the author of *Kissinger: A Biography*, and a coauthor of *The Wise Men: Six Friends and the World They Made*. He lives in Washington, D.C., with his wife and daughter.

Brushing Up on Vocabulary

intransigence state of being uncompromising; inflexible. When Queen Isabella of Spain was deposed in 1868, the throne remained vacant for two years until Prince Amadeo of Savoy agreed to rule. However, after just three years on the throne, he abruptly resigned. A group of individuals calling themselves the "volunteers of liberty" attempted to establish communism in Spain. They were known as *los intransigentes* because they refused to compromise with any other political entity. In the English and American press, their name was simply given as the *intransigents*. In Latin, *in* means "not," and *transigo* means "to come to an agreement."

Ben Franklin—Declaring Independence

"*I hold it that a little rebellion now and then is a good thing, and as necessary in the political world as storms in the physical.*"

—Thomas Jefferson

1   As the Continental Congress prepared to vote on the question of American independence in 1776, it appointed a committee for what would turn out, in hindsight, to be a momentous task, but one that at the time did not seem so important: drafting a declaration that explained the decision. It included Franklin, of course, and Thomas Jefferson and John Adams, as well as Connecticut merchant Roger Sherman and New York lawyer Robert Livingston.

2   How was it that Jefferson, at 33, got the honor of drafting the document? His name was listed first on the committee, signifying that he was the chairman, because he had gotten the most votes and because he was from Virginia, the colony that had proposed the resolution. His four colleagues had other committee assignments that they considered to be more important, and none of them realized that the document would eventually become viewed as a text akin to the Scripture. As for Franklin, he was still laid up in bed with boils and gout when the committee first met. Besides, he later told Jefferson, "I have made it a rule, whenever in my power, to avoid becoming the draughtsman of papers to be reviewed by a public body."

3   And thus it was that Jefferson had the glorious honor of composing, on a little lap desk he had designed, some of the most famous phrases in history while sitting alone in a second-floor room of a home on Market Street in Philadelphia just a block from Franklin's house. "When in the course of human events . . ." he famously began. Significantly, what followed was an attack not on the British government (i.e., the ministers) but on the British state incarnate (i.e., the King). "To attack the King was," as historian Pauline Maier notes, "a constitutional form. It was the way Englishmen announced revolution."

4   The document Jefferson drafted was in some ways similar to what Franklin would have written. It contained a highly specific bill of particulars against the British, and it recounted, as Franklin had often done, the details of America's attempts to be conciliatory despite England's intransigence. Indeed, Jefferson's words echoed some of the language that Franklin had used, earlier that year, in a draft resolution that he never published: "Whereas, whenever kings, instead of protecting the lives and properties of their subjects, as is their bounden duty, do endeavor to perpetrate the destruction of either, they thereby cease to be kings, become tyrants, and dissolve all ties of allegiance between themselves and their people."

5   Jefferson's writing style, however, was different from Franklin's. It was graced with rolling cadences and mellifluous phrases, soaring in their poetry and powerful despite their polish. In addition, Jefferson drew on a depth of philosophy not found in Franklin. He echoed both the language and grand theories of English and Scottish

Enlightenment thinkers, most notably the concept of natural rights propounded by John Locke, whose *Second Treatise on Government* he had read at least three times. And he built his case, in a manner more sophisticated than Franklin would have, on a contract between government and the governed that was founded on the consent of the people. Jefferson also, it should be noted, borrowed freely from the phrasings of others, including the resounding Declaration of Rights in the new Virginia constitution that had just been drafted by his fellow planter George Mason, in a manner that today might subject him to questions of plagiarism but back then was considered not only proper but learned.

6   When he had finished a draft and incorporated some changes from Adams, Jefferson sent it to Franklin on the morning of Friday, June 21. "Will Doctor Franklin be so good as to peruse it," he wrote in his cover note, "and suggest such alterations as his more enlarged view of the subject will dictate?" People were much more polite to editors back then.

7   Franklin made only a few changes, some of which can be viewed written in his hand on what Jefferson referred to as the "rough draft" of the Declaration. (This remarkable document is at the Library of Congress and on its website.) The most important of his edits was small but resounding. He crossed out, using the heavy backslashes that he often employed, the last three words of Jefferson's phrase "We hold these truths to be sacred and undeniable" and changed them to the words now enshrined in history: "We hold these truths to be self-evident."

8   The idea of "self-evident truths" was one that drew less on Locke, who was Jefferson's favored philosopher, than on the scientific determinism espoused by Isaac Newton and the analytic empiricism of Franklin's close friend David Hume. In what became known as "Hume's fork," the great Scottish philosopher had developed a theory that distinguished between "synthetic" truths that describe matters of fact (such as "London is bigger than Philadelphia") and "analytic" truths that are so by virtue of reason and definition ("the angles of a triangle total 180 degrees"; "all bachelors are unmarried"). Hume referred to the latter type of axioms as "self-evident" truths. By using the word "sacred," Jefferson had implied, intentionally or not, that the principle in question—the equality of men and their endowment by their creator with inalienable rights—was an assertion of religion. Franklin's edit turned it instead into an assertion of rationality.

9   Franklin's other edits were less felicitous. He changed Jefferson's "reduce them to arbitrary power" to "reduce them under absolute despotism," and he took out the literary flourish in Jefferson's "invade and deluge us in blood" to make it more sparse: "invade and destroy us." And a few of his changes seemed somewhat pedantic. "Amount of their salaries" became "amount and payment of their salaries."

10   On July 2, the Continental Congress finally took the momentous step of voting for independence. Pennsylvania was one of the last states to hold out; until June, its legislature had instructed its delegates to "utterly reject" any actions "that may cause or lead to a separation from our Mother Country." But under pressure from a more radical rump legislature, the instructions were changed. Led by Franklin, Pennsylvania's delegation joined the rest of the colonies in voting for independence.

11   As soon as the vote was completed, the Congress formed itself into a committee of the whole to consider Jefferson's draft Declaration. They were not as light in their editing as Franklin had been. Large sections were eviscerated, most notably the one that criticized the King for perpetuating the slave trade. Congress also, to its credit, cut by more than half the draft's final five paragraphs, in which Jefferson had begun to ramble in a way that detracted from the document's power. Jefferson was distraught. "I was sitting by Dr. Franklin," he recalled, "who perceived that I was not insensitive to these mutilations." Franklin did his best to console him.

12   At the official signing of the parchment copy on August 2, John Hancock, the president of the Congress, penned his name with his famous flourish. "There must be no pulling different ways," he declared. "We must all hang together." According to the early American historian Jared Sparks, Franklin replied, "Yes, we must, indeed, all hang together, or most assuredly we shall all hang separately." Their lives, as well as their sacred honor, had been put on the line.

Excerpted with slight changes from Walter Isaacson, *Benjamin Franklin: An American Life*. Copyright © 2003 by Walter Isaacson. Used by permission of Simon & Schuster Adult Publishing Group.

Comprehension Checkup

Vocabulary in Context

Insert the appropriate word from the list below in the spaces provided (one letter per space). After completing all seven problems, use the number key to decipher the saying by Benjamin Franklin.

akin	gout	incarnate	mellifluous	tyrant
cadence	hindsight	intransigence	peruse	whereas

1. In — — — — — — — — 1 4 X 9 6 4 X 1 2 I now know I should have studied more for the final exam.

2. Julie Andrews had a — — — — — — — — — — 5 7 X X 4 8 X X 3 X 6 voice.

3. You may — — — — — — 10 7 13 X 6 7 the document at your leisure.

4. They marched in a slow — — — — — — — 15 20 9 7 X 15 7 throughout the funeral procession.

5. A tangerine is — — — — 20 19 4 X to an orange.

6. He has a lot of money — — — — — — — 30 1 7 13 7 20 6 I have none.

7. My boss is such a — — — — — —; 2 25 13 20 X 2 he never lets me have a day off.

Benjamin Franklin says:

— — — — —   — — —   — — — —   —   — — — — — —
2 1 13 7 7   5 20 25   19 7 7 10   20   6 7 15 13 7 2

— —   — — —   — —   — — — —   — — —   — — — —.
4 8   2 30 3   3 8   2 1 7 5   20 13 7   9 7 20 9

Vocabulary Practice

Below are groups of words, three of which have similar meanings. Write the letter of the word that does not belong in this group in the space provided.

_____ 1. a. sparse   b. abundant   c. meager   d. scanty

_____ 2. a. wither   b. shrivel   c. decay   d. flourish

_____ 3. a. flood   b. trickle   c. deluge   d. inundate

_____ 4. a. wander   b. focus   c. ramble   d. digress

_____ 5. a. felicitous   b. well-chosen   c. apt   d. clumsy

_____ 6. a. eloquent   b. pedantic   c. affected   d. stilted

In Your Own Words

1. Franklin says in paragraph 2, "I have made it a rule, whenever in my power, to avoid becoming the draughtsman of papers to be reviewed by a public body." How does this statement explain the anecdote he told Jefferson (in the previous selection) about the hatter?

2. How did people feel about "borrowing words" in Jefferson's time? Did it earn the borrower respect or condemnation? Do we have a different attitude about borrowing words today?

The Art of Writing

In a brief essay, respond to one of the items below.

1. How does Franklin's account of the writing of the Declaration of Independence compare to Jefferson's and Adams's accounts as described in the previous selection? State specific differences and similarities.

2. Describe the differences between synthetic and analytic truths and give an example of each.

Annotating: An Example

Getting the Picture

The following is an annotated version of the Declaration of Independence. The annotations are based on information provided by Stephen E. Lucas, a professor of communication arts at the University of Wisconsin—Madison.

The Declaration of Independence

INTRODUCTION	1	When in the course of human events, it becomes necessary for one people to dissolve the political bands	Key word
A general statement		which have connected them with another, and to assume	Impersonal tone
		among the Powers of the earth, the separate and equal station to which the Laws of Nature and Nature's God entitle them, a decent respect to the opinions of mankind requires that they should declare the causes which	
		impel them to the separation.	Purpose stated
PREAMBLE	2	We hold these truths to be self-evident, that all men are	Five propositions given
		created equal, that they are endowed by their Creator with certain unalienable Rights, that among these are Life, Liberty and the pursuit of Happiness.	
General philosophy of gov.	3	That to secure these rights, Governments are instituted among Men, deriving their just powers from the consent of the governed.	

4   That <u>whenever any Form of Government becomes destructive of these ends, it is the Right of the People to alter or to abolish it</u>, and to institute a new Government laying its foundation on such principles and organizing its powers in such form, as to them shall seem most likely to effect their Safety and Happiness. Prudence, indeed, will dictate that Governments long established should not be changed for light and transient causes; and accordingly all experience hath shown that mankind are more disposed to suffer, while evils are sufferable, than to right themselves by abolishing the forms to which they are accustomed. But when a long train of abuses and usurpations pursuing invariably the same Object evinces a design to reduce them under absolute Despotism, it is their right, it is their duty, to throw off such government, and to provide new Guards for their future security.

5   Such has been the patient sufferance of these Colonies; and such is now the necessity which constrains them to alter their former Systems of Government. The history of the present King of Great Britain is a history of repeated injuries and usurpations, all having in direct object the establishment of an absolute Tyranny over these States. *To prove this, let Facts be submitted to a candid world.*

6   He has <u>refused his Assent to Laws</u>, the most wholesome and necessary for the public good.

7   He has forbidden his Governors to pass Laws of immediate and pressing importance, unless <u>suspended in their operation</u> till his Assent should be obtained; and when so suspended, he has utterly neglected to attend to them. He has refused to pass other Laws for the accommodation of large districts of people, unless those people would relinquish the right of Representation in the Legislature, a right inestimable to them and formidable to tyrants only.

8   He has called together legislative bodies at places unusual, uncomfortable, and distant from the depository of their public Records, for the sole purpose of fatiguing them into compliance with his measures.

9   He has <u>dissolved Representative Houses repeatedly</u>, for opposing with manly firmness his invasions on the rights of the people.

10   He has refused for a long time, after such dissolutions, to cause others to be elected; whereby the Legislative powers, incapable of Annihilation, have returned to the People at large for their exercise, the State remaining in the mean time exposed to all the dangers of invasion from without, and convulsions within.

11   He has endeavoured to prevent the population of these States; for that purpose obstructing the Laws for Naturalization of Foreigners; refusing to pass others to encourage their migrations hither, and raising the conditions of new Appropriations of Lands.

12   He has <u>obstructed the Administration of Justice</u>, by refusing his Assent to Laws for establishing Judiciary powers.

Side notes:

Fifth is most crucial— asserts right of revolution

INDICTMENT OF GEORGE III

Four groups of facts listed

Proof : 28 grievances

Group I charges 1–12: describe the abuse of king's executive power

Word *candid* implies an appeal to fair and unbiased

Charges are arranged by topics, not chronologically

Charges are purposely ambiguous: no names, dates, or places are identified

13   He has made Judges dependent on his Will alone, for the tenure of their offices, and the amount and payment of their salaries.

14   He has erected a multitude of New Offices, and sent hither swarms of Officers to harass our People, and eat out their substance.

15   He has <u>kept among us, in times of peace, standing Armies</u> without the Consent of our legislatures.

16   He has affected to render the Military independent of and superior to the Civil power.

Group II charges 13–22: subjected America to unconstitutional measures

17   He has combined with others to subject us to a jurisdiction foreign to our constitution, and unacknowledged by our laws; giving his Assent to their Acts of pretended Legislation:

18   For Quartering large bodies of armed troops among us:

19   For protecting them, by a mock Trial from punishment for any Murders which they should commit on the Inhabitants of these States:

20   <u>For cutting off our Trade with all parts of the world:</u>

21   <u>For imposing Taxes on us without our Consent:</u>

22   <u>For depriving us in many cases of the benefits of Trial by Jury:</u>

23   For transporting us beyond Seas to be tried for pretended offences:

24   For abolishing the free System of English Laws in a neighboring Province, establishing therein an Arbitrary government, and enlarging its Boundaries so as to render it at once an example and fit instrument for introducing the same absolute rule into these Colonies.

25   <u>For taking away our Charters</u>, abolishing our most valuable Laws, and altering fundamentally the Forms of our Governments:

26   For suspending our own Legislatures, and declaring themselves invested with power to legislate for us in all cases whatsoever.

Group III charges 23–27: the king is charged with violence and cruelty

27   He has abdicated Government here, by declaring us out of his Protection and waging War against us.

28   He has <u>plundered</u> our seas, <u>ravaged</u> our Coasts, <u>burnt</u> our towns, and <u>destroyed</u> the Lives of our people.   emotionally charged verbs

29   He is at this time transporting large Armies of foreign Mercenaries to compleat the works of death, desolation and tyranny, already begun with circumstances of Cruelty & perfidy scarcely paralleled in the most barbarous ages, and totally unworthy of the Head of a civilized nation.

30   He has constrained our fellow Citizens taken Captive on the high Seas to bear Arms against their Country, to become the executioners of their friends and Brethren, or to fall themselves by their Hands.

31   He has excited domestic insurrections amongst us, and has endeavoured to bring on the inhabitants of our frontiers, merciless Indian savages, whose known rule of warfare, is an undistinguished destruction of all ages, sexes, and conditions.

Group IV final charge   32   In every stage of these Oppressions We have Petitioned for Redress in the most humble terms: <u>Our repeated Petitions have been answered only by repeated injury.</u> A Prince, whose character is thus marked by every act which may define a Tyrant, is unfit to be the ruler of a free people.

Colonies have appealed in vain

DENUNCIATION OF THE   33   Nor have We been wanting in attentions to our British
BRITISH PEOPLE   brethren. We have warned them from time to time of attempts by their legislature to extend an unwarrantable jurisdiction over us. We have reminded them of the circumstances of our emigration and settlement here. We have appealed to their native justice and magnanimity, and we have conjured them by the ties of our common kindred to disavow these usurpations, which would inevitably interrupt our connections and correspondence.

This section finishes the   <u>They too have been deaf to the voice of Justice and of</u>
case for independence   <u>consanguinity.</u> We must, therefore, acquiesce in the neces-
                                      sity, which denounces our Separation, and hold them, as
                                      we hold the rest of mankind, Enemies in War, in Peace

Use of metaphor

CONCLUSION   Friends.
                          34   We, therefore, the representatives of the united States of America, in General Congress, Assembled, appealing to the Supreme Judge of the world for the rectitude of our intentions, do, in the Name, and by Authority of the good People of these Colonies, solemnly publish and declare, That these United Colonies are, and of Right ought to be Free and Independent States; that they are absolved from all Allegiance to the British Crown, and that all political connection between them and the State of Great Britain, is and ought to be totally dissolved; and that as Free and Independent States, they have full Power to levy War, con- clude Peace, contract Alliances, establish Commerce, and to do all other Acts and Things which Independent States

Personal tone

may of right do. And for the support of this Declaration, with a firm reliance on the protection of divine Providence, <u>we mutually pledge to each other our Lives, our Fortunes and our sacred Honor.</u>

A solemn vow from men of honor

Annotation of the Declaration of Independence is based on information from Stephen E. Lucas, *The Stylistic Artistry of the Declaration of Independence,* 1989.

Comprehension Checkup

Short Answer

In one or two sentences, answer the questions below.

1. In the very first sentence, Jefferson makes a claim that people are entitled by "the Laws of Nature and Nature's God" to separate and equal stations. What does this claim mean?

   _____

   _____

   _____

2.   According to Jefferson's reasoning in the second paragraph, what truths does he claim are self-evident? What is meant by the term *self-evident?*

_____

_____

_____

3.   According to paragraph three, what is the purpose of governments? From where do governments derive their power?

_____

_____

_____

4.   In paragraph four, Jefferson responds to those who would throw off governments for "light and transient causes." What sort of cause does he say you need to "throw off governments"?

_____

_____

_____

5.   Jefferson hopes that a listing of specific acts of tyranny by George III will convince others that the American colonies are justified in separating themselves from England. List some factual evidence given by Jefferson to justify independence. What are the most serious complaints?

_____

_____

_____

6.   To whom is Jefferson addressing his declaration?

_____

_____

_____

7.   What is Jefferson referring to in the next-to-the-last paragraph? Do you think the British Parliament accepted Jefferson's claim?

_____

_____

_____

8.   What does Jefferson announce in the last paragraph?

_____

_____

_____

9.   Many reform movements have been inspired by Jefferson's Declaration. Do you think that Jefferson was aware that he was speaking to future generations?

_____

_____

_____

10. What is the overall tone of Jefferson's argument?

_____

_____

_____

Brief Chronology of the American Campaign for Independence

1775—The first battle of the Revolutionary War (Battles of Lexington and Concord) fought.
1776—Declaration of Independence signed.
1787—Constitution of the United States signed.
1789—George Washington inaugurated as first president of the United States.
1790—Washington D.C. founded as the nation's capital.
1791—Bill of Rights ratified by the states.
1801—Thomas Jefferson inaugurated as the third president.

In Your Own Words

The following painting is John Trumbull's *The Declaration of Independence*, which dates from 1818. It was commissioned by President James Madison to hang in the U.S. Capitol Rotunda in Washington, D.C. Trumbull, who fought in the Revolutionary War, also painted three other pictures illustrating the fight for American independence. In addition, he did a series of portraits of famous people from that period.

Study the composition of the painting. To portray the scene as realistically as possible, Trumbull consulted with Thomas Jefferson. All of the signers of the Declaration are present in the painting. The tallest figure, Jefferson, is handing a copy of the Declaration to John Hancock. To Jefferson's left is Benjamin Franklin, and to his right in the foreground is John Adams. What is the overall tone of the painting? What is the significance of the flags on the wall? Which figure is given the most importance?

*To see this work of art in color, turn to the color insert following page 260.

Architect of the Capitol

The Declaration of Independence (1818), by John Trumbull*

The Art of Writing

In a brief essay, respond to the items below.

1.   The phrase "that all men are created equal" has caused considerable contro-
     versy. What do you think Jefferson meant by it? What is your interpretation
     of the phrase?

2.   Do you think that the sort of rebellion advocated by Jefferson in the Declara-
     tion could ever be justified in today's world? In what circumstances?

Internet Activity

To learn more about Thomas Jefferson, go to

>   www.monticello.org

Click on "A Day in the Life of Jefferson" to follow Jefferson through a typical
24 hours during his retirement at Monticello. Then learn more about Jefferson's role
in the Lewis and Clark expedition and click on "Jefferson and the Expedition."
Peruse this portion of the site to find a page of interest to you; print it and briefly
summarize your findings.

To learn more about the Declaration of Independence and to view material from
the collections of the Library of Congress go to

>   http://lcweb.loc.gov/exhibits/declara/declara1.html

Click on either "Chronology of Events" or "Objects in the Exhibition." If you select
the chronology, create a short time line of the events leading up to the signing of
the Declaration. Or select an object in the current exhibition and briefly describe it.

SELECTION

Excerpt from *The Majesty of the Law*   *by Sandra Day O'Connor*

*"The Bill of Rights was drafted intentionally in broad, sweeping terms, allowing meaning
to be developed in response to changing times and current problems."*

Getting the Picture

Opinion on the ratification of the U.S. Constitution was almost evenly divided
between those who favored its passage and those who did not. Many were opposed
because they feared that a strong federal government would usurp the power of
the states and individual citizens. As a result, a compromise was reached, declaring that if the Constitution were approved, amendments would be added at a later
date that would safeguard individual liberties. The ten amendments adopted later
became the Bill of Rights.

Bio-sketch

Sandra Day O'Connor, the first woman justice on the U.S. Supreme Court, was
appointed by President Ronald Reagan in 1981. Raised on a ranch in Arizona, she
is the author, with her brother Alan, of the bestseller *Lazy B*, which describes her
formative years. A graduate of Stanford University and Stanford University Law
School, O'Connor, who graduated near the top of her class, initially could not find
employment as a lawyer because of her sex. Instead, she was offered jobs as a legal

secretary. In her book *The Majesty of the Law,* from which the following excerpt is taken, she discusses notable cases and reminisces about changes in the law since she first became an attorney and then a judge.

Brushing Up on Vocabulary

Federalists   persons who favored a strong central government and the creation of a national bank. *The Federalist Papers* were a series of essays written primarily by Alexander Hamilton, James Madison, and John Jay to convince the voters of New York to adopt the Constitution.

Anti-Federalists   persons who favored a weak central government and emphasized individual and states' rights. The Bill of Rights is considered a major accomplishment of the Anti-Federalists.

The Evolution of the Bill of Rights

1   The Bill of Rights is truly a remarkable document. Upon reading it, one cannot help but be struck by how concise it is. Countless thousands of pages have been written about it, but the Bill of Rights itself sums up our most precious freedoms—more than two dozen fundamental rights—in fewer than five hundred words. And its brevity is not accidental. Before James Madison rose in Congress to read his first draft, he pored over hundreds of provisions suggested by various state ratifying conventions. He could have compiled them all into a lengthy document, but chose not to. He decided, quite deliberately, to single out only a handful of fundamental principles. His view was that enumerating additional rights of less significance would risk diminishing the document's importance. After all, a laundry list of lesser rights, such as the right to wear powdered wigs in public, would sit uneasily beside such fundamental liberties as freedom of speech and religion.

2   Madison was keenly conscious of the language he used in framing the Bill of Rights. The proposals offered by the various state conventions used tentative terms. An earlier state version of what became our Eighth Amendment provided that "excessive bail *ought not* to be required." Madison replaced the tentative terms with stronger ones, transforming suggestions into bold declarations. Thus, the Eighth Amendment declares in no uncertain terms that "excessive bail *shall not* be required." This kind of language does not *request* that the government afford the people certain freedoms; it *demands* it. It declares that they exist as a matter of natural law, and that the government has no authority to interfere with their exercise.

3   Likewise, the First Amendment does not *ask* the government to refrain from intervening in religious matters. It declares unflinchingly that "Congress *shall make no law* respecting an establishment of religion, or prohibiting the free exercise thereof." This strong language serves two purposes. It inspires and reassures those of us who hold the rights, and it warns any who would dare violate these rights that they may not do so.

4   The Bill of Rights is both simple and eloquent. The ten amendments are written in language that any literate American can understand and many can recite from memory. And at the same time that they are forcefully written, they are neither rigid nor inflexible. The Bill of Rights was drafted intentionally in broad, sweeping terms, allowing meaning to be developed in response to changing times and current problems. In many ways the Bill of Rights is like a novel by Faulkner or a painting by Monet: it does not change, but our understanding and perception of it may. Had the Bill of Rights been written in less broad terms, it might not have withstood the passage of time. The world today is a much different place than it was two centuries ago. We have different problems, different priorities, and different technologies than our ancestors had.

5   As a result, several of the amendments are as vital today—or more so—than when they were adopted. Consider the First Amendment's declaration that "Congress shall make no law . . . abridging the freedom of speech." In drafting this provision, the primary concern was to protect political speech: specifically, criticism of the government. In England, outspoken critics of the king had sometimes been labeled traitors and severely punished. It was thus of immense importance to the early Americans, in setting up their own government, to permit all kinds of political speech. More than two hundred years later, we continue to value the importance of speech on political topics and afford it constitutional protection, no matter how controversial or despised its substance may be. Indeed, the First Amendment has been relied on to permit even neo-Nazis to march and speak in a city that included Holocaust survivors.

6   At the same time, the First Amendment has been invoked to protect speech on all sorts of topics far removed from politics—topics that its drafters could never have imagined. This has required the Supreme Court to grapple with a host of difficult issues. One case, for instance, questioned whether the First Amendment prohibits a high school principal from keeping stories about pregnancy and birth control out of the school paper. Another asked whether pharmacies must be permitted to advertise their prices for over-the-counter drugs. We have even had to decide whether New Hampshire residents who disagree with the state motto, "Live Free or Die," can use tape to cover that part of their license plates.

7   Nevertheless, the guarantee of "the freedom of speech" contained in the Bill of Rights is not absolute. The Court has held, for example, that obscene speech is not protected.

8   Further removed from the drafters' vision of the First Amendment are cases holding that the First Amendment protects conduct that conveys a particular message. Thus, the Court has ruled that a junior high school could not prohibit its students from wearing black armbands to protest the nation's involvement in the Vietnam War. And, more recently, the Court held that the First Amendment invalidates a statute criminalizing the burning of the American flag as a form of protest, although it does not invalidate a prohibition on nude dancing in public places.

9   Another constant and inexhaustible source of litigation has been the Fourth Amendment, which protects Americans against "unreasonable searches and seizures." This amendment was included in the Bill of Rights to outlaw in this country the much despised British practice of conducting unannounced house-to-house searches, pursuant to so-called writs of assistance.

10   But the Fourth Amendment has come to stand for much more. Technological advancements that Madison and his contemporaries could never have foreseen have made it possible for the government to conduct a search without ever entering a person's home. For example, wiretaps allow people's conversations to be monitored and recorded without their knowledge. The Court has held that to be a search. It has also determined that a search occurs when police officers use thermal imaging devices to "see" through walls. But this leads to further questions. Does it matter whether the technology is generally available to the public? How available is generally available? Do Fourth Amendment protections decrease as technology becomes even more advanced?

11   Questions like these are difficult, and no amount of study of James Madison's private notes will yield a conclusive answer.

12   Just as technology has made the Fourth Amendment a murkier area than our forebears could have suspected, biological science has complicated application of the Fifth Amendment. The Fifth Amendment guarantees that no one "shall be compelled in any criminal case to be a witness against himself." We all know from watching TV police shows what the Fifth Amendment means: "You have the right to remain silent." The government cannot force you to testify against yourself if you are accused

of a crime. The inspiration for this amendment can be traced all the way back to the Inquisition, where heretics were routinely tortured until they confessed their sins.

13 But today the government can often tell whether someone is guilty without an oral confession. It can test drivers' blood to see if they have been driving while intoxicated. Or it can analyze defendants' DNA structure to determine conclusively whether a single hair or body-fluid sample found at the scene of the crime belongs to them. The question for the Court has become whether the Fifth Amendment allows the government to compel the extraction and use of such evidence.

14 These amendments—the First, Fourth, and Fifth—were adopted in the infancy of our republic, but they remain a constant source of litigation, controversy—and inspiration—even in a new millennium. Time and technology have advanced, yet these provisions remain vital because our ancestors recognized the importance of framing our most basic rights in broad terms.

15 On the other hand, other of the amendments are little remembered today. Cited very rarely is the Third Amendment, which declares: "No soldier shall, in time of peace be quartered in any house, without the consent of the Owner, nor in time of war, but in a manner to be prescribed by law." This had been a very real problem in eighteenth-century England. Soldiers were put in people's homes, and the homeowner was made responsible for providing room and board. But this has never been a policy in our country. While the government may, in times of war, take young people out of their homes and draft them into the military, it rarely tries to put soldiers *into* people's houses.

16 There are two other amendments that do not enumerate any specific freedoms, but which were nonetheless of vital significance to those who drafted the Bill of Rights. They are the Ninth and Tenth Amendments.

17 The Ninth Amendment provides that the rights enumerated in the Bill of Rights are not the *only* rights possessed by the people. Probably the most famous example of an unenumerated right is the right to privacy. In *Griswold* v. *Connecticut,* the Court held that the Constitution protects a right of privacy, including the right of married couples to use contraceptives. The nature and description of unenumerated rights, and the extent to which they are subject to the highest level of judicial scrutiny, is hotly debated. But there is little doubt that some such rights do exist. And there is little doubt that we will see more litigation to test and define them.

18 The Tenth Amendment sets out in a single sentence the Anti-Federalists' main concern about the Constitution: that the new government not be permitted to usurp the sovereign authority of state governments: "The powers not delegated to the United States by the Constitution, nor prohibited by it to the States, are reserved to the States respectively, or to the people." The amendment makes clear that the power of the federal government is derived from the states, and that the Constitution is not construed to convey any more power to the government than is absolutely necessary to carry out its enumerated functions. All other power belongs to the states.

19 This understanding is consistent with the sentiments of the Anti-Federalists, who recognized that state legislatures were closer to the people than the new national government and more accurately reflected the people's wishes. It is also consistent with the sentiments of the Federalists, who, while desiring a strong central government, wanted to preserve strong state governments to prevent the federal government from abusing its power.

20 Of course the Ninth and Tenth Amendments are not often relied upon by litigants. Like the Third Amendment, they have been largely ignored, at least for the time being. But this does not mean that they will not become more vital in the future. One would think that, after two centuries, we would have figured it all out. But we have not. More than two hundred years after the Bill of Rights was adopted, courts still grapple with many of the same questions. Thus, even though the First

Amendment's freedom of speech clause and the Fourth Amendment's prohibition of unlawful searches have been subjects of litigation since the Framer's days, we their descendants are still working out the details.

21   And new questions are always being raised—questions that no one could have foreseen in our nation's earliest years. That is the beauty of the Bill of Rights. Along with the new questions come new understandings of what the amendments mean. For while the text of the Bill of Rights does not change, our perspective on it has evolved with the passage of time. The adoption of the Bill of Rights deserves our praise and thanksgiving. It is part of our American contribution to the notion of freedom and justice.

From Sandra Day O'Connor, *The Majesty of the Law*, pp. 59–76. Copyright © 2003 by Arizona Community Foundation. Used by permission of Random House, Inc.

Comprehension Checkup

Multiple Choice

Write the letter of the correct answer in the blank provided.

_____   1.   The author's main idea is:
                 a. Some amendments in the Bill of Rights are no longer as relevant today as they were in earlier times.
                 b. The Bill of Rights is a remarkable document deserving of our praise and thanksgiving.
                 c. The Fourth Amendment has a broader meaning today than when it was originally adopted.

_____   2.   The author's purpose and mode of writing is
                 a. purpose in writing: to entertain; mode of writing: narrative
                 b. purpose in writing: to inform; mode of writing: expository
                 c. purpose in writing: to entertain; mode of writing: persuasive

_____   3.   The author's tone is
                 a. angry
                 b. indifferent
                 c. instructive

_____   4.   The reader can logically infer that the author
                 a. values the forcefulness of the Bill of Rights
                 b. values the flexibility of the Bill of Rights
                 c. Both of the above

_____   5.   Who is the author's intended audience?
                 a. high school and college students
                 b. the general public
                 c. teachers and other educators

_____   6.   The title of the selection implies that
                 a. several amendments are just as vital today as they were in the past
                 b. the Third Amendment will become more vital in the future
                 c. while the wording of the Bill of Rights remains the same, its meaning has changed over time

_____   7.   The words *simple, eloquent,* and *remarkable* in reference to the Bill of Rights have a
                 a. positive connotation
                 b. negative connotation
                 c. neutral meaning

_____ 8. As used in paragraph 2, *tentative* most nearly means
  a. experimental
  b. temporary
  c. weak

_____ 9. Complete the following analogy: ought not : shall not : : request : _____ (paragraph 2)
  a. demand
  b. gift
  c. ask

_____ 10. In paragraph 4, the author compares the Bill of Rights to a painting by Monet, implying that
  a. the Bill of Rights is a beautiful document
  b. the Bill of Rights is subject to varying interpretations
  c. the writing of the Bill of Rights was painstaking

_____ 11. In paragraph 15, the transition phrase *on the other hand* indicates
  a. cause and effect
  b. contrast
  c. comparison

_____ 12. Which of the following does the excerpt support as true?
  a. The Supreme Court grapples with difficult issues that could not have been foreseen by the framers.
  b. Advances in technology have had little effect on the justices' interpretation of the Bill of Rights.
  c. Unenumerated rights are those that the Supreme Court views as having little importance.

_____ 13. Which of the following statements from the selection represents a fact rather than an opinion?
  a. "Questions like these are difficult, and no amount of study of James Madison's private notes will yield a conclusive answer."
  b. "The Bill of Rights is both simple and eloquent."
  c. "Indeed, the First Amendment has been relied on to permit even neo-Nazis to march and speak in a city that included Holocaust survivors."
  d. "One would think that, after two centuries, we would have figured it all out."

_____ 14. Which of the following statements is correct?
  a. The Ninth Amendment provides that citizens have more rights than those specified in the first eight amendments.
  b. Unlike the first eight amendments, the Ninth and Tenth Amendments do not identify specific rights.
  c. The Tenth Amendment places limits on the powers of the federal government.
  d. All of the above.

The Art of Writing

In a brief essay, respond to the item below.

Discuss some of the ways the Bill of Rights protects people who are wrongfully accused of a crime.

Internet Activity

The texts of opinions and transcripts of oral arguments appear on the Supreme Court's website at

> www.supremecourtus.gov

Visit the site, choose an opinion of interest to you, and summarize it briefly.

The Bill of Rights

Articles in Addition to, and Amendment of, the Constitution of the United States of America, Proposed by Congress, and Ratified by the Legislatures of the Several States, Pursuant to the Fifth Article of the Original Constitution.

AMENDMENT I

Congress shall make no law respecting an establishment of religion, or prohibiting the free exercise thereof; or abridging the freedom of speech, or of the press; or the right of the people peaceably to assemble, and to petition the Government for a redress of grievances.

AMENDMENT II

A well-regulated Militia, being necessary to the security of a free State, the right of the people to keep and bear Arms, shall not be infringed.

AMENDMENT III

No soldier shall, in time of peace be quartered in any house, without the consent of the Owner, nor in time of war, but in a manner to be prescribed by law.

AMENDMENT IV

The right of the people to be secure in their persons, houses, papers, and effects, against unreasonable searches and seizures, shall not be violated, and no Warrants shall issue, but upon probable cause, supported by Oath or affirmation, and particularly describing the place to be searched, and the persons or things to be seized.

AMENDMENT V

No person shall be held to answer for a capital, or otherwise infamous crime, unless on a presentment or indictment of a Grand Jury, except in cases arising in the land or naval forces, or in the Militia, when in actual service in time of War or public danger; nor shall any person be subject for the same offence to be twice put in jeopardy of life or limb; nor shall be compelled in any criminal case to be a witness against himself; nor be deprived of life, liberty, or property, without due process of law; nor shall private property be taken for public use, without just compensation.

AMENDMENT VI

In all criminal prosecutions, the accused shall enjoy the right to a speedy and public trial, by an impartial jury of the State and district wherein the crime shall have been committed, which district shall have been previously ascertained by law, and to be informed of the nature and cause of the accusation; to be confronted with the witnesses against him; to have compulsory process for obtaining witnesses in his favor, and to have the Assistance of Counsel for his defence.

AMENDMENT **VII**

In Suits at common law, where the value in controversy shall exceed twenty dollars, the right of trial by jury shall be preserved, and no fact tried by a jury, shall be otherwise reexamined in any Court of the United States, than according to the rules of the common law.

AMENDMENT **VIII**

Excessive bail shall not be required, nor excessive fines imposed, nor cruel and unusual punishments inflicted.

AMENDMENT **IX**

The enumeration in the Constitution, of certain rights, shall not be construed to deny or disparage others retained by the people.

AMENDMENT **X**

The powers not delegated to the United States by the Constitution, nor prohibited by it to the States, are reserved to the States respectively, or to the people.

Comprehension Checkup

Fill in the Blank

Identify the correct amendment and fill in the blank provided.

1. Lt. Col. Oliver North frequently cited the _____ amendment privilege against self-incrimination when he refused to testify about the Iran-Contra scandal.

2. Rap artist Snoop Dogg (real name: Calvin Broadus) believes his lyrics are constitutionally protected by the _____ amendment.

3. Today's debate over handgun control is based on the _____ amendment.

4. The constant noise and glare of military planes at an airport interfered with the normal use of adjoining land as a chicken farm. The owner protested and was awarded just compensation because of the _____ amendment.

5. A Jehovah's Witness feels his child is not required to salute the flag at school because of the _____ amendment.

6. The _____ amendment exists to answer the objections of those who thought that naming some rights but not all results in the government's claiming the power to prevent a person from "lying on his left side on a long winter's night."

7. Bail of $200,000 for a person who has robbed a store is prohibited under the _____ amendment.

8. The Supreme Court let stand a Georgia decision that bans organized prayers before public school football games because of the _____ amendment.

9. Under the _____ amendment, a confession cannot be considered voluntary unless preceded by proper warnings (Miranda).

10. Because of amendment number _____, the national government can't place a soldier in a private citizen's home to live without the owner's permission (during peacetime).

11. Because of amendment number _____, a person cannot be made to wait years with a charge hanging over his or her head.

12. In 1971, the federal government sought to prohibit *The New York Times* from publishing the "Pentagon Papers." However, the Supreme Court ruled such a prohibition was a violation under the _____ amendment.

In Your Own Words

1. Why do you think these particular rights were considered important by the framers of the Constitution? If you were to write a contemporary Bill of Rights, what other rights would you include?

2. Phrases such as "due process of law" and "cruel and unusual punishment" are always open to interpretation. What are the advantages of such abstract language? Would more specific language have been better? Why?

The Art of Writing

In a brief essay, respond to one of the items below.

1. Rewrite the 10 amendments in modern colloquial English, and illustrate each with a relevant example.

2. The second amendment is complicated and open to multiple interpretations. Do you think this amendment grants today's citizens the right to own guns? Or does it only grant them the right to carry guns in militias?

Internet Activity

Visit the Constitution Center website at

www.constitutioncenter.org

You can take a tour of the museum, review Supreme Court cases, or explore the Constitution and the Bill of Rights.

Five Tests of Your Freedoms

Getting the Picture

Speech. Religion. Press. Petition. Assembly. You learned all those First Amendment rights in basic civics class. But how well do you *really* understand them?

The *USA WEEKEND* First Amendment Center Poll

The USA, the first nation to be founded on principles of liberty and justice, is fueled by freedom, particularly the rights guaranteed in the First Amendment to the Constitution. But how well do we understand these basic rights? To find out *USA Weekend* Magazine and the First Amendment Center commissioned a scientific online poll consisting of a series of hypothetical scenarios. Each was designed to challenge one of the five freedoms set out in the First Amendment: freedom of speech, press and religion, and the right to assemble and to petition government for constructive change.

The poll results clearly show some serious confusion among Americans about their First Amendment protections and how they apply to a diverse and sometimes divided society.

Here, take the poll yourself (or in a group) and test your own answers against the survey respondents'—and those of Lee C. Bollinger, one of the nation's leading First Amendment experts, president of Columbia University and the author of *The Tolerant Society and Eternally Vigilant: Free Speech in the Modern Era.*

1. A high school student wears a T-shirt to public school with the words "International Criminal" framing President Bush's picture on the front. The principal tells the student to put on a different shirt, turn the shirt inside out, or go home. If those requests are refused, the student will face immediate suspension.

Does the principal have the right to ban the T-shirt?

2. A town strapped for funds enters an agreement with the community's largest church by which the church will operate the town's failing convention center. The church agrees to raise the money itself to run the center and promises it will not discriminate against any religious, political, racial, or other groups that might want to rent it for a fee.

Do you think such an arrangement is allowed under the First Amendment?

3. A recent decision by the city council to reduce trash pickup from twice weekly to once a week upset one citizen so much that he has posted comments on a local Internet site, using the alias "Angry Citizen." In his comments the citizen accuses one council member of being a "lying communist." When the councilman learns the identity of the writer, he contacts Angry Citizen, who quickly offers to post another comment apologizing for his remark. ("Angry Citizen" says he was just upset at that moment.) Dissatisfied, the accused councilman threatens to sue him for libel.

Does the First Amendment protect "Angry Citizen" if the councilman files the lawsuit?

4. County officials recently have been hounded and harassed at commission meetings by a small number of activists who oppose a county tax increase. In response, the officials have established new rules governing all public appearances before the county commission. Specifically, citizens wishing to speak at commission meetings now must apply seven days in advance for permission to do so and must limit their comments to two minutes.

Do county officials have the right to establish these new rules?

5. A citizen who participates in a neighborhood antiwar march learns that the local police department has secretly videotaped the rally and created a file with the names of everyone who participated. Police officials defend their actions by citing the increased possibility of terrorist threats and the needs of national security.

Do you think the police department has the right to videotape the marchers and keep files on them?

SURVEY RESPONDENT RESULTS

1. **America says: Yes** 62% **No** 38%

The expert says: The majority has it wrong. Most people may want to ban the offending T-shirt, but they can't in this case. The First Amendment protects the right of "speech" even when it's symbolic, as when the message is in the form of an image on a piece of clothing. And although many may think the constitutional right of freedom of speech does not reach minors, the Supreme Court has held otherwise.

The landmark case on this point (from the 1960s) recognized the free speech rights of a 13-year-old to wear a black armband in class in protest against the war in Vietnam. As a society, we have staked our future on a robust right of freedom of expression (even for neo-Nazis and the Ku Klux Klan), and it is inconsistent with that commitment, the court has held, to make it available only when you turn 18 or 21.

Still, nothing in life is absolute, and, contrary to what even a few Supreme Court justices have said, that is true of the First Amendment as well. If a principal can show significant "disruption" as a result of the speech, courts will give more leeway to restrict the speech. The mere fact that other students take offense would not be enough, but spontaneous fighting or outbursts making class discipline impossible very well might be.

A final note: The First Amendment applies only to "state action" and hence to public schools. A principal in a private school can set whatever limits on speech he or she wishes.

2.   **America says: Yes** 70%   **No** 30%
The expert says: The answer is no. This is not a good idea for the town, the public, the church, or the First Amendment. The amendment's guarantees of religious freedom and free speech prevent the government from favoring one religion over another, so the choice itself may have involved improper bias against other groups who also sought to operate the center. Beyond that, appearances matter enormously here. Just imagine if Central Park were leased to a particular church to "operate." The First Amendment long has required the state to make available certain public property—most notably, streets and parks—for citizens to exercise their right of free speech. Although reasonable restrictions can be imposed (for instance, the time, place, and manner of expression), the state cannot favor particular speakers or points of view over others.

Furthermore, under the Establishment Clause, the Supreme Court has refused to permit relationships between church and state where there is the appearance of religious endorsement and where the prospects of "entanglement" are great. In this case, despite the church's assurances that it will not discriminate among speakers, we would have to expect an endless series of conflicts and disagreements over whether the church has administered this "public forum" with a religious bias.

What can seem perfectly reasonable in the abstract, as it does to 70 percent of the respondents, can be filled with latent constitutional problems.

3.   **America says: Yes** 60%   **No** 40%
The expert says: The majority got it right this time. The First Amendment's guarantee of a free press does not apply only to professional journalists—it protects every citizen.

It is exceedingly difficult for a public official to force a citizen to pay damages for a libelous statement. Under the Supreme Court's verdict in *The New York Times* v. *Sullivan,* the council member would have to show that the statement is false (Maybe he *is* a "lying communist"), that the statement was one of fact rather than "opinion" (Would the reasonable reader assume this accusation was just the speaker's interpretation of generally known facts, or perhaps just hyperbole?), that the false statement actually injured the council member's reputation, and that the injurious statement was made with knowledge of its falsity or with "reckless disregard of the truth" (i.e., with "actual malice").

Those criteria are nearly insurmountable barriers to a successful lawsuit for defamation. Is this justified? The court's rationale is not a lack of concern for the reputations of public servants, nor a high regard for falsehoods. Rather, the idea is that, because we are committed to living in a democracy where the citizens are sovereign, we need to provide ample space for citizens to engage in public debate without being intimidated about speaking their minds by the prospect of having to defend themselves against lawsuits.

In an imperfect world, someone's rights or interests often have to give way. Here it's the reputation of public officials.

Neither the fact that this statement was made on the Internet nor the fact that it was made anonymously changes the outcome. Generally speaking, the rules in this area of First Amendment protections do not change, whether you are communicating with millions or speaking across the fence to a neighbor.

4. **America says: Yes** 56% **No** 44%
The expert says: Yes, the new rules appear to be fine on their face. Certainly, the county can require speakers to sign up in advance and impose a time limit on each speaker. Nothing in the First Amendment's right to petition for a redress of grievances or freedom of speech prohibits the state from bringing some order to a forum.

What are prohibited, however, are regulations that discriminate against speakers because of the content of their messages. This is where I have concerns. We are not told what the "activists" did that "hounded and harassed" the officials, nor are we told why and how the new rules are a response to that behavior.

So here's the caution: If the activists only criticized the county officials, even if harshly, and if the officials believe that they can use the new rules to treat the "activists" differently because of their criticisms, then we have a very real problem under the First Amendment. The officials may (constitutionally, at least) hope the activists won't have the foresight to apply and to limit their critiques to two minutes at a time—and thereby give county officials the right to prohibit them from speaking at commission meetings. But they must pursue these wishes in a content-neutral way, applying the same rules to everyone, not just the activists.

5. **America says: Yes** 54% **No** 46%
The expert says: Yes, it is permissible under the First Amendment's rights of free speech and assembly. As citizens we have the right to march and to express our views—however sound, however outrageous. But the government may watch and keep information on us, for good or for bad reasons.

That's not to say doing so under any and all circumstances is a good idea. There is much, in fact, to be said against it, not least because it may have a chilling effect on the exercise of constitutional liberties. But not all government actions that chill speech are unconstitutional, and thus far, at least, the Supreme Court has not declared keeping files on marchers to be an abridgement of the First Amendment.

Everything depends on how the government uses the files. A systematic campaign to discredit its opponents through the partisan use of videos and other information selectively gathered, accompanied by baseless intimations of terrorist connections, could raise an interesting new case under the First Amendment. Certainly, it would be a violation of the spirit of democracy.

From *USA Today*. Copyright © June 27–29, 2003. Reprinted with permission.

Internet Activity

The survey was conducted April 21–28, 2003. A total of 517 surveys were completed online by adults age 18 or older. To view the entire survey, visit the website at

TEST-TAKING TIP

Key Words That Often Appear in Essay Questions

Following is a list of key words that often appear in essay questions. If you are going to write a good answer to an essay question that uses one of these terms, you need to know what the term means.

analyze to break down the subject into parts and discuss each part. You will discuss how the parts relate to each other.

comment on to discuss or explain

compare to show differences and similarities, but with the emphasis on similarities

contrast to show differences and similarities, but with the emphasis on differences

criticize The narrow meaning of *criticize* is to examine something for its weaknesses, limitations, or failings. Does the theory, article, or opinion make sense? If not, why not? In a more general sense, criticize means to find both strengths and weaknesses. In this sense, the meaning of *criticize* is similar to the meaning of *evaluate*.

define to state the meaning of a term, theory, or concept. You will want to place the subject in a category and explain what makes it different from other subjects in the category.

describe to explain what something is or how it appears. You will need to draw a picture with words.

diagram to make a chart, drawing, or graph. You will also want to label the categories or elements, and maybe provide a brief explanation.

discuss to go over something fully. You will want to cover the main points, give different perspectives, and discuss strengths and weaknesses.

enumerate to make a list of main ideas by numbering them

evaluate to examine for strengths and weaknesses. You will need to give specific evidence and may wish to cite authorities to support your position.

Evaluating the Evidence

12

The Thinker (1880)*
BY AUGUSTE RODIN

Auguste Rodin, French 1840–1917. *The Thinker*, c. 1880. Bronze, green patina, 182.9 × 98.4 × 142.2 cm.
© The Cleveland Museum of Art, Gift of Ralph King, 1917.42

Rodin originally sculpted *The Thinker* as part of his unfinished masterpiece *The Gates of Hell*. From his lofty perch at the top of the gate, *The Thinker* was meant to look down and ponder the sins of humanity. At the request of many patrons, Rodin increased the size of the original sculpture and made it free standing. Today, it is one of the most widely recognized pieces of art in the world.

1 In this sculpture, Rodin tried to create a man "who did not just think with his head, but thought with his entire body." What do you think Rodin meant by this comment? Do you think he succeeded?

2 In 1970, a bomb was set at the base of an original Rodin *Thinker*, badly damaging the statue's feet. The museum decided against encasing the statue in protective glass or having it repaired. Do you think the museum made the right decision?

Evaluating Persuasive Writing

Instead of sticking with neutral, objective language, authors sometimes use language with strong connotations, language designed to arouse the reader emotionally. This is often a sign of bias on the author's part and serves as a signal that the author is trying to influence you. Authors might exploit any or all of the following persuasive techniques:

1. Emotionally loaded language designed to appeal directly to your feelings rather than your reasoning abilities

In the example below, notice Dr. William Nolan's use of loaded words in his description of a severely disabled 90-year-old woman who has developed pneumonia. A decision must be made on whether to treat the pneumonia with penicillin or withhold the medication, which would likely cause death within three or four days.

> On the one hand, you cannot bear to see your **once vivacious** mother living the **painful, limited** life to which the stroke has **condemned** her. On the other hand, you hate to be the one to decide to let nature take its course. Until you are actually faced with such a decision, you probably won't be able to predict which course you would take.
>
> I'll tell you what choice I would make. I'd say, "Don't give her any penicillin. Keep her as comfortable as possible and let's see what happens. Maybe she'll have the resistance to fight off the pneumonia on her own and if she doesn't, she'll die a **peaceful** death. I don't want to be responsible for **condemning** my mother to a **living hell.**"

From William Nolen, "Deciding to Let Your Parents Die," permission from Blassingame, McCauley, and Wood. Reprinted from Deanne Milan, *Improving Reading Skills*, 2nd ed., New York: McGraw-Hill, 1992, p. 345.

2. Tear-jerking stories or references to people and causes that you empathize with

In the following paragraph, the author describes the plight of the men and women, many of whom are immigrants making hourly wages one-third lower than other employees, who clean the nation's slaughterhouses and have "arguably the worst job in the United States."

> A brief description of some cleaning-crew accidents over the past decade says more about the work and the danger among slaughterhouse sanitation crews than any set of statistics. At the Monfort plant in Grand Island, Nebraska, Richard Skala was beheaded by a dehiding machine. Carlos Vincente, a twenty-eight-year-old Guatemalan who'd been in the United States for only a week, was pulled into the cogs of a conveyor belt at an Excel plant in Fort Morgan, Colorado, and torn apart. Salvador Hernandez-Gonzalez, an employee of DCS Sanitation, had his head crushed by a pork-loin processing machine at an IBP plant in Madison, Nebraska. The same machine had fatally crushed the head of another worker, Ben Barone, a few years earlier. At a National Beef plant in Liberal, Kansas, Homer Stull climbed into a filthy blood-collection tank to clean it. Stull was overcome by hydrogen sulfide fumes. Two co-workers climbed into the tank and tried to rescue him; all three men died. Eight years earlier, Henry Wolf had been overcome by hydrogen sulfide fumes while cleaning the very same tank; Gary Sanders had tried to rescue him; both men died; and the Occupational Safety and Health

Administration (OSHA) later fined National Beef for its negligence. The fine was $480 for each man's death.

From Eric Schlosser, *Fast Food Nation*, pp. 83–85, 2001 Houghton Mifflin. Reprinted with permission from the publisher.

3. Figurative analogies

In the example below, the author draws on figurative language to describe what's wrong with popular culture.

> The popular culture, in its hierarchy of values, puts the joys of sex far above the happiness of motherhood. The women's magazines, the soaps, romance novels, and prime-time TV all celebrate career, sex, and the single woman. "Taking care of baby" is for Grandma. **Marriage and monogamy are about as exciting as a mashed potato sandwich.** That old triumvirate "the world, the flesh, and the devil" not only has all the best tunes, but all the best ad agencies.

From Patrick J. Buchanan, *The Death of the West*, New York: St. Martin's Press, 2002, p. 43.

4. Manipulation of tone

In the first paragraph, the author assumes an ironic tone when she says the United States has the safest food supply. In the second paragraph, she explains the problems inherent in the food production system by making an analogy.

> One of the most insistent marketing messages we hear, trumpeted by both industry and regulators, is that the United States has the safest food supply in the world. Yet according to the Center for Disease Control's best calculations, each year 76 million Americans—nearly one in four, and that's a lowball estimate—become infected by what they eat. Most find themselves for a few days dolefully memorizing a pattern of bathroom floor tiles. About 325,000 land in the hospital. Two million suffer drawn-out, sometimes lifelong, medical complications from unwittingly eating a contaminated morsel. More than 5,000—about 14 a day—die from indulging in what should be one of life's great pleasures. The "world's safest food supply" regularly doles out *E. coli* O157:H7 in hamburgers, *Salmonella* in alfalfa sprouts, *Listeria* in hot dogs, *Campylobacter* in Thanksgiving turkeys.
>
> The site of modern meat production is akin to a walled medieval city, where waste is tossed out the window, sewage runs down the street, and feed and drinking water are routinely contaminated by fecal material. Each day, a feedlot steer deposits 50 pounds of manure, as the animals crowd atop dark mountains composed of their own feces. "Animals are living in medieval conditions and we're living in the twenty-first century," says Robert Tauxe, chief of the CDC's foodborne and diarrheal diseases branch. "Consumers have to be aware that even though they bought their food from a lovely modern deli bar or salad bar, it started out in the sixteen hundreds."

From Madeline Drexler, *Secret Agents: The Menace of Emerging Infections*, pp. 75, 86. Copyright © 2002 by the National Academy of Sciences. Courtesy of the National Academies Press, Washington, D.C. Reprinted with permission.

5. Propaganda techniques such as bandwagon, plain folks, name calling, testimonial

In his final book before his death, noted historian Stephen Ambrose wrote about our founding fathers. He had less than positive feelings about Thomas Jefferson, our third president and author of the Declaration of Independence. He described Jefferson as having "a great mind and a limited character." In the following paragraph, Ambrose "name-calls" Jefferson "an intellectual coward."

> Thomas Jefferson, the genius of politics, could see no way for African Americans to live in society as free people. He embraced the worst forms of racism to justify slavery, to himself and those he instructed. The limitations he displayed in refusing both to acknowledge the truth of his own observations on the institution, and his unwillingness to do something, anything, to weaken and finally destroy it, brand him an intellectual coward. . . .

From Stephen Ambrose, *To America: Personal Reflections of an Historian*, New York: Simon & Schuster, 2002, p. 4.

In the following example, David Sadker turns to a testimonial to demonstrate his point that there has always been criticism of the nation's public schools.

> "Everyone is aware today that our educational system has been allowed to deteriorate. It has been going downhill for some years without anything really constructive having been done to arrest the decline, still less to reverse its course. We thus have a chronic crisis: an unsolved problem as grave as any that faces our country today. Unless this problem is dealt with promptly and effectively, the machinery that sustains our level of material prosperity and political power will begin to slow down."
>
> Does this sound familiar, as though you just read it in today's newspaper? Actually, this was written in the 1950s by Admiral Hyman Rickover, a frequent critic of U.S. schools. And that's the point that a growing number of educators are making: School bashing is nothing new; it is as American as apple pie, an old tradition that has reached a new peak in recent years. In fact, these educators believe that not only is the current crescendo of criticism old hat, but it is terribly misguided, because today's schools are doing as well as they ever have—maybe, just maybe, they are doing better.

From Myra Pollack Sadker and David Miller Sadker in *Teachers, Schools, and, Society*, 5th ed., New York: McGraw-Hill, 2000, p. 251. Copyright © 2000 McGraw-Hill. Reprinted by permission of The McGraw-Hill Companies, Inc.

When an author cites a testimonial, ask yourself the following questions:

- Is the writer an authority in that particular field?
- Is this the writer's specific area of competence?
- Is the writer biased?
- Is the writer likely to gain some advantage from the testimonial?

6. Psychological appeals

The media frequently employs this technique to create ads that appeal directly to our desire for safety, power, prestige, sex, or popularity.

> For example, for Thanksgiving 2002, People for the Ethical Treatment of Animals (PETA) used a "turkey terror" campaign that appealed to Americans' fear of terrorism. The commercial depicts a terrorist takeover of a supermarket by a turkey. The store manager is shown "bound and gagged," with grocery shoppers cowering as the turkey warns that "innocent creatures will be beaten, scalded, and dismembered if anyone resists." The commercial ends with a plea to stop eating meat.

PETA ad (Thanksgiving 2002)
Courtesy of People for the Ethical Treatment of Animals.

Fear induction is one of the most effective persuasive techniques. It is commonly used in advertisements and public service announcements, such as the one in the advertisement below that was commissioned by the U.S. Department of Transportation. For fear tactics to work (1) the appeal must engender a lot of fear, (2) the audience must believe the message, and (3) specific instructions for avoiding the danger must be presented.

From Karen Huffman, et al., in *Psychology in Action*, 4th ed., pp. 59, 590. Copyright © 1994 John Wiley & Sons, Inc. This material is used by permission of John Wiley & Sons, Inc.

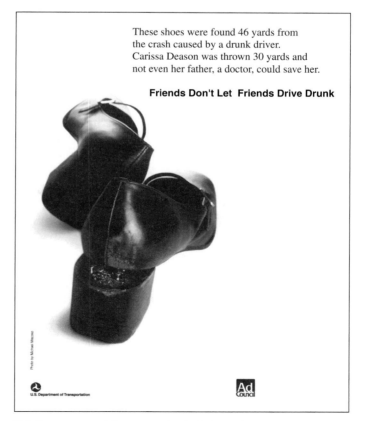

These shoes were found 46 yards from the crash caused by a drunk driver. Carissa Deason was thrown 30 yards and not even her father, a doctor, could save her.

Friends Don't Let Friends Drive Drunk

U.S. Department of Transportation/Ad Council

7. Moral appeals

Authors may seek to appeal to your sense of morality or fair play:

> In his book *Living a Life That Matters*, Rabbi Harold Kushner discusses the views of Kenneth Blanchard and the Reverend Norman Vincent Peale. Blanchard and Peale call for integrity in the business world both as a tactical advantage and as a matter of principle. If a company encourages employees to increase sales by dishonest means, that company might find its employees padding expense accounts or taking trade secrets to other companies when they move on. Both Blanchard and Peale urge their readers to ask themselves: "If we have to cheat to win, shouldn't we think twice about what business we're in?"

From Harold S. Kushner, *Living a Life That Matters*, New York: Anchor Books, 2001, p. 91.

8. Appeals to authority

Authors may call attention to the integrity, intelligence, or knowledge of themselves or others to convince you to trust their judgment and believe them, as the following excerpt by James Steyer illustrates:

> If another adult spent five or six hours a day with your kids, regularly exposing them to sex, violence, and rampantly commercial values, you would probably forbid that person to have further contact with them. Yet most of us passively allow the media to expose our kids routinely to these same behaviors—sometimes worse—and do nothing about it.
>
> If we don't start taking responsibility—as parents first, but also by demanding it from the huge media interests, as well as the government officials who are supposed to regulate them on behalf of the public interest—then we put our children at continued risk. We will raise generations of kids desensitized to violence, overexposed to reckless sex, and commercially exploited from their earliest years. And our culture will pay an ever-increasing price.
>
> As a parent, as a national child advocate, as someone who teaches constitutional law and civil liberties courses at Stanford University, and as the head of one of the few independent children's media companies in the United States, I've had a unique vantage point. And from where I stand, the world of media and children is not a very pretty picture. In fact, I'm convinced that the huge influence of the "other parent" should be a matter of national concern for parents, policymakers, and responsible media executives alike.

From James P. Steyer, *The Other Parent*, New York: Atria Books, 2002, pp. 5, 10, 16.

To evaluate persuasive writing, you want to become better at recognizing the techniques we have just discussed. You should also pay attention to the following topics:

1. *Background:* Learn what you can about the author. What other books or articles has the author written? Is the author known for representing certain viewpoints? Is the author involved in advocacy organizations?

2. *Assumptions:* Try to identify the values and principles that form the author's basic outlook. Do you agree with this outlook? Contrast the author's basic outlook to other possibilities. What are the values and principles behind opposing outlooks?

3. *Organization:* Pay attention to how a piece of writing is organized. How is the author structuring the argument? Where are the reasons or explanations? Do the reasons support the conclusion?

In summary, authors who are trying to persuade do not usually write material that is entirely objective and meant solely to inform. Instead, they tend to make use of factual material to bolster their opinions and conclusions. By recognizing persuasive techniques and understanding the author's motives and underlying assumptions, you will be better able to avoid emotionalism and manipulation and to evaluate the persuasiveness or worth of the argument the author is making rationally and critically. Are some people easier to persuade than others? In the next section, we will look at four major factors that make certain audiences susceptible to persuasion: personality traits, vulnerability, involvement, and reactance (resistance to persuasion). After reading the paragraphs, complete the outline that follows.

Characteristics of the Audience

1. *Personality traits*   The relationship between personality and persuasion is complex. Consider, as an example, self-esteem. Research shows that people with low self-esteem may be less confident of their opinions, but they also tend to be less attentive to persuasive arguments and are therefore harder to persuade. On the other hand, people with high self-esteem tend to be more confident of their opinions and are therefore harder to persuade. Interestingly, people with moderate self-esteem tend to be the easiest to influence. Because they pay attention to the message and they are somewhat unsure of their opinions, they tend to change their attitudes the most.

2. *Vulnerability*   Young children and adolescents are particularly vulnerable to certain appeals. Parents and health officials are thus understandably concerned about cigarette advertisements that apparently target these groups with "cool" cartoonlike characters. Adults are particularly susceptible to persuasive appeals if they are lonely, depressed, inexperienced, poorly educated, or physically isolated.

3. *Involvement*   The more actively an individual becomes involved in an idea or product, the more likely he or she is to be persuaded. If you can get someone to sign a petition or write a letter to a candidate, they are likely to become committed to your cause or product.

4. *Reactance*   Regardless of individual differences in personality, vulnerability, and involvement, most recipients of persuasive messages share a common need to believe they are free to choose and free to disagree. When people feel pressured, they often increase their resistance to persuasion—a phenomenon known as **reactance.** They may even rebel and do just the opposite. In one experiment, children were allowed to choose any brand of candy on display, except Brand X. Can you guess what the children did? Those who were told not to choose Brand X chose it significantly more often than those who were given a free choice.

   Having concluded our brief look at persuasion, we encourage you to use what you have learned to critically evaluate the persuasive messages that bombard all of us every day. Many people needlessly worry about the dangers of subliminal advertising, hypnosis, and brainwashing, and then overlook the ordinary techniques that are used *effectively* to sell everything from toothpaste to presidential candidates. Developing your critical thinking skills and applying your new knowledge better equips you to deal with our complex, message-dense culture.

Outlining

Below is an outline of the first two characteristics discussed above. Complete the outline for the remaining two characteristics.

I. Four major characteristics of an audience that affect ease of persuasion.
    A. Personality traits
        1. Because people with low self-esteem are less confident of their opinions and less attentive to persuasive arguments, they are harder to persuade.
        2. Because people with high self-esteem are more confident of their opinions, they are harder to persuade.
        3. Because people with moderate self-esteem pay attention to the message and are somewhat unsure of their opinions, they are the easiest to persuade.
    B. Vulnerability
        1. Young children and adolescents are vulnerable to persuasive appeals.
        2. Adults may also be susceptible to persuasive appeals.
            a. If they are lonely.
            b. If they are depressed.
            c. If they are inexperienced.
            d. If they are poorly educated.
            e. If they are physically isolated.
    C. _____
        1. _____
            _____
        2. _____
            _____
    D. _____
        1. _____
            _____
        2. _____
            _____
        3. _____

Introduction to Deductive and Inductive Reasoning

Drawing Conclusions: Deductive and Inductive Reasoning

In the final step of analyzing a selection, the reader must evaluate the soundness of the author's reasoning. Often our evaluation is based on **deductive** or **inductive** reasoning.

Deductive Reasoning

The word *deduction* comes from the Latin *de*, meaning "from" and *duc*, meaning "to lead." In **deductive reasoning,** we move from a general principle and a specific example to reach a conclusion.

Here's an example of a deductive argument:

Major premise: All of Stephen King's books are enjoyable.

Minor premise: *From a Buick 8* is a book by Stephen King.

Conclusion: Therefore, *From a Buick 8* is enjoyable.

This deductive argument has two premises: First, the general principle (also called the *major premise*): "All of Stephen King's books are enjoyable." Second, the specific instance (or minor premise): "*From a Buick 8* is a book by Stephen King." Finally, the conclusion: "*From a Buick 8* is enjoyable." This type of deductive argument—with a major premise, a minor premise, and a conclusion—is called a **syllogism.** If both the major and minor premises are true, and the conclusion follows from the premises, then the conclusion must be true, and we have a *sound* argument. Since the conclusion follows from the premises, the argument is also *valid*.

Here's another example:

Major premise: If I have the flu, I won't feel good.

Minor premise: I feel good.

Conclusion: Therefore, I don't have the flu.

Again, we have both a major and a minor premise. If both of these premises are true, then the conclusion must be true because, again, the argument is valid.

Here's a third example:

Major premise: If I go to the store now, I'll miss the start of the basketball game on TV.

Minor premise: If I miss the start of the basketball game on TV, I'll be in a bad mood.

Conclusion: If I go to the store now, I'll be in a bad mood.

Again, if both premises are true, then the conclusion is also true, since it does follow from the two premises. (The argument is valid.)

But not all deductive arguments are valid. Look at this example:

Major premise: All of Stephen King's books are enjoyable.

Minor premise: The book I'm reading now is enjoyable.

Conclusion: Therefore, the book I'm reading now is a Stephen King book.

This argument is *invalid* because, while both premises may well be true, the conclusion does not follow from these premises. The book you're reading now might not be a Stephen King book. It might be an enjoyable book by another author.

Here's something else about deductive arguments. A deductive argument is only sound when both the premises are true. Let's go back to our second example.

Major premise: If I have the flu, I won't feel good.

Minor premise: I feel good.

Conclusion: Therefore, I don't have the flu.

What if this second premise is false. It says you feel good. But what if you really don't feel good. What if you really feel sick. If you don't really feel good, then you can't conclude that you don't have the flu. You very well might have the flu.

We can say this about deductive arguments: You can rely on the conclusion only if the argument is both sound and valid.

In the previous chapter, you read the Declaration of Independence. The Declaration as a whole is considered a classic deductive argument. If pared down to its basic parts—major premise, minor premise, and conclusion—the syllogism would look like this:

> **Major premise:** When a government becomes tyrannical in its treatment of its people, the people have a right to overthrow it and create a new government.
>
> **Minor premise:** The government of Great Britain has become tyrannical in its treatment of Americans.
>
> **Conclusion:** Therefore, Americans have a right to overthrow the British government and create a new government.

If these premises are true then the conclusion must be true.

You can see that explaining deductive arguments can get complicated. What we have just said could only be called an introduction to deductive arguments. To learn more about them, you should take a course in logic.

Inductive Reasoning

Like *deduction,* the word *induction* comes from the Latin root *duc* meaning "to lead" and *in* meaning "into." In **inductive reasoning,** specific examples, evidence, or propositions lead to a more general conclusion.

Here's an example of inductive reasoning:

> It's Wednesday, and you're trying to decide what restaurant to go to this weekend. You're thinking about three possibilities: Great Flavors, Hot and Spicy, and Healthy Stuff. So you start talking to your friends. Bill tells you that Great Flavors is all right, but nothing special. Tanya says that Hot and Spicy is too hot and spicy. Lisa says that she enjoyed Healthy Stuff. You talk to some other people too. They all tell you about the same thing. The food at Great Flavors is mediocre. Hot and Spicy goes overboard. And Healthy Stuff serves food that is nutritious *and* delicious. So you decide that you will probably have a good time at Healthy Stuff, and that's where you will go.

The argument here moves from specific information about three restaurants to a general conclusion about which restaurant would be most enjoyable.

As this example shows, a conclusion reached by inductive reasoning is only as sound as the quality of the information on which it is based. If the information on which you based your conclusion is bad, so will be your conclusion.

One problem with your conclusion might be that it was based on too little information. Perhaps you didn't ask enough people about your three restaurant options. Maybe if you had talked to more people, you would have started hearing negative opinions about Healthy Stuff. And maybe you would have started hearing positive opinions about Great Flavors or Hot and Spicy. From talking to more people, you might have reached a different conclusion. You might have concluded that you would likely have a good time at Hot and Spicy.

So inductive arguments lead to conclusions that are only probably true. You couldn't conclude from your survey that you would *certainly* have a good time at Healthy Stuff. You could only conclude that you would *probably* have a good time there. The better your information is, the more probable your conclusion will be true.

You can now see one important difference between deductive and inductive reasoning. Deductive reasoning produces conclusions that are either true or false. But inductive reasoning produces conclusions that are only probably true or false.

The Scientific Process

Inductive and deductive reasoning are both involved in the scientific process. Scientists conduct research, which involves collecting data and analyzing it, and then they seek to draw a general conclusion or *hypothesis* from their research. This process of formulating hypotheses from research involves inductive reasoning. Scientists then use deductive reasoning to test their hypotheses. A hypothesis tells a scientist what should happen when the scientist collects further data or performs a further test. If the new data or test is consistent with the hypothesis, the hypothesis is confirmed; if not, the hypothesis needs to be modified. Scientists often have to revise a hypothesis in response to new research.

For example, imagine you are thinking about using a computer dating service, but you aren't sure you really want to do it. So you start collecting information about computer dating by talking to people you know who have tried it. Nearly all of these people tell you that it didn't work out. The person found through the computer didn't show up or wasn't at all like what was expected. You reason inductively from this data and conclude that computer dating services almost always fail to deliver good dates. This becomes your hypothesis. You know your hypothesis has limitations because you didn't talk to all that many people. But still it makes sense on the basis of what you've heard so far.

Reasoning deductively from your hypothesis, you decide that if you do make use of a computer dating service, you will likely not have a good experience. But you are willing to take the chance. You make the arrangements through the dating service and go on the date. To your surprise, everything goes well. You liked the person you met and had a good time.

Now you will want to revise your hypothesis. You now have more data, and this new data runs contrary to the thrust of your previous data. Your view of computer dating is now more optimistic. Rather than saying it almost always doesn't work out very well, you now want to say that sometimes it does and sometimes it doesn't. This becomes your new hypothesis, one you reached through a further process of inductive reasoning. It too will be subject to further revision as you collect more data about computer dating.

Exercise: Identifying Inductive and Deductive Arguments

After studying each example, indicate whether the argument is inductive or deductive by writing I or D in the blank provided. Be prepared to discuss whether the conclusion is valid or invalid.

         1. The only passenger train running between Tucson and Los Angeles is operated by Amtrak. Wynona is taking a passenger train from Tucson to Los Angeles. So Wynona must be traveling on an Amtrak train.

         2. I was at Mall of America this morning, and it was crowded with shoppers carrying shopping bags filled with recent purchases. So the economy must be doing well.

         3. When I don't eat breakfast I start feeling weak around 10:30. I missed breakfast this morning, so I know I'm going to start feeling weak around 10:30.

_____ 4. Frida likes all kinds of jazz music. Marco gave Frida a jazz CD. Frida is going to like her new CD.

_____ 5. When the principal visited Lois Johnson's classroom, the children were running around the classroom talking and playing with each other, while Ms. Johnson yelled at them to take their seats and be quiet. The principal concluded that Ms. Johnson did not know how to maintain discipline.

_____ 6. Yomiko has noticed that many of the speakers at the seminars she attends are dull. Yomiko will be going to a seminar tomorrow. Yomiko expects that some of the speakers at the seminar will be dull.

In the pages that follow, you will need to evaluate the author's reasoning to see how valid or persuasive it is. What you've learned here about inductive and deductive reasoning will help you become a more critical reader.

Death and Dying

The next three selections focus on death and dying. Carefully evaluate the evidence in each selection so that you can answer the questions that follow it.

The Tragedy (1903)* by Pablo Picasso

Chester Dale Collection, Image © 2004 Board of Trustees, National Gallery of Art, Washington, D.C.

*To see this work of art in color, turn to the color insert following page 260.

1. In what ways does Picasso convey sadness through this picture?
2. What does the young boy seem to be doing?
3. What do you think has happened to this family to make them so sad?

SELECTION

Dreaming of Disconnecting a Respirator   *by Elissa Ely*

"Some will eventually be 'weaned' back to their own lung power. Others will never draw an independent breath again."

Getting the Picture

In the United States today, deciding how to treat the terminally ill or those in chronic pain is harder than ever because of the existence of life-prolonging medical technology. As a result, the whole concept of a "good death" has been called into question. One of the top fears of many Americans is dying in a hospital hooked up to machines. The author of this article, a physician, describes the dilemma of caring for a patient who has no realistic chance of recovery.

Bio-sketch

Elissa Ely graduated magna cum laude in 1978 from Wesleyan University and earned her M.D. from Harvard Medical School in 1988. Today she is a psychiatrist at the Massachusetts State Hospital. She is also a regular contributor to the *Boston Globe* and a featured commentator on *All Things Considered* aired by National Public Radio. In addition, she has been a psychiatrist at Tewksbury Hospital and given lectures in psychiatry at Harvard Medical School.

Brushing Up on Vocabulary

cardiac   pertaining to the heart.

respirator   an apparatus to produce artificial breathing. Originally this word came from the Latin word parts *re* meaning "again" and *spirare* meaning "to breathe."

chintz   cotton fabric with bright colors, borrowed from Hindi *chint* and Sanskrit *citra-s* meaning "distinctive, bright, clear." The cheetah also gained its name from these words.

1   Late one night in the intensive care unit, one eye on the cardiac monitor and one on the Sunday paper, I read this story:

2   An infant lies in a hospital, hooked to life by a respirator. He exists in a "persistent vegetative state" after swallowing a balloon that blocked the oxygen to his brain. This "vegetative state," I've always thought, is a metaphor inaccurately borrowed from nature, since it implies that with only the proper watering and fertilizer, a comatose patient will bloom again.

3   One day his father comes to visit. He disconnects the respirator and, with a gun in hand, cradles his son until the infant dies. The father is arrested and charged with murder.

4   In the ICU where I read this, many patients are bound to respirators. I look to my left and see them lined up, like potted plants. Some will eventually be "weaned" back to their own lung power. Others will never draw an independent breath again.

5   In Bed No. 2, there is a woman who has been on the respirator for almost two months. When she was admitted with a simple pneumonia, there were no clues she would come apart so terribly. On her third day, she had a sudden and enigmatic seizure. She rolled rapidly downhill. Her pneumonia is now gone, but her lungs refuse independence: She can't come off the machine.

6   I know little about this patient except that she is elderly and European. (It is the peculiar loss of hospital life that patients often exist here with a medical history, but not a personal one.) I sometimes try to picture her as she might have been: busy in a chintz kitchen smelling of pastries. She might have hummed, rolling dough. Now there is a portable radio by the bed, playing Top Ten, while the respirator hisses and clicks 12 times a minute.

7   The family no longer visits. They have already signed the autopsy request, which is clipped to the front of her thick chart. Yet in their pain, they cannot take the final step and allow us to discontinue her respirator. Instead, they have retired her here, where they hope she is well cared for, and where she exists in a state of perpetual mechanical life.

8   I have dreamed of disconnecting my patient's respirator. Every day I make her death impossible and her life unbearable. Each decision—the blood draws, the rectal temperatures, the oxygen concentration—is one for or against life. No action in the ICU is neutral. Yet many of these decisions are made with an eye toward legal neutrality—and this has little to do with medical truth. The medical truth is that this patient exists without being alive. The legal neutrality is that existence is all that is required.

9   Late at night, reading in the ICU, the story of that father—so dangerous and impassioned—puts me to shame. I would never disconnect my patient from her respirator; it is unthinkable. But this is not because I am a doctor. It is because I feel differently toward her than the father toward his son.

10   I do not love her enough.

Elissa Ely, "Dreaming of Disconnecting a Respirator," *Boston Globe*, July 1, 1989. Copyright © 1989 by Globe Newspaper Co. (MA). Reproduced with permission of Globe Newspaper Co. (MA) in the format Textbook via Copyright Clearance Center.

Comprehension Checkup

Evaluating the Evidence

1. Is the author's primary purpose to inform or to persuade? What evidence do you have to support your conclusion?

    _____

    _____

    _____

    _____

2. What is the author's background? Does the author have the qualifications to write seriously about this topic? _____

3. Does the article contain primarily facts or opinions?

_____

_____

A. List below some facts from the article:

_____

_____

_____

_____

B. List below some opinions from the article:

_____

_____

_____

_____

4. If the author has a strong bias, write it below. Can you give some examples of emotionally loaded language or material that has been included to create an emotional response on your part?

_____

_____

_____

_____

_____

5. What is your opinion on the topic of euthanasia (mercy killing, assisted suicide)? Do you think that your opinion is biased? If so, does your bias interfere with your ability to evaluate what the author is saying fairly?

_____

_____

_____

_____

6. Does the author use any specific propaganda devices? List them below. How did you react to these techniques?

_____

_____

_____

_____

7. How would you describe the author's tone? What does the tone tell you about the author's bias?

_____

_____

_____

The Good Death: Embracing a Right to Die Well   *by Sheryl Gay Stolberg*

"There is no blueprint, however, for a good death. Death can't be neatly packaged with a red bow. It is messy, irrational . . . "

Getting the Picture

The article below explores some fundamental questions about death and dying in the United States today.

Bio-sketch

Sheryl Gay Stolberg, a Washington correspondent for *The New York Times*, spent five years covering science and health policy, but now covers Congress. Previously, she worked at the *Los Angeles Times* and *The Providence Journal* in Providence, Rhode Island. She graduated from the University of Virginia in 1983 and presently lives in Chevy Chase, Maryland, with her husband and two daughters.

Brushing Up on Vocabulary

melatonin   a hormone important in regulating biorhythms.

hospice   a health care facility or series of home visits for the terminally ill. Originally a hospice was a rest house for travelers.

palliative   relieving a person from an illness without necessarily curing the disease.

"The art of living well and the art of dying well are one."

—Epicurus

1   The cold bare facts of Barbara Logan Brown's death are these: on July 17, 1996, Mrs. Logan Brown, a 38-year-old mother of two from Rochester, New York, died of AIDS, another statistic in an epidemic that has killed more than 362,000 Americans. Cancer had seeped into her brain; thrush had clogged her throat, making swallowing impossible. An intravenous diet of morphine had rendered her comatose.

2   Those are the cold bare facts. But there are other facts—achingly poignant, indeed, beautiful, some might argue—about Barbara Logan Brown's death. They are recounted here by Roberta Halter, herself a mother of four who cared for her dying friend and is today the guardian of Mrs. Logan Brown's son and daughter:

3   "The last time Barbara was able to go outside, she sat on the front porch. The girls and I went upstairs and took poster paint and painted a big huge smiley face above her bed. The next day, everyone put hand prints all over the wall. The children called it 'The Hands of Love,' and they started to paint messages on the wall. After the paint had dried, we let visitors come. By the end of the day, there were messages everywhere. It was kind of a tribute to her while she was still living. And it was wonderful."

4   It was in Mrs. Halter's view, a good death.

5   A good death. It is a provocative phrase.

A MYSTERY PROFANED

6   The Supreme Court has weighed in on one of the most divisive moral, legal, and medical questions of the day: whether the Constitution gives Americans a fundamental right to a physician's help in dying. The justices said it does not, leaving the

battle over whether to permit or prohibit assisted suicide to rage on among lawyers and legislators, doctors and ethicists across the country.

7   While the court ruled on the constitutional issue, what remains unsettled—indeed, unsettling—is the idea at the heart of the assisted-suicide question: that for most Americans, modern medicine has made dying worse.

8   America is often called a "death-denying" society; each year the United States spends millions on efforts to conquer death, or at least to postpone it. The self-help shelves of bookstores overflow with such pearls as "Stop Aging Now!" and "Stay Young the Melatonin Way."

9   If Americans don't deny death, they often trivialize it, said Joan Halifax, a Zen Buddhist priest who founded the Project on Being with Dying in Santa Fe, New Mexico. "By the time a kid gets into high school, he has seen 20,000 homicides on television," she said. "Death as a mystery to be embraced, entered into and respected has been profaned in our culture."

10   Courtesy of the assisted-suicide debate, the concept of a good death has now emerged, though many experts reject the phrase as simplistic. Dr. Ira Byock, president of the Academy of Hospice and Palliative Medicine, prefers "dying well." Dr. Timothy Keay, an end-of-life care expert at the University of Maryland, says "the least worst death."

11   There is no blueprint, however, for a good death. Death can't be neatly packaged with a red bow. It is messy, irrational, most often filled with sorrow and pain. More than two million Americans die each year; there are as many ways to die as to live. And so unanswerable questions arise: Not only what constitutes a good death and how can it be achieved, but who, ultimately, it is for—the person dying, or those going on living?

12   "I'm a little cynical about this whole notion of good death," said Dr. David Hilfiker, the founder of Joseph's House in Washington, which cares for homeless men dying of AIDS. "Death is really hard for most people. Why should people who are dying have to have a beautiful death? That's putting the burden on them to have some kind of experience that makes us feel good."

13   Indeed, said Dr. Sherwin B. Nuland, the author of "How We Die," the patient's needs often get lowest priority. "A good death," he said, "is in the eye of the beholder."

14   In centuries past, a good death was celebrated in art and literature as *ars moriendi,* the art of dying. Death marked salvation of the soul, neither an ending nor a beginning but, like birth, part of the cycle of life. "True philosophers," Plato wrote, "are always occupied in the practice of dying."

15   Buddhism is filled with stories of Zen masters who write poems in the moments before death, embracing it as the only time in life when absolute freedom may be realized. In the Middle Ages, Christian monks greeted one another with the salutation *Momento mori*, remember that you must die.

16   Today, it seems, most Americans would rather forget. Asked their idea of a good death, they say, "quick." Keeling over in the garden, trowel in hand, is one ideal, going to bed and not waking up another.

17   That is a reaction against medical technology; if Americans want anything from death, they want to remain in control, to avoid making their exits tethered to a machine. It is fear of a painful, lonely and protracted high-tech death that has fueled the movement to make assisted suicide legal.

18   "The classic idea of the good death is the sudden death," Dr. Nuland said, "but if you think seriously about it, that isn't what you want." "What you really want is a tranquil, suffering-free last few weeks where you have the opportunity for those near you to express what your life has meant to them."

19   A century ago such opportunities could be elusive. Infectious disease caused most deaths; cholera struck, and there was a burial two days later. Dr. Joanne

Lynn, director of George Washington University's Center to Improve Care of the Dying, said: "When people went to bed and said 'If I should die before I wake,' they meant it."

"Death, the last   20   Today the leading causes of death are heart disease, cancer, and stroke. For
voyage, the longest,   older people, disproportionately affected by these ailments, dying can drag on for
the best."   months or years. Most women, Dr. Lynn said, have eight years of disability before
                                 they die; most men, five or six. It might seem, then, that people have time to plan
—Thomas Wolfe   for their deaths, but many don't take advantage. A study to be published in this
                                 week's *Annals of Internal Medicine* found that most seriously ill adults in the hos-
                                 pital do not talk to their doctors about being kept alive on life-support machines.
                                 They prefer not to discuss it.

21   Americans have been reticent to talk about death; only recently have doctors and families felt obliged to tell a terminally ill person that he was, in fact, dying. Often the truth simply went unremarked, like an elephant in the dining room.

22   In 1969, Elisabeth Kubler-Ross shattered the silence with "On Death and Dying." In it, she described the progression of a patient's coping mechanisms in five stages of dying: denial, anger, bargaining, depression and finally acceptance.

23   Dr. Byock, the author of "Dying Well," offers what he calls the "developmental model" of dying. When he began caring for the terminally ill 20 years ago, he noticed that when he asked patients how they were feeling, often the reply was something like this: "Despite it all, doctor, I am well."

24   The juxtaposition of wellness and dying seemed a paradox, but he has concluded that the two can exist side by side. "In dying," he said, "there are opportunities to grow even through times of severe difficulty, which we would label suffering."

25   In his view, dying well includes love and reconciliation, a settling of worldly affairs and a life's summing up, as stories are recounted and passed to new generations. By these standards, Barbara Logan Brown most certainly had a good death. "Barbara," Mrs. Halter said, "had an opportunity to put her life here on earth in order."

IN THE END, LIBERATION

26   Conventional wisdom holds that people die as they have lived; a crotchety old man in life will be a crotchety old man in death. Not so, say experts in end-of-life care: death can be both transforming and liberating.

27   Dr. Halifax, the Buddhist priest, tells of a woman whose daughter was a hospice nurse. Throughout her life, the mother had adhered to strict codes of politeness and propriety. A few days before her death, she began screaming in rage and pain.

28   As a nurse, her daughter knew that narcotics could subdue her mother's pain. But she chose to do nothing; the screaming, she believed, was her mother's way of finally expressing herself. "The screaming went on for four days and four nights," Dr. Halifax said. "And about an hour before she died, she lit up, and became extremely peaceful, and relaxed completely. And then she died."

29   Was it a good death? Dr. Halifax paused.

30   "A good death," she finally allowed, "sounds a little polite. It's like death with manners. I don't want to adorn death. Death is death."

From Sheryl Gay Stolberg, "The Good Death: Embracing a Right to Die Well," from *The New York Times,* June 29, 1997, section 4, pp. 1, 4. Copyright © 1997 by The New York Times Co. Reprinted with permission.

Content and Structure

Choose the best answer for each of the following questions. You may refer back to the article.

1. The mode of rhetoric in this selection is primarily _____. (Explain the answer you give.) _____

2. The pattern of organization in paragraph 3 is primarily
   a. comparison-contrast
   b. example
   c. chronological order
   d. cause and effect

3. In paragraphs 14–16, two types of death are contrasted. Describe the two types below.

   a. _____

   _____

   b. _____

   _____

4. Explain the cause and effect relationship in paragraph 17.

   Cause: _____

   Effect: _____

5. In paragraphs 18–20, Stolberg implies several contrasts. State two specific things being contrasted.

   1. _____

   _____

   2. _____

   _____

   3. _____

   _____

6. In paragraph 21, Stolberg uses a figure of speech to describe Americans' reluctance to speak of death. Identify and then explain the meaning of this figure of speech.

   _____

   _____

7. According to Dr. Byock, what does "dying well" include?

   a. _____

   b. _____

   c. _____

8. Explain the meaning of the phrase "death with manners" in the last paragraph.

   _____

9. Write the overall main idea of the selection below.

   _____

   _____

10. The author's purpose is to _____. (Explain the answer you give.)

_____

11. To support her conclusion, the author primarily relies on
    a. statistics from research studies
    b. expert opinion from health-related fields
    c. her own observations and opinions

12. The author's tone throughout the article is
    a loving
    b. angry
    c. serious
    d. humorous

Vocabulary in Context

For each italicized word from the article, use your dictionary to find the best definition according to the context.

1. other facts—achingly *poignant* (paragraph 2) _____

2. they often *trivialize* it (9) _____

3. has been *profaned* in our culture (9) _____

4. exits *tethered* to a machine (17) _____

5. lonely and *protracted* high-tech death (17) _____

6. a *tranquil,* suffering-free last few weeks (18) _____

7. such opportunities could be *elusive* (19) _____

8. *reticent* to talk about death (21) _____

9. *juxtaposition* of wellness and dying (24) _____

_____

10. *crotchety* old man (26) _____

11. *adhered* to strict codes (27) _____

12. politeness and *propriety* (27) _____

13. *subdue* her mother's pain (28) _____

14. to *adorn* death (30) _____

In Your Own Words

1. Do you think dying today is more dehumanizing than in the past? Why or why not?

2. Do you have a living will? Why are so many Americans reluctant to make provisions for death?

3. Dr. Jack Kevorkian, the so-called "Dr. Death," insists that those in chronic pain with no chance of recovery have a right to a physician-assisted suicide with the administration of mercy-killing drugs. The Supreme Court has decided that no such general right can be found in the Constitution. Do you think that laws should be passed authorizing physician-assisted suicide? Or do you think that laws should be passed banning it?

4. The June 1997 issue of the *Journal of the American Medical Association* reported that "a new analysis of doctor-assisted suicide in the Netherlands suggests that caregivers there have increasingly taken the next, troubling step: ending patients' lives without their permission." The Netherlands has long been considered a model by advocates of assisted suicide in the United States. This new information seems to confirm the fears of U.S. opponents of assisted suicide, which remains illegal in most states. In the political cartoon below, Steve Benson, an opponent of assisted suicide, addresses this troubling issue. Do you think that the acceptance of euthanasia would lead to a more relaxed attitude toward the taking of life in general, and toward taking the lives of those in need of constant attention in particular? What effect would this have on patients' ability to trust their doctors?

STEVE BENSON reprinted by permission of Newspaper Enterprise Association, Inc.

The Art of Writing

In a brief essay, respond to one of the items below.

1. Compare and contrast the experience of dying described at the beginning of the selection to that described at the end. From the perspective of the patient, which one would you call a "good death"? From the perspective of the family? Be sure to provide arguments that support your position.

2. The Greek word parts *eu* meaning "good" and *thanatos* meaning "death" appear in the word *euthanasia*, so the literal meaning of this term is "good death." Euthanasia is also thought of as "mercy killing." Euthanasia may be either active or passive: in the first case, death is deliberately inflicted, sometimes by a relative; in the second, life-support systems are withdrawn and the patient dies naturally. Controversy surrounding the morality of euthanasia has increased in recent years because of advances in medical technology that make it possible for human beings, both newborn and old, to be kept alive almost

indefinitely, even when severely impaired. Where do you stand on euthanasia? Do you think life is sacred, so that euthanasia is always wrong? Do you think that the patient's ability to continue to enjoy life should influence the decision? Who should make the decision? The patient? The family? The doctor? The courts? Be sure to provide arguments that support your position.

Internet Activity

Below are two websites (with very similar URLs) that discuss euthanasia from radically different perspectives. Visit the two sites and browse through their web pages and links. After determining the point of view of each, list the various persuasive techniques they employ.

www.euthanasia.com

www.euthanasia.org

SELECTION

Excerpt from *Core Concepts in Health*   *by Paul M. Insel and Walton T. Roth*

"In the Mexican worldview, death is another phase of life, and those who have passed into it remain accessible."

Getting the Picture

In Mexican culture, the skeleton or skull is viewed as a symbol of resurrection, rather than as a symbol of death. Papier-mache figures like the one below commonly

© Spike Mafford/Getty Images

poke fun at particular people from many walks of life. In the United States, *el Dia de los Muertos* is often confused with Halloween, but unlike Halloween, the Mexican holiday is not considered scary or macabre. Actually, *el Dia de los Muertos* most closely resembles U.S. Memorial Day because both holidays show honor and respect for the dead.

Brushing Up on Vocabulary

indigenous   originating from a particular country or region.

dogma   specific tenet or doctrine.

El Dia de los Muertos: The Day of the Dead

"A solemn funeral is inconceivable in the Chinese mind."

—Lin Yutang

"As men, we are all equal in the presence of death."

—Publilius Syrus

(A) In contrast to the solemn attitude toward death so prevalent in the United States, a familiar and even ironic attitude is more common among Mexicans and Mexican Americans. In the Mexican worldview, death is another phase of life, and those who have passed into it remain accessible. Ancestors are not forever lost, nor is the past dead. This sense of continuity has its roots in the culture of the Aztecs, for whom regeneration was a central theme. When the Spanish came to Mexico in the sixteenth century, their beliefs about death, along with such symbols as skulls and skeletons, were absorbed into the native culture.

(B) Mexican artists and writers confront death with humor and even sarcasm, depicting it as the inevitable fate that all—even the wealthiest—must face. At no time is this attitude toward death livelier than at the beginning of each November on the holiday known as *el Dia de los Muertos,* "the Day of the Dead." This holiday coincides with All Souls' Day, the Catholic commemoration of the dead, and represents a unique blending of indigenous ritual and religious dogma.

(C) Festive and merry, the celebration in honor of the dead typically spans two days—one day devoted to dead children, one to adults. It reflects the belief that the dead return to Earth in spirit once a year to rejoin their families and partake of holiday foods prepared especially for them. The fiesta usually begins at midday on October 31, with flowers and food—candies, cookies, honey, milk—set out on altars in each house for the family's dead. The next day, family groups stream to the graveyards, where they have cleaned and decorated the graves of their loved ones, to celebrate and commune with the dead. They bring games, music, and special food—chicken with molé sauce, enchiladas, tamales, and *pande muertos,* the "bread of the dead," sweet rolls in the shape of bones. People sit on the graves, eat, sing, and talk with the departed ones. Tears may be shed as the dead are remembered, but mourning is tempered by the festive mood of the occasion.

(D) During the season of the dead, graveyards and family altars are decorated with yellow candles and yellow marigolds—the "flower of death." In some Mexican villages, yellow flower petals are strewn along the ground, connecting the graveyard with all the houses visited by death during the year.

(E) As families cherish memories of their loved ones on this holiday, the larger society satirizes death itself—and political and public figures. The impulse to laugh at death finds expression in what are called *calaveras,* a word meaning "skeletons" or "skulls" but also referring to humorous newsletters that appear during this season. The *calaveras* contain biting, often bawdy, verses caricaturing well-known public figures, often with particular reference to their deaths. Comic skeletal figures march or dance across these pages, portraying the wealthy or influential as they will eventually become.

(F) Whenever Mexican Americans have settled in the United States, *el Dia de los Muertos* celebrations keep the traditions alive, and the cultural practices associated with the Day of the Dead have found their way into the nation's culture. Books and museum exhibitions have brought to the public the "art of the dead," with its striking blend of skeletons and flowers, bones and candles. Even the schools in some areas celebrate the holiday. Students create paintings and sculptures depicting skeletons and skulls with the help of local artists.

(G) Does this more familiar attitude toward death help people accept death and come to terms with it? Keeping death in the forefront of consciousness may provide solace to the living, reminding them of their loved ones and assuring them that they themselves will not be forgotten when they die. Yearly celebrations and remembrances may help people keep in touch with their past, their ancestry, and their roots. The festive atmosphere may help dispel the fear of death, allowing people to look at it more directly. Although it is possible to deny the reality of death even when surrounded by images of it, such practices as *el Dia de los Muertos* may help people face death with more equanimity.

From Paul M. Insel and Walton T. Roth, *Core Concepts in Health*, 9th ed., New York: McGraw-Hill, 2002, p. 579. Copyright © 2002 McGraw-Hill. Reprinted by permission of The McGraw-Hill Companies, Inc.

Comprehension Checkup

Write the letter of the correct answer in the blank provided.

_____ 1. Which sentence best expresses the main idea of the selection?
   a. The festival of the Day of the Dead typically begins on October 31.
   b. The Mexicans view death as part of life and have a yearly celebration to remember and honor their loved ones who have died.
   c. Mexican artists treat death with humor and sarcasm
   d. The souls of deceased children and deceased adults return on separate days.

_____ 2. The author's tone could best be described as
   a. arrogant
   b. pessimistic
   c. incredulous
   d. objective

_____ 3. The author's primary purpose is to
   a. persuade Americans to interact more with family members
   b. entertain the reader with personal stories celebrating a unique ritual
   c. inform the reader of the ways in which death is dealt with around the world
   d. explain the Day of the Dead celebration

_____ 4. In paragraph B, the author says that Mexican artists and writers depict death as something "that all—even the wealthiest—must face." This means that
   a. "For certain is death for the born" (Gita)
   b. "As men we are all equal in the presence of death" (Syrus)
   c. "Death is certain to all; all shall die" (Shakespeare)
   d. all of the above

_____ 5. The author of this selection probably feels that
  a. a graveyard is no place for a celebration
  b. poking fun at death is in poor taste
  c. yearly celebrations such as the Day of the Dead may help people cope with their own inevitable death
  d. unlike the lighthearted attitude toward death reflected in U.S. culture, Mexicans exhibit an exceedingly solemn attitude

_____ 6. _Indigeneous_ ritual, as described in paragraph B, is likely to be
  a. native
  b. inborn
  c. unnatural
  d. creative

_____ 7. From this selection you could conclude that
  a. the Day of the Dead celebrations continue to be popular with many Mexican immigrants to the United States
  b. the Day of the Dead celebration is only popular with non–Christians
  c. family and community members participate in the Day of the Dead celebration
  d. both (a) and (c)

_____ 8. A synonym for the word _equanimity_ as used in paragraph G is
  a. excitability
  b. indifference
  c. composure
  d. evasion

_____ 9. The word _tempered_ as used in paragraph C means
  a. property mixed
  b. tuned
  c. made less intense
  d. having a pleasant disposition

_____ 10. The Mexican celebration features all of the following _except_
  a. bread of the dead
  b. a mournful attitude throughout
  c. aromatic flowers
  d. vigils to honor loved ones

Topics and Supporting Details

Using the paragraph letters in the text, match each paragraph with its topic.

1. Uses for the "flower of death" _____
2. Satirical elements of the holiday _____
3. Psychological and social benefits of the holiday _____
4. Continuation of aspects of the holiday by Mexican immigrants to the United States _____
5. Introduction and origin of the holiday _____
6. Description of food and activities that comprise the celebration _____
7. Lively depiction of death by artists and writers _____

Below are additional sentences about _el Dia de los Muertos_. Write the paragraph number in which the sentence is most likely to fit in the blank provided.

1. Mexican marigolds, called zempascuchitl, are particularly suited for the Days of the Dead festivities because of the strong, pungent aroma. _____

2.   Concepts of death and the afterlife existed in the ancient Maya and Aztec cultures. _____

3.   Mexican poets often write about death, comparing the fragility of life to a dream, a flower, a river, or a passing breeze. _____

4.   These *calaveras* often show individuals dancing with their own skeletons. _____

5.   A teacher at a Phoenix elementary school had her seventh-grade students create ofrendas during the Day of the Dead holiday. _____

Internet Activity

To learn more about the Day of the Dead celebrations consult the following websites:

www.public.iastate.edu/~rjsalvad/scmfaq/muertos.html

www.dayofthedead.com/html/traditions.htm#skullsandskeletons

Animal Rights

The three articles that follow focus on animal rights. As with the preceding section, evaluate the evidence in each of these selections to answer the questions that follow.

The Peaceable Kingdom (1834)* BY EDWARD HICKS

*To see this work of art in color, turn to the color insert following page 260.

Photo: Art Resource, NY

Edward Hicks, a Quaker preacher, based the painting on the facing page on this passage from the Bible: "The wolf also shall dwell with the lamb, and the leopard shall lie down with the kid; and the calf and the young lion and the fatling together; and a little child shall lead them." The background scene is meant to illustrate William Penn's treaty with the Native Americans with whom he had friendly relations. Penn, a Quaker, was owed money by the British government. In lieu of cash, he received title to what is now Pennsylvania, a colony that was noted for religious tolerance. Why do you think Hicks entitled this painting *The Peaceable Kingdom?* What groups are peacefully coexisting? Write a sentence that summarizes your interpretation of this picture.

SELECTION

Excerpt from Animal Experimentation Raises Ethical Questions
by Eli C. Minkoff and Pamela J. Baker

"Over forty Nobel Prizes have been awarded in medicine or physiology for research using experimental animals."

Getting the Picture

The following excerpt from a biology textbook discusses the use of animals in our society for food, labor, recreation, companionship, and scientific research. The excerpt then discusses the animal rights movement and its goal of improving the status of animals in relation to humans.

Bio-sketches

Eli C. Minkoff and Pamela J. Baker are professors of biology at Bates College in Lewiston, Maine. Minkoff received his B.A. degree from Columbia University and his M.A. and Ph.D. from Harvard Uiversity. He has published numerous articles and encyclopedic reference works and is the author of the textbook, *Evolutionary Biology*. Baker received two B.S. degrees, from the University of Wales at Swansea and from Bates College, and her M.A. and Ph.D. from the State University of New York (Buffalo). She has published many articles and is the author of a children's sign language dictionary, *My First Book of Sign*.

Brushing Up on Vocabulary

Luddites   originally members of various bands of workers in England (1811–1816) who destroyed industrial machinery in the belief that the use of machines would lead to diminished employment. Today the term *Luddite* refers to an opponent of any new technology.

sadists   people who receive pleasure from being cruel.

utilitarian   a person who believes that a person's conduct should be directed towards the greatest happiness for the greatest number of people.

deontologist   a person interested in ethics dealing with moral obligation and right action.

Uses and Abuses of Animals

1   Human societies have kept animals at least since the origin of agriculture. There are few societies of any kind that do not have some tradition of keeping animals as pets, as workmates, or as food. Most societies that practice agriculture use animals for all three purposes. Love of animals and use of animals can go hand in hand.

"All animals are equal, but some animals are more equal than others."

—George Orwell

2   By far the largest number of animals used by any society are raised for use as food for humans. Animal products are used for clothing. Animals are also used, even in many industrial societies, for recreational hunting, fishing, and trapping. An estimated 7 percent of the United States population has a hunting or fishing license. Many people keep pets or "companion" animals. Pets can offer benefits beyond companionship. For example, studies have shown that heart attack victims who are pet owners live longer and suffer fewer repeat attacks than heart attack victims who do not own pets. Work animals include animals that are used for riding, for pulling and carrying loads, for police work, and for helping handicapped people in various ways, such as seeing eye dogs for the blind and also a small but growing number of monkeys and other animals trained to assist patients confined to wheelchairs. Finally, animals are often used in research, although the number of animals used annually in research is only a tiny fraction of numbers used each day as food and for other purposes.

Justifications for the use of animals

3   A variety of reasons have been given to justify the use of animals by humans, including (1) saving human lives (e.g., serving as stand-ins for humans in dangerous situations), (2) improving human health (e.g., testing medical and surgical procedures), (3) providing food for people, (4) providing nonmedical information, (5) serving our recreational needs (hunting other than for food, entertainment uses such as circus acts), and (6) serving as status symbols (e.g., wearing furs). A large number of people will accept reasons 1 to 4 as adequate to justify the use of animals, or their more extensive use, while fewer people will accept reasons 5 and 6.

Animals as test subjects

4   Nearly all new drugs, cosmetics, food additives, and new forms of therapy and surgery are tested first on animals before they are tested on humans. The use of animals in research is considered critical to continued progress in human health. Over forty Nobel Prizes have been awarded in medicine or physiology for research using experimental animals. Organ transplants, open-heart surgery, and various other surgical techniques were first performed and perfected on animals before they were performed on humans. All major vaccines, including those for smallpox, polio, mumps, measles, rubella, and diphtheria, were tested on animals before they were used on human patients. Despite the vociferous opposition of the animal rights movement, the general concept of using animals in research has received widespread support in most industrial societies.

5   In most cases, animals are used in research as stand-ins for humans. If we were to abolish the use of animals for these purposes, we would be using many more procedures on humans without benefit of prior animal testing. In effect, the first few dozen or few hundred human patients would be serving as human guinea pigs—the experimental subjects on which the new technique is tested. Most people favor the use of animals as substitutes for humans in those cases where the use of animals can lessen the suffering of human beings. This is especially true in those cases (the majority) in which the animal testing is limited to the initial development of a drug but the human benefit continues for many generations or longer.

Regulation of animal use

6   Very few people would object to the use of animals if human lives were saved as a consequence. Most people would also agree that we should alleviate unnecessary suffering among animals, whether the animals are pets, work animals, or research animals. It is in the best interest of science for scientists to conduct their tests on healthy, well-treated animals, and the U.S. Guide for the Care and Use of Laboratory Animals reflects this concern. The United States Department of Agriculture keeps statistics on the use of experimental animals in research. According to these statistics, 62 percent of the animals used in research experienced no pain, and another 32 percent were given anesthesia, painkillers, or both, to alleviate pain. Only in 6 percent of cases were animals made to suffer pain without benefit of anesthesia. Federal law in the United States requires the use of anesthesia and/or painkillers in animal research whenever possible. Exceptions are allowed only when the experimental design would be compromised by the use of anesthesia and when no other alternative method is available for conducting the test. Each such exception must be approved by the same institutional animal care and use committee that supervises animal research in general. All research using live animals must, by law, be scrutinized and approved by such committees, and the committees are required to minimize both the number of animals used and the amount of pain that those animals experience. Although it is assumed that researchers will design their experiments with these criteria in mind. the review process ensures that the researcher(s) are not the ones making the final decision on whether their experiments conform to ethical guidelines.

THE ANIMAL RIGHTS MOVEMENT

7   Like many other movements, the animal rights movement is a heterogeneous mixture of believers, partial believers, zealots, and sympathizers. Bernard Rollin, a philosopher on the faculty at the College of Veterinary Medicine at Colorado State University, focused on the animal rights issue in a 1992 book:

8   The main problem, which continues to concern me the most . . . is polarization and irrationality on the animal ethics issues by both sides. . . .
        The American Medical Association's recent paper on animal rights labels all
        animal advocates as "terrorists," and scientific and medical researchers
        continue to equate animal rights supporters with lab trashers, Luddites,
        misanthropes, and opponents of science and civilization. Animal rights
        activists continue to label all scientists as sadists and psychopaths. Thus
        an unhealthy *pas de deux* is created that blocks rather than accelerates
        the discovery of rational solutions to animal ethics issues.

9   Those concerned with animal rights vary from traditional humane societies like the Society for the Prevention of Cruelty to Animals (SPCA) and various national, state, and local humane societies, through groups like People for the Ethical Treatment of Animals (PETA, founded in 1980), to groups like the Animal Liberation Front (ALF, founded in 1972). From the start, the ALF concentrated on such tactics as breaking into animal research labs, wrecking their facilities and equipment (often beyond repair), and "liberating" the animals. Because these activities are illegal, leading members of the ALF are sought by law enforcement authorities, and most of them are now in hiding. This is the organization most often labeled as "terrorist."

10   Some animal rights activists use a utilitarian ethic to support their position; others write as deontologists. An example of a deontological position would be that animals have inviolable rights, or that it is always wrong to do harm to them, regardless of the circumstances or consequences. A utilitarian animal rights position might

insist on a comparison of costs and benefits (or good and bad consequences) but with equal value placed on the lives (or the pain) of humans and animals.

CURRENT DEBATES

Fur clothing

11   The wearing of furs has long been one of the major targets of animal rights activists, and the elimination of fur clothing has consistently been one of their strongest aims. In most cases, fur clothing is made from very small animals like mink or chinchilla, so it takes many dozens of animals to produce a jacket and many more to produce a coat. These animals are either trapped in the wild or are ranch-raised.

12   What would a cost-benefit analysis of fur clothing reveal? In addition to the death and suffering of the fur-bearing animals themselves, the death and suffering of animals inadvertently caught in the traps must be calculated on the cost side. On the benefit side, there is the utility for humans of having warm clothing. A number of people (fur trappers, shippers, processors, salespeople) are economically dependent on the fur industry, but many of these people could use their skills equally well in other jobs.

13   None of these costs and benefits are easily measured in a way that permits comparison in the same units. Pain and suffering are particularly difficult to measure or quantify. As in many other cases, after listing all the costs and all the benefits, we then leave it up to each of us as individuals to decide whether or not the benefits outweigh the costs. If we approach this question instead from a rights perspective, we must balance the rights of animals to go on living and to be free from pain against the rights of people to wear whatever they please.

14   Among the alternatives to animal-derived clothing are synthetic fabrics such as polyester, which are made from, and therefore use up, nonrenewable petroleum products. Other forms of warm clothing may not require using a nonrenewable resource. For example, wool can be obtained as a renewable resource from sheep; the shearing causes them no apparent harm, and they simply regrow a new coat of wool. Other fibers for fabrics can be made from plants such as cotton. Leather is generally obtained from animals that are killed for other purposes (such as food). Most of these are much less expensive than fur and raise none of the ethical issues mentioned here.

Testing of pharmaceuticals

15   Of all the types of experiments to which animals are subjected, none are as often justified in the eyes of the public as the testing of medicines intended for human use. In fact, a pharmaceutical company would be considered remiss if it marketed a new drug without first testing it on animals. In many countries, including the United States, animal testing is required by law before a new drug can be brought to market. If a drug causes adverse effects in even a small fraction of humans who use it, then the failure of the drug company to identify such adverse effects in animal testing could be used against them in a very expensive lawsuit.

16   New drugs are tested every year, and most of the tests use experimental animals. In fact, a good deal of the expense involved in bringing a new drug to market is the cost of animal testing. In addition to the lives of the animals, the costs of the experimental testing of new drugs include the salaries of the experimenters and animal handlers. On the other side of the cost-benefit equation are the human lives saved or symptoms relieved. If the drug is successful, its benefits may continue far into the future.

17   Those people who value human life above the lives of animals are only being consistent when they insist that drugs or new procedures be tested on animals before they are used on humans. Some animal rights advocates, such as Ingrid Newkirk of PETA, have adopted the viewpoint that a human life is no more valuable than an

animal life, or, in her words, "a rat is a pig is a dog is a boy." A direct logical consequence of this viewpoint is that the pain and suffering of animals in any experiment can no more be justified than an equivalent amount of pain and suffering for a human subject. On this issue, as on many others, the cost-benefit equation can come out differently according to the relative values placed on the lives of humans and the lives of nonhuman animals.

IMPROVING THE TREATMENT OF ANIMALS

18 Attempts to improve the status of animals in research include attempts to prevent animal abuse and neglect and to minimize pain and suffering. Most current legislation deals with the prevention of abuse and neglect by setting minimum standards for housing and care. For example, the U.S. Animal Welfare Act sets standards for the housing of various species (including minimum cage sizes and similar details); the provision of adequate food, water; and sanitation; and such other matters as ventilation, protection from temperature extremes, veterinary care, and the use of anesthetics, painkillers, and tranquilizers whenever it is appropriate.

19 Animal rights groups have advocated what are known as the three Rs: reduction, refinement, and replacement. *Reduction* would mean using methods that require fewer animals; such measures would also in most cases reduce costs. *Refinement* would mean using methods that get more information from a given amount of experimentation. Among other refinement measures, researchers should always make sure they are not repeating earlier work. *Replacement* would mean using tissue culture and other in vitro methods in preference to whole animals, or avoiding the use of animals entirely whenever this can be done without compromising experimental goals.

From Eli C. Minkoff and Pamela J. Baker, "Animal Experimentation Raises Ethical Question," in *Biology Today,* 7th ed., New York: McGraw-Hill, 1996, pp. 25–30. Copyright © 1996 McGraw-Hill. Reprinted by permission of the authors.

 ### Comprehension Checkup

1. In paragraph 3, the author lists reasons for the use of animals. Which ones do you agree with? _____

    _____

    _____

FRANK & ERNEST reprinted by permission of Newspaper Enterprise Association, Inc.

2. Look at the cartoon above. Can this cartoon be seen as making an argument in favor of animal testing? In what way? _____

    _____

    _____

3. Summarize the information on animals as research subjects in paragraph 4. Define the term *vociferous* according to the context of the sentence. Does the

use of that particular word indicate a bias on the author's part? If so, what is the bias?

_____

_____

_____

4. Summarize the author's arguments in paragraph 5. Were any propaganda or persuasive techniques used? If so, what are they? _____

_____

_____

_____

5. What persuasive or propaganda techniques are used in paragraph 6? Can you see any problems with the safeguards currently in place for the treatment of animals?

_____

_____

_____

6. In paragraph 8, Bernard Rollin discusses the polarization of those favoring and opposing the use of animals in research. What propaganda technique does each group use in referring to the other? _____

7. Explain the differences, as described in paragraph 10, between the utilitarian and deontological animal rights' positions. _____

_____

_____

_____

_____

The Art of Writing

In a brief essay, respond to one of the items below.

1. After reading the information on the fur industry, do you favor or oppose raising animals for fur clothing? List your arguments.

2. Do you agree or disagree with Ingrid Newkirk of PETA on the issue of drug testing? Explain your reasoning.

3. Do you think improving the treatment of experimental animals is a valid goal? What, if any, additional safeguards for their treatment should be put in place? Do you think an outside agency would be better able to monitor the care of the animals?

SELECTION

The Monkey Wars _____ _by Deborah Blum_

"Using monkeys, scientists have created vaccines for measles, learned to fight leprosy, developed anti-rejection drugs that make organ transplants possible."

Getting the Picture

Read the following article by Deborah Blum for a more personal perspective on the debate on animal rights. Blum wrote the Pulitzer Prize winning series "The Monkey Wars" while working as a reporter for the *Sacramento Bee*. The excerpt that follows is the lead article in that series, which was first published in 1991 and has since been republished as a book.

Bio-sketch

Deborah Blum received her education at the University of Wisconsin, where she was trained specifically as a science writer. Although she writes in a novelistic style, her essays are the product of a great deal of research on her part. Originally rebuffed by both sides, Blum ultimately gained the confidence of both the scientists engaged in animal research and the animal rights activists. Because she was perceived as fair, she was given unlimited access to the notes of long-time animal activist Shirley McGreal. Dr. Allen Merritt, over his department chair's objections, also allowed Blum full access to his lab. Blum herself likened her reporting on primate research as something similar to a "religious quest." At the outset, the questions that drove her were, "Who are we?" and, "How do we treat our fellow species?"

Brushing Up on Vocabulary

leprosy   a chronic slowly progressing disease, usually mildly infectious, outwardly characterized by inflamed skin or dry patches.

centrifuge   an apparatus that rotates at high speed and separates different substances.

vigils   periods of watchful attention.

vivisectionists   people in favor of cutting into or dissecting live animals in order to advance medical knowledge.

1   On the days when he's scheduled to kill, Allen Merritt summons up his ghosts.

2   They come to him from the shadows of a 20-year-old memory. Eleven human babies, from his first year out of medical school. All born prematurely. All lost within one week when their lungs failed.

3   "We were virtually helpless," said Merritt, now head of the neonatal intensive care unit at the University of California—Davis Medical Center.

4   "There's nothing worse than being a new physician and standing there watching babies die. It's a strong motivator to make things different."

5   On this cool morning, he needs that memory. The experiment he's doing is deceptively simple: a test of a new chemical to help premature babies breathe. But it's no clinical arrangement of glass tubes. He's trying the drug on two tiny rhesus monkeys, each weighing barely one-third of a pound. At the end of the experiment, he plans to cut their lungs apart, to see how it worked.

6   Even his ghosts don't make that easy. Nestled in a towel on a surgical table, eyes shut, hands curled, the monkeys look unnervingly human. "The link between people and monkeys is very close," Merritt said. "Much closer than some people would like to think. There's a real sense of sadness, that we can only get the information we need if we kill them."

7   Once, there was no such need to justify. Once, American researchers could go through 200,000 monkeys a year, without question. Now, the numbers are less— perhaps 20,000 monkeys will die every year, out of an estimated 40,000 used in experiments. But the pressures are greater.

8   These days, it seems that if researchers plan one little study—slicing the toes off squirrel monkeys, siphoning blood from rhesus macaques, or hiding baby monkeys from their mothers—they face not just questions, but picket signs, lawsuits and death threats phoned in at night.

9   The middle ground in the war over research with monkeys and apes has become so narrow as to be nearly invisible. And even that is eroding.

10   Intelligent, agile, fast, but not fast enough, these nonhuman primates are rapidly being driven from the planet, lost to heavy trapping and vanishing rain forests. Of 63 primate species in Asia—where most research monkeys come from—only one is not listed as vulnerable.

11   Primate researchers believe they are making the hard choice, using nonhuman primates for medical research because they must, because no other animal so closely mirrors the human body and brain. During the 1950s, American scientists did kill hundreds of thousands of monkeys for polio research, using the animals' organs to grow virus, dissecting their brains to track the spread of the infection. But out of those experiments came a polio vaccine. Using monkeys, scientists have created vaccines for measles, learned to fight leprosy, developed antirejection drugs that make organ transplants possible.

12   Outside the well-guarded laboratory wall, that choice can seem less obvious. Animal rights advocates draw a dark description of research. They point out that AIDS researchers have used endangered chimpanzees, without, so far, managing to help people dying of the disease. Further, conservationists fear that the research is introducing dangerous infection into the country's chimpanzee breeding program, badly needed to help counter the loss of wild animals.

13   "They're guzzling up money and animals, and for what?" asked Shirley McGreal, head of the nonprofit International Primate Protection League. "Why not use those resources in helping sick people, why infect healthy animals?"

14   Her argument is that of animal advocates across the country—that scientists are sacrificing our genetic next-of-kin for their own curiosity, dubious medical gains and countless tax dollars.

15   No one is sure exactly how much money scientists spend experimenting on monkeys, although the National Institutes of Health alone allocates almost $40 million annually to its primate research programs, including one in Davis. Overall, more than half of NIH's research grants—approaching $5 billion—involve at least some animal research.

16   Rats and mice are the most abundant, some 15 million are used in experiments every year. But primates are the most expensive; monkeys cost a basic $1,000, chimpanzees start at $50,000.

17   For people such as McGreal, these are animals in a very wrong place. McGreal's long-term goal for monkeys is simple: out of the laboratory, back into what remains of the rain forests.

18   "I used to think that we could persuade those people to understand what we do," said Frederick King, director of the Yerkes Regional Primate Research Center in Atlanta. "But it's impossible. And that's why I no longer describe this as a battle. I describe it as a war."

19   The rift is so sharp that it is beginning to reshape science itself.

20   "Science has organized," marveled Alex Pacheco, founder of the country's most powerful animal rights group, People for Ethical Treatment of Animals. "Researchers are out-lobbying us and outspending us. They've become so aggressive that it puts new pressure on us. We're going to have to fight tougher too."

21   In the past year, researchers have made it clear just how much they dislike the role of victim. If Pacheco wants to call scientists "sadistic bastards"—which he does frequently—then Fred King is more than ready to counter with his description of PETA: "Fanatic, fringe, one of the most despicable organizations in the country."

22   But beyond name-calling, the research community is realizing its political power. Its lobbyists are pushing for laws that would heavily penalize protesters who interfere with research projects. And this year, to the fury of animal rights groups, primate researchers were able to win a special exemption from the public records laws, shielding their plans for captive monkey care.

23   For researchers, the attention focused on them is an almost dizzying turnabout. Not so long ago, they could have hung their monkey care plans as banners across streets and no one would have read them.

24   "When I first started 20 years ago, monkeys were $25 each," said Roy Henrickson, chief of lab animal care at the University of California, Berkeley. "You'd use one once and you'd throw it away. I'd talk to lab vets who were under pressure about dogs and I'd say, I'm sure glad I'm in nonhuman primates. Nobody cares about them."

25   He can date the change precisely, back to 1981, the year Pacheco went undercover in the laboratory of Edward Taub. Taub was a specialist in nerve damage, working in Silver Springs, Maryland. To explore the effects of ruined nerves, he took 17 rhesus monkeys and sliced apart nerves close to the spinal column, crippling their limbs. Then he studied the way they coped with the damage.

26   Pacheco left the laboratory with an enduring mistrust of scientists and an armload of inflammatory photographs: monkeys wrenched into vices, packed into filthy cages. Monkeys who, with no feeling in their hands, had gnawed their fingers to the bone. Some of the wounds were oozing with infection, darkening with gangrene.

27   Many believe those battered monkeys were the fuse, lighting the current, combative cycle of animal rights. In the fury over the Silver Springs monkeys, Pacheco was able to build People for Ethical Treatment of Animals into a national force, and across the country, the movement gained power. Today, membership in animal advocacy groups tops 12 million; the 30 largest organizations report a combined annual income approaching $70 million.

28   And primate researchers have suddenly found themselves under scrutiny of the most hostile kind.

29   There are experiments, such as Allen Merritt's work to salvage premature infants, that the critics will sometimes reluctantly accept. The compound that Merritt is testing on young monkeys is a kind of lubricant for the lungs, a slippery ooze that coats the tissues within, allowing them to flex as air comes in and out.

30   Without the ooze—called surfactant—the tissues don't stretch. They rip. The problem for premature babies is that the body doesn't develop surfactant until late in fetal development, some 35 weeks into a pregnancy. Although artificial surfactants are now available, Merritt doesn't believe they're good enough. Two-thirds of the tiniest premature babies, weighing less than a pound at birth, still die as their lungs shred. He's trying to improve the medicine.

31   "There could be a scientific defense for doing that, even though it's extremely cruel," said Elliott Katz, head of In Defense of Animals, a national animal rights group, headquartered in San Rafael.

32   But Katz finds most of the work indefensible. He can rapidly cite examples of a different sort: a U.S. Air Force experiment, which involved draining 40 percent of the blood from rhesus macaques and then spinning them on a centrifuge, to simulate injured astronauts; a New York University study of addiction in which monkeys were strapped into metal boxes and forced to inhale concentrated cocaine fumes.

33   Last year, animal advocates rallied against a proposed study at the Seattle center, a plan to take 13 baby rhesus macaques from their mothers and try to drive them crazy through isolation, keeping them caged away from their mothers and without company. The scientists acknowledged that they might drive the monkeys to self-mutilation; rhesus macaques do badly in isolation, rocking, pulling out their hair, sometimes tearing their skin open.

34   This year, protesters have been holding candlelight vigils outside the home of a researcher at a Maryland military facility, the Uniformed Services University of the Health Sciences. That project involves cutting the toes from kittens and young squirrel monkeys and then, after they've wobbled into adjustment, killing them to look at their brains.

35   In both cases, there are scientific explanations. The Washington scientists wanted to analyze the chemistry of a troubled brain, saying that it could benefit people with mental illness. The Maryland researchers are brain-mapping, drafting a careful picture of how the mind reorganizes itself to cope with crippling injury.

36   But these are not—and may never be—explanations acceptable to those crusading for animal rights. "This is just an example of someone doing something horrible to animals because he can get paid for it," said Laurie Raymond, of Seattle's Progressive Animal Welfare Society, which campaigned against the baby monkey experiment and takes credit for the fact that it failed to get federal funding.

37   Researchers are tired of telling the public about their work, documenting it in public records—and having that very openness used against them. The Washington protesters learned about the baby monkey experiment through a meeting of the university's animal care committee—which is public. The Maryland work came to light through a listing of military funded research—which is public.

38   When the U.S. Department of Agriculture, which inspects research facilities annually, complained about the housekeeping at the Tulane Regional Primate Research Center in Louisiana, the director wrote the agency a furious letter. Didn't administrators realize that the report was public—and made scientists look bad?

39   "The point I am making is that USDA, without intending to do so, is playing into the hands of the animal rights/antivivisectionists whose stated goal is to abolish animal research," wrote center head Peter Gerone, arguing that the complaints could have been handled privately. "If you are trying to placate the animal rights activists by nitpicking inspections . . . you will only serve to do us irreparable harm."

40   When Arnold Arluke, a sociologist at Boston's Northeastern University, spent six years studying lab workers and drafted a report saying that some actually felt guilty about killing animals, he found himself suddenly under pressure. "I was told putting that information out would be like giving ammunition to the enemy," he said.

41   He titled his first talk "Guilt among Animal Researchers." The manager of the laboratory where he spoke changed "guilt" to stress. When he published that in a journal, the editors thought that stress was too controversial. They changed the title to "Uneasiness among Lab Workers." When he gave another talk at a pharmaceutical company, he was told uneasiness was too strong. They changed the title to "How to Deal with Your Feelings." Arluke figures his next talk will be untitled.

42   "People in animal research don't even want to tell others what they do," he said. "One woman I talked to was standing in line at a grocery store, and when she told the person next to her what she did, the woman started yelling at her: 'You should be ashamed of yourself.'"

43   And when new lab animal care rules were published this year, it was clear that researchers were no longer willing to freely hand over every record of operation.

44   The new regulations resulted from congressional changes in 1985 to the Animal Welfare Act. They included a special provision for the care of laboratory primates; legislators wanted scientists to recognize that these were sociable, intelligent animals.

45   The provision—perhaps the most controversial in the entire act—was called "psychological well-being of primates." When the USDA began drafting rules, in response to the new law, it received a record 35,000 letters of comment. And 14,000 consisted of a written shouting match over how to make primates happy. It took six years before the agency could come up with rules that the research community could accept.

46   Originally, the USDA proposed firm standards: Laboratories would have to give monkeys bigger cages, let them share space, provide them with puzzles and toys from a list.

47   Researchers argued that was unreasonable. Every monkey species was different, the rigid standards might satisfy one animal and make another miserable. Now, each institution is asked to do what it thinks best for its monkeys; USDA inspectors will be free to study, criticize and ask for changes in those plans.

48   But animal rights groups will not. Research lobbyists persuaded the USDA to bypass the federal Freedom of Information Act; the president of the American Society of Primatologists told the agency that making the plans public would be like giving a road map to terrorists. Under the new rules, the plans will be kept at the individual institutions rather than filed with the federal government, as has been standard practice. That makes them institutional property—exempted from any requests for federal records.

49   Tom Wolfle, director of the Institute for Laboratory Animal Resources in Washington D.C., the federal government's chief advisory division on animal issues, said the research community simply needed some clear space. "The idea was to prevent unreasonable criticism by uninformed people," he said.

50   Advocacy groups have sued the government over the new rules, saying they unlawfully shut the public out of research that it pays for. "In the end, they just handed everything back to the researchers and said, here, it's all yours," said Christine Stevens, an executive with the nonprofit Animal Welfare Institute.

51   Stevens, daughter of a Michigan physiology researcher, finds this the ultimate contradiction, as well as "foolish and short-sighted." She thinks that science, of all professions, should be one of open ideas.

52   On this point, she has some unlikely allies. Frederick King, of Yerkes, no friend to the animal rights movement, is also unhappy with the research community's tendency to withdraw. "I don't know about the law," he said. "But our plans for taking care of our primates will be open."

53   "We are using taxpayers' money. In my judgment, we have an obligation to tell the public what we're about. And the fact that we haven't done that, I think, is one of the greatest mistakes over the last half-century, hell, the last century, that scientists have made."

54   Against that conflict, Allen Merritt's decision to make public an experiment in which he kills monkeys was not an easy one. His wife worried that antiresearch fanatics would stalk their home. His supervisors worried that animal lovers would be alienated; one administrator even called the Davis primate center, suggesting that Merritt's work should not be publicly linked to the medical school's pediatrics department.

55   But Merritt, like King, believes that his profession will only lose if it remains hidden from the public. "People need to understand what we're doing. If I were to take a new drug first to a nursery, and unforeseen complications occurred, and a baby died—who would accept that?"

56   So, on a breezy morning, he opens the way to the final test of lung-lubricating surfactants that he will do this year, a 24-hour-countdown for two baby monkeys. Those hours are critical to whether these drugs work. If human premature babies last from their first morning to the next one, their survival odds soar.

57   The tiny monkeys—one male, one female—taken by C-section, are hurried into an intensive care unit, dried and warmed with a blow drier, put onto folded towels, hooked up to ventilators, heart monitors, intravenous drip lines. During the experiment, they will never be conscious, never open their eyes.

58   "OK, let's treat," Merritt says. His technician gently lifts the tube from the ventilator, which carries oxygen into the monkey's lungs. A white mist of surfactant fills the tube, spraying into the lungs. And then, through the night, the medical team watches and waits.

59　　　The next morning, they decide to kill the female early. An intravenous line going into her leg is starting to cause bleeding problems. The monkey is twitching a little in her unconsciousness, as if in pain. Merritt sees no point in dragging her through the experiment's official end.

60　　　But the male keeps breathing. As the sun brightens to midday, the scientists inject a lethal dose of anesthesia. Still, the monkey's chest keeps moving, up and down, up and down with the push of the ventilator. But, behind him, the heart monitor shows only a straight green line.

61　　　For a few seconds, before they shut the machines down and begin the lung dissection, Allen Merritt stands quietly by the small dead monkey, marshaling the ghosts of the babies he couldn't save, a long time ago.

Note: As a postscript, after the publication of this article, Dr. Allen Merritt received threatening phone calls and for his children's protection was forced to send them away from home for a short time. Though he has no real regrets about participating in the interviews, he has not spoken to Blum since the article's publication.

From Deborah Blum, "The Monkey Wars," from *The Sacramento Bee*, 11–24–91. Copyright © 2004 The Sacramento Bee. Reprinted with permission.

Comprehension Exercises

Multiple Choice

Write the letter of the correct answer in the blank provided.

_____　1.　Allen Merritt was motivated to pursue his experiments with the baby rhesus monkeys because of
　　　　　　　a. pressure from the animal rights activists
　　　　　　　b. the deaths of premature human infants
　　　　　　　c. the amount of money involved in animal experimentation

_____　2.　A likely title for this selection would be
　　　　　　　a. "Animal Research—The Controversy Continues"
　　　　　　　b. "Allen Merritt's Animal Research"
　　　　　　　c. "The Increased Cost of Animal Research"
　　　　　　　d. "Animal Research—Too Much Red Tape"

_____　3.　Animal rights activist Shirley McGreal feels it would make more sense to
　　　　　　　a. spend more money on experiments with monkeys
　　　　　　　b. spend money to help sick people get better rather than infect healthy animals with disease
　　　　　　　c. send the chimpanzees to zoos around the country

_____　4.　Researchers won a major victory against animal rights activists because their plans for the care of their primates
　　　　　　　a. will be open to inspection by animal activists
　　　　　　　b. will be kept hidden from public view at the individual research institutions
　　　　　　　c. will apply the same standards to each monkey species.

_____　5.　From this selection, you could infer that the term "animal advocates" refers to people who
　　　　　　　a. want more animal research
　　　　　　　b. believe that animal research should be both humane and limited
　　　　　　　c. do not take a position in relation to animal experimentation

True or False

Indicate whether the statement is true or false by writing T or F in the blank provided.

_____ 6. Today fewer animals are used in animal experiments and fewer animals lose their lives.

_____ 7. In the past, animal researchers faced considerably more protest than they do today.

_____ 8. The USDA has enacted strict standards to improve the mental health of primates.

_____ 9. The condition of the animals at the Silver Springs Lab helped spur a national movement to improve the treatment of animals.

_____ 10. Research on animals is relatively inexpensive and is paid for by private donations.

1. Look at paragraph 8. Explain why the phrase "one little study" is used ironically.

   _____

   _____

2. Responding to objections from the research community, Arnold Arluke had to continually change the title of his speech "Guilt among Animal Researchers." What does this demonstrate about the attitudes of the research community as a whole?

   _____

   _____

   _____

   _____

Vocabulary in Context

Using the context clues provided in the essay, match each word in column I with the correct definition from column II. Write the letter of the definition in the blank provided.

Column I

_____ 1. agile

_____ 2. alienated

_____ 3. despicable

_____ 4. dissecting

_____ 5. dubious

_____ 6. fanatic

_____ 7. inflammatory

_____ 8. lethal

_____ 9. neonatal

_____ 10. placate

_____ 11. sadistic

_____ 12. unnervingly

Column II

A. to stop from being angry; appease

B. fatal or deadly

C. relating to newborn children

D. with a feeling of weakness or nervousness

E. nimble

F. to cut apart for purpose of study

G. questionable

H. taking pleasure from inflicting pain

I. zealous beyond reason (a person)

J. contemptible

K. likely to rouse anger, violence

L. estranged; withdrawn from

In Your Own Words

1. How do the beliefs of the animal rights activists and the animal researchers conflict?

2. Are you convinced by the arguments of the animal rights activists that there is too much animal experimentation today?

3. Do you think Deborah Blum is truly neutral? Where do you think she would draw the line killing animals?

4. Do you think that it is morally acceptable to experiment on humans who possess extremely low intelligence?

5. Would it be morally acceptable to experiment on persons incarcerated for particularly heinous crimes such as murder?

6. What is the main idea in the picture below?

Rick Giase/AP/Wide World Photos

The Art of Writing

In a brief essay, respond to one of the items below.

1. Summarize the arguments made by Shirley McGreal. Summarize Fred King's attack on animal rights activists. Which side's arguments do you believe are more persuasive? Why?

2. Which issues do you think Dr. Merritt argues most persuasively? Summarize his reasons for publicizing an experiment in which he kills monkeys.

3. Some people believe that it is acceptable to experiment on animals such as rats and rabbits, but that it is unacceptable to experiment on animals such as dogs, cats, or monkeys. How do you feel about this issue? Explain your reasoning.

Internet Activity

Using a search engine like Google <www.google.com> or Ask Jeeves <www.askjeeves.com>, find a website that deals with animal experimentation and analyze the website by answering the following questions.

1. *Author's Purpose* Is the author's primary purpose to inform or to persuade? Why do you think so?

2. *Emotional Appeals* Where does the author use language that is intended to arouse the reader emotionally? Give two examples of material that is included for its emotional appeal.

3. *Ethical Appeals* What information does the author include to persuade the reader to consider her (or him) an authority in this area or to trust his (or her) judgment on this subject?

4. *Logical Appeals* What logical or reasonable arguments does the author use? Is the author using inductive or deductive reasoning?

5. *Psychological Appeals* Is the author trying to manipulate the reader psychologically by appealing to the need for acceptance, power, prestige, etc.?

6. *Propaganda Techniques* What propaganda techniques does the author use? Are the techniques appropriate to his (or her) purpose? Cite specific examples.

7. *Tone* What is the author's tone? Is the tone meant to influence or manipulate the reader? Give specific examples of how the author uses tone to affect the reader.

8. *Bias* What is the author's specific bias? Where is the bias presented? At the beginning? The middle? The end?

Print one or two pages from the website.

SELECTION

An excerpt from **Dominion**   *by Matthew Scully*

"Animals are so easily overlooked, their interests so easily brushed aside."

Getting the Picture

In the following excerpt, Matthew Scully presents a classic argument for compassion toward the animals with whom we share the planet. He condemns what he considers the commonplace maltreatment of animals in the name of factory farming, sport, and science. He describes the mass slaughter of animals in Britain and Western Europe following the outbreak of foot-and-mouth disease in 2001.

Bio-sketch

Matthew Scully, a vegetarian since 1974, is a former editor at *National Review,* and a former special assistant and senior speechwriter to President George W. Bush. In 2003, he published *Dominion: The Power of Man, the Suffering of Animals, and the Call to Mercy,* from which this excerpt is taken.

Brushing Up on Vocabulary

epidemic a disease affecting many at the same time. An epidemic is widespread but temporary. The foot-and-mouth epidemic described below is considered to be one of the world's worst.

phoenix   according to mythology, the *phoenix* was a legendary bird that was consumed by fire every 500 years. A new, young bird sprang from its ashes. The *phoenix* is considered a symbol of both rebirth and immortality.

1   It began with one pig at a British slaughterhouse. Somewhere along the production line it was observed that the animal had blisters in his mouth and was salivating. The worst suspicions were confirmed, and within days borders had been sealed and a course of action determined. Soon all of England and the world watched as hundreds, and then hundreds of thousands of pigs, cows, and sheep and their newborn lambs were taken outdoors, shot, thrown into burning pyres, and bulldozed into muddy graves. Reports described terrified cattle being chased by sharpshooters, clambering over one another to escape. Some were still stirring and blinking a day after being shot. The plague meanwhile had slipped into mainland Europe, where the same ritual followed until, when it was all over, more than ten million animals had been disposed of. Completing the story with the requisite happy ending was a calf heard calling from underneath the body of her mother in a mound of carcasses to be set aflame. Christened "Phoenix," after the bird of myth that rose from the ashes, the calf was spared.

2   The journalist Andrew Sullivan discerned in these scenes a "horrifying nothingness," something about it all that left us sick and sad and empty. More than a year has passed since the last ditch was covered over. But probably you can still recall your own reactions because it was one of those events that made us all pause and question basic assumptions. One knew that something had gone terribly wrong, something deep and serious and beyond the power of vaccines or borders or cullings to contain. We saw in all of their simplicity the facts of the case: Here were innocent, living creatures, and they deserved better, and we just can't treat life that way. We realized, if only for an instant, that it wasn't even necessary, that we had brought the whole thing upon them and upon ourselves. Foot-and-mouth disease is a form of flu, treatable by proper veterinary care, preventable by vaccination, lethal neither to humans nor to animals. These animals, millions of them not even infected, were all killed only because their market value had been diminished and because trade policies required it—because, in short, under the circumstances it was the quick and convenient thing to do. By the one measure we now apply to these creatures, they had all become worthless. For them, the difference between what happened and what awaited them anyway was one of timing. And for us the difference was visibility. This time, we had to watch.

3   Silent while all of this was unfolding in early 2001 were people usually quick to caution against "sentimentality" toward animals. Looking out upon those fields of burning pyres, no one could claim that mankind is going soft. The images bore witness, instead, to an incredible hardness and abandon. It was an "economic disease," as one writer put it, revealing attitudes there all along and now, in desperation, grimly carried out to their logical conclusion.

4   The drama had a familiar feel to it, for in a strange way mankind does seem to be growing more sentimental about animals, and also more ruthless. No age has ever been more solicitous to animals, more curious and caring. Yet no age has ever inflicted upon animals such massive punishments with such complete disregard, as witness scenes to be found on any given day at any modern industrial farm. These places are hard to contemplate even without the crises that now and then capture our attention. Europe's recurring "mad cow" scares have all come about from the once unthinkable practice of feeding cattle the ground-up remains of other cattle. Livestock farmers around the world are becoming "growers," their barns "mass confinement facilities," and slaughterhouses vast "processing plants" dispatching animals—"production units"—at a furious pace of hundreds per minute.

5   When a quarter million birds are stuffed into a single shed, unable even to flap their wings, when more than a million pigs inhabit a single farm, never once stepping into the light of day, when every year tens of millions of creatures go to their death without knowing the least measure of human kindness, it is time to question old assumptions, to ask what we are doing and what spirit drives us on. "Our inhumane treatment of livestock," as Senator Robert C. Byrd warned in July 2001, in remarks without precedent in the Congress of the United States, "is becoming widespread and more and more barbaric. . . . Such insensitivity is insidious and can spread and be dangerous. Life must be respected and dealt with humanely in a civilized world."

6   The attitude Senator Byrd describes has already spread into sport hunting, which is becoming colder and more systematic even as the ranks of hunters decline. In our day hunting has taken on an oddly agricultural aspect, with many wild animals born, bred, and held in captivity just to be shot, and even elephants confined within African game parks to be "harvested" by Western sportsmen in a manner more resembling execution. Wildlife across the world live in a state of perpetual retreat from human development, until for many species there is nowhere else to go, as we have seen for a generation in mankind's long good-bye to the elephants, grizzlies, gorillas, tigers, wolves, pandas, and other creatures who simply do not have the room to live and flourish anymore.

7   Even whales are still hunted, long after an international moratorium was declared and longer still after any credible claims of need have passed away. Employing weapons and methods ever more harsh and inescapable, the hunt goes on for many other animals one might have thought were also due a reprieve, as new substitutes are found for their fur and flesh. From Africa to the western United States to the storied rain forest of the Amazon, it is the fate of many wild creatures either to be unwanted by man or wanted too much, despised as a menace to progress or desired as a means to progress—beloved and brutalized all at once, like the elephant and whale and dolphin.

8   In our laboratories, meanwhile, we see the strange new beings of mankind's own creation, genetically engineered, cloned, and now even patented like any other products ready for mass production. Even with all its possibilities for good, this new science of genetic engineering carries the darkest implications of all for animals, conferring on us the power not only to use them as we will but to remake them as we will. It comes at an inconvenient moment, too, just as research of a very different kind has revealed beyond a reasonable doubt the intelligence of many animals, their emotional sensitivity, their capacities for happiness and suffering alike.

9   The care of animals brings with it often complicated problems of economics, ecology, and science. But above all it confronts us with questions of conscience. Many of us seem to have lost all sense of restraint toward animals, an understanding of natural boundaries, a respect for them as beings with needs and wants and a place and purpose of their own. Too often, too casually, we assume that our interests always come first, and if it's profitable or expedient that is all we need to know. We assume that all these other creatures with whom we share the earth are here for us, and only for us. We assume, in effect, that we are everything and they are nothing.

10   Animals are more than ever a test of our character, of mankind's capacity for empathy and for decent, honorable conduct and faithful stewardship. We are called to treat them with kindness, not because they have rights or power or some claim to equality, but in a sense because they don't; because they all stand unequal and powerless before us. Animals are so easily overlooked, their interests so easily brushed aside. Whenever we humans enter their world, from our farms to the local animal shelter to the African savanna, we enter as lords of the earth bearing strange powers of terror and mercy alike.

11   Dominion, as we call this power in the Western tradition, today requires our concentrated moral consideration. Though reason must guide us in laying down standards and laws regarding animals, and in examining the arguments of those who reject such standards, it is usually best in any moral inquiry to start with the original motivation, which in the case of animals we may without embarrassment call love. When we wince at the suffering of animals, that feeling speaks well of us even when we ignore it, and those who dismiss love for our fellow creatures as mere sentimentality overlook a good and important part of our humanity.

12   It is true, as we are often reminded, that kindness to animals is among the humbler duties of human charity—though for just that reason among the more easily neglected. And it is true that there will always be enough injustice and human suffering in the world to make the wrongs done to animals seem small and secondary. The answer is that justice is not a finite commodity, nor are kindness and love. Where we find wrongs done to animals, it is no excuse to say that more important wrongs are done to human beings, and let us concentrate on those. A wrong is a wrong, and often the little ones, when they are shrugged off as nothing, spread and do the gravest harm to ourselves and others. I believe this is happening in our treatment of animals. The burning pyres of Europe were either a sign to us, demanding an accounting for humanity's treatment of animals, or else they were just a hint of things to come.

13   After the foot-and-mouth crisis, Matthew Parris, a former member of Parliament writing in the conservative *Spectator,* observed that "a tide of moral sentiment is slowly turning. It turns first in the unconscious mind. We feel—not opposed to something, but vaguely uncomfortable about it." I hope he is right. I hope that more of us might pass from moral discomfort to moral conviction. I hope that animal welfare will receive more of the public concern it warrants, leading over time to legal reforms not only in our treatment of the creatures now raised and slaughtered by the billions, but of all within the reach of human recklessness, greed, cowardice, and cruelty.

Comprehension Checkup

Multiple Choice

Write the letter of the correct answer in the blank provided.

_____ 1.   In paragraph 1, the author states that "soon all of England and the world watched . . ." This is an example of
a. overstatement
b. understatement
c. exaggeration
d. both a and c

_____ 2.   In paragraph 1, the author uses all of the following persuasive techniques *except*
a. emotionally loaded language
b. tear-jerking stories
c. figurative language
d. manipulation of tone

_____ 3.   According to paragraph 2, which values is the author likely to endorse?
a. The lives of innocent creatures should not be treated so cavalierly.
b. Animals are an expendable commodity.

        c. It makes no difference how an animal dies.

        d. none of the above

_____ 4. The word *sentimentality* in paragraph 3 implies

        a. fastidiousness

        b. emotionalism

        c. softheartedness

        d. both (b) and (c)

_____ 5. When the author refers to an "economic disease" in paragraph 3, he means

        a. the slaughter of the animals wasn't necessary for health reasons

        b. the animals were slaughtered because their economic value had fallen

        c. trade policies required that the animals be slaughtered

        d. all of the above

_____ 6. A **paradox** can be a statement that seems contradictory but that actually presents a truth. What is the essential paradox in paragraph 4?

        a. Humans are overly concerned with the well-being of animals.

        b. Meat is no longer a priority in the U.S. diet.

        c. Humans treat animals in both a ruthless and caring fashion.

        d. Millions of animals are killed a day.

_____ 7. Referring to slaughterhouses as "processing plants" in paragraph 4 is an example of

        a. simile

        b. metaphor

        c. euphemism

        d. personification

_____ 8. The author's reference to Senator Byrd in paragraph 5 is an example of what propaganda device?

        a. testimonial

        b. plain folks

        c. slogan

        d. faulty cause and effect

_____ 9. The word *harvested* in paragraph 6 is an example of

        a. literary allusion

        b. symbolism

        c. euphemism

        d. personification

_____ 10. In paragraph 6, the author concludes that sport hunting and agriculture are alike in that

        a. both agriculture and hunting are in decline

        b. both animals and plants are bred to be harvested

        c. both animals and plants wither and die without proper nutrition

        d. both animals and plants need arable lands in which to thrive

_____ 11. In paragraph 7, the phrase *unwanted by man or wanted too much* and the phrase *despised as a menace to progress or desired as a means to progress* make use of

        a. homonyms

        b. synonyms

        c. antonyms

        d. none of the above

_____ 12. In paragraph 9, Scully asserts that the care of animals is problematical because of
   a. conscience and economics
   b. ecology and science
   c. all of the above
   d. none of the above

_____ 13. The main idea of paragraph 10 is
   a. humans should not hesitate to exploit animals
   b. the loss of the large mammals like grizzlies and pandas will prove to be irreparable
   c. animals must be treated decently because they are powerless
   d. there will always be injustice in the world

_____ 14. The author in paragraph 12 sees the burning pyres of the hoof-and-mouth epidemic as a possible
   a. harbinger of things to come
   b. reckoning for our callous disregard of the rights and feelings of animals
   c. source of pollution
   d. both (a) and (b)

_____ 15. In the final paragraph, the author expresses a hope that
   a. people will become increasingly concerned to protect the welfare of animals
   b. more people will become vegetarians
   c. people will give up wearing fur coats and hunting for sport
   d. cloning of animals will become more prevalent

True or False

Indicate whether the statement is true or false by writing T or F in the blank provided.

_____ 1. According to the author, humans are pushing back the boundaries of wildlife habitats.

_____ 2. An international moratorium was declared to stop the hunting of whales.

_____ 3. New research has revealed that animals are incapable of suffering.

_____ 4. Scully implies that the needs of humans should not always be paramount where animals are concerned.

_____ 5. While recognizing the positive accomplishments of genetic engineering, Scully feels that it could have dire consequences for animals.

_____ 6. There is a correlation between mad cow disease and feeding cows the ground up parts of other cows.

Vocabulary in Context

Read the following sentences and select a word from the list below that best matches a concept expressed in the sentence. (Not all words will be used.)

barbaric	culled	expedient	grimly	requisite
clambering	discerned	finite	precedent	solicitous
contemplate	empathy	flourish	reprieve	wince

1. Most plants grow luxuriantly with enough plant food and water.
   _____

2. Their behavior was completely lacking in civilizing influences.
   _____

3. After her daughter's death, Mara's friends were especially anxious and concerned for her well-being. _____

4. After paying for Mike's education for the last six years, his parents wanted him to know that any further money was subject to limits and conditions.
   _____

5. Jenna needed to consider her options thoroughly before deciding to return to school. _____

6. After Francisco had fulfilled all required and necessary classes, his counselor told him that he would be eligible to graduate in January. _____

7. The pain of the blow was so sharp that it made him recoil. _____

8. When looking for a job, it is advantageous to network with people in your chosen field. _____

9. After her mother's death, Katrina gathered from her mother's possessions only the choice objects that she wanted for her own home. _____

10. Walker received a two-month delay in his impending execution while the governor considered giving him clemency. _____

In Your Own Words

1. Have you ever seen animals slaughtered on a farm or in a stockyard? Did the experience affect your attitude toward eating meat?

2. Can you think of any advantages of the modern industrial farm as described by Matthew Scully?

The Art of Writing

In a brief essay, respond to one of the items below.

1. Matthew Scully says that about 80 million of the 95 million hogs slaughtered each year in the United States are raised "without benefit of soil or sunshine" in mass-confinement farms. These hogs are "genetically designed by machines, inseminated by machines, fed by machines, monitored, herded, electrocuted, stabbed, cleaned, cut, and packaged by machine—themselves treated by machines from birth to bacon." Discuss your reaction to this description of how hogs are treated in modern industrial farms.

2. According to Matthew Scully, the typical trophy hunter today is hunting "captive animals." Many of the animals are rejects from zoos or are raised to be killed in a hunt. Many hunters prefer killing captive animals because they "make better-looking trophies." What do you think about the concept of the canned hunt?

Internet Activities

1. For a history of the foot-and-mouth epidemic of 2001, consult the following website:

   www.pighealth.com/fmdoutbreaks.htm

   Make a brief time line of key events.

2. For an interview with Matthew Scully by Kathryn Jean Lopez of *National Review* Online, consult

    www.nationalreview.com/interrogatory/interrogatory120602.asp

    Think of five questions that you would like to ask Scully.

3. Use a search engine such as Google <www.google.com> or Yahoo <www.yahoo.com> to locate information about recent developments in the field of cloning. Summarize your findings.

TEST-TAKING TIP

Key Words That Often Appear in Essay Questions (Continued)

explain	to make clear, to give reasons. An explanation often involves showing cause-and-effect relationships or steps.		reflect the main ideas and supporting details.
illustrate	to use a diagram, chart, or figure, or specific examples to explain something further.	**prove**	to demonstrate that something is true by means of factual evidence or logical reasoning.
interpret	to say what something means. A question that asks for an interpretation usually wants you to state what something means to you. What are your beliefs or feelings about the meaning of the material? Be sure to back up your position with specific examples and details.	**relate**	to discuss how two or more conclusions, theories, or opinions affect each other. Explain how one causes, limits, or develops the other.
		review	to summarize or sometimes to summarize and then analyze critically.
justify	to give reasons in support of a conclusion, theory, or opinion.	**summarize**	to put down the main points; to state briefly the key principles, facts, or ideas while avoiding details and personal comments.
list	to put down your points one-by-one. You may want to number each of the points in your list.	**trace**	to follow the course of development of something in a chronological or logical sequence. You will want to discuss each stage of development from beginning to end.
outline	to organize information into an outline, using headings and subheadings. Your outline should		

Part 5

Study Skills

Organizing Textbook Information

Photo by Wolfgang Volz © Christo, 1995.

Wrapped Reichstag, Berlin
(1995)
BY CHRISTO AND JEANNE-CLAUDE

The wrapping of the Reichstag required 1,076,000 square feet of fabric. It took 90 climbers and 120 installation workers to complete the project, which remained in place for only two weeks. All of the projects done by Christo and Jeanne-Claude are temporary, paid for by the artists, and completed with recycled materials. The two have been called "environmental artists" because they work in both rural and urban environments. They force people to view familiar locations in new and different ways.

1   What do you imagine the building here would look like without the wrappings?

2   The Reichstag is Germany's parliament building. Do you think the wrapping of the Reichstag comments on politics? How?

3   Do you consider the wrapping of a large structure like the Reichstag art? Why or why not?

Studying Textbook Chapters

In previous chapters of this book, you were introduced to various study techniques. You also practiced applying many of these techniques. In this chapter, we will review those techniques and introduce you to others that will help you study for your college classes. You will also have a chance to practice your newly acquired skills with a complete chapter on the arts from a cultural anthropology textbook.

Skimming

Skimming is a study technique very similar to SQ3R (see page 56). Skimming involves reading material quickly in order to gain a quick overview and identify the main points. As in SQ3R, you read the introduction to the chapter, the summary at the end of the chapter, the section titles and subtitles, and the first sentence of each section and many paragraphs. You also look at the illustrations and read the captions. Once you have skimmed the chapter, you should be able to state its main idea.

Now skim through the textbook chapter on pages 466–482 and then answer the true/false questions below.

True or False

Indicate whether the statement is true or false by writing T or F in the blank provided.

_____   1.   Many cultures don't have a specific word for "art."

_____   2.   "The Arts" usually include visual arts, music, literature, and theater.

_____   3.   Art is static and changes little.

_____   4.   Throughout the ages, art has rarely been associated with religion.

_____   5.   Folk art is representative of ordinary people.

_____   6.   What is aesthetically pleasing is often dependent upon one's culture.

_____   7.   Art is a recent phenomenon that only goes back several hundred years.

Scanning

Scanning is a technique for quickly finding answers to specific questions. People use scanning techniques daily in order to find information quickly. When you go to the phone book, you scan down through the list of names or businesses until you find the one you are looking for. You don't actually take the time to read every name. You may also scan through the TV guide, the dictionary, and newspaper ads.

Now that you have skimmed through this chapter on art, scan through it to find the answers to specific questions. Scan titles and subtitles of sections to determine which sections are likely to have the answers. Once you have located the appropriate section, move your eyes rapidly across the information to locate the answers to the questions that follow.

Fill in the Blank

1. In what section would you probably find a definition for "art"? _____

    According to the chapter, what does art include? _____

    _____

2. Where might you go to locate works of art? _____

    _____

    In what section did you find this information? _____

3. In what section would you probably find a discussion of whether art is more of an individual or social activity? _____

4. Do most artists in nonindustrialized societies work full time or part time at their artistic careers? _____

    In what section did you find the answer to this question? _____

5. What does the author of this chapter have to say about continuity and change? _____

    _____

Annotating

In Study Technique 1 (page 32), you learned how to underline or highlight information and then make notes to yourself in the margins. In the sample textbook chapter that follows, we have demonstrated these skills for you in the introductory section entitled "What Is Art"? Study this example and use it as a guide. Then practice your annotating skills on the section entitled "Art and Religion" (pages 467–468).

Outlining

In Study Technique 4 (page 117), we introduced you to outlining, an important study technique for organizing textbook information. Here we will illustrate the proper outlining format by giving you a sample outline for the section entitled "Locating Art." You can then practice outlining the sections entitled "Art and Individuality" and "The Work of Art" (pages 470–471 and 471–472).

In a formal outline, main, first-level headings are enumerated with Roman numerals (I, II, III, etc.), second-level headings are enumerated with capital letters (A, B, C, etc.), third-level headings are enumerated with Arabic numbers (1, 2, 3, etc.), and fourth-level headings are enumerated with lowercase letters (a, b, c, etc.). Each level contains information that is more specific than the level above it.

Another rule for making a formal outline is that you cannot have a single subsection: You must have either no subsections or at least two. So, for example, section I cannot have only subsection A; it must either have no subsections or at least subsections A and B.

It takes time to outline textbook material, but the process of outlining helps you to organize and learn the material. If you have done a good job with your outline, you should be able to study from it without having to return to the original textbook material.

Study the outline below for the portion of the textbook chapter "Locating Art." Compare the outline with the text.

I. What is art?
    A. Art often is in the eye of the beholder.
        1. Andy Warhol and others have made common items such as Brillo pads and soup cans into art.
        2. Other artists such as Christo have tried to make people and buildings into a form of artistic expression.
    B. Objects may become art by being placed in a museum—art by transformation or art by destination. For example, the Olivetti typewriter was transformed into art by placing it in a museum.
    C. There are unresolved questions.
        1. If something is mass-produced, can it be art?
            a. Prints are usually considered art.
            b. What about mass-produced works made in a factory?
        2. Does a book or movie become art when it receives a major award?
II. Who decides what is art?
    A. State societies—people have disagreements about what's art
    B. Non-Western societies
        1. We expect regular standards.
        2. We shouldn't necessarily apply our own standards.
        3. Religious sculpture is not always art—example, Kalabari art.
            a. Sculpture must represent its spirit.
            b. Carvers must base their sculpture on past models.
            c. Sculpture is done for religious purposes, not artistic ones.

Mapping

You were introduced to mapping in Study Technique 6 (page 157). Mapping is similar to outlining in that it includes main categories and subcategories. But in contrast to outlining, it is more visual and free-form. Look at the map based on the section entitled "Art, Society, and Culture" on pages 472–474. After studying the sample map, try to map the section entitled "Cultural Transmission." Your goal in mapping is to create a good study guide.

Comparison-Contrast Chart

In Study Technique 5 (page 151), you were introduced to the comparison-contrast chart. Some material lends itself nicely to a comparison-contrast chart, and this is the case with the section "I'll Get You, My Pretty, and Your Little R2" (pages 476–478). In this section the author discusses myths and legends by comparing and contrasting the movie *The Wizard of Oz* with the original *Star Wars* movie. Read this section and complete the chart on page 464. In the first column, list the categories to be compared and contrasted; in the second and third columns, record the information for each movie that pertains to the category. We have completed the first row for the first category as a sample, and we have listed two more categories to help you get started. You may or may not use all the rows, depending on how you establish your categories. When you finish completing the chart, answer the question that follows the chart.

Mapping: Art, Society, and Culture

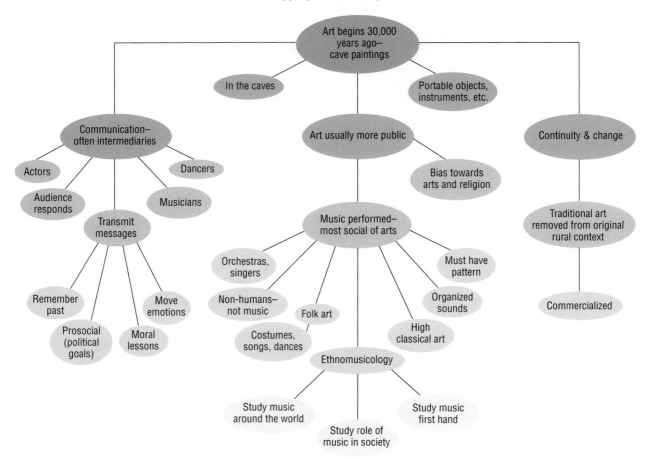

Comparison-Contrast Chart

Category	*Wizard of Oz*	*Star Wars*
Beginning of movie	Set in arid Kansas	Set in desert planet Tatooine
Names of main characters		
Relationship of characters with familiy		

Comparison-Contrast Chart (*continued*)

Category	*Wizard of Oz*	*Star Wars*

What similarities did you discover about these two movies through the process of filling in this chart? Give specific examples to substantiate your conclusions.

Venn Diagram

In Study Technique 9 (page 385), you learned to make a Venn diagram. Like the comparison-contrast chart, Venn diagrams are helpful for showing similarities and differences. As you will recall, the Venn diagram is made up of two interlocking circles. In the outside parts of the circles, you list the traits that are unique to each subject being discussed, while in the overlapping area you list the traits the two subjects share. The following textbook chapter discusses similarities and differences between Western and non-Western art. Complete the Venn diagram below with information from the textbook chapter. We have given you a few sample items to get you started.

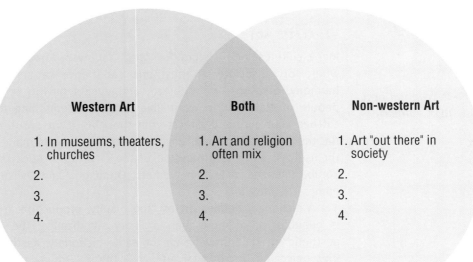

Western Art

1. In museums, theaters, churches
2.
3.
4.

Both

1. Art and religion often mix
2.
3.
4.

Non-western Art

1. Art "out there" in society
2.
3.
4.

Chapter 13

The Arts

by Conrad Phillip Kottack

"People in all cultures do seem to associate an aesthetic experience with certain objects and events."

Overview

Is art, like religion, a cultural universal? People in all cultures do seem to associate an aesthetic experience with certain objects and events. Experiencing art involves feelings as well as appreciation of form. The arts, sometimes called "expressive culture," include the visual arts, literature, music, and theater arts.

Students of non-Western art have been criticized for ignoring individual artists, and for focusing too much on the social nature and context of art. Many non-Western societies do recognize the achievements of individual artists. Community standards judge the completeness and mastery displayed in a work of art. Standards may be maintained informally in society, or by specialists, such as art critics.

Folk art, music, and lore refer to the expressive culture of ordinary, usually rural, people. The arts are part of culture, and aesthetic judgments depend, at least to an extent, on cultural background. Growing acceptance of the anthropological definition of culture has helped broaden the study of the humanities from fine art and elite art to popular and folk art and the creative expressions of the masses and of many peoples. Myths, legends, tales, and storytelling play important roles in transmitting culture and preserving traditions.

The arts go on changing, although certain art forms have survived for thousands of years. In today's world, a huge "arts and leisure" industry links Western and non-Western art forms in an international network with both aesthetic and commercial dimensions.

WHAT IS ART?

Def.
Art—is beautiful or more than ordinary

Many cultures lack a word for "art." Yet even without such a word, people everywhere do associate an aesthetic experience—a sense of beauty, appreciation, harmony, pleasure—with objects and events having certain qualities. The Bamana people of Mali have a word (like "art") for something that attracts your attention, catches your eye, and directs your thoughts (Ezra 1986). Among the Yoruba of Nigeria, the word for art, *ona,* encompasses the designs made on objects, the art objects themselves, and the profession of the creators of such patterns and works. For two Yoruba lineages of leather workers, Otunisona and Osiisona, the suffix *-ona* in their names denotes art.

Def.
Aesthetics— mind, emotion, beauty

A dictionary defines **art** as "the quality, production, expression, or realm of what is beautiful or of more than ordinary significance; the class of objects subject to aesthetic criteria." Drawing on the same dictionary, **aesthetics** involves ". . . the qualities perceived in works of art . . . ; the . . . mind and emotions in relation to the sense of beauty." However, it is possible for a work of art to attract our attention, direct our thoughts, and have more than ordinary significance without being judged as beautiful by most people who experience that work. Pablo Picasso's *Guernica,*

Copyright © 2005 by The McGraw-Hill Companies, Inc.

a famous painting of the Spanish Civil War, comes to mind as a scene that, <u>while not beautiful, is indisputably moving, and thus a work of art</u>.

George Mills (1971) notes that, in many cultures, the role of art lover lacks definition because art is not viewed as a separate activity. But this doesn't stop individuals from being moved by objects and events in a way that we would call aesthetic. Our own society does provide a fairly well-defined role for the connoisseur and collector of the arts, as well as a sanctuary, the museum, into which such people may occasionally retreat with their refined tastes.

M.I.

"Arts"—visual, music, lit., theater

<u>"The **arts"** include the visual arts, literature (written and oral), music, and theater arts</u>. These manifestations of human creativity are sometimes called **expressive culture.** <u>People express themselves creatively</u> in dance, music, song, painting, sculpture, pottery, cloth, storytelling, verse, prose, drama, and comedy.

This chapter will not attempt to do a systematic survey of all the arts, or even their major subdivisions. Rather, the approach will be to examine topics and issues that apply to expressive culture generally. "Art" will be used to encompass all the arts, not just the visual ones. In other words, the observations to be made about "art" are generally intended to apply to music and narratives as well as to painting and sculpture.

<u>That which is aesthetically pleasing is perceived with the senses.</u> Usually, when we think of art, we have in mind something that can be seen or heard. But others might define art more broadly to include things that can be smelled (<u>scents, fragrances</u>), tasted (recipes), or touched (<u>cloth textures</u>). How enduring must art be? Visual works and written works, including musical compositions, may last for centuries. <u>Can a single noteworthy event</u>, such as a feast, which is not in the least eternal, except in memory, <u>be a work of art?</u>

Art and Religion

Some of the issues raised in the discussion of religion also apply to art. Definitions of both art and religion mention the "more than ordinary" or the "extraordinary." Religious scholars may distinguish between the sacred (religious) and the profane (secular). Similarly, art scholars may distinguish between the artistic and the ordinary.

If we adopt a special attitude or demeanor when confronting a sacred object, do we display something similar when experiencing a work of art? According to the anthropologist Jacques Maquet (1986), an artwork is something that stimulates and sustains contemplation. It compels attention and reflection. Maquet stresses the importance of the object's form in producing such artistic contemplation. But other scholars stress feeling and meaning in addition to form. The experience of art involves feeling, such as being moved, as well as appreciation of form, such as balance or harmony.

Such an artistic attitude can be combined with and used to bolster a religious attitude. Much art has been done in association with religion. Many of the high points of Western art and music had religious inspiration, or were done in the service of religion, as a visit to a church or a large museum will surely illustrate. Bach and Handel are as well known for their church music as Michelangelo is for his religious painting and sculpture. The buildings (churches and cathedrals) in which religious music is played and in which visual art is displayed may themselves be works of art. Some of the major architectural achievements of Western art are religious structures. Examples include the Amiens, Chartres, and Notre Dame cathedrals in France.

Art may be created, performed, or displayed outdoors in public, or in special indoor settings, such as a theater, concert hall, or museum. Just as churches demarcate religion, museums and theaters set art off from the ordinary world, making it special, while inviting spectators in. Buildings dedicated to the arts help create the

This photo was taken in Phnom Penh, Cambodia, in 1988. On the grounds of a Buddhist temple, artisans make religious artifacts. We see a young man carving a Buddha, along with several completed Buddha statues.

© Philip Jones-Griffiths/Magnum Photos

artistic atmosphere. Architecture may accentuate the setting as a place for works of art to be presented.

The settings of rites and ceremonies, and of art, may be temporary or permanent. State societies have permanent religious structures: churches and temples. So, too, may state societies have buildings and structures dedicated to the arts. Nonstate societies tend to lack such permanently demarcated settings. Both art and religion are more "out there" in society. Still, in bands and tribes, religious settings can be created without churches. Similarly, an artistic atmosphere can be created without museums. At particular times of the year, ordinary space can be set aside for a visual art display or a musical performance. Such special occasions parallel the times set aside for religious ceremonies. In fact, in tribal performances, the arts and religion often mix. For example, masked and costumed performers may imitate spirits. Rites of passage often feature special music, dance, song, bodily adornment, and other manifestations of expressive culture.

In any society, art is produced for its aesthetic value as well as for religious purposes. According to Schildkrout and Keim (1990), non-Western art is usually, but wrongly, assumed to have some kind of connection to ritual. Non-Western art may be, but isn't always, linked with religion. Westerners have trouble accepting the idea that non-Western societies have art for arts' sake just as Western societies do. There has been a tendency for Westerners to ignore the individuality of non-Western artists and their interest in creative expression. According to Isidore Okpewho (1977), an oral literature specialist, scholars have tended to see religion in all traditional African arts. Even when acting in the service of religion, there is room for individual creative expression. In the oral arts, for example, the audience is much more interested in the delivery and performance of the artist than in the particular god for whom the performer may be speaking.

Locating Art

Aesthetic value is one way of distinguishing art. Another way is to consider placement. The special places where we find art include museums, concert halls, opera houses, and theaters. If something is displayed in a museum, or in another socially accepted artistic setting, someone at least must think it's art. But decisions about what to admit as a work of art may be political and controversial. In our own society, museums often have to balance concern over community standards with a wish to be as creative and innovative as the artists and works they display. Although tribal societies typically lack museums, they may maintain special areas where artistic expression takes place. One example, discussed in the section entitled "The Artistic Career," is the separate space in which ornamental burial poles are manufactured among the Tiwi of North Australia.

Will we know art if we see it? Art has been defined as involving that which is beautiful and of more than ordinary significance. But isn't beauty in the eye of the beholder? Don't reactions to art differ among spectators? And, if there can be secular ritual, can there also be ordinary art? The boundary between what's art and what's not is blurred. The American artist Andy Warhol is famous for transforming Campbell's soup cans, Brillo pads, and images of Marilyn Monroe into art. Many recent artists, such as Christo (see the photo at the beginning of this chapter) have tried to erase the distinction between art and ordinary life by converting the everyday into a work of art.

If something is mass-produced or industrially modified, can it be art? Prints made as part of a series may certainly be considered art. Sculptures that are created in clay, then fired with molten metal, such as bronze, at a foundry, are also art. But how does one know if a film is art? Is *Star Wars* art? How about *Citizen Kane?* When a book wins a National Book Award, is it immediately elevated to the status of art? What kinds of prizes make art? Objects never intended as art, such as an Olivetti typewriter, may be transformed into art by being placed in a museum, such as

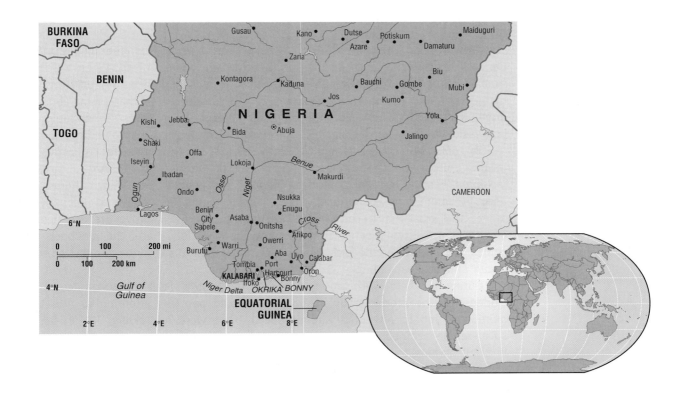

New York's Museum of Modern Art. Jacques Maquet (1986) distinguishes such "art by transformation" from art created and intended to be art, which he calls "art by destination."

In state societies, we have come to rely on critics, judges, and experts to tell us what's art and what isn't. A recent play titled *Art* is about conflict that arises among three friends when one of them buys an all-white painting. They disagree, as people often do, about the definition and value of a work of art. Such variation in art appreciation is especially common in contemporary society, with its professional artists and critics and great cultural diversity. We'd expect more uniform standards and agreement in less-diverse, less-stratified societies.

To be culturally relativistic, we need to avoid applying our own standards about what art is to the products of other cultures. Sculpture is art, right? Not necessarily. Previously, we challenged the view that non-Western art always has some kind of connection to religion. The Kalabari case to be discussed now makes the opposite point: that religious sculpture is not always art.

Among the Kalabari of southern Nigeria, wooden sculptures are not carved for aesthetic reasons, but to serve as "houses" for spirits (Horton 1963). These sculptures are used to control the spirits of Kalabari religion. The Kalabari place such a carving, and thus localize a spirit, in a cult house into which the spirit is invited. Here, sculpture is done not for art's sake but as a means of manipulating spiritual forces. The Kalabari do have standards for the carvings, but beauty isn't one of them. A sculpture must be sufficiently complete to represent its spirit. Carvings judged too crude are rejected by cult members. Also, carvers must base their work on past models. Particular spirits have particular images associated with them. It's considered dangerous to produce a carving that deviates too much from a previous image of the spirit or that resembles another spirit. Offended spirits may retaliate. As long as they observe these standards of completeness and established images, carvers are free to express themselves. But these images are considered repulsive rather than beautiful. And they are not manufactured for artistic but for religious reasons. For these reasons, they probably should not be classified as art.

Art and Individuality

Those who work with non-Western art have been criticized for ignoring the individual and focusing too much on the social nature and context of art. When art objects from Africa or Papua New Guinea are displayed in museums, generally only the name of the tribe and of the Western donor are given, rather than that of the individual artist. It's as though skilled individuals don't exist in non-Western societies. The impression is that art is collectively produced. Sometimes it is; sometimes it isn't.

To some extent, there *is* more collective production in non-Western societies than in the United States and Canada. According to Hackett (1996), African artworks (sculpted figures, textiles, paintings, or pots) are generally enjoyed, critiqued, and used by communities or groups, rather than being the prerogative of the individual alone. The artist may receive more feedback during the creative process than the individual artist typically encounters in our own society. Here, the feedback often comes too late, after the product is complete, rather than during production, when it can still be changed.

During his field work among Nigeria's Tiv people, Paul Bohannan (1971) concluded that the proper study of art there should pay less attention to artists and more attention to art critics and products. There were few skilled Tiv artists, and such people avoided doing their art publicly. However, mediocre artists would work in public, where they routinely got comments from onlookers (critics). Based on critical suggestions, an artist often changed a design, such as a carving, in progress.

There was yet another way in which Tiv artists worked socially rather than individually. Sometimes, when an artist put his work aside, someone else would pick it up and start working on it. The Tiv clearly didn't recognize the same kind of connection between individuals and their art that we do. According to Bohannan, every Tiv was free to know what he liked and to try to make it if he could. If not, one or more of his fellows might help him out.

In Western societies, artists of many sorts (e.g., painters, sculptors, actors, classical and rock musicians) have reputations for being iconoclastic and antisocial. Social acceptance may be more important in the societies anthropologists have traditionally studied. Still, there are well-known individual artists in non-Western societies. They are recognized as such by other community members and perhaps by outsiders as well. Their artistic labor may even be conscripted for special displays and performances, including ceremonies, or palace arts and events.

To what extent can a work of art stand apart from its artist? Philosophers of art commonly regard works of art as autonomous entities, independent of their creators (Haapala 1998). Haapala argues the contrary, that artists and their works are inseparable. "By creating works of art a person creates an artistic identity for himself. He creates himself quite literally into the pieces he puts into his art. He exists in the works he has created." In this view, Picasso created many Picassos, and exists in and through those works of art.

Sometimes little is known or recognized about the individual artist responsible for an enduring artwork. We are more likely to know the name of the recording artist than of the writer of the songs we most commonly remember and perhaps sing. Sometimes we fail to acknowledge art individually because the artwork was collectively created. To whom should we attribute a pyramid or a cathedral? Should it be the architect, the ruler or leader who commissioned the work, or the master builder who implemented the design? A thing of beauty may be a joy forever even if and when we do not credit its creator(s).

The Work of Art

Some may see art as a form of expressive freedom, as giving free range to the imagination and the human need to create or to be playful. But consider the word *opera*. It is the plural of *opus,* which means a work. For the artist, at least, art is work, albeit creative work. In nonstate societies, artists may have to hunt, gather, herd, fish, or farm in order to eat, but they still manage to find time to work on their art. In state societies, at least, artists have been defined as specialists—professionals who have chosen careers as artists, musicians, writers, or actors. If they manage to support themselves from their art, they may be full-time professionals. If not, they do their art part time, while earning a living from another activity. Sometimes artists associate in professional groups such as medieval guilds or contemporary unions. Actors Equity in New York, a labor union, is a modern guild, designed to protect the interests of its artist members.

Just how much work is needed to make a work of art? In the early days of French impressionism, many experts viewed the paintings of Claude Monet and his colleagues as too sketchy and spontaneous to be true art. Established artists and critics were accustomed to more formal and classic studio styles. The French impressionists got their name from their sketches—*impressions*—of natural and social settings. They took advantage of technological innovations, particularly the availability of oil paints in tubes, to take their palettes, easels, and canvases into the field. There they captured the images of changing light and color that hang today in so many museums, where they are now fully recognized as art. But before Impressionism became an officially recognized "school" of art, its works were perceived by its critics as crude and unfinished. In terms of community standards, the first impressionist paintings were evaluated as harshly as were the overly crude and incomplete Kalibari wood carvings of spirits, as discussed previously.

To what extent does the artist—or society—make the decision about completeness? For familiar genres, such as painting or music, societies tend to have standards by which they judge whether an artwork is complete or fully realized. Most people would doubt, for instance, that an all-white painting could be a work of art. Standards may be maintained informally in society, or by specialists, such as art critics. It may be difficult for unorthodox or renegade artists to innovate. But, like the impressionists, they may eventually succeed. Some societies tend to reward conformity, an artist's skill with traditional models and techniques. Others encourage breaks with the past, innovation.

ART, SOCIETY, AND CULTURE

Art goes back at least 30,000 years, to the Upper Paleolithic period in Western Europe. Cave paintings, the best-known examples of Upper Paleolithic art, were, in fact, separated from ordinary life and everyday social space. Those images were

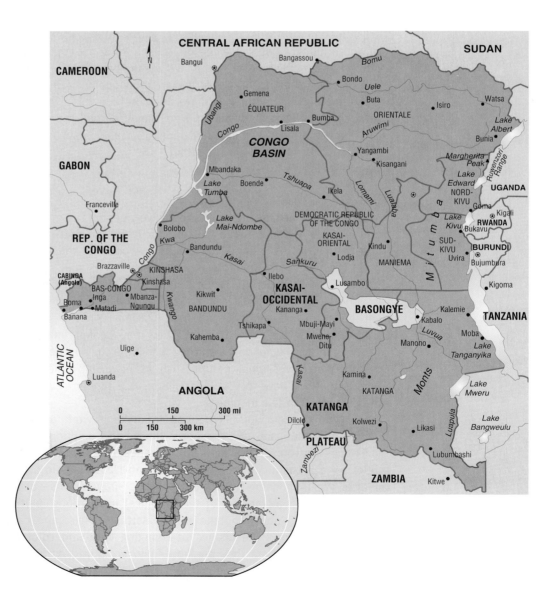

painted in true caves, located deep in the bowels of the earth. They may have been painted as part of some kind of rite of passage, involving retreat from society. Portable art objects carved in bone and ivory, along with musical whistles and flutes, also confirm artistic expression during the Upper Paleolithic.

Art is usually more public than the cave paintings. Typically, it is exhibited, evaluated, performed, and appreciated in society. It has spectators or audiences. It isn't just for the artist.

Ethnomusicology is the comparative study of the musics of the world and of music as an aspect of culture and society. The field of ethnomusicology thus unites music and anthropology. The music side involves the study and analysis of the music itself and the instruments used to create it. The anthropology side views music as a way to explore a culture, to determine the role—historic and contemporary—that music plays in that society, and the specific social and cultural features that influence how music is created and performed.

Ethnomusicology studies non-Western music, traditional and folk music, even contemporary popular music from a cultural perspective. To do this there has to be field work—firsthand study of particular forms of music, their social functions and cultural meanings, within particular societies. Ethnomusicologists talk with local musicians, make recordings in the field, and learn about the place of musical instruments, performances, and performers in a given society (Kirman 1997). Nowadays, given globalization, diverse cultures and musical styles easily meet and mix. Music that draws on a wide range of cultural instruments and styles is called World Fusion, World Beat, or World Music—another topic within contemporary ethnomusicology.

Music, which is often performed in groups, would seem to be among the most social of the arts. Even master pianists and violinists are frequently accompanied by orchestras or singers. Alan Merriam (1971) describes how the Basongye people of the Kasai province of Congo use three features to distinguish between music and other sounds, which are classified as "noise." First, music always involves humans. Sounds emanating from nonhuman creatures, such as birds and animals, are not music. Second, musical sounds must be organized. A single tap on the drum isn't music, but drummers playing together in a pattern is. Third, music must continue. Even if several drums are struck together simultaneously, it isn't music. They must go on playing to establish some kind of sound pattern. For the Basongye, then, music is inherently cultural (distinctly human) and social (dependent on cooperation).

Originally coined for European peasants, **"folk"** art, music, and lore refer to the expressive culture of ordinary people, as contrasted with the "high" art or "classic" art of the European elites. When European folk music is performed, the combination of costumes, music, and often song and dance is supposed to say something about local culture and about tradition. Tourists and other outsiders often perceive rural and "folk" life mainly in terms of such performances. And community residents themselves often use such performances to display and enact their local culture and traditions for outsiders.

Art says something about continuity and change. Art can stand for tradition, even when traditional art is removed from its original (rural) context. The creative products and images of folk, rural, and non-Western cultures are increasingly spread—and commercialized—by the media and tourism. A result is that many Westerners have come to think of "culture" in terms of colorful customs, music, dancing, and adornments—clothing, jewelry, and hairstyles.

A bias toward the arts and religion, rather than more mundane, less photogenic, economic and social tasks, shows up on TV's Discovery Channel, and even in many anthropological films. Many ethnographic films start off with music, often drum beats: "Bonga, bonga, bonga, bonga. Here in (supply place name), the people are very religious." We see in such presentations the previously critiqued assumption that the arts of nonindustrial societies usually have a link with religion. The (usually unintended) message is that non-Western peoples spend much of their time wearing colorful clothes, singing, dancing, and practicing religious rituals. Taken to an extreme, such images portray culture as recreational and ultimately unserious, rather than as something that ordinary people live every day of their lives—not just when they have festivals.

Art also functions in society as a form of communication between artist and community or audience. Sometimes, however, there are intermediaries between the artist and the audience. Actors, for example, are artists who translate the works and ideas of other artists (writers and directors) into the performances that audiences see and appreciate. Musicians play compositions of other people along with music they themselves have composed. Using music written by others, choreographers plan and direct patterns of dance, which dancers then execute for audiences.

How does art communicate? We need to know what the artist intends to communicate and how the audience reacts. Often, the audience communicates right back to the artist. Live performers, for instance, get immediate feedback, as may writers and directors by viewing a performance of their own work. Artists expect at least some variation in reception. In contemporary societies, with increasing diversity in the audience, uniform reactions are rare. Contemporary artists, like businesspeople, are well aware that they have target audiences. Certain segments of the population are more likely to appreciate certain forms of art than other segments are.

Art can transmit several kinds of messages. It can convey a moral lesson or tell a cautionary tale. It can teach lessons the artist, or society, wants told. Like the rites that induce, then dispel, anxiety, the tension and resolution of drama can lead to **catharsis,** intense emotional release, in the audience. Art can move emotions, make us laugh, cry, feel up or down. Art appeals to the intellect as well as to the emotions. We may delight in a well-constructed, nicely balanced, well-realized work of art.

Art can be self-consciously prosocial. It can express community sentiment, with political goals, used to call attention to social issues. Often, art is meant to commemorate and to last. Like a ceremony, art may serve a mnemonic function, making people remember. Art may be designed to make people remember either individuals or events, such as the AIDS epidemic that has proved so lethal in many world areas.

What is art's social role? To what extent should art serve society? Should the arts reflect, or question, community standards? We've seen that art has entered the political arena. Today, no museum director can mount an exhibit without worrying that it will offend some politically organized segment of society. The United States has an ongoing battle between liberals and conservatives involving the National Endowment for the Arts. Artists have been criticized as aloof from society, as creating only for themselves and for elites, as out of touch with conventional and traditional aesthetic values, even as mocking the values of ordinary people.

The Cultural Transmission of the Arts

Because art is part of culture, appreciation of the arts depends on cultural background. Watch Japanese tourists in a Western art museum trying to interpret what they are seeing. Conversely, the form and meaning of a Japanese tea ceremony, or a demonstration of origami (Japanese paper folding), will be alien to a foreign observer. Appreciation for the arts must be learned. It is part of enculturation, as well as of more formal education. Robert Layton (1991) suggests that whatever universal principles of artistic expression may exist, they have been put into effect in a diversity of ways in different cultures.

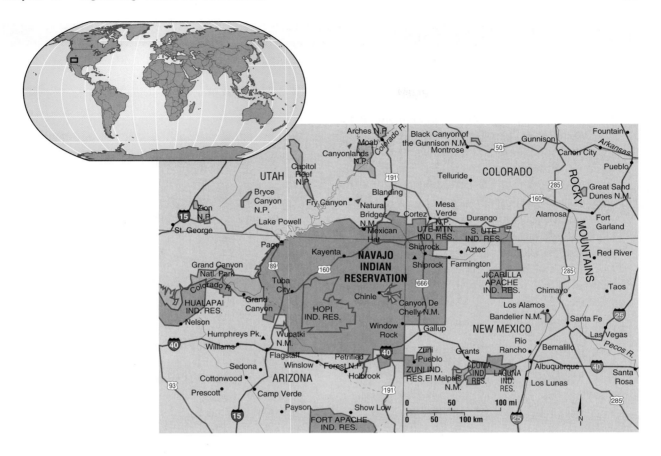

What is aesthetically pleasing depends to some extent on culture. Based on familiarity, music with certain tonalities and rhythm patterns will please some people and alienate others. In a study of Navajo music, McAllester (1954) found that it reflected the overall culture of that time in three main ways: First, individualism is a key Navajo cultural value. Thus, it's up to the individual to decide what to do with his or her property—whether it be physical property, knowledge, ideas, or songs. Second, McAllester found that a general Navajo conservatism also extended to music. The Navajo saw foreign music as dangerous and rejected it as not part of their culture. (This second point is no longer true; there are now Navajo rock bands.) Third, a general stress on proper form applied to music. There is, in Navajo beliefs, a right way to sing every kind of song.

People learn to listen to certain kinds of music and to appreciate particular art forms, just as they learn to hear and decipher a foreign language. Unlike Londoners and New Yorkers, Parisians don't flock to musicals. Despite its multiple French origins, even the musical *Les Miserables,* a huge hit in London, New York, and dozens of cities worldwide, bombed in Paris. Humor, too, a form of verbal art, depends on cultural background and setting. What's funny in one culture may not translate as funny in another. When a joke doesn't work, an American may say, "Well, you had to be there at the time." Jokes, like aesthetic judgments, depend on context.

At a smaller level of culture, certain artistic traditions may be transmitted in families. In Bali, for example, there are families of carvers, musicians, dancers, and mask makers. Among the Yoruba of Nigeria, two lineages of leather workers are entrusted with important bead embroidery works, such as for the king's crown and the bags and bracelets of priests. The arts, like other professions, often "run" in families. The Bachs, for example, produced not only Johann Sebastian, but several other noted composers and musicians.

Interesting Issues

I'll Get You, My Pretty, and Your Little R2

Myths, legends, and tales express cultural beliefs and values. Sometimes they offer hope, adventure, and pleasure. Sometimes, as cautionary tales, they warn against certain kinds of behavior. They also teach lessons that society wants taught. On encountering the word *myth,* most people probably think of stories about Greek, Roman, or Norse gods and heroes. However, all societies have myths. Their central characters need not be unreal, superhuman, or physically immortal. Such tales may be rooted in actual historical events.

> The popular notion that a "myth" is . . . "untrue"—indeed that its untruth is its defining characteristic—is not only naive but shows misunderstanding of its very nature. Its "scientific truth" or otherwise is irrelevant. A myth is a statement about society and man's place in it and the surrounding universe. (Middleton 1967, p. x)

Myths are hallowed stories that express fundamental cultural values. They are widely and recurrently told among, and have special meaning to, people who grow up in a particular culture. Myths may be set in the past, present, or future or in "fantasyland." Whether set in "real time" or fictional time, myths are always at least partly fictionalized.

Techniques that anthropologists have used to analyze myths and tales can be extended to two fantasy films that most of you have seen. *The Wizard of Oz* has been telecast annually for decades. The original *Star Wars* remains one of the most popular films of all time. Both are familiar and significant cultural products with obvious mythic qualities. The contributions of the French structuralist anthropologist Claude Lévi-Strauss (1967) and the neo-Freudian psychoanalyst Bruno Bettelheim (1975) to the study of myths and fairy tales permit the following analysis of visual fairy tales that contemporary Americans know well.

Examining the myths and tales of different cultures, Lévi-Strauss determined that one tale could be converted into another through a series of simple operations, for example, by doing the following:

1. Converting the positive element of a myth into its negative.

2. Reversing the order of the elements.

3. Replacing a male hero with a female hero.

4. Preserving or repeating certain key elements.

Through such operations, two apparently dissimilar myths can be shown to be variations on a common structure, that is, to be transformations of each other.

We'll see now that *Star Wars* is a systematic structural transformation of *The Wizard of Oz*. We may speculate about how many of the resemblances were conscious and how many simply reflect a process of enculturation that *Star Wars* writer and director George Lucas shares with other Americans.

The Wizard of Oz and Star Wars both begin in arid country, the first in Kansas and the second on the desert planet Tatooine (Table 13.1). *Star Wars* converts *The Wizard*'s female hero into a boy, Luke Skywalker. Fairy-tale heroes usually have short, common first names and second names that describe their origin or activity. Thus Luke, who travels aboard spaceships, is a Skywalker, while Dorothy Gale is swept off to Oz by a cyclone (a gale of wind). Dorothy leaves home with her dog, Toto, who is pursued by and has managed to escape from a woman who in Oz becomes the Wicked Witch of the West. Luke follows his "Two-Two" (R2D2), who is fleeing Darth Vader, the witch's structural equivalent.

Dorothy and Luke each starts out living with an uncle and an aunt. However, because of the gender change of the hero, the primary relationship is reversed and inverted. Thus, Dorothy's relationship with her aunt is primary, warm, and loving, whereas Luke's relationship with his uncle, though primary, is strained and distant. Aunt and uncle are in the tales for the same reason. They represent home (the nuclear family of orientation), which children (according to American culture norms) must eventually leave to make it on their own. As Bettelheim (1975) points out,

TABLE 13.1

Star Wars as a Structural Transformation of *The Wizard of Oz*

Star Wars	The Wizard of Oz
Male hero (Luke Skywalker)	Female hero (Dorothy Gale)
Arid Tatooine	Arid Kansas
Luke follows R2D2:	Dorothy follows Toto:
R2D2 flees Vader	Toto flees witch
Luke lives with uncle and aunt:	Dorothy lives with uncle and aunt:
Primary relationship with uncle	Primary relationship with aunt
(same sex as hero)	(same sex as hero)
Strained, distant relationship with uncle	Warm, close relationship with aunt
Tripartite division of same-sex parent:	Tripartite division of same-sex parent:
2 parts good, 1 part bad father	2 parts bad, 1 part good mother
Good father dead at beginning	Bad mother dead at beginning
Good father dead (?) at end	Bad mother dead at end
Bad father survives	Good mother survives
Relationship with parent of opposite sex	Relationship with parent of opposite sex
(Princess Leia Organa):	(Wizard of Oz):
Princess is unwilling captive	Wizard makes impossible demands
Needle	Broomstick
Princess is freed	Wizard turns out to be sham
Trio of companions:	Trio of companions:
Han Solo, C3PO, Chewbacca	Scarecrow, Tin Woodman, Cowardly Lion
Minor characters:	Minor characters:
Jawas	Munchkins
Sand People	Apple Trees
Stormtroopers	Flying Monkeys
Settings:	Settings:
Death Star	Witch's castle
Verdant Tikal (rebel base)	Emerald City
Conclusion:	Conclusion:
Luke uses magic to accomplish goal	Dorothy uses magic to accomplish goal
(destroy Death Star)	(return to Kansas)

fairy tales often disguise parents as uncle and aunt, and this establishes social distance. The child can deal with the hero's separation (in *The Wizard of Oz*) or the aunt's and uncle's deaths (in *Star Wars*) more easily than with the death of or separation from real parents. Furthermore, this permits the child's strong feelings toward his or her real parents to be represented in different, more central characters, such as the Wicked Witch of the West and Darth Vader.

Both films focus on the child's relationship with the parent of the same sex, dividing that parent into three parts. In *The Wizard,* the mother is split into two parts bad and one part good. They are the Wicked Witch of the East, dead at the beginning of the movie; the Wicked Witch of the West, dead at the end; and Glinda, the good mother, who survives. The original *Star Wars* reversed the proportion of good and bad, giving Luke a good father (his own), the Jedi knight who is proclaimed dead at the film's beginning. There is another good father, Ben Kenobi, who is ambiguously dead when the movie ends. Third is the evil father figure, Darth Vader. As the good-mother third survives *The Wizard of Oz,* the bad-father third lives on after *Star Wars,* to strike back in the sequel.

The child's relationship with the parent of the opposite sex also is represented in the two films. Dorothy's father figure is the Wizard of

Oz, an initially terrifying figure who later is proved to be a fake. Bettelheim notes that the typical fairy-tale father is disguised as a monster or giant. Or else, when preserved as a human, he is weak, distant, or ineffective. Dorothy counts on the wizard to save her but finds that he makes seemingly impossible demands and in the end is just an ordinary man. She succeeds on her own, no longer relying on a father who offers no more than she herself possesses.

In *Star Wars* (although emphatically not in the later films), Luke's mother figure is Princess Leia. Bettelheim notes that boys commonly fantasize their mothers to be unwilling captives of their fathers. Fairy tales often disguise mothers as princesses whose freedom the boy-hero must obtain. In graphic Freudian imagery, Darth Vader threatens Princess Leia with a needle the size of the witch's broomstick. By the end of the film, Luke has freed Leia and defeated Vader.

There are other striking parallels in the structure of the two films. Fairy-tale heroes often are accompanied on their adventures by secondary characters who personify the virtues needed in a successful quest. Such characters often come in threes. Dorothy takes along wisdom (the Scarecrow), love (the Tin Woodman), and courage (the Lion). *Star Wars* includes a structurally equivalent trio—Han Solo, C3PO, and Chewbacca—but their association with particular qualities isn't as precise. The minor characters are also structurally parallel: Munchkins and Jawas, Apple Trees and Sand People, Flying Monkeys and Stormtroopers. And compare settings—the witch's castle and the Death Star, the Emerald City and the rebel base. The endings are also parallel. Luke accomplishes his objective on his own, using the Force (mana, magical power). Dorothy's goal is to return to Kansas. She does that by tapping her shoes together and drawing on the Force in her ruby slippers.

All successful cultural products blend old and new, drawing on familiar themes. They may rearrange them in novel ways and thus win a lasting place in the imaginations of the culture that creates or accepts them. *Star Wars* successfully used old cultural themes in novel ways. It did that by drawing on the American fairy tale, one that had been available in book form since the turn of the 20th century.

Anthropology has extended the definition of "cultured" well beyond the elitist meaning of "high" art and culture. For anthropologists, everyone acquires culture through enculturation. In academia, growing acceptance of the anthropological definition of culture has helped broaden the study of the humanities from fine art and elite art to popular and folk art and the creative expressions of the masses and of many cultures.

In many societies, myths, legends, tales, and the art of storytelling play important roles in the transmission of culture and the preservation of tradition. In the absence of writing, oral traditions may preserve details of history and genealogy, as in many parts of West Africa. Art forms often go together. For example, music and storytelling may be combined for drama and emphasis, much as they are in films and theater.

At what age do children start learning the arts? In some cultures, they start early. Sometimes children's participation in arts or performance, including sports, exemplifies forced enculturation. It may be pushed by parents rather than by kids themselves. In the United States, performance, usually associated with schools, has a strong social, and usually competitive, component. Kids perform with their peers. In the process, they learn to compete, whether for a first place finish in a sports event or a first chair in the school orchestra or band.

The Artistic Career

In nonindustrial societies, artists tend to be part-time specialists. In states, there are more ways for artists to practice their craft full time. The number of positions in "arts and leisure" has mushroomed in contemporary societies, especially in North

America. Many non-Western societies also offer career tracks in the arts: For example, a child born into a particular family or lineage may discover that he or she is destined for a career in leather working or weaving. Some societies are noted for particular arts, such as dance, wood carving, or weaving.

An artistic career also may involve some kind of a calling. Individuals may discover they have a particular talent and find an environment in which that talent is nourished. Separate career paths for artists usually involve special training and apprenticeship. Such paths are more likely in a complex society, where there are many separate career tracks, than in band or tribal societies, where expressive culture is less formally separated from daily life.

Artists need support if they are to devote full time to creative activity. They find support in their families or lineages if there is specialization in the arts involving kin groups. State societies often have patrons of the arts. Usually members of the elite class, patrons offer various kinds of support to aspiring and talented artists, such as court and palace painters, musicians, or sculptors. In some cases, an artistic career may entail a lifetime of dedication to religious art.

Goodal and Koss (1971) describe the manufacture of ornamental burial poles among the Tiwi of North Australia. Temporary separation and detachment from other social roles allowed burial pole artists to devote themselves to their work. The pole artists were ceremonially commissioned as such after a death. They were granted temporary freedom from the daily food quest. Other community members agreed to serve as their patrons. They supplied the artists with hard-to-get materials needed for their work. The burial pole artists were sequestered in a work area near the grave. That area was taboo to everyone else.

The arts are usually defined as neither practical nor ordinary. They rely on talent, which is individual, but which must be channeled and shaped in socially approved directions. Inevitably, artistic talent and production pull the artist away from the practical need to make a living. The issue of how to support artists and the arts arises again and again. We've all heard the phrase "struggling artist." But how should society support the arts? If there is state or religious support, something is typically expected in return. There is inevitably some limitation of the artist's "free" expression. Patronage and sponsorship also may result in the creation of artworks that are removed from public display. Art commissioned for elites is often displayed only in their homes, perhaps finding its way into museums after their deaths. Church-commissioned art may be closer to the people.

Continuity and Change

The arts go on changing, although certain art forms have survived for thousands of years. The Upper Paleolithic cave art that has survived 30,000 years was itself a highly developed manifestation of human creativity and symbolism, with an undoubtedly long evolutionary history. Monumental architecture along with sculpture, reliefs, ornamental pottery, and written music, literature, and drama have survived from early civilizations.

Countries and cultures are known for particular contributions, including art. The Balinese are known for dance; the Navajo for sand paintings, jewelry, and weaving; and the French for making cuisine an art form. We still read Greek tragedies and comedies in college, as we also read Shakespeare and Milton, and view the works of Michelangelo. Greek theater is among the most enduring of the arts. The words of Aeschylus, Sophocles, Euripides, and Aristophanes have been captured in writing and live on. Who knows how many great preliterate creations and performances have been lost?

Classic Greek theater survives throughout the world. It is read in college courses, seen in the movies, and performed live on stages from Athens to New York. In today's world, the dramatic arts are part of a huge "arts and leisure" industry, which links Western and non-Western art forms in an international network that has both aesthetic and commercial dimensions. For example, non-Western musical traditions and instruments don't function apart from the modern world system. We've seen that local musicians perform for outsiders, including tourists who increasingly visit their villages. And "tribal" instruments such as didgeridoos are now exported worldwide. At least one store in Amsterdam, the Netherlands, specializes in didgeridoos, the only item it carries. Dozens of stores in any world capital hawk "traditional" arts, including musical instruments, from a hundred Third World countries.

We've seen that the arts typically draw in multiple media. Given the richness of today's media world, multimedia are even more marked. As ingredients and flavors from all over the world are combined in modern cuisine, so, too, are elements from many cultures and epochs woven into contemporary art and performance.

Our culture values change, experimentation, innovation, and novelty. But creativity also may be based on tradition. The Navajo, remember, can be at once individualistic, conservative, and attentive to proper form. In some cases and cultures, it's not necessary for artists to be innovative as they are being creative. Creativity can be expressed in variations on a traditional form. We see an example of this in "Interesting Issues", in which *Star Wars,* despite its specific story and innovative special effects, is shown to share its narrative structure with a previous film and fairy tale. It isn't always necessary for artists, in their work, to make a statement separating themselves from the past. Often, artists pay fealty to the past, associating with and building on, rather than rejecting, the work of their predecessors.

Summary

1. Even if they lack a word for "art," people everywhere do associate an aesthetic experience with objects and events having certain qualities. The arts, sometimes called "expressive culture," include the visual arts, literature (written and oral), music, and theater arts. Some issues raised about religion also apply to art. If we adopt a special attitude or demeanor when confronting a sacred object, do we display something similar with art? Much art has been done in association with religion. In tribal performances, the arts and religion often mix. But non-Western art isn't always linked to religion.

2. The special places where we find art include museums, concert halls, opera houses, and theaters. However, the boundary between what's art and what's not may be blurred. Variation in art appreciation is especially common in contemporary society, with its professional artists and critics and great cultural diversity.

3. Those who work with non-Western art have been criticized for ignoring individual artists and for focusing too much on the social context and collective artistic production. Art is work, albeit creative work. In state societies, some people manage to support themselves as full-time artists. In nonstates artists are normally part time. Community standards judge the mastery and completion displayed in a work of art. Typically, the arts are exhibited, evaluated, performed, and appreciated in society. Music, which is often performed in groups, is among the most social of the arts. "Folk" art, music, and lore refer to the expressive culture of ordinary, usually rural, people.

4. Art can stand for tradition, even when traditional art is removed from its original context. Art can express community sentiment, with political goals, used to call attention to social issues. Often, art is meant to commemorate and to

last. Growing acceptance of the anthropological definition of culture has guided the humanities beyond fine art, elite art, and Western art to the creative expressions of the masses and of many cultures. Myths, legends, tales, and the art of storytelling often play important roles in the transmission of culture. Many societies offer career tracks in the arts; a child born into a particular family or lineage may discover that he or she is destined for a career in leather working or weaving.

5. The arts go on changing, although certain art forms have survived for thousands of years. Countries and cultures are known for particular contributions. Today, a huge "arts and leisure" industry links Western and non-Western art forms in an international network with both aesthetic and commercial dimensions.

Critical Thinking Questions

1. Think of something visual that you consider to be art, but whose status as art is debatable. How would you convince someone else that it is art? What kinds of arguments against your position would you expect to hear?

2. Think of a musical composition or performance you consider to be art, but whose status as such is debatable. How would you convince someone else that it is art? What kinds of arguments against your position would you expect to hear?

3. Where did you last witness art? In what kind of a setting was it? Did people go there to appreciate the arts, or for some other reason?

4. Is *Star Wars* art? If so, what kind of art? How would you analyze it as art?

5. Based on your own experience, how may the arts be used to buttress religion?

6. Can you think of a political dispute involving art or the arts? What were the different positions being debated?

7. Should society support the arts? Why or why not? If so, how?

Internet Exercises

1. *Body Art:* Visit the National Museum of Natural History's online exhibit of "Canela body adornment," http://www.nmnh.si.edu/naa/canela/canela1.htm. Read all three pages of the exhibit and answer the questions below:

   a. In this example, how interrelated are art and world view? How is art being used by the Canela?

   b. What individuals among the Canela get their ears pierced, and what does it signify? Who participates in the piercing? How does this practice compare to ear piercing in Western society?

   c. Cultures can change through time. What kinds of changes have occurred in the Canela practices of ear piercing since the 1950s? In the same way, what kinds of changes have occurred in ear piercing practices in Western society? What do these changes signify?

2. *Comparing Art:* Go to the Metropolitan Museum of Art's Collection page, www.metmuseum.org/collections/index.asp and browse their collections of Egyptian Art, www.metmuseum.org/collections/department.asp?dep=10, European

Paintings, www.metmuseum.org/collections/department.asp?dep=11, and Modern Art, www.metmuseum.org/collections/department.asp?dep=21. For each of these collections, address the following questions:

a. By whom is this art produced, and for whom is it produced?

b. For what purpose is this art being produced (e.g., religious, aesthetic, political, monetary)?

c. What themes and subjects are portrayed in the art?

d. By just looking at the art, what can you learn about the culture that produced it?

From Conrad Phillip Kottack in *Cultural Anthropology*, 9th ed., New York: McGraw-Hill, 2002, pp. 334–356. Copyright © 2002 McGraw-Hill. Reprinted by permission of The McGraw-Hill Companies, Inc.

TEST-TAKING TIP
Preparing for Standardized Tests

At some point, many of you are likely to have to take standardized exams like the SAT, ACT, and GRE. Most standardized exams require you to read passages of varying lengths and then answer questions about the passages. Many of the passages come from literary works, textbook selections, essays, news magazines, and documents similar to those you have been reading in *The Art of Critical Reading*. As with most exams, preparation for standardized exams is the key to doing well. Here are some tips:

1. Familiarize yourself with the types of directions you're likely to encounter.

2. Familiarize yourself with the types of questions that will be on the exam.

3. If possible, take a practice exam or answer sample questions allotting yourself the same amount of time you will have during the actual test.

4. Consider the scoring system. Should you guess? Most experts say that if you can eliminate at least two of the four choices, it's in your best interest to make an educated guess if you don't know the answer.

5. Experiment with the following methods for reading a passage. Determine which method works best for you before taking the big exam.

- Read the passage carefully and then answer the questions.

        OR

- Skim the passage, glance at the questions, reread the passage carefully, and then answer the questions.

        OR

- Read the questions first, then read the passage carefully, and finally answer the questions.

Part 6

Vocabulary

Vocabulary Units

The Great Figure
Among the rain
and lights
I saw the figure 5
in gold
on a red
fire truck
moving
tense
unheeded
to gong clangs
siren howls
and wheels rumbling
through the
dark city

William Carlos Williams,
"The Great Figure" in
*The Collected Poems of
William Carlos Williams:
1909–1939,* Volume I,
Litz & MacGowan, eds.
Copyright © 1938 by New
Directions Publishing Corp.
Reprinted by permission of
New Directions Publishing
Corp.

**I Saw the Figure 5
in Gold** (1928)*
BY CHARLES DEMUTH

The Metropolitan Museum of Art, Alfred Stieglitz Collection, 1949. (49.59.1)

*To see this work of art in
color, turn to the color
insert following page 260.

The title of the painting is taken from the poem above by William Carlos
Williams, a friend of the artist.

1 Can you find three places where the friend's name (or initials) are
incorporated into the painting?

2 How many times do you see the number 5 repeated in the painting?

3 The red shape represents the fire truck. Does the repetition of the
number 5 help to give the fire truck a feeling of moving quickly down
a city street? What other elements in the painting add to the feeling of
movement?

4 How closely did the artist come to interpreting the description of the
fire truck in the poem?

Vocabulary Units 1–8

Each of the following eight units will introduce you to important prefixes, suffixes, and root words, and give you vocabulary words using these word parts. Each unit will draw on what you learned in the previous units. You will find an exercise and a crossword puzzle at the end of each unit to reinforce your learning.

Unit 1

The following prefixes all indicate numbers:

uni—one	qua(d)—four	sept—seven
mono—one	tetra—four	hept—seven
bi—two	quint—five	oct—eight
di—two	pent—five	
du(o)—two		nov—nine
	hex—six	
tri—three	sex—six	dec, dek—ten

unify	to make or become a single unit.
unicameral	-*cam*- means "chamber." *Unicameral* is a legislative body made up of only one house or chamber.
bicameral	having two groups in the lawmaking body. The *bicameral* U.S. Congress is made up of the Senate and the House of Representatives.
univalve	having a shell composed of a single piece, such as a snail.
bivalve	having a shell composed of two parts hinged together, such as a clam or oyster.
monochromatic	of or pertaining to only one color, as in *monochromatic* pottery. It was obvious that Regis, who wore a gray tie, gray shirt, and gray slacks, preferred a *monochromatic* style of dress.
monogram	initials of a person's name in a design, such as are used on articles of clothing or stationery.
monolith	-*lith* means "stone," so a monolith is a single block or piece of stone of considerable size, sometimes carved into a column or large statue. The sphinx of Egypt is a *monolith*.
monotonous	sounded or uttered in one unvarying tone; lacking in variety. At the graduation ceremony, many were displeased with the keynote speaker because of his *monotonous* speaking style.
monocle	an eyeglass for one eye.
monorail	a single rail serving as a track for cars. Taking the *monorail* at Disneyland adds to the excitement.
monosyllabic	having only one syllable like "what" or "how."
biracial	consisting of or representing members of two separate races. Tiger Woods, whose mother is Asian and father is black, is *biracial*.
bipartisan	made up of or supported by two political parties. Support for education is *bipartisan*.

bifocals	eyeglasses in which each lens has two parts, one for reading and seeing nearby objects and the other for seeing things further away. Benjamin Franklin invented *bifocals* in 1784.
bisect	*-sect* means "to cut," so *bisect* means to cut or divide into two equal parts.
bigamy	the act of marrying one person while already legally married to another.
dichotomy	division into two parts or kinds. *-tomy* is derived from the Latin word *temnien*, meaning "to cut." In the United States, there is a *dichotomy* of viewpoints on the issue of the death penalty.
duplex	a house having separate apartments side by side.
duplicate	to make an exact copy of; to double.
triplicate	to make three copies of; to triple.
triple	made up of three. He ordered a *triple* cone with vanilla, strawberry, and chocolate. A hit in baseball that lets the batter get to third base.
triannual	done, occurring, or issued three times a year, as in a *triannual* magazine.
trilogy	a set of three plays, novels, or other creative works, which form a group, although each is a complete work on its own. *Star Wars*, *The Empire Strikes Back*, and *The Return of the Jedi* make up a *trilogy*.
quadrangle	an open area surrounded by buildings on all four sides such as is often seen on college campuses; a plane having four sides.
quatrain	a stanza or poem of four lines, such as in this example by Emily Dickinson: "Hope" is the thing with feathers That perches in the soul And sings the tune without the words And never stops—at all.
quadriceps	a large, four-part muscle at the front of the thigh.
quadricentennial	*cen-* means "100" and *-enn-* means "year," so a *quadricentennial* is a 400th anniversary. The United States will celebrate its *quadricentennial* in 2176.
tetrapod	*-pod* means "foot," so a *tetrapod* is a vertebrate having four legs or one that is descended from a four-legged ancestor.
quintessence	the fifth element; a perfect type or example of something. Works by Picasso are the *quintessence* of modern art.
pentathlon	an athletic contest with five different track and field events.
hexagram	a six-pointed starlike figure. The Star of David is a *hexagram*.
sextet	a group of six singers or players.
heptagon	a seven-sided figure.
octet	a group or stanza of eight lines; a company of eight singers or musicians.
decimate	to destroy or kill a large part of. Florida was *decimated* by the hurricane. In the sixteenth century, the word *decimate* meant to kill every tenth man arbitrarily as punishment for mutiny.

September	originally the seventh month. Our calendar evolved from the original Roman calendar, which began in March instead of January. You can see that making March the first month makes *September* the seventh month.
October	originally the eighth month.
November	originally the ninth month.
December	originally the tenth month.

Completing Verbal Analogies

The easiest type of analogy question involves synonyms, or words that have the same meaning. Analogy questions involving synonyms can be expressed as "*A* means the same as *B*; *C* means the same as *D*." An example is shown below.

```
         A   B      C     D
  b    bi : duo : : sept : _____
         a. hex
         b. hept
         c. nov
         d. sex
```

You must first look at the relationship between A and B. The relationship between A and B is one of sameness. *Bi* and *Duo* both mean "two." They are synonyms; they mean the same thing. This means that the relationship between C and D must also be one of sameness. *Sept* means "7." We learned previously that *hept* also means "7." Therefore *hept*, or choice (b), is the correct answer.

The complete analogy reads as follows:
    bi : duo : : sept : hept
    "bi" is to "duo," as "sept" is to "hept."

Complete the following analogies.

```
_____   1.  sex : hex : : quad : _____
             a. uni
             b. quint
             c. pent
             d. tetra

_____   2.  uni : mono : : bi : _____
             a. di
             b. nov
             c. tri
             d. dec

_____   3.  quint : pent : : sex : _____
             a. hept
             b. hex
             c. dec
             d. dek

_____   4.  dek : dec : : di : _____
             a. duo
             b. ped
             c. pod
             d. mono
```

Now that you have studied the vocabulary in Unit 1, practice your new knowledge by completing the crossword puzzle on the following page.

Vocabulary 1

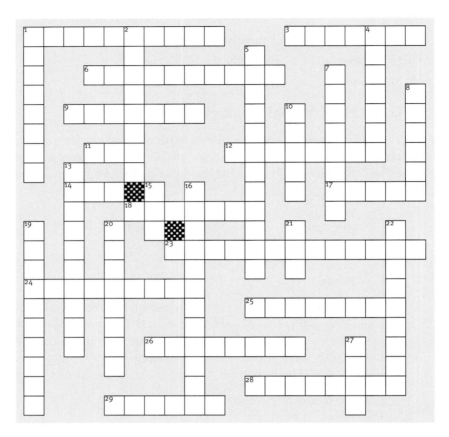

ACROSS CLUES

1. A one-house legislature.
3. Was once the eighth month.
6. At work he does the same thing every day. His job is _____.
9. Tolkien's *The Fellowship of the Ring*, *The Two Towers*, and *The Return of the King* make up the _____ of *The Lord of the Rings*.
11. A word part meaning "eight."
12. An earthquake can _____ an entire city.
14. A word part meaning "one."
17. A group of eight musicians.
18. Agatha Christie's murder mysteries feature a detective who uses a _____ to inspect for clues.
23. Maria Martinez is famous for her black-on-black _____ pottery.
24. There is a _____ of viewpoints on the issue of cloning.

25. The Star of David is a _____.
26. The poet Emily Dickinson is famous for her four-line _____.
28. When you're at Disneyland, be sure to ride on the _____.
29. You will _____ a circle if you draw a line through the middle.

DOWN CLUES

1. A snail has a _____ shell.
2. Each of the stone figures on Easter Island is a _____.
4. Oysters have _____ shells.
5. Michelangelo's statue of David is considered to be the _____ of sculpture.
7. The four-legged horse is an example of a _____.
8. A group of six musicians is a _____.
10. On the reality show *Survivor*, first the two teams are pitted against each other and then they _____ and become one tribe.
13. Too much running and jumping caused him to injure his _____.
15. An abbreviation for what was once the ninth month.
16. There are no _____ vocabulary words in this unit. All of the words have more than one syllable.
19. Figure having four angles or sides.
20. Many people begin wearing _____ to see better after the age of 50.
21. A word part meaning "three."
22. Congress is a _____ legislature.
27. A word part meaning "four."

Unit 2

In this unit, we will be working with words having opposite meanings, such as "love" and "hate." We will also introduce you to the word parts *meter*, *equi*, and *a(n)*.

phil(o)—love

bibliophile	Since *biblio-* means "book," a *bibliophile* is a person who loves or collects books.
philanderer	a man who makes love to a woman he can't or won't marry. *Ander* means "male."
philanthropist	a person who shows love for others by donating money or services to help them. Bill and Melinda Gates are both *philanthropists*.
philosopher	a person who offers views and theories on profound questions; "a lover of wisdom." Socrates, Plato, and Aristotle were ancient Greek *philosophers*.
philharmonic	loving music; a symphony or orchestra. The *Philharmonic* Orchestra performs once a month.
philately	the collection and study of postage stamps and postmarks.

mis—hate; bad(ly)

misanthrope	a person who hates or distrusts people. Ebenezer Scrooge, a character in *A Christmas Carol* by Charles Dickens, was the town *misanthrope*.
misogynist	Since *-gyn-* means "woman," a *misogynist* is a person who hates or is hostile toward women.
miscreant	a vicious or depraved person.
misconstrue	to think of in a wrong way, to misunderstand. Taryn *misconstrued* Brad's response because to her a grunt indicates a sign of displeasure.
misnomer	a wrong name; an error in naming a person or thing. It is a *misnomer* to call a whale a fish.

eu—good or well; dys—bad, abnormal, difficult

eulogy	a speech or composition praising a person or thing, especially a person who has just died.
euphemism	a word or phrase that is used in place of another that is considered to be offensive. "Adult entertainment" is a *euphemism* for "pornography."
euphoria	a feeling of great joy or excitement.
euthanasia	the act of putting someone to death painlessly or allowing them to die by withholding medical assistance. *To euthanize* means to subject to *euthanasia*.
dysentery	infectious disease of the large intestine marked by diarrhea. *Dysentery* literally means "bad bowel."
dyslexia	any of a variety of reading disorders.

meter—measure

speedometer	an instrument to measure the rate of travel in miles or kilometers.
odometer	an instrument for measuring distance traveled, as in a car.
pedometer	an instrument that measures the distance walked or run by recording the number of steps taken.
barometer	an instrument that measures atmospheric pressure.

macro—large or long; micro—small

macrocosm	the universe considered as a whole. *Cosmo* means "universe."
microcosm	a little world, a world in miniature; a group thought of as representing a larger group. The 100 representatives to Boys' State were a *microcosm* of the U.S. high school population.
microbe	a disease-causing bacterium; a small bit of life.
microfilm	film bearing a miniature photographic copy of graphic or textual material.

equi—equal

Don't confuse *equi* with *equus*, which means "horse." (An *equestrian* competition involves horse riding.)

equity	fairness; justice. Also the value of a piece of property after subtracting the amount owed on it in mortgages and liens. How much *equity* do you have in your home?
equitable	fair or just. Maria's will made sure that her assets were distributed in an *equitable* fashion among her three sons.
equivalent	equal in value, measure, force, or significance. Eat five servings of fresh fruits and vegetables or their *equivalent* every day.

a(n)—not, without

atypical	not typical; irregular; abnormal.
amoral	without a sense of moral responsibility.
aseptic	free from the living germs of disease.
atrophy	a wasting away or a shrinking up of a part of the body. Muscles can *atrophy* from lack of use. Can the mind also *atrophy* from lack of use?
anomaly	not following the usual rule or pattern; abnormal. The penguin, which cannot fly, is an *anomaly* among birds.
amorphous	without a definite shape or form. When Carlos examined the amoeba through the microscope, he discovered that it had an *amorphous* shape.
anemia	a condition in which a person's blood does not have enough red blood cells.
asymmetrical	having or showing a lack of symmetry; not balanced. Because the design in the painting was *asymmetrical*, it was not pleasing to the eye.

poly—many

polychromatic	having or exhibiting many colors.

| polysyllabic | consisting of four or more syllables. *Pol-y-syl-lab-ic* has five syllables. |
| polytechnic | pertaining to or offering instruction in a variety of industrial arts, applied sciences, or technical subjects. |

Completing Verbal Analogies

Analogy questions involving antonyms (opposites) can be expressed as "A means the opposite of B; C means the opposite of D." An example is shown below.

```
        A     B     C     D
__c__  early : late : : ahead : _____
       a. before
       b. prior
       c. behind
       d. never
```

You must first look at the relationship between A and B. Since the relationship between A and B is one of opposition, the relationship between C and D must also be one of opposition. *Behind* is the opposite of *ahead*. Therefore *behind*, which is choice (c), is the correct answer.

Complete the following analogies.

_____ 1. asymmetrical : symmetrical : : unbalanced : _____
     a. abnormal
     b. paranormal
     c. unequal
     d. balanced

_____ 2. typical : atypical : : regular : _____
     a. normal
     b. equal
     c. irregular
     d. equitable

_____ 3. macrocosm : microcosm : : whole : _____
     a. measure
     b. universe
     c. world
     d. part

_____ 4. equitable : arbitrary : : just : _____
     a. authentic
     b. unjust
     c. fair
     d. considerate

_____ 6. septic : aseptic : : dirty : _____
     a. putrid
     b. clean
     c. rotted
     d. free

_____ 7. polychromatic : monochromatic : : many : _____
     a. color
     b. one
     c. two
     d. varied

Now that you have studied the vocabulary in Unit 2, practice your new knowledge by completing the crossword puzzle on the following page.

Vocabulary 2

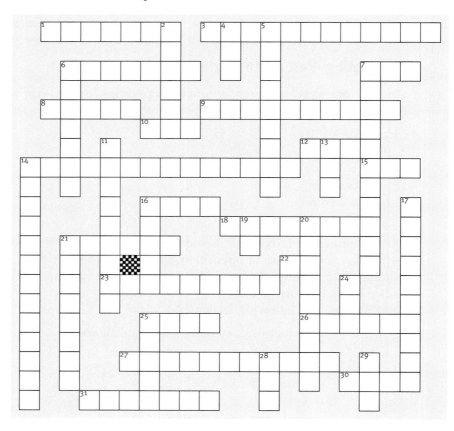

ACROSS CLUES

1. Pneumonia and strep throat are caused by a _____.
3. Her features were not perfectly aligned. Instead they were _____.
6. The roadrunner is an _____ among birds because it rarely flies.
7. A word part meaning "hate or bad."
8. A word part meaning "measure."
9. A confirmed _____ will probably not enjoy the company of women.
10. A word part meaning "bad or difficult."
12. A word part meaning "one."*
14. The _____ made a large monetary contribution to the new science building.
15. The abbreviation for what was once the ninth month.*
16. A word part meaning "four."*
18. An instrument measuring how many miles you have traveled in your car.
21. Condition when a person is lacking sufficient red blood cells.
22. A word part meaning "good or well."
23. The vet said that our dog Bandit was so sick that we should _____ him.
25. A word part meaning "many."
26. A person who lacks moral standards is _____.
27. Thomas Jefferson, a true _____, had over 6,000 volumes of books in his private collection.
30. A word part meaning "five."*
31. A muscle can _____ from lack of use.

DOWN CLUES

2. After Pat's mother died, he delivered a stirring _____ at her memorial service.
4. A word part meaning "six."*
5. A world in miniature is a _____.
6. Surgical instruments must be maintained in _____ condition.
7. Did the reporter _____ the president's remarks or did he quote him accurately?
11. A _____ is used to forecast changes in the weather.
13. The abbreviation for what was once the eighth month.*
14. According to the Bible, Jacob gave his son Joseph a coat of many colors, or a _____ garment.
16. A word part meaning "five."*
17. A liter is almost _____ to a quart.
19. A word part meaning "two."*
20. The judge rendered a decision considered to be _____ by both parties to the dispute.
21. It would be _____ for an *A* student to fail a test.
24. A word part for two.*
25. A word part meaning "love."
28. A word part meaning "six."*
29. An abbreviation for what was once the tenth month.*

*From a previous unit.

Unit 3

In Unit 3, you will be introduced to word parts related to direction and motion.

vert—turn; con—with; in—not, opposite, into, within

avert	*a* means "from," and *vert* means "turn," so the literal meaning of *avert* is "to turn from." Martha *averted* her eyes during the violent parts of the movie *Road to Perdition*. *Avert* also means "prevent," as in she narrowly *averted* an accident.
invert	Here *in* means "opposite", so when you *invert* something you are turning it upside down. She could tell that Marco did not know how to read because he had the newspaper *inverted*.
vertigo	a dizzy feeling, especially the feeling that everything is spinning around. After Katrina got off the merry-go-round, she experienced a bout of *vertigo*.
subvert	to overturn or undermine something established. In the 1950s and 1960s, rock 'n' roll was thought likely to *subvert* the wholesome values of American teenagers.
convert	to turn from one form, use, or belief to another. Missionaries around the world try to *convert* people to Christianity. As a noun, *convert* (pronounced *con'-vert*, with the stress on the first syllable) means a person who has changed from one belief or religion to another.
divert	to turn aside. Trapped by the Doberman, Alicia tried to *divert* the dog's attention by throwing a bone across the yard.
versatile	able to turn with ease from one thing to another. The basketball player was very *versatile* in that he could play many positions.
vertebra(e)	any one of the bones that make up the spinal column, or backbone. The backbone enables us to turn our bodies.

mis, mit—send; re—back, again; dis—apart, away; ad—toward

mission	a special duty or errand that a person or group is sent to do by a church, government, or other entity. A place where a group of missionaries or diplomats live and work. The diplomatic *mission's* goal was to facilitate peace in the Middle East. *Mission* Santa Clara is marked by a California state historical marker.
admit	*ad-* means "toward," so the literal meaning of *admit* is to "send toward, or to let go." When you buy a ticket to a movie, you are *admitted* to the theater. Carol *admitted* that she had not told the truth to Rob.

submissive	willing to give in or obey another; humble or obedient. For years, Shawna had been *submissive* to her husband; finally, after too much abuse, she decided to file for divorce.
remit (remission)	*Re-* means "back" or "again." *Remit* means "to send back," or "to let go." Mark needs to *remit* his car payment by the first of each month. Cerise's breast cancer is currently in *remission*.
intermission	stopping for a time; an interruption. There is a twenty-minute *intermission* between Act I and Act II of the play. The original meaning of the word was "to send between."
intermittent	stopping and starting again from time to time. During a baby's first year of life, pediatricians recommend *intermittent* checkups or well-baby visits.
dismiss	*Dis-* means "away," so the literal meaning of *dismiss* is "to send away," or "to tell or allow to leave." He was *dismissed* from the army after failing to report for duty.
emissary	A person sent on a special mission. The *emissary* was sent to Cuba to arrange a meeting with the president.
emit	to send out or give forth. The owl *emitted* a shrill screech before attacking its prey. Motor vehicles *emit* toxic fumes that contribute to air pollution.

ven—come; circum—around

prevent	to keep from happening, to stop. The literal meaning is "to come before" or "to act in anticipation of." Vaccinations *prevent* the spread of disease.
convention	a meeting of members or delegates from various places. The literal meaning is "coming with." The Republican Party held its *convention* in New York in 2004.
circumvent	to get around, often by using sly or tricky methods. Warren thought we should deal with the problem directly; Sylvia thought we should try to *circumvent* it.

se—apart, away from

separate	to keep or put apart. Tina's job at the cannery required her to *separate* the good peaches from the bad ones.
seclude	to keep away from others; to remove from social contact. *-clude* is derived from *claudere*, meaning "to shut, or close." The literal meaning of *seclude* is "to close away from."
segregation	the practice of keeping people of different religious, racial, or ethnic groups apart from each other.

sequ (secut)—following

consecutive	following in a regular order without a break. In Phoenix, Arizona, it is unusual to have rain for two *consecutive* days.

sequence	one thing following after another. A bizarre *sequence* of events led to his apprehension and arrest.
sequel	a literary or film work that takes up and continues the narrative of a preceding work. The *sequel* to the movie *Star Wars* is *The Empire Strikes Back*.
consequence	the effect, result, or outcome of something occurring earlier. When you are under oath in a court of law, you must tell the truth or face the *consequences*.

dia—through, across, apart, thoroughly; pro—forward; log(ue)—speech, word

diagonal	*-gonia* means "angle," so *diagonal* means "connecting two nonadjacent angles." It also means "slanting." Martina's dress had *diagonal* stripes.
dialect	a form of language that is used only in a certain place or with a certain group. *-lect* means "to speak," so the literal meaning is "to speak across." Because of television, regional *dialects* in the United States are in danger of disappearing.
dialog(ue)	conversation between two or more persons; an exchange of ideas or opinions on a particular issue with a view to reaching a friendly agreement.
diagnosis	*-gnosis* means "to know," so a *diagnosis* means "a thorough examination or learning of all the facts in order to determine the nature of a disease." The doctor's *diagnosis* was that the patient suffered from heat exhaustion.
prognosis	*pro-* is a prefix meaning "forward," so a *prognosis* is a forecast or prediction of how a disease will develop in a person and what the chances are that the person will get well. After undergoing radiation treatments for prostate cancer, his *prognosis* for a full recovery was excellent.
progressive	moving forward. His *progressive* improvement in math is impressive.

duc—lead; in—into

reduce	to lead back; to decrease. Kristin wanted to *reduce* her intake of caffeinated drinks.
abduct	to take someone away forceably; to kidnap. The literal meaning is "to lead away." Most missing children are abducted by a parent in a custody dispute.
conduct	to lead or guide. The meeting was *conducted* by the vice president.
conducive	helping to bring about; contributing. The quiet in the library is *conducive* to studying.

seduce	to lead away, lead astray. In the *Star Wars* movies, Darth Vader was *seduced* by the dark side of the Force.
deduct	to lead away; subtract. If I save my receipt, the store will *deduct* 10 percent from the price of a new pair of shoes.
induce	to lead or move by persuasion or influence; to bring about or cause. Can't I *induce* you to stay a little longer?

Completing Verbal Analogies

The following verbal analogies include antonyms and synonyms. Consider the relationship between the first pair carefully before selecting your answer.

Complete the following analogies.

_____ 1. prevent : avert : : allow : _____
   a. prevail
   b. observe
   c. harm
   d. permit

_____ 2. include : seclude : : integration : _____
   a. intermission
   b. segregation
   c. conducive
   d. progressive

_____ 3. submissive : obedient : : prevent : _____
   a. delegate
   b. send toward
   c. hinder
   d. allow

_____ 4. reduce : decrease : : conduct : _____
   a. abandon
   b. overturn
   c. subtract
   d. lead

_____ 5. dismiss : discharge : : admit : _____
   a. allow
   b. renew
   c. turn
   d. send

_____ 6. intermittent : constant : : off-and-on : _____
   a. tentative
   b. concerned
   c. permanent
   d. timely

Now that you have studied the vocabulary in Unit 3, practice your new knowledge by completing the crossword puzzle on the following page.

Vocabulary 3

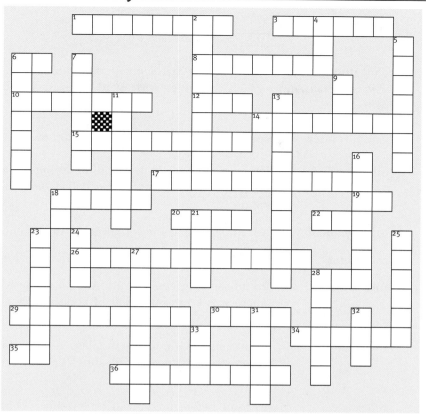

ACROSS CLUES

1. A line slanting from one corner to the opposite corner of a rectangle is a _____ line.
3. If I trade in my old camera, the store will _____ $25 from the price of a new one.
6. A word part meaning "away from."
8. The power failure at the college caused instructors to _____ classes early.
10. It had been his lifelong dream to _____ an orchestra.
12. A word part meaning "with."
14. The two parties were brought together in the hope that they could resolve the dispute with a civil _____.
15. For many students, talking by other students is not _____ to taking a quiz.
17. The _____ of taking drugs could be addiction.
18. A peace agreement was signed between the two countries to _____ further hostilities.
19. A word part meaning "back or again."
20. A word part meaning "following."
22. A word part meaning "send."
26. There was _____ rainfall every few hours all afternoon.
28. A word part for two.*
29. The doctor's _____ was that Ray had chicken pox.
30. A word part meaning "turn."
34. Should you _____ the number of hours that you work so that you can concentrate on your classes?
35. A word part meaning "into."
36. The doctor said that Anna had a good _____ for a complete recovery.

DOWN CLUES

2. The _____ and murder of Charles Lindbergh's son in 1932 led to stronger federal laws against kidnapping.
4. A word part meaning "apart or away."
5. The actress Reese Witherspoon had to speak in a Southern _____ for her role in *Sweet Home Alabama*.
6. If you have a contagious disease, it might be necessary to _____ you from others.
7. After her child swallowed a strange pill, the doctor told the mother to _____ vomiting immediately.
9. A word part meaning "forward."
11. When Taryn married Mike, she agreed to _____ to his religion.
13. Have you ever tried to _____ a rule by finding a way to get around it?
16. Christina's ear infection caused her to lose her balance and experience feelings of _____.
18. A word part meaning "toward."
21. Cars _____ carbon monoxide and other harmful gases.
23. A group of doctors were sent on a humanitarian _____ to help with a medical crisis.
24. A word part meaning "across."
25. In the movie *The Lord of the Rings*, the Hobbit Frodo must fight against the power of the "one ring" to _____ him.
27. Former President Jimmy Carter has been an active _____ for peace around the globe.
28. The police were trying to _____ traffic away from the scene of the accident.
31. Please _____ your payment no later than the fifteenth of each month.
32. A word part meaning "lead."
33. A word part meaning "come."

*From previous unit.

Unit 4

This unit begins with the word parts *inter, -intra* and *-medius, ped-, -capt* and *-cept,* and *cap-* and *corp-*. It concludes with word parts for blood relations and the suffix *-cide.*

inter—between, among; intra—within, inside; medius—middle

interpersonal	between persons. In hopes of bettering his relationships with his peers, he is taking a class called *Interpersonal* Communication.
intrapersonal	self-knowledge as in *intrapersonal* intelligence.
interloper	a person who intrudes into the affairs or business of others.
interlude	an intervening episode; an interval in the course of action. There was a brief *interlude* of good weather between the two storms.
interject	to interrupt with; to insert. Class is much more interesting when students *interject* questions or comments during the lecture.
intercede	to come between or plead on another's behalf. Because the mother was unable to refrain from taking drugs, the state *interceded* and placed the young child in foster care.
intervene	to come between. When the two boys got into a fight, the teacher *intervened* to settle the dispute.
intermediate	coming between two other things or events; in the middle. Adolescence is an *intermediate* stage that comes between childhood and adulthood.
intermediary	*medius* means "middle." An *intermediary* is a go-between or mediator. The airline hired an *intermediary* to write a contract acceptable to both labor and management.

ped—child

The Latin prefix *ped-* also means "foot" as in *pedal* and *pedestrian.* Don't get the two meanings confused.

pediatrician	a doctor who takes care of babies and children.
pedagogy	comes from the Greek word part *paidos,* meaning "child," and *agogos,* meaning "leader." In Latin, a *pedagogue* was a slave who escorted children to school and then was responsible for supervising them. Later the term came to refer to a teacher. Today, the word refers to teaching or the study of teaching.
pedophile	an adult who has a sexual desire for a child. In California, a suspected *pedophile* was charged in the rape and murder of a five-year-old girl.

pedantic	showing off learning in a boring way or attending too closely to the minute details of a subject. The term originally referred to a schoolmaster.

capt, cept—hold, seize, take

captivity	the condition of being held by force. There are very few giant pandas held in *captivity*.
capability	the power to do something.
capacious	able to hold much. The best features of the house were the *capacious* walk-in closets.
deception	If we practice *deception*, we are "taking" something from someone by fraud.
intercept	to take or seize on the way (between). He *intercepted* the quarterback's pass and ran 30 yards for the touchdown.

cap—head; corp—body

decapitate	to cut off the head. During the French Revolution, people were *decapitated* by the guillotine.
caption	a title at the head of an article or below a photo in a newspaper or magazine. Sonia quickly scanned the *captions* to determine whether or not the articles were relevant to her research paper.
capital punishment	the killing of someone by law as punishment for a crime.
corporal punishment	physical punishment (of the body) as in whipping or spanking.
corpulent	fat and fleshy; stout body build.
corporation	a business, city, college, or other body of persons having a government charter, which gives it some of the legal powers and rights of a person.
corps	a group of people joined together in some work; a section or special branch of the military. *Corps* has the same pronunciation as apple "core." After graduation from college, Jeremy joined the Peace *Corps*. At age fifty-five, Kirk retired from the Marine *Corps*.
corpse	the dead body of a person.

mater, matri—mother; pater, patri—father; soror—sister; frater, fratri—brother; homo—man; genus—birth, begin, race; cide—kill

This section discusses "blood" relations and the suffix -*cide*, which means "kill."

maternal	relating to a mother. The *maternal* instincts of a lioness make it dangerous to get caught playing with the cubs.

maternity	the state of being a mother. The new mothers were in the *maternity* ward of the hospital.
matricide	The suffix *-cide,* as in insect*icide* and pest*icide,* means "kill," so *matricide* means murdering one's mother.
paternal	relating to a father. Your father's father is your *paternal* grandfather.
paternity	the state of being a father. The mother brought a *paternity* suit against her child's father.
patricide	murdering one's father.
fraternity	a brotherhood. College *fraternities* are groups of young men who live together like brothers.
fratricide	murdering one's brother.
sorority	a sisterhood. College *sororities* are groups of young women who live together like sisters.
sororicide	murdering one's sister.
homicide	the murder of one human being by another. *Homo-* means "same," but *homo-* also has a second meaning of "man," which is the meaning that applies to the word *homicide* and other words. The *homo-* meaning "same" has a different derivation than the *homo-* meaning "man."
Homo sapiens	mankind; human beings. *Sapiens* means "wisdom," so *Homo sapiens* are humans with wisdom. This is the scientific term for all human beings.
genius	A *genius* is a person with very high intelligence. The word *genius* has an interesting etymology. It comes from *genus,* meaning "birth." The ancient Romans believed that each person was assigned a guardian spirit at birth.
genocide	the systematic killing of a national or ethnic group. The word *genocide* was first applied to the attempted extermination of the Jews by the Nazis.
Genesis	the beginning, the origin. The first book of the Bible is called *Genesis* because it gives an account of the Creation.
genealogy	a history of a person's descent from ancestors. Your "family tree" or birth history shows your *genealogy*.

Completing Verbal Analogies

Another common type of analogy can be expressed as "A is by definition a person who does B or has characteristics of B or is B; C is by definition a person who does D or has characteristics of D or is D." An example is shown below.

	A	B	C	D
b	thief : steals : : spectator : _____			

    a. thinks
    b. observes
    c. mediates
    d. whines

The answer is (b). A *spectator* is by definition someone who *observes*, just as a *thief* is by definition someone who *steals*.

Complete the following analogies.

_____ 1. pedagogue : teaches : : intermediary : _____
    a. punishes
    b. deceives
    c. mediates
    d. flatters

_____ 2. interloper : intrudes : : interceptor : _____
    a. cuts off
    b. mediates
    c. seizes
    d. hires

_____ 3. homicide : killing a human : : genocide : _____
    a. sororicide
    b. killing an ethnic group
    c. killing one's brother
    d. killing one's mother

_____ 4. father : paternal : : mother : _____
    a. authentic
    b. maternal
    c. fair
    d. considerate

_____ 5. fraternity : brotherhood : : sorority : _____
    a. motherhood
    b. fatherhood
    c. sisterhood
    d. adulthood

Now that you have studied the vocabulary in Unit 4, practice your new knowledge by completing the crossword puzzle on the next page.

Vocabulary 4

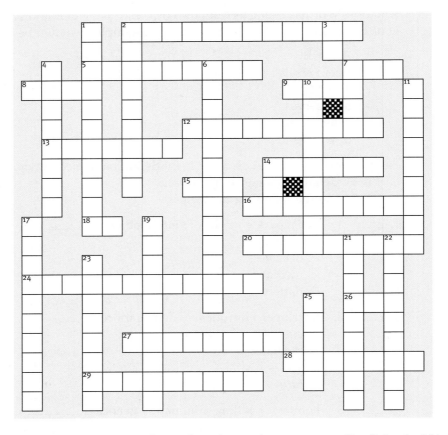

ACROSS CLUES

2. Roberta's _____ advises going easy in toilet-training toddlers.
5. An act of _____ has a mother as a victim.
7. A word part meaning "head."
8. A word part meaning "man."
9. A word part meaning "kill."
12. Kill by beheading.
13. The newspaper issued a retraction because the _____ had mistakenly identified the wrong person as the arsonist.
14. A dead body.
15. A word part meaning "child."
16. There was a brief musical _____ between the first and second acts of the play.
18. A word part meaning "apart."*
20. The defensive back tried to _____ the pass.
24. The school board hired an _____ to work on conflicts between the parents and the faculty.
26. A word part meaning "forward."*

27. I was pleased to receive stationery with my _____.*
28. The first book of the Bible.
29. Virginia, who traces her family history back to the Mayflower, is an expert in _____.

DOWN CLUES

1. "humans with wisdom." (Don't leave a space between the two words.)
2. DNA tests were conducted to determine the child's _____.
3. A word part meaning "toward."*
4. If his victim dies, he will be charged with _____.
6. Conflict management and assertiveness are _____ skills that can help you become a more effective person.
7. A word part meaning "seize."
10. The U.S. decided to _____ in the dispute between the two nations in the hope of preventing a war.

11. Bob raised his hand to _____ a question, but the teacher ignored him.
14. A word part meaning "with."*
17. A 3 ounce bourbon and soda and a twelve ounce light beer have an _____ amount of alcohol.*
19. Is Marie Barone on *Everybody Loves Raymond* an _____ because she meddles in Ray and Debra's life without being asked?
21. The doctor told the _____ man that he needed to go on a diet.
22. The _____ was sentenced to life in prison for the rape and murder of the young child.
23. Students who major in education take classes in _____.

25. A word part meaning "between."

*From a previous unit.

Unit 5

This unit begins with word parts relating to law, politics, and power. It then looks at word parts relating to religious beliefs. The last section covers word parts relating to time.

legis—law; demos—people; polis—city; graph—write

legal	of or based on law; lawful. Comes from the Latin *legis* meaning "law." Cynthia needed to see a lawyer to find out if her marriage to Paul was *legal*.
legislature	a group of people who meet together to write and enact laws. The Florida state *legislature* played an active role in the battle for Florida's electoral votes during the presidential election between Al Gore and George W. Bush.
legitimate	allowed by law or custom; being justifiable. He had a *legitimate* claim to ownership of the land.
illegitimate	against the laws or rules.
democracy	*Demos* means "the people" in Greek, so *democracy* means "government by the people."
demography	Literally *demography* means "writing about people." It is the science of vital and social statistics, concerned with such things as the births, deaths, diseases, marriages, and the educational level of a population. A *demographer* gathers data, such as in the census we take every 10 years, and then compiles that data into maps and charts. A *demographic* map might show income levels in different areas of a city or county.

The following words come from the Greek word *polis*, which means city-state. In ancient Greece, each city was a state unto itself because there was no greater political authority.

political	In ancient Greece, each city-state was responsible for its own *political* or governmental affairs. Today, the word also refers to *political* parties, such as Libertarian, Republican, Democratic, or Green.
politician	a person who is active in politics as a career; a seeker or holder of public office.

cracy—rule, strength, power; archy—rule; auto—self, by one's self; theo—god

anarchy	the complete absence of government or the rule of law.
monarchy	government by one person, usually a king, queen, or emperor. Monaco is an example of a *monarchy*.
autocracy	government in which one person has all the power. *auto-* means "self or by one's self." Germany under Adolf Hitler was an *autocracy*. Hitler was an *autocrat*.

oligarchy	a form of government in which power is vested in a few persons.
plutocracy	a government in which the wealthy class rules.
patriarchy	an institution or organization in which power is held by males and passed on through males, quite often from father to son.
matriarchy	a family, society, or state governed by women or where a woman is the dominant member of the group. The Navajo nation is a *matriarchy*.
theocracy	*theo* means "god," so a *theocracy* means "rule by God." A *theocracy* is a government that claims to be based on divine authority.

agogos—lead, bring together, excite; potis—powerful; syn—same

demagog(ue)	according to its word parts, a *demagogue* is a person who leads and excites people, or a person who gains power by arousing people's emotions and prejudices. The word usually has a negative connotation. Hitler was a *demagogue*.
synagogue	a building where Jews gather for worship and religious study. The literal meaning is "a place to which people are brought together or led to." The origin of the word *synagogue* may date back to the sixth century B.C.E. when the Jewish people were in exile in Babylon. Formal worship in a temple was impossible, so the Jewish people began to meet in member's homes. These homes became the first *synagogues*.
potent	having great power; having a strong effect on the body or mind; producing powerful physical or chemical effects. The doctor told the patient that she needed some *potent* medicine.
potential	capable of coming into being but not yet actual. He had the *potential* to become a great swimmer.
potentate	a person having great power; a ruler or monarch. The sultan was a very wealthy *potentate*.

deus—god; sanct—holy; sacri—holy; ology—study of; -ism, doctrine, or theory

theology	the study of God and religious beliefs.
atheism	the belief that there is no god.
monotheism	the belief that there is only one god. Judaism, Christianity, and Islam are *monotheistic* religions.
polytheism	the belief in more than one god. The ancient Greeks were polytheists. Their gods included Zeus, Athena, and Apollo.
deity	a god or goddess. The ancient Greeks and Romans believed in many *deities*.

deify	to make a god of. In ancient Rome, the emperors were often *deified*.
sanctuary	a sacred or holy place; a place of protection, shelter, or refuge. The World Wildlife *Sanctuary* was created to provide a home for animal species in danger of extinction.
sanctify	to make saintly or holy.
sanction	approval given by someone in authority. The students formed a club with the *sanction* of the school administration.
sacred	holy or set apart for some religious purpose; not to be broken or ignored. She took a *sacred* vow to become a nun.
sacrament	a sacred ceremony in Christian churches, such as baptism and Holy Communion. A *sacrament* was originally an oath of allegiance taken by a Roman soldier.

chrono—time; temp—time, moderate; ana—back, up, again

chronology	the science or study of measuring time; arranging events in the sequence in which they happened. What was the *chronology* of events for the assassination of President Kennedy?
synchronize	According to its word parts, *synchronize* means "at the same time." We need to *synchronize* our watches so that we can meet at the restaurant at the same time. *Synchronized* swimming is an Olympic event.
anachronism	The literal meaning is "back in time"; anything that is out of its proper time in history is an *anachronism*. Using a horse and buggy for transportation is an *anachronism* in the United States today.
chronicle	to tell or write the story of; a *chronological* record of events; a history. Lewis and Clark *chronicled* their adventures as they made their way to the Pacific Northwest.
chronometer	a device for measuring time; a clock or watch. A stop watch is one kind of *chronometer*.
temporary	lasting or effective for a short time only. She worked at Macy's as *temporary* help during the Christmas holidays.
contemporary	existing or happening in the same period of time; a person living in the same period as another. George W. Bush and Bill Clinton are *contemporaries*.
temper	a mood or state of mind; also, to moderate. He was in a foul *temper* after he wrecked his brand new car. The passing years *tempered* his rashness.
temperate	neither very hot nor very cold; moderate. Hawaii has a *temperate* climate.
temperance	moderation in one's actions, appetites, or feelings; drinking few, if any, alcoholic beverages. Is a lifestyle that emphasizes *temperance* healthier?

Completing Verbal Analogies

One type of analogy involves examples: "A is an example of B; C is an example of D." Look at the sample below.

               A   B   C   D
___c___   red : color : : oak : _____
          a. bright
          b. large
          c. tree
          d. clothing

As always, you must first look at the relationship between A and B. *Red* is an example of a color. And *oak* is an example of a tree. Therefore, *tree*, or choice (c), is the correct answer.

Complete the following analogies.

_____   1.   United States : democracy : : Vatican City : _____
               a. god
               b. theocracy
               c. pope
               d. matriarchy

_____   2.   Hitler : autocrat : : Queen Elizabeth : _____
               a. democrat
               b. politician
               c. monarch
               d. deity

_____   3.   Navajo nation : matriarchy : : ancient Hebrews : _____
               a. men
               b. women
               c. patriarchy
               d. Arizona

_____   4.   Islam : monotheism : : ancient Greeks : _____
               a. polytheism
               b. atheism
               c. Christianity
               d. deity

_____   5.   baptism : sacrament : : stop watch : _____
               a. chronology
               b. chronometer
               c. theology
               d. sanction

_____   6.   President : executive branch : : Congress : _____
               a. judiciary
               b. laws
               c. legislative branch
               d. George W. Bush

Now that you have studied the vocabulary in Unit 5, practice your new knowledge by completing the crossword puzzle on the next page.

Vocabulary 5

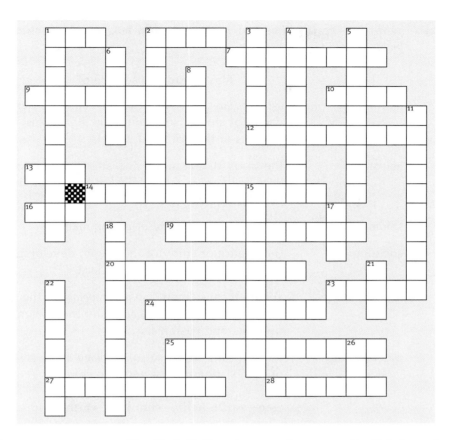

ACROSS CLUES

1. A word part meaning "with."*
2. A word part meaning "god."
7. Rule by one person, usually a king or queen.
9. A person with great power; a ruler.
10. A word part meaning "many."*
12. The climate in Vilcabamba, Ecuador, is a _____ 70 degrees Fahrenheit all year long.
13. A word part meaning "child."*
14. The U.N. considered the dictator's government to be _____ because he seized power from the lawfully elected president.
16. A word part meaning "come."*
19. Alex would like to run for political office. Many people think he would be a good _____.

20. The belief in only one god.
23. To make a god of.
24. A country governed by a few people is an _____.
25. A typewriter is an _____ today.
27. Churches have historically given _____ to those in trouble.
28. A word part meaning "time."

DOWN CLUES

1. A wristwatch is an example of a _____.
2. A person who "leads and excites people."
3. Snow White ate an apple that contained a _____ poison that put her into a deathlike sleep.
4. Zachary received the _____ of baptism when he was two months old.

5. Rule by god.
6. A word part meaning "holy."
8. It is not _____ to park close to a fire hydrant.
11. The literal meaning is "to write about people."
15. Where a woman is the dominant member of the society.
17. A word part meaning "head."*
18. _____ advocates proposed laws that would outlaw the sale of alcohol.
21. A word part meaning "across."*
22. The belief that there is no god.
25. A word part meaning "back."
26. A word part meaning "same."

*From a previous unit.

Unit 6

This unit begins with the word parts *-ology; geo-, helio-,* and *terr-;* moves on to *path-; ten-* or *tin-; fid-* and *cred-; tact-* and *tang-;* and concludes with *-ject* and *locut-.*

logy—study or science of

astronomy	*astro-* means "pertaining to the stars," so *astronomy* is the science that studies such things as the origins, composition, and motions of the stars and planets.
astrology	the study that assumes and attempts to interpret the influence of the heavenly bodies on human affairs. Horoscopes are based on *astrology.*
seismology	the science and study of earthquakes.
sociology	the science or study of the origin, development, organization, and functioning of human society.
anthropology	*anthro-* means "man," so *anthropology* is the science that studies human beings, especially their origin, development, division, and customs.
paleontology	*paleo-* means "old," so *paleontology* is the science of the forms of life existing in past geologic periods.

geo—earth; helio—sun; terr—earth, land

geology	the science that deals with the dynamics and physical history of the earth. A *geologist* studies the earth's crust and the way in which its layers were formed.
geography	the study of the surface of the earth, its division into continents and countries, and the climate, natural resources, and inhabitants of the regions.
geocentric	having or representing the earth as the center, as in the *geocentric* theory of the universe.
heliocentric	having or representing the sun as the center of the universe.
apogee	*apo-* means "off" or "away," so the *apogee* is the point in the orbit of the moon at which it is farthest from the earth; the highest point or most exalted point. Is Tiger Woods at the *apogee* of professional golf?
perigee	*Peri* means "near," so the *perigee* is the point in the orbit of the moon at which it is nearest to the earth; the lowest point.
territory	any large stretch of land or region.
terrain	a tract of land with reference to its natural features or military advantages. He purchased a home with five acres of hilly *terrain.*

terra firma	Latin for firm or solid earth. After the long ocean voyage, Shawn was grateful to be back on *terra firma*.
terrestrial	pertaining to, consisting of, or representing the earth. Coyotes are *terrestrial* animals.

path(o), pathy—feeling, suffering, emotion

antipathy	an aversion; strong feeling against. Although Adella liked animals, she had a real *antipathy* toward cats.
apathy	lack of strong feeling, interest, or concern. Because of public *apathy*, no real reform was likely to occur.
pathos	the quality in life or art of evoking a feeling of pity or compassion. As the heroine lay dying, the musical score turned to *pathos*.
pathetic	causing or evoking pity either sympathetically or contemptibly. The fireman was haunted by the victim's *pathetic* cries for help.
pathological	characterized by an unhealthy compulsion; habitual; concerned with diseases. Unfortunately, you cannot trust her word because she is a *pathological* liar.

ten(t), tin—hold, cling, keep

tenacious	gripping firmly; holding fast. Despite their separation, he cannot rid himself of his wife; she has a *tenacious* hold on his feelings.
retentive	able to hold, keep, remember. Calla has an extremely *retentive* mind for facts and figures.
tenure	the length of time something is held; the status of holding a job permanently. Professors work hard to achieve *tenure*.
detention	holding back; forced delay or confinement. Because of Mike's behavior, he has a *detention* every day this week.
tenant	a person who pays rent to use land; to hold, occupy, or dwell in.
pertinent	relevant, holding to the point. Don't bother me with trivial details; I only want the *pertinent* information.

fid—faith(ful); cred—believe

fidelity	loyalty. The subjects pledged *fidelity* to their new king.
infidel	a person who does not believe in a particular religion, an unbeliever; a person who disbelieves a particular theory or belief.
confident	sure, certain, assured; a strong belief in oneself. Nina was utterly *confident* she would pass the bar exam and become a lawyer.
diffident	lacking faith in one's own ability, worth or fitness; timid, shy.

credulous	willing to believe things even without proof; easily convinced. It is easy to play tricks on Charlotte; she is so *credulous* that she'll believe anything.
incredulous	not willing or able to believe; doubtful. Mona gave Sam an *incredulous* look when she found out he'd won the lottery.

tact, tang—touch

intangible	not able to be touched or grasped; vague, elusive. He has many fine *intangible* qualities like compassion and forthrightness.
tactile	perceptible to the touch.
intact	untouched; remaining sound or whole. When Juan found his wallet, it was still *intact* and held all of his credit cards and money.

ject—throw

dejected	to depress the spirits. The literal meaning of *deject* is "to throw down."
eject	to drive or force out; to throw out.
inject	The literal meaning of *inject* is "to throw in." She *injected* some humor into a dreary situation.
interject	*Inter* means "between," so an *interjection* is a remark "thrown into" a conversation, often abruptly. To interject means "to interrupt."
project	to throw forward; to predict; to cause to be heard clearly. The teacher easily *projected* her voice so that those sitting in the back of the class had no trouble hearing.

locut (loqu)—speak, talk

eloquent	graceful and forceful in speech. *e-* means "out," and *loqu-* means "speak," so the literal meaning is to "speak out." At the trial's end, the defense attorney gave an *eloquent* summation of the evidence favoring his client's innocence.
loquacious	talkative. Some people are more *loquacious* when they are nervous or uncomfortable.

Completing Verbal Analogies

One type of analogy can be expressed as "A is the study of B; C is the study of D." An example is given below.

```
        A          B       C          D
  a    astronomy : stars :: seismology : _____
       a. earthquakes
       b. dinosaurs
       c. rocks
       d. oceans
```

The answer is (a). *Astronomy* is the study of the stars, and *seismology* is the study of earthquakes.

Complete the following analogies.

_____ 1. sociology : human society : : geology : _____
    a. the lowest point
    b. the highest point
    c. the zodiac
    d. the earth

_____ 2. anthropology : human beings : : geography : _____
    a. the sun
    b. surface of earth
    c. the moon
    d. heavenly bodies

The following questions review previous analogy types. Some questions may contain vocabulary from previous units.

_____ 3. heliocentric : sun : : geocentric : _____
    a. stars
    b. atmosphere
    c. earth
    d. ocean

_____ 4. zenith : apogee : : nadir : _____
    a. distance
    b. moon
    c. perigee
    d. earth

_____ 5. interject : remark : : inject : _____
    a. intravenous
    b. vaccine
    c. person
    d. talking

_____ 6. anarchy : lawlessness : : apathy : _____
    a. military
    b. government
    c. people
    d. indifference

_____ 7. astrology : astronomy : : _____ : _____
    a. science : pseudoscience
    b. pseudoscience : science
    c. pseudoscience : horoscopes
    d. stars : planets

Now that you have studied the vocabulary in Unit 6, practice your new knowledge by completing the crossword puzzle on the next page.

Vocabulary 6

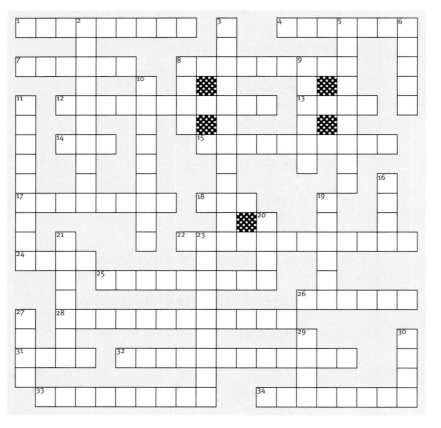

ACROSS CLUES

1. After the bitter custody battle, Sarah had _____ for her ex-husband.
4. She used her _____ sense to read the braille letters with her fingers.
7. Because of public _____, the voter turnout was low.
8. Because Jerry cut classes, he had to serve a _____ after school.
12. Samantha gave Matt an _____ look when she learned he had spent all his hard-earned money gambling in Las Vegas.
13. A word part meaning "throw."
14. A word part meaning "faith."
15. Susie is so _____ that her friends wonder when she pauses to breathe.
17. The Miami Hurricanes became _____ when they lost the college national championship game after the second overtime.
18. Abbreviation for what was once the eighth month.*
22. If you are interested in dinosaurs, you might want to take a course in _____.
24. A word part meaning "god."*

25. Oregon was a _____ before it became a state.
26. The landlord had to evict the _____ because he wasn't paying his rent.
28. Margaret Mead revolutionized the field of _____ with her research on the customs of the people of Samoa.
31. A word part meaning "hold."
32. The theory that regards the sun as the center of the universe.
33. If you are interested in social organization, you might study _____.
34. At the wedding ceremony, the couple pledged their undying _____ to each other.

DOWN CLUES

2. There are many _____ qualities like patience that go into making a successful leader.
3. A _____ liar might be able to pass a polygraph test.
5. Holding her son's head above the water, she maintained a _____ grip until they reached safety.

6. He did not want to _____ the annoying student from the class, but he finally had to tell him to leave.
8. A word part meaning "god."*
9. A baby rattlesnake can sometimes _____ more poison than a full-grown rattlesnake.
10. He wanted a summary report with only the _____ details on his desk by 5:00.
11. She felt _____ that she would do well on the test because she had studied hard.
16. A word part meaning "touch."
19. Was his election as president the _____ of his political career?
20. A word part meaning "science of."
21. The _____ was considered to be too rocky for any crops to grow.
23. The science of _____ is not to be confused with the pseudoscience of astrology.
27. A word part meaning "feeling."
29. A word part meaning "believe."
30. A word part meaning "many."*

*From a previous unit.

Unit 7

Unit 7 covers vocabulary with the following word parts: *belli-, -cede* and *-ces; -gnostos* and *cogni-; cur-; bene-* and *mal-; pos-* and *pon-; -trac(t); viv-; voc-.*

belli—war

bellicose	inclined or eager to fight; aggressively hostile. The situation worsened daily as each nation sounded more *bellicose* and less inclined to a peaceful resolution.
belligerent	engaged in warfare; showing readiness to fight; hostile. Amanda thought that Todd's increasingly *belligerent* behavior must be due to using drugs. *Bellicose* and *belligerent* are synonyms.
rebel	a person who rises in arms against a ruler or government; a person who resists authority, control, or tradition. During the teenage years, many young people are *rebels:* They just can't tolerate their parents' authority.

cede, ces—go (back), yield, withdraw

cede	to yield or formally surrender to another. After the battle, the disputed land was *ceded* to the victorious party.
accede	to give one's consent or approval; to give up, agree. Mona refused to *accede* to her parents' wishes and give her child up for adoption. Instead, she vowed to raise him all by herself.
precede	to go or come before. In a traditional wedding ceremony in the United States, the bridesmaids *precede* the bride up the aisle.
recession	the act of receding or withdrawing; a period of economic decline.
secede	to stop being a member of a group. During the Civil War, Alabama was one of the states that *seceded* from the Union.

gnostos—know; cogni—know

agnostic	a person who believes that it is impossible to know whether or not there is a God.
cognitive	pertaining to the act or process of knowing; perception.
incognito	with one's identity hidden or unknown. Many movie stars, not wishing to be recognized by fans, travel *incognito.*
cognizant	being aware or informed of something. Were the parents *cognizant* that their child was suffering from depression?

cur(r)—run

concurrent	occurring or existing simultaneously or side by side. The literal meaning is running together. What is the likelihood of an earthquake and a tornado happening *concurrently?*

cursive	handwriting in flowing strokes with the letters joined (running) together. While I can read his printing, his *cursive* writing is often illegible.
cursory	going rapidly over something without noticing details; hasty; superficial. Eva gave the memo a *cursory* reading; she will review it again later when she has more time.
discursive	passing aimlessly from one subject to another; rambling. Because I hadn't seen Marilyn for a long time, our conversation was *discursive*, ranging from our health and our children to new books and movies.
incursion	an invasion of a place or territory; a raid. Has there been another *incursion* into enemy territory?
precursor	a person or thing that comes before and makes the way ready for what will follow; forerunner. Was the typewriter a *precursor* to the computer?
recur	to occur again. The literal meaning is to run back. As soon as Sonia finishes her antibiotic, her ear infection *recurs*.

bene—well; mal—bad

benefactor	a person who has given money or other help as to a charity or school. An anonymous *benefactor* paid Truman's tuition to a private school.
beneficiary	a person or group that receives benefits. In his mother's will, Marco was named as her primary *beneficiary*.
benediction	a blessing; an utterance of good wishes.
benevolent	characterized by expressing goodwill or kindly feelings; kind; generous. Sascha's *benevolent* uncle paid for her trip to the United States.
malcontent	not satisfied with current conditions; ready to rebel.
malevolence	the quality or state of wishing evil or harm on others. In the fairytale "Snow White and the Seven Dwarfs," the *malevolent* stepmother plots Snow White's death.
malfeasance	misconduct or wrongdoing committed by someone holding a public office. The congressman was accused of *malfeasance* for accepting expensive gifts from a lobbyist.
malign	to speak harmful untruths about someone; slander. Now that she is no longer around to defend herself, it seems unfair to *malign* her.

pos, pon—put, place

imposition	the laying on of something as a burden or obligation. Would it be too much of an *imposition* for you to watch Colby every day after school for the next two weeks?

depose	to remove from office or position, especially high office. The rebels did not succeed in *deposing* the tyrant.
deposition	the written statement of a witness, made under oath, but not in court, to be used later at a trial.

trac(t)—pull, draw

retract	to draw back; to withdraw. Threatened by the senator's attorneys, the paper was forced to *retract* a statement that it had made earlier in the week about the senator's extramarital affairs. A turtle can *retract* its head.
detract	to take something away, especially something worthwhile or attractive. Josie wanted to get contacts because she believed that her glasses *detracted* from her appearance.
traction	the power to grip or hold to a surface, moving without slipping; the act of drawing or pulling. When the tires lost *traction* on the wet road, the car began to skid.

viv—live

vivid	strikingly bright or intense; realistic; full of life; lively. The flower paintings of Georgia O'Keeffe are famous for their *vivid* colors.
revive	renew; restore to life or consciousness. After pulling the two-year-old from the swimming pool, the paramedics worked frantically to *revive* her.
convivial	enjoying a good time with other people, such as at a party; sociable; friendly; jovial. Her new in-laws were so *convivial* that Kelly looked forward to spending the holidays with them.
vivisection	the action of cutting into or dissecting a living body. *Antivivisectionist* groups have caused many university researchers to abandon experiments on rhesus monkeys.

voc—call

vocal	having a voice; inclined to express oneself with words. The teacher told the class that she wanted them to be *vocal* and participate.
revoke	to call back or withdraw; to cancel. Because Tim failed to come home by midnight, his mother *revoked* his driving privileges for the next two weeks.
advocate	to support or urge by argument. *ad-* means "to," and *voc-* means "call," so the literal meaning is "to call to." The financial adviser was a strong *advocate* for staying out of debt.
vocation	a person's regular occupation or calling.
avocation	something a person does in addition to a principal occupation, especially for pleasure; hobby. His *vocation* is teaching, but his *avocation* is surfing.

Completing Verbal Analogies

Another common type of analogy can be expressed as "A is associated with B; C is associated with D." An example is shown below.

　　　　　　A　　　B　　　C　　　D
__b__　　lawyer : legal : : chef : _____
　　　　a. fasting
　　　　b. culinary
　　　　c. comfort
　　　　d. dieting

　　　The answer is (b). A *lawyer* is associated with the *legal* field, in the same way that a *chef* is associated with the *culinary* field.
　　　Complete the following analogies.

_____　　1.　malefactor : bad : : benefactor : _____
　　　　　　　a. good
　　　　　　　b. money
　　　　　　　c. possessions
　　　　　　　d. poverty

_____　　2.　belligerent : hostility : : convivial : _____
　　　　　　　a. aggressiveness
　　　　　　　b. eagerness
　　　　　　　c. rebelliousness
　　　　　　　d. friendliness

_____　　3.　incognito : hidden : : cognizant : _____
　　　　　　　a. contented
　　　　　　　b. perceived
　　　　　　　c. withdrawn
　　　　　　　d. serious

_____　　4.　accede : giving up : : recede : _____
　　　　　　　a. accepting
　　　　　　　b. moving back
　　　　　　　c. pleading
　　　　　　　d. believing

_____　　5.　avocation : hobby : : vocation : _____
　　　　　　　a. prayer
　　　　　　　b. yelling
　　　　　　　c. occupation
　　　　　　　d. trip

　　　Now that you have studied the vocabulary in Unit 7, practice your new knowledge by completing the crossword puzzle on the next page.

Vocabulary 7

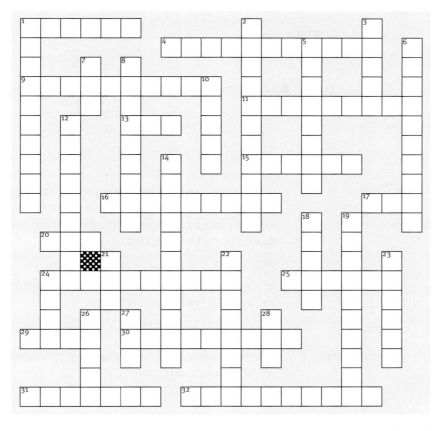

ACROSS CLUES

1. You _____ someone when you spread a false, mean-spirited story about that person.
4. The legislator committed _____ when he accepted a bribe.
9. The judge sentenced the defendant to _____ sentences of three and five years.
11. Prince William, dressed in casual clothes, traveled _____ throughout the United States.
13. A word part meaning "run."
15. Because Sascha had only been underwater for a minute, the paramedics were able to _____ her.
16. The supervisor was _____ of the fact that Carrie and Guillermo were leaving early every Friday.
17. A word part meaning "earth."*
20. A word part meaning "call."
24. An unknown _____ gave Maria enough money to complete her education.

25. Should we _____ a driver's license after only one DUI offense?
29. A word part meaning "yield."
30. His _____ of photography was more important to him than his vocation as a computer programmer.
31. The minute the legislator made the comment, he wished he could _____ it.
32. Kind people are considered to be _____.

DOWN CLUES

1. The employee complained all the time and was known as a _____.
2. The _____ countries were at war with each other.
3. A word part meaning "war."
5. Josh said he was an _____ because he did not know whether or not God exists.
6. The lawyer took the _____ of the witness to the car accident.
7. The abbreviation for what was once the eighth month.*

8. Was the icebox a _____ to the refrigerator?
10. A word part meaning "pull."
12. He sounded increasingly _____ and less likely to find a peaceful resolution.
14. After the funeral service, the priest delivered a short _____.
18. The _____ army could sense that victory was near.
19. It was a real _____ to have her mother-in-law stay for two months in their tiny house.
21. The abbreviation for what was once the tenth month.*
22. Snow tires have better _____ on snow than regular tires.
23. South Carolina was the first state to _____ from the Union.
24. A word part meaning "good."
26. Darcy's allergies _____ every fall and spring.
27. A word part meaning "bad."
28. A word part meaning "put."

*From a previous unit.

Unit 8

This is the last vocabulary unit. The first group of words in this unit concerns water, air, and life. The second group concerns sleep and light. The final group includes words using the prefix *in-*, but in several variant forms.

aqua, hydro—water; pneu—air, breathe, wind

aquarium	a tank or container filled with water in which collections of animals and plants live; also the building where these collections are placed on exhibit.
aqueduct	*-duc* means "to lead," so this word means literally "to lead water." An *aqueduct* can be a pipe for bringing water from a distant place, or it can resemble a canal or tunnel. The Romans built *aqueducts* throughout their empire; many of these are still used today.
Aquarius	This is the constellation that looks like a man carrying water. If you were born between January 20 and February 18, your zodiac sign would be *Aquarius*.
hydrant	a large pipe with a valve for releasing water from a water main.
hydroelectric	electricity generated by the energy of running water, usually water falling over a dam.
hydrologist	a person who studies water, including the cycle of evaporation and precipitation.
hydraulic	The literal meaning is "water tube." Today, *hydraulic* is a term used to describe a system operated by the movement of fluid, such as a *hydraulic* jack or *hydraulic* brakes.
pneumatic	containing wind, air, or gases; filled with or worked by compressed air. The tires on your car are *pneumatic* because they hold pressurized air.
pneumonia	*Pneumonia* is an inflammation of the lungs that causes difficulty in breathing.

nat—birth; bio—life

nature	the essential character of something; what has always been there from birth.
native	*Native* has two meanings: First, your *native* state or country is where you were born. Second, *native* plants, animals, and people are the ones that originally came from an area. Eucalyptus trees are not *native* to the United States; they were brought here from Australia.
nativity	A *nativity* scene is a birth scene, such as you might see at Christmas when the birth of Jesus is celebrated.
innate	*in-* here means "within," so your *innate* characteristics are those you were born with.

prenatal	before birth.
postnatal	after birth.
biography	an account of a person's life written by someone else.
autobiography	Because *auto-* means "self," an *autobiography* is the story of one's own life written by oneself.
biochemistry	the study of the chemistry of life processes in both plants and animals.
biopsy	the removal of bits of living tissue for analysis.
biodegradable	matter that is capable of breaking down or decomposing so that it can return to the life cycle.
symbiotic	the living together of two different organisms for mutual benefit.

lum, luc—light; photo—light

luminary	a body or object that gives off light; a person who has attained eminence in a field or is an inspiration to others. Maya Angelou, Rita Dove, and other literary *luminaries* were invited to attend a conference on writing held at Vanderbilt University.
illuminate	to supply or brighten with light; to enlighten. Sylvia used a flashlight to *illuminate* the boxes in the cellar.
translucent	permitting light to pass through but not allowing things on the other side to be seen clearly; easily understood, clear. The glass on most shower doors is *translucent*.
lucid	easily understood; intelligible; sane; glowing with light. After the driver's *lucid* explanation of the events leading to the traffic accident, the police officer had no further questions.
photography	the art or method of making pictures by means of a camera.
photogenic	forming an appealing subject for photography; producing or emitting light. A *photogenic* politician has an advantage.
photosynthesis	the process by which green plants form sugars and starches from water and carbon dioxide: This process occurs when sunlight acts upon the chlorophyll in the plant.

hypno(s), dorm, coma—sleep

hypnosis	an artificially induced trance resembling sleep that is characterized by a heightened susceptibility to suggestion.
dormitory	a building, as at a college, containing rooms for residents; a large room containing a number of beds and serving as communal sleeping quarters.
dormant	inactive, as in sleep; undeveloped. Although the volcano has been *dormant* for fifty years, scientists predict an eruption sometime this century.

coma	a state of prolonged unconsciousness including a lack of response to stimuli.
comatose	lacking vitality or alertness; torpid.

Additional meanings of *in*

As you learned in Unit 3, the Latin prefix *in-* has two distinct meanings: "not" as in the word *inactive*, and "within" or "into" as in the word *incarcerate* (meaning to put in jail or prison). In some English words, *in-* acts as an intensifier, with the meaning "very" or "completely."

infamous	This word does not mean "not famous." Rather, it means "famous but for the wrong reasons." *Infamous* refers to people who have a bad reputation or are notorious, such as Jesse James, Bonnie and Clyde, or Charles Manson.
invaluable	*Invaluable* does not mean "not valuable," but instead means something so extremely valuable that it is priceless. Original copies of the Constitution, your mother's advice, and your grandmother's ring might all be considered *invaluable*.
inflammable	This word means "very flammable." If something is inflammable, it will burn easily. This word is related to the word *inflame*, which means "to catch fire." If something does *not* burn, it would be *non*flammable.
ingenious	*Ingenious* does not mean that a person is not smart. Instead, it means that a person is clever and creative. Inventors such as Thomas Edison and Alexander Bell were *ingenious*.
ingenuous	being naïve about a subject; a childlike candidness. A spy cannot afford to be truly *ingenuous*, although at times she might want to pretend to be *ingenuous*.

Completing Verbal Analogies

Another common type of analogy can be expressed as "A is primarily concerned with B; C is primarily concerned with D." An example is shown below.

```
      A        B        C              D
  d   dentist : teeth :: ophthalmologist : _____
      a. ears
      b. feet
      c. insects
      d. eyes
```

The answer is (d). A *dentist* is primarily concerned with *teeth*, just as an *ophthalmologist* is primarily concerned with *eyes*.

Complete the following analogies.

```
_____  1.  terrarium : plants :: aquarium : _____
             a. dirt
             b. fish
             c. air
             d. water
```

_____   2.   pneumatic : air : : hydraulic : _____
a. fluid
b. tires
c. nature
d. wind

_____   3.   geologist : earth : : hydrologist : _____
a. air
b. nature
c. dirt
d. water

_____   4.   biography : someone else's life : : autobiography : _____
a. one's horoscope
b. one's own life
c. one's birth date
d. one's health

_____   5.   prenatal : events before birth : : postnatal : _____
a. events leading up to birth
b. innate characteristics
c. events after birth
d. state of alertness

_____   6.   sun : solar energy : : dams : _____
a. hydroelectric power
b. wind energy
c. water resource
d. thermonuclear energy

Now that you have studied the vocabulary in Unit 8, practice your new knowledge by completing the crossword puzzle on the next page.

Vocabulary 8

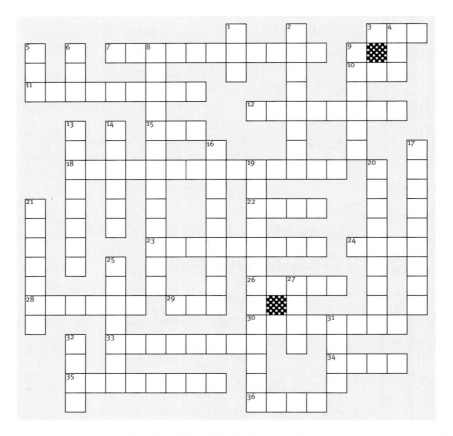

ACROSS CLUES

3. A word part meaning "call."*
7. Bathroom windows are often _____.
10. A word part meaning "born."
11. A relationship of mutual dependency.
12. Picasso, who attained great eminence in the field of art, is an artistic _____.
15. A word part meaning "life."*
18. _____ occurs when sunlight acts upon chlorophyll in a plant.
22. A word part meaning "sleep."
23. Hospital patients who lie in bed too long sometimes develop _____.
24. A word part meaning "air."
26. His writing was very _____ and clear.
28. It is in her _____ to be kind and caring.
29. A word part meaning "put or place."*

30. The driver hit his head on the windshield of the car and became _____.
33. The ancient Romans used an _____ system to move water from one city to another.
34. A word part meaning "water."
35. A birth scene.
36. A word part meaning "believe."*

DOWN CLUES

1. A word part meaning "run."*
2. Jeffrey Dahmer, a serial killer, became _____.
4. An abbreviation for what was once the eighth month.
5. A word part meaning "yield."*
6. A word part meaning "light."
8. The life story of your life written by you.
9. Researchers have concluded that shyness is an _____ characteristic that tends to stay with people throughout their lifetime.

13. A person under the influence of _____ is more susceptible to suggestion.
14. The _____ showed that the growth was benign.
16. Marilyn Monroe often played innocent, childlike, _____ roles.
17. The _____ brakes on your car contain a liquid.
19. The dams along the Colorado River produce _____ power.
20. The iMac computer has an _____ design.
21. In most states, if you park too close to a fire _____, you will get a ticket.
25. The volcano is currently _____, but is expected to erupt within the next decade.
27. A word part meaning "sleep."
31. A word part meaning "pull."*
32. A word part meaning "good."*

*From a previous unit.

TEST-TAKING TIP

Taking Standardized Tests

Here are some more tips for performing well on standardized tests:

1. Read actively. Think carefully about what you are reading.

2. Immediately determine the topic and the central theme or main idea of the passage you have read. Read to determine main ideas and to understand concepts. You can go back and look for details later.

3. The first paragraph of a passage is extremely important, so make sure you understand it. It often gives an overview of the passage, and the main idea is often located there.

4. Mark key parts of the passages or make short notes in the margins if permissible. For instance, you might write *MI* by the main idea and circle key transition words like "in contrast," or "in summary." But be careful not to overmark.

5. Be sure to read all the possible answers carefully before choosing one. Remember that several answers may be partially correct; the correct answer is the one that most accurately and completely answers the question.

6. If the exam has more than one reading passage, you might want to start with a passage that is about something with which you are already familiar. It is also permissible to tackle the easier questions first.

7. If you must read a passage that you have little interest in, ask yourself what you might learn from the passage.

8. Your exam is likely to include all of the following:

   - Main idea questions that test your ability to identify the central point.
   - Detail questions that test your ability to locate specific pieces of information.
   - Inference questions that test your ability to understand the implications of the material.
   - Purpose questions that test your ability to understand why the author wrote the passage and who the intended audience is.
   - Vocabulary questions that test your ability to decipher the meaning of words from context clues.
   - Tone questions that test your ability to describe the author's attitude.

Appendices

Visual Aids

Bar Graphs

Bar graphs use vertical (top to bottom) or horizontal (left to right) bars to show comparisons. Usually, longer bars represent larger quantities. The title of the bar graph below is "Annual Earnings and Education." In this graph, the vertical bars represent the average earnings for the U.S. population in 1999 for increasing levels of education. The source of the bar graph is the U.S. Census Bureau, U.S. Department of Commerce.

Annual Earnings and Education

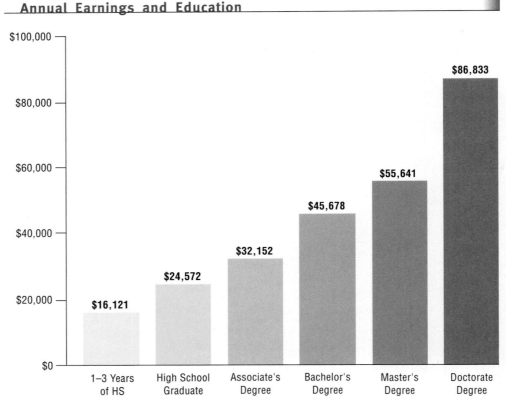

Source: Census 2000, U.S. Census Bureau, U.S. Department of Commerce.

After studying the graph, answer the questions below.

1. What is the average annual income for somebody with a Bachelor's Degree?

     45678

2. What is the average annual income for somebody with an Associate's Degree?

     32152

3. What is the average annual income for somebody with a high school diploma?
   24,572

4. What is the difference in average annual income between someone with an Associate's Degree and someone with a high school diploma? *7,580*

5. What is the relationship between level of education and average annual income?
   More education higher pay

6. Would you expect the lifetime earnings of someone with a Doctorate Degree to be greater on average than for someone with a Master's Degree? *Yes*

From Sharon K. Ferrett in *Peak Performance*, 4th ed., New York: McGraw-Hill, 2003, pp. 2–9. Copyright © 2003 McGraw-Hill. Reprinted by permission of The McGraw-Hill Companies, Inc.

Tables

Tables display information in rows (across) and columns (up and down). The table below demonstrates how two people (Joe and Roscoe) respond differently to the same stressors. Joe encounters a stressor, perceives it as stressful, and winds up with stress. Roscoe, on the other hand, encounters the same stressor, but perceives it in such a way as to avoid stress. Thus, we can see that an event only has potential for eliciting a stress reaction. Whether it actually does elicit a stress reaction depends on how it is perceived.

The Chronic Stress Pattern versus the Healthy Stress Pattern

Stressor	Joe (Chronic Stress Pattern)	Roscoe (Healthy Stress Pattern)
Oversleeps—awakes at 7:30 instead of 6:30	Action: Gulps coffee, skips breakfast, cuts himself shaving, tears button off shirt getting dressed	Action: Phones office to let them know he will be late; eats a good breakfast
	Thoughts: I can't be late again! The boss will be furious! I just know this is going to ruin my whole day.	Thoughts: No problem. I must have needed the extra sleep.
	Result: Leaves home anxious, worried, and hungry	Result: Leaves home calm and relaxed
Stuck behind slow driver	Action: Flashes lights, honks, grits teeth, curses, bangs on dashboard with fist; finally passes on blind curve and nearly collides with oncoming car	Action: Uses time to do relaxation exercises and to listen to his favorite radio station
	Thoughts: What an idiot! Slow drivers should be put in jail! No consideration of others!	Thoughts: Here's a gift of time—how can I use it?
Staff meeting	Action: Sits in back, ignores speakers, and surreptitiously tries to work on monthly report	Action: Listens carefully and participates actively

(Continued)

The Chronic Stress Pattern versus the Healthy Stress Pattern (Continued)

Stressor	Joe (Chronic Stress Pattern)	Roscoe (Healthy Stress Pattern)
	Thoughts: What a waste of time. Who *cares* what's going on in all those other departments? I have more than I can handle keeping up with my own work. Results: Misses important input relating to his department; is later reprimanded by superior	Thoughts: It's really good to hear my coworkers' points of view. I can do my work a lot more effectively if I understand the big picture of what we're all trying to do. Results: His supervisor compliments him on his suggestions.
Noon—behind on deskwork	Action: Skips lunch; has coffee at desk; spills coffee over important papers Thoughts: That's the last straw! Now I'll have to have this whole report typed over. I'll have to stay and work late.	Action: Eats light lunch and goes for short walk in park Thoughts: I'll be in better shape for a good afternoon with a little exercise and some time out of the office.
Evening	Action: Arrives home 9 P.M., family resentful; ends up sleeping on couch; does not fall asleep until long into the morning Thoughts: What a life! If only I could run away and start over! It's just not worth it. I'll never amount to anything. Results: Wakes up late again, feeling awful; decides to call in sick	Action: Arrives home at usual time; quiet evening with family; to bed by 11 P.M., falls asleep easily Thoughts: A good day! I felt really effective at work, and it was nice reading to the kids tonight. Results: Wakes up early, feeling good

Indicate whether the statement is true or false by writing T or F in the blank provided. If you can't tell based on the information provided in the table, write CT. You may refer to the table.

_____ 1. Roscoe, stuck behind a slow driver, listens to the radio.

_____ 2. Joe, stuck behind a slow driver, causes an accident.

_____ 3. Roscoe is chastised by a superior.

_____ 4. Roscoe eats a salad before his walk in the park.

_____ 5. Joe openly tries to work on his monthly report at the staff meeting.

From Jerrold Greenberg, *Comprehensive Stress Management*, 6th ed., New York: McGraw-Hill, 1999, p. 11. Copyright © 1999 McGraw-Hill. Reprinted by permission of The McGraw-Hill Companies, Inc.

Flowcharts

Flowcharts are often used in textbooks to show cause-and-effect relationships and the sequence of events. The action moves, or flows, in the direction of the arrows. The following flowchart which appears in a psychology textbook shows how stress triggers bodily effects, upsetting thoughts, and ineffective behavior. Notice how each element worsens the others in a vicious cycle.

Stress: The Vicious Cycle

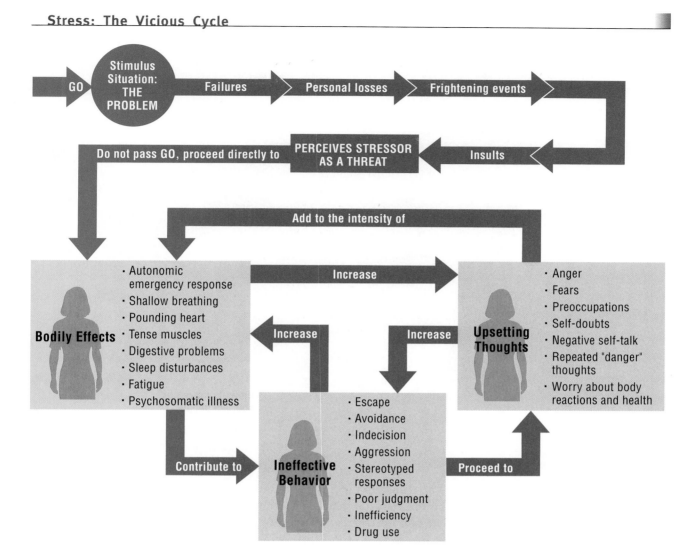

Indicate whether the statement is true or false by writing T or F in the blank provided. If you can't tell based on the flowchart, write CT.

_____ 1. Avoidance decreases the bodily effects of stress.

_____ 2. Sleep disturbances contribute to ineffective behavior.

_____ 3. Shallow breathing increases upsetting thoughts like anger.

_____ 4. Poor judgment can lead to negative self-talk.

_____ 5. Anger can intensify digestive problems.

_____ 6. Exercise can reduce the bodily effects of stress.

Maps

Maps are useful for presenting information visually. The legend, which indicates what color or shading represents, is the key to understanding the map. Maps may also have endnotes that explain the specific details. The following map, based on data from the *Statistical Abstract of the United States 1999,* shows the number of violent crimes that occurred in the United States as of 1999. Study the map, using the legend and the endnotes as a guide.

Some States Are Safer: Violent Crime in the United States

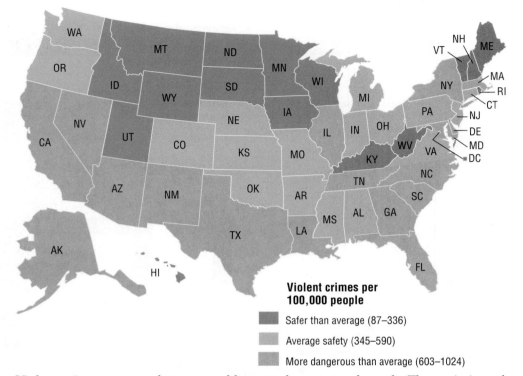

Violent crimes per 100,000 people

- Safer than average (87–336)
- Average safety (345–590)
- More dangerous than average (603–1024)

Violent crimes are murder, rape, robbery, and aggravated assult. The variation of violence among the states is incredible. Some states have a rate that is ten times higher than that of other states. With a rate of 87 per 100,000 people, North Dakota has the lowest rate of violence, while Florida, at 1,024, has the highest rate. The U.S. average rate is 424 (the total of the states' average rates of violence divided by 50). This total does not include Washington, D.C., whose rate is 2,024, 23 times as high as North Dakota and almost five times the national average.

Source: Statistical Abstract 1999: Table 344.

Using the information in the map and legend, answer the following questions.

1. According to the information given, violent crimes are _____ ____, _____, and _____.

2. _____ is the state with the lowest rate of violent crime.

3. The state with the highest rate of violent crime in the United States is _____.

4. How many states are considered to be safer than average? _____

5. California, Alaska, and Nevada all have _____ rates of violent crime.

6. West Virginia has a safer than average rate, but Virginia has only an _____ safety rate.

From U.S. Government: *Statistical Abstract 1999:* Table 344.

Pie Graphs

Pie graphs are illustrations that show percentages or proportions as pie-shaped sections of a circle. The whole interior of the circle represents 100 percent. The pie graph that follows illustrates the percentage of employees who feel that their company encourages unethical conduct or exerts pressure on them to engage in unethical behavior. The figures are based on a 1997 business ethics survey. The source is the Ethics Resource Center/Society for Human Resource Management.

Percentage of Employees Who Believe That Their Company Encourages Unethical Conduct

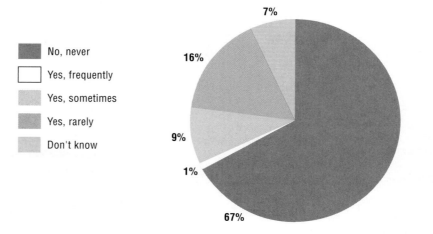

Legend:
- No, never
- Yes, frequently
- Yes, sometimes
- Yes, rarely
- Don't know

7%
16%
9%
1%
67%

Source: Ethics Resource Center/Society for Human Resource Management, 1997, Business Ethics Survey Report, p. 19.

Using the information in the pie chart, answer the following questions.

1. What percentage of employees believe that their company frequently encourages unethical conduct? _____

2. What percentage of employees believe that their company never encourages unethical conduct? _____

3. What percentage of employees say "Yes" when asked whether they believe their company encourages unethical conduct? _____

4. How important do you think it is for a company to have ethics policies and standards that draw a line between ethical and unethical conduct?

_____

_____

Is it a good idea for companies to have an ethics training program for employees? If so, why?

_____

_____

Whistle-blowing occurs when an employee exposes an employer's wrongdoing to outsiders such as the media or a government oversight agency. Whistle-blowers are often treated harshly by their employers and sometimes may lose their jobs. Do you think whistle-blowers should be given legal protection?

_____

_____

From O.C. Ferrell, *Business Ethics Survey Report*, 3rd ed., New York: McGraw-Hill, 2000, p. 65. Copyright © 2000 McGraw-Hill. Reprinted by permission of The McGraw-Hill Companies, Inc.

Consumer Labels

Consumer labels are designed to help consumers make wise choices about specific products. Since March 1999, the FDA has required the labels of dietary supplements to carry a "supplements facts" panel. In addition, because most supplements have not been evaluated by the FDA for safety or effectiveness, the label must carry a disclaimer.

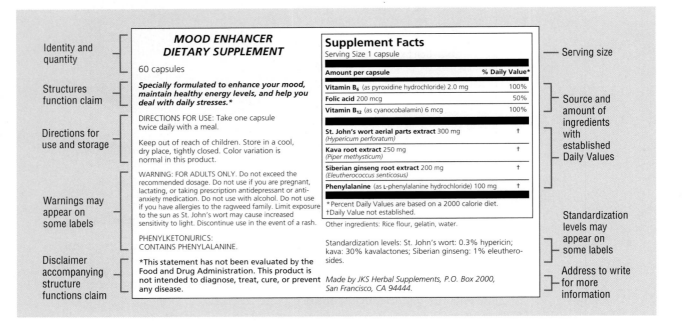

Using the information in the dietary supplement label, answer the following questions.

1. What is the meaning of *disclaimer?* _____
   a. a statement that reveals or lays open
   b. a statement that expresses disapproval
   c. a statement that repudiates or denies

2. One capsule of this product contains _____ mg of St. John's wort.

3. Is this product something that should be given to children? _____

4. What is the meaning of *warning?* _____
   a. notification of possible dangers
   b. directions about how much medicine to give
   c. praise of the product

5. What is the recommended dosage for this product?
   _____

6. Does this product claim to help you if you are suffering from stress?
   _____

7. Should you take this product if you are going to be in the sun for prolonged periods? _____
   a. Yes, there should be no adverse effect.
   b. No, the product increases the skin's sensitivity to sunlight.

8. Is it safe to take this product with alcohol? _____

From Paul M. Insel, *Core Concepts in Health,* 9th ed., New York: McGraw-Hill, 2002, p. 343. Copyright © 2002 McGraw-Hill. Reprinted by permission of The McGraw-Hill Companies, Inc.

Line Graphs

A **line graph,** which takes the form of a line drawn in an L-shaped grid, shows the relationship between two variables. One of these variables will be defined along the bottom, on the horizontal (across) axis of the grid. The other variable will be defined along the side, on the vertical (up and down) axis of the grid. The line need not be straight, and, in fact, it is often jagged or curved. Often the bottom scale of the grid measures time (for example, minutes, years, decades), and so the line graph shows changes over time. The line graph below shows the percent of Americans who believe the federal government listens carefully to them before deciding what to do. The horizontal axis gives the years covered, and the vertical scale gives the percentage of those who answered "a good deal."

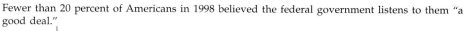

Few Americans Think Government Listens

Fewer than 20 percent of Americans in 1998 believed the federal government listens to them "a good deal."

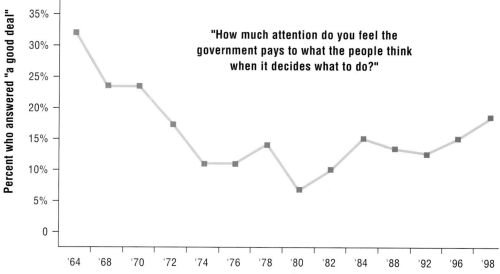

Using the information in the line graph, answer the following questions.

1. In what year was the percentage of people who answered "a good deal" the highest? _____

2. In what year was the percentage of people who answered "a good deal" the lowest? _____

3. What was the general trend from 1964–1974? _____

4. What was the general trend from 1980–1984? _____

5. What is the source of the information? _____

_____

From U.S. Government, *Congressional Quarterly*, February 18, 2002, p. 17.

Exercise: Visual Aids

On this page and the next are a **bar graph**, a **line graph**, and a **map.** The bar graph depicts life expectancy by year of birth. The line graph and the map depict the "graying of America," that is, the increasing proportion of elderly people in the U.S. population.

Life Expectancy by Year of Birth

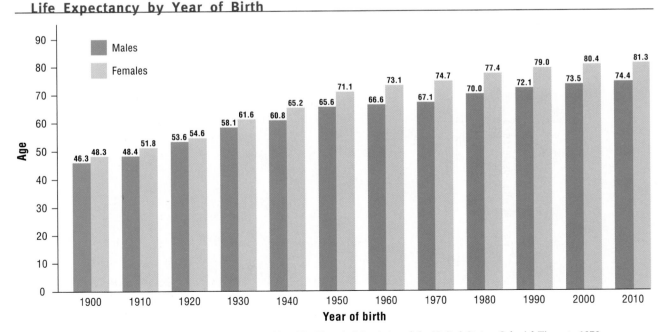

Source: Statistical Abstract of the United States, 1991; Table 105; Historical Statistics of the United States, Colonial Times to 1970, Bicentennial Edition, Part 1, Series B, 107–115.

Median Age of U.S. Population

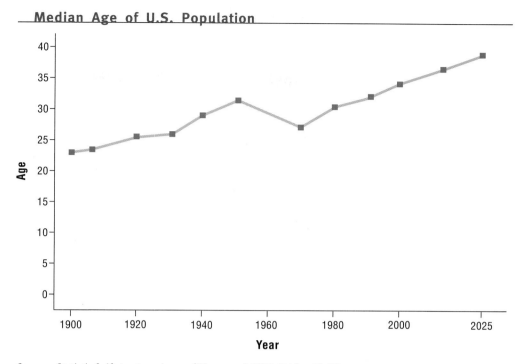

Sources: Statistical Abstract, various editions, and 1999: Tables 13, 24.

As Florida Goes, So Goes The Nation: The Year 2025

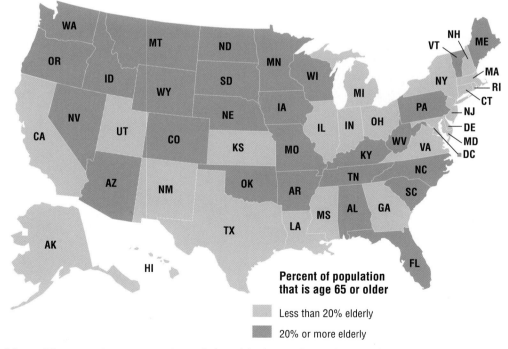

Percent of population that is age 65 or older

Less than 20% elderly

20% or more elderly

Note: The growing proportion of the elderly in the U.S. population is destined to have profound effects on U.S. society. By the year 2025, one-fifth of the population of 27 states is expected to be 65 or older. Today, at 19 percent, only Florida comes close to this.

Source: U.S. Bureau of the Census, 1996, U.S. Department of Commerce, PPL-47.

Using the information in these three visual aids, answer the questions below:

1. The average life expectancy of a man born in 1980 is _____.

2. The average life expectancy of a woman born in 2000 is _____.

3. In one hundred years, 1900–2000, the life expectancy of males has increased from _____ to _____ years.

4. In 1900, the median age of the U.S. population was approximately _____.

5. In 1940, the median age of the U.S. population was approximately _____.

6. In 2000, the median age of the U.S. population was approximately _____.

7. What do these visual aids tell us about the percentage of people age 65 or older in California? _____.

8. What do they tell us about the percentage of people age 65 or older in Oregon? _____

From U.S. Government, *Statistical Abstract of the United States, 1991, 1999,* and *U.S. Bureau of the Census, 1996.*

Using a Thesaurus

The word *thesaurus* is derived from the Greek *thesauros,* meaning "treasure or treasury." A **thesaurus** is a "treasury" of related words. It is a dictionary of synonyms and antonyms presented alphabetically in categories. Unlike a dictionary, a thesaurus does not give the definition, pronunciation, or etymology of a word.

The purpose of a thesaurus is to enable you to be more precise in the words that you use so that you can express your thoughts exactly. It also enables you to choose alternate words so that you don't just repeat the same word over and over again. Many students find a thesaurus to be an invaluable resource in helping them select just the right word to use in an essay or homework assignment.

As an example, imagine that you have just written the following sentences:

Worn out by evading her pursuers, she now lay prostrate in the desert sand. Trying to conserve her insufficient supply of water, she drank sparingly from her canteen, fully aware that only a few insufficient drops remained.

Notice that the word *insufficient* has been used twice. Replacing the word with a synonym might improve the sentence and help to clarify your meaning. Turning to *Roget's College Thesaurus,* you find the following entry:

INSUFFICIENCY

Nouns—**1,** insufficiency; inadequacy, inadequateness; incompetence, IMPOTENCE; deficiency, INCOMPLETENESS, IMPERFECTION, shortcoming, emptiness, poorness, depletion, vacancy, flaccidity; ebb tide; low water; bankruptcy, insolvency (see DEBT, NONPAYMENT).

2, paucity; stint; scantiness, smallness, none to spare; bare necessities, scarcity, dearth; want, need, deprivation, lack, POVERTY; inanition, starvation, famine, drought; dole, pittance; short allowance *or* rations, half-rations.

Verbs—**1,** not suffice, fall short of (see FAILURE); run dry, run *or* give out, run short; want, lack, need, require; be caught short, be in want, live from hand to mouth; miss by a mile.

2, exhaust, deplete, drain of resources; impoverish (see WASTE); stint, begrudge (see PARSIMONY); cut back, retrench; bleed white.

Adjectives—**1,** insufficient, inadequate; too little, not enough; unequal to; incompetent, impotent; weighed in the balance and found wanting; perfunctory (see NEGLECT); deficient, wanting, lacking, imperfect; ill-furnished, -provided, *or* -stored; badly off.

2, slack, at a low ebb; empty, vacant, bare; out of stock; short (of), out of, destitute (of), devoid (of), denuded (of); dry, drained; in short supply, not to be had for love or money, not to be had at any price; empty-handed; short-handed.

(Continued)

INSUFFICIENCY (Continued)

3, meager, poor, thin, sparing, spare, skimpy, stinted; starved, half-starved, famine-stricken, famished; jejune; scant, small, scarce; scurvy, stingy; at the end of one's tether; without resources (see MEANS); in want, poor (see POVERTY); in DEBT. *Slang,* shy of, fresh out of.
Adverbs—insufficiently, *etc.;* in default, for want of; failing.
Antonyms, see SUFFICIENCY.

From *The New American Roget's College Thesaurus* by Phillip D. Morehead and Andrew T. Morehead. Copyright © 1958, 1962 by Albert H. Morehead. Copyright © 1978, 1985, renewed 1986 by Phillip D. Morehead and Andrew T. Morehead. Used by permission of Dutton Signet, a division of Penguin Group (USA) Inc.

Notice that the synonyms are presented by parts of speech: nouns, verbs, adjectives, and adverbs. At the end of the entry, antonyms are listed.

Depending on the meaning you are trying to convey, you might choose to replace the word *insufficient* with *inadequate* or *meager*. For instance, your new sentence might now look like this:

Worn out by evading her pursuers, she now lay prostrate in the desert sand. Trying to conserve her insufficient supply of water, she drank sparingly from her canteen, fully aware that only a few meager drops remained.

Exercise: Using a Thesaurus

Use a thesaurus to find two synonyms for each of the words below.

1. insufferable: _____   _____
2. frugal: _____   _____
3. enervate: _____   _____

Exercise: Recognizing Synonyms

Can you recognize the following well-known proverbs? They have been rewritten with synonyms for key words. Rewrite the proverbs to bring them back to their familiar form.

1. Birds of similar plumage assemble.

   _____

2. Sanitation is next to piousness.

   _____

3. An examined kettle does not bubble.

   _____

   Now use your thesaurus, to rewrite the following proverbs. Find synonyms for at least two words in each proverb.

4. You can't teach an old dog new tricks.

   _____

5. Where there's smoke, there's fire.

   _____

6. Look before you leap.

    _____

7. People who live in glass houses shouldn't throw stones.

    _____

Peter Mark Roget (1779–1869), an English physician, wrote the first thesaurus in 1852 at the age of 73. Since Roget's death, many editions of his thesaurus have been published, including editions that are now on the Internet, such as *Roget's International Thesaurus* <www.bartleby.com/110/>. Most computer word processing programs, such as MS Word also feature a thesaurus.

MS Word Thesaurus

The thesaurus that accompanies MS Word groups words into categories based on meaning. In MS Word, to find a synonym, you highlight the word in your typed text that you want to replace, click on Tools, click on Language, and then click on Thesaurus. Below is a sample search for the word "art" as found in the title of this textbook, *The Art of Critical Reading.* The first MS Word Screen that appears is the one below.

Two meanings for "art" are given. The one that is highlighted refers to art as painting. Since this meaning does not apply, you have to select "skill," and the following box appears.

You now have three more words related to "art." You can use any of these words, or if you want to look further, you can highlight one of these words, and check on Look Up to bring up additional words. For example, if you highlight "ability," and click on Look Up, the following screen will give you additional words related to "skill."

Screens from MS Word Thesaurus. Reprinted by permission of Microsoft Corporation.

You can continue to highlight words until you find a word that suits your needs. If you can't find something close enough, consult *Roget's International Thesaurus* or the following website: www.refdesk.com.

Roget's International Thesaurus

Roget's International Thesaurus is organized by categories. To search for a word, first consult the index found at the back of the book. The following is how the word "art" appears in the index of the *International Thesaurus*:

art

representation 349.1
knack 413.6
science 413.7
cunning 415.1
stratagem 415.3
visual arts 712.1
artistry 712.7
vocation 724.6
science 927.10

The numbers after each category indicate where that particular category is located in the *Thesaurus*. Probably the best category for our purposes is 413.7, which appears as follows:

413 Skill

7 art, science, craft; skill; technique, technic, **technics,** technology, technical knowledge or skill, technical know-how <nonformal>, field-work, **mechanics,** mechanism, method

From *Roget's International Thesaurus,* 5th ed., Robert L. Chapman (ed.), pp. 781, 413, & 303. Copyright © 1992 by HarperCollins Publishers. Reprinted by permission of HarperCollins Publishers, Inc.

The words are listed in order of their relationship to the general classification, in this case "skill." The words in bold are the most common words for each variation of use. If none of these words meet your needs, you can look in other sections of the general classification or return to the index to locate another general category.

Exercise: Using a Thesaurus

What synonyms can you find for the word "critical" as used in *The Art of Critical Reading?*

Look up "critical" in the thesaurus that is associated with your word processor. Follow the same procedure that we completed above with the word "art." Write the appropriate words that you locate on the line below.

Look up "critical" in the index of *Roget's International Thesaurus*. Find words that could be substituted for "critical" as it is used in *The Art of Critical Reading*. Write those words below.

Spelling Tips

Here are a few simple rules to help you become a better speller. However, remember that there are always exceptions.

1. When the suffixes -*ness* and -*ly* are added to a word, the spelling of the word usually does not change. However, when adding -*ness* or -*ly* to a two-syllable word ending in *y*, change the *y* to *i* before adding the suffix.

    Examples:

    open + ness = openness

    quick + ly = quickly

    sly + ness = slyness

    silly + ness = silliness

    happy + ly = happily

2. When words end in a -*y* preceded by a consonant, change the -*y* to -*i* when adding a suffix that does not begin with *i*.

    Examples:

    sunny + er = sunnier

    defy + ed = defied

    study + ing = studying

3. A word that ends in -*y* preceded by a vowel keeps the -*y*.

    Example:

    employ + er = employer

4. Drop the final -*e* before a suffix beginning with a vowel, but keep it before a suffix beginning with a consonant.

    Examples:

    share + ing = sharing

    hope + ful = hopeful

5. For a one-syllable word that ends in a consonant, double the final consonant when adding a suffix.

    Examples:

    plan + ing = planning

    stop + ing = stopping

6. Nouns ending in -*ch*, -*sh*, -*s*, -*ss*, -*x*, and -*z* add -*es* to form the plural.

   Examples:

   fax/faxes

   buzz/buzzes

   bush/bushes

   mattress/mattresses

7. For most words that end in -*f* or -*fe*, change the -*f* or -*fe* to a -*v* and add -*es*.

   Examples:

   wife/wives

   knife/knives

8. Most nouns ending in an -*o* preceded by a consonant add -*es* to form the plural.

   Examples:

   hero/heroes

   tomato/tomatoes

9. If you have trouble remembering the spellings of particular words, make up sayings to fix the spellings in your mind.

   Examples:

   Ma is in *grammar* and *pa* is in *separate*.

   Does *lipstick* make a girl *irresistible*?

After two years of college, students still frequently misspell the following words:

absence	definitely	government	privilege
accidentally	dependent	grievance	procedure
achieve	descendant	irresistible	proceed
aggravate	desirable	knowledge	pronunciation
amateur	despair	laboratory	receive
appearance	develop	losing	recommend
argument	disappear	maintenance	repetition
athlete	disappoint	marriage	responsibility
believe	dispensable	mischievous	restaurant
benefited	embarrass	occasion	rhythm
cemetery	environment	occurred	schedule
committee	exaggerate	occurrence	separate
competition	exceed	omitted	superintendent
conscientious	exercise	parallel	supersede
convenience	existence	permissible	tragedy
correspondence	foreign	precede	villain
criticize	forty	prejudice	weird

Sample Summary

The following paragraph summarizes the plagiarism scandal described in Jody Wilgoren's article "School Cheating Scandal Tests a Town's Values" (pages 164–167).

A plagiarism scandal at Piper High School in Kansas caused deep divisions in a once close-knit community. Students in Christine Pelton's sophomore biology class were required to complete a leaf project worth 50 percent of their grade. Upon reviewing the projects, Ms. Pelton discovered with the aid of computer software that 28 of 115 students had plagiarized parts of their reports. Ms. Pelton gave those students zeros on the assignment. Both the principal and the superintendent initially backed Ms. Pelton, but after parental protests, the superintendent intervened and reduced the assignment from 50 percent of the final grade to only 30 percent. He also directed Ms. Pelton to deduct only 600 points instead of 1,500 points from those who were accused of plagiarizing. In protest, Ms. Pelton resigned her position. The resulting scandal pitted parent against parent. Some parents asserted that the leniency unfairly penalized those who did the assignment correctly, and that students were being robbed of a valuable lesson in values. Others said that those who plagiarized did not fully understand the meaning of plagiarism. Teachers worried that their authority had been seriously undermined. And because of the media attention focused on Piper, residents feared the incident made the entire community look bad.

Vocabulary Word Parts

Following is a list of the vocabulary word parts you studied in Chapter 14. The prefixes indicating numbers are listed first. The other word parts are listed in alphabetical order.

Word Parts	Meaning	Examples
uni	one	unify
mono	one	monogram
bi	two	bivalve
di	two	dichotomy
du(o)	two	duplex
tri	three	triplicate
qua(d)	four	quadrangle
tetra	four	tetrapod
quint	five	quintessence
pent	five	pentathlon
hex	six	hexagram
sex	six	sextet
sept	seven	September
hept	seven	heptagon
oct	eight	October
nov	nine	November
dec, dek	ten	December
a(n)	not, without	asymmetrical
ad	toward	admit
agogos	lead; bring together; excite	demagogue
ana	back; up; again	anachronism
aqua	water	aquarium
archy	rule	monarchy
auto	self, by one's self	autocracy
belli	war	belligerent
bene	well	benefactor
bio	life	biography
cap	head	caption
capt, cept	hold; seize; take	captivity
cede, ces	go (back); yield; withdraw	precede
chrono	time	chronology
cide	kill	genocide
circum	around	circumvent
cogni	know	cognitive
coma	sleep	comatose
con	with	convert
corp	body	corporation

Word Parts	Meaning	Examples
cracy	rule; strength; power	plutocracy
cred	believe	incredulous
cur(r)	run	recur
demos	people	democracy
deus	god	deity
dia	through; across; apart; thoroughly	diagonal
dis	apart; away	dismiss
dorm	sleep	dormant
duc	lead	induce
dys	bad; abnormal; difficult	dysentery
equi	equal	equitable
eu	good; well	eulogy
fid	faith(ful)	fidelity
frater, fratri	brother	fraternity
genus	birth; begin; race	genealogy
geo	earth	geocentric
gnostos	know	agnostic
graph	write	demography
helio	sun	heliocentric
homo	man	homicide
hydro	water	hydroelectric
hypno(s)	sleep	hypnosis
in	not; opposite; into; within	invert
inter	between; among	interpersonal
intra	within; inside	intrapersonal
ism	doctrine; theory	polytheism
ject	throw	inject
legis	law	legislature
locut (loqu)	speak, talk	loquacious
log(ue)	speech; word	dialogue
logy	science of; study of	seismology
lum, luc	light	translucent
macro	large, long	macrocosm
mal	bad	malign
mater, matri	mother	maternity
medius	middle	intermediate
meter	measure	pedometer
micro	small	microfilm
mis	hate; bad(ly)	misconstrue
mis, mit	send	mission
nat	birth	native
pater, patri	father	paternity
path(o), pathy	feeling; suffering; emotion	apathy
ped	child	pediatrician
phil(o)	love	philanthropist
photo	light	photography
pneu	air; breathe; wind	pneumonia
polis	city	politician
poly	many	polytechnic
pos, pon	put; place	depose
potis	powerful	potent
pro	forward	progressive
re	back; again	remit
sacri	holy	sacred
sanct	holy	sanctuary
se	apart; away from	separate
sequ, secut	following	sequence

Word Parts	Meaning	Examples
soror	sister	sorority
syn	same	synagogue
tact, tang	touch	tactile
temp	time; moderate	temperate
ten(t), tin	hold; cling; keep	detention
terr	earth, land	territory
theo	god	theocracy
trac(t)	pull; draw	traction
ven	come	prevent
vert	turn	divert
viv	live	revive
voc	call	vocal

Internet Site Evaluation Sheet

1. Topic: _____

2. Search engine used _____

3. Website address (URL) _____

4. Summary of information found _____

   _____

   _____

   _____

   _____

5. Date of information, if found _____ (Does the date of the
   information seem appropriate for the topic? Explain.)

   _____

6. Go to the home page or basic URL (delete all the information after the
   type of site—.com, .edu, .org) and find out information about the
   organization or author.

   _____

   _____

7. Organization name _____

8. How qualified is the person or organization responsible for the website?

   _____

9. Purpose of website (information, selling a product or person, etc.)_____

   _____

10. Viewpoint of website/organization _____

11. Information indicating point of view _____

    _____

12. Is there an easy way of contacting the author or organization? If so, how?

    _____

13. Are sources for claimed facts clearly cited so you can easily find them?
    Explain.

    _____

14. Reliability of organization (Do you think that this organization or person
    has given consistent quality information over a period of time? Explain.)

    _____

    _____

548

15. Validity of Internet material (Does the information given in this website seem to be consistent with other information you have read? Explain.)

_____

_____

16. Evaluation of information based on answers to the previous questions ___

_____

_____

17. Usefulness of information for paper on topic (Give reasons) _____

_____

_____

(Print out and attach one or two typical pages from website.)

Index

Index of Artists and Art Works